A History of Israel

From the Beginnings to the Bar Kochba Revolt, AD 135

J. Alberto Soggin

A HISTORY OF ISRAEL

From the Beginnings to the Bar Kochba
Revolt, AD 135

SCM PRESS LTD

Translated by John Bowden from the Italian
Storia d'Israele, dalle origini alla rivolta di Bar-Kochba, 135 d.C.,
published by Casa Editrice Paideia, Brescia 1985.

DS 117
S 6413
1984

Soggin, J. Alberto
   A history of Israel : from the beginnings
   to the Bar Kochba Revolt, AD 135.
   1. Jews——History——To 70 A.D.   2. Jews——
   History——168 B.C. - 135 A.D.   3. Israel——
   History
   I. Title
   933   DS117

   ISBN 0-334-02043-3

334 02043 3

First British edition published 1984
by SCM Press Ltd
26-30 Tottenham Road, London N1

Photoset by Input Typesetting Ltd
and printed in Great Britain by
Redwood Burn Ltd
Trowbridge

לָאוּנִיבֶרְסִיטָה הָעִבְרִית בִּירוּשָׁלַיִם,
שֶׁבְּמָכוֹן לְלִימוּדִים מִתְקַדְּמִים שֶׁלָּהּ,
בִּשְׁנַת תשמ״ג, הֶעֱנִיקָה לִי זְמַן וּמָקוֹם, עֶזְרָה וּשְׁלֵוָה;
בִּלְעֲדֵיהֶם מֶחְקָר זֶה לֹא הָיָה בָּא לָעוֹלָם.

To the Hebrew University of Jerusalem which,
in its 'Institute of Advanced Studies',
during the academic year 1982-83
provided me with quiet, space, time and
co-operation, without which this book
would never have been written.

Contents

Plates   339

Preface

This book could never have been written without a series of circumstances which have helped it on in a number of ways:

1. The invitation I received from the Institute of Advanced Studies
in the Hebrew University of Jerusalem to be Fellow at the Institute for
the academic year 1982-83 and the many facilities put at my disposal
and at that of my colleagues.

2. The study leave which was immediately granted by the Rector of
the University of Rome on the recommendation of the Faculty of Arts
and Philosophy, and the readiness of my colleagues in the Institute of
Near Eastern Studies to support me.

3. The brotherly welcome from the École biblique et archéologique
française of the Dominican Convent of St Stephen in Jerusalem, whose
superb library I could enjoy at my leisure.

4. The collaboration of my colleagues in the Waldensian Faculty in
Rome.

Many colleagues, in Italy and abroad, have discussed with me
important parts of this work and I have profited enormously from the
time that I have spent with them. I cannot even list their names.
However, in particular I would like to recall the staff of the Hebrew
University in Jerusalem, some of whom continued to discuss issues
with me while making no bones about their disagreement over a
number of the positions put forward here. qin'at sōperīm tarbeh ḥokmāh,
'the zeal (and sometimes indeed the jealousy) of scholars increases
wisdom', as the ancient 'father' of the Talmud remarked.

The reader will often notice, here and there in this book, a certain
disproportion between the attention given to some features which are
clearly not of primary importance and the lesser attention given to
others which are obviously more important. I offer no excuses for this
in advance; things sometimes work out like this, and only constant
refinement can remedy the proportions or eliminate the disproportions.

In the course of this work I have not spent time discussing the books
of the Bible. For this I would refer the reader to my *Introduction to the
Old Testament*, London and Philadelphia ²1980. I should also point out
that the bibliographies are almost always select ones. To provide

complete bibliographies (which in effect would mean listing every title) would not only be to embark on pointless toil (there are plenty of bibliographical studies to which the reader could refer), but would also turn an attempt at a history into a bibliographical manual which would have virtually nothing to do with a history.

This book ends with the events of AD 74 and 135, which led to the destruction of Judaism in Judaea and the dispersion of the survivors. It does not seem to me so significant that after the period covered by this *History*, many groups succeeded in remaining in the Holy Land, especially in the plain of Jezreel, in Galilee and in the hill-country to the south (as we know from the very fine synagogues discovered in this region); after the destruction of the temple (which has never been rebuilt) by Titus and the failure of the Bar Kochba revolt, the cultural and religious centre of Judaism in Palestine ceased to exist, and it was the Diaspora, which from now on even included some parts of the Holy Land, which was to be the determinative element.

So here we find ourselves confronted with one of those breaks in history which in all respects can be compared with the 'official' end of the Roman empire as marked by the deposition of Romulus Augustulus in 476. Therefore it seems to me legitimate to break off the investigation at this point. Although they were heir to biblical and immediately post-biblical Judaism, Talmudic Judaism, mediaeval Judaism and the Judaism of the great philosophers are necessarily something different, as different as the Judaism of the Enlightenment, the Emancipation, the Holocaust and finally of the restored state of Israel.

The reader will note that from the period of the Maccabees onwards the account becomes more synthetic, more sparse. The truth of the matter is that after the discovery of the Qumran manuscripts in 1947, little or nothing new can be said in this field. So for a detailed account the reader should refer to the various *Histories of Israel* which deal with it, sometimes at length: G.Ricciotti, M.Noth, A.H.J.Gunneweg, J.H.Hayes and J.M.Miller, J. Bright (below, II, 6.2ff.), and all the monographs indicated in the bibliography. For two highly specialized themes, the chronology of the period of the monarchy and Palestinian archaeology, I have felt it necessary to make use of the works of particularly competent scholars, D.Conrad of the University of Marburg and H.Tadmor of the Hebrew University of Jerusalem. While the contribution by the former was written specially for this work, the latter's study is a reprint of a chapter of the *World History of the Jewish People*, by kind permission of the publisher, Massada Press in Jerusalem.

This history leaves one very substantial question open, that of relationship of the two Hebrew kingdoms (and later the kingdom of Judah) to Assyria and later Babylon on the one hand, and Egypt on the other. Here we are confronted with a strange tripartite relationship which none of the sources in any of the nations mentioned manage to clarify. It should be noted that neither Israel nor, more particularly, Judah ever succeeded in freeing themselves totally from at least a nominal vassalship under Egypt. Granted, there were periods in which the power of Egypt seems to have been non-existent, but this did not mean a change in the legal situation.

We have a series of direct interventions on the part of Egypt, the chief of which were as follows:

1. The invasion of Shishak/Shoshenk I at the end of the tenth century BC;

2. The invasion of 701 BC;

3. The invasion of 609 BC;

4. The invasion of 600 BC;

5. The only intervention which was asked for, and never took place, in the last years of the kingdom of Judah.

In cases 1,3 and 4, there is nothing surprising in the fact that Egypt should have tried and indeed succeeded, at least for a short time, in re-establishing its own effective sovereignty over the region. In cases 2 and 5 these will have been interventions asked for by Judah, just as similar interventions were asked for by the Syro-Palestinian vassals in the fifteenth and fourteenth centuries BC as recorded in the el-'Amarna vassals. The *kittīm* mercenaries mentioned in the letters of 'Arad could also have been mercenaries in the pay of the Egyptians, stationed in the Negeb, to whose maintenance Judah had to contribute (an oral communication by G.Garbini).

Obviously these are questions of considerable complexity, so much so that I have not felt that I could even attempt a solution here. However, I think that I have indicated a line of research for the next few years, which either I myself or others, simultaneously or after me, should be able to develop in a useful way.

I would like to thank those who have put photographs, diagrams and other materials at my disposal, some of it unpublished:

The Department of Antiquities of the State of Israel, Jerusalem;

The Hebrew Union College of Jerusalem (Professor A.Biran);

The Israel Exploration Society of Jerusalem (Professor N.Avigad);

The Institute of Archaeology of the University of Tel Aviv (Professor R.Gophna).

Once again, the Revd Richard Coggins of King's College, London, has provided invaluable help in verification of details for the English edition.

One last word. It is clear that this history, like all histories, is no more than an attempt. The traditions which Israel handed down about itself are also no more than an attempt, even if, in Christian doctrine, they are regarded as an inspired attempt. And that is the limit of this work, which is now open to discussion.

Jerusalem, summer 1983

Rome, autumn 1983

Abbreviations

AASOR	Annual of the American Schools of Oriental Research
AB	The Anchor Bible
ABLAK	M.Noth, Abhandlungen zur biblischen Landes- und Altertumskunde, Neukirchen 1974
ADPV	Abhandlungen des Deutschen Palästinavereins
AfO	Archiv für Orientforschung
AHw	W. von Soden, Akkadisches Handwörterbuch, Wiesbaden 1965-1981
AION	Annali dell'Instituto Orientale di Napoli
AJBI	Annual of the Japanese Biblical Institute
AnBibl	Analecta Biblica
ANET	J.B.Pritchard (ed.), Ancient Near Eastern Texts relating to the Old Testament, Princeton ³1969
ANEP	J.B.Pritchard (ed.), The Ancient Near East in Pictures, Princeton ³1969
ANL-M/R	Atti dell'Accademia nazionale dei Licei – Memorie/Resconti
AOAT	Alter Orient und Altes Testament
AOF	Altorientalische Forschungen
ARM	Archives royales de Mari
ASNSP	Annali della Scuola Normale Superiore di Pisa
ASOR	The American Schools of Oriental Research
ASTI	Annual of the Swedish Theological Institute
ATANT	Abhandlungen zur Theologie des Alten und Neuen Testaments
ATD	Das Alte Testament Deutsch
AustBR	Australian Biblical Review
BA	The Biblical Archaeologist
Bab	Babylonian Talmud
BASOR	Bulletin of the ASOR
BBB	Bonner biblische Beiträge
BeO	Bibbia e Oriente
BHH	Biblisch-historisches Handwörterbuch, 4 vols, Göttingen 1962-1975

BHK	*Biblia Hebraica*, ed. R.Kittel
BHS	*Biblia Hebraica Stuttgartensia* (= *BHK*[4])
Bibl	*Biblica*
BiblOr	Biblica et Orientalia
BiblRes	*Biblical Research*
BJRL	*Bulletin of the John Rylands Library*
BK	Biblischer Kommentar zum AT
BN	*Biblische Notizen*
BO	*Bibliotheca Orientalis*
BTB	*Biblical Theology Bulletin*
BWANT	Beiträge zur Wissenschaft vom Alten und Neuen Testament
BZ	*Biblische Zeitschrift*
BZAW	Beiheft zur *ZAW*
CAH	*Cambridge Ancient History*
CB-OTS	Coniectanea Biblica – Old Testament Series
CBQ	*Catholic Biblical Quarterly*
CTA	A.Herdner, *Corpus des tablettes alphabétiques découvertes à Ras-Shamra-Ugarit 1929-39*, Paris 1963
DBAT	*Dielheimer Blätter zum Alten Testament*
DOTT	*Documents from Old Testament Times*, ed. D.Winton Thomas, London and New York 1958
EI	*'Eres Iśra'el*
EncBibl	*Encyclopedia Biblica* (in Hebrew)
EncJud	*Encyclopedia Judaica*
ETL	*Ephemerides Theologicae Lovaniensis*
EvTh	*Evangelische Theologie*
ExpT	*Expository Times*
FRLANT	Forschungen zur Religion und Literatur vom Alten und Neuen Testament
FS	Festschrift
GA	Gesammelte Aufsätze
GS	Gesammelte Schriften
HAT	Handbuch zum Alten Testament
HKAT	Handkommentar zum Alten Testament
HSM	Harvard Semitic Monographs
HTR	*Harvard Theological Review*
HUCA	*Hebrew Union College Annual*
IASHP	*Israel Academy of Sciences and Humanities – Proceedings*
ICC	International Critical Commentary
IDB-SV	Interpreter's Dictionary of the Bible – Supplementary Volume
IEJ	*The Israel Exploration Journal*
Int	*Interpretation*

JANESCU	*Journal of the Ancient Near Eastern Society*, Columbia University
JAOS	*Journal of the American Oriental Society*
JBL	*Journal of Biblical Literature*
JCS	*Journal of Cuneiform Studies*
JEA	*Journal of Egyptian Archaeology*
JESHO	*Journal of the Economic and Social History of the Orient*
JJS	*Journal of Jewish Studies*
JNES	*Journal of Near Eastern Studies*
JNWSL	*Journal of North-Western Semitic Literature*
JPOS	*Journal of the Palestine Oriental Society*
JQR	*Jewish Quarterly Review*
JSOT-SS	*Journal for the Study of the Old Testament* – Supplementary Studies
JSS	*Journal of Semitic Studies*
JTS	*Journal of Theological Studies*
KAI	W.Donner and W.Röllig, *Kanaanäische und Aramäische Inschriften*, Wiesbaden ²1966-70
KB	L.Köhler and W.Baumgartner, *Lexicon in Veteris Testamenti Libros*, Leiden ³1967-83
KS	Kleine Schriften
KuD	*Kerygma und Dogma*
LA-SBF	*Liber Annuus – Studii Biblici Franciscani*
LXX	Septuagint: Greek translation of the Old Testament
NKZ	*Neue Kirchliche Zeitschrift*
OA	*Oriens Antiquus*
OAW-Sitzb	Österreichische Akademie der Wissenschaften-Sitzungsberichte
OBO	Orbis Biblicus et Orientalis
OLZ	*Orientalische Literaturzeitung*
Or	*Orientalia*
OTL	Old Testament Library
OTOS	J.A.Soggin, *Old Testament and Oriental Studies*, BibOr, Rome 1975
OTS	*Oudtestamentische Studiën*
OTW	Martin Noth, *The Old Testament World*, ET London 1966
PEQ	*Palestine Exploration Quarterly*
PJB	*Palästina-Jahrbuch*
PL	Patrologia Latina, ed. J.P.Migne
PP	*La Parola del Passato*
Prot	*Protestantesimo*
RA	*Revue d'Assyriologie*
RB	*Revue Biblique*
RGG	*Die Religion in Geschichte und Gegenwart*

RHPR	*Revue d'Histoire et de philosophie religieuse*
RHR	*Revue d'histoire des religions*
RiBib	*Rivista biblica*
RIDA	*Revue internationale des droits de l'antiquité*
RSF	*Rivista di studi fenici*
RSLR	*Rivista di storia e di letteratura religiosa*
RSO	*Rivista di studi orientali*
RTP	*Revue de théologie et de philosophie*
SBL DS/MS	Society of Biblical Literature – Dissertation Series/ Monograph Series
SBS	Stuttgarter Bibelstudien
SBT	Studies in Biblical Theology
ScrHier	*Scripta Hierosolymitana*
SDB	*Supplément au Dictionnaire de la Bible*
SEA	*Svensk Exegetisk Arsbok*
SNTS-MS	Society for New Testament Studies – Monograph Series
SOTS-MS	Society for Old Testament Studies – Monograph Series
SSI	J.C.L.Gibson, *Textbook of Syrian Semitic Inscriptions*, Oxford I, 1971; II, 1975; III, 1982
SSR	*Studi di Storia delle Religioni*
StSem	Studi semitici
SVT	Supplement to *Vetus Testamentum*
Targ	Targum: Aramaic translation of the Old Testament
TDOT	*Theological Dictionary of the Old Testament*
TLZ	*Theologische Literaturzeitung*
TRE	*Theologische Realenzyklopädie*
TS	*Theological Studies*
TZ	*Theologische Zeitschrift*
VuF	*Verkündigung und Forschung*
WHJP	B.Mazar (ed.), *The World History of the Jewish People*, Jerusalem 1964ff. (cf. II.6.4.10)
WMANT	Wissenschaftliche Monographien zum Alten und Neuen Testament
WuD	*Wort und Dienst*
WUS	J.Aistleitner, *Wörterbuch der ugaritischen Sprache*, Berlin 1963
ZAW	*Zeitschrift für die Alttestamentliche Wissenschaft*
ZDMG	*Zeitschrift der Deutschen Morgenländischen Gesellschaft*
ZDPV	*Zeitschrift des Deutschen Palästinavereins*
ZNW	*Zeitschrift für die Neutestamentliche Wissenschaft*
ZTK	*Zeitschrift für Theologie und Kirche*

Works quoted frequently in abbreviated form

*= History of Israel

Y.Aharoni, *The Land of the Bible*, Philadelphia ²1979 (cf.I.10.2.5)
W.F.Albright*, *From the Stone Age to Christianity*, Baltimore 1940, ²1957 (cf.II.6.4.1); unless indicated otherwise, quotations come from the second edition
J.Bright*, *A History of Israel*, Philadelphia and London ³1981 (cf.II.6.4.3)
.G.Buccellati, *Cities and Nations of Ancient Syria*, StSem 26, Rome 1967
W.M.Clark*, cf. Hayes-Miller*
R. de Vaux*, *The Early History of Israel*, London 1978 (cf.II.6.4.4)
W.G.Dever*, cf. Hayes-Miller*
H.Donner*, cf. Hayes-Miller*
G.Fohrer*, *Geschichte Israels*, Heidelberg ³1982 (cf.II.6.4.7)
G.Garbini, *I Fenici – Storia e religione*, Naples 1980
N.K.Gottwald, *The Tribes of Yahweh*, Maryknoll 1979 - London 1980
A.H.J.Gunneweg*, *Geschichte Israels bis Bar Kochba*, Stuttgart ³1979 (cf.II.6.4.5)
J.M.Hayes and J.M.Miller (eds.)*, *Israelite and Judaean History*, OTL, London and Philadelphia 1977 (cf.II.6.4.8)
S.Herrmann*, *A History of Israel in Old Testament Times*, London and Philadelphia ²1981 (cf.II.6.4.6)
T.Ishida (ed.), *Studies in the Period of David and Solomon*, Tokyo 1982
H.Jagersma*, *A History of Israel in the Old Testament Period*, London and Philadelphia 1982 (cf. II.6.4.9)
K.A.Kitchen, *The First Intermediate Period in Egypt*, Warminster 1973
A.R.C.Leaney*, cf. Hayes-Miller*
A.Lemaire*, *Histoire du peuple hébreu*, Paris 1981 (cf. II.6.5.3)
A.D.H.Mayes*, cf. Hayes-Miller*
J.Neusner*, cf. Hayes-Miller*
M.Noth*, *The History of Israel*, London ²1959 (cf.II.6.4.2)
id., *A History of Pentateuchal Traditions*, Englewood Cliffs, NJ 1972 reprinted Chico, Ca 1982
B.Oded*, cf. Hayes-Miller*

G.Ricciotti*, *The History of Israel* (1932), ET Milwaukee 1955 (cf.II.6.3.2)

P.Schäfer*, cf. Hayes-Miller*

P.Sacchi*, *Storia del mondo giudaico*, Turin 1976 (cf. II.6.4.13)

J.A.Soggin, *Das Königtum in Israel – Ursprung, Spannungen, Entwicklung*, BZAW 10, Berlin 1967

id., *Introduction to the Old Testament*, London and Philadelphia ²1980

id., *Joshua – A Commentary*, OTL, London and Philadelphia 1972

id., *Judges – A Commentary*, OTL, London and Philadelphia 1981

id.*, cf. Hayes-Miller*

Stern, M., *Greek and Latin Authors on Jews and Judaism*, Jerusalem I, 1974; II, 1980; III in preparation

T.L.Thompson*, cf. Hayes-Miller*

Weippert, M., *The Settlement of the Israelite Tribes in Palestine*, SBT II 21, London 1971

G.Widengren*, in Hayes-Miller*

PART ONE

Introductory Problems

'The methods of criminal detection are not at every point identical with those of scientific history, because their ultimate purpose is not the same...

So long as this is borne in mind, however, the analogy between legal methods and historical methods is of some value for the understanding of history...'

(R.G.Collingwood, *The Idea of History*, Oxford and New York 1946, 268)

I

CONTEXT

1 Up to AD 135, the history of Israel mostly takes place in the small territory situated on the south coast of the eastern Mediterranean, south of the Lebanon and Syria, west of the Jordan and north-east of Egypt. Here and there Israelite settlements are attested east of the Jordan, and parts of the region were under Israelite rule on various occasions from the beginning of the first millennium BC onwards.

Select bibliography. G.Dalman, *Arbeit und Sitte in Palästina*, Gütersloh I, 1928 – VII, 1942 and reprint (the classic work of the great German philologist and ethnologist which records the agricultural techniques, crafts, products and foods to be found in Palestine before Zionism introduced modern techniques); A.Moscati, *I predecessori d'Israele*, Rome 1957; M.Noth, *The Old Testament World*, London and Philadelphia 1966; H.Donner, *Einführung in die biblische Landes- und Altertumskunde*, Darmstadt 1976; Y.Aharoni, *The Land of the Bible*, London and Philadelphia [2]1979. For the geographical and climatic problems cf. the recent study by J.Sapin, 'La géographie humaine de la Syrie-Palestine au deuxième millénaire avant Jésus Christ', *JESHO* 24, 1981, 1-62; 25, 1982, 1-49, 114-86. For the complex ethnic and sociological problems cf. the studies by M.B.Rowton, 'The Physical Environment and the Problem of the Nomads', in *La civilisation de Mari, XVe Rencontre assyriologique internationale*, Louvain 1967, 110-21; id., 'Autonomy and Nomadism in Western Asia', *Or* 41, 1973, 247-58; id., 'Urban Autonomy in a Nomadic Environment', *JNES* 32, 1973, 201-15; id., 'Enclosed Nomadism', *JESHO* 17, 1974, 1-30; id., 'Dimorphic Structure and the Problem of the 'Apiru-'Ibrīm', *JNES* 35, 1976, 13-20; id., 'Dimorphic Structure and the Tribal Elite', *Anthropos* 28, 1976, 219-57; id., 'Dimorphic Structure and the Parasocial Element', *JNES* 36, 1977, 181-98; D.C.Hopkins, *Agricultural Subsistence in the Early Iron Age Highlands of Canaan*, Diss.

Vanderbilt University, Nashville 1983, to be published Sheffield, England 1984 (I have not been able to use this work).

1.1 The territory we shall be considering is ecologically, ethnically and linguistically part of Syria, so that we can distinguish between a 'Syria major', which also includes the present-day territories of Lebanon, Israel and Jordan, and a Syria in the narrower sense, comprising only present-day Syria together with the sanjak of Alexandretta, ceded to Turkey in the 1920s because most of the present population are Turks.

1.2 'Syria Major' in turn is part of the region which we call the 'Near East' (a more appropriate designation than the usual 'Middle East', which should be kept for Iran, Afghanistan and Pakistan). It is also known by the more colourful title 'the Fertile Crescent', arising from the fact that pictorially it can be depicted enclosed within two arcs of different radii, one broader than the other, and joined at the ends to produce the shape of a crescent moon.

2.1.1 However, the earliest and most authentic name known to us is certainly Canaan, written with the consonants *kn'n* and vocalized in Hebrew as *k^ena'an*.[1] It perhaps appears in cuneiform texts as early as Ebla (at the end of the third millennium BC and certainly from the first half of the second millennium BC onwards in the form *kinaḫḫu* and orthographic variants;[2] it was used in Roman North Africa among the population of Punic origin as late as the fourth and fifth centuries AD, as is attested by St Augustine.[3]

2.1.2 The origin of this name is connected with the production of purple dye,[4] in antiquity one of the main sources of income in the region. However, this took place in Phoenicia, and the Greek word φοῖνιξ and its derivatives refer to Phoenicia in the narrower sense rather than to the region in general. Still, the use made of 'Canaan' by the biblical texts and other ancient Eastern texts suggests that at least in origin the name denotes the whole region and not just the small part that we know as Phoenicia.[5] Moreover, in Isa.19.18, a text which, while probably late, refers back to events that took place at the end of the eighth century BC, Hebrew itself is called the 'language of Canaan', *s^epat k^ena'an*, which is philologically a correct definition.

2.2 Another very frequent name, 'Palestine', goes back to the settlement of the Philistines, an alien population whose origins have still not been completely explained (below, III.5.2); they settled mainly in the southern part of the region from the twelfth century onwards.[6] However, since the official name *Palaestina* was introduced by the Romans after the events of AD 132-135 in place of the traditional *Judaea*, it has been often been rejected in Jewish circles, which tend to use the name discussed in the next paragraph (cf. below XIV.7.2). Today it serves as a general designation of the region as distinct from Syria and the Lebanon, regardless of who is in power there. It appears for the first time in Herodotus (fifth century BC) as an adjective (ἐν τῇ Παλαιστίνῃ Συρίᾳ, I, 105), and as a noun (ἡ Παλαιστίνη, III, 91 and elsewhere), and is meant to distinguish the region from Phoenicia, which tended to be termed Canaan.

2.3 Another name which is closely bound up with the region, this time as the scene of the history of Israel, is 'land, country of Israel', Hebrew *'ereṣ iśrā'ēl*, though it is hardly used in the Bible (I Sam.13.13). It appears in rabbinic literature and today is used as the official name of the region within the Zionist movement and by the state of Israel.[7]

2.4 Other designations are of a theological kind, like 'Promised Land', 'Holy Land', and so on.

3 A first characteristic of the region is its extremely small size: the country is roughly equivalent to Belgium or the state of Vermont in length and breadth. In antiquity, inhabited Palestine extended 'from Dan to Beersheba', in the Negeb, i.e. a distance of a little less than 150 miles as the crow flies; its breadth from the Mediterranean to the Jordan is not more than 36 miles as the crow flies. This makes its physical structure, especially its hills and mountains, all the more remarkable, producing a series of regions with very different climates and therefore very different ecologies. From east to west we find successively the following features:

3.1 The plateau of Transjordan, which on the average is about 2100 feet above sea level, is furrowed by a number of rivers and streams which run westwards and flow down into the Jordan. Towards the east the plateau merges into the desert of northern Arabia; towards the west, however, as we gradually move in the direction of the Jordan valley, it becomes increasingly fertile because it is favoured by the rain. There was good reason why in ancient times this was the granary of the region. The predominant climate is continental, hot and dry in the summer, though tempered by the altitude, and cold and wet in the winter, with frequent and heavy falls of snow. Today it comprises the greater part of the Hashemite Kingdom of Jordan whose capital, Amman, has retained the second part of the name used in antiquity by the Ammonites and the Hebrews, Rabbath-ammon. As I mentioned earlier, Transjordan was occupied on and off by Israelite populations, but only came under Israelite sovereignty at the beginning of the first millennium BC, at the time of the united kingdom of David and Solomon, and in the years immediately following it.

3.2.1 The depression formed by the Jordan runs from north to south. It is part of a greater geological fault, which begins in the *beqaʿa* of Syria and Lebanon, well above sea level, and reaches its greatest depth below sea level in the region of the Dead Sea; it then continues in the valley of the *ᵃrābāh* and again reaches sea level in the Gulf of Aqaba. However, the geological system continues right through the Red Sea, to become the Rift Valley in East Africa (Ethiopia, Kenya and Tanzania), and beyond. Its origins are to be sought in a prehistoric seismic cataclysm; even today the whole of the region is sensitive to earthquakes.

3.2.2 From above sea level at the border between Israel and Lebanon, the Jordan valley soon reaches Lake Huleh, a marsh not more than ten or twelve feet deep and about eight square miles in surface area; it was drained in the 1950s and all that is now left of it is a small pool in a national park. From there, after a few miles the valley descends to the Sea of Galilee, just over 600 feet below sea level, and then, at the level of the Dead Sea, reaches the lowest point of the land: over 1000 feet below sea level. Throughout the depression the climate is tropical and humid, springlike and therefore gentle in winter, and very oppressive in summer. About twelve miles south of the Sea of Galilee the rains tend to become increasingly sparse and then cease almost altogether; this produces a desert zone which can only be cultivated where there are oases (like those of Jericho and En-gedi), or where it is possible to get water in other ways.

3.2.3 The river Jordan, closely confined between steep banks which are often prone to landslides a few miles beyond the Sea of Galilee, cannot be used for agriculture without the installation of irrigation systems which would be so expensive as to make the produce uneconomical; furthermore, the river is not navigable and has hardly any fish in it. It is therefore of little benefit to the economy of the region and divides rather than unites those who live on its banks.

3.2.4 However, where there is water, or where it is possible to convey the water needed for irrigation, the Jordan valley is extremely fertile, and it produces early crops on the stretch around the Sea of Galilee and tropical fruit along its southern reaches.

3.3.1 The plateau on the west bank of the Jordan has been the main scene of the history of Israel. From north to south it is divided in turn by the mountain chains in upper Galilee and by the hill country, in the centre, and in the south.

3.3.1.1 The mountain chains in Galilee reach a maximum height of about 3500 feet above sea level and have particularly fertile valleys. The mountains are covered with woods, some original and some the result of modern forestation. They are divided by the two plateaus of the plain of Jezreel, in Hebrew *yizrᵉʿʾēl* (below, 3.4).

3.3.1.2 The plateau rises from this plain and extends as far as the northern limits of present-day Jerusalem; its maximum height is just over 3000 feet above sea level. To the traveller it appears generally barren; the vegetation is sparse: sometimes it is still original, but usually it is the result of modern afforestation; round the villages there has been intensive cultivation, using terraces.

3.3.1.3 The southern hill-country begins south of Jerusalem and reaches its greatest height in the region of Hebron, at about 3500 feet above sea level; it then merges into the Negeb, the southern steppe, with a northern part which can be cultivated after particularly wet winters and now with modern systems of irrigation. The southern hill-country has more woods than that in the centre; again they are partly the result of afforestation, and there is also intensive cultivation around the villages.

3.3.2 The western area of the mountains of Galilee and of the two plateaux, exposed to the winds from the Mediterranean, has a moderate mountain climate: healthy, cold in winter and moderately warm in summer, with abundant falls of rain and even snow in the winter. The eastern area tends to become increasingly dry the further east one goes.

3.4 Between Galilee and the central plateau in the north we have the extremely fertile plain of Jezreel and its surroundings; to the east it drops towards the Jordan valley and to the west it extends as far as the Mount Carmel chain, which runs from the south-east to the north-west, maintaining an average height of about 1000 feet, with a summit 1500 feet above sea level. It ends at the city and port of Haifa, Hebrew *ḥēpāh*, Arabic *ḥayfāh*.

3.5.1 Between the plateaux and the Mediterranean coast is an intermediary hilly zone, called *šᵉpēlāh* in Hebrew; this, too, is fertile where there is water and it is not eroded.

3.5.2 The coasts are generally sandy and little suited either for agriculture or for the construction of ports. This last feature explains why the ancient Israelites mistrusted the sea, which they considered to be a relic of ancient chaos; unlike their neighbours the Phoenicians, they were no sailors.

4.1 We have seen how the mountainous structure of the region makes it very varied in climate, even over a relatively short distance. However, all the regions (with the exception of Transjordan) lie in an area which has a sub-tropical Mediterranean climate. There is a regular sea breeze from the south-west, which brings coolness in the summer and rain in the winter. In spring and in autumn, more rarely a wind comes off the Eastern desert, a kind of dry sirocco, called *ḥamsīn* in Arabic and *šārāb* in Hebrew. This causes trouble for both human beings and domestic animals, and its ruinous consequences for agriculture are also noted in the Bible (Isa.40.7). The north wind, which blows especially in winter and tends to brings rain, is also more rare.

4.2 Despite all the local variations, one of the main characteristics of the climate of the region is the division of the year into two main seasons: the winter, with abundant though intermittent rain, which can often turn into cloudbursts, and snow on the high ground, followed by many calm days; and the summer, a completely dry season. The spring and the autumn tend to be very brief.

4.2.1 It is the occurrence of rain, in particular, that makes a fundamental difference between Palestine and the other civilizations in the region, Mesopotamia and Egypt. These two latter civilizations had been aware of the benefits of irrigation from time immemorial. This irrigation was carried out by making canals for water from rivers which could be exploited by the techniques of construction and maintenance in use at the time. By contrast, in Canaan, which was a region of sparse and meagre watercourses, until only a few decades ago agriculture was dependent on the volume of the winter rains, which were preceded in October by the 'first rains' (Hebrew *yōreh*) and followed in April-May by the 'latter' rains (Hebrew *malqōš*). One or more dry winters, or winters with insufficient rain, could easily lead to ecological catastrophe: the springs and the wells dried up, and the cisterns emptied. It was asking a lot for domestic animals, who were also deprived of fodder, to survive in such conditions; sometimes even the very survival of human beings was in danger. There is a reference to a particularly serious drought, lasting for three years, in I Kings 17.1ff. (cf. IX.3.4.1.2.1; 1983-1984 was a particularly dry year). Today, with a centralized plan for the use of water and the possibility of constructing canals on a national scale, such catastrophes no longer happen, though a prolonged drought could still have serious consequences for agriculture.

4.2.2 However, on the plateaus and in the valleys of the mountain chains the rain was never enough to ensure the permanent settlement of human beings and animals, except of course where there were springs: it was necessary to be able to save water from the winter rains for the use of human beings and animals during the dry season. Only with the discovery of a special mortar for coating cisterns and thus making them impermeable did it become possible, in the last centuries of the second millennium BC, to populate the mountainous regions and the hill-country (cf. below VII.3.3).

4.2.3 This dependence on factors beyond human control explains why agriculture has always been so precarious in the region until recent decades. As J.Sapin pointed out in his basic study (1981-82, I, 13), 'It is a marginal world without defences or autonomy', an easy prey either for the ambitions of the cities or for the rapacious depredations of the nomads.

4.3 The further east we go, especially east of the watershed on the plateaus, the more the rains, which average about 15-19 inches in the west, diminish and then cease almost completely in the Jordan valley and the region of the Dead Sea.

4.4 With the onset of the rainy season in the autumn the vegetation grows again and the cycle of agricultural work begins once more with ploughing and sowing. The end of the rain in the spring leads to the death of all the vegetation other than trees and bushes, though the seed germinates again in the autumn. The trees and bushes usually survive the burning heat of summer, provided that they have received enough water during the winter. This natural cycle also explains the nature of Canaanite religion: Baʻal, the god of the fertility of the soil and the crops, dies in the spring and is buried; now Lord Mot reigns, the god of death and the underworld. In autumn Baʻal rises again; first he fertilizes the soil with the rain (the classical authors described this as τὸ σπῆρμα τοῦ βααλ, 'the seed of Baʻal'), and then, at the end of the winter, he also fertilizes the flocks and the herds, again dying at the end of the spring. This religion is obviously a reproduction of the natural cycle, in an attempt to guarantee its regular occurrence.

5 Naturally the climate of the season also determines the flora and the fauna. Along with the climatic variety we therefore have a large variety of original vegetation and animals, within a very limited space.

Bibliography: Fauna and Flora of the Bible (Helps for Translators), The United Bible Societies, London and New York ²1980 (this book also provides a complete general bibliography on the subject); M.Zohary, *Plants of the Bible*, Cambridge 1982. Cf. also B.S.J.Isserlin, 'Ancient Forests in Palestine: Some Archaeological Indications', *PEQ* 86, 1955, 87f.; J.V.Thirgood, *Man and the Mediterranean Forest*, London 1981, 107-22.

5.1 As one might expect, the wild trees are usually to be found in the woods and the scrubland. In ancient times a good deal of the mountains and the plateaus seems to have been wooded, though we should never imagine ancient Palestine as having been one great forest, as was the case e.g. with central and northern Europe and North America. At all events the progressive exploitation of even the hill-country and the mountains for agriculture and pasturage, from the last centuries of the second millennium BC, along with a rapacious use of the resources provided by the forests, soon led to a marked reduction in the ancient woodland, and now it can be found in its original form only over a limited area of Upper Galilee and on Carmel. This original woodland is now rare, and the typical Mediterranean scrub, combined with some trees with tall trunks, is much more common.

5.1.1 Among the original trees of the region one might mention some kinds of oaks, the more widespread of which are the *quercus coccifera* and the *quercus aegilops*; the terebinth, *pistacia terebinthus*; and a local type of conifer, *pinus halepensis*. In the steppes we also find the tamarisk, *tamarix*, and various kinds of shrubs.

5.1.2 In the course of the last half-century enormous work has been done on reforestation, sponsored first by the British under the mandate and then by the Jewish National Fund; it has made a remarkable difference in the appearance of many areas and in the number of trees in them. One only has to travel from Jerusalem to Tel Aviv one way in a bus and the other in a train: in the bus one goes through an area which has been completely reforested, as far as the entry into the mountains through the *bab el-wād* (Arabic) or *ša'ar haggay* (Hebrew: coord. 136-152; for an explanation of this reference see 10.1 below); in the train one follows the picturesque and winding course of the old Ottoman railway, finished in 1892, which goes through areas which have not been reforested. The difference is amazing!

5.1.3 This work has introduced other kinds of plants into the area which are more resistant to drought, more suited to the climate, and therefore more economical from an agricultural point of view. Thus there are new forms of conifer and cypress, and in the marshy regions eucalyptus trees, imported from Australia. The original flora of the region have therefore been substantially changed.

5.1.4 Again, various kinds of shrubs and grasses are indigenous. The shrubs, which are often spiny (the so-called 'thorns' of the Bible) flower again at the end of the rainy season and then dry out once more in the summer; the grass begins to sprout during the rain, and then finally dries up during the course of the last siroccos, at the end of the spring.

5.2 As was evident from agricultural discoveries made during the excavations at Jericho in the 1950s, the region has been cultivated at least from the eighth millennium BC. Although it is not particularly fertile (there is nothing to match the 'black earth' of the Ukraine or the plains of North and South America), it has always produced what was needed to sustain its inhabitants, despite the interruption of the rains by the summer. In some cases it has provided an abundance of crops.

5.2.1 Native fruit trees include the classical olive, fig, almond and vine, this last being hung between other trees or cultivated on the ground. Nowadays wine is produced by Arab Christians and Israelis, since, like all alcoholic drinks, it is forbidden to Moslems. Apple and pear trees, sycamores, pistachio, walnut and almond trees can also be found.

5.2.2 Again, there are many different kinds of cereal crops, mainly barley and wheat, which are grown almost everywhere. As I mentioned above, in ancient times Transjordan was the granary of the region. The harvest takes place between March and May, the threshing at the beginning of the summer.

5.2.3 In the tropical regions of the Jordan valley there are date-palms and bananas, both intensively cultivated: in ancient times Jericho was even called the 'City of Palms' (Deut. 34.3; Judg.3.13; I Chron. 28.15). In recent decades mangoes and avocados have also been introduced.

5.2.4 The cultivation of citrus fruits, lemons, oranges, tangerines and grapefruit is a relatively recent development; nowadays they are one of the main agricultural riches of the region. They are cultivated especially along the coast, hence the trademark 'Jaffa' for Israeli fruit; today the ancient city has become a southern suburb of Tel Aviv. According to legend citrus fruits were introduced into the country, along with the tomato, by Italian Franciscans in the seventeenth century.

5.2.5 The introduction of the prickly pear (sabra) also seems to be fairly recent; the Arabs use it for fencing, like people in the south of Italy. The fruit is eaten and the 'peel', treated properly, can be used as food for livestock in times of drought.

5.2.6 Agriculture has been radically transformed over the last half-century, first in the Jewish agricultural colonies and then in the state of Israel. The smallholdings, usually consisting of farms run by families, have disappeared, giving place to large-scale undertakings which were granted land at one time by the Jewish National Fund and later by the state: this has produced co-operatives (Hebrew *mōšāb*), some of which have a socialist structure (Hebrew *qibbūṣ*). However, the ancient farm, originally run by a family or the property of the village, which assigned land in rotation to those who had a right to it, has remained in areas where the population is predominantly Arab. Its productivity per acre is usually inferior in quantity and often also in quality, unless the crop is a specialist one or is particularly valuable, calling for a good deal of manual work by individuals.

5.2.7 On the Jewish co-operative farms the traditional crops have largely been replaced by crops which on the one hand resemble those in central and southern Europe, and on the other hand resist the heat and can be harvested mechanically. On the Arab farms, however, the traditional crops are still produced on a large scale.

6 The differences in climate favour a difference in fauna, as they do in flora.

6.1.1 The marked increase in the Israeli and Arab population over the last half-century and the intensification of agriculture has had serious consequences for wild animals; it has increasingly limited their habitat and therefore reduced their numbers, where it has not made them completely extinct. That is the case, for example, with the wolf, the hyena, the wild dog and the wild cat, the fox, the wild boar, the hare, the wild goat and the badger. Other animals of the Bible are now extinct, like the bear and the Asiatic lion; a few bears still survive in the scant protection of the Syrian and Lebanese mountains. In Israel the threatened species are now adequately protected, but little can be done about conserving their habitat, in a situation similar to that in any industrialized country.

6.1.2 The birds have also suffered from the reduction in their natural habitat. Among the birds of prey there are the falcon, the vulture, and, very occasionally, the eagle, while the others include the quail, the guinea fowl and other game birds; however, the fact that Moslems and Jews usually only eat meat which has been ritually slaughtered much reduces the effect of hunting and favours the preservation of the species.

6.1.3 There are abundant reptiles: snakes, lizards and tortoises. Down to the end of the last century there was even evidence of crocodiles on the tributaries to the left of the Jordan.

6.1.4 From time immemorial fish have been part of the wealth of the Sea of Galilee. Today, on ground which is not really suitable for agriculture, artificial pools have been made and stocked with fresh-water (or, rarely, with salt-water) fish. As is well known, there is virtually no form of animal life in the Dead Sea because of the high level of its salinity.

6.1.5 Among insects, the best known is the locust because of the damage which it has caused over the centuries (cf. Joel 1). Today it is possible to take effective measures against it, neutralizing or at least containing the damage it causes. However, even at the beginning of the First World War a particularly serious plague of locusts reduced the countryside to famine, contributing not a little to the success of the English army on the Turkish front in 1917-1918. (For this occurrence see the classical article, with copious documentation, by J.D.Whiting, *National Geographic Magazine* 28, 1915, 511-50.)

6.2.1 Until very recently the ox and the ass were the main domestic animals; the horse appears more rarely, being considered a luxury. In biblical times the ox and the ass were the working animals, as they often still are today for the Arab peasant (*fellah*). Nowadays they are limited essentially to regions which are hardly accessible to motorized vehicles. Otherwise, these traditional friends and collaborators of mankind are being condemned to progressive extinction as mechanized agriculture is also spreading among the Arabs.

6.2.2 The same also goes for the camel (the dromedary with the single hump); it is now used almost exclusively in the steppes and in adjacent regions, where it is reared by the Bedouin; hence it is possible to come across herds of camels in the central and southern Negeb. However, in those areas where agriculture is intensive, while the camel appeared frequently in the 1960s, it is becoming increasingly rare; it, too, tends to be replaced where possible by motorized vehicles.

6.2.3 The main domestic animals kept nowadays are the cow, the sheep and the goat, all for their milk, meat and hides; the sheep and the goat are also kept for their wool. The cow is now generally reared on mechanized farms in order to increase production; however, sheep and goats have to be put out to pasture if they are to produce good-quality wool, so Arab and Israeli shepherds can often be found in the scrub. In the biblical period the cow was usually a luxury and the most common beasts west of the Jordan were the 'small cattle', Hebrew *ṣōʾn;* however, in Bashan, present-day Hauran, in northern Transjordan, the rearing of cattle was common and their quality was proverbial (cf. Amos 4.1).

6.2.4 Among domestic animals which have recently been imported mention might be made of various kinds of poultry, ducks, geese and turkeys. Here, too, breeding has been rationalized among the Israelis and has a more traditional form among the Arabs, though there the new techniques are also making increasing strides.

7 The Old Testament provides a good deal of information about the peoples of Canaan at the time of the Israelite conquest; it is said that there are seven of them.

7.1 However, three of the seven are generic designations for the inhabitants of the whole region, i.e. 'Canaanites', 'Amorites' and 'Hittites'; the last two probably derive from nomenclature in Mesopotamia, where at various times the region is denoted by *amurru, ḥatti* and derivatives, as is rightly pointed out by scholars today (above n.5 and below, n.8).

7.2 There remain the names of four other populations, listed in varying order: Hivites, Perizzites, Girgashites and Jebusites.[8] Of these only the Jebusites and the Hivites are connected with particular cities, the former with Jerusalem and the latter with Shechem (below, VII.2.3); however, these are associations which appear only in the Hebrew Bible and not in other texts. In extra-biblical texts the two places are never associated with these peoples.[9] The Hivites have been sometimes connected with the Hurrians, a population from Asia Minor whose language is not Semitic; of the others we know nothing as research now stands. We do not even know whether the names are real and therefore recall peoples which actually existed, or whether they are mythical designations, or indeed purely imaginary, as was the case, for example, with the Rephaim, whom we shall discuss below (VII.2.10.6).

7.3 However, there is mention of one alien people, the Philistines, who were hostile to Israel from the start; as we have seen, they also gave a name to the region. We shall consider them below (III.5.2-3).

7.4 Around Israel we find peoples with whom the Hebrews had dealings over the centuries: to the north the city-states of Phoenicia; to the East, in Transjordan, the Ammonites, the Moabites and the Edomites, all, along with Israel, speaking variant dialects of the same language. The people of Transjordan settled in their region rather later than Israel. In Syria, however, we find the Aramaeans, who spoke a different language, Aramaic, even if they too were part of the Western Semitic group.

8 Given the present state of research it is impossible to reconstruct the ethnic composition of the region at the time of the arrival of the Israelites; however, we do have important first-hand information about its political structure and economy, in sources which are a little earlier than the conquest. This appears first of all in the archives of el-'Amarna, a place in Egypt about half-way between Cairo and Luxor. These archives contain the correspondence which came to the court of the Pharaohs Amenophis III and IV (Akhenaten), between the end of the fifteenth and the middle of the fourteenth century BC from Egyptian vassals in the Near East; a large number of them were Canaanite. The correspondence has been collected and published in what is now a classic critical edition by J.A.Knudtzon, *Die El-Amarna Tafeln*, Leipzig I, 1908; II, 1915; after more than half a century, the work needs to be revised in many respects. Some texts discovered later were published by A.F.Rainey, *The El-Amarna Tablets*, AOAT 8, Neukirchen ²1978. The texts from Ugarit, a Syrian city-state just north of Latakia and destroyed in the twelfth century are also important; the ruins of Ugarit, near to present-day *raś eš-šamrā*, were excavated from 1929 onwards. The material relevant to this analysis has been collected and analysed by M.Heltzer, *The Rural Community in Ancient Ugarit*, Wiesbaden 1976; id., *The Internal Organization of the Kingdom of Ugarit*, Wiesbaden 1982; cf. also M.Liverani, 'Ras Shamra-Ugarit', in 'Territoire et population – 2', *SDB* IX, 1979, 1316-23.

8.1 The social and political picture which emerges from the el-'Amarna letters is particularly interesting. It shows various city-states, all governed by a ruler who is often a foreigner, though he never bears the title king (perhaps out of respect for the Pharaoh). From Ugarit, where that title does, however, occur, we have texts which provide information on the internal social and economic situation. Below the person of the monarch, around the palace, we have a structure rather like a pyramid: there are the noblemen, who constitute an assembly, an institution which seems to have had considerable power even over against the crown; then there are landowners, merchants and craftsmen (organized into 'guilds'), manual workers and unskilled labourers, and finally slaves. There seems to have been a similar structure around the temple, which thus formed an alternative centre of power. From el-'Amarna we also know that the city-states were for the most part located in the plains and commanded only very small territories (the cities themselves were very small compared with modern ones: Hazor, regarded as one of the largest, measured less than thirty-five acres!); however, they were densely populated and intensively cultivated. In the hill-country the city states could be counted on the fingers of one hand: we know of the existence only of Hebron, Jerusalem and Shechem; Hazor, mentioned above, was on the border between the two zones.

8.2 The capital cities were surrounded by countryside in which there could be lesser centres. It seems that on the one hand there was no effective power in the country to counter the actions of the city-state and that on the other hand it was the greatest producer of goods in the principal economic sectors of the time, namely agriculture and cattle.

8.3 In other words, the capital of the city-state exercised economic and political power through the palace and the army, and its riches were based on crafts developing the products of the countryside and trading in its products. The inhabitants of the countryside themselves do not seem to have had any power in decision-making.[10]

8.4 A situation of this kind might suggest a vigorous and continuing conflict between the city, which did the exploiting, and the countryside, the productive region which was exploited. However, the reality seems to have been different: in the el-'Amarna texts, although we find accounts of rebellions and of kings forced to flee, none of these movements arises in the country, in an attempt to throw off the yoke of the city; they occur actually within the city, usually between the assembly of the nobility and the monarch, i.e. between groups which already held power in one way or another, or as a result of groups of refugees.

8.5 One of the most tangible results of these conflicts was the emergence of various kinds of refugees, a development to which we shall return in more detail (V.3.2.4). Those exiled from one city-state took refuge in another one nearby and with their intrigues endangered not only the place from which they had originally come but often also the place which had taken them in; as a result this was involved against its will in conflicts which originally had nothing to do with it.

8.6 It is not surprising that the combination of these factors - fragmentation and often conflict at a political level, hostilities within the city-state, the remarkable economic prosperity and the presence of sparsely populated territories in the hill-country and on the steppes – encouraged the settlement of those groups which formed the ancestors of Israel, and, in the neighbouring regions, of those from whom the peoples of Syria and Transjordan descended.

9 There is one last point. As can be seen here and there from what I have already said, the region of Syria and Palestine has always been the bridge between Africa and Asia, and therefore between Egypt on the one side and the Hittite and Mesopotamian empires on the other. Every power therefore sought to control it. So from the end of the second millennium BC to the middle of the first millennium we find almost constant conflict between Egypt on the one hand and successi-

vely the Hittites, Assyria and Babylon on the other. This is another of the objective features which have characterized the region, almost down to the present day.

10 For a better knowledge of the region it is necessary to use the many working tools which are now at our disposal.

10.1 The best map is that made by the Survey of Israel. It exists in an edition of two sheets on a scale of 1: 250,000, and is supplemented by another two sheets on the same scale to cover Sinai. There are two editions, one physical and one political; the former is more useful for the student. The physical and political map on a scale of 1:100,000, on 22 sheets, is much more detailed. Both are available in Hebrew and English editions. Then there is a series of maps on a scale of 1:50,000, only in Hebrew; only some of them are available commercially. They are edited by the Israeli Society for the Protection of Nature. Finally, there is a series of maps on a scale of 1:25,000 which are not available commercially, but can be consulted in libraries. The 1:100,000 series is regularly brought up to date; the 1:50,000 series is often relatively old. Another, extremely good, map is published as an appendix to *BHH* IV, 1979; it is in two leaves, on a scale of 1:300,000, and is edited by E. Höhne.[11]

10.2 Other indispensable working tools are the various geographies of the Bible, which enable one to follow the discussions and the various theories about the identification of ancient places (below VII.5.1.1). However, some of these do not give the co-ordinates on the maps mentioned above, and this is an obvious limitation. I would refer to the following:

10.2.1 F.-M. Abel, *Géographie de la Palestine*, Paris I, 1933; II, 1938, recently reprinted;

10.2.2 M. du Buit, *Géographie de la Terre Sainte*, Paris I-II, 1958;

10.2.3 J. Simons, *The Geographical and Topographical Texts of the Old Testament*, Leiden 1959;

10.2.4 D. Baly, *The Geography of the Bible*, New York [2]1974;

10.2.5 Y. Aharoni, *The Land of the Bible*, Philadelphia and London [2]1979;

10.2.6 Y. Karmon, *Israel. Eine geographische Landeskunde*, Darmstadt 1983;

10.2.7 O. Keel and H. Küchler, *Orte und Landschaften der Bibel*, Zurich and Göttingen I, 1985; II, 1982; III is planned for 1986. This is the most complete guide, and is up to date on geography, climate, topography and archaeology.

10.2.8 E. K. Vogel and B. Holtzclaw, 'Bibliography of Holy Land Sites', *HUCA* 42, 1971, 1-98 and 52, 1981, 1-92.

10.2.9 Of the many archaeologies, the most recent and up-to-date is

Y. Aharoni, *The Archaeology of the Land of Israel*, Philadelphia and London 1982.

10.3 Of these works, the first is now a classic even if in some respects it is out of date; the second is a supplement to *La Bible de Jérusalem* and is very useful because of its brevity; the third is complete, but has an awkwardly large format and is produced in a luxurious edition, which makes it very expensive. The book by Baly is one of the most useful studies available, and the same can be said of the two books by Aharoni. The recent volumes by Keel and Karmon are scholarly and up-to-date.

10.4 In this book I have largely followed the details given by Aharoni (1979).

II

METHODOLOGY, BIBLIOGRAPHY
AND SOURCES

1 There are now many scientific and critical histories of Israel, up-to-date in method and bibliographies (below, 6.2-5). Many biblical scholars have produced such works from the Second World War onwards, and as one might expect, few Near Eastern scholars have failed to incorporate the history of Israel into their works. To judge from the number of histories of Israel which have been published, the years between 1940 and 1980 have been the most productive.

Select bibliography: H.Schulte, *Die Enstehung der Geschichtsschreibung im Alten Israel*, BZAW 128, Berlin 1972; M.Weippert, 'Fragen des israelitischen Geschichtsbewusstseins', *VT* 23, 1973, 415-42; J.M.Miller, *The Old Testament and the Historian*, Philadelphia 1976; Z.Kallai, 'The United Monarchy of Israel – A Focal Point in Israelite Historiography', *IEJ* 27, 1977, 130-9; J.A.Soggin, 'The Davidic-Solomonic Kingdom', in J.H.Hayes-J.M.Miller*, 332-80; id., 'The History of Israel – A Study in Some Questions of Method', *EI* 14, 1978, 44*-51*; W.W.Hallo, 'Biblical History in its Ancient Near Eastern Setting: The Contextual Approach', in *Scripture in Context – Essays on the Comparative Method*, ed. C.O.Evans, W.W.Hallo, J.B.White, Pittsburgh 1980, (1-26) 9ff., 14ff.; M.Liverani, 'Le "origini" d'Israele – progetto irrealizzabile di ricerche etnogenetica', *RivBib* 28, 1980, 9-32; J.M.Sasson, 'On Choosing Models for Recreating Israelite Pre-Monarchical Israel', *JSOT* 21, 1981, 3-24; J.A.Soggin, 'Problemi di storia e di storiografia nell'antico Israele', *Hen* 4, 1982, 1-10; A.Lemaire, 'Recherches actuelles sur l'origine de l'ancien Israël', *Journal Asiatique* 270, 1982, 5-24; A.Malamat, 'The Proto-History of Israel', in *The Word of the Lord Shall Go Forth. Essays... D.N.Freedman*, Philadelphia 1983, 303-13; B.J.Diebner, 'Kultus, Sakralrecht und die Anfänge des Geschichtsdenkens in "Israel"' - Denkansatz zu einer Hypothese', *DBAT* 17, 1983, 1-20, and for a critical survey of the

history of Israel, its methodology, and the basic approach to it cf.
Hayes-Miller* (below, 6.4.8) and H. Cazelles* (6.4.11), 1ff.

1.1 Paradoxically, it now seems increasingly difficult to write a history
of Israel, especially from its beginnings, after more than a century of
scientific studies in historical criticism. Almost all the histories of Israel
produced over this period have the same basic approach, as a result of
which they all arrive at virtually analogous results. The history by
Martin Noth* is slightly different and methodologically important; it
begins in the last centuries of the second millennium BC. However,
there are signs in some most recent work, e.g. the *History** edited by
J.H.Hayes and J.M.Miller and the monographs by J.Van Seters and
T.L.Thompson, that this consensus leaves much to be desired. Some
basic assumptions are not as firm as they might seem. The problems
and possible solutions can only become clear if we look at questions of
method and sources all over again. Here we must begin by asking, in
what circumstances, where and when, do we find the origins of the
people which in the Bible bears the name of Israel?

1.2 One thing seems certain. At the time of the letters contained in
the el-'Amarna archives (above I.8), not only is there no reference to a
group which bears this name; there is not even a place for it in the
region. Then, in the last decades of the second millennium BC, there,
unexpectedly, is Israel, which rapidly develops into an empire. Those
are the accredited facts in the present state of research.

1.3 However, as M.Liverani (1980) has recently confirmed, the
problem of the birth of a people does not have a solution from the
inside, in Israel or anywhere else. Only when a people already exists
and has acquired certain structures does it begin to ask about its own
origins, and wants to know how it has come to be what it now is; it is
not difficult to realize that even centuries can pass between the
beginning of this process of ethnogenesis and the awareness of a people
which makes it ask such questions, and it will become aware of its
particular ethnic character only in the final phase of that long process.
Only then, as it looks back, will the people try to explain the factors
which caused or shaped its own formation.

1.4 Now we must accept one fact (and I want to stress this, to avoid
any misunderstanding and any *a priori* assertions to the contrary). In
the historical period, traditions, whether oral or written, can still exist
which go back to particular phases in this process and therefore allow
us to reconstruct part of the development, even if only in outline and
in particular areas. However, when we look at those traditions that we
do possess, the facts that are there tend to be very few. At the beginning
of his career, the great American archaeologist and philologist W.F.Al-
bright[1] gave a warning: 'The long memory possessed by semi-civilized

peoples for historical fact is a pious fiction of over-zealous apologists...!'
– a view which, however, was soon to be replaced by other much more
optimistic ones.

1.5 It has been said that the work of the historian can be usefully
compared to that of a detective. I would like to develop the simile to
include the whole function of the court in a criminal trial: it cross-
examines the witnesses, examines the evidence, and evaluates the
circumstances, and in this way arrives at a verdict that may be
considered to be based on an authentic and normative reconstruction
of events. However, we should also recall that while they were being
handed down, the traditions, whether oral or written, were often
subjected, like the evidence in a trial, to the phenomenon which in
legal jargon is called 'contamination'. This happens quite simply
because, even leaving aside carelessness or forgetfulness, errors or
omissions, those who originally handed down the traditions were
influenced by different interests from the ones that motivated their
successors; and the latter interests determined what information was
collected and handed down when other information, probably most of
it, was discarded. Added to that, it may well be that some statements
are the product of later theological or philosophical reflection, of
psychologizing, or in extreme cases, even products of the imagination,
for apologetic or polemical purposes.

1.6 Rome under Augustus is a good illustration, because it is much
less controversial. Livy and Tacitus as historians, and Virgil as an epic
poet, have handed on information about the migration of Aeneas from
Troy to Italy, about the foundation of Rome, the growth of the Roman
republic, and the time of the Punic wars. Often, as we know, these are
legends, like the migration of Aeneas and the stories of Romulus and
Remus; at other times we find elements which are historically probable,
even if as things are there is no way of trying to prove their truth, as in
the case of the relationship between Rome and Alba Longa in the early
days (Liverani, 1980). We also have material which seems to be more
concrete, especially in the works of Livy and Tacitus, but often the
particular concern of these historians is with famous men and women,
either as examples with whom others can identify and whom they can
therefore imitate, or sometimes as deterrents, arousing aversion and
therefore not to be imitated in any way.[2] Now we should certainly not
reject *a priori* the possibility that this material goes back through ancient
traditions to real experience and therefore provides factual information.
However, the problem seems to me to be rather different. It arises
when the historian is on longer a pedagogue but concerned for
historiography in the modern sense. What possible importance could
stories of heroes like Horatius Coclites and Mucius Scaevola, of virtuous
women like Cornelia and Lucretia, of Cincinnatus the dictator, who

returned quietly to country life after having successfully held supreme office in the state, have for someone seeking to write a modern history of ancient Rome? What is he to make of the death of the consul Attilius Regulus for keeping his word, finding himself in an irresolvable conflict with loyalty to his country? These last two episodes in particular have an obvious place in traditional pedagogy as edifying episodes worthy of imitation (and they were probably meant as polemic against later politicians whose morality was very different); but what importance could they have for a reconstruction of the institution of the dictatorship at the beginning of the Republic or for a study of the duties of the consuls during the Punic wars? The same goes for the virtuous women whom I have mentioned. To know that there were heroes and heroines at the end of the period of the monarchy and in the earliest days of the Republic may well produce good teaching and amount to an implied negative judgment on other, later periods, but it does not help much with a reconstruction of political and economic history and of the institutions of the period. Thus to argue as a historian that the gesture by Mucius Scaevola persuaded Porsena to return to his own territory is no more than congenial naivety, congenial because it is prompted by memories of school-days.

1.7 What we have here, then, are positive heroes and heroines, examples which could inspire later generations (and they have performed these functions admirably, right down to the present day) and which their successors could be exhorted to imitate; they are probably also embodiments of the hope of the more enlightened members of the court at the time of Augustus that, for his greater glory, the ancient virtues, the *pietas* of days gone by, might be reborn in a return of conditions not dissimilar from those of the golden age. Certainly it seems more difficult to set out to clarify, for example, the relations between Rome as a growing power and the Etruscans, to see how things came to a final break, and why Rome chose a rather unusual form of government instead of the more usual form of the monarchy, which it had had for some centuries, or to explain how the new institutions worked. However, despite these rather negative considerations we can usually discover a good deal about a number of institutions: the composition and functioning of the senate, the organization of the patricians and the plebeians, the first 'class struggles' in ancient Rome, the treatment of the Italici, and so on. Still, this comes from other sources.

2 Despite the basic differences, which obviously relate to religion, in a number of ways the situation over the origins of Israel seems remarkably similar.

2.1 Here, too, we find a tradition according to which the distinctive feature of the nation is to be found in a group of alien origin, which arrived in its new homeland through a migration following a basically negative experience. Ancient Israel (and to a large extent 'historical', later Israel, too) also abounded in figures whom we might call examples: what happened to them, more or less precariously connected with the historical and narrative plots and then collected into larger, more coherent cycles, served as an inspiration and example for later generations (the Puritans of North America in the seventeenth century seem an obvious parallel, even if this is a limiting case), and for the 'edification' of the civil and religious community. So it is that we find Abraham, who believes and hopes against any rational hope; Moses, who frees his own people and leads them through many dangers to the promised land, having renounced a tranquil, easy and cultured life; Jacob, whose lies and deceits brought him immediate advantages, though in the long run they created a good deal of embarrassment and difficulty. Here, then, is a series of traditions about 'exemplary' figures from the prehistory of Israel which were also collected, edited and transmitted in their present form (the only one that we possess) by redactors living many centuries after the events to which they relate: the J and E sources of the Pentateuch, the 'collector' of Joshua and Judges, the author of the 'succession narrative' (below III.1.5.3) in II Samuel and I Kings. These are sources which are traditionally dated from the time of the early monarchy, with the eighth century as a *terminus ante quem*, even if today there are some writers who would prefer to make these dates much later,[3] even bringing them down to a time shortly before the Babylonian exile (below, XI.7). Others go so far as to reject the documentary hypothesis in the form in which it has been presented[4] – and that does not seem at all improbable in the case of E. However, in turn these sources, too, were collected and re-edited in still larger complexes, during the exile and afterwards: foremost among them is the Deuteronomistic historian (Dtr), who was also responsible for a first edition of the first four books of the Pentateuch and for the books of some pre-exilic prophets like Amos, Hosea, Jeremiah, and perhaps also Proto-Isaiah[5] and Micah; then there is also P for all the Pentateuch and fragments of Joshua, and finally the 'Chronicler' for the historical books.

2.2 So it seems clear that the horizon of the redactors of the Pentateuch, the historical books and the prophetic books is chiefly the exilic and the post-exilic period, even when the texts are dealing with earlier themes, and that the problems with which they are concerned chiefly reflect the consequences of that first, fundamental break in the history of Israel represented by the exile in Babylon and the end both of political independence and of the dynasty which reigned by divine promise and to which an eternal kingdom had been promised (II Sam.7). They were also concerned with the new political and religious problems which arose from this new situation: above all the rise of a regime which, following Josephus' definition (below 7.2.1), is often defined as a 'theocracy', though in reality it will have been a 'hierocracy'. Little or no difference is made to these reflections by the fact that such a 'hierocratic' regime only emerged two centuries later than is commonly supposed, at the end of Persian rule or even later, rather than at the time of the return from the exile. This is indicated by the sources discovered during the 1970s (cf. below XII.5.3.6).

2.3 Here and there the accounts of the migrations of the patriarchs to the Promised Land or within its boundaries certainly reflect features from the time of the united monarchy (below, V.1), so it is possible to look for an earlier phase in the collection of traditions during this period; however, these traditions fit even better into the exilic and post-exilic period, when Israel's political independence was over and the Davidic dynasty had fallen, never to rise again, and when the people found themselves first deported far from their own country and then strangers in a homeland under alien occupation. And it is precisely in this context that the migration of the family of Abraham from 'Ur of the Chaldaeans' to Haran would fit perfectly. Instead of looking for improbable explanations, would it not be much better to see here the narrative of the itinerary followed by the exiles on their return home? The mention of Ur, which is otherwise anachronistic, would then become perfectly logical, given that the exiles settled in the south-eastern region of Mesopotamia.

2.3.1 A substantial diaspora took shape abroad, first in Babylon and Persia, then also in Egypt and in the Western world. In this new situation of oppression and dispersion, the divine promises originally made to the patriarchs, that Israel would become a great nation and would have its own land, took on a new existential value for those who had been deprived of all these things. And the exodus from Egypt, the journey through the desert, the conquest of their own land, the period of the judges, events now presented in an essentially theological rather than a political and historical light, together with the formation of the tribal league and its stress on common worship as a factor of political as well as religious unity, fit well into the context of the return of the exiles to their homeland; it is no coincidence that Second Isaiah (chs.40-55) presents this return in terms of a 'second exodus'. All this would explain why there is never any firm reference to the Pharaohs of whom the Bible speaks here, and who lived before the end of the tenth century BC. The absence of this detail poses usually insurmountable problems in identifying them, suppose that we accept that the redactors who began to hand down these traditions were interested in such dates. As to the exodus, P.A.H. de Boer put forward a very interesting theory, though it still has to be verified:[6] in his view the negative phase in the evaluation of Egypt characteristic of the accounts of the exodus only begins with the exile; to begin with, that country is seen, rather, as the land of refuge *par excellence* (below V.1.2.2), a view which also appears in the infancy narratives of the Gospels (cf. Matt.2.13ff.).

2.4 By contrast, the tribal league, with its eminently theocratic content, appears not only as a valid precursor of the post-exilic hierocracy, thus serving to legitimate it, but also as an authentic alternative which preceded the fallen monarchy; in both cases, in fact God himself and not yet or no longer an instrument of human origin appears as the effective sovereign, who exercises his own power through the central sanctuary and the human instruments at its head. In both cases we still have the complete identity of the people as a religious community with the people as an ethnic and political entity, governed by the priesthood ('the kingdom of priests', the 'holy nation', of which Ex.19.1ff. speaks, below XIII.11.3.5). As to the pre-exilic period, from the little that we know we can say that the situation was more complex: all the Canaanites of Palestine and the peoples of the surrounding lands occupied by the united monarchy or later by Israel or Judah were, politically speaking, subjects in one way or another of the sovereign of the united kingdom and, later, of the sovereign of one or other of the two Hebrew kingdoms, even if they were obviously not part of the religious community of Israel.

2.5 We find similar methods of reassessment and reinterpretation in the treatment of the institution of the monarchy. The biblical tradition (and we shall be returning to the subject, III.4.1 below) is unequivocal: once there was a time when Israel was not governed by a monarchy but ruled by a tribal league. For those who handed down this tradition, this was the normative period, and ideal from many points of view (as was that of the earlier Republic for the Roman historians). Then the monarchy was introduced (all the indications are that this was in the last decades of the second millennium BC) under the pressure of specific military and political events, especially the need to offer strong resistance in the south-west to the Philistines, and to the neighbours which threatened Israel from the east. So the monarchy came into being in circumstances not unlike those which led to the institution of the dictatorship in the Roman republic; paradoxically, in Israel, too (as in imperial Rome), the monarchy arose through the transformation of what was originally an office held for life into a hereditary one.[7] Now, however, in the biblical narrative the institution of the monarchy appears as apostasy from the true faith, expressed in the form of rule through the God of Israel: those who desire an earthly king in fact reject the divine kingship (I Sam. 8.7). The situation seems very much the same in Judg.19-21; here we cannot fail to note the contrast between the pro-monarchical affirmations in 18.1; 17.6; 19.1; 21.25 on the one hand, which attribute the anarchy prevalent at the time to the lack of a monarchical power, and on the other the presence of the tribunal of the tribal league, quite capable of resolving any problems, even the most serious – if necessary with force, where persuasion was not enough. Here the institution of the monarchy clearly seems superfluous, given that the tribal organization functioned perfectly; hence the impiety in the request for a king.[8]

Now clearly we cannot rule out the possibility that here we encounter two basic tendencies which coexisted in Israelite society down the centuries, one theocratic and hierocratic, and the other favourable to the monarchy. We have impressive evidence of the former in the apologia of Jotham (Judg.9.7ff.), while elsewhere, too, we hear of criticism and rebellion against the institution on the part of the prophets. However, in this case it seems more reasonable to see in the narrative the hand of a later redactor, probably belonging to the last, exilic, phase of Deuteronomy, who is concerned to show the basically negative character of the Israelite monarchy, the institution and the aberration to which the catastrophe of the exile was chiefly attributed. This clearly confuses what had been wrong political choices (albeit in a situation which did not allow much room for manoeuvre) with a considerable degree of impiety on the level of faith.

2.6 One final feature clearly emerges from these considerations. The picture that we have of the earliest period of Israel is that presented by the pre-exilic period generally and profoundly influenced, not to say determined, by the exilic and post-exilic re-reading and redaction of the texts.[9] Any critical *a priori* evaluation of post-exilic Judaism in favour of a supposed purity in the pre-exilic period, any negative reflections on the 'legalism' of the former as compared with the 'prophetic' and therefore positive character of the latter therefore seems no longer tenable historically. The Hebrew Bible as it has been transmitted is for the most part the product of the thought and work of that post-exilic period of which a number of scholars, including J.Wellhausen,[10] the founder of modern historical criticism of the Bible, have had such a negative view.

2.7 Since these are the circumstances in which the majority of the books of the Bible came into being, it is always a difficult undertaking to establish the antiquity of individual traditions. In any case, even when traditions do seem to be early, it is clear that they have been separated from their original context and inserted into a new context. This is a redactional procedure which inevitably had a marked effect on the interpretation of these traditions, modifying their content, even where the form seems to have remained the same.

2.8 Finally, what has been said so far should have made one thing clear; when we begin to write a history of Israel, we too shall be writing an essentially secular history, a history which therefore leaves out views which Israel had of itself, like 'people of God' or 'elect people'. The religion of Israel and its sacred history are an integral part of Israelite thought, and therefore they too are an element in the history of the people.[11]

3 Where, then, does a history of Israel begin? In other words, is there a time after which the material in the tradition begins to offer credible accounts, information about individuals who existed and events which happened or are at least probable, when it indicates important events in the economic and political sphere, and their consequences?

3.1 Such questions are not new; they have been asked for more than a century. In 1869 the Dutchman Abraham Kuenen and in 1885 the German Bernhard Stade put them in exactly the same terms,[12] and each presented his own solution. Moreover, the legitimacy of such demands is generally recognized. The North-American Assyriologist W.W.Hallo, who is very critical of the comments which I shall go on to make, accepts them fully. Now over the course of the last decade I have come to the conclusion that the answer should be to point to the united kingdom of Judah and Israel under David and Solomon, a kingdom which included most of the neighbouring countries as well (see below III.5; this theory was also put forward earlier by B.Stade). It was in fact from that time on that Israel began to exist not only as an ethnic group (which would be formed by the tribes once they had settled in their own territories, as A. Malamat, 1983, following M.Noth, wants to suggest), but also as a political group, in that it was constituted as a state. From then on, therefore, reflection on its own past began to be both possible and significant, and it would appear disconcerting (even if the example of ancient Rome shows us that this is neither a unique nor an isolated phenomenon) that Israel (or at least its basic nucleus) was not originally part of the indigenous population of Palestine, but arrived in the region by means of a migration from abroad: the tradition points to Egypt and Babylonia. At the end of this process it was involved in a conflict with the native population.

3.2 It was with the formation of the state, first as a nation and then as a territory, that for the first time Israel was faced with the problem of its own national identity, its own right to exercise a decisive function in the region, and its own legitimacy to be what it had meanwhile become. It seems to be no coincidence that it is only from then on that we have the first political, administrative and economic information (below, IV.3 and 5). To go back to the time of the exodus from Egypt as the period in which Israel acquired its own 'group identity', 'the awareness of a collective destiny', which is what W.W.Hallo would prefer, would be to use these somewhat rhetorical formulas to cloak a remarkable degree of naivety, if we look at the proposal in the light of what I have said so far.[13]

3.3 However, there are many problems even over the empire of David and Solomon, certainly more than we can solve.

3.3.1 First of all there is the fact, which I have already mentioned, that the sources for our knowledge of the united kingdom were themselves also edited at a late date; thus they reflect the problems of later periods in which the people had undergone some extremely disturbing experiences. At that time reflection on the valour and the victories of David, on the wisdom, the riches and the magnificence of Solomon, the frontiers and the imperial character of the new state, could have had a special significance.

3.3.2 Then there is one clearly disconcerting point: it is a well known fact (which has recently been confirmed by J.M.Sasson[14]) that there is no trace of the empire of David and Solomon in any of the ancient Near Eastern texts of the period, which is all the more strange when we think of the importance attributed to it not only by the Hebrew Bible but also by the New Testament tradition.

3.3.3 Is it then possible that this, too, is a pseudo-historical, artificial tradition aimed at glorifying a past which never existed in order to compensate for a dull and grey present? This has recently been argued by M.C.Astour,[15] who thinks that here we have texts which even date from the Persian period, given that the northern boundary of the empire would be that of the satrapy of Transeuphrates (below, XII.3.1.1). As I have already pointed out, a similar theory has been put forward by G. Garbini: on the best of interpretations, David and Solomon will have ruled over a much reduced territory, including Judah, Israel and Philistine and Moabite areas. These are questions which are neither absurd nor wrong-headed, but show the obvious limitations we come up against in seeking to deal with periods the sources for which present so many difficulties.

3.3.4 One thing remains certain. If we leave aside the stele of Pharaoh Merneptah from the second half of the thirteenth century BC, the significance of which is not always clear (cf. 7.3.1), Israel appears in ancient Near Eastern texts only from the second half of the ninth century onwards, in the stele of Mesha king of Moab, and a little later in the Assyrian annals. The toponyms given by Pharaoh Shoshenk or Shishak I in the course of his expedition to Palestine, shortly after the break-up of the empire (below IX.1.4), do not provide us with any information about Israel as a political entity.[16] Is it possible, then, that here we have accounts which, if not imaginary, are at least considerably exaggerated, to compensate for Israel's dull present? That is certainly possible, but improbable: in fact there are too many details of a political, economic, administrative and commercial kind, too many features bound up with the culture of the time, not to mention the negative elements which are introduced to make the narratives in question anything but a romanticized glorification of the past, even if, as we shall see, romanticized elements are also present.

3.4 Beginning with the empire of David and Solomon also allows us to take up the discussion where it was left some decades ago by the German scholar Albrecht Alt, who was followed by the Italian Sabatino Moscati.[17] For these scholars the contrast between the territorial and political aspects of the region at the time of the el-'Amarna letters and those of a few centuries later, at the time of the united monarchy, is a very real one. Therefore it is between these two extremes that we must look for what is usually called the Israelite 'conquest' of Palestine, in whatever way it may have taken place.

3.4.1 So it is not rash to continue to argue, albeit with the qualifications I have already made, that the period of the united monarchy is a point of reference from which to begin a historical study of ancient Israel. And unless appearances are deceiving, this was also the period when Israel itself felt the need to make a first collection of its own earliest traditions. Here the proto-history[18] was understood, probably not without reason, as the formative period of Israel as an ethnic and national entity. This process may have lasted for quite a long time, extending as far as the exile and beyond.

4.1 At this point I want to try to make a preliminary evaluation of the character of the traditions which Israel narrated about its own proto-history. The whole of Part Two will be devoted to a more detailed examination.

4.1.1 It should be remembered that even where investigation reveals the substantial antiquity of a tradition or collection of traditions, the material has in all cases been detached from its original context and is now inserted into a new context, that planned by the redactor. Moreover what we now have is the result of a selection, a sifting of materials, made for motives quite independent of those which originally led to their being handed down. Of course this process happens in all history writing; obviously the historian should not and cannot describe everything. In this case, though, the result is a kind of anthology made at particular times – those of J, Dtr, the Chronicler – of the material which was considered to be the earliest and most important traditions. It is clear that in the course of this operation (or these operations) the collectors and redactors have shown themselves to have had quite remarkable artistic skills, creating out of the small units substantial major works which at first sight are a coherent unity, and this justifies a purely literary analysis of the documents as a work of art. However, it is hardly relevant to a historical investigation.

4.1.2 What does seem improbable, though, is that the redactors created a considerable number of texts from scratch, presenting them as though they were ancient and thus filling in gaps in the content with their imagination. Certainly there are texts the late character of which is now generally recognized: Gen.14 and 24; Ex.19.1ff., and a great many others like I Sam.17; however, it is not easy to show that these were created by the redactors. At all events we need to recognize that even these texts are the exception and not the rule, and it would not be strange if the redactors had drawn from contemporary temple traditions or popular traditions the material which our analyses prove to be late.

4.2 Where the creative bent of the redactors could be exercised freely and sometimes capriciously was in the choice and restructuring of the material that had come down to them. However, in such cases, choosing and restructuring – as I have said – meant far more than introducing some changes in form: changing the context tends also to change the substance.

4.2.1 It is now generally accepted that the arrangement of the persons of the patriarchs in a genealogical sequence is the work of the J redaction or at most of those who edited the first cycles immediately before or immediately after him (for further details cf. below, V.2.3.1). Therefore on the historical level there is no basic objection to supposing that all or some of the patriarchs might have existed contemporaneously, or, for that matter, that they may never have existed at all! Moreover, the sequence of patriarchs, exodus, conquest seems to be a simplification introduced by the redactors to cope with the problems raised by more complex features. Their work is well reflected in those summaries of the sacred history which in the past have sometimes been called 'creeds' or, better, 'confessions of faith', as in Deut.26.5b-9; 6.21-26 and, in a longer form, in Josh. 24.1-14. The restructuring of the material by the redactors also reduces the biographical and ideological information about the patriarchs, Moses, Joshua and to a large extent the judges to texts supporting the theories of the redactors, or to pericopes aimed at 'edifying' present and future generations.

4.2.2 Again, the redactors describe the 'conquest' narrated in the book of Joshua in terms drawn from the liturgy of public worship, stressing the fact that this is a divine gift to the people. (In current scholarship there are at least two other theories about this conquest, that it was a peaceful infiltration of barely inhabited territories or, less probably, that it was a revolt of the country peasants against exploitation by the city-state, cf. VII.4.2.) This explains why the first part of the book is a ritual procession and celebration rather than being warlike and political.[19] This characteristic fits well into the context of a post-exilic re-reading of the material, especially in the light of the failure of the institution of the monarchy at the time of the exile on the political level (and indeed on the theological and ethical level, to judge from the texts). A return to the origins (or to the institutions that were presumed to be the origins) in which the people of God accepted humbly and passively what God offered them in his mercy, without ever trying to take their destiny into their own hands, seemed to be a quietistic alternative compared with a policy whose failure had become all too manifest.

4.2.3 The representation of Israel at the end of the second millennium BC as a sacred league of twelve tribes united in common worship around the central sanctuary, the supreme institution not only in the religious field but also in establishing the norms of behaviour for individual members, also fits into this context. The texts do not always agree on the identity of the individual members, but their number appears constant: twelve, never more and never less, though with the sole (but remarkable!) exception of Judg. 5, the Song of Deborah (below VIII.3). This presentation of the organization of Israel in the pre-monarchical period is not manifestly absurd nor anachronistic, but could very well correspond to reality.[20] However, it also fits in very well with the rethinking and reflections of the post-exilic period, when the monarchy had been succeeded by the hierocratic order and the temple of Jerusalem had become not only the spiritual but also the ethnic and political centre of Israel, down to its final destruction by the soldiers of Titus in AD 70.

4.2.4 To present the 'liberators' of Israel in this way (below VIII.1) in a chronological sequence which foreshadows that of the kings, and to extend their sovereignty to all Israel, when they could very well be (and indeed probably were) for the most part contemporaries, each in his own territory, giving each of them the title 'judge' (Hebrew *šōpēṭ*, evidently identical with that of the Phoenician and Punic *suffetes* from the sixth century BC onwards), seems to be the work of the redactors rather than the reflection of an ancient tradition.

4.2.5 In their present version, the narratives about the reign of Saul (below, III.4.1-6), which was probably only an episode of short duration, have been supplemented with material drawn from the narrative of David's rise to power. This makes someone who must have been a skilful but rough warrior, without blemish or fear, and who ends his career in glory, falling in battle against an enemy superior in numbers and in arms, into a hero of Greek tragedy, in the grip of his God (who here takes the place of fate) and of events greater than he is. As a result he is eaten up by insecurity, and jealousy, a prey to attacks of hypochondria[21] and homicidal moods. This is a case where the redactor becomes an artist in our sense of the word, creating a work which has inspired dramatists over the centuries.

4.2.6 Many of the episodes in the life of David, too, are presented more as scenes of family life than as public or political events, as though the monarchy were an institution in the private sphere; this is a feature which already begins to fade into the background with Solomon. However, with David and Solomon we now have important information about politics, economics and administration: military expeditions with territorial conquests; local rebellions; building works, often purely for show and prestige; foreign trade, international treaties; economic measures to finance or even to rescue public enterprises which cannot always have been very profitable. In the end all this gives us a rather grim picture in which, behind the language of the court and the praise of later times, we can see a nation whose resources have been strained beyond all reasonable limits and which is therefore economically close to collapse, together with the emergency measures put into effect to cope with the situation thus created: forms of taxation which bear particularly heavily on the population, like the conscription for forced labour of those who were incapable of paying in cash or in kind (below IV.5). And according to our sources, it was precisely this situation which led to various forms of protest, then to open rebellion, and finally to the secession of the north from the united kingdom at the death of Solomon, with its subsequent break-up (below, IX.1). Here, behind the facade of family life, we begin to find important information which the historian can use, all of which seems very plausible. That is why I think that the united reign of David and Solomon is a good point from which to begin the history of Israel.

4.3 To sum up: the biblical sources responsible for the collection and redaction of the traditional material could have taken a great many liberties with the texts at their disposal. However, in essentials these seem to have been limited to the insertion of the texts into new contexts. It is improbable, and in any case difficult to prove, that the redactors invented fictitious episodes and presented them as being ancient: that seems to have been the exception rather than the rule. Thus a large number of modern scholars are ready to recognize e.g. the objectivity of Dtr in the presentation of its sources.[22] The situation already seems to be different in the post-exilic sources: P and the Chronicler associate people and episodes from the proto-history and the early history with specific acts of worship, like the institution of circumcision and the temple liturgy which they are supposed to have initiated and founded. In a time when antiquity was a sign of authority, that demonstrated at least the dignity, if not the validity, of the acts which the faithful were asked to perform. Here, too, however, despite the apparently artificial aspect of the presentation, we can never be certain that the text has not retained an authentic recollection, within the tradition, of concepts and practices which were in fact much older than their present context.[23]

5.1 It follows, therefore, that any history of Israel, especially one which starts from its origins, that seeks to deal with the period before the monarchy simply by paraphrasing the biblical texts and supplementing them, where possible, with alleged parallels from the ancient Near East, is not only using an inadequate method but ends up by offering a distorted picture of those events which can be ascertained. That is because it accepts uncritically the picture which Israel had of its own origins (this is the case, for example, with the work by Giuseppe Ricciotti, below 6.3.2).

5.2 The attempts to go back to a particular period of the second millennium BC, usually to the second quarter or the beginning of the second half, or even to the last centuries, the end of the millennium, and to start with the so-called tribal league to which I referred earlier (above 4.2.3), are much more relevant, but they also produce somewhat problematical results. This is the approach taken by M.Noth and his disciples (see below 6.4.2 and VII.7), cf. now A.Malamat (1983), who speaks of the period when the tribes were now definitively settled in their territories. However, the material provided by the texts does not lend very much support to an enterprise of this kind. So even in the light of this research, with all the uncertainties to which I have referred, it is more appropriate to keep to the context of the united monarchy, classifying the materials which relate to the period before the monarchy as 'traditions about Israel's proto-history'. Part Two of this book is devoted to them.

5.3 What I have said so far clearly obliges me to revise considerably what I have said in many of my earlier writings, especially those from the 1960s and the beginning of the 1970s.[24] However, this revision does not go so far as a repudiation: these are studies whose theories and results represent not so much a faithful reconstruction of earlier times as an account of what the later redactors and those who handed down the traditions affirmed about such periods.

6 We have seen that the critical discipline of writing the history of Israel has now existed for more than a century. Before that the tendency was to accept the texts in a basically uncritical way, paraphrasing them or at best only criticizing them superficially.

6.1 Evidently there can be no question here of reviewing the histories of Israel published over this century and more; I shall confine myself simply to indicating the most important of them which appeared before the Second World War. I shall, however, comment in more detail on those which appeared after the Second World War: after all, these are the ones which have determined the course of the debate.

6.2 After the works of A.Kuenen (1869) and B.Stade (1885), mentioned in 3.1 (n.12) above, I would list the following works, all of which are very important:

6.2.1 J.Wellhausen, *Israelitische und jüdische Geschichte*, Berlin 1894,⁷1914 and reprints. This is a systematic recapitulation of the consequences of the documentary hypothesis and other studies by the author for the history of Israel. These results were already expounded systematically in the now classical contribution to the *Encyclopaedia Britannica*, Vol. XIII (1881), 'Israel', 369-431. For Wellhausen the history of Israel began during the second millennium BC.

6.2.2 R.Kittel, *Geschichte der Hebräer*, Gotha 1888 (ET *A History of the Hebrews*, London, Edinburgh and New York 1888),²1909, as *Geschichte des Volkes Israel*, Stuttgart ⁷1932. This is an important work because from the second edition onwards it makes systematic use of the information coming from the archaeological discoveries in the ancient Near East. So we can regard R.Kittel as the instigator of the comparative historical method. The work is still worth reading today.

6.2.3 M.Weber, *Ancient Judaism* (1921), ET Glencoe 1952; this is the first attempt at a sociological and historical analysis of early Israel, and it is still largely valid.[25] It is interesting that Weber was neither an orientalist or a biblical scholar, so that the sources are always quoted at second hand.

6.3. Reference is still often made to the works of:

6.3.1 A.Lods, *Israel: From its Beginnings to the Middle of the Eighth Century* (1930), ET London ²1946, followed and completed by *The Prophets and the Rise of Judaism* (1935), ET London 1937; these two books develop Wellhausen's theories.

6.3.2 G.Ricciotti, *The History of Israel* (1932), two vols., ET Milwaukee 1955. This represents a very conservative approach and is for the most part an uncritical work which ends up by paraphrasing the texts, supplementing them with extra-biblical material where that is available. Ricciotti is very good at synthesis and exposition, which is also well demonstrated by his two well-known works on Jesus and Paul; however, the method he uses ignores most of the problems and gives the reader the evidence available as though it were clear and obvious. Perhaps this is why the book was so successful, and it was translated into at least three languages (above 5.1).

6.3.3 W.O.E. Oesterley and T.H.Robinson, *A History of Israel*, two vols, London 1932 and reprints, is a solid work, carried out in the best British humanist tradition, which is still useful today for seeing how the problems were raised about fifty years ago.

6.4 During and after the Second World War the following works were published, which I list in chronological order:

6.4.1 W.F.Albright, *From the Stone Age to Christianity*, Baltimore 1940,²1957. In a bold historical, philosophical and theological approach (though in fact he was neither a historian, a philosopher or a theologian), the author sees the history of Israel as a typical example of the evolution of humanity towards monotheism, following the Hegelian pattern of thesis, antithesis and synthesis. The author's theories appear in a rather shorter work, *The Biblical Period from Abraham to Ezra*, New York 1949, ³1963, which originated as an introduction to J.J.Finkelstein (ed.), *The Jews* I, New York 1949.

6.4.2 M.Noth, *The History of Israel* (1950), ET ²1959; as I have pointed out (above 5.2), this begins with the tribal alliance (and thus with the last centuries of the second millennium BC), which Noth describes (probably wrongly) as 'amphictyonic', thinking of the ancient Hellenic and Italian tribal alliances.The work remains a classic and cannot be ignored. The important works by M.Liverani, *Introduzione alla storia dell'Asia orientale antica*, Rome 1963 (published only as a university mimeograph), in its section on Israel and the Philistines, 259ff., and M.Metzger, *Grundriss der Geschichte Israels*, Neukirchen 1963, ⁵1979, still seem mainly to follow the lines of Noth's work.

6.4.3 J.Bright,*A History of Israel*, Philadelphia and London 1959, ³1981; this is the history of Israel from a conservative perspective, deriving from the school of W.F.Albright. It attributes substantial historical value to the biblical texts, not for religious reasons (Bright is not a fundamentalist) but because it considers that they have been adequately substantiated by what is said in ancient Near Eastern texts and by archaeological discoveries. At any rate it is always up-to-date over the problems raised by the Bible, which it does not seek to press; it is familiar with the details of the important texts and discoveries.

6.4.4 R. de Vaux OP, *The Early History of Israel* (two vols, 1971, 1973), ET London 1978; this was planned as a monumental work in three volumes, along the lines of that by Kittel (above 6.2.2). At the time of his premature death the author had completed Vol.I and fragments of Vol. II have been published following the lines indicated by the text begun by the author and his notes. Volume I deals with the problems of the patriarchal period, the exodus and the conquest; Volume II begins with the period of the judges, but has the limitations that I have pointed out.

6.4.5 A.H.J. Gunneweg, *Geschichte Israels bis Bar Kochba*, Stuttgart 1973, ⁴1982; all in all, like the work which follows, this is a substantial presentation of modern problems, with some original solutions.

6.4.6 S.Herrmann, *A History of Israel in Old Testament Times* (1973, ²1980), ET London and Philadelphia 1975, ²1981. This is important for its contribution in the sphere of Egyptology, in particular in connection with the proto-history of Israel, arising out of earlier studies by the author. The first edition ends with Ezra and Nehemiah, the second with the Roman occupation.

6.4.7 G.Fohrer, *Geschichte Israels*, Heidelberg 1977, ³1982. Another useful synthesis of the problems and solutions that have been put forward. A last chapter deals, though very briefly, with the history of Judaism from AD 70/134 to the present day.

6.4.8 J.H.Hayes and J.M.Miller (eds.), *Israelite and Judaean History*, Philadelphia and London 1977; this is a composite work by various scholars specializing in particular material and particular periods. It provides a complete and up-to-date picture of the state of the question and of the solutions proposed, and also produces original arguments. And it is the indispensable starting point for any later investigations.

6.4.9 H.Jagersma, *A History of Israel in the Old Testament Period* (1979), London and Philadelphia 1982. A succinct work, but full of important and original ideas; it begins at the second millennium BC, but argues that we do not have any certain information before the monarchy; it ends with Ezra and Nehemiah, i.e. with the Jewish canon. A second volume is in preparation.

6.4.10 B.Mazar (ed.), *The World History of the Jewish People*, Jerusalem and London, 8 vols., 1964-1984.This work sets out to be a kind of monumental history of the Jews, a fact which explains its essential conservative approach. It is to go down to our own day. A similar work in approach, results and contributors, though on a much smaller scale, is that edited by H.H.Ben Sasson, *History of the Jewish People*, London 1976, 3 vols., of which Vol.1 relates to our period. It has been translated from modern Hebrew. The contributions, in both cases by different authors, all with established reputations, vary in quality, depending on the author and his competence, but the level is generally high.

6.4.11 H.Cazelles, *Histoire politique d'Israël*, Paris 1982, is a work which I have not been able to use.

6.4.12 A brief history of Israel has been inserted into the recent work by R.Rendtorff, *The Old Testament. An Introduction* (1983), ET London and Philadelphia 1985, which I have not been able to use. See too H.Donner, *Geschichte Israels* I, Göttingen 1984 (a second volume is in preparation).

6.4.13 For post-exilic Judaism we have:

P.Sacchi, *Storia del mondo giudaico*, Turin 1976, a basic work for the study of Judaism from the Babylonian exile to the destruction of the temple in AD 70 under Titus.

6.5 Works on a smaller scale which are conceived scientifically and are a useful introduction to the problems are:

6.5.1 H.M.Orlinsky, *Ancient Israel*, Ithaca NY 1954, ²1960;

6.5.2 E.L.Ehrlich, *A Concise History of Israel*, ET London and New York 1963;

6.5.3 A.Lemaire, *Histoire du peuple hébreu*, Paris 1981.

6.6 Whereas the histories of Israel before the end of the last century often doubted the possibility of going back beyond the united monarchy (A. Kuenen even thought it was impossible to go back beyond the eighth century BC, a theory which has been put forward again today by J.M.Sasson, above 3.3.2), for reasons of principle J.Wellhausen and

R. Kittel (on the basis of the Near Eastern material which was continually being discovered) broadened the horizon beyond the middle of the second millennium BC; A.Lods, T.H.Robinson, G.Ricciotti, W.F.Albright, J. Bright, G.Fohrer, J.H.Hayes, J.M.Miller and H.Jagersma moved in the same direction (though the latter recognized the problems, above 6.4.9). By contrast, M.Weber and M.Noth (and his pupils) would prefer to go back to the period of the tribal league. The approach of G.Buccellati (1967, above 4.2.3) is similar, as is recently that of A.Malamat (1983, cf. the bibliography, above 1). W.F.Albright and J.Bright (and today the *Archaeology* by Y.Aharoni, above I, 10.2.5) even begin with the Stone Age. However, this approach regards Palestine as an entity in itself, regardless of whether Israel were present or absent. The present work aims to begin with the empire of David and Solomon; material earlier than this period appears in Part Two, as traditions from the proto-history of the people.

7 As I have already explained, one thing should have become clear: for the period down to the end of the ninth century BC the sources for the history of Israel are for the most part the biblical texts, the historical problems of which I have tried to point out. At a later stage the Bible is supplemented by other sources, from Israel and the ancient Near East, and they give us a more complete picture of the situation (though it is still full of gaps). As to the biblical texts, we have seen that while they are numerous, their quantity is as it were negatively counter-balanced by their doubtful value as history, because they are presented in terms of problems which are often centuries away from the events which they appear to describe.

7.1.1 In the first place we have a historical collection of fundamental importance, the 'Deuteronomistic History' (Dtr), so called because it gathers together the traditions according to criteria which are clearly inspired by the book of Deuteronomy. To this we owe the redaction and editing of at least two and perhaps three phases of the fifth book of the Pentateuch (with the exception of Deut.32; 33; 34) and of the books of Joshua, Judges, I & II Samuel, and I & II Kings.[26] For the patriarchal narratives, and the accounts of the exodus and the journey through the wilderness, we have the J and E sources of the Pentateuch, or, rather, of only the first four books of the Pentateuch; there is only rare evidence of E, so much so that some scholars doubt whether it existed. After Genesis, it is in any case difficult to distinguish J and E, so that the relevant analyses are usually made on the first book of the Bible. Some ancient collections of laws like the so-called 'Book of the Covenant' (Ex.21-23) and early epic and heroic compositions (Judg. 5) and patriarchal sayings (Gen.49; Deut.33) come from a time probably earlier than the seventh century BC (the date of Josiah's reform, below XI.4). From the collections of laws we can deduce some interesting information about the rural community in Israel; however, it is difficult, if not impossible, to date these texts with even a minimum of certainty. The epic and heroic songs only rarely provide features which the historian can use, not least because these too cannot be dated with any precision.

7.1.2 J and E seem to have been combined shortly before the exile; however, they too have been subjected to a revision of a Deuteronomic or Deuteronomistic kind: this has introduced, always at key points (e.g. Gen.15; Ex.13.1-10; 19.3-8; 34.10-13, etc.), sections obviously intended to provide the key to reading the whole of the passages which follow. A Deuteronomic redaction is usually also presupposed in the case of the prophets Hosea, Jeremiah and Ezekiel, and it has recently also been proposed in an extreme form for Isaiah[27] by O.Kaiser; a redaction of this kind also seems probable for passages of Amos.[28] We are again given sparse information about the end of the pre-exilic period by the prophets mentioned above (in those passages which we can extract from the Deuteronomistic redaction) and by Nahum, Habakkuk and Zephaniah.

7.1.3 The first four books of the Pentateuch then received a final redaction in the early post-exilic period at the hand of P, the last source of the Pentateuch. In all these cases it is clear that we have reached the late exilic or early post-exilic period, i.e. not before the second half of the sixth century BC.

7.1.4 Another complex of history writing is that of Chronicles, to which until recently it has been usual to add the books of Ezra and Nehemiah. Here sacred history decisively gains the upper hand over secular history, so that these books are of relatively little use to the historian; here and there, however, they hand on information which is authentic and therefore important.

7.1.5 The facts that can be deduced from the Psalter seem sparse; they usually amount to information also contained in other works and, moreover, those which had a late redaction. We can deduce virtually nothing from the wisdom books, whether canonical or deutero-canonical; the little that is said about patterns of behaviour allows us to reconstruct tiny features of the milieu, but we always have the problems posed by the difficulty of dating. The book of Lamentations gives us information about Jerusalem shortly after the destruction of 587/86 (below XI.6.4); from the post-exilic period, however, we have the books of Ezra and Nehemiah, mentioned above, and those of the prophets Haggai, Zechariah 1-8, Obadiah and Malachi. All of these provide interesting information, but it must be taken with a pinch of salt. We have no information of a historical kind from the prophets Joel and Jonah, from the books of Ruth and Esther, the deutero-canonical books of Judith and Tobit, or from the additions to Esther and Daniel. Even the information provided by the book of Daniel is interesting only for a study of the *modus operandi* of an apocalyptic writer, no more. However, the deutero-canonical book of I Esdras does give us some interesting information about the period of the exile.

7.1.6 The deutero-canonical books of Baruch, I Esdras and I & II Maccabees are also important for the period with which we are concerned.

7.2.1 Outside the Bible but within the Jewish tradition we have the historian Joseph, who later took the name Flavius and became Flavius Josephus; he was a Jewish priest who at first commanded the rebel Jewish troops in Galilee; however, he then went over to the Romans during the war with Vespasian and Titus, AD 67-70. His works are the *Antiquities* (*Antt.*), an important source partly parallel to the Hebrew Bible; the *Jewish War* (*BJ*), which deals with the revolt of 67-70, and an apologetic work, *Contra Apionem*. There is a useful edition of Josephus edited by H.St-J.Thackeray, *Josephus*, in the Loeb Classical Library, nine volumes, London and Cambridge, Mass. 1926-65, a Greek critical text with an English translation opposite. It is not always easy to make proper historical use of the material which Josephus provides. First of all he writes to vindicate himself before the Romans, and then to defend Judaism over against paganism. Then he often cites lost texts of Phoenician and Greek authors; when he cites these works we are therefore in no position to check the accuracy, the completeness, or – and this is much more serious – the sheer trustworthiness of the texts. In any case, the apologetic character of his work makes it suspect and some scholars now think that Josephus provides only second- or third-hand material, of little value to the historian and strongly prejudiced by the apologetic character of his writings.[29] Most pagan authors, some of them quoted by Josephus, have also been collected in the anthology by M.Stern, *Authors*.

7.2.2 We find other information in Philo of Alexandria and, later, in Eusebius of Caesarea and among other ancient authors, pagan or Christian.[30] This material is often very interesting, but at other times it is not very valuable because of its apologetic or edifying approach or its polemical character; in the last instance these are often texts which reflect a marked ignorance of the subject-matter; they are interesting only because they show us what were already the prejudices against Judaism.

7.3 Israel is mentioned regularly, as I have indicated, in ancient Near Eastern sources from the ninth century BC onwards (above 3.3.2). The important texts have been collected and translated in *Ancient Near Eastern Texts. Relating to the Old Testament*, edited by J.B.Pritchard, Princeton [3]1969, which has a companion volume, *The Ancient Near East in Pictures*. The Western Semitic texts which are particularly important for their ethnic and linguistic affinities with Israel appear in a critical edition in H.Donner and W.Röllig, *Kanaanäische und aramäische Inschriften*, three vols., Wiesbaden ³1968ff. and J.C.L.Gibson, *Syrian Semitic Inscriptions*, three vols, Oxford 1971-82 (a work which has to be used with a degree of caution because of the many reconstructions of the text made by the author). These are abbreviated as *KAI* and *SSI* respectively.

7.3.1 The earliest text which makes explicit mention of Israel is the stele of Pharaoh Merneptah from the second half of the thirteenth century BC, found at Thebes with a copy at Karnak. The fact that the text exists in duplicate copies makes its literary form certain. Dated in the fifth year of the monarch (*c.* 1237-35 according to the 'intermediate' chronology and *c.* 1224-04 in the 'low chronology'); it therefore dates from about 1231 or 1219. The end of it reads as follows (my rendering is based on the translation by S.Moscati:[31]

> The princes lie prostrate, saying 'Salaam!'
> No one lifts his head among the 'nine bows'.
> Tehenu is destroyed, Hatti pacified,
> Canaan is plundered with every evil.
> Ashkelon is deported, Gezer captured,
> Yanoam is annihilated, Israel is devastated, its seed is no more!
> Hurru has become a widow for Egypt.

The 'nine bows' is an expression which denotes people allied to Egypt in a vassal relationship, here evidently rebels who have been tamed. Tehenu is a name for Libya; Ashkelon, Hebrew '*ašqᵉlon* (coord.107-118) is in the south-west of Canaan and soon afterwards became a Philistine city; Gezer is in the centre, to the West (coord.142-140); Yanoam is probably to be identified with *tell en na'am*, according to the convincing proposal by A.Alt, and situated to the south-east of the Sea of Galilee (coord.236-197; H.Engel, cf. n.30).

7.3.2 In the stele Israel appears to be located in Canaan, but the determinative with the name indicates a 'tribe' or 'non-sedentary population' as opposed to the 'sedentary population' indicated in the other cases. So it seems that according to this text Israel was in a transitional phase between a non-sedentary and a sedentary situation.[32] This is an acceptable interpretation of the text, even if, as we shall see later, it is not the only one.

7.3.3 The problems begin as soon as we subject the text to a closer examination. First of all, it mostly refers to a campaign against Libya ('Tehenu'), i.e. to the west; so how is it that the Pharaoh and his troops suddenly find themselves in the East, in Asia? Again, the Egyptologists generally point out the vagueness of the Egyptian scribes of the time, a feature also substantiated by some inconsistencies within the text.

Finally, there are doubts about the historicity of a campaign by Pharaoh in Canaan in this period; J.A.Wilson, who edited the translation for _ANET_, considers the text 'a poetic eulogy of a universally victorious pharaoh'. And apart from these intrinsic difficulties, we should note that the text gives only scanty information about the Israel that it mentions: basically, we know only of its presence and that it was not yet sedentary; otherwise we learn nothing. Was it an ethnic group in process of formation and not yet a political entity? Where exactly was it? How was it governed? What were its relationships with Egypt and its own neighbours? If we accept that the places mentioned on the stele are listed in a sequence running from south to north (as would seem logical to anyone coming from Egypt), we might locate 'Israel' in central or upper Galilee. This is not improbable in itself, as we shall see (below VII.4.1.2). Finally, the stele does not give us any information that we can connect with the biblical texts, but this is probably because of the historical deficiencies of the latter. Perhaps the name of Merneptah is still reflected in the name of a spring a little way north of the present Western exit from Jerusalem, 'the waters of Nephtoah' (Josh.15.9; 18.15)[33], but this seems far from certain.

7.3.4 Again, since it seems impossible to reconcile the indication of the presence of an entity called Israel with the traditional chronology of the exodus, some scholars supposed that there was an Israelite group present in Palestine independent of the one involved in the exodus.[34] However, we shall see in due course (see V.1ff.; VI.1ff.) that the chronological sequence of the biblical books of Genesis and Exodus is the work of the redactors, for whom the problem was in fact non-existent. Nor does there seem to me to be anything in favour of the recent attempt by E.Otto[35] to connect the mention of Israel on the stele with the presence of Jacob and his group in the region of Shechem (Gen.33.18-35.1); according to the text Israel would be more to the north.

7.4 Another very important text is the stele of Mesha, king of Moab, from the second half of the ninth century BC.[36] This gives an account which is partly parallel to, but largely supplements, that in II Kings 1.1; 3, but from the perspective of the other side. At that time Moab succeeded in freeing itself from Israelite occupation, under the 'son of Omri' (according to II Kings 3, though, this was Joram, son of Ahab and therefore grandson of Omri; the occasion for the rebellion will have been the death of Ahab, below IX.3.3.3). It also emerges from the stele that the 'men of Gad had long dwelt in the land of Ataroth' (line 10); this is present-day _ḥirbet el 'aṭṭārūs_ (coord.213-109).

All this indicates why some authors would prefer to make the history of Israel begin from the eighth century BC onwards (above 3.3.1-4).

III

DAVID

1 The biblical tradition is unanimous in affirming that in the last years of the second millennium BC and the first years of the first millennium a single monarchical state was formed in Palestine and the surrounding territories, modelled on the great empires of the ancient Near East. The origins of this state were modest: the original nucleus was formed of the tribe of Judah and groups affiliated to it; soon afterwards they were joined by Israel in the narrower sense of the term, i.e the north, made up chiefly of the tribes of Ephraim and Manasseh from the central hill-country and those of Galilee. Benjamin, a very small tribe with few economic resources (though it was renowned for its prowess in the military sphere), wedged between the borders of Judah and Ephraim, belonged sometimes to the south and sometimes to the north, as often happens to territory in this situation.

1.1 Now it is important to note that the division between north and south (i.e. between 'Israel' in the narrower sense, also called 'house of Joseph', and Judah or 'house of Judah') seems to have been originally an ethnic and political division in that it probably existed before the dissolution of the united monarchy on the death of Solomon (below, IX.1). It probably also existed at the religious level. Despite the obvious affinities between the two groups, it seems to have been an intrinsic difference.[1] This needs to be stressed because the tendency of the biblical tradition is rather to show the two groups as being fundamentally united, if not identical, at least on a religious level and as far as their common aims were concerned, and this unity is said to have been disturbed only because of the impiety of the north and its kings. Politically, however, it seems that here were two distinct entities which the empire never succeeded in unifying: as we shall see (7.4.3), the empire was ruled, as A. Alt has shown, by a form of government known as a 'personal union', in which the sovereign of two or more nations is the same, but the structures of government are distinct. The affirmation that the two groups are one should in fact be treated with great caution, seeing that this is a religious and not a political affirmation. It is rather like the way in which ecumenically minded Christians today confess the unity of the church despite its obvious divisions. Only with the emergence of the Samaritan community at an indeterminable time in the post-exilic period (below XIII.4) does it seem that this unity which had been felt so far, against all appearances, gave place to the awareness that there were now two monotheistic communities in the region, each defining itself as 'Israel' and both appealing to the *tōrāh* and to Moses.

1.2 Joshua 17.12f.//Judges 1.27-35[2] relate to a period which we can no longer determine with any certainty, but which is probably to be put in the time of David (see also below IV.5.2). In Judges 1.28 we read explicitly that Israel, apparently peacefully, succeeded in subjecting and making into vassals (this is to be preferred to the improper translation 'subject to forced labour') the city-states in the northern plains which at the time of the conquest had succeeded in maintaining their own independence; and these are the cities already mentioned for the most part in the archives of el-'Amarna. Thus the region was unified for the first and last time in its history, though only for a short while, under a single sceptre, instead of being divided into dozens of autonomous entities. Jerusalem, too, was conquered and incorporated into the united kingdom, becoming its capital; later, with the division of the kingdom, it passed to Judah.

1.3 During the following years, thanks to the political ability and military skill of David, the united kingdom was able to expand in a remarkable way; this expansionist dynamics seems indeed to have constituted its original power. So within a short time we can see how, either by conquest or by voluntary submission, the whole of Transjordan (Ammon, Edom and Moab) and the major part of Syria, including various Aramaean kingdoms, came under the rule of David. Like Israel, the peoples of the two regions had also been formed recently. Once the capacity of the kingdom for expansion began to decline (and this process already begins at the time of Solomon, below IV.3.3; 4.3), ceasing almost entirely after the break-up of the personal union, the fate of Israelite sovereignty in the region was sealed.

1.4.1 As I pointed out earlier, and have often repeated (above, II.3.3.2), the existence of the empire is not confirmed anywhere in the sources from the period so far available. However, we have seen that it is quite probable.

1.4.2 Certainly external circumstances favoured its development: the Assyrian empire was not yet involved in the region and Egypt was going through one of its many periods of political eclipse.[3] There is obviously no proof here, but these factors indicate the possibility of an Israelite empire; moreover, the detailed information about politics and

economics is often so relevant that it is hard tc   it could
have been invented.

1.5 However, precisely because of this abse   .al from the
ancient Near East, we are forced to refer exclı   ɔiblical texts,
the problems of which we have already cc   ɔ.3). The texts
are contained in what we can regard as th   ollections.

1.5.1 The 'history of the rise of Davi⁻   ne' (I Sam.16 – II
Sam.4) collects together material whicl   ɔnsider in detail in
due course (2-3), about relations betw   .d David.

1.5.2 We shall examine the 'ark narı   .1.2 below. They begin
in I Sam.4, with the capture by the ˈ   of the sacred ark after a
defeat which is followed by the int   ɔf the monarchy in Israel.
In ch.5 there is an account of the da.   ɩone among the Philistines
because of their careless treatment of thɛ ark, and in ch. 6 we are told
how they send it away, evidently in order to avoid other disasters. In
this way it reaches Beth-shemesh (coord.147-128), and then Kiriath-
jearim (coord.159-135), from where, a generation later, David has it
brought to Jerusalem (II Sam.6). This account is interwoven with
legendary and even humorous elements.

1.5.3 The 'succession narrative' is particularly important.[4] It
comprises II Sam.9-20 and I Kings 1-2, perhaps preceded by II Sam.21.1-
14. This importance is, however, markedly reduced by a series of
factors, especially the difficulty in establishing its literary genre and
aim, features on which scholars are not yet agreed. Certainly until
recently the narrative was hailed as a magnificent example of ancient
Israelite historiography, perhaps even the earliest example of historiography ever produced. Today scholars have become more prudent, if
not more shrewd;[5] a study by Whybray rightly calls the work a historical
novel, pointing out that the scenes which take place in the bedroom
are clearly a fiction (II Sam.13), but at the same time typical of the
narrative, as is also the way in which the narrative is related as a family
saga. By contrast, the impressive scene in II Sam.12 is a legend. Still,
as I have said, even the aim of the work has yet to be sufficiently
clarified. However, among the various theories proposed the most
probable seems to be that of T.Ishida, who argues that the narrative
was originally intended to legitimate Solomon's accession to the throne
over against the direct dynastic line, through which the throne might
have been expected to go to his older brother Adonijah. In this context
David appears as a figure in a state of complete physical and moral
decadence, who has left affairs of state in the hands of his general Joab.
And to avoid the prolongation of such a situation (indeed Adonijah
also seems to be a puppet of Joab), the intervention of Solomon was
the lesser of two evils, even if it was accompanied by proscriptions

and political assassinations. Here the political element predominates, although the account still has its setting in the family of David.

1.5.4 In II Sam.5; 8 we find a summary account of the campaigns of David, which can be added to 1.5.1 or made to precede 1.5.3, a course which scholars often take. In origin, the account of the conquest of the Ammonite capital, now completely incorporated into the story of David's adultery (II Sam.10-12), may also have belonged here.

1.5.5 In Chronicles David appears as a stained-glass-window saint, when the texts are not simply parallel to Samuel and Kings; they therefore only rarely retain the real sources.

1.5.6 On an archaeological level, the discoveries which can be certainly attributed to the time of David are few and controversial. We shall be considering them along with those from the time of Solomon (below, IV.1.4).

2.1 In the world of the ancient Near East, then, there was nothing at this time to oppose the rise of an empire in Palestine and in Syria. However, as soon as the great empires began to turn their attention to the region, the crisis for what remained of the united kingdom began to intensify. However, in the meantime, it succeeded in maintaining its power for another seventy years after the beginning of the tenth century.

2.2 The biblical tradition presents David as being crowned first king of Judah, i.e. the south, at Hebron. This was the place which, according to II Sam.2.1-3, he had occupied on his move from the Negeb, where he had a kind of fief given to him by the Philistines, whose vassal he had become. However, the fact that Hebron was clearly under his occupation raises the suspicion that 'the men' were not so much acting of their own free will but were recognizing and legitimizing a *de facto* situation which was now in fact now irreversible, and which must have reduced somewhat their power of decision-making.

2.3 At the same time, the north, Israel in the narrower sense, was slowly recovering from the defeat inflicted on it by the Philistines shortly beforehand at the battle of Mount Gilboa, in which their king Saul and three of his sons had been killed.[6] It seems that there were about five years of disorders and difficulties of various kinds, after which Abner, Saul's uncle and his general, decided to put the surviving son of the dead monarch, Eshbaal on the throne (the name, caricatured in II Sam., appears in its correct form in I Chron. 8.33; 9.39). He established the provisional seat of the kingdom at Mahanaim in Transjordan, probably present-day *tell-hajjiaj* (coord.214-177), outside the Philistine sphere of activity. The texts here also speak of struggles between Israel and Judah, and in one case of an episode of single-handed combat between champions of the south and champions of the north (II Sam.2.12-3.11), some aspects of which recall the struggles in

Rome between the Horatii and the Curati. However, what remained of the house of Saul soon fell: Eshbaal, described by the texts as a weak and irresolute figure, soon found himself in conflict with Abner, by whom he felt insulted; and the general went over to David (3.7ff.). The killing of both Eshbaal and Abner for reasons apparently connected with feuds and private vendettas (3.22ff.; 4.1ff.) cleared all the remaining obstacles from David's path; after reigning for seven and a half years in Hebron, he also had the insignia of rule over the north conferred on him by 'all the elders of Israel' (II Sam.5.1-4).

3 We have a series of narratives about the origins and early career of David, a Judaean of modest birth, though not of a poor family (it had its own flocks); for the most part they are legendary or even novelistic, and in some instances they are also contradictory.

Select bibliography: A.Alt, 'The Formation of the Israelite State in Palestine' (1930), *Essays on Old Testament History and Religion*, Oxford 1966, 173-237; H.-U.Nübel, *Davids Aufstieg in der Frühe israelitischer Geschichtsschreibung*, Diss. Bonn 1959; F.Mildenberger, *Die vordeuteronomistische Saul-David Überlieferung*, Diss.-Tübingen 1962; B.Mazar, 'David's Reign in Hebron and the Conquest of Jerusalem', in *In the Time of Harvest. Festschrift A.H.Silver*, New York 1963, 235-44; R.A.Carlson, *David the Chosen King*, Stockholm 1964; A.Weiser, 'Die Legitimation des Königs David', *VT* 16, 1966, 325-54; J.A.Soggin, *Das Königtum in Israel*, BZAW 104, Berlin 1967, 53ff. (with bibliography); M.Kessler, 'Narrative Technique in I Sam. 16.1-13', *CBQ* 32, 1970, 543-54; J.H.Grønbaek, *Die Geschichte von Davids Aufstieg (I Sam.15 – 2.Sam.5)*, Copenhagen 1971; J.Conrad, 'Zum geschichtlichen Hintergrund von Davids Aufstieg', *TLZ* 97, 1972, 321-32; F.Schicklberger, 'Die Davididen und das Nordreich', *BZ* 18, 1974, 255-63; T.N.D.Mettinger, *King and Messiah*, CB-OTS 8, Lund 1976; W.Dietrich, 'David in Überlieferung und Geschichte' *VuF* 22, 1977, 44-64 (with a long annotated bibliography); T.Ishida, *The Royal Dynasties in Ancient Israel*, BZAW 142, Berlin 1977; J.Conrad, 'Der Gegenstand und die Intention der Geschichte von der Thronnachfolge Davids', *TLZ* 108, 1983, 161-76; A. Malamat, *Das davidische und salomonische Königreich und seine Beziehungen zu Ägypten und Syrien*, ÖAW-Sb 402, Vienna 1983; H.Donner, 'Israel und Tyrus im Zeitalter Davids und Salomos', *JNWSL* 10, 1982, 43-52; G.Garbini, 'L'impero di David', *ASNSP* III, 13, 1983, 1-20. For the name cf. A.Hoffman, *David*, Stuttgart 1973; for a history of Jerusalem written in a popular style see recently E.Otto, *Jerusalem – Geschichte der Heiligen Stadt*, Stuttgart 1980.

3.1.1 The tradition is unanimous in affirming that David began his career as a follower of Saul, and in a sense continued it and crowned it at Saul's expense. In the story of David's rise to the throne (above

1.5.1), a work which favours David and is therefore hostile to Saul, the merits of the first king of Israel in both the political and the military sphere are quite evident; however, the prejudice in favour of David presents the final phase of Saul's reign as having been characterized by a series of wrong choices; the reader is meant to have the impression that the king was now incompetent on the political level, unworthy on the religious level, and psychologically unbalanced, which is why he was eaten up with suspicion and afflicted with persecution mania, often falling victim to homicidal moods and states of depression. So there was nothing more logical than that other more competent and worthy people should take his place; and who was better qualified than his able general?

3.1.2 The account uses a series of arguments in trying to demonstrate its own thesis that Saul was now incapable of reigning, and that David therefore had a right to the crown.

3.1.2.1 In I Sam.16.1-13, a predominantly Deuteronomistic passage, David is directly designated by God and 'anointed' king by Samuel to replace Saul, who is rejected.[7] Only M.Kessler (1970) now considers this passage ancient.

3.1.2.2 In 18.17-27 David marries Michal, Saul's daughter, after being subjected to epic proofs of bravery. It is far from impossible that the whole passage is a fiction; in I Sam.25.44 the woman is given by Saul to a certain Palti(el) as his wife and Paltiel is later forced to suffer what he finds an intolerable indignity: to give Michal back to David (II Sam.3.15). The theory that the woman was first given to David and then, while he was still alive, to someone else, is hard to reconcile with what we know to have been the law and the practice in Israel at a later stage (cf. Deut.24.1-4; Jer.3.1). At all events, whatever the historical value of the narrative, once Saul and his three sons were dead and only Meribbaal remained, in default of any other heirs, marriage to the daughter of Saul put David automatically in the line of succession to the throne. (In the case of Meribbaal, too, we find the exact name only in the passages of Chronicles mentioned above; he was the son of Jonathan and grandson of Saul, and unsuited to kingship because he was lame as a result of an incident which happened when he was small, II Sam.4.4.)

3.1.2.3 Two features are well known in popular traditions; the attribution to David of extraordinary prowess in battle (I Sam.17, the 'giant' Goliath,[8] a text which at some points contradicts the information given in the preceding 16.17ff.; 18.20-27 and elsewhere), as a result of which it is said that people maliciously sang under Saul's window the refrain:

Saul has slain his thousands
and David his ten thousands! (I Sam.18.7; cf. 22.12; 29.5)

and later, the phrase pronounced by the elders of the north who came to crown David: 'In times past, when Saul was king over us, it was you that led out and brought in Israel' (II Sam.5.2, a statement which does not in fact correspond with the sources). The gist of them is that the better (David) was called to take the place of the less good (Saul).

3.1.2.4 Another reason why the kingdom is said to have gone as of right to David and not to a survivor from the house of Saul is that he was designated king by the assembly in a procedure that we might call democratic.

3.2 For the final Deuteronomistic redactor, the first element, the divine designation, was clearly decisive. It is interesting that this is a theme which we can also find elsewhere in the ancient Near East: direct divine designation as a legitimation of someone who ascended the throne outside the legitimate line of succession. Also in the Old Testament we have the case of Jehu, king of Israel, designated and 'anointed' by a prophet (II Kings 9); in the ancient Aramaean world we have the case of Zakkur, king of Hamath, whose stele says, 'I am Zakkur, king of Hamath and of L'S, a humble man [...] Ba'al ŠMYN; and he has raised me up to him and... has made me king over Hazrak...'; the inscription then continues with a description of the struggles he had to undergo with neighbouring peoples (*KAI* 202; *SSI* II, 5: line 2). And we find similar examples in the royal inscriptions of Assyria.[9]

3.3 However, the continual offers of friendship to the house of Saul and the remarks which seek to dissociate David from any responsibility for its extermination or even for the death of Abner are also aimed at legitimizing him (II Sam.1.13-16; 4.9-12; 9.1ff., cf. the poems in 1.19-27 and 3.33f., regardless of whether or not David wrote them). That accusations of this kind were made against David is explicitly stated in II Sam.16.5-14.

3.4 The oracles which David is said to have received (II Sam.2.1-4; 3.9f.,18 and 5.2b) also point in this direction: they are meant to show that not only human might but the will of God himself was at work in David's elevation to the throne; so these complement the first theme.

4 This having been said, we must now deal briefly with the reign of Saul.

Select bibliography: J.A.Soggin, *Das Königtum...*, 22f. (with bibliography); B.C.Birch, *The Rise of the Israelite Monarchy: the Growth and Development of I Samuel 7-15*, SBL-DS 27, Missoula, Montana 1976; V.Fritz, 'Die Deutungen des Königtums Sauls in den Überlieferungen von seiner Entstehung, I Sam.9-11', *ZAW* 88, 1976, 346-62; C. Grottanelli, 'Possessione carismatica e razionalizzazione statale nella Bibbia ebraica', *SSR* 1, 1977, 263-88; D.M.Gunn, *The Fate of King Saul*, JSOT-SS 14, Sheffield 1980; P.K.McCarter, 'The Apology of

King David', *JBL* 99, 1980, 489-93; T.R.Preston, 'The Heroism of Saul
– Patterns of Meaning in the Narratives of Early Kingship', *JSOT* 24,
1982, 27-46.

4.1 The reason why I have not done this before, indeed why I did
not begin this history with him, is simply because the sources are
inadequate. In fact they show very little direct interest in the first king
of Israel. On the one hand he is mentioned only to support the theory
that his election had been an impious act (I Sam.8; 10.17-27), the
rejection by some of the people of the divine sovereignty. The former
text provides the key for reading two others (chs.9; 11), which are
earlier and more favourable to Saul's election; in the first we have a
romanticized account of the designation of Saul by Samuel on the
command of God; in the second we have his first decisive victory over
the Ammonites in the East, by lifting the Ammonite siege of Jabesh-
gilead, in Transjordan (its location is uncertain; perhaps it is *tell el-
maqlub*, coord.214-201, on *wādī yābiś*, which has kept the ancient
name). This achievement will then have been followed by the popular
acclamation which proved him to be a charismatic in the sense proposed
by M.Weber.[10] Now, however, all this is seen as the development of
the previous section, markedly anti-monarchical and also personally
unfavourable to Saul. On the other hand, Saul is spoken of only in
relationship to David, the man in the ascendant.

4.2.1 The argument is presented in what seems to us rather a
transparent way, by inserting into those texts which deal with the
glorious achievements of Saul passages which tend to put them in a
bad light: cf.I Sam.13-14, where the protagonists are Saul and his son
Jonathan. In this section the two achieve a decisive military victory
over the Philistines, who in fact seem to have been driven out of the
hill-country. Again in an addition (ch.15), Saul leads an expedition
against the Amalekites, here probably not the nomadic people of the
south with whom Israel is said to have had difficulties even at the time
of the exodus, but an autochthonous people, settled in the north-
western region of the central hill-country,[11] around *pir'ātōn*, the name
of which has been kept in present-day *far'atā* (coord.165-177). II Samuel
4.2f.; 21.14 refer to an expedition against other natives of the hill-
country (the Gibeonites, with whom Israel is said to have had an
alliance). Hence Saul will have succeeded not only in driving out the
Philistines, but also in subjecting at least two Canaanite populations in
the hill-country.

4.2.2 Now, however, chs.13-15 are disfigured by insertions or revi-
sions aimed at demonstrating the guilt of Saul and his sons on the
theological level and therefore his unworthiness to continue as king:
in 13.7b-14 Saul intervenes in the liturgy, which was considered

sacrilege, while in 14.24-34 he and Jonathan violate a solemn oath, albeit quite unconsciously. In 15.1ff. we have another complex connected with a ban which should have been implemented totally, according to the Deuteronomistic concept of the holy war, but which Saul carries out only partially. The result is that the king is now unworthy to continue his royal functions and a replacement seems inevitable; this is what in effect happens in ch.16.

4.2.3 Again, from 16.14ff. onwards Saul is presented as suffering from serious psychological disturbances; he is victim to attacks of melancholy which only David can calm by playing the harp, while in 18.10-16; 20.33 he seems to be the victim of homicidal fits, caused by his jealousy.

4.3 As far as we can reconstruct it, the real state of affairs seems to have been rather more prosaic. Saul is elected to the monarchy to serve the needs of a political and military situation which we can still appreciate perfectly today: the attacks of the Philistines from the south-west and the Ammonites from the east. In I Sam.8.20b, which as we have seen is Deuteronomistic or even later, we in fact find the people using a symptomatic phrase, intended to counter the anti-monarchical arguments of Samuel: 'That our king may govern (root *špṭ*) us and go out before us and fight our battles!' So if we accept the view, presented by all the biblical traditions, that Israel, unlike the other people in the region (Mesopotamia, Egypt, Syria and Palestine), did not originally have a king, it is also evident that the monarchy does not seem to have been the spontaneous product of the internal development of the nation. It came about under the stimulus of external needs, the concentric attacks of the Philistines and the Ammonites, against which the groups that made up Israel had no effective defence, and which put in question the very existence of the people. The existing centripetal organization which had prevailed so far had not succeeded in concentrating the various resources of Israel for its defence. And that also explains how there was always a strong anti-monarchical tendency in Israel, with the result that the fall of the reigning house in 587/6 was simply seen as proof on a historical level of the correctness of its own views. The national catastrophe was the just punishment for the sin of the people. We also find anti-monarchical views in Hos.8.4; 9.15-17, though they are limited to the northern kingdom.[12]

4.4 The reign of Saul seems to have been only of brief duration; in fact Saul fell in battle against the very Philistines whom he had first succeeded in conquering (I Sam.31; II Sam.1). However, the chronological information presented by the texts seems uncertain: I Sam.13.1 is a very obscure text, the first part of which is certainly corrupt, but the second part states, albeit with a suspect syntactical construction, that he had reigned only 'two years'[13] (that is, provided that we should not translate the passage, 'More than a year, indeed, two years, Saul reigned over Israel',[14] which would give a similar meaning). At all events, it seems to me that the information should be taken seriously, not least because the figure is not a stereotype;[15] and two years are not too short, in view of what I have said. There is another obscure text, I Sam. 27, where we have the expression '*yāmīm* and four months'; the first term is often used not only for 'day' but also for 'year', but in that case what does the plural signify? 'A year and four months'? If that is what it does mean, the statement would fit in well with the second part of 13.1.

4.5 Were we to accept this figure, it would in fact follow that Saul, the second part of whose history coincides with that of the rise of David to the throne, has now been supplanted by David on the literary level as well. What we now have is, as we have seen, a narrative favourable to David, in which the person of Saul and his relationship with David have been romanticized and dramatized; the first king of Israel emerges as a figure from Greek tragedy: unworthy without being really to blame (here the God of Israel clearly takes the place of fate), unbalanced psychologically as a result of events greater than he was, and which he was incapable of facing up to adequately, in continual struggle wih the very God who had first chosen him and later rejected him, his replacement was now only a matter of time. That was all the more certain since the person destined to succeed him was at hand: David, first a brave warrior of legendary prowess, and later a skilful commander. And given the mental instability of the king, the break between the two could only lead to the ruin of Saul, the weaker in character and the less skilful politician. Despite David's friendship with the hereditary prince Jonathan (I Sam.18.1ff.; 19.1ff.; 20.1ff.), his marriage to the princess Michal (we have already examined the problems over its historicity, above 3.1.2.2), which made him the king's son-in-law (I Sam.18.17ff.), the unjustified suspicions of the monarch soon forced David to make a total break. First he fled, and then took to the wilds in the desert of Judah, finally going over to the Philistines with the troops whom he had collected in the meantime and formed into a kind of private army (though originally these were essentially fugitives, insolvent debtors and other people in all kinds of difficulty, 22.1ff., eventually they formed the nucleus of David's own personal troops). To mark his status as a vassal, he received from the Philistines the locality of Ziklag, with which we shall be concerned in due course (7.4.2.1). Then, on the death of Saul, David was able to exploit skilfully his own position of strength, the chaos prevailing in the north and the benevolent neutrality of the Philistines towards him by having himself crowned successively king of Judah and then of Israel.[16] The tripartite division proposed by Humphreys - Saul as tragic hero in the earliest version of the narrative, Saul in the role of the 'wicked man' and finally Saul as the 'reject' -[17] thus seems essentially to fit the facts, even if his treatment of the texts is unconvincing. In other words, as Lemche rightly points out,[18] David comes out on top, and by coming out on top is the one who 'writes the history'!

4.6 However, all this is not history but historical romance. What little seems to be capable of historical verification shows a very different Saul: the commander who with a few, well-conducted military operations seems to have succeeded first in driving back the Ammonite threat from the east and then in liberating the hill-country from Philistine occupation and subjecting the hostile native populations. The defeat of his army and his death in battle at the edge of the hill-country marked the end of his work. The view of the narrative of David's rise to the throne that a madman, a maniac, prey to profound melancholy, to homicidal moods and other irrational fits (which is how the text describes Saul) could have continued to hold the supreme office of kingship seems improbable, even if history does give evidence of various cases of this kind. Now these considerations, if they are valid, cast considerable doubt on the original character of the motive which combines the rise of David with the psychological decline of Saul; indeed it is only Saul's madness which brings David to court, to practise a kind of music therapy (I Sam.16.14ff.), and which is later the cause of the future king's flight. It also substantiates the intrinsically disconcerting fact that David was to be found among the Philistines while Israel was fighting for its own survival, though the text stresses (I Sam.28.1f.; 29.1-11) that David and his troops never took up arms against their brothers in the north, albeit for involuntary reasons. So the end of Saul was due to his defeat and death in battle rather than to any other factors, whether celestial or terrestrial.

4.7 Contrary to my arguments of some years ago,[19] all this produces a notably different picture from the traditional one. David leaves Ziklag in the Negeb and settles in Hebron, where he is crowned king. Then, skilfully manoeuvring between the position of strength which he has achieved through his relationships with the victorious Philistines and the military decay of the north, after seven and a half years he also succeeded in becoming king of Israel. In both cases this probably happened with the connivance of the Philistines (it is difficult to imagine that they would have allowed their vassal to grow so strong without their permission); in this way they saw the possibility of exercising indirect control over the region through an intermediary. The rest seems to be the stuff of historical romance, a literary work of artistic strength and remarkable drama (which has not failed to inspire dramatists down the centuries), with at least as its main purpose the aim of legitimating the rise of David to the throne in place of an heir of Saul.

It does not seem historically improbable that David and Saul did know each other and for some time had a direct relationship, nor is there any reason to doubt that David had begun his own career under Saul, breaking with him later. We do not know why this happened, nor do we know why he thought he had to go over to the Philistines, against whom I Sam.23.1-5 even says that he won a battle with his private troops. Later, a remarkable work of art was constructed from all these episodes, which makes Saul the tragic hero, destined to fail because he represents the past, while David, the man in the ascendant, represents the future. The story describes in lyric tones the noble relationships (albeit in improbable circumstances) which bound together David and Jonathan and which made the first king a tormented figure, at odds with God and his own vocation, who fell victim to the tensions thus created, losing his psychological balance. Here his death in battle seems to be the deciding element in a situation from which not even the poet and dramatist could see a way out! We shall probably never know where history ends and the poetic transfiguration begins.

5.1 Having come to power, first over Judah and soon afterwards over Israel, two very modest political and ethnic groups, the second of which was emerging from a war which had ended in disaster and years of anarchy, David's first task clearly was that of restoring order and beginning reconstruction. However, there was also a basic need to maintain good relationships with the Philistines, with whose permission his ascent to the throne had become possible, as we have seen. As I pointed out, this relationship (above 4.7) was one of the strong points in David's position and allowed him remarkable freedom for manoeuvre: the thought that the hill-country which they sought to control, the seat of a hostile population, was in the hands of a vassal who had often given convincing proofs of his fidelity, must have been enticing to the Philistines, allowing them to exercise *de facto* power without using men and materials.

5.2 In this history we also need to devote some space to the Philistines themselves; they had proved a hard nut for Israel to crack in its earliest days, and even at a later date they were subject to Israel only for brief periods. As was acutely observed about twenty years ago,[20] they 'constituted so to speak a dialectical element in the history of Israel. Indeed it could be said that had there had not been such a strong adversary against which they had to defend themselves, the Hebrews might perhaps never have succeeded in achieving political unity' (above, 4.3).

Select bibliography: G.A.Wainwright, 'Some Sea-Peoples', *JEA* 47, 1961, 71-90; B.Brouda, 'Die Einwanderung der Philister in Palästina', in *Studien und Aufsätze... Anton Moortgat*, Berlin 1965, 126-35; M.-

L. & H. Erlenmeyer and M.Delcor, 'Philistins', *SDB* VII, 1966, 1233-88; K.A.Kitchen, 'The Philistines', in D.J.Wiseman (ed.), *Peoples from Old Testament Times*, Oxford 1973, 53-78; A.Strobel, *Der spätbronzezeitliche Seevölkerrsturm*, BZAW 145, Berlin 1976 (for the phenomenon in general and the Philistines in particular); T.Dothan, *The Philistines and their Material Culture*, New Haven 1982.

5.2.1 One thing should be said in advance: we do not have any written documents going back directly to the Philistines, but only mention of them by others, in Egyptian texts, and later in the Hebrew Bible and in Assyrian and Babylonian texts. It is only in the last few years that archaeological excavations have begun to provide first-hand discoveries; so far, however, there are no texts; here I should mention the excavations at Ashdod (coord.117-129, from the 1960s onwards) and on *tell qaṣīle* (coord.161-131), now on the northern periphery of Tel Aviv (we do not know to what Philistine locality this corresponds). We have no direct inside knowledge of the Philistines: we are forced back entirely on indirect evidence.

5.2.2 According to biblical information in the period identified according to conventional chronology with the last centuries of the second millennium BC, and specifically at the time of their clashes with Saul in the last decades of the millennium, the Philistines were now for the most part assimilated to the Western Semitic world. They had accepted its religion (I Sam.5-6 speaks of the cult of the god Dagon or Dagan, a deity of the harvest, probably identical to Ba'al in Syria and Palestine) and its language, so much so that their dealings with Israel and the other populations do not seem to have presented difficulties in this respect. However, they must have kept some technical terms, like *sᵉrānīm*, of uncertain origin, for their rulers. Here, too, however, we must seriously consider the possibility that these texts no longer reflect realities at the end of the second millennium but the situation of those who later handed down the tradition, when assimilation was now an accomplished fact.

5.3.1 Egyptian texts give us information about the origins of the Philistine settlement in the region. First, we know that throughout the second half of the second millennium BC, but particularly acutely at the time of the Pharaohs Merneptah (1237-25 or 1224-11) and Ramses III (1198-66 or 1184-43), groups of peoples coming from the Anatolian and Aegean worlds, commonly, though inaccurately, referred to as 'sea peoples', poured into the Eastern Mediterranean, Egypt and Libya by land and sea. At the end of the thirteenth century and the beginning of the twelfth they were the effective cause of the fall of the Hittite empire and of the Syrian city-states of Ugarit and Alalakh (the texts we have from these places are an important source of direct information about the region at this time, above, I.8). From Syria they pressed on towards Egypt by land and sea, but were thrust back by Ramses III (texts in *ANET*, 262ff.). The same Pharaoh then settled them in the southern coastal region of Palestine, which in fact took its name from them. They continued to live there, for some time at least nominally the vassals of Egypt. This is information which can easily be reconciled with that in the Bible, which sees the Philistines as being settled to the south-west of the hill-country, organized into a pentapolis comprising the places Ekron (perhaps *ḫirbet el-muqanna*, coord.136-131), Ashdod (mentioned above), Ashkelon (coord.107-118), Gath (perhaps *tell eṣ-ṣafī[t]*, coord.135-123), and Gaza (coord.099-101). The evidence for this is Josh 13.3, though this is a late text; each one of these places will have been ruled over by one of the *sᵉrānīm* (there is no instance of the singular **seren*).

5.3.2 Another group of 'sea peoples' had settled at Dor (present-day *ḫirbet el-burj*, near the abandoned Arab village of *tantūra*, coord.142-224) a few miles south of Carmel, again along the coast, and its presence here is confirmed by the story of the Egyptian official Wen-Amon at the end of the twelfth century (*ANET*, 25-29); there is no mention of this group in the Old Testament. The influence of the 'sea peoples' seems to have extended as far as Beth-shean, present-day *tell el-ḥuṣn*, a few yards to the north of the modern city (coord.197-212). This was another Egyptian stronghold, this time on the eastern edge of the plains which divide Galilee from the centre. And in fact the Philistines who defeated Saul and his sons on the heights of Gilboa (I Sam.31.8) were operating some way away from the pentapolis, which might suggest that they also had good relationships with the Canaanite city-states there, depending on them for their supplies. Perhaps Sisera, whom we see as the head of a Canaanite (and Philistine, if the information is correct) coalition, was also a Philistine; the coalition was defeated by Israel in the battle mentioned in Judg.4-5, which we shall deal with in due course (VIII.3).

5.3.3 Although they were victorious over the north, the strategic position of the Philistines remained weak. They did not have control of the hill-country, which they lost after their battles with Saul at the beginning of his career and never reconquered. That they had succeeded in occupying the area before Saul cannot follow from I Sam.13.19-23, which indicates that they had something like a monopoly in the working of iron; the monopoly would obviously have given them superiority over Israel and the Canaanites, even in the Bronze Age, not only in weapons but also in agriculture and crafts. And the rise of David to power seems to have resolved this problem for them in a favourable way.

6.1 II Sam.5;8 tell us of David's first enterprises; these chapters form a kind of annalistic summary of the king's undertakings (cf. above, 1.5.4).

6.1.1 If we accept the sequence of events and the description of the facts presented in ch. 5, we have a picture of the situation which, at least in broad outline, is not improbable, even if we take into account the possibility that the chronological order of the text does not necessarily correspond with actual events. Thus e.g. in his 1963 study B.Mazar suggests the following sequence of events: David king of Judah at Hebron; conquest of Jerusalem; continuation of the war with Eshbaal; his death and proclamation of David as king of Israel; defeat of the Philistines; restoration and rebuilding of Jerusalem and its proclamation as capital of the united kingdom. David's first enterprise thus seems to have been the conquest of Jerusalem, the territory of which was wedged between Judah and Benjamin and made communications difficult between the centre and the south. According to the sources, he will have managed this by a stratagem: a group of volunteers (5.8) will have crept in by the water conduit, either penetrating the city by stealth, or cutting off the water supply from the besieged. As the text puts it, what happened is unclear, but the reference is to the conduit which brought water to the upper city from the spring of Gihon in the Kidron valley.[21] This water course, restored and improved by King Hezekiah at the end of the eighth century with the prospect of an Assyrian siege, is still in existence and can be traversed on foot; we shall be dealing with its construction later (XI.2.3.3.2).

6.1.2 According to the sources, David then established his own residence in the citadel, from then on called 'the city of David' (5.9), which he restored and fortified; soon afterwards he had the ark, which the Philistines had captured and then abandoned (above, 1.5.2), brought to Jerusalem in solemn procession; the king himself joined in the procession (II Sam.6). In Jerusalem, the ark, an object which probably served as the throne of the invisible God of Israel, was given a provisional home in the expectation that its final resting-place would be somewhere more worthy of it, a temple (6.17ff.). As a result of all this the city, whose population belonged neither to Israel nor to Judah, had become the capital of the united kingdom, in that it was equidistant from its two components and at the same time independent of them and of tribal rivalry. However, this also a population which did not belong to the tribes of Israel and which was of a different religion into part of the kingdom.

6.1.3 For the Deuteronomistic history, David's action in bringing the ark to Jerusalem indicates on the one hand the continuity of the united kingdom with the past and on the other a completely new beginning, the new era which would end only with the destruction of the first temple in 587/86 BC, probably along with the ark. However, the ark tends to lose virtually all importance with the inauguration of the monarchy, becoming, in Solomon's temple, just one of the many furnishings of the sanctuary.[22]

6.2 This is the period in which the sources place David's first dealings with the Phoenicians of Tyre, even if everything does not seem to be as clear as it might appear on a first superficial reading. The mention of Hiram (probably Ahiram I, *c.* 970/69 – 936 or 926) in 5.11 raises considerable difficulties in terms of chronology. This ruler was in fact a contemporary of Solomon, with whom he had frequent dealings, so that if there was any overlap at all between his reign and that of David, it will have been at the end of David's reign, not at the beginning; nor does the narrative indicate any dealings with 'Abiba'al, Hiram's father. Is it possible that there were two rulers of the same name, the first of them a contemporary of David and the second a contemporary of Solomon? We do not know, but it seems improbable; it is more likely that here the sources are very confused over the chronology. That explains Garbini's scepticism about the historicity of these reports, even those about Solomon. Moreover, we know little about Phoenicia at this time: our scant information is based on extracts from the list of the kings of Tyre in a work by a certain Menander of Ephesus, quoted by Josephus;[23] I have dealt with the problems of these quotations earlier (II.7.2.1).

6.2.1 Relations with Tyre proved to be enduring: they continued to be excellent for more than a century, first between Tyre and the united kingdom, and then between Tyre and Israel, which had borders with it. It was only with Jehu's *coup d'état* and the overthrow of the dynasty of Omri, when the ruling house of Israel was exterminated and the queen mother, a princess of Tyre, was killed (below IX.4.1.2), that relationships were unilaterally broken off. The permanence of these relationships, which is quite unusual on the international scene, can be well explained from the fact that Israel and Phoenicia had complementary economies; Phoenicia helped Israel, which in antiquity was never a sea-faring people, in its overseas enterprises.

6.3 By now David, still nominally a Philistine vassal, had made himself so independent that a conflict was inevitable sooner or later. In other words, the Philistine hope of dominating the hill-country through an intermediary had been dashed, and the problems which decades earlier had ended in conflicts between the Philistines and Israel (giving rise to the monarchy in Israel) returned, magnified by the fact that now Judah and Israel had been reunited in a single kingdom under the leadership of a man who had proved to be very able. And the best pretext for opening hostilities was clearly provided by the alliance with Tyre:[24] nowhere in the region – as we know from almost all the treaties the texts of which have come down to us – was the vassal allowed to pursue a foreign policy independent of that of the king.[25] So David's action constituted a real *casus belli*.

6.4.1 The sources indicate two campaigns by the Philistines to subjugate David, the first in 5.17-21 and the second in 5.23-25. Both took the form of an attack against Jerusalem through the valley of the Rephaim, generally identified with the present-day *baq'a* (coord.127-167), through which the railway now enters the city. Both times the attackers were defeated. In this way the existing relationship between David and the Philistines was in effect overthrown: he had progressed from vassal to great king, and the Philistines were his subjects.

6.4.2 This does not seem to have caused any notable resentment among the Philistines as far as we know: it is generally accepted that they continued to provide mercenary contingents for David which the text calls 'Cherethites and Pelethites' (8.18; 15.18) and 'Hittites' (15.18),[26] while relationships with Achish of Gath, his first mentor when he went over to the Philistines, remained excellent until the beginning of the reign of Solomon (I Kings 2.39f.).

6.5 In the space of a few years, what the tradition calls a league of tribes, essentially in the north, united only in case of danger (and it was in a situation of extreme danger that Saul was elevated to the monarchy), had been substantially transformed. Earlier it had been governed by organs which barely existed, usually taking the form of an assembly with leaders elected by acclamation (i.e. a structured society which we might call democratic in the broadest sense of the term), an order which in recent years has often been compared with the so-called 'segmentary' society of black Africa, ethnically homogeneous. Now Israel, too, like the neighbouring nations, had become a state with a monarchy, hereditary and therefore dynastic, united and centred on the palace (and later, with Solomon, also on the temple). Its structure was more similar to that of the Canaanite city-state than to its former structure (cf. above, I.8). Probably the ancient tribal structures continued in force, at least theoretically; in practice the new system ended by displacing all other forms of government. Of course it was much more efficient at the administrative level and in providing defence, but it was also much less tolerant at a personal and economic level!

7 After the unification of Israel and Judah in one kingdom,[27] the conquest of Jerusalem and the neutralization of the Philistines, David went on to a series of military campaigns which led in succession to the conquest of Transjordan and a large part of Syria.

7.1 The information given in II Sam.5 and 8 is of an annalistic kind and could go back to an ancient source. However, it does not say anything about the precise order of events and the chronological intervals between them: the few dates that we do have (for example, the seven and a half years of David's reign in Hebron and the two years' reigns of Saul and Eshbaal respectively) are not only often uncertain but also inadequate as a basis for the reconstruction of a chronology of David's reign, whether relative or absolute: the same goes, as we shall see shortly, for the reign of Solomon (below IV.1ff.).

7.1.1 As we have seen, chs.5 and 8 should probably be taken with the narrative in ch.12 about the capture of Rabbath-ammon; these accounts have now been inserted into the 'succession narrative' (above 1.5.3) and filled out with the story of David's first relations with Bathsheba and the reproof of him from the prophet Nathan.

Bibliography: M.F.Unger, *Israel and the Aramaeans of Damascus*, London 1957 and reprints; B.Mazar, 'Geshur and Maacah', *JBL* 80, 1961, 16-28; id., 'The Military Elite of King David', *VT* 13, 1963, 310-20; A.Malamat, op.cit., at 3.1 (with bibliography); G.Garbini, art.cit.

In ch.8 David again fights with the Philistines and then defeats the Moabites (v.2), in effect decimating them; next come the Aramaean kingdoms of Zobah (v.3, cf.10.6) and Damascus (v.5), while the kingdom of Hamath submits of its own accord (vv.9f.). Then the Edomites are also defeated (vv.13ff.).

7.1.2 In chs.10-12//I Chron.19-20 there is an account of how the Ammonites were subjected, along with the Aramaeans of Beth-rehob, Ma'acah and Tob (10.6).

7.1.3 The incorporation into the empire of the Canaanite city-states of the central and northern plains must also have taken place in this period, probably before the campaigns in Transjordan and Syria, since it is reasonable to suppose that they had to be occupied so that the flanks of tribal territory could be protected. Judges 1.27ff. (cf. Josh.17.11ff.) explicitly says that the areas had not been conquered, but notes that 'they were subjected to tribute' 'when Israel became powerful' (Josh.17.13//Judg.1.28); this is a piece of information which could easily be connected with the rise of the Davidic empire. Solomon then incorporated them, some decades later, into the new system of districts into which the north was divided (I Kings 4.7-19; cf. IV.5.1).

7.1.4 *Bibliography*: A. Malamat, op.cit. (above 3), 31-42.

In II Sam.3.3 it is said that David had married the daughter of the king of Geshur, another Aramaean kingdom of Syria, so that for many years there was a close alliance between this small state and the empire. And it was in fact to Geshur, to his maternal grandmother, that tradition made Absalom flee after the facts narrated in II Sam. 13.37-39 (cf. 14.23,32). This must originally have been an alliance between equals, as in the case of Tyre.

7.2 At a constitutional level (to use a modern expression which is not completely appropriate), the kingdom of David thus seems to have been a remarkably complex structure.

7.2.1 First of all we have the traditionally Israelite territories: Judah in the south, the first seat of the monarchy, and Israel in the centre and to the north, over which David reigned by the decision of the respective popular assemblies (above 2.2).

7.2.2 At least two places seem to have enjoyed a special status by belonging to the dynasty in a personal form. Ziklag, in the south, was given by the Philistines to David when he submitted to them (I Sam.27.5f., cf. above 4.5); the terminology indicates that this status was maintained. David was ruler of Jerusalem by right of conquest (but cf. above, 6.1.1), becoming king of the city-state and residing in its citadel (5.9).

7.2.3 Then there were the Canaanite city-states in the central and northern plains which, for want of direct information, we can only suppose to have been incorporated into the empire, as we saw, by some form of treaty which left their administration intact.

7.2.4 There were also the kingdoms of Transjordan, corresponding in territorial terms more or less to the present-day Hashemite Kingdom of Jordan (without the territory west of the Jordan), namely Ammon, Edom and Moab. Edom seems to have been annexed directly, if it is true, as II Sam. 8.13f. affirms, that David had governors there: the other two, however, probably became vassals of the empire.

7.2.5 The various Aramaean kingdoms, a territory comprising the greater part of present-day Syria and eastern Lebanon (the coastal region, however, belonged to the Phoenician city states), had partly accepted a vassal relationship and had partly been subjected. Only Geshur was a long-standing ally of David.

7.3 Such a complex structure obviously gave rise to equally complex and often contradictory situations, which therefore could lead to conflict at a legal level. In fact substantially different and partly almost incompatible institutions had come together and been superimposed. There were: the personal union between the two Hebrew groups, a problem to which we shall return in due course (7.4.3); the special status of Ziklag and Jerusalem; the nations of Transjordan and Syria, allies, vassals or just annexed; the city-states of the plains, of which we have virtually no precise knowledge and about which we can only make guesses; and the treaties and intimate alliances with Geshur and Tyre, the second certainly much freer than the first, which was completely surrounded by territory belonging to the empire. However, such a structure, which seems to agree with the main lines of the census taken by David (II Sam.24//I Chron.21, a text of uncertain date but certainly a different tradition from the other sources) is not unusual in the ancient Near East; it also recalls the structures first of the Assyrian empire and then of Babylonia and of Persia. Like these, it had incorporated substantial territory inhabited by alien populations and extended far beyond the original boundaries of the mother country; and like these it was difficult to administer, given its ethnic diversity and the natural tendency of the people who made it up to seek to regain their independence (this had already begun to happen under Solomon, below, IV, 3-4). This process accelerated and even became irreversible after the break in the personal union on the death of Solomon. Moreover, the united kingdom was a large one: according to the sources, from the traditional boundary with Egypt (the *wādī el 'arīš*, the 'brook of Egypt') it extended to the northern bank of the Euphrates, a feature which (above II, 3.3.3) some scholars would still like to see as a sign of the late character of the whole tradition.

7.4.1 This reconstruction of the legal and constitutional situation of the Davidic empire has followed and amplified the basic study of the question made by A.Alt.[28] However, its results were put in question during the 1960s by the important work of Giorgio Buccellati.[29]

7.4.2 For Buccellati, the first doubtful feature is the special status of Ziklag and Jerusalem respectively: Alt argued that the two places had a special status; for Buccellati this theory seems without foundation.

7.4.2.1 The situation of Ziklag, according to Buccellati, was simply governed by the fact that the territory was never restored to those who had a right to it, the Philistines, who had given it to David (161). The text states: 'In those days Achish gave Ziklag to him (David); therefore the place has belonged to the kings of Judah to this day' (I Sam.27.6); this is a formula the ultimate implications of which are not completely clear. A further difficulty is that the location of the place has not been identified precisely, so that it is not easy to see what function it had in the sphere of the Philistine pentapolis. According to traditional opinion,[30] it is to be identified with present-day *tell el-ḥuweilife* (coord.136-088), about thirty miles NNE of Beersheba; in that case the territory in the area was not strictly Philistine but was part of an area occupied by them only in the periods of their maximum expansion. And it seems to have been assigned to David in one of these periods: in that way the Philistines were still able to control it without extending their own lines of communication too far, an attempt like the one they made earlier in the case of the hill country (above 4.7). However, another authoritative attempt to identify the place is that proposed recently by Y.Aharoni;[31] this connects it with *tell eš-šarī'ah* (coord.119-088), about thirty miles NNW of Beersheba; in that case it would be a typical frontier post, subject to frequent changes of sovereignty depending on circumstances. Here too, however, it does not seem appropriate to talk of restitution: once independent of the power of the

Philistines, David continued his own career without allowing the Pentapolis to expand further. Therefore the redaction, certainly later than the time of Solomon, had to limit itself to noting that the place belonged to the crown in a personal form, we might say as an ancient possession of the state, independently of the sovereignty of the house of David and Judah and their order. However, where Buccellati is right is in pointing out that there is nothing to show that before it was assigned to David, Ziklag will once have been a city-state governed by a hereditary monarchy whose place was then taken by David and his successors: the text does no more than affirm that the city 'belonged' to the dynasty without specifying how or under what legal regime.

7.4.2.2 The question of Jerusalem, on the other hand, seems much more complicated, not least because of the infinitely greater importance of the capital, whether on the immediate political level or within the sphere of the religious tradition of Israel. Here, as we have seen (above I.8), its character as a city-state is firmly attested in the pre-Israelite period, since we also hear of the sovereign who governed it, who was at least nominally a vassal of Egypt. There is no reason to doubt that this will have been its situation at the time of the occupation by David's troops. This raises the question: did Jerusalem continue to keep its status after its conquest and incorporation into the kingdom? For lack of any direct evidence, here too we must base ourselves on indirect and implicit evidence, which is all we have at our disposal. David and his successors never bore the title 'king of Jerusalem', unlike the Crusader kings and their successors, but we have seen that in the el-'Amarna letters the sovereigns never had this title either. On the other hand, the texts never speak of Jerusalem as an ancient administrative or topographical entity belonging to Judah, or of Judah as including the city; that would have been obvious had the city been incorporated into the northern part of the kingdom. The phrase used is always 'Judah and Jerusalem', which suggests a special administrative situation, autonomous over against both the tribal institutions and those of the state, and governed directly by the crown. Indirect confirmation of this appears in Josh.15.7b-19, where the unexpected wealth of frontier points as soon as we reach the area of the capital seems meant to indicate the separation between the territory of the south and that of the ex-city-state.[32] In my contribution to Hayes-Miller*, 1977, I have therefore suggested as a parallel the federal districts and the 'federal capitals' of Australia and so many American states. This would indicate that, apart, of course, from the republican form of government in the modern parallels, Jerusalem was at the same time united and yet separate from the kingdom, as they are.

7.4.2.3 Again according to Alt, the status of Samaria in the North, founded at the end of the ninth century BC, does not seem to have been very different (below, IX.3.3.2, but see the well-founded objections made here). The only difference was that it never had the tradition of a city-state behind it; the similarity lay essentially in the fact that the model seems to have been that of Jerusalem.[33] In the light of what has been said it therefore seems reasonable to maintain Alt's theory in the present state of research, at least for Jerusalem.

7.4.3 However, Buccellati has again put in question the very idea of a personal union. This is the form of government by which two or more nations, politically independent of one another, have the same sovereign; otherwise each has its own political and administrative organization. One modern instance is that of Denmark and Iceland before the Second World War; each country had its own legislative, executive and judiciary powers, but only one ruler, the king of Denmark.

7.4.3.1 On the one hand, Buccellati is certainly ready to recognize that there are a number of features in favour of the theory of a personal union between Judah and Israel under David and Solomon; on the other hand, he points out that this seems to be in marked contrast with the image of a state heavily centralized on the capital, Jerusalem, and on the court. Is it possible to maintain such an image?

7.4.3.2 A number of features would seem to militate against it: to begin with, we have the enthronement of David first over one and then over the other of the two entities, followed by the 'secession' of the latter on the death of Solomon, after the laborious negotiations between the assembly and his nominated successor Rehoboam (below, IX.1.1); further, there is the division of the North into districts each responsible for maintaining the court and the state cult, along with the bureaucracy, for one month of the year (I Kings 4.7-19), while there is no indication of anything of this kind in the South (below, IV.5.1). However, what seems probable is that in Judah and Israel there was considerable tension between traditional centrifugal tendencies and centripetal tendencies focussed on the court; the former were led by the ancient tribal organs, now partly superseded (and we shall see some examples of this even during the reign of David, 9.1.2-3), but always ready to make a comeback in times of crisis, when the central power was eclipsed. That is not to say that these forces were intrinsically opposed to the monarchy; after all, it brought peace, order, security and indeed prosperity (with the exceptions that we shall consider below). It was opposed only when it took the form of bad government and oppression, excessive and therefore unjust taxation, personal services with no relation to real need, and a tendency to wipe out local autonomy. In the present state of research, then, the concept of personal union seems to be the most suitable one for describing relationships which at the same time both united and separated Israel and Judah.

8 The complexity of the new kingdom obviously tended to make its administrative structure complex as well. This explains why it is only with David that we begin to feel that we can talk of what might be called a real public administration, a bureaucracy, with trained officials for the various and mostly new tasks that had to be performed.

8.1 *Bibliography*: T.N.D.Mettinger, *Solomonic State Officials*, CB-OTS 5, Lund 1971, with bibliography; J.A.Soggin*, 1977, 336ff. I have not been able to use U.Rütersworden, *Die Beamten der israelitischen Königszeit*, Diss. Bochum 1981.

Two texts give us information about government officials at the time of David: II Sam.8.15-18//I Chron.18.14-17 and II Sam.20.23-26, with no parallel in Chronicles, probably slightly later. A third list appears in I Kings 4.1-6 for the period of Solomon. In the first of these lists, v.17//16 should probably read: '... and Zadok, and Abiathar, son of Ahimelech, son of Ahitub...' These are in fact the names of the father and the grandfather of Abiathar (I Sam.22.20); originally Zadok appears as no one's son, and only in I Chron.6.34 is he given a genealogy, generally considered to legitimate him. It is therefore of little historical value (below XII.5.3.1).

8.2 The following officials appear in the list:

8.2.1 Joab, commander of the army (8.16; 20.24);

8.2.2 Jehoshaphat (8.16; 20.24), who has the title *mazkīr*;

8.2.3 Zadok and Abiathar (8.17; 20.25), priests;

8.2.4 Seraiah (8.17), who has the title *sōpēr*; but in 20.25 he appears as *š^eyā'* in K, and *š^ewā'* in Q, as *šawšā'* in I Chron., while in I Kings 4.6 we have *šīšā'*. This is probably the corruption of the original title of an Egyptian official: *sš.š'.t* or *sh š'.t*, i.e. 'scribe' plus 'letter'.[34]

8.2.5 Benaiah, commanding the 'Cherethite and Pelethite' mercenaries (8.18; 20.23, cf. above 6.4.1).

8.2.6 The 'sons of David', indicated generically as 'priests' (8.18), whereas in I Chron. 18.17 they are called 'the first beside the king', perhaps a deliberate correction by someone who could not accept priests who were not levites.

8.2.7 Adoniram (only 20.24), in charge of forced labour (*mas*).

8.2.8 Ira, 'priest for David' (only 20.25), whatever this expression is meant to indicate.

8.2.9 These offices and the people who perform them reappear in I Kings 4.1-6, where we also find a 'prefect of the palace', whose name is Ahishar (4.6).

8.3 The titles *sōpēr* and *mazkīr* (above, 8.2.2-4) are translated into Greek as γραμματεύς and ὑπομνηματόγραφος respectively; in modern translations they often appear as 'scribe' and 'secretary'. In reality, the former seems to be 'secretary', contrary to later Hebrew usage; his office is the one which is in fact referred to by the Egyptian title which usually denotes it. However, we know little of the latter, and there are those who think that he had a representative function.

9.1.1 We have already seen that the complexity of the Davidic empire, and the institutions of which it was evidently a real centralized public administration, inevitably led to tensions, if not to real conflicts on a local level, especially when it was involved in clashes with the traditional tribal institutions and forced otherwise free citizens to curtail their own freedoms for reasons which cannot in any way have seemed connected with public good and public order. Moreover, it conscripted them for works whose utility was either misunderstood or non-existent (we shall be concerned with this in more detail below, IV.5.3.1 – 5.4.2). Even today, in the so-called segmentary societies of Black Africa, there are similar conflicts in analogous situations.

9.1.2 The sources have handed down information about at least two rebellions, which chiefly involved the North (the tribes most affected by the new fiscal policy of the empire, below, IV.5.2). In anticipation I should say that the paradox of the empire of David and Solomon is that it did not fall under the pressure of external factors, as was the case with the empires of Assyria, Babylon and Persia, but dissolved from within because the North, one of the two constituent elements in the personal union, detached itself and until its fall became completely independent, a fact with which the South could never come to terms.

9.1.3 The texts of II Sam.15-19 mention a first rebellion which produced a real crisis for the empire. In fact David had to flee the capital, together with all the apparatus of state and religion, indeed even abandoning his harem. This rebellion was begun and led by Absalom, the crown prince, and, as is the wont of the 'succession narrative', everything is described in terms of the family. We are told that the prince had avenged the honour of his sister Tamar, who had been enticed, raped, rejected and insulted by her half-brother Amnon: he had killed Amnon. Absalom had had to flee abroad and had taken refuge with his mother's family at Geshur (above 7.1.4); then, however, after being pardoned by his father, he had returned home. The texts (cf. 15.2-6) present him as a man with remarkable personal gifts, capable of exploiting with great skill the popular discontent which the sources show to have been quite widespread. After spending some time making preparations, he went to Hebron, where he had himself proclaimed king, immediately obtaining the support of 'all the tribes of Israel' to whom he had sent messengers. The text does not say whether 'Israel' means only the North, as is often the case, or whether it refers to the whole Israelite part of the empire, thus including Judah; however, the latter alternative appears more probable, despite what I have said in earlier works. The meeting place is in the South and was also the original seat of David's kingdom; moreover, the almost catastrophic dimensions of the event suggest happenings which must have involved almost everyone. Be this as it may, David succeeded in gaining the upper hand thanks to his own personal army, which put to flight the popular militia of the rebels and also killed the prince in his flight. Other details narrated in the 'history' are not relevant here.

9.1.4 A second case, of what seem much more modest proportions, limited to the North and probably never really dangerous, is the rebellion of the Benjaminites, soon joined by Ephraim and Manasseh. It is reported that the rebels had as their war-cry:

> 'We have no portion in David,
> and we have no inheritance in the son of Jesse;
> every man to his tents, O Israel!' (II Sam.20.1).

The phrase is important because it appears on the lips of the secessionists a generation later, with the addition of a fourth line:

> 'Look now to your own house, David' (I Kings 12.16).

This shows that the North had spontaneously entered the empire through the personal union, and decided to leave when the original reasons for its involvement no longer existed.

This time, too, David succeeded in gaining the upper hand; the chief of the rebels, a certain Sheba, was killed in the city in which he had taken refuge, and the rebels were pardoned by David.

9.2 The 'succession narrative' ends with the accession of Solomon to the throne on the death of David (I Kings 1-2). Here the king seems totally senile, incapable of taking decisions and therefore of governing, at the mercy of the intrigues of the harem and the court. It is not surprising that there were those who attempted to exploit a situation of this kind. The crown prince Adonijah tried to secure the succession which in any case he might reasonably expect as the next in line to the throne. He was aided by Joab, the commander of the army, and Abiathar the priest. Solomon, however, the second in the line, had been designated by David himself at the instigation of his mother Bathsheba; he was supported by David's private army, a group which once again proved its efficiency, and Zadok the priest. He managed to get the better of his opponents, and used the first period of his new power to proscribe or even eliminate on various pretexts all those who might have been a danger to him. So this is actually a *coup d'état*, though the author of the 'succession narrative' describes the political ability of the new ruler in laudatory terms. Whether or not he supported these acts of government, he clearly considered them the lesser evil, if not actually a good thing; as I have already pointed out, David, at least in the latter part of his life,[35] in fact seems to have been in a decline: the victim of his own passions, puppet of his own general Joab, whom he allowed to intervene in affairs of government as he liked, and senile during the last years of his reign. Nor can we suppose that Adonijah, who was also completely dependent on the general, would have conducted the affairs of state with greater skill; because he owed power to Joab, he too would have been Joab's puppet. The succession narrative hardly has an objective approach to the problem: it tries to discredit the dying sovereign (as we can see, not without reason) and his successor in line to the throne, thus legitimating the one who was only second in line of succession and his seizure of power. Thus, *mutatis mutandis*, what happened to David was very like what happened to Saul, a feature which we can perhaps also see as a didactic aim of the 'succession narrative'.

10 One of the most complex problems of the period, which is virtually insoluble in the present state of research, is that of the nature and development of Israelite religion from this time onwards, down to the time of Josiah (below, XI.4). The sources paint the following picture, but this is clearly the theory of the 'succession narrative', later taken up and developed by Deuteronomy.

10.1 David will have marked the beginning of what I have called a 'state syncretism'.[36] With the aim of unifying the various populations which made up the empire, at least on the religious level, since this was obviously impossible at an ethnic or political level, David had recourse to a series of religious measures, which were taken over and completed by his successor Solomon. So his will have been a planned and coherent political action, not just the kind of unity which people arrive at, even if they are different, by the continued contact which results from living in the same territory and being subjected to the same political régime. Rather, these were measures emanating from on high, from the competent instruments of government. And as I have said, with the building of the temple at Jerusalem, Solomon only took to its conclusion the approach which had already been begun by providing a real central sanctuary for the whole of the empire. David, too, wanted to build the temple, but II Sam.7.1-3 describes how the prophet Nathan, having first given his consent, suddenly prohibited the implementation of the plan. I have tried to explain this unexpected *volte face* in terms of the opposition of more active theological elements to a manifest attempt on the part of the king to claim authority in the religious sphere, an authority which could in no way be his right in Israel. Saul, too, is said to have met his downfall attempting to do the same thing. And the opposition will have shown itself as soon as Nathan saw the implications of David's project. However, it seems simpler, and nearer to reality, to think that the tradition registered what at that time will certainly have been a disconcerting fact, that it was not the victorious king David (according to the widespread custom) who built the temple, but his successor Solomon; and tried to find a plausible reason.

10.2 A first move by David in the direction of this syncretistic policy will have been the recovery of the ark and its transfer to Jerusalem, to a temporary resting place (II Sam.6). In succession a series of Canaanite elements will have been incorporated into the religion of Israel by means of the state cult: the royal ideology, including among other things the divine promise that the dynasty would last for ever (II Sam.7.15; Ps.2.7; 110.4; Isa. 9.6f. and other passages). In Israel, too, the king was thus presented as the 'adopted son' of the deity, a feature well attested in Ugarit (*CTA* 15, II.25-27; 16.10f.), but unknown in Israel on the secular level; adoption evidently brought the monarch close to the divine sphere (cf. Ps.45.7, where the cantor addresses to the king the invocation 'O God', or I Kings 21.11-14, where anyone who blasphemes 'God and the king' is said to deserve death). This is an approach which is not mentioned in any of the collections of laws in the Hebrew Bible and there is evidence of it only in Isa.8.21 as a sign of desperation. Cf. also Ps.21.4, where the king obtains 'eternal life', a typical divine prerogative, and II Sam.23.1, in the emended text, where Elyon, a Canaanite deity also attested elsewhere (and later identified with Yahweh) raises the king above all other men. The functions of protection and promotion in the social sphere also form part of the royal ideology (II Sam.21.17; Lam.4.20), as do his connections with the fertility of the soil, the flocks and the herds (Ps. 72.5-6,16 and the Ugaritic texts cited above). Again, the king appears to perform real priestly functions, as guardian and patron of the ark; Solomon, as we shall see later (IV.2.3ff.), intercedes for the people in prayer and offers sacrifice when he inaugurates the temple. The king also seems to have exercised similar functions in Phoenicia.[37]

10.3 This is what our sources and the reconstruction of events on the basis of them seemed to tell us until about ten years ago. However, contrary to what I have argued in earlier works, the problem which emerges is much more complex.

10.3.1 First of all, the view that Israelite religion was originally pure and orthodox (at this point we could well ask: judged by what criteria?) and later contaminated, first by contact with the Canaanites during and immediately after the conquest, and then through the syncretism of the state (and also, of course, by the sinfulness of the people, who are often said to have 'stiff necks') is a reconstruction which is too reminiscent of the myth of the golden age, of noble and pure origins subsequently followed by decay, to be adequate as a historical explanation of the phenomenon of paganism and syncretism in Israel. However, this is the view of the first redactors of the Old Testament, especially of Deuteronomy and Dtr, who used it to explain the (well-deserved) divine judgment on the people, manifest first in the fall of the monarchy, which by divine decree had been destined to be eternal, and then in the loss of political independence, which put in doubt the divine promise of the land.

10.3.2 Nor is that all. As I have tried to demonstrate elsewhere,[38] it is very difficult, if not impossible, to go back on the historical level to the content, rites and beliefs of Israelite religion in pre-exilic times. The little that we can discover with any certainty shows the broad diffusion of features little different from those existing in the Canaanite world around, the only difference being that YHWH was the national deity. These are features which later historiography criticized severely, presenting them as the cause of the divine judgment. Certainly, even before the exile there were people and groups who argued the need for Israel to worship one God, YHWH, and not to recognize others, and we can probably find these features among the prophets and their disciples.It seems only reasonable to suppose that the authors of Deut and Dtr could have been able to draw abundantly on the sources and that they will have had their spiritual roots there.

10.4 Thus, if, for example, we look at ancient Hebrew nomenclature, we find some particularly revealing features. The tradition gave Gideon another name, Jerubbaal; a son of Saul is called Eshbaal and one of his grandsons Merib-baal or Mepi-baal; a son of David bears the name Ba'aliada (I Chron.14.7). These are names which evidently indicate either a devotion to this Canaanite deity or his identification with the God of Israel; later, when this deity had become the opponent of YHWH *par excellence*, the redactors distorted the names to *bōšet*, 'shame' (in II Sam.11.21 *Jerubbaal* has become *Jerubbeset*!). And we may well also ask whether many personal names ending in *'ēl* or beginning with *'ēl* do not rather refer to the supreme deity of the Canaanite pantheon before he was put on a level with YHWH and identified with him.

10.5 What seems to have happened, then, is that increasingly influential groups, led by the prophets, struggled down the centuries to impose on the religion of Israel absolute monotheistic forms of faith of a very high spiritual level; and these struggles were crystallized in the religious reforms first of Hezekiah (below XI.2) and then of Josiah (below, XI.4.2.2).

11 The economic and political problems which arose with the emergence of the new form of government, with its demands in the form of personal and collective taxation, claims for contributions in kind and for compulsory, often forced, labour, are also particularly complex. We shall deal with them next (IV.5), lock, stock and barrel, in the context of the reign of Solomon. I have already alluded to them above (9.1.1).

IV

SOLOMON

1 As we have seen (above, 9.2), the history of Solomon begins with the epilogue to the 'succession narrative' and continues as far as I Kings 11.

1.1 In I Kings 11.41 there is mention of a 'Book of the Acts of Solomon', which some regard as the official chronicle of the court and others, given the lack of any objective means of verification, as one of the many references to documents with which all ancient literature, including classical literature, is so often furnished. The same thing still appears in relatively recent times in the form of fictitious letters; one need only recall the manuscript from which Alessandro Manzoni claims to have taken *I promessi sposi*. For Josephus and his references to ancient sources, cf. above II.7.2.1.[1] So the mention of the existence of this 'book' needs to be treated with caution, taking into account the possibility that it is fictitious, especially as the biblical text does not give extracts from it, but only makes quite general references to it.

1.2 If we are to accept the existence of a work of this kind and the transmission of extracts from it in the text that has come down to us, we must try, at least hypothetically, to identify the extracts; and we can only do this by attempting to isolate what seems to be relevant information at a political, administrative and economic level, in which family saga, legends, anecdotes or stories are either completely absent, or at least secondary. These are:

1.2.1 The list of state officials in I Kings 4.1-6, like the other two which appear in the David narratives (above III.8).

1.2.2 The list of districts and governors appointed over them (I Kings 4.7-19).

1.2.3 The very brief note on forced labour (below, 5.3) in I Kings 5.13, in clear contrast to the other longer note in 9.15-22, revised by Dtr and with an interesting addition by the LXX.

1.2.4 Sparse references to commercial enterprises launched by Solomon (10.11ff., 22, 28ff.).

These are some texts which could be extracts from the 'Book of the Acts of Solomon', provided that we accept its existence: more than that it is impossible to say.

1.3 *Bibliography*: H.G.M.Williamson, 'The Accession of Solomon in the Books of Chronicles', *VT* 26, 1976, 351-61.

As in the case of David (cf. above III.1.5.5), the books of Chronicles give a description in which the authors are controlled by hagiographical interests: the person of the monarch is no longer seen in realistic terms, but he appears as a combination of national hero and saint. He is essentially the wise man, dedicated to the organization of the cult, of which he is largely the founder, in succession to his father. On the basis of the information provided by Chronicles, the request of the tribes from the north (II Chron.10.1ff.//I Kings 12.1ff.) for the tribute imposed on them under Solomon to be reduced would seem almost absurd, gratuitous and therefore impious, given that the texts have said little or nothing about it. But we may conjecture that in cases like this, as elsewhere, the Chronicler would presuppose that his readers had access to the information given in I-II Samuel and I-II Kings. At all events, Chronicles is to be used with special care in reconstructing the history of the period, if we suppose it can be used at all.

1.4 In terms of archaeology, however, we are better informed than we were with David (above III.1.5.6), though here, as I pointed out in 1977*, 340ff., the information is 'disappointingly scarce'. In the early 1960s the North American archaeologist G.E.Wright pointed out – and I quote his very words:[2] 'No discovery has been made in Jerusalem which can be dated with a minimum of certainty to the time of David and Solomon.' Today this situation has partly changed, but only in certain sectors, after about twenty years of archaeological campaigns, in particular in the Jewish Quarter of the Old City.

1.4.1 The difficulties of making excavations under Jerusalem are easy to explain: it has always been a complicated, not to say impossible task to carry out archaeological explorations under an inhabited centre, at least in every-day conditions. Only in special cases like the restoration of the Jewish Quarter in the Old City of Jerusalem or the building of the seminary of the Armenian Patriarchate south of the Jaffa Gate has it become partially possible, and then only in very limited areas. At all events, the English expeditions led by K.M.Kenyon in 1964 and 1974[3] have thought that they have identified an ancient filling of ground with man-made objects that the texts call *millō'* (literally 'filling up'). David is said to have extended and restored this, and Solomon is said to have reinforced it and strengthened it (II Sam.5.9; I Kings 9.24; 11.27). Remains of Solomon's walls have also been identified here and there under the Herodian walls which supported the ancient esplanade of the temple, now the Moslem sanctuary of *harām eš-šarīf*.[4] Here and there, during the reconstruction of the Jewish Quarter, ancient walls from the time of the monarchy have surfaced, even if they do not go back as far as the united monarchy.

1.4.2 On *tell el-mutesellim* (coord.167-221), the ancient Megiddo, we find a more favourable situation, even if a number of over-optimistic affirmations from the past have had to be revised. The most famous of these was the claim to have discovered 'Solomon's stables', which the king is said to have built (I Kings 9.15-19); in the first place, this is a complex which recent checks have shown to be a century or two later, and perhaps they are not even stables. For a study of two Solomonic palaces at Megiddo, see now the exhaustive article by B.Gregori.[5]

1.4.3 The situation seems to be similar with Hazor (*tell el qedah*, coord. 203-269) and Gezer (coord.142-140), places which, like Megiddo, are said to have been 'built' (root *bānāh*), by Solomon. However, this may mean that Solomon 'restored it', 'rebuilt it', or 'fortified' the existing structures (I Kings 9.15). In all these places a construction has been found which has been identified with the gate of the city. It has a distinctive form, typical of this period: beside the passage-way we find three rectangular niches; these are usually taken to be guard-rooms. At Megiddo, the excavations show that this kind of gate is to be found at the end of the development of a particular technique, attested in Canaan in previous centuries. However, the gates of Dan (*tell el-qadi*, coord.211-294, in the extreme north) and Beersheba (*tell es-saba'*, coord.134-072, in the Negeb) show a similar construction, but one that is later and considerably simplified, with only two spaces, one on each side of the passage.[6]

1.4.4 A ruin near the shore of the Red Sea, between the present-day localities of Aqaba and Eilath, on the Jordanian side near the frontier, *tell el-ḥeleife* (coord.147-884), which in the 1930s had been identified by archaeologists with the biblical Ezion-geber, the port for loading copper at the time of Solomon, has meanwhile proved, after more accurate checks, to be a warehouse with an adjacent small fortress. The port in question is now located more to the south-south-east, perhaps in the bay south of the Coral Isle or the Isle of the Pharaohs (Arabic *jazīrat al-far'ūn*, Hebrew *'y ha'almōgīm*, coord.133-871), the ancient Egyptian port for transporting minerals. What are known as 'Solomon's pillars' or 'Solomon's mines' at Timnah, north of Eilath (coord.145-909), were abandoned between the twelfth and the tenth centuries BC, so they cannot have been used by Solomon.[7]

2 At the end of the 'succession narrative', Solomon thus seems to be firmly seated on his own throne, now with no enemies who could have thwarted the operation.

2.1 Moreover it is clear, as we have seen, that for the author of the 'succession narrative' it was good that things worked out like this.

2.1.1 However, whereas to judge from the sources the twin themes of divine designation and popular acclamation thus appear to have been basic, first for Saul and then for David, neither of them appears in the history of Solomon, who ascended the throne after a palace conspiracy and a *coup d'état*. The fact that the author of the 'succession narrative' takes a favourable view of these events does not alter this situation in any way.

2.1.2 Thus there arose the problem of the legitimation of the new king, a problem which was evidently felt deeply by the writer who continued the 'succession narrative': the fact that an irregular act of government proved in particular conditions to be opportune and thus beneficial did not make it legitimate. And the sources found the legitimation of Solomon in the account of a pilgrimage which he made to the 'high place' of Gibeon, probably located near to the present-day village of *ej-jīb* (coord.167-139, I Kings 3.14f.). The text does not say whether this was a Canaanite or an Israelite sanctuary, but the fact that I Chron. 21.29 and II Chron 1.3-5 ostentatiously locate the tabernacle and the altar from the wilderness period here, thus trying to make the place an Israelite sanctuary, seems at least suspicious; the excuse offered in I Kings 3.2 that the place served as a sanctuary for Israel because the temple had not yet been built points in the same direction: why offer an excuse if this was an Israelite sanctuary?

2.2 Now according to the text, Solomon had a dream in the sanctuary of Gibeon. YHWH appeared to him and asked him to make a wish, which would be granted. The king asked for 'an understanding mind [literally 'heart'] to govern (*špṭ*) your people, that I may discern between good and evil' (v.9). In the final phase of the redaction, the narrative seeks to substantiate the legend of Solomon as the wise king; however, originally the passage will have related to more important characteristics: in Ps.2, a text which is connected with the enthronement ceremony of the king of Judah and which is perhaps already connected with the enthronement ceremony of the united kingdom, we find a phrase which is semantically equivalent to the one quoted in I Kings 3.5:

I Kings 3.5: *š'l mh w'tn lk*
Ps. 2.8 : *š'l mmny w'tn*
(LXX *w'tnk*),

the translations of which are:

I Kings 3.5: 'Ask what (you will) and I will give (it)'
Ps.2.8 : 'Ask me (what you will) and I will give (it) (LXX to you)'.

Here, too, we find the formula according to which God himself promises help to the king quite generally, making him formulate a request – here, as a usurper (above III.3.2). So it is clear that Solomon, too, was legitimated in this way (cf. above III.3.2). 'In other words,' I wrote in 1977*, 367, 'Solomon tried to keep the shell of ancient institutions, where things look much as they did before, but at the same time Solomon made substantial changes in institutional content.' So now, thanks to the divine support, the usurper had been newly legitimated.

2.3 Solomon has gone down in history essentially as the wise king (a theme to which we shall return in due course, 2.4) and as the builder of the temple in Jerusalem, the building which through changing circumstances was the spiritual centre of Judaism for about a thousand years. In AD 70 it was destroyed in the course of the final assault on Jerusalem by the soldiers of Titus, and was never rebuilt (below XIV.4.5).

The fact that three whole chapters out of a total of nine which speak of the reign of Solomon are devoted to the building and the inauguration indicates the importance which the whole narrative attributes to the event.

2.3.1 It is now virtually impossible, on the basis of the information provided in the Hebrew Bible (cf. I Kings 6), to reconstruct the appearance of the outside and inside of the temple, the way it was built and its structure, even if its topography is sufficiently well known. The proof of this is that writers who have been concerned with the problem have arrived at very different conclusions, none of which can be considered definitive. Still, it must have been extremely large by the standards of the time (over 100 feet by 35 feet).

However, from the information which seems historically probable we learn that Solomon made use, for example, of Phoenician craftsmen, hired out to him by Hiram of Tyre (5.15-31; 7.13f.), while Israel provided the unskilled manual labourers. Now this information should *not* be understood to mean that Israel, a people who had settled relatively recently, did not yet possess the technique, the know-how, to construct a monumental building like the temple by themselves; we have seen that Solomon was capable of having fortified cities of substantial size built or restored, and this will have called for advanced techniques (above 1.4). Rather, the note indicates that Solomon planned to build a sanctuary of a Canaanite type and for it also to be recognized as such by the non-Israelite population of the empire. So for a reconstruction of the temple we need to look in the area of sacred buildings in Syria and Palestine, and excavations over the last half century have brought some to light, enough to reconstruct the pattern and topography of the Temple. It should be stressed, as has recently been demonstrated by A.V.Hurovitz in his doctoral thesis (1983, cf. the bibliography to the next section), that the procedure followed is identical to that attested in Mesopotamia from the time of Gudea of Lagash onwards: (*a*) decision by the king, validated by divine approval (I Kings 5.17-19); (*b*) preparation of the material and the labour force, etc. (5.20-32); (*c*) description of the building (chs.6-7); (*d*) its dedication (I Kings 8.1-11, 62-66); (*e*)the king's prayer (I Kings 8.12-61, cf. below, 2.3.6).

2.3.2 The best-known temple is that of *tell-tayinat* in ancient northwestern Syria, present-day Turkey, near to Alexandretta (on the Orontes, about twelve miles north of Antioch), opposite *tell alalaḥ*.

Select bibliography: A.Alt, 'Verbreitung und Herkunft des syrischen Tempeltypus' (1939), *KS* II, 100-15; T.A.Busink, *Der Tempel von Jerusalem*, Leiden I, 1970; II, 1980; D. Ussishkin, 'Building IV in Hamat and the Temple of Solomon and Tell Tayinat', *IEJ* 16, 1966, 104-10; A.Kuschke, 'Der Tempel Salomos und der "syrische Tempeltypus"', in *Festschrift L.Rost*, BZAW 105, 1967, 124-32; id.,'Tempel', *BRL* [2]1977, 333-42 (with thirty-four plans of different temples); H.-D.Hoffmann, *Reform und Reformen*, ATANT 66, Zurich 1980, 47ff.; and A.V.Hurovitz, *Temple Building in the Bible, in the Light of Mesopotamian and North-West Semitic Writings*, Diss. Hebrew University, Jerusalem 1983 (in Hebrew, with an English summary). For the question of royal patronage of the temple cf. the basic article by K.Galling, 'Königliche und nicht-königliche Stifter beim Tempel von Jerusalem', *ZDPV* 68, 1949-51, 134-42.

In addition to this building there is now another, discovered near Hamath; cf. also the pre-Israelite temples of Shechem and Hazor.[8] It also seems probable that Solomon had other temples built outside the capital; e.g. the earliest phase of the small temple of *tell-'ārād* in the eastern Negeb (coord.162-076)[9] is dated from this period, even if, for obvious reasons, the Deuteronomistic history is silent about this fact.

2.3.3 Characteristically, the covered Syro-Palestinian sanctuary (the open-air one obviously has a different structure) has a basically tripartite structure: a vestibule surrounded by a covered veranda but otherwise open; the building proper, and within it the holy of holies, the place for the statue of the deity who was worshipped. In Israel, as the sources tell us, because the cult was aniconic, the ark took the place of the statue. Then, when the ark disappeared (Jer.3.16),[10] there was nothing at all in the Holy of Holies, a feature which always caused amazement and perplexity to foreign invaders (below XIII.10.7).

2.3.4 The dates of the beginning and end of the construction work, which took a full eight years (I Kings 6.1,37f.; 8.2) coincide not only with the two Israelite agricultural festivals but also with celebrations connected with Ba'al worship. (We should also note the ancient Canaanite names recorded for the months in the narrative: Ziv [later Iyyar] = April/May, that of Pentecost; and Etannim [later Tishri] = September/October, that of the feast of Tabernacles.) The latter festival seems to be connected with the Ba'al festival in particular; here his resurrection at the beginning of the autumnal New Year festival was celebrated, after which he proceeded to build his heavenly temple. Now though the Israelite feast of Tabernacles seems to be quite remote from concepts of this kind, remarkably it is connected with building the temple for YHWH.[11] Moreover, it is worth noting that the temple was not inaugurated until almost a year after the end of the work, so as to coincide with the date of Solomon's coronation, or perhaps so that both coincided with the festivities of Ba'al!

2.3.5 As in Mesopotamia, a characteristic feature of the work seems to have been the continual intervention of the king in questions which we should suppose to be strictly connected with the cult. First and foremost, the priest Abiathar, David's collaborator when he was still in the wilderness (above III.8.1), but guilty of having supported Adonijah, was exiled to Anathoth (present-day *tell ḥarrube*, coord. 174-135); the name is preserved in the neighbouring village of *'anāta* (below VII, 5.1.1: 2.26). Zadok, who appears first of all in connection with the conquest of Jerusalem, is invested with all the prerogatives (2.35). Again at Gibeon, at the 'high place', Solomon personally offers 'burnt offerings and complete sacrifices',[12] and he acts similarly in 9.25.

2.3.6 However, it is precisely in connection with the temple that Solomon exercised functions which can only be defined as priestly, if we accept the descriptions of them in I Kings 8.

2.3.6.1 Solomon solemnly introduces the ark into the temple and thus carries through the work begun by David (8.1-13).

2.3.6.2 Solomon 'blesses all the congregation of Israel...' (*qᵉhal yiśrā'ēl*; the first term is characteristic of the cultural community and is suppressed by LXX, which has only 'all Israel'. This suppression may have been deliberate, because the translators thought it wrong that the king should bless the community assembled for worship, 8.14.)

2.3.6.3 Solomon pronounces a first, short prayer, elaborated by Dtr (8.15-21), and then

2.3.6.4 A second prayer, with a very complex structure (8.22-52), again with marked Deuteronomistic expansions.

2.3.6.5 Again, in 8.54-61, 'with his hands raised to heaven, ...he blessed the whole assembly in a loud voice...', then

2.3.6.6 Solomon sacrifices to YHWH along with all the people.

2.3.6.7 Finally, in vv.64ff. we have a summary of the proceedings, from which it clearly emerges that Solomon had exercised priestly functions.

2.3.6.8 Now if we recall what was said above (III.10.2), that the Phoenician kings also seem in all probability to have been priests in the state cult, the picture becomes clearer, particularly in the light of the close relationship existing between Israel and the Phoenicians at this time: Solomon did not simply assume priestly functions *ad hoc*, during the building of the temple, but exercised them legitimately. Ps.110.4, an archaic composition, one phrase of which is not completely clear, conveys this when it calls the king 'priest for ever' (cf. further below V.3.2.2).

2.3.7 Only towards the end of his reign do the texts mention enemies of Solomon, abroad in 11.14-25, and at home in 11.26-40. The Deuteronomistic historian connects this (v.33) in quite general terms with Solomon's syncretism in the cult; this is his well-known doctrine of retribution for the sinner. Moreover, it does not emerge that these were reactions to Solomon's exercise of such functions, a sign that the royal priesthood was considered to be quite obvious and normal.

2.4 Now Solomon has also gone down in history for his wisdom, which soon became proverbial, so much so that traditionally the majority of the wisdom literature, from Proverbs to the deutero-canonical Wisdom of Solomon, has been attributed to him.

2.4.1 In the texts the king's wisdom is usually described in an anecdotal way, often reminiscent of folk-lore; we are reminded of the way in which, a millennium later, the Thousand and One Nights describes the wisdom of Harun el-Rashid and Saladin. The tradition of the wise and benevolent sovereign is in any case an old established feature in the Near East, and contrasts pleasantly with the character of the modern politician, in the region and elsewhere, who is usually bereft of such virtues.

2.4.2 Wisdom and ability in the political sphere, albeit totally unscrupulous, appear in I Kings 2, where, as I have pointed out, the king succeeds in ridding himself of his opponents, both potential and real, by skilful pretexts which absolve him of all blame.

2.4.3 In 3.16, as a direct consequence of the wisdom which he chose and obtained in his vision at Gibeon, we have the famous 'judgment of Solomon', more a proof of cleverness than of wisdom.

2.4.4 In 4.29-39 Solomon is said to have had a remarkable capacity for composing proverbs and discourses on various subjects, usually connected with the plant and animal world. We shall not go far wrong in supposing that the authors had in mind the literary genre of the fable, which had plants and animals as its subjects. However, no examples of this work by Solomon have been handed down to us: in the wisdom writings attributed to him, and especially in Proverbs, we find no mention of 'trees, from the cedar that is in Lebanon to the hyssop that grows out of the wall' (4.33), nor 'of beasts, and of birds, and of reptiles, and of fish' (4.34, cf. below 6).

2.4.5 The wisdom discussions with the solving of riddles which Solomon is said to have had with the same Hiram and with the Queen of Sheba belong to the same literary genre of legend (10.1-13).

2.5 Solomon is also said to have built the royal palace, thus continuing a course already evident with David. The palace stood right beside the temple, so near that some centuries later, in the sixth century BC, Ezek.43.6-9 harshly criticized the fact that the two stood as close as a pair of feet. This made the temple in effect something like a Palatine chapel. In I Kings 9.10 we are told that the building of the temple and the palace took about twenty years, and 7.1ff. calculates the time needed to build the temple as being thirteen years. So it seems clear that the time taken to build the palace was markedly longer than that devoted to the temple; the subordinate function of the latter could hardly be better expressed.

2.6 The basis laid by Solomon for the organization of the cult, the temple and the palace, in other words, if one can put it that way, the relationships between church and state, proved to be very solid: they survived in Judah down to the fall of the kingdom in 587/86.

2.6.1 In Judah, while the monarchy existed, the sovereign there was the legitimate patron of the state cult, with the right to intervene directly in its performance and its organization. Thus we see first King Hezekiah and then King Josiah (below XI.2 and 4) acting as genuinely reforming sovereigns (and it is no coincidence that in the late Renaissance Philip II of Spain put their statues among the others which adorned the front of the Escorial, north of Madrid). Little or nothing seems to have distinguished the functions of the king of Judah from those which were exercised by the Phoenician kings in the cult, though clearly we cannot establish whether this was an original feature in Israel or whether it was not rather the result of an involuntary process, which is what the texts would suggest (above III.10.2).

2.6.2 In the post-exilic period we see the high priest taking over these prerogatives (below XII.5.3.1), and also assuming the few which remained to Judah in the political sphere. However, as we shall see, we cannot yet properly speak of a 'hierocracy'.

3 Just as the biblical tradition presents David, at least to begin with, as a skilful leader, so it stresses Solomon's skill in the political sphere, especially in international relationships (cf. above III.7.1-2).

3.1 This is by no means obvious in itself: in the previous chapter (III.1.3) I spoke of the expansionist, indeed one might even call it imperialist, dynamic inherent in the united kingdom, merely stating the fact without any other implications. However, we should consider whether, if the strength of the empire lay in this expansionist dynamic, the transition to a more passive policy involving complex and subtle international political relationships, with the need for negotiations that this called for, did not prove to be alien to the character of the empire and therefore contributed to its break-up. However, it could also be that Solomon succeeded, to turn Clausewitz's dictum upside down, in waging war in international politics by other means, obtaining more than war could have brought him by means of treaties, contracts and commercial enterprises. This latter view seems to be the one supported by the biblical sources, if we take into account the triumphalist tone with which they refer to the king's commercial enterprises.

3.2 Every enterprise of Solomon in the international and commercial field is in fact presented as having been crowned with success. However, this view, clearly too laudatory by far, which is presented by the court historian and later hagiography concerned to idealize the age of Solomon, needs to be put to the proof.

3.2.1 Among other things, Solomon is presented as a shipowner,[13] albeit not directly (ancient Israel was never a seafaring people; among other things it lacked natural ports from which to sail, above I.3.5.2), but in conjunction with Hiram of Tyre. In 9.26f., it is stated that 'he built a fleet of ships at Ezion Geber' (above, 1.4.4, south of present-day Eilath on the Red Sea), in the land of Edom. And Hiram sent with the fleet 'his subjects (literally 'servants'), seamen who were familiar with the sea, together with the subjects of Solomon'.

3.2.1.1 We are not in a position to establish precisely where these expeditions in the Red Sea went; the texts (9.28; 10.11) refer to Ophir, a place or region which has not been identified;[14] we cannot rule out the possibility that Ophir, together with Tarshish (like Atlantis and the earthly paradise) formed part of a purely mythical and symbolic geography with no bearing on reality.[15]

3.2.1.2 In 10.22 it is said that 'a fleet of Tarshish' (a place which some scholars locate on the Eastern coast of Spain and others in Cilicia, while yet others suppose it to be part of the mythical and symbolic geography just mentioned), joined the fleet of Hiram of Tyre in making voyages lasting for three years! The dealings with the Queen of Sheba (above 2.4.5) which are mentioned could be a recollection of such voyages. This would mean that the region could be situated either in southern Arabia or on the African coast opposite, in Eritrea or Somalia.

3.2.1.3 In I Kings 9.28; 10.11, 22 there are again reports that the ships brought back gold, precious stones and precious wood (of *'almuggīm*, in Chronicles always *'algummīm*, an unknown wood; the traditional translation 'sandal wood' is unsatisfactory, even more so the modern Hebrew rendering, which connects the term with 'coral'), a curiosity like apes and peacocks.[16] Evidently this was merchandise obtained in trading.

3.2.1.4 At all events, if we consider that the seafaring techniques of the period allowed only short coastal voyages, it is impossible that the ships would have gone far from the African or Asiatic coasts of the Red Sea or much beyond the *bab el-mandīb*, the strait which separates Eritrea from Arabia, even if the figure of 'three years' suggests rather longer voyages.

3.2.2 Another text (10.28f.) shows Solomon as a trader in war chariots and horses between Egypt and Cilicia (the region of Qüé); it is now clear that the first place mentioned is Egypt and not the region of Musri in the Taurus, as has often been suggested.[17] To judge from the texts, this commerce also involved some minor sovereigns in the north-north-east: 'Hittites (the term usually applied to Syria and Palestine, from the neo-Assyrian texts onwards, above I.7.1) and the king of Aram.' The position of Palestine as a bridge nation (above I.9) between Asia and Africa evidently favoured these commercial operations.

3.3 As I have stressed, the account suggests that all these enterprises were crowned with success, obviously meaning to indicate that there was a significant influx of capital into the royal coffers. Indeed 9.28; 10.25-27 speak of the riches which flowed into the royal treasury under Solomon. However, a closer examination of the facts indicated here necessarily leads us to an initially more sober, less optimistic and later largely negative evaluation of the situation. What is now a marginal note in fact reports that at one time there was a danger that the good relations between Solomon and Hiram would be disrupted because Solomon was unable to pay, or at least to give adequate collaterals for, his debts to Hiram who, it appears, had allowed him unlimited credit (9.10-14). So, unable to do either, Solomon will have found himself forced to cede to Hiram about twenty places, probably situated in Western Galilee (their exact location is not clear) in a region which was later called the 'country of Kabul'. However, Hiram considered this action inadequate to pay, or at least to guarantee, the debts that Solomon had contracted. This must have seemed scandalous at a later date, and II Chron.8.1-16 reverses the terms of the arrangement: it was Hiram who assigned the places to Solomon. Still, the view in I Kings seems the more probable; it fits in well with what we shall discover soon (below 5.3) about the problem of the financial resources of a nation exploited to the limit.[18]

3.4 If Solomon thus proved so heavily in debt that he had to cede part of what was originally the territory of his nation in payment of or at least as a guarantee for the debts that he had contracted, we clearly have to ask whether his commercial enterprises, unconditionally praised in the texts, were really crowned with success and therefore contributed actively to the revenue or whether they were not purely prestige operations or, even worse, a form of trade controls, appropriating the practice of trade for the crown by way of a state monopoly. Obviously these two things are not mutually exclusive.

4 This cession of territory is the first indication of the break-up of the empire on a territorial level.

4.1 The expansionist trend of the empire, which had been its strength, began to diminish, and further territories soon had to be surrendered.

4.2 Edom in the south-east, beyond the Dead Sea (11.14-22),rebelled under the leadership of a certain Hadad, a member of the royal family; not without Egyptian support, as the texts tell us. In the circumstances Egypt seems to have played something like a double game (cf.4.6 below). The text ends succinctly: '...and Hadad... ruled over Edom.'

4.3 In Syria, which, as we have seen, David had also subjugated, movements with the aim of regaining lost liberty began to develop in a number of city-states. 11.23-25 tells us that a certain Rezon, a former official of the king of Zobah, founded a state at Damascus (and, according to the probable addition in the LXX, also in his own country), so this place will have regained its own autonomy. The text continues by indicating that from then on he 'was an enemy of Solomon for the rest of his life'. This did away with part of the conquests of David mentioned in II Sam.8.3ff., 13ff. (cf. above III.6.1.1-4). For these two episodes cf. S.Abramski, 'The Resurrection of the Kingdom of Damascus and its Historiographical Record', *Mᵉhaqqᵉrīm bammiqrā' ūbᵉmizraḥ haqqadmōn*, Jerusalem 1978, 1, 189ff. (= FS S.E.Loewenstamm, in Hebrew with an English summary); A.Malamat, *Königsreich*, 26, 31ff.

4.4 However, as I pointed out earlier (2.3.7), the North, too, was disturbed. I Kings 11.26-40 reports a revolt led by a certain Jeroboam, formerly an important official in the state bureaucracy, who also took refuge in Egypt. From there, as we shall see later (IX.1.2.1.3.3), he re-entered the country on the death of Solomon. The tradition even reports something like a divine investiture of him (vv.29ff.) at the hands of a prophet.

4.5 In this way, a far from favourable economic trend was combined with a political situation of considerable danger. Moreover, it would not be far from the truth to say that this political situation was closely connected with the economic one; the empire was now insolvent and also crumbling at its frontiers, especially towards the north, in the north-east and towards the south-east.

4.6 By contrast, one international success of notable dimensions seems to have been Solomon's marriage to a daughter of the Pharaoh (I Kings 3.1; 7.8; 9.16,24; 11.1). The alliance brought with it as a dowry the town of Gezer, conquered and destroyed for Solomon by the Pharaoh, and rebuilt and refortified by Solomon (above 1.4.3). The texts do not give the name of the Pharaoh, and scholars suggest either Siamun (*c.*978-959) or his successor Psausennes II (*c.* 959-945).[19] In the present state of sources and research it is not easy to check the truthfulness of the information (the Pharaohs virtually never married their daughters to the sovereigns of other countries) and, if the information is indeed true, in what circumstances such a marriage could have taken place. However, the fact that the Pharaoh conquered and destroyed Gezer demonstrates that he was not a particularly weak and lazy person; and the fact that he gave the place as a dowry for his daughter again demonstrates that he cannot have been hostile to the marriage or to his son-in-law, and that this was therefore an agreement between equals.[20] However, this stands in marked contrast to the information that the Pharaoh had given political asylum to Solomon's enemies exiled from the empire (above 4.4).

4.7 The texts also tell us that Solomon took as wives or concubines princesses of allied or subject peoples, so that he had a considerable harem (11.3); Moabite, Ammonite, Edomite, Syrian ('Hittite') and Sidonian women are mentioned. If the information is correct, it shows that Solomon continued his foreign policy by treaties with his own vassals and allies; however, in the historical theory put forward by Dtr these women are said to have 'seduced' Solomon on the religious level, causing him to lapse into idolatry and religious syncretism. This is one way of explaining the fact which, moreover, the tradition does not conceal, that Israelite religion was then little different from the Canaanite religion of the time, at the same time maintaining the theory of religious degeneration from a primitive purity (cf. above III.10).

5 One feature particularly worth noting and about which the texts give us a good deal of information is a complex system of taxation that we can still reconstruct with some degree of precision on the basis of the information that has come down to us. Such a possibility of reconstruction is quite rare; certainly there are few cases in which we have information of this sort, and that, as we have seen, makes it difficult to produce a history of ancient Israel.

5.1 An important text to which I referred briefly above (1.2.1-2) speaks of the division of the North into twelve districts or provinces (but cf. also 5.1.2), each with a governor or superintendent (Hebrew $n^e sib$) at its head (I Kings 4.7-19).[21] The text explicitly states that each district was responsible for providing provisions for 'the king and his house' (v.7) one month in each year, a way of stating that the expenses of public administration and the worship of the state fell in equal parts on the twelve districts of the north. One reasonable explanation of the list is that proposed some years ago by D.B.Redford:[22]

5.1.1 The most obvious parallel to the list is to be found in Egypt at the time of Pharaoh Shoshenk (the biblical Shishak) I, a younger contemporary of Solomon, who invaded Palestine shortly after Solomon's death (below IX.1.4). In the Egyptian example we have places and officials responsible for procuring certain kind of provisions, each for one month of the year, plus one for those days at the end of the year which were necessary to complete the solar year.

5.1.2 In I Kings 4 the accent falls, as with the Egyptian source, more on the officials than the districts, so that Redford does not want to talk in terms of districts or provinces at all; we may deduce something like districts, but that does not follow directly from the texts.

5.1.3 Furthermore, according to 5.2 it seems that Solomon received all the allocation for a month, including that for the temple, on the same day.

5.1.4 Solomon will also have used the system for provisioning his garrisons stationed in border areas, following the evidence for the practice in Egypt.

5.1.5 Redford's analysis here clearly takes us a good way further forward; however, it seems unimportant whether or not we should speak of districts or provinces: in Egypt, too, the list first mentions the person, followed by the territorial area for which he is responsible. And in whatever way we define this territory on the legal and administrative level, its duties were evidently fiscal, whether the contribution was made in money or in kind.

5.2 However, what seems to be of undoubted interest is that, as I have indicated, the system operated within the Israelite empire exclusively for the North. There is no mention of any analogous institution in the South. It is indeed the case that Josh.15.21-61 gives a list of twelve districts for Judah,[23] but the most ancient parts of it are dated in the early period of the monarchy and its later parts belong to the time of Josiah (second half of the seventh century BC, below, XI.4.4.1). However, some scholars would see this list as a text from Judah giving the system in the South corresponding to the twelve districts of Israel, perhaps produced from the census made by David mentioned in II Sam.24//I Chron.21, the boundaries of which are largely those given above (III.7.3). This would allow us to say that the South, too, was subjected to similar fiscal measures to those in the North.[24] However, this is an unconvincing argument: first of all the list of the twelve districts in the South is never connected with any fiscal measure, while the text about the census never stresses either any kind of taxation, or a division into districts, even if it is recognized that in the ancient Near East the census was regularly connected with fiscal measures. Again, for decades the hostility and resentment of the North towards the house of David seems to have been much stronger than what we see in the South. On the other hand, we have to recognize that none of the texts says that the south treated the North as conquered territory to exploit.[25] So if the texts are rather obscure, we must keep this characteristic in mind: to sum up, it is said that the North was divided administratively into districts for the purpose of taxation; nothing of this kind is reported of the South.

5.3.1 One characteristic element of the way in which the tribute was collected by the administrations of David and Solomon is that communities and individuals were conscripted for forced labour. There are parallels to this throughout the region, but in Israel under Solomon it must have assumed abnormal proportions.

Bibliography: J.A.Soggin, 'Compulsory Labor under David and Solomon', in T.Ishida (ed.), *Studies*, 259-67.

5.3.2 The system does not seem to have been limited to demanding tribute in coin or in kind or to personal services for recognized motives of public utility, from the community or from the individual; and where contributions in the former category were not considered adequate, conscription was introduced in a form very similar to the corvées which during the European Middle Ages supplied the needs of the feudal lords, even if the fundamental difference in the structures of ancient Near Eastern society must make us cautious about looking for analogies of this kind. The Hebrew term used is *mas*; later, when the word increasingly took on the meaning of 'tax' (a meaning which it still has in modern Hebrew), the term *'ōbēd* was added to it, to indicate that it was provided in the form of labour.

5.3.2.1 The distinguishing mark of this work was that it was compulsory and therefore forced. Many societies have recognized, and still recognize today, the place of work exacted from free citizens for projects of public utility or in a case of emergency, and this labour, and the taxation it implies, is therefore accepted; not always willingly, but also without great resistance. In this case, however, the public utility of the work was either not perceived or not accepted; that is why it had to be performed by forced labour.

5.3.2.2 Now it is interesting to note that whereas one of the texts affirms that 'Israel' was conscripted for the forced labour (I Kings 5.27f.// II Chron.2.16, cf. Josephus, *Antt.* VIII, 58), another text (9.15a,20-22 [LXX 10.22a-c]//II Chron 8.8-10) says that only the Canaanites were subjected and that the Israelites were not employed in the work (v.22). However, this text is generally recognized to be Deuteronomistic or even later.

5.3.2.3 So I shall keep to the first text, which follows, even if not immediately, the text about the division of the north into districts: does 'Israel' here, too, indicate only the North and not also the South? That is difficult to say, but from what we know the former seems probable.

5.3.2.4 In other words, as the tradition gradually moves away from its immediate theme and a hagiographical view begins to take over, the descriptions of the united kingdom lose those elements which are more obviously critical; and a system which involved all the people becomes instead the well-deserved(!) fate reserved for the surviving Canaanites.

5.3.3.1 It is not easy to determine exactly when and how the system entered Israel, but II Sam.20.24 already speaks of the 'man over the forced labour' as an obvious function, even if this does not appear in the preceding list of royal officials. So it would not be strange if the system had already begun under David. Moreover, it must have begun quite early: II Sam.12.31 in fact says that David conscripted forced labour from the people of Transjordan – the best explanation of this otherwise difficult text. Under Solomon the system then seems to have been developed to the point of taking in a large part of the population, including Israelites.

5.3.3.2 David and Solomon did not need to go far or stretch their imaginations to find models. The institution is firmly attested at Alalakh and in Ugarit, as also in the el-'Amarna letters, and the Accadian term used, *massu*, is recognizably of Western Semitic origin.[26]

5.4 According to our sources, the introduction of forced labour and especially the conscription of free Israelites for it was one of the main factors, first of disorders and later often of open revolts. As time went on, it became one of the features which made a major contribution to the dissolution of the personal union on the death of Solomon and therefore to the collapse of the united kingdom from within, as I have already indicated (above III.9.1.2; cf. also below IX.1.2ff.).

5.4.1 If at this point it is permissible to make some conjectures, for want of direct information, it would seem evident that under David the institution had been kept within reasonable and tolerable limits. With Solomon, on the other hand, in pursuit of a financial policy which in the most favourable circumstances we could call adventurous, and treating the North and the South differently, the institution seems to have assumed intolerable proportions for the individual, the community and the economy in general. It was also probably the economy that suffered most: it was deprived of the greater part of its productive forces, which were used for undertakings that provided little or no income because they were purely for purposes of prestige. And it is precisely at this point that those forces entered the united kingdom which were to cause its collapse from within.

6 One last piece of information. During recent decades, the not particularly happy term 'the Solomonic enlightenment' has often been used to define this period, in connection with the wisdom of Solomon (above 2.4.4).[27] One characteristic element of the wisdom of the ancient Near East (as of culture generally, down to the present day), has been its international and cosmopolitan character. So there is nothing strange in the fact that during the reign of the sovereign who passed into history and legend for his wisdom, Israel would have been open to

international culture, to the great currents of the wisdom of the time. The consequence of this openness will have been the birth of literary historical works like the J source of the Pentateuch and the succession narrative, the beginnings of proverbial wisdom and a great many other elements, for example the composition of the Joseph stories at the end of Genesis.

6.1 However, we do not have any specific and precise information about all this, but only speculation and inference, which we need to consider with the greatest caution.[28] This seems even clearer in the case of a hypothesis which has been repeated often during recent years. It argues that wisdom schools will have emerged in this period, schools in which future officials will have received the training that they needed for their work in public administration. But given the silence of the sources, it is quite probable that first David and then Solomon simply incorporated the existing Egyptian and Canaanite bureaucracies of the various city-states into the administrative apparatus of the state.[29] And there is nothing to indicate that the officials in question bore the title of 'sages', $h^a k\bar{a}m\bar{\imath}m$.[30] The age of Solomon could therefore also very well have been a time of an openness which was also favoured by the international contacts produced through commerce and travel and the remarkable riches that were in circulation. As to the rest, we can say little or nothing, given the silence of the sources. The obscure character of the phrases which attribute a particular wisdom to Solomon also prevents us from drawing any certain conclusion and at all events counsels great prudence.[31]

PART TWO

Traditions about the Proto-history of the People

'The scribes... were not interested in the history of the land, but in the traditions of their own people, which they accepted as implicitly as the modern Soudanese believes in his tribal legends... The long memory possessed by semi-civilized peoples for historical fact is a pious fiction of over-zealous apologists...'

W.F.Albright, 1918

V

PATRIARCHS

Select bibliography: P.W.Lapp, *The Dhar Mirzabanēh Tombs*, New Haven 1966, 86ff.; J.Scharbert, 'Patriarchentradition und Patriarchenreligion', *VuF* 19, 1974, 2-22 (with an exhaustive annotated bibliography); T. L.Thompson, *The Historicity of the Patriarchal Narratives*, BZAW 133, Berlin 1974; J.Van Seters, *Abraham in History and Tradition*, New Haven and London 1975; G.W.Coats, *From Canaan to Egypt*, Washington 1976; W.McKane, *Studies in the Patriarchal Narratives*, Edinburgh 1977; A.R.Millard and D.J.Wiseman (eds.), *Essays on the Patriarchal Narratives*, Leicester 1980. A recent attempt to antedate at least the theme of the promise to the patriarchs has been made by H.Seebass, 'Gehörten Verheissungen zum ältesten Bestand der Väter-Erzählungen?', *Bibl* 64, 1983, 189-210.

1 There is an evident relationship between some of the texts in the patriarchal narratives, especially those transmitted by the J source, and texts which refer to the united kingdom of David and Solomon. In fact it seems clear that at least in an earlier phase of the collection, J, which has brought together most of the material which is certainly pre-exilic, saw some texts about the patriarchs functioning as a 'divine promise' and 'fulfilment'; in them the empire was the fulfilment of the ancient prophecies. That is particularly evident where the patriarchal texts refer to the possession of the land of Canaan and to numerous descendants, and also to the descendants of the patriarchs as a 'nation', Hebrew *gōy*.

1.1 Of course, as I have stressed, these considerations relate to the earliest phase of the collection and do not exclude re-readings of the same texts at a substantially later period, even during the exile or afterwards – in less happy times, when the community had become tiny, the nation had collapsed and it seemed increasingly problematical how it could ever possess the land.

1.1.1 The first of these similarities appears in the almost verbal parallel between the divine promise addressed to Abraham at the time of his calling (Gen.12.2a) and the divine promise addressed to the dynasty of David (II Sam.7.9b):

Gen.12 has: ...*wa'ᵃgaddᵉlāh šᵉmēkā '*...I will make your name great',

II Sam.7 has:...*wᵉ'āśītī lᵉkā šēm gādōl '*...I will make you a great name'.

It is not difficult to see the affinity of the two phrases on the semantic level; their programmatic content seems clear, despite the slightly more prolix (and, one might feel, less elegant) form of the second. So David appears as the antitype of Abraham.[1]

1.1.2 Again, not only in Gen.12.2, but also in 18.18 and Num.14.12, Israel is defined as *gōy gādōl*, where the first term has the meaning of 'nation' in the political sense of the word. For nation in the ethnic sense the Hebrew Bible prefers *'am*, also because *gōy* soon takes on negative connotations. Now, it seems evident that only at the time of David and Solomon was Israel 'a great nation'; neither before nor afterwards was it clearly a nation in the political sense of the expression. Of course, that does not exclude the possibility that these concepts were read into the text at a later date, e.g. from a messianic perspective at a time when the people lived in hope that the kingdom of David would be established, if not as a great earthly empire, at least as an eschatological heavenly kingdom.

1.1.3 However, that is not the whole story. One of the values of the studies by Thompson and Van Seters[2] has been their discovery that the mention of ethnic groups, places and individuals in the patriarchal narratives makes sense only at the time of the united monarchy and afterwards (for Van Seters as late as the post-exilic period), and certainly never before! The theme is too vast for me to be able to deal with it here, so I must refer the reader to their studies.

1.1.4 So we must conclude that, leaving aside the possibility of re-readings and later reinterpretations, the nucleus of the patriarchal narratives can be traced back without any difficulty to the time of the united monarchy. There are, however, problems in establishing and, in the present state of the sources, demonstrating in practice whether we can go back beyond this period, and if so in what instances, e.g. to ethnic migratory movements attested in the course of the second millennium BC. Any attempt in this direction should in any case begin with an evaluation of each individual tradition, and never with the complex in which it is now included.[3]

1.2 The texts about the patriarchs are concentrated in the section of the Pentateuch which extends from Gen.11.10ff. to the end of ch.50. We again find allusions to episodes in the life of Jacob in Hos.12.4-5,13, cf. 10.11. In Genesis, as we know, the patriarchs appear in a genealogical sequence, passing from Abraham to Isaac and Jacob, and from him to the ancestors of the twelve tribes: chs.37; 39-48, however, are dedicated to the figure of Joseph.

1.2.1 In 11.10-27,30-31 we have the genealogy of Shem according to P, followed by a note according to which Abraham and his forebears emigrated from 'Ur of the Chaldaeans' in south-eastern Mesopotamia to the region of Ḥarrān in north-west Mesopotamia (cf. also Gen.11.28, where J also alludes to the journey). The place was an important caravan centre, attested as such from the beginning of the second millennium BC.

1.2.2 At the beginning of Gen.12.1ff., Abraham obeys the divine call which bids him leave Ḥarrān, his homeland, to go to an unknown country which God will show him at the right time (later, 12.5, this proves to be Canaan). We find that once he has arrived at his destination, Abraham travels essentially in the southern region of the country: Hebron and the northern Negeb. Because of a famine (a favourite theme with the biblical writers) we see him making a stay in Egypt (12.10-20); the narrative paints the picture of an organized Egypt, without a famine, since water is assured by the Nile, and a safe refuge for anyone in difficulty. This description of Egypt lasts down to the New Testament (Matt.2.13-23), where the infancy narratives speak of the 'flight into Egypt'. However, it is soon joined by another, attested from the exodus narrative onwards: here Egypt is a land of oppression and slavery, from which only the powerful hand of the God of Israel has been able to free his people.[4] The theme seems to have been developed fully by Deut and Dtr, who made it one of the focal points of Jewish piety down the centuries: from time immemorial it has been the foundation for the celebration of the Hebrew passover.

1.2.3 Some scholars have tried to connect Abraham's migration to Canaan with a hypothetical 'Amorite migration', said to have taken place in the same direction at the beginning of the second millennium BC;[5] in this way they think that they can recover the historical context of the narrative. However, such theories no longer seem tenable in the light of most recent research: they are based too much on doubtful interpretations of archaeological discoveries, and in fact there are no consistent traces of new arrivals in Canaan at this period. There are also problems over chronology (Lapp, Thompson). So Bright's assertion, still repeated in the latest edition of his *History*, seems all the more rash: 'We conclude, then, that the patriarchs were historical figures, a part of that movement of Northwest-Semitic (Amorite) people which brought a new infusion to the population of Palestine toward the beginning of the second millennium BC'(95).

1.2.4 The patriarchal narratives lack any specific details connected with the journey to Canaan, and the same goes for their account of the stay in Egypt: there are no itineraries, stopping places, indications of how long the journey took. There are even more problems over the journey from Ur of the Chaldaeans, since the designation relates to the first millennium BC, when the Chaldaeans had settled in the region, and certainly not to the second millennium. However, as we saw above (II.2.3), this mention of Ur and of the peoples of Chaldaea becomes quite probable once we accept that the patriarchal traditions were re-read at the end of the exile and in the early post-exilic period: the itinerary of Abraham then became the itinerary of those who were returning home, from south-eastern Mesopotamia, passing through Ḥarrān, the usual route between the two regions.

Abraham's stay among the Philistines at Gerar (Gen.20.1-18) evidently presupposes their arrival and settlement in the region, and that did not take place before the twelfth century BC (above III.5.2). Again, for millennia it was a regular phenomenon for 'Asiatics' (as the Egyptians called them) to cross the isthmus of Suez and settle in Egypt for various reasons; there is an illustration of a typical instance in the frescoes on the tomb of Ḥnum Hotep at Beni Hassan (*ANEP*, no.3) from the nineteenth century BC. The texts do not give the name of the Pharaoh with whom they had dealings, nor does it mention the places that they will have visited;[6] this must have been information which was of little or no interest to those who first handed down the traditions, or they simply had none. To use a modern expression, their historical interest must have been virtually nil. Moreover, the same is true of the exodus (cf. also VI.3), and we find a very similar problem over the identification of the Pharaoh who was Solomon's father-in-law (above IV.4.6). The name of the Philistine king of the area of Gerar, Abimelech, is a good Western Semitic name, already attested in the writings from Ugarit and el-'Amarna, as well as being that of four other people in the Hebrew Bible. Another interesting feature is that Gerar does not appear even in the cities making up the Philistine pentapolis (above III.5.3.1). All this evidently makes it very doubtful whether the narrative in fact corresponds with historically ascertainable fact.

1.3 When Isaac makes an appearance he has similar, if not identical characteristics, but the account is on a much smaller scale. Here the whole story is overshadowed by the divine promise, a promise endangered first by the barrenness of Sarah, then by God's demand that Abraham should sacrifice his only son (Gen.22.1ff.), and again by his relations with Sarah's maidservant Hagar. The other information does not seem to be original: Isaac is born, marries, has children, grows old and dies. Shortly before his death he is deceived by his wife Rebecca and his son Jacob. At Gerar, Isaac has a similar experience to that of Abraham in Egypt, in connection with the same ruler, Abimelech (Gen.26.1-11). It is easy to deduce from these few facts that the figure of Isaac has been played down in favour of his father Abraham and his son Jacob, who were evidently thought to be more important.

1.4.1 We learn much more about Jacob than about the others, but the details are always essentially characteristic of family folk-lore and anecdote. The young Jacob is particularly good at manipulating people and events to his own advantage, even stooping to real deceit of those who have contact with him: his old father, his brother Esau (supplanted from the time of his birth, and later in various other ways), his father-in-law and kindred (cheated of their riches in dealings which always exploit the agreement to its limit). Here again, however, the divine promise ultimately wins through, despite the dubious ethics of the hero of the narrative.

1.4.2 Jacob is presented as the man who, to escape the understandable wrath of his cheated brother, makes something like the reverse of Abraham's journey, returning to the region of Ḥarrān (Gen.28.10ff.) and his own Aramaean kinsfolk (cf. 31.20,24, where Laban is called 'the Aramaean'; Gen.25.20 is from P). The region of Ḥarrān is often called *'ārām naharayīm* (Gen.24.10, though this is a late text,[7] even if it is often attributed to J), while in P we often find the term *paddān 'ārām*. The first designation refers to the region called *naḥ(a)rina* (and also, from the beginning of the second millennium *birīt narīm*, 'between the rivers', and from the middle of the millennium *naḥrīma, na'rīma* or *narīna*) in cuneiform and Egyptian texts; it is situated between the Euphrates and its left-bank tributary, the Balikh. It has nothing to do with Mesopotamia generally, as some scholars have argued on the basis of the apparent dual in Hebrew ('between, or of the two rivers'). The second expression denotes 'the plain of Aram' in Aramaic and later in Syriac, and is semantically identical to the Hebrew *śedēh 'ārām* (Hos.12.13, EVV 12.12). This last text maintains the idea that during the exile Israel had to repeat the experience of Jacob in his flight, but in much more difficult circumstances. As we have seen above (1.1.3), other texts were probably also rewritten in the exilic and post-exilic periods.

1.4.3 In all these texts the basic problem is the frequent mention of Aram and the Aramaeans, which presupposes that they were settled in the region of Syria and north-western Mesopotamia. However, that did not happen until the twelfth century BC or even later.[8] A second problem is presented by the fact that we do not find the names of the above-mentioned regions in any of the extra-biblical sources at our disposal.

1.5 The patriarchal cycle ends with the story of Joseph, sold as a slave to Egypt by his jealous brothers, but soon rising, after changes of fortune, by a combination of integrity, personal ability and the divine blessing, to the post of Pharaoh's vizier (again the Pharaoh is not mentioned by name). It is precisely through Joseph's good offices that his father and brothers arrive in Egypt, again to escape yet another famine, and there they stay. So the cycle of patriarchal narratives is linked to that of the exodus from Egypt.

2.1 Now the patriarchal narratives, with the exception of the Joseph story, have two distinguishing features. First, the narrative themes which occur in them are always the same. They make exhaustive use of a variety of migrations (it should be noted that these *are* migrations and not forms of semi-nomadism of the kind that can still be found today on the steppes of the Near East at the borders of agricultural civilization, even if socially and economically the patriarchs clearly resemble very closely the semi-nomadic populations attested in north-Western Mesopotamia and later in Syria in the eighteenth and seventeenth centuries BC).[9] Attempts are made by foreign kings to seduce the wives of the patriarchs, who are thought of as being very beautiful; these kings introduced them into the harem (increasing levity can be seen in these stories: Gen.12.10-20; 20.1-18; 26.1-14). Relations with Syria in the north-east and Mesopotamia in the north-west are close and constant even after the move away from that area: Abraham comes from the region, and Isaac and Jacob take their wives from there (cf. the concern, a reflection from much later times, that they did not choose their wives from among the women of Canaan, Gen.23.3; 24.1ff.; 27.46, also called 'Hittite' wives according to the designation current in the neo-Assyrian and neo-Babylonian period; cf. again 23.1ff; 27.34); it is emphasized that the kinsfolk in Mesopotamia are Aramaean. And the ancestors of the person making the offering in Deut.26.3bff., a kind of confession of faith to be recited at the time of the offering of the first-fruits, is called a 'wandering...' or 'lost Aramaean'.

2.2 So it seems clear that, even if the biblical tradition means to put the patriarchs a long time before the institution of the monarchy (the figures given in Gen. 15.13 and I Kings 6.1 are 400 and 480 years respectively, making a total of about 880 years), the model that the writers or those who handed down the tradition have in mind is not that of semi-nomads as they are attested e.g. in northern Mesopotamia at the end of the first half of the second millennium BC. As I have often stressed (Soggin, *Das Königtum*, ii and passim), the comparison with these groups which has often been made in recent years is fully valid at a social and economic level, but it is not the model that the authors of the biblical narrative have in mind: for them the patriarchs are, rather, migrants.[10] The actual model for them is certainly later, and nowhere is it possible to establish whether or not it is based on an ancient tradition. It also follows that it was ideal for using again in the exilic and post-exilic period to indicate those Israelites who had returned to the country from which they had been deported. Be this as it may, the model of the semi-nomads cannot be regarded as an absolute, either: we should recall that down the millennia, constant economic and social conditions tend to produce very similar social structures and modes of production because they are suited to the circumstances, and that happens even today.

2.3 So there is nothing that obliges us to consider the genealogical line proposed here by the texts as being the primary, original element, and much that tells against it: I discussed this problem at the beginning of the present book (above II. 4.2) and would like to return to it briefly.

2.3.1 Throughout the ancient Near Eastern world, over much of the Western world and even now in the modern Near East, the genealogy seems to be the most effective way of explaining the origins of ethnic groups. A people is imagined as the product of the increase, through varying fortunes, of the progenitor, the patriarch, the eponymous hero. In the context of Western antiquity it is enough to recall the relationship between Aeneas and the *gens Julia*, and in the modern Arab world descent from the prophet or at least from his tribe, a matchless and legitimizing status symbol, especially when combined with political power. However, this approach seems totally inadequate on the historical level, both generally and in this instance: Gottwald[11] lists a series of basic inconsistencies resulting from the genealogy indicating the succession of the patriarchs as soon as we try to take into account not only the main characters but also their wives, sisters and daughters. However, the genealogy seems more than adequate for the aims it is meant to fulfil, whether political, religious or otherwise,[12] though certainly not on the level of history and ethnology.

2.3.2 Again, the scarcity of the information, as I indicated above, and the stereotyping of themes which is a characteristic of the narratives, taken with the way in which figures are typed by being associated with different locations (Abraham in the region of Hebron,[13] Isaac usually in the Negeb, Jacob in the centre, around Shechem), makes it quite possible that the three figures all existed at the same time, or even, if one wants to be more critical, that they never existed at all.[14] Scholars have been aware of these possibilities for some time. In other words, probably as early as the monarchical era and certainly in exilic and post-exilic times, Israel confessed that there was what we might call a 'theological' relationship between itself and its land, the 'holy land'; this land had been given freely by God for Israel to enjoy, though God continued to be its absolute sovereign. Human beings could constantly jeopardize this relationship between Israel and its own land; the dangers ranged from the expeditions of foreign rulers who claimed possession of it (e.g. the expedition of Shishak/Shoshenk I of Egypt at the end of the tenth century BC, soon after the death of Solomon, I Kings 14.25-28//I Chron.12.8-11, below IX.1.4), through the wars with neighbouring people (those with Israel's Aramaean neighbours which lasted for virtually the whole of the ninth century BC seem to have been particularly serious, cf. below IX.2.2ff.) and the deportations first by the Assyrians and then by the Babylonians, down to the return to the homeland in conditions of extreme hardship and the complete loss of political independence (below XII.3ff.).

2.3.3 However, one can hardly call this discourse on Israel's past 'history', regardless of whether it refers to real historical figures or only supposedly historical figures; rather, it is a theology of history, an attempt to explain by means of a confession of faith what had in fact been a catastrophe on both the political and the ethnic level. This attitude might seem unrealistic to some, but no one would want to deny a certain greatness. Here Israel set over against the inescapable reality of political and economic facts its faith in the work of God in its own history, in grace and in judgment; it confessed the sovereignty of the creator and the Lord of history over whatever might happen, despite all appearances to the contrary. This argument is an essential, albeit late, element in the religion of Israel and therefore in the spiritual heritage of those who confessed themselves to be the people of God chosen from of old and heir to the ancient promises.

2.3.4 These observations are certainly not new: they have been made many times from the end of the last century onwards (cf. above, II.3.2); then, decades afterwards, by scholars like H.Gunkel and his pupil H.Gressmann[15] and, a few decades later again, by K.Galling.[16] Like Thompson, I would like to quote Gressmann's final comment on the Abraham traditions: 'The migration or, as one should say, the nomadism of this patriarch is not therefore based on any historical remembrance but is an artificial composition by the narrator of legends (*Sage*), intended to hold different traditions together. This observation, an elementary one in connection with the study of legends, *a priori* rules out any modern attempt to argue that the "migration of Abraham from Ur in Chaldaea to Hebron" is something that happened in real life, even with the support of the imagination.'[17]

2.3.5 So it is rather surprising that during and after the Second World War there was a new, apologetic development, in which scholars sought to demonstrate that the biblical traditions about the proto-history of Israel have a credible historical background, despite the objections which had been made against such attempts decades earlier. In his works, the American archaeologist and explorer Nelson Glueck often refers to what he calls 'the astonishing historical memory of the Bible',[18] and a similar view has been put forward by some North American scholars, usually archaeologists and philologists, and pupils of W.F.Albright.[19] The school of Albright and his immediate disciples has also been the training ground for a new generation of Israeli archaeologists, philologists and historians – which would explain their sometimes similar approach to problems. However, shortly before his death, the most distinguished of Albright's pupils, G.E.Wright, tried to revise views in this tradition quite substantially.[20] For these scholars, the difference between the history of Israel as confessed by the people of God and that reconstructed by historical criticism over the last century is only an apparent one; and is supposed to be being bridged by the progressive convergence of the two histories as a result of new archaeological discoveries. Consequently they do not dramatize the problem in any way (below, VII.5). By contrast, on the continent of Europe the majority of scholars have indicated the depth of the difference, and some even see it as a serious problem for scholarly work on the Bible.[21] However, this divergence is a typical one, and only to be expected in the circumstances, as I have tried to demonstrate elsewhere.[22]

2.3.6 Over the years, then, what we might call 'the American school' has tried to argue for the substantial historical authenticity of the narratives about the patriarchs and about the Exodus, the conquest and the time of the Judges, while accepting the existence of dubious features in matters of detail. So we find frequent references to 'the patriarchal age' or equivalent expressions, as if we had to do with a clear and definite historical period like that of Ur-III or Hammurabi in Mesopotamia. However, the reality is much less promising: even a superficial look at those works which argue that the traditions are essentially authentic immediately shows that these scholars place the patriarchs in periods ranging from the beginning of the second millennium (more rarely as early as the end of the third millenium) to the end of its first half (or even after the first half of the millennium or, indeed, at its end), and it is precisely this vagueness on a chronological level (a vagueness which arises from inadequate sources) that is the best proof of the dubious historical character of the materials at our disposal. Therefore even without *a priori* assuming a sceptical attitude towards them, we need to take the utmost care in evaluating them or using them. And sometimes we have to be so careful that it seems doubtful whether the sources are of much value to the historian. So while Bright*, 69, may call for 'a new and more sympathetic evaluation of the traditions', it must also be pointed out that what might seem a lack of sympathy is not due so much to preconceptions, still less to cynicism or nihilism, as is sometimes said, as to the very nature of the sources. On the European continent, the German scholars A.Alt and M.Noth have certainly made more than sympathetic (to use Bright's term) evaluations, even if they have not always been thought of as such; the latter[23] was in fact ready to accept in broad outline that in the context of the patriarchal narratives '...there are real and manifest features, and, moreover, of such a specific kind that it is necessary to connect them with some historical element' (here the author is thinking of the semi-nomads attested around the city-state of Mari, above 2.2, especially in connection with nomenclature and customs and their relation to the patriarchal world). And that is certainly a good deal more than we are disposed to admit today, about twenty years after the publication of these remarks: the parallels which seemed to exist between patriarchal customs and those attested especially in legal texts (and which do not appear later in other texts of the Bible) have meanwhile proved for the most part spurious, because they were either based on erroneous interpretation of the texts or made illegitimate connections between different sociological and legal situations.[24] As for patriarchal nomenclature, here again all we can say is that the names of the patriarchs, or names with a similar formation, are widespread throughout the ancient Near East, from the Ebla texts (at the end of the third millennium BC) to the beginning of the first millennium BC. So when we also take into account the fact that names tend to persist down the generations within a constant linguistic context, it seems impossible to use them as a criterion for dating; there is in fact a span of more than a thousand years.[25] Then other names, like *térah, nāhōr, sērūg*, are all names of places attested around Ḥarrān, the contemporaneous existence of which has been proved only for the period spanning the end of the second and the beginning of the first millennium BC; as we have seen, this is the time when references to the Aramaeans also make sense.[26]

2.4 So the problem seems to have remained the same, and decades of studies with an apologetic slant, based on archaeological discoveries, have failed not only to resolve it, but even to smooth over the difficulties raised by the clash between the biblical account and modern historical research. As I have already said, I do not intend *a priori* to rule out the possibility that individual traditions may be ancient and therefore go back to actual memories about people who existed and to facts which happened; however, what is lacking in the present state of research is any possibility of even comparative, let alone direct, historical corroboration. What we can affirm, though, is what Israel confessed in faith, many centuries afterwards, as its own proto-history; and this proto-history appeared so interesting because in it the people of God saw a foreshadowing, an explanation and even a reason for its own present situation.[27] And at this point, of course, the problem remains whether these last factors were not the ones which more often than not determined the tradition! It seems difficult to say much more.

3 That having been said, I now want to reduce this analysis of the individual traditions to their essential elements, at the same time trying

to show the way in which they came to be inserted into the new contexts in which they were recited.

3.1 The itinerary of the migration of Abraham's ancestors from 'Ur of the Chaldeans' (Gen.11.28,31; 15.7; Neh.9.7) to Ḥarrān presents no problems: the two extreme points are well known, and the itinerary must have followed one of the banks of the Euphrates, probably the western one.

3.1.1 Ur is usually identifed with *tell el-muqāyyar*, the site of ancient Sumerian Ur, today about half-way between Baghdad and the Persian gulf,[28] about thirty miles from the Euphrates, and east of the railway. Of course there is nothing to prove that the biblical Ur was identical with the ancient Sumerian Ur,[29] at least in the mind of the author of the story, so it is not surprising that modern authors have directed their researches towards another possible place of the same name situated in the north-west of Mesopotamia, near to Ḥarrān.[30] As we have already seen, the mention of the Chaldaeans also seems anachronistic in this context: the Old Testament itself mentions them only from Hab.1.6 and Jer.21.4 onwards, i.e. not before the second half of the seventh century BC. It so happens, however, that the LXX has an interesting variant: in v.11 it reads ἐκ τῆς χώρας τῶν Χαλδαίων, and in v.28 ἐν τῇ χώρᾳ τῶν Χαλδαίων. The variant presupposes an original Hebrew *mēʾereṣ* and *bᵉʾereṣ* instead of *mēʾūr/bᵉʾūr*, i.e. with an extra ṣ in the consonantal text; and this is a general reference to an area which could be situated further north. W.F.Albright[31] conjectured an original reading *mēʾūr, bᵉʾereṣ kaśdīm*, of which the Hebrew text will have omitted the second word and the LXX the first, but this proposal does not seem to have found much of a following.

3.1.2 But why migrate from Ur to Ḥarrān? One plausible explanation for the journey has been thought to be that both places were the sites of important sanctuaries dedicated to the moon god Sin, and there seems to be evidence of a lunar cult in the names of members of the group: Terah and Laban are both certainly lunar names, while Sarah and Milcah are also connected with the moon, through the goddess Sin.[32] That would lend probability to a journey like that of Abraham's ancestors.[33] However, a closer examination of the question produces different results. The detail was introduced, first by J at a late stage and then by P: as we have seen, conditions in Judah in the second half of the sixth century BC would seem very appropriate at the time of the Priestly writer, and the mention of the Chaldaeans fits then.[34] In that case the journey from the south-east of Mesopotamia to the north-west, and then on to the Promised Land, is the itinerary of the exiles on their return to their homeland (below XII.3.2).

3.1.3 Explanations of this kind become even more probable if we suppose that the Deuteronomistic history writer wanted not only to explain the cause of the national catastrophe which befell Israel in its history but also to lay the foundations for the restoration,[35] while Deutero-Isaiah (below, XII.1.4.3) saw the return home of those who had been deported as a second exodus, a theme which Isa.41.8-10 specifically connects with the election of the patriarchs. The brief mention by J of the migration from Ur in 11.28 could therefore be the product of a late, exilic re-reading: the theme appears again in another late text, Gen.15.4 (probably Deuteronomistic), and was then current in the post-exilic period (Neh.9.7). It is also interesting that in Gen.12.1ff., Abraham's 'homeland' (he is summoned to leave ...*mimmōlad^etēkā...*) appears to be Ḥarrān and not Ur; this also seems to be the view of the Jacob traditions and of ch.24, which is late: the paraphrases at vv.4 and 7 can refer only to Ḥarrān.

3.2 Genesis 14 is the only text which connects Abraham with an event which is said to have thrown Syria and Palestine, or at least a large part of them, into confusion: the expedition of the four kings of four great nations against the five cities situated in the Jordan valley, in the region of the Dead Sea (the 'Valley of Siddim').

Select bibliography: the commentaries on Genesis and especially E.A.Speiser, *Genesis*, AB 1, Garden City, NY 1965; C.Westermann, *Genesis*, BK I, 2, Neukirchen 1981, both ad loc.; J.A.Emerton, 'Some False Clues in the Study of Gen.XIV', *VT* 21, 1971, 24-47; and 'The Riddle of Gen.XIV', ibid., 403-39; W.Schatz, *Genesis 14. Eine Untersuchung*, Berne 1972; T.L.Thompson, *The Historicity...*, ch.9; Y. Muffs, 'Abraham the Noble Warrior', *JJS* 33, 1982, 81-107.

3.2.1 Two of the countries of the four kings, Mesopotamia and Elam, can be identified; of the countries of the other two, the identity of the first (Elassar) is disputed and the name of the second is generic (*gōyīm*, 'of the nations'). The cities of the valley have yet to be identified; it is interesting that the lower valley of the Jordan and that of the Dead Sea are imagined as being extremely fertile, as round the oasis of Jericho (cf. Gen.13.10). This was before the region was destroyed by an enormous cataclysm in the course of which Sodom and Gomorrah met their end (Gen.18-19). However, the description of the great fertility and dense population in the lower valley of the Jordan, with cities, also savours of myth: we do not in fact have any evidence whatsoever for affirming that the region will once have been fertile and densely populated, and then destroyed by a combination of earthquakes and volcanic eruptions, even if such phenomena have been repeated from time to time.[36] The expedition of the four kings will then have involved Abraham through his nephew Lot, who came with him from Ḥarrān and parted company with him to go and live at Sodom, because the kings had taken Lot prisoner. Abraham emerged victor from a battle which was probably with the rearguard of the four kings, freed Lot, and followed the enemy as far as Dan (v.14), a gross anachronism if we compare the note with Judg.19.19 (below VII. 2.6). On his return Melchizedek, the king of Salem (usually identified with Jerusalem) and priest of *'ēl-elyōn*, offered him supplies, receiving from him in turn a tithe of the captured booty.

3.2.2 Now countless studies have been published on this question, and I have given only a selection of them above. However, these efforts have produced only essentially negative results. The same may be said of attempts to derive the content of the chapter from an unknown Mesopotamian cuneiform text. In fact, even on the most sympathetic of readings, the picture which emerges from the chapter seems very confused. In the case of the Eastern nations and kings we have either too many possible identifications or not enough, while we know nothing at all about the kings of the cities of the valley and the cities themselves![37] This includes the figure of the king of Salem, who was later to play so large a part in Christian liturgy and the doctrine of priesthood, and whose name reappears in the archaic Ps.110.4, albeit in an obscure context: the psalm in fact seeks to make the king of Jerusalem a 'priest for ever' (cf. above IV.2.3.5). However, we know nothing of his royal priesthood from the el-'Amarna texts, which mention the king of Jerusalem, while the names known to us are only in part western Semitic (e.g. *abdi-ḫepa*, the first part of which is Semitic, 'servant of', 'devotee of', but which is followed by the name of a deity who does not belong to the area).[38]

3.2.3 Thompson's proposal seems to me to be correct and in many respects definitive. He points out the similarity in form between this account and a series of Serbo-Croat epics dating from the middle of the nineteenth and the beginning of the twentieth centuries AD. Figures in them which are intrinsically historical (sultans, kings and queens, emperors and voivodes) and events which are intrinsically real (conquests, treaties, cessions of territory) are synchronized in one and the same context, though they in fact belonged to different periods, sometimes centuries apart. From this parallel he correctly deduces that the figures denoted in the chapter could very well have been historical, but that it is neither demonstrable nor necessary (*a*) that they were contemporaries; (*b*) that they fought against each other; and (*c*) that they had had contacts with Abraham. Therefore their identification seems to be quite irrelevant on the historical level generally and on that of the patriarchs in particular.

3.2.4 The fact that in Gen.14.13 Abraham is called 'the Hebrew' (*hā'ibrī*) recalls a discussion which began during the 1930s and was broken off, without being really resolved, in the 1970s. This discussion was about the relationships between this term and quite a major ethnic

and political phenomenon attested throughout the second millennium
BC, which became acute especially in the latter part of the millennium,
that of the groups called '*prw* in Egypt, '*prm* in Ugarit, and *ḫabīru* or
ḫapīru in Mesopotamia; these are transcriptions of the logogram SA-
GAZ, which also means 'brigand', 'outlaw', transcribed *ḫabbātu(m)*. For
this reason the phenomenon was for a while confused with some form
of brigandage, and its real nature was only discovered at a relatively
late stage.

Select bibliography. The texts have been brought together in two
useful collections: J.Bottéro, *Le problème des Habiru*, Paris 1954;
M.Greenberg, *The Hab/piru*, New Haven 1955. Monographs:
B.Landsberger, 'Habiru und Lulaḫḫu', *Kleinasiatische Forschungen* 1,
1930, 321-34 (this is the pioneer study on the question); R.Borger,
'Das Problem der 'Apiru (Habiru)', *ZDPV* 74, 1958, 121-32; M.P.Gray,
'The Habiru-Hebrew Problem in the Light of the Source Material
Available at Present', *HUCA* 29, 1958, 135-202; M.Liverani, 'Il fuoru-
scitismo in Siria nella tarda età del bronzo', *Rivista storica italiana* 77,
1965, 315-36; M.B.Rowton, 'The Topological Factor in the *Hapiru*
Problem', in *Studies in Honor of B.Landesberger*, Chicago 1965, 375-
87; N.A.van Uchelen, *Abraham de Hebreeër*, Assen 1965, 71-105;
M.Weippert, *The Settlement*, 63-102; R. de Vaux, 'Le problème des
Hapiru après quinze années', *JNES* 27, 1968, 221-8; M.Weippert,
'Abraham der Hebräer?', *Bibl* 52, 1972, 407-32; G.E.Mendenhall, *The
Tenth Generation*, Baltimore and London 1973, ch.V; W.Thiel, *Die
soziale Entwicklung Israels in vorstaatlicher Zeit*, Berlin DDR 1980, 76-9;
H.Jagersma*, 10-13.

3.2.5 In Accadian, *ḫ* usually transcribes the semitic ', while in all the
languages of the region the change between *b* and *p* seems frequent,
as it is in some Indo-European languages.[39] Therefore it is obvious that
the various designations which I have cited relate to a single term;
moreover, it has often been suggested that when the Hebrew term '*ibrī*
is not just a synonym for 'Israelite' but indicates some form of social
stratification, it should be connected with these groups and put in the
context of the disturbances which they caused to the life of the city-
states, especially in the late Bronze Age. This could be a confirmation
of, or at least an allusion to, the Israelite conquest of Palestine in the
same era (below VII.4.2). Consequently, the conquest would at least
be touched on in the documentation of the period, even if it is not
attested in the text. Special attention has to be paid to the el-'Amarna
archive, where in the correspondence between the lordlings of the city-
states and the Pharaohs many of the former complain that their
territorial integrity and political supremacy are threatened precisely by
these *ḫapiru*. Clearly here is not the place even to attempt to resume

the discussion on this complex problem. It should be enough to indicate that the following details can be taken to be firm:

3.2.5.1 The people indicated by the name in question do not seem ever to have been an ethnic group or part of an ethnic group; rather, this is a social group characterized by the lack of any rights. They are typical outlaws, as in Anglo-Saxon jurisprudence. Normally people were not reduced to this state (and we clearly have to talk of 'being reduced') of their own free will; for an exception cf. 3.2.6 below.

3.2.5.2 Their very condition made them a disturbing, destabilizing element, and in the most serious cases even a threat to the existing order of the city-states in whose territory they happened to be, a threat which could lead to crisis. That explains the frequent charges of brigandry even in ancient times, a fact which is also supported by the possibility that here we have a transcription of the logogram SA-GAZ.

3.2.5.3 Finally, as M.Liverani seems to me to have demonstrated convincingly,[40] these people owed their particular situation of being outlaws to the fact that they had been forced to leave their own country, mostly for political or economic reasons, less frequently by their own choice. That also explains quite easily how they came to be the leading forces behind certain disorders. The case of David fleeing from Saul (above III.4.5) is a legitimate example in the context of the Bible;[41] in fact 'every one who was in distress, and every one who was in debt, and every one who was discontented' came to join the future king (I Sam.22.1f.). So I do not see the viability of Rowton's theory (1965), which seeks to divide the *ḥapīru* 'ecologically', putting them in particularly suitable territories.

3.2.6 These features could explain the use of the term '*ibrī* in the Old Testament where it is not the ethnic designation of an Israelite, but denotes a particular social condition. Thus we have the case of the 'Hebrew slave' (Ex.21.2-6; Deut.15.12-18; cf. also Jer.34.9-14), a member of society in need of particular protection because he or she had probably entered into slavery voluntarily. A parallel, this time a real one, comes from the legal texts of the north-eastern Mesopotamian city-state of Nuzi, where we have the case of people who voluntarily go into slavery because they are *ḥapīru* and this is the only way in which they can keep alive. This was an institution which obviously lent itself to a variety of abuses, in Israel as elsewhere; hence the need for it to be regulated adequately.[42] However, first the Egyptians and then the Philistines use the term with disparaging connotations, with that derogatory attitude which many people have towards the poor stranger. Then the term went on to denote, in Israel, the condition of the people under foreign oppression, while at a late stage (cf.Jonah 1.9; Gen.14.13) it became synonymous with Israelite, a meaning which it has kept down to the present day. For all the relevant passages, the reader must be referred to a concordance.

3.2.7 There can only be one conclusion: despite some authoritative affirmations to the contrary,[43] in the present state of researh the *'prm/ ḥapīru* have nothing to do with the ancient Israelites at the time of the conquest or at any other time. That is, provided that we do not accept the theory of G.E.Mendenhall, developed by N.K.Gottwald,[44] that the Israelite 'conquest' of Palestine will have taken place not from the outside but from within (below VII.4.2) by means of a revolt of oppressed peasantry, as opposed both to the theory of the Hebrew Bible and the very different views of A.Alt and M.Noth. These rebellions on the part of peasants are said to have been caused by the oppression of the city-state and the exploitation of the riches produced by the rural populations. They were accompanied by what Gottwald calls the 'conversion' to Yahwistic faith introduced into the region by groups coming from the desert (cf. above, I.8.4).[45] However, to speak of a religious 'conversion' in this context raises the problem of the religion of the patriarchs. This is a theme on which much has been written; I begin with a famous study by A.Alt in 1929.

3.3 In his study Alt affirmed that it is possible to establish the type of religion practised by the patriarchs of Israel on the basis of certain statements made by the sources and a kind of religion attested in the ancient Near East, especially among non-sedentary peoples.

Select bibliography: A.Alt, 'The God of the Fathers' (1929), in *Essays on Old Testament History and Religion*, Oxford 1966, 3-77; J.Lewy, 'Les textes paléo-assyriens et l'Ancien Testament', *RHR* 110, 1934, (26-65) 50-59; H.S.Nyberg, 'Studien zum Religionskampf im Alten Testament', *AfR* 75, 1938, 329-87; A.Alt, 'Zum "Gott der Väter"', *PJB* 36, 1940, 93-104; J.P.Hyatt, 'Yahweh as "The God of My Father"', *VT* 5, 1955, 130-6; J.Hoftijzer, *Die Verheissungen an die drei Erzväter*, Leiden 1956, 84-96 (important for the bibliography, with comments on earlier studies); F.M.Cross, 'Yahweh and the God of the Patriarchs', *HTR* 55, 1962, 225-59; *Canaanite Myth and Hebrew Epic*, Cambridge, Mass. 1973, 1-2; K.T.Andersen, 'Der Gott meines Vaters', *ST* 16, 1962, 170-88; M.Haran, 'The Religion of the Patriarchs', *ASTI* 4, 1965, (30-55) 51f.; O.Eissfeldt, 'El and Yahweh', *JSS* 1, 1956, 25-37; H.Seebass, *Der Erzvater Israel*, Berlin 1966, 49-55; H.Cazelles, 'La religion des Patriarches', *SDB* VII, 1966, 141-55; H.Weidmann, *Die Patriarchen und ihre Religion*, FRLANT 94, Göttingen 1968; R.de Vaux, 'El et Baal, le Dieu des pères et Yahweh', *Ugaritica* 6, 1969, 501-17, and *Early History* I, 267-82; G.Fohrer, *History of Israelite Religion*, London and Nashville 1973, 27-42; H.Vorländer, *Mein Gott*, AOAT 23, Kevelaer 1975, (184-215) 224ff.; B.Diebner, 'Die

Götter der Väter – eine Kritik der "Vatergott"-Hypothese', *DBAT* 9, 1975, 21-51; R.Albertz, *Persönliche Frömmigkeit und offizielle Religion*, Stuttgart 1978, 77-81; N.Wyatt, 'The Problem of the "God of the Fathers"', *ZAW* 90, 1978, 101-4; J. Van Seters, 'The Religion of the Patriarchs in Genesis', *Bibl* 61, 1980, 220-33; J.Bright*, 95ff.

3.3.1 The sources of the Pentateuch all present the religion of Israel as having been continuous from the time of the patriarchs to that of the individual redactors, though they use different and sometimes contradictory arguments. J makes the worship of YHWH begin right back in prehistory (Gen.4.26); E and P (Ex.3;6) by contrast regard the divine revelation made to Moses as the decisive factor, though they too suppose faith and cultic practices to have been continuous. However, another text, this time independent of the Pentateuchal sources (Josh.24.2,14, one of the texts of the so-called 'confession of faith') presents the religion of the patriarchs as having been polytheistic: 'Beyond the river (Euphrates)... your ancestors... worshipped other deities'. Their descendants are now invited to eliminate these deities from their cult, and to be converted to YHWH alone. It is obviously difficult to say how the ancient authors envisaged this conversion of their ancestors (a conversion which their descendants are also called on to undergo), or how they imagined the original polytheism. For N.K.Gottwald[46], this will have been a conversion in the more or less modern sense of the term: the rebel rural masses will have accepted belief in YHWH, the liberator God brought to them by groups coming out of the eastern desert (cf. below VII.4.2).

3.3.2 On the basis of the scant conclusions that can be drawn from a few passages in the biblical tradition, in his pioneer work A.Alt tried to study the religion of the patriarchs, those groups from which Israel claimed to descend. These are the premises of his study:

3.3.2.1 'The origin of the people of Israel is based, historically speaking, on the union of its tribes in the common worship of the God YHWH', a development which does not seem to have taken place before the settlement in Canaan.

3.3.2.2 It is impossible to obtain from the ancient traditions and legends an adequate picture of this process, which on the one hand was extremely complex, and on the other has been considerably simplified and schematized by the tradition.

3.3.3 Now the discovery on which Alt bases his own conclusions is that the patriarchs are never presented in the act of worshipping deities connected with the fertility of the soil or their flocks, or with the cycles of nature, nor do they appear in any way associated with the sanctuaries near which they settle or which belong to the region in which they live: Shechem, Bethel, Hebron (Mamre). The deity or deities which they worship (in the texts these are now identified with YHWH on the basis of the concept of continuity to which I referred above, 3.3.1) are given titles and designations indissolubly connected with the person of the patriarch who offers worship to them. So these are authentic personal deities, in the sense that they are identified through the person who is their follower.

3.3.4 The most important titles are:

3.3.4.1 'The God of my father' (Gen.31.5b; Ex.15.2, in the second case parallel to 'my God').

3.3.4.2 'The God of your father' (Gen.31.29b, with Sam. and LXX; MT has the plural; 46.1; 50.17).

3.3.4.3 'Your God and the God of your father' (Gen.43.33).

3.3.4.4 'The God of Abraham' (Gen.31.53); however, it should be noted that he is called on together with the deity of the other partner to the alliance!

3.3.4.5 'The God of your father Abraham and your father Isaac' (Gen.28.13).

3.3.4.6 'The God of your Father Abraham' (Gen.26.24).

3.3.4.7 'The same as in 3.3.4.5 but with the first person suffix (Gen.32.10).

3.3.4.8 Again, in the passage cited above, Gen.31.42,53, we read that Jacob swore 'by "the terror of Isaac" his father', *bᵉpaḥad ʾabī...*, a very strange expression. In 1940 W.F.Albright understood this to mean 'kinsman of Isaac',[47] and he was followed by a number of scholars, some of them distinguished.[48] His interpretation was based on the Palmyrene Aramaic *paḥdāʾ*, 'family', 'clan', 'tribe', cf. the Arabic *faḥd* or *fāḥid*, femur, loin, hence 'tribal branch from which the family originates'. This suggested explanation of an expression which otherwise is very strange seems reasonable, even if so far it has not succeeded in gaining general acceptance.

3.3.4.9 The title 'the mighty one of Jacob' (*ʾabīr yaʿᵃqōb*, or perhaps 'the bull', but then we have to read *ʾabbīr*) seems to be on the same lines (Gen.49.24f., where the expression seems parallel to 'God of your father'). In the same, ancient passage we also find, in parallelism, the expression 'of the shepherd of the rock of Israel' (*rōʿeh ʾeben yiśrāʾēl*), but the text seems corrupt and therefore it is difficult to know what to make of the term: as it stands, the expression does not make much sense. In the same phrase we also find a reference to *ʾēl šadday*, a divine designation of a kind typical of P, but which here appears in a very ancient text.

3.3.5 Now for Alt, these expressions are a sign that here we have that particular form of the deity which in the history of religion is called θεὸς πατρῷος: he is not connected either to the agricultural cycle or to a sanctuary, but is closely associated with the group of his own worshippers; he is usually anonymous and is called after the person at the head of the tribe. Moreover, in Genesis, in this context he is often given the title 'ēl instead of the more frequent 'elōhīm, which suggests the possibility that he was originally connected in some way with the sovereign of the Western Semitic pantheon, called 'ēl or ilu; we know that in Israel this deity was assimilated to YHWH. In 1929 Alt had only a few parallel texts at his disposal, usually late; in fact he had to limit himself to the Nabataeans, who lived more than a millennium after the patriarchs, in southern Transjordan. However, in 1934 J.Lewy, setting out with the intention of criticizing Alt's theory, instead provided a series of ancient Assyrian texts coming from Caesarea in Cappadocia, present-day Kültepe.[49] In them there are not only references to the national deity 'aššur but also to a deity called 'god of your father', often without any other designation or specification, although this is a deity who intrinsically could have borne a name. A few other examples were then discovered at Mari, where Aplaḫanda, ruler of Carchemish, writes to Ismaḫ-Addu, viceroy of Mari,[50] saying such things as: 'If you have not sent me anything because of the god of my father, my heart will be afflicted' (lines 15ff.). Another later example (second half of the ninth century BC) is that of rakīb-'ēl, patron (b'l byt) of the reigning house of sam'āl in northern Syria, cf. the statue of bar-rakīb.[51]

3.3.6 The reason why I have devoted perhaps somewhat dispropor-tionate space to this problem is that here we could have a surviving recollection of what might have been the type of religion professed by the ancestors of Israel before the settlement, or, better, what Israel later thought that this religion was. Of course it is uncertain because it is remote and dim. In fact the texts connect this form of religion with the non-sedentary sojourn of the patriarchs in Canaan, and it is a type which also has good parallels elsewhere in the ancient Near East. However, here too one cannot be too careful: already more than twenty-five years ago J.Hoftijzer (1956) pointed out that in the Bible the mention of the God of the fathers is not limited to the time before the revelation of the name of YHWH (cf. Ex.18.4; I Chron.28.9; II Chron.17.4), so that it cannot serve to identify pre-Yahwistic religion. And recently Diebner (1975) has pointed out polemically that the excavations made at Mamre show that the sanctuary did not yet exist in the pre-exilic period. In his most recent study, Van Seters (1980) would prefer to date the concept about the time of the exile, when in Israel, as we know, there was a debate on the problem of individual responsibility and the relationship of the individual to God.

3.4 Finally, the patriarchs are also said to have worshipped deities localized at particular sanctuaries, now all identified with YHWH, also with composite titles which include 'ēl: Gen.31.13;35.7 mention an 'ēl-bet'ēl, probably to be connected with the sanctuary of the same name; Gen.21.33 attests worship of an 'ēl 'ōlām at Beer-sheba; Gen.16.13 an 'ēl-

$r^e\bar{i}$ in an unspecified place in the Negeb. Then we have *'ēl 'elyōn*, which Gen.14.18 (above 3.2.2) associates with the pre-Israelite cult of Jerusalem but which is probably a late amalgamation of two different deities, then combined in the person of YHWH, since classical sources also indicate that there was an ἐλιοῦν in Syria. Mention of this deity tends to give Gen.14 an archaizing flavour. *'ēl šadday*, to be found essentially in P, also has no specific location. Lastly, in Judg.9.4,46, i.e. outside the context of the patriarchs,[52] we find an *'el b^erīt* and a *ba'al b^erīt*, connected with the sacred places of Shechem. Cross (1962) makes the interesting comment that the God of the fathers has the same attributes as *'ēl*, head of the Ugaritic pantheon, 'bull', 'eternal', etc.

VI

EGYPT AND EXODUS

1 In the official biblical chronology, the migrations of the patriarchs are followed by the stay in Egypt, and this in turn is followed by the oppression and the exodus. The Joseph story now serves as the connecting link between the two cycles, but as we shall see in more detail below (2.1.2), there are traditions which seem to be unaware of it. From time immemorial the material connected with the exodus from Egypt has been of central importance for the faith and piety of Israel, and it is certainly no coincidence that the Christian tradition also makes a close connection between the redemptive death of Jesus, and especially his resurrection, and the Jewish passover.

1.1 *Select bibliography*: H.H.Rowley, *From Joseph to Joshua*, Oxford [2]1951 (important because of its bibliography with comments on previous works); P.Weimar and E.Zenger, *Exodus – Geschichten und Geschichte der Befreiung Israels*, SBS 75, Stuttgart 1975; H.Engel, *Die Vorfahren Israels in Ägypten*, Frankfurt am Main 1979 (annotated bibliography on the subject and on the history of research); T.N.D.Mettinger, *The Dethronement of Sabaoth*, CB-OTS 18, Lund 1982, 72-9. For material either from folklore or connected with popular tradition cf. D.Irvin, *Mytharion*, AOAT 32, Kevelaer 1978, passim.

Given the importance of the events narrated in the exodus for the religion of Israel and also indirectly for Christianity, it is not surprising that over the past century research into their possible historicity has been constant and zealous. This is demonstrated by Hellmut Engel's useful and learned dissertation (1970). Studies of this kind have often concluded that the traditions are substantially historical.[1] John Bright*'s exclamation is famous because it is often quoted with approval: 'It is not the sort of tradition any people would invent! Here is no heroic epic of migration, but the recollection of shameful servitude from which only the power of God brought deliverance.'[2] The argument sounds fine; but can it be maintained in the light of what we know of people in similar conditions? The Roman tradition also has its recollection, of Aeneas, who emigrated after a crushing defeat with his old father on his shoulders and holding the hand of his little son: these are certainly pathetic figures, arousing our pity, but they are hardly glorious. The tradition that newly-founded Rome had become a city of refuge for all kinds of doubtful people, so that no one wanted to give their daughters to the Romans in marriage, hardly seems to celebrate the dignity of the protagonists, and it is in this kind of narrative that we find mention of Israel's 'slavery', or at least conscription to forced labour in Egypt. The problem is at the same time different and much more complex: it is not in fact about what people invented or did not invent, but about what the traditions report and about their historical authenticity, about the possibility of the verification of such material. And in this task of verification we find some points worth noting.

1.2.1 The Israelite traditions about the 'conquest' stress that the invaders did not arrive from the north, which was the normal route followed by anyone invading the region; it was also used by Abraham (when Jacob returned to the country, he passed through Transjordan; this is a variant, but is still basically the same). They certainly came from the east and probably also from the south (see VII.2.1; 2.4). This makes it at least probable that they had started from Egypt.[3]

1.2.2 Other features are less important, but also contribute towards reinforcing the tradition of a stay in Egypt on the part of at least some of the groups from which Israel originated; later, and especially among the priestly class, we find a number of names of Egyptian origin. So we have Hophni and Phinehas, the unworthy sons of Eli, the priest of Shiloh and teacher of the boy Samuel at the end of the second millennium BC; later we have Assir and Pashur: the first name has probably been vocalized wrongly and should be pronounced '*ōsīr*, 'Osiris',[4] while Moses' own name (Hebrew *mōšeh*) is evidently Egyptian, though in Egyptian it is always combined with the name of a deity: *ah-*, *ka-*, *ra'-*, *tut-*, i.e. 'son of NN'. That is the case despite the attempt to give a Hebrew etymology to the name in Ex.2.10, rather a clumsy attempt from a philological point of view; on the other hand, it fits well in the kind of popular tradition with which it is associated. However, the argument from nomenclature does not seem conclusive, as we have also seen on other occasions: down to the rise of the Davidic monarchy, the region of Canaan and southern Syria was, as we know, at least nominally under the ruler of Egypt, as clearly emerges from the el-"Amarna letters; we know from other sources that Egypt had a garrison at Beth-shean (present-day *tell el-ḥuṣn*, coord. 198-213, a few hundred yards north of the place itself), while under Solomon (above IV.4.6), with a few exceptions, relationships seem to have been constant and cordial. In these conditions the presence of linguistic islands is quite likely, and it is quite legitimate to suppose that there was a marked influence on both language and names. Moreover, we have seen that one of David's officials (above III.8.2.4) had a name which in reality is probably his title in Egyptian, distorted in the Hebrew transcription.

1.2.3 On the other hand, here too the biblical material is such that it cannot be verified in any way, a fact which is generally accepted. The only reliable feature seems to be the brief note acording to which 'Israel' was employed on the building of the cities of Pithom and Raamses (Ex.1.11). The first place probably corresponds to the Egyptian *pr 'tm*, 'house (temple) of Atum' (with the omission of the *r* typical of the pronunciation of the New Kingdom) and is certainly in the region of the *wādī et-tumeilat*, probably on either *tell er-retābeh* or *tell el-mašḫūta*. *t̲kw* was a few miles to the east; it is probably the Succoth of Ex.12.37. The site of Raamses is none other than the old Hyksos capital Avaris, rebuilt in the reigns of Sethos I (*c.*1318-1304 or 1305-1290) and Ramses II (*c.* 1304-1237 or 1290-1224); the second of these rulers, under whom the work was finished, gave his name to the city. It became *pr-r'mššw*, 'house of Ramses'; later it was called Tanis, though we cannot discover whether here we have the same place under different names or two different places.[5]

1.2.4 This identification is now usually accepted and would put the date of the servitude[6] towards the beginning of the thirteenth century BC. In Hebrew the cities, whether built or rebuilt, have the title *'ārē miskᵉnōt*, a term probably to be connected with the Accadian *maškantu* or *maškattu*, 'store', 'provision', so that it is often translated as 'store cities' or 'warehouse cities' (*AHw* II, 627).[7] This is confirmed by Aquila and Symmachus, while LXX has πόλεις ὀχυράς, 'fortified cities'.[8] It is interesting that this is a term of Eastern Semitic and not Egyptian or Western Semitic origin; moreover, it is used quite rarely. It appears only in I Kings 9.19//I Chron 8.6, cf. also II Chron. 16.4; 17.1; 32.28. The first quotation takes us back, like J, to the earliest period of the monarchy as a *terminus a quo*.

2.1 The end of Genesis connects the arrival of the patriarchs in Egypt closely with the person of Joseph, one of the younger sons of Jacob.

2.1.1 However, this tradition is not without internal tensions: in Gen.35.16-20 Jacob's youngest son is Benjamin, born after Joseph of the same mother, who died bringing him to birth; however, in 37.3f. Joseph is the 'son of Joseph's old age'. Again, in 37.25b; 39.1b (J), he is sold to the Ishmaelites, but in 37.28,36 to the Midianites: this is one of the classical passages for source analysis. The story is well known and here we can only pause over the essentials. Having arrived in Egypt in a wretched state, Joseph is sold to an Egyptian nobleman. At first his fortunes go from bad to worse, but ultimately he succeeds in becoming the imperial vizier, the highest post open to anyone who is not a member of the royal family. The narrators see in his spectacular career a well-deserved reward for his piety, honesty, integrity and hard work (cf.Gen.39.7ff., and especially 45.5b, where after the dramatic reunion Joseph says to his brothers: 'God sent me before you to preserve life...; it was not you who sent me here but God; and he has made me a father to Pharaoh, and lord of all his house and ruler over all the land of Egypt!') Exodus 1.8ff. (J) makes explicit reference to all the vicissitudes of Joseph: 'Now there arose a new king over Egypt, who did not know Joseph...', thus implying that the Egyptians owed a debt of recognition to Joseph, a debt which the new Pharaoh chose to ignore.

2.1.2 However, there is another tradition about the migration of the patriarchs to Egypt, much terser, which is contained in the 'confession of faith'. I have already mentioned it in connection with the patriarchs (above V.1.6; 2.1). Deuteronomy 26.5b affirms: 'A wandering Aramaean was my father; and he went down into Egypt and sojourned there, few in number...'; and in Josh.24.4 we read: '...but Jacob and his children went down to Egypt.'

2.1.3 In other words, we have at least a second version of the origins of the sojourn of the patriarchs in Egypt. While the first is the best known, because it is dealt with better on a narrative level, the second is not aware of the figure of Joseph, and sees Jacob as the main character in the migration; and while the first is rich in details from folklore, topography and chronology, the second has none of these features and confines itself to stating the fact of the migration. From the second version it is hard to see why a Pharaoh should have been grateful to Joseph.

2.1.4 Against this duplication of versions in the biblical tradition, however, we have to set the total silence of the Egyptian sources as we know them. There is no information which could be connected with the migration of the patriarchs, nor do we know anything about an Asiatic vizier who could be associated with the figure of Joseph. Moreover, as always happens down to the death of Solomon, there is no mention of the name of the Pharaoh connected either with Joseph or with the oppression; here, too, we find ourselves in the same situation as with the other patriarchal traditions, because of the inadequacy and vagueness of the sources at our disposal.

2.2 *Select bibliography*: J.Vergote, *Joseph en Égypte*, Louvain 1959, and the important review by S.Morenz, *TLZ* 84, 1959, 401-16; G.von Rad, 'The Joseph Narrative and Ancient Wisdom', in *The Problem of the Hexateuch*, 292-300; id., *Die Josephsgeschichte*, Neukirchen 1956 (a popular account); O.Eissfeldt, *Stammessage und Menschheitserzählung in der Genesis*, Berlin 1965; L.Ruppert, *Die Josepherzählung*, Munich 1965; R.N.Whybray, 'The Joseph Story and Pentateuchal Criticism', *VT* 18, 1968, 512-28; D.B.Redford, *A Study in the Biblical Story of Joseph*, SVT 10, Leiden 1970; R.Martin-Achard, 'Problèmes soulevés par l'étude de l'histoire biblique de Josèphe (Génèse 37-50)', *RTP* 105, 1972, 94-102; G.W.Coats, 'The Joseph Story and Ancient Wisdom: An Appraisal', *CBQ* 35, 1973, 285-97; H.Donner, *Die literarische Gestalt der alttestamentlichen Josephsgeschichte*, Heidelberg 1976; I.Willi-Plein, 'Historiographische Aspekte der Josephsgeschichte', *Hen* 1, 1979, 305-31; J.B.Geyer, 'The Joseph and Moses Narratives: Folk Tale and History', *JSOT* 15, 1980, 51-56; T.L.Thompson, 'History and Tradition', ibid., 57-61.

2.2.1 Martin Noth and Gerhard von Rad have always expressed their scepticism about the historicity of the Joseph story. Besides, it does not aim to relate history but has a predominantly narrative function: it serves as a connecting link between the patriarchal traditions and those of the oppression and the exodus.[9] Backwards, the connection is purely genealogical, in that Joseph is the son of Jacob, and it produces the tensions that we have noted earlier (2.1.1); however, for the historical worth of such connections cf. above V, 2.3.1-3. Forwards, the connection seems to be an extremely general one. Moreover, in terms of form the Joseph story seems to be a self-sufficient literary entity, which presupposes neither what goes before nor what comes afterwards. So it is not surprising that a number of modern scholars would want it to be studied leaving aside the question of the Pentateuchal sources. Noth regarded it essentially as a novelistic amplification of a predetermined theme, namely the migration of Jacob and his sons to Egypt. The development is achieved by means of the insertion of a thematic narrative, elements of which are on occasion drawn from the ample store of popular tradition and fable. There are the motives of the younger brother who is privileged and therefore envied; of Joseph as a 'goodly child' who is also unsympathetic because he 'tells tales' (Gen.37.2b); of the man fallen on hard times who ends up by triumphing over adversity because he is virtuous and pious; of the unfaithful wife who accuses the honest young man who has spurned her advances (there is a very similar Egyptian story, that of the 'Two Brothers', *ANET* 23ff.); and of the hostility of the brothers and their reconciliation after the triumph of the hero (a theme which also appears in the text of the statue of Idrimi, king of Alalakh, *ANET*, 557ff.).[10]

2.2.2 G.von Rad again notes[11] that Joseph, his brothers and their father are given such individual characteristics that it is impossible to begin to think of them as eponymous heroes or heads of tribes.

2.2.2.1 In fact, the narrative develops in a domestic context (while that may be said of a high proportion of the patriarchal narratives, here it seems to be taken to the limit).

2.2.2.2 Moreover, here the nuclear family 'is' all Israel, so that while the narrative element, the delight in storytelling, becomes the keynote of the narrative, the narrative also has a clear paradigmatic function. However, this is also the very point at which it fails us, in that it is minimally preoccupied with real factual details, even supposing that these were available to the authors or that they thought them interesting. In any case, had information of this kind been available, it must have been in the north, in Israel in the narrower sense, seeing that Joseph is the father of Ephraim and Manasseh, the two leading tribes of the North.

2.2.2.3 However, we should also note another feature: leaving aside the initially unsympathetic tone (which is an essential element, providing a reason for the violent reaction of Joseph's brothers), in the rest of the story Joseph appears as the hero without fault or blemish, rather like David and Solomon in the Chronicles version. There are none of those cynical or even brutal overtones which have always been a feature of political life and which are well represented in the stories about the first kings and indeed partly even in the patriarchal narratives of the J source. It is precisely this somewhat hagiographical approach which might suggest a rather late redaction, although of course there is no way of providing definitive proof.

2.2.2.4 Von Rad then tries to connect the evident interest of the narrative in the practices and customs current in Egypt with what he calls the orientation of the narrative on wisdom. He cites references to the court and its ceremonial, the embalming of corpses, the buying of corn by the crown cheaply in times of plenty and its resale at an advantageous price in times of famine. The basic principle behind this wisdom is in fact the fear of God (cf. Gen.39.9; 42.18b with Prov. 1.7a). O.Eissfeldt sees an indirect confirmation of this characteristic in the use made of the story in children's catechisms down the centuries.

2.2.3 However, von Rad's study, important though it may be (and many scholars have hailed it as a basic turning-point), leaves some problems open.

2.2.3.1 What von Rad claims to be a connection with wisdom seems rather tenuous: what he regards as features of wisdom can very easily be attributed to the narrator's interest in original features, in unusual details, by which he can attract the attention of the reader or the hearer.[12] This has little or nothing to do with wisdom.

2.2.3.2 At this point, by way of a provisional conclusion, we can be sure of at least one thing: clearly the Joseph story is a historical novel and not a historical work.

3 Thus because of the preponderance in the Joseph story of narrative

elements reminiscent of folk-lore, for want of any comparative Egyptian historical material it proves to be an inadequate source for a reconstruction of the events which are supposed to have led to the settlement of the ancestors of Israel in Egypt and which, after a certain time, also led to the exodus.

3.1 So we must direct our researches elsewhere. And down to the present day, the settlement of the ancestors of Israel in Egypt has often been associated with the seizure of power by the so-called Hyksos.

3.1.1 Again for A.Alt in 1939,[13] it seemed possible to connect the migration of Jacob and his sons with the seizure of power in Egypt by a group called Hyksos, who were then thought to have come from northern Mesopotamia and to have been made up of Semitic and Indo-European elements. However, in 1954 Alt himself[14] arrived at almost opposite conclusions: that the rise to power of this group (whose name had first been translated as 'shepherd kings', but which probably means something like 'foreign rulers') had not been the result of migrations, nor even of an invasion. The origins of the group are still largely obscure, though it seems increasingly probable that these were Semitic and Hurrian nuclei which had already been settled for some time in the eastern Delta. At the end of the first quarter of the second millennium BC they will have succeeded in seizing power, profiting from the disorders of the so-called 'Second Intermediate Period', and held it for about 200 years.

3.1.2 So just as the theory of an 'Amorite' invasion in the wake of which Abraham is supposed to have arrived in Canaan from north-western Mesopotamia has proved to be unfounded (above V.1.2.3), so too the similar theory of a migration by the Hyksos from Canaan, Syria and northern Mesopotamia to Egypt, a migration which will have involved Jacob and his sons, proves to rest on fragile foundations. Of course, in the absence of a migration of the Hyksos to Egypt it is also difficult to assume that they were expelled, even if scholars still seem fond of using the expression;[15] indeed, many of them have wanted to connect this event with the figure of the 'Pharaoh who did not know Joseph'.[16]

3.2.1 To give some idea of the complexity of the problems connected with the texts of the story of Jacob, it is enough to recall that the Belgian Egyptologist J.Vergote, in his important 1959 study, succeeded in bringing together a remarkable series of parallels and agreements in the linguistic field between the Joseph story and Egyptian texts dating from the XIXth Dynasty (*c*.1320-1200 or 1306-1200). Moreover, not only does Vergote see nothing against putting the stories in this period; he also finds much in favour of such a dating.[17] The German Egyptologist Siegfried Morenz, in his review of Vergote's work, seems more prudent and less enthusiastic, yet he too is extremely favourable towards Vergote's theory.

3.2.2 In confirmation of these theories, scholars refer to various instances in which foreigners who rose to 'positions of great power'.[18] So this does not seem to have been at all unusual in the second half of the second millennium BC. Nor does the story of the famine seem improbable: a prolonged and severe drought at the source of the Nile was enough to lower the level of the waters, thus restricting considerably the possibility of using them for irrigation.

3.2.3 On the other hand there are scholars who would prefer to date the account round about the time of Solomon,[19] i.e. at the beginning of the first millennium BC, and therefore very much later than Vergote's proposal. They claim that at the beginning of the first millennium there is a reference to Joseph's Egyptian name, ṣap‘nat pa‘nē‘ḥ in Gen.41.45, a possible Hebrew version of the Egyptian ḏd NN iw.f‘nḥ: 'NN has declared: "May he live"!'[20] However, the expression with which the Egyptians are said to have saluted Joseph's carriage as he went by would seem to be very different: ’abrēk (Gen.41.43). This was first often understood as being the equivalent of 'Attention!',[21] and then associated with the root bārak₁, 'kneel', taken to be an invitation to pay homage; however, Lipiński's proposal seems more probable.[22] Adopting the suggestion made by Franz Delitzsch in 1881, he thinks, rather, of a connection with the Accadian *abarakku*, 'high official'[23] (*AHw* 3), cf. the analogous Phoenician *hbrk b‘l* in the first inscription of Karatepe (*KAI* 26), to be understood probably as: 'I am Azitawadda, the vizier of Baal...'. This is perhaps an allusion to the priesthood of the king, or, more simply, to his particular devotion to this god. In that case, however, this term, like the designation of the two cities in Ex.1.11 (above 1.2.4), points to the Western Semitic area and would also be relatively late.

The texts tell us that the ancestors of Israel were allotted a residence in what is called the 'land of Goshen'.

4.1 The practice of assigning land to Asiatic peoples like the patriarchs is well attested in Egypt. Papyrus Anastasi VI[24] gives us important information; it contains the report of an official appointed to a post on the eastern frontier towards the end of the thirteenth century BC. Among other things, it says: '...we have finished passing the tribes of the shepherds[25] through the fortress... which is near *tkw* (probably the Succoth of Ex.12.37) to the cisterns of Per Atum (*pītōm*?) which are near *tkw*, to keep them and their animals alive by means of the *ka* of the Pharaohs...'. There are also other texts of this kind, even if they are not so explicit.

4.2 So it is in this direction that we must look for the country of Goshen,[26] an area which from time immemorial down to the beginning of major reclamation work in modern times, to make it suitable for intensive agriculture, has been chosen for the extensive rearing of cattle. Gen.46.28ff. again tells us that Joseph, travelling in a carriage, could cover the distance betwen this region and the capital in a relatively short time; this is an indication that the tradition does not locate the capital at Memphis, but at Avaris-Tanis (above 1.2.3), which was the capital first under the Hyksos and then at the time of the Nineteenth Dynasty, who rebuilt it. Of course it is difficult to say to which of these two periods the account is meant to refer, but we have seen that Vergote thinks the Nineteenth Dynasty a suitable time.

5 So we come to the problem of the chronology of the narrative, which is also very complicated. In Gen.15.13ff.(Dtr) and Ex.12.40ff.(P) there is mention of 400 and 430 years respectively between the time of Abraham and that of the Exodus, but Gen.15.16 mentions only four generations, i.e. a period of at most between 60 and 120 years. The chronology of I Kings 6.1 takes up the first of the two figures (400 and 430 years); here the date of the beginning of work on the building of the temple is put at 480 years after the Exodus (cf. also above IV.2.3). However, all these figures seem problematical on a historical level, and they cannot be used to reconstruct a chronology of the earliest history of Israel. The 480 years must be explained from other perspectives, which are ideological and theological rather than historical,[27] whereas the first two figures do not as yet seem to have any certain meaning. So it would be better to give up trying to reconstruct a chronology and accept that the information at our disposal is not enough to calculate one. We can, however, argue that during the period of the early monarchy Israel (and the reference is probably to the tribes of the North) handed down the memory of its own direct relationships with those groups which, at the beginning of the thirteenth century, under the Nineteenth Egyptian Dynasty, will have built or rebuilt the two cities of the Delta, and will have been conscripted for forced labour by the very authority which at one time will have settled them in the region. So there is no point in asking what was the relationship between these groups and the tribes of Israel in Palestine centuries later: not only do we now have no plausible information, but we also know (below VII.6) that the tribes of Israel came into being in Canaan, and not before they arrived there, though that is what the tradition maintains. So we shall never know which of the ancestors of Israel had been slaves in Egypt, nor can we even confirm the intrinsic probability of the information, even if, as we have seen, some passages make things inherently possible. So we are in the same position as that in which we find ourselves with the traditions of Aeneas in the Rome of Augustus: we know what the people believed about their own past, but we have no certain information which we can put to the proof.

6 We have seen (2.1.1 above) that at the beginning of the book of Exodus the slavery of the ancestors of Israel is connected with a change at the highest levels of Egyptian power: a Pharaoh ascended the throne who no longer felt bound to the person and the work of Joseph and who was also afraid that the people, who had meanwhile become numerous and therefore powerful, might be a danger to Egypt in case of war (1.8-10 J).

6.1 This fear was soon translated into hostile acts: first of all, we are told, Israel was employed in forced labour, but the administration gave them the materials (1.12ff.). At a later stage, however, the Israelites had personally to go in search of the necessary materials without the quotas being reduced (5.6-23). But in 1.15-23, probably E, a second element appears: this is the order given by the king to the midwives to kill all the newborn males so as to cause a dramatic drop in the growth of the population. However, the attempt failed because of the piety and the religion of the two midwives assigned to Israel, whose names have a sound Western Semitic etymology.[28] But again, as we have already seen several times, the realism in the names cannot be any proof of their authenticity or of the authenticity of the tradition; it is only an indication, as in the patriarchal narratives (above V.2.3.5).

6.1.1 Anyone who wants to be very precise could then point out that there is a certain tension, perhaps even incompatibility, between the two types of persecution. The forced labour in fact has a twofold aim: surveillance of the suspects and at the same time intensive economic exploitation of them. There is no mention of any form of genocide; indeed, again given the logic of the narrative, one might suppose that they would be freed once the building work was finished and the danger had passed. By contrast, killing the newborn males and thus condemning the male Hebrew population to growing old and therefore to extinction would obviously in time diminish the second of the two aims of the forced labour, its productivity. On the other hand, we can hardly see the theme of the attempted genocide as a secondary addition: it now introduces the birth of Moses, who will soon be the main character in the majority of the stories which follow.

6.1.2 However, the story of the birth of Moses, to which the note about the extermination of the children forms a kind of prologue, is also not without its problems. It is an obvious parallel to the 'autobiography' of Sargon I of Accad (c. 2334-2270 BC), who was also conceived and borne by his mother in secret; she then 'put him in a basket of reeds, with the covering sealed with pitch', and left it to float on the river. However, the basket, made and treated in a skilful way, does not sink, and is rescued by a water carrier. He brings up the child (*ANET*, 119). In the biblical narrative, too, we are told that the basket is made watertight, an apparently otiose detail because it is not meant to float, but is abandoned among the reeds. So at all events it is evident that, while on the one hand the story of Moses fits in with the theme of the attempted genocide, on the other hand it is a narrative feature which is well attested in the ancient Near East and was therefore probably well known.

6.2 The comment that the anonymous Pharaoh of the oppression 'did not know Joseph' shows that the tradition thought in terms of a substantially different dynasty, characterized by a marked lack of confidence on the part of those who had come to power in one who had been favoured by the previous dynasty, especially since he was a foreigner.

6.2.1 However, only two of these changes qualify for our narrative: the one that took place at the time of the 'expulsion' of the Hyksos about 1550 by the Pharaohs of the Eighteenth Dynasty, especially Ah-Moses I (*c.*1570-1546) and the one which took place about 1306 with the beginning of the Nineteenth Dynasty under Sethos I (*c.*1318-1304 or 1305-1290).

6.2.1.1 The former might seem probable in terms of content: in fact nothing is more obvious than that a new dynasty, taking the place of an earlier one which had been felt to be foreign, should have imposed its own programme of government in a markedly nationalistic and xenophobic way and therefore have sought to put a brake on what could easily have appeared as an abuse on the part of the former government, namely the settling of alien, if not hostile, peoples in regions which were peripheral and therefore dangerous in any conflict. However, if we accept these suggestions, Israel will have been subjected to forced labour for about 250 years, an improbably long period, and the building of the two cities mentioned in 1.11 will have taken place only at the end of the period.

6.2.1.2 The second period would work much better on the chronological level, but if we accept it, it is impossible to explain the unexpected mistrust of the new regime towards a population which had now lived in the region for quite some time, and which had never so far caused trouble. On the contrary, it had been a notable benefit in an area which was otherwise unpopulated and unproductive. So the mistrust does not seem to have been motivated by any objective features.

6.2.1.3 To that must be added a factor that we have already encountered on other occasions: the almost total silence of the Egyptian sources. On one solitary occasion, in fact, in Pap. Anastasi V from the end of the thirteenth century BC (*ANET*, 259b), there is mention of the pursuit of two (n.b. two!) fugitive slaves beyond the frontier; we hear nothing of any conscription to forced labour of entire foreign groups living in the area.[29] So it is not the case that the Egyptian sources are not concerned with a theme like the one with which we are concerned; they do not know of it, but they do record other similar instances.

6.3 So the study of the oppression and slavery of Israel in Egypt and of the Exodus brings us up against a series of initial difficulties not dissimilar to those which we encountered in our study of the patriarchs.

Select bibliography: O.Eissfeldt, *CAH* II, 2, ³1975, 318ff.; W.H.Schmidt, 'Jahwe in Ägypten', in *Sefer Rendtorff*, Dielheim 1975, 94-112; R. de Vaux, *Early History* I, 324ff.; G.von Rad, 'Beobachtungen an der Moseerzählung Exodus 1-14', *EvTh* 31, 1971, 579-88, *GS* II, 189-98; G.W.Ramsey, *The Quest of the Historical Israel*, Atlanta and London 1981, ch.III; J.-L.Ska, 'La sortie d'Égypte (Ex.7-14) dans le récit sacerdotal (P^g) et la tradition prophétique', *Bibl* 60, 1979, 171-215.

6.3.1 As we have already seen to be so often the case, the biblical sources are rich in anecdotes, popular traditions and elements of folklore; however, they lack information which is capable of verification by historical criticism: the Pharaohs or important officials are never named, and the chronological information is sparse and imprecise. We have only a few topographical notes that we can use.

6.3.2 The Egyptian texts are also virtually silent on anything other than, for example, those mentions which we have already come across (above 4.1) of the crossing of the Eastern frontier by shepherds or the pursuit of fugitive slaves (above 6.2.1.3). One argument which keeps recurring is that the Egyptian annals do not concern themselves with minutiae of this kind; however, that does not seem plausible in the light of what we have seen so far. Similarly, the argument according to which the Pharaohs, especially the nationalistic Pharaohs of the Nineteenth Dynasty, were not accustomed to record their own defeats, hardly appears relevant. In this connection one might quote the instance of the battle of Kadesh on the Orontes (in present-day Lebanon), about 1285, which resulted in a Hittite victory. The Hittites succeeded in occupying the whole of the northern part of Syria, but the battle was presented by Ramses II as an Egyptian victory. What actually happened was that the Pharaoh managed with some difficulty to avoid being encircled and therefore losing all his troops by beating a hasty retreat; so on the most favourable of readings we have a tactical success, and certainly not a victory. Now it is said that the flight through the Red Sea with the annihilation of the pursuing troops was evidently a defeat, precisely the sort of thing about which the Pharaohs kept quiet. However, to note that some Pharaohs concealed certain facts and even lied about their defeats in their propaganda or their war bulletins clearly does not amount to a proof, nor is it a valid alternative to the silence of the Egyptian sources about the facts in which we are interested; with the best will in the world it is no more than a possible explanation.

6.3.3 However, there is more to come. Even the non-specialist reader cannot fail to marvel at the wealth of detail provided in the texts, and this wealth can readily appear suspect.

6.3.3.1 First of all we have a series of formal encounters between the Pharaoh, surrounded by his own dignitaries and soothsayers, and Moses, accompanied by Aaron and possibly by the elders of the people. Now the improbability of these scenes has often been noted, in connection both with the meetings and the negotiations which make up their content. To say the least, it seems improbable to suppose that Pharaoh, the god-king, should have met on equal terms representatives of a group of foreign cattle-breeders suspected of being a potential fifth column and therefore conscripted to forced labour, even if according to the tradition Moses had been educated at court.

6.3.3.2 Furthermore, the narrative seems to be too schematic, too well constructed, to be a record of real events, even one that has been modified to meet the demands of a narrative. To begin with, Pharaoh regularly grants the requests of Moses and his followers; then his heart is 'hardened' by God himself and he goes back on everything. Time and again, under the impact of the successive plagues, he again yields, and then, once the plague has passed, he has second thoughts. Only with the last plague does he finally yield once and for all, and when yet again he has second thoughts it is too late: Israel has already gone.

6.3.3.3 At all events, it seems difficult to establish whether the narratives contain material which goes back to ancient traditions, and if so what these might have been; we cannot tell how much belongs to the narrative stage of the discourse and how much again proves to be reflections of an ethical and religious kind. For example, this last category might include the concept that God might deprive the sinner even of the possibility of repenting of his guilt if in his action he went beyond a certain limit. Finally, we do not know how much is purely and simply part of the passover liturgy.

6.3.3.4 The theory that in the final analysis this narrative is part of the Jewish passover liturgy and that it can therefore be explained only in that context was authoritatively put forward in the 1930s by the Danish scholar J.Pedersen,[30] who for precisely this reason stresses that the account is substantially a unity.

6.4 This is what brings us to consider the account of the 'plagues' which struck Egypt following the refusal of the Pharaoh to let the people of God go. The texts appear in Ex.7.14-11.10 and all present serious problems. I shall devote perhaps a disproportionate amount of space to this theme, but it does seem to me to be worth the trouble, to look at an example of the way in which the Israelite tradition functioned.

Select bibliography: G.Hort, 'The Plagues of Egypt', ZAW 69, 1957, 84-103; 70, 1958, 45-59; G.Fohrer, Überlieferung und Geschichte des Exodus, BZAW 91, Berlin 1964, 60-97; M.Greenberg, 'The Redaction in the Plagues Narrative in Exodus', in Near Eastern Studies in Honor of W.F.Albright, Baltimore and London 1971, 243-52; S.E.Loewenstamm, 'An Observation on Source Criticism of the Plague Pericope', VT 24, 1974, 374-8; E.Otto, 'Erwägungen zum überlieferungsgeschichtlichen Ursprung und "Sitz im Leben" des jahwistischen Plagenzyklus', VT 26, 1976, 3-27; A.Ademollo, 'I morbi nel racconto biblico delle piaghe d'Egitto e nella loro rispodenza scientifica', Rivista di storia della medicina, 20, 2, 1976, 137-67; M.Gilula, 'The Smiting of the First-Born – An Egyptian Myth?', TA 4, 1977, 94f.; S.I.L.Norin, 'Er spaltete das Meer', CB-OTS 9, Lund 1977, 13ff., 128ff.; J.-L.Ska, art.cit. (6.3).

6.4.1 Hebrew has five terms for what we usually translate as 'the plagues': niplā'ōt, 'wonders'; 'ōt, 'natural sign'; mōpet, 'miraculous sign'; nega', 'blow'; and negep, 'affliction'. Furthermore, it is possible to divide the plagues into two categories, depending on their character: the first nine belong in the sphere of natural phenomena and the miraculous element consists only in the fact that they coincide and are of such severity; by contrast, the last clearly transcends the natural order of events and is definitive and irreversible.

6.4.2 Moreover, despite the apparent unity and schematic character of the narrative, a remarkable amount of redactional and editorial activity has led up to its present form. M. Greenberg (1971) has seen two strata in the narrative, one JE and the other P, partly overlapping and partly diverging, while S.E.Loewenstamm (1974) sees two traditions within J. As if that were not enough, two mentions of the plagues outside the exodus narrative (Ps. 78.43-51; 105.27-36) list them in different orders. De Vaux reasonably remarks:[31] 'It would appear, then, that a great deal was in fact said about these "plagues", and that only one tradition, providing one selection, is contained in Exodus.'

6.4.3 Not all the sources have all the plagues.

6.4.3.1 The first, the pollution of the water, appears in the three sources (cf. 7.14-25); but only J connects the pollution with the death of the fish, whereas E and P have the water miraculously turned into blood; this is probably a variant of the theme of the pollution.

6.4.3.2 The second plague, the frogs, appears only in J and P (cf. 7.26-8.11).

6.4.3.3 The third, the mosquitoes, appears only in P (8.12-15).

6.4.3.4 The fourth, the flies (probably the musca canina, an insect which attacks domestic animals more than man, cf. Zorrell's Lexicon s.v. 'ārōb), appears only in J (8.16-28).

6.4.3.5 The fifth, the death of the livestock, is attested only in J (9.1-7).

6.4.3.6 The sixth, the ulcers, appears only in P (9.8-12).

6.4.3.7 The seventh, the hailstorm, appears in J and E (9.13-35).

6.4.3.8 The eighth, the locusts, also in J and E, appears in 10.12-20.

6.4.3.9 The ninth, the darkness, appears only in E (10.21-27).

6.4.3.10 The tenth plague, the killing of the firstborn of men and animals, appears in all three sources (12.29-34).

Therefore in J we have seven plagues, and in E and P only five each.

6.4.4 So we may take into account the possibility that some of the plagues are simply variants or even duplications of others (nos.3-4, 5-6, 7-8 – these last in the sense that the hail and the locusts are both visitations from the heavens which destroy the crops). That could give us something like seven specific plagues, of which the first five are usually considered to be the earliest in terms of the tradition.[32]

6.4.5 This analysis, which perhaps seems rather extensive given the overall framework of the present work, allows of only one conclusion. As de Vaux already points out, the tradition is a literary composition, not a historical or legendary text; it is a work conceived at the writing desk, not a collection of ancient traditions going back to reminiscences of past events.

6.5 It is natural that attempts are constantly made to connect the plagues with natural phenomena attested in the region.[33]

6.5.1 The results of these labours are very modest, compared with the resources used and the profound knowledge of those who engage in them. So far the most interesting argument is that of Hort in 1957-58, and for details I refer the reader to it. For Hort the only inexplicable element is the hailstorm, the seventh plague, since hail is virtually unknown in Egypt, whereas it is frequent in Palestine during the winter. The killing of the firstborn would be based on an early error: the *bikkūrīm* will not have been the firstborn but the firstfruits of the produce of the soil, which had been destroyed as a result of the other, earlier plagues. However, the term was later understood, and therefore misinterpreted, to mean that the 'firstborn' of human beings and animals had been killed. The explanation by Gilula (1977) differs: the detail is supposed to derive from an ancient Egyptian myth on a similar theme, incorporated into the passover narrative and inserted among the others as the last plague.

6.5.2 Now however probable these arguments may be in individual details (and we have seen how rarely this is in fact the case), they do not take account of the fact that in the narrative the effect is cumulative; it does not depend on individual plagues but on the whole series of them. It is only this last feature which makes the first nine a series of divine signs, miracles. Obviously it is useless to seek to rationalize something that is irrational, and the story loses its point here, without the doubters being convinced. What the text confesses (and this *is* a confession of faith, as the passover context indicates) is the divine intervention on the side of the humble and the oppressed, and their triumph over the greatest power of the time along with its ruler, who was considered to be a divine being.

7 Chapters 12-14, followed by the epic song in ch.15, narrate the central event of the Exodus: the miraculous departure from Egypt through the stretch of water which is known as the *yam sūp*.

Select bibliography: G.R.H. Wright, 'The Passage of the Sea', *Göttinger Miscellen* 33, 1979, 55-68; J.Scharbert, 'Das "Schilfmeerwunder"' in den Texten des Alten Testaments', in *Mélanges bibliques et orientaux en l'honneur de M.Henri Cazelles*, AOAT 212, Kevelaer 1981, 395-417; B.F.Batto, 'The Reed Sea: Requiescat in pace', *JBL* 102, 1983, 27-35 (in favour of the traditional rendering 'Red Sea' and against 'Reed Sea'); J.A.Soggin, 'Das Wunder am Meer und in der Wüste, Exodus cc.14-15', in *D'Ugarit à Qumrân. Mélanges bibliques et orientaux en l'honneur de M.Mathias Delcor*, AOAT, Kevelaer 1985, 379–85; my last two studies have detailed bibliographies.

7.1 The translation 'Red Sea' is conventional and dates from the time of the LXX, which has ἐρυθρὰ θάλασσα, and the Vulgate, which has *Mare Rubrum*. However, it is wrong: the Hebrew *sūp* means 'rush', or 'reed'; also in Ex.2.3,5, where the two ancient translations are in fact correct. The rendering 'Red Sea' probably arises from the fact that in at least two certain texts, I Kings 9.26 and Jer.49.21, the expression refers to the eastern arm of the Red Sea, the present-day Gulf of Aqaba. So Israel arrived at the Sea of Reeds or Sea of Rushes, having finally succeeded in leaving Egypt, caught between the waters in front of them and the army behind. This is the high point of the narrative. Pharaoh went back on his word for the umpteenth time and began the pursuit with his troops. But as we know, the waters opened to allow the Israelites to pass through and then closed again over their pursuers.

7.2 However, the narrative is not so much a unity as might appear at first sight; it is possible to recognize at least three strata in the account which we could, if we wished, identify as the three sources of the Pentateuch,[34] each with its own version of the event.

7.2.1 What is evidently the earliest stratum, which we could attribute to J, appears in 14.21abba: 'The Lord made the sea withdraw (*wayyōlek*, hiphil) by a strong east wind all night, and made the sea dry land.' This version of the facts is evidently meant to present a natural phenomenon, in which the miraculous element consists exclusively in the perfect synchronization of events, which helped Israel and hindered the pursuers. For Noth, the phenomenon could have historical roots.[35] At the end of the second millennium BC the Gulf of Suez was still partially connected with the Bitter Lakes; the link was broken only by a narrow tongue of land and, depending on the tide and the wind, this could either be above the water or submerged. In that case the crossing would have taken place in the southern region of the isthmus.

7.2.2 The stratum that we can attribute to P occurs in 14.21a*abb*-22b and runs: 'Then Moses stretched out his hand over the sea; and the waters were divided. And the people of Israel went into the midst of the sea on dry ground, the waters being a wall to them on their right hand and on their left...' The waters then closed in on the pursuers (vv.23,26ff.). Here we have a miracle pure and simple: any part of the Mediterranean or the Red Sea could fit the phenomenon; it becomes impossible and indeed unnecessary to provide a topographical location.

7.2.3 However, there is a third version of events which is difficult to harmonize with the other two; so much so that the redactors have preferred to indicate this as a later event, independent of the other two. Exodus 14.24f., which could perhaps be attributed to E, reads: 'And in the morning watch the Lord in the pillar of fire and of cloud looked down upon the host of the Egyptians, and discomfited the host of the Egyptians, braking (to be read with Sam, LXX and Syr *wayye'esōr*, root *'sr*, for the Massoretic *wayyāsar*, root *swr*, 'remove' or 'upset') their chariot wheels so that they drove heavily; and the Egyptians said: "Let us flee from before Israel; for the Lord fights for them against the Egyptians."' In the narrative style peculiar to E (if we can attribute this section to that source), the Egyptians see the miracle and note that something is going radically wrong, so they decide to retreat. In this version the waters do not even appear, thus presupposing a tradition substantially different from the other two. Moreover, as I have pointed out, this tradition cannot be harmonized with the others, especially with the second: in v.23 the Egyptians have already rashly begun to pursue the Israelites between the two walls of water, whereas in vv.24f. they are still within the camp, at the time of the reveille, and having seen that things are about to take a turn for the worse, break off the pursuit and return to their bases. For the first two versions the catastrophe is caused by the continuation of the pursuit; in the third, a prudent retreat enables the Egyptians to avoid it.

7.2.4 However, perhaps there is even a fourth version, that of the heroic hymn handed down in ch.15. This is a composition which some scholars consider to be very old, even if its conclusion (15.13b,17) suggests the existence of Solomon's temple, and the peoples mentioned in 15.14f. seem to presuppose the wars of David.[36] According to this version, YHWH 'cast into the sea Pharaoh's chariots and his host; and his picked officers are sunk (LXX has: 'YHWH has sunk...') in the Sea of Reeds!' This could be a simple poetic variant of the second version;

it could represent a heightening of the event by means of the introduction of mythical elements like the 'abysses' (*t^ehōmōt*) and the 'depths of the sea' (*m^esōlōt*).

8 However, the three or four descriptions of the phenomenon given by the tradition do not say anything about its topography. For this see the following select bibliography:

> O.Eissfeldt, *Baal Zafon, Zeus Kasios und der Durchzug der Israeliten durch das Meer*, Halle 1932 (a basic study); M.Noth, 'Der Schauplatz des Meereswunders', in *Festschrift O. Eissfeldt zum 70. Gehurtstag*, Halle 1947, 181-90 = *ABLAK*, 102-110; W.F.Albright, 'Baal Zephon', in *Festschrift für A.Bertholet*, Tübingen 1950, 1-14; H.Cazelles, 'La localisation de l'Exode et la critique littéraire', *RB* 62, 1955, 321-64; B.Mazar, 'The Exodus and the Conquest', *WHJP* III, 1971, 69-79; M.Haran, 'Exodus, The', in *IDB-SV* 1976, 308-10; Y.Aharoni, *The Land*, 195ff. and map 13; G.I.Davies, *The Way of the Wilderness*, SOTS-MS 5, Cambridge 1979, 70ff.; M.Har-El, *The Sinay Journeys*, San Diego, Ca 1983, 169-71 (against Eissfeldt), and the works by G.R.H.Wright 1979, J.Scharbert 1981, and J.A.Soggin 1985 cited at 7.

8.1 A reconstruction of at least the first part of the itinerary of the exodus is a necessary preliminary to any attempt to locate the miracle of the Red Sea.

8.1.1 How, then, did the people arrive at the place which Israel considered as central for its belief? Moreover, given that some identification is possible, is this an ancient tradition or merely a later attempt to locate the event and therefore to historicize it? It seems that all the sources have their own topographical theories.

8.1.2 The texts begin by stating that Israel did not take the 'Way of the Philistines' (13.17). Apart from the obvious anachronism which presupposes at least a later redaction, this is the coastal route which under the Romans was called the *via maris*. However, from what we can reconstruct of the first part of the journey it seems that Israel did simply choose to follow the coastal route and not a route more to the interior of the peninsula.[37] Moreover, the designation 'Sea of Reeds' refers to the northern coast; only along the Mediterranean coast, either in the eastern part of the Delta or further east in Lake Sirbonis, are there the stretches of fresh water which are essential for the growth of reeds or rushes! So that seems to exclude the region of the Bitter Lakes, now incorporated into the Suez Canal system, and the coast of the Gulf of Suez.[38] On the other hand there is one fact that we have to accept: any on-the-spot investigations in the region of the canal are now pointless. The topography has been irremediably changed by the building of the waterway, and also, though to a much lesser extent, by the wars of 1956 and 1973.

8.1.3 The stages between the departure from Egypt and the scene of the miracle are given in 13.17-14.9 (cf. also Num.33.5-8). From Raamses (above, 1.2.3) the first stopping place is Succoth (12.13), perhaps the *tkw* which I have already mentioned (4.1). This could have been the meeting place with the group from further south, from Pithom. From Succoth the group went by Etam (13.20), a place which has still not been identified, then arriving 'in front of Pi-ha-hiroth, between Migdol and the sea, in front of Ba'al-zephon' (14.2,9). It was here that the pursuing army caught up with them. Now the last two places are known, thanks to Eissfeldt's study (1932), even if the identification is not universally accepted (e.g. Haran 1976 and Har-El 1983, and also Noth 1947 and Albright 1950 cited above).

8.1.3.1 As the name indicates, Migdol is a fortress with a tower and is usually identified with the Egyptian *mktr*, present-day *el-her* (coord. 912-048).

8.1.3.2 Ba'al-zephon has been identified by Eissfeldt with a well-known seafarers' sanctuary, a place of worship for the deity of that name, for whom there is also evidence at Ugarit. The sanctuary was on the central part of the western end of the tongue of land which shuts off the lagoon, in ancient times called Lake Sirbonis, and now *sabhat el-bardawīl* (coord.967-072). The area has been carefully explored (cf. M.Dothan, 'The Exodus in the Light of Archaeological Survey in Lake Sirbonis', in *Proceedings of the Fifth World Congress of Jewish Studies, Jerusalem 1969* I, Jerusalem 1972, 18-20, in Hebrew, with an English summary).

8.1.4.1 From there, according to some scholars,[39] the group will have made a turn of about 150 degrees, moving south and following more or less the present-day eastern bank of the Suez Canal (13.18, cf. 14.2).

8.1.4.2 However, the expression used by the first of these two texts is not clear: in fact it reads *derek hammidbār yam sūp*, an expression which cannot in any way be translated 'the way of the desert of the sea of reeds', as often happens. *hammidbār* does not occur, nor can it occur, in the construct state; in reality the second expression seems to be a gloss on the first, which was thought to be incongruous. O.Eissfeldt[40] thinks that the text is corrupt and suggests reading *derek hammidbāderek yam sup*, i.e. 'in the direction of the desert' and 'in the direction of the Sea of Reeds' respectively. He supposes, however, that here the name must actually mean the Red Sea, the Gulf of Akaba, and not the Sea of Reeds. In that case the route would be that traditionally followed by the pilgrims going to Mecca, parallel to the horizontal coordinates 940/920; this is also the suggestion which Haran makes for the various sources. But the objection is clear enough: the expression *yam sūp*, which is hardly a frequent one, would be used here with two different meanings.

8.1.4.3 We can only come to one conclusion on the basis of what I have said so far: we know some stages on the itinerary of the first part of the exodus and not others. It is sufficiently certain that the ancient author thought that the miracle should be located either in the eastern Delta or in Lake Sirbonis; there was probably no other information even at that time, and M.Noth[41] seems to be right in concluding that here we have essentially rationalizing attempts to give a precise historical and topographical context to the miracle, a feature which is clearly absent from the original traditions.

8.2.1 The account of the first stage after the miracle, from the Sea of Reeds to Kadesh, is full of the names of places touched on during the journey, but again they are all, without exception, unknown.

Select bibliography: V.Fritz, *Israel in der Wüste*, Marburg 1970; G.W.Coats, 'The Wilderness Itinerary', *CBQ* 34, 1972, 135-72. Attempts have been made to reconstruct the itinerary by G.I. Davies, 1979, and M.Har-El, quoted above, 7-8.

8.2.1.1 The attempts to identify the individual stages[42] can be considered for the most part to be failures, not only because of the vagueness of the information in the Bible, but also because they always want to see the journey as a route which will have led from the Sea of Reeds to Mount Sinai, a route which would largely coincide with the way to the ancient turquoise and copper mines in the mountains of southern Arabia.

8.2.1.2 However, the journey of the fugitives does not lead directly to Sinai, as we might suppose (and as many of the biblical atlases indicate); were that the case, topographically it would indeed be likely that they followed the route to the mines, though the probability is reduced by the fact that this route must have been well guarded. Rather, the journey leads to the oasis of Kadesh. This is probably to be identified with present-day *'ein el-qudeirat* (coord.098—007), situated just on the Egyptian side of the frontier with Israel, on the Egyptian side, towards the north-north-west. Near here, about six miles SSE, there is still an *'ein qudeis* which has preserved the name.[43]

8.2.1.3 We must also look in the area of Kadesh for Massah and Meribah, mentioned in Ex.17.5-7 and Num.20.1,13f., where the two localities are identified by means of an onomastic aetiology (cf. also the combination Meribat-kadesh in Num.27.14; Deut.32.51; Ezek.47.19; 28.28). So it seems evident that here we have a single complex of various oases, all interconnected.

8.2.1.4 Moreover, on the basis of Num.27.14, where Kadesh is located in the Desert of Sin, M.Noth[44] rightly asks whether the various designations of this desert, which seem to denote the various regions into which it is divided, are not in reality phonetic variants of the same designation for a single region. In reality *sinay, sin* and *ṣin* (this last is a name still attested in Arabic, as *arḍ* or *wādī es-ṣinī*) would seem to be the same name; that is obvious in the first two instances and probably also holds for the third. So the differentiation between them would be the product of a late and artificial attempt to give the region of each great stopping-place a different name: from the Sea of Reeds to Kadesh this was *sīn*; from Kadesh to Sinai, *sīnay*; from Kadesh onwards, *ṣīn*. At all events, one thing seems certain: the first part of the journey goes from the Sea of Reeds to Kadesh and nowhere else. So it is along this itinerary that we must look for[45] the various stages of the journey, and not elsewhere.

8.2.1.5 However, the reality seems to be even more simple; there is basically only one itinerary with an interruption in the middle: from the Sea of Reeds to Kadesh and from Kadesh to the Promised Land. The pilgrimage to Sinai has been inserted into it, along with the promulgation of the *tōrāh* there. It should be noted that this last theme is apparently independent, at least in origin, of the journey through the wilderness and the exodus generally; it could have taken place in any other locality or region and on any other occasion; all the more so since, as we shall soon see, it is difficult, if not impossible, to locate the sacred mountain.

8.3 *Select bibliography*: W.Beyerlin, *The Origins and History of the Oldest Sinaitic Tradition*, Oxford 1965; J.Jeremias, *Theophanie. Geschichte einer alttestamentlichen Gattung*, WMANT 33, Neukirchen 1965, 7ff. 38ff.; H.Gese, Τὸ δὲ Ἁγὰρ Σινὰ ὄρος ἐστιν ἐν τῇ Ἀραβίᾳ (Gal.4.25)', in *Das ferne und das nahe Wort. Festschrift L.Rost*, BZAW 105, Berlin 1967, 81-94 = *Von Sinai zum Zion*, Munich 1974, 49-62; G.W.Coats, *Rebellion in the Wilderness*, Nashville 1968; K.H.Walkenhorst, *Der Sinai*, BBB 33, Bonn 1969; G.I. Davies, 'Hagar, el-Hagra and the Location of Mount Sinai', *VT* 22, 1972, 152-63; B.Zuber, *Vier Studien zu den Ursprüngen Israels*, OBO 9, Freiburg-CH 1976, 15ff.; G.I.Davies, 'The Significance of Deuteronomy 1.2 for the Location of Mount Horeb', *PEQ* 111, 1979, 87-101; E.Zenger, *Israel am Sinai*, Altenberge 1982; M.Har-El, op.cit. (7). For the archaeological problems cf. B.Rothenberg, 'An Archaeological Survey of South Sinai', *PEQ* 102, 1970, 4-29.

In the biblical tradition, the promulgation of the *tōrāh* on the holy mountain is now presented as a self-contained episode, included in the section which runs from Ex.19 to Num.9.

8.3.1 As we have seen, the pilgrimage to Sinai now interrupts the itinerary from the Sea of Reeds to Kadesh and from Kadesh to the Promised Land, an itinerary which is otherwise coherent and characterized by stereotyped episodes, like the lack of drinking water, the manna and the quails (Ex.16.13-16; Num.11.7-9); the institution of tribunals in Ex.18 and their functioning in Num.11.16; the leave-taking of Moses by his wife's relatives (cf. below 9): his father-in-law (Ex.18.27); and his brother-in-law (Num.10.29).[46] In these narratives, moreover, we find with some frequency the theme of 'murmuring in the wilderness and nostalgia for Egypt'.

8.3.2 So the Sinai episode is probably an interpolation into the present context of the journey through the wilderness, which as a result is divided into two parts. However, the section about Sinai, too, is far from being a unity; indeed it is one of the most complex sections in the whole of the Hebrew Bible. So the apparent unity should not deceive us. I cannot deal with the problem of the literary structure here, and must refer the reader to the *Introductions to the Old Testament* and the commentaries. It must suffice to point out that it is possible to distinguish between pre-exilic material (though this is not necessarily connected with Sinai), material of a Deuteronomic or Deuteronomistic type, and finally material from the P redaction.

8.3.3 These difficulties are not only on the literary level but also over geography and topography. In fact we do not even know where the sacred mountain was located in the ancient traditions, assuming that they were in fact interested in a location and did not simply consider the place as part of a myth! The tradition which connects Sinai with the southern part of the peninsula of the same name is relatively late: it goes back to the fourth century AD.[47] Here we have a group of mountains culminating in two peaks, *jebel musa* (7293 feet, coord.778-048) and *jebel qaṭarīn* (8456 feet, coord.771-047), a few miles apart: Justinian had the convent of St Katherine built at their feet.[48] However, other locations have been authoritatively proposed in addition to those which are now traditional: in the neighbourhood of Kadesh, which would limit the interpolation to the promulgation of the *tōrāh*, avoiding a special journey; or in northern Arabia, where a tradition reported by St Paul in Gal.4.25 also locates it; here some extinct volcanoes suggest that the phenomena which accompany the theophany should be identified as an eruption.[49] If we connect the location of Sinai with these volcanoes, we are led to the region of *tebūk*, once a station on the southbound track of the Hegiaz railway, dismantled during the Second World War and then abandoned, about 160 miles south of *ma'an*, one of the last stations on the line before it was extended to Akaba. It is interesting that some texts which are certainly pre-exilic. and in some instances even older, point precisely in this direction. These include Deut.33.2; Judg.5.4-5 (where we find the parallelism between Sinai and Se'ir), and also Hab.3.3 (where we find the parallelism betwen Se'ir and Paran); in both cases we are in Edom, specifically in northern Arabia. This is indicated by the passage from St Paul, which is otherwise difficult to understand. However, though things might seem clear, a number of difficulties remain. For example, while it could be claimed that here we have the recollection of events connected with terrifying natural phenomena like eruptions or earthquakes, might this not also be an instance of a literary genre which is also well attested elsewhere in the Hebrew Bible, that of the 'theophany'? The characteristics of the theophany seem to be constant, even in passages where volcanic eruptions are not mentioned (cf. Gen.15.17; II Sam.22//Ps.18.8f.). Only in Isa.6.1ff. do we hear of phenomena which can be connected with an earthquake; and here there is no indication of an eruption. Scholars are more inclined towards the second of the proposed alternatives.[50]

8.3.4 To these difficulties is added yet one more, which is obvious even to the reader who does not know Hebrew. The holy mountain has two names. J consistently uses Sinai, but E, Dtn and Dtr use Horeb. And as if that were not enough, a *har pā'rān*, 'Mount Paran', also appears in Deut.33.2, the passage cited above, where it is parallel to Sinai and Se'ir, and in Hab.3.3, where it is parallel to Teman, a place near Petra. And it is from here that YHWH comes to the aid of his people. Now in different languages it is quite normal for there to be a number of names for the same object (e.g. Cervino/Cervin and the Matterhorn in the Alps), but this variety has never been explained in the context of the same language in a tradition which must go back to the same archetype. Finally, the Hebrew tradition is completely unaware of the present location of Sinai, so it has never considered this mountain as a holy place.

8.3.5 To sum up, the tradition which identifies Mount Sinai with the present-day Mount Sinai in the south of the peninsula is relatively late; it dates from about 1500 years after the events; moreover it is a tradition which is unknown in Judaism and grew up in a Christian context. On the other hand, these objections are not insurmountable: place names, especially those of sanctuaries, tend to be retained over a long period, especially in cases like this, where the name is closely connected with the name of the wilderness (above, 8.2.1.4). However, we might ask whether here, too, we do not have a later attempt to historicize the events of the sacred history by giving them a location.

8.3.6 Certainly, if we want to try to locate at least some of the places mentioned in the itinerary of the exodus, our best bet would be to include those places which still exist today in the Arabic nomenclature of the region.[51] I follow the proposals of Y. Aharoni, who makes these parallels the main argument for the identification of the biblical Sinai with the Sinai of tradition, situated in the south of the peninsula of the same name. However, this does not say much: we have the Hebrew *pā'rān*, corresponding to the Byzantine φαράν and the Arabian *wādī fir'ān* (Deut.1.1, coord.791-012); the Hebrew *yotbātāh*, corresponding to the

Byzantine ἰωτάβη, Arabic *ṭābah* (Num.33.33f.; Deut.10.7, coord. 879-139), on the frontier situated a few miles south of Eilath, disputed in the modern peace treaty between Israel and Egypt; *ḥⁿṣērōt*, corresponding to the Arabic *'ein ḥaḍra* (Num.11.35; 12.16; 33.17f.; Deut.1.1, coord.182-095); and *dī-zāhāb*, corresponding to the Arabic *ḏāhab* (Deut.1.1, coord.768-101). However, here too it should be noted that not only do we have just a few names, but the identification of the localities is rather dubious, so that even Aharoni seems to have a basically precarious position.

8.3.7 We find mentions of a pilgrimage to Sinai in the Elijah traditions, though we cannot be sure whether the texts are not simply intended to describe a flight (and therefore an extraordinary, not a normal action). In I Kings 19 some features are described, and Beersheba is said to have been one of the resting places. However, the figure of 'forty days and forty nights' (cf. 19.8) is a typical round figure, indicating 'many' in both Old and New Testaments, so it cannot be taken as an indication of the supposed duration of the journey.

8.4 From Kadesh to the Promised Land we have what the texts now take to be third major stage of the Exodus.

Select bibliography: M.Noth, 'Der Wallfahrtsweg zum Sinai', *PJB* 36, 1940, 5-28 = *ABLAK*, 55-74; R. de Vaux, 'L'itinéraire des Israélites de Cadès aux plaines de Moab', in *Hommages à M.A.Dupont-Sommer*, Paris 1971, 331-42; G.W.Coats, art.cit. (8.2.1); B.Mazar, *The Exodus and Conquest*', in *WHJP* III, 1971, 69-79; E.Cortese, *La terra di Canaan nelle storia sacerdotale del Pentateuco*, Brescia 1972; M.Haran, 'Exodus, The', *IDB-SV*, 1976, 304-10; Z.Kallai, 'The Wandering Traditions from Kadesh Barnea to Canaan: a Study in Biblical Historiography', *JJS* 33, 1982, 175-84; M.Har-El, op.cit. (7.1), 230ff., 252ff.

8.4.1 The text of Num.33.1-49, which some scholars do not want to attribute to any of the Pentateuchal sources, though it is probably to be attributed to P (Cortese), was studied in detail by M.Noth shortly before the Second World War and understood in a completely new way. The basic validity of his interpretation has recently been confirmed, though with a number of modifications, in Kallai's study. The starting point is the superscription of v.1: 'These are the stages (*masᵉ'e*, the construct of a word which is not found in the plural, root *nāsa'*, 'travel') of the people of Israel, when they left Egypt...' This text is meant to present to the reader a summary of the itinerary covered from Raamses (v.2) to the 'plains of Moab' (v.49), the region of the Transjordan opposite Jericho, present-day *gōr el-kafrīn* (coord.140/44 – 202/10). That this list is late is evident from the fact that it combines the various narratives of the sources of Exodus and Numbers, also including part of the information in Deuteronomy. This would suggest that the authors had the complete text of the Pentateuch in front of them. It is interesting to note that the names of the places included in the list are almost twice as many as those which appear in Exodus and Numbers,[52] while some also appear in Deuteronomy and in other books of the Bible. Noth concludes from this information that here we have a text based on an autonomous source which could evidently be arrived at independently of the texts indicated in the sources. He also notes how by reversing the second part of the list we arrive at what he calls the itinerary for pilgrims from Canaan to Sinai, an itinerary which had many stages in common with the traditional route of the Exodus.

8.4.2 However, the picture presented by Noth is in fact more complex.

8.4.2.1 First of all, the text which he produces also already has a long history behind it. This is evident, not least, from the inexplicable fact that between the arrival at Kadesh and the departure from it, we have only one mention of the 'desert of Sinai' (in v.16), where Israel is supposed to have camped, and that there is no mention of the journey to and from the holy mountain. Noth's explanation of this disconcerting phenomenon (a deliberate substitution of two unimportant places, *dopqāh* and *'ālūš*, lacking in the other texts, with the intention of giving the list an original character), appears doubtful, to say the least.

8.4.2.2 Again we need an explanation of how, in an itinerary of this kind, the pilgrims could have passed through Transjordan (v.40), i.e. going eastwards, only to turn towards the south and the west in order to to go through Arad in the Negeb (*tell 'ārād*, coord.162-076, or *tell el-milḥ*, coord.152-069).[53]

8.4.2.3 Finally, we need to know how the itinerary attributed to the prophet Elijah follows a more direct route, through Beersheba.

9 The exodus from Egypt, the journey through the wilderness and the promulgation of the *tōrāh* on Mount Sinai are now features which the biblical tradition connects inextricably with the figure of Moses. He embodies a number of figures: the founder of a religion, the legislator, the prophet, the model believer who is severely punished in the few cases where his faith fails. It is not surprising that there is a vast bibliography on someone who seems to be a key figure in the origins of Israel and its religion; as has so often been the case, I can only give a selection from it.

G.von Rad, *Moses*, Neukirchen 1958 (popular, but well informed); H.Cazelles, 'Moîse', *SDB* V, 1957, 1308-37; M.Buber, *Moses*, New York 1946; R.Smend, *Das Mosebild von H.Ewald bis M.Noth*, Tübingen 1959; E.Osswald, *Das Bild Mose*, Berlin DDR 1962 (both with annotated bibliographies); K.Koch, 'Der Tod des Religionsstifters', *KuD* 8, 1962, 100-23; F.Baumgärtel, *KuD* 9, 1963, 223-33; A.H.J. Gunneweg, 'Moses in Midian', *ZTK* 61, 1964, 1-9; H.Schmid, *Moses. Überlieferung und Geschichte*, BZAW 110, Berlin 1968; G.Widengren, 'What do we know about Moses?', in *Proclamation and Presence* (FS G.Henton Davies), ed. J.I.Durham and J.R.Porter, London and Richmond, Va. 1970, 21-47; E.F.Campbell Jr, 'Moses and the Foundations of Israel', *Int* 19, 1975, 141-54 (especially on the discussion between M.Noth and J.Bright); for a presentation of the theories of W.F.Albright cf. id., 'Moses in Historical and Theological Perspective', in *Magnalia Dei... Essays in Memoriam G.E.Wright*, Garden City, NY 1976, 120-31. For a more recent discussion cf. J.B.Geyer, 'The Joseph and Moses Narratives: Folk Tale and History', *JSOT* 15, 1980, 51-6, and the response by T.L.Thompson, 'History and Tradition', ibid., 57-61; and G.Sauer, 'Vom Exoduserleben zur Landnahme', *ZTK* 80, 1983, 26-32. For Moses as prophet see L.Perlitt, 'Mose als Prophet', *EvTh* 31, 1971, 579-88.

9.1 So Moses appears as the key figure who unites and interprets the events narrated in the last four books of the Pentateuch: the liberation of 'Israel' from slavery in Egypt, its journey through the wilderness towards the Promised Land, and its constitution as a religious community around the word of God given on Sinai.

9.1.1 We have seen that Moses' name is Egyptian in origin (above, 1.1.2), even if it does not have the necessary theophoric element and is therefore incomplete; we can also see how the account of his birth and rescue has its roots in the popular tradition of the ancient Near East and especially of Mesopotamia (above 6.1.2); we have also examined the problem of his meetings with the Pharaoh and the plagues which ensue (above 6.4). The result of these studies is that at all events the texts are very complex, whether as literary compositions or as history. So it is not surprising that M.Noth and G.von Rad[54] have indicated their doubts whether the texts are an adequate basis for reconstructing the most important events on a historical level and can therefore help towards a biography of Moses. In his article cited above (1962), K.Koch seems more critical still, even denying that Moses ever existed as a historical figure.

9.1.2 We can see the reasons for an attitude which in the United States has often been called 'nihilistic' as soon as we consider not only the complexity and the generally late character of the traditions which have come down to us but also the mentions of Moses in texts outside the Pentateuch. In fact, taking into account the importance of Moses in the Pentateuch and especially in the narratives of the exodus and the journey through the wilderness, we would expect him to be mentioned frequently right through the Hebrew Bible, rather as happens in the New Testament with the figure of Jesus of Nazareth. In the New Testament, episodes from the life of Jesus are narrated in the Synoptic Gospels, commented on in the Fourth Gospel, and are the object of continuous reflections and references in Acts, the Epistles and Revelation. However, we find precisely the opposite with Moses in the Hebrew Bible: the narrative texts outside the Pentateuch in which Moses is mentioned can be counted on the fingers of one hand and are for the most part Deuteronomistic: Josh.9.24; 24.5; I Sam.12.68; I Kings 8.53; the Psalms in which he appears are all exilic or post-exilic: 77.21; 90.1 (only the title); 103.7; 105.26; 106.16,23,32. There are only a few certainly pre-exilic texts which mention Moses: Judg.1.16; 4.11 (with an obscure reference to 'father-in-law' or 'son-in-law', perhaps meant to be a generic designation, 'kinsman of Moses'[55]); II Kings 18.4, where Hezekiah has the relic of the 'serpent of Moses' (cf. Num.21.4-9) removed from the temple in the course of his religious reform (below XI. 2.1). And in the prophetic books we find the same phenomenon. There are only three texts which mention Moses: Micah 6.4 (late!); Jer.15.1 (probably Dtr) and Isa.63.11-12 (exilic or post-exilic). So it would seem that only with the Babylonian exile did the figure of Moses acquire the importance that people are accustomed to attribute to it, while the references to him before this period are scarce and stereotyped. We can deduce from this that there were certainly traditions about Moses, but at the same time we may doubt whether they were considered very important. In other words, only with Deuteronomy and Dtr does the figure of Moses seem to have begun to assume a pre-eminent position in the biblical tradition.

9.1.3 According to M.Noth,[56] it is only in Dtr that the traditions of Moses were revised on a large scale, thus becoming the great bond which combines the most disparate documents in a single text, the guideline through the most diverse episodes. However, this does not happen before Dtn and P; in the traditions that we can still recognize as being early, e.g. Ex.24.1-2, 9-11, the figure of Moses appears as a clear rival to the 'elders of Israel', who are more authentically primitive and certainly the representatives of the people, whom Moses is meant to replace. However, for Noth Moses appears to be in place in the traditions during the journey from Kadesh to the 'plains of Moab', especially in Transjordan.

9.2 The validity of these considerations has been contested from 1956 onwards (down to the present day) by J.Bright, one of the most distinguished disciples of W.F.Albright in the United States.[57]

9.2.1 In his study *Early Israel in Recent History Writing*, Bright works with examples taken from the history of the American Civil War. Around this, especially in local folklore, a series of elements has grown up which can easily be compared with those about the exodus and the journey through the wilderness. However, apart from the fact that the heroes of the Civil War move in quite a precise historical context, so that most of the time it is possible to distinguish between history and popular tradition, even Bright arrives at a conclusion which must seem disconcerting to those who want to follow him: 'The trouble is that one cannot by direct argument prove Noth wrong... But neither can Noth prove himself right. We move in a realm where we can no longer lay hold of objective evidence; we can only contradict one another. But the burden of proof is definitely on Noth!'

9.2.2 Thus even J.Bright is forced to admit the inadequacy of the sources for a historical reconstruction of the persons and events involved, even if, like Noth, he accepts the substantial historicity of the figure of Moses. On the other hand, it is obvious that once it is admitted that there are no adequate proofs, it is also impossible to speak of a 'burden of proof' which lies on someone.

9.2.3 So if we want to begin from the presupposition that the figure of Moses is substantially historical, we are basically confronted with a problem rather like that of Romulus in the earliest history of Rome. The only difference is that, given the character of the religion of Israel, Moses was not taken up into heaven or divinized; nor do we have a tradition that sees him lynched by the Senators. We have only a few authentic features:

9.2.3.1 The contacts with the Midianites, the people of Moses' father-in-law.

9.2.3.2 The introduction of the cult of YHWH (Ex.3 E and 6 P).

9.2.3.3 The theme of Moses' foreign wife, the daughter of the Midianite priest (Ex.2.16ff.), cf. the independent tradition in Judg.1.16; 4.11 (cf. nn.46, 55 above). In Num.12.1, however, Moses has a wife from Kush, classical Ethiopia, now the Sudan; some scholars think that this is still the same woman.

9.2.3.4 Local features connected with the journey from Kadesh onwards.

9.2.3.5 A tradition about the tomb of Moses, though its location is not mentioned, so that it remains unknown (cf. Deut.34.6). Is this an Israelite parallel to the theme of the assumption of Romulus to heaven?

9.3 There is also a dispute over the figure of Moses as the founder of the religion of Israel. M.Noth[58] hesitated to assign him this role, whereas J.Bright observes:[59] 'Events like those of the Exodus and Sinai call for the presence of a great personality. And a unique faith like that of Israel demands, calls for a founder, just like Christianity or Islam. To deny this role to Moses would oblige us to postulate the presence of another person with the same name!' He could also have added Buddha to the list. Now if we look at the end of this quotation, which is an obvious witticism, we find that the basis of the argument in fact begs the question. It seems more reasonable to keep within the limits of descriptive statements, as in e.g. the suggestion made by

E.Osswald,[60] who confines herself to indicating 'the decisive role played by Moses' in the events described.

10 The final part of the itinerary, through Transjordan, introduces incidents which happened to Israel in its first contacts with the king of Moab and the Midianites (Num.22-25; 31).

10.1 On the historical plane the main difficulty lies in the fact that the settlement by the peoples of Transjordan cannot have happened earlier than the twelfth century BC, according to archaeological discoveries, and probably falls in the eleventh century or perhaps even later. That would compel us to date the events mentioned a good deal later than the thirteenth century.

10.2 This is another example of how, in Bright's words, 'The evidence is ambiguous (and incomplete), so that we cannot come to any certain conclusions.'[61] The same thing holds for the places mentioned, which are often hard to identify, while even the traditions 'are often difficult to harmonize'. These problems recur in connection with the 'conquest', so I shall discuss them in the next chapter (VII.2.10).

VII

CONQUEST

1 The biblical tradition is unanimous in affirming that Israel was not native to the land of Canaan but arrived there from abroad and conquered it. Only in Chronicles, according to S.Japhet's study (cf. the following bibliography, 1979) do we seem to have the theory that Israel always lived in its own land.

Select bibliography: A.Alt, 'The Settlement of the Israelites in Palestine', in *Essays on Old Testament History and Religion*, Oxford 1966, 133-69; id., 'Erwägungen über die Landnahme der Israeliten in Palästina' (1939), *KS* I, 126-75; 'Josua' (1936), *KS* I, 176-92; 'Israel', *RGG* III([2]1929), 439ff. and [3]1959, 936ff.; W.F.Albright, 'The Israelite Conquest of Canaan in the Light of Archaeology', *BASOR* 74, 1939, 11-22; R. de Vaux, 'Israël, Histoire d'', *SDB* IV, 1949, 738f.; H.H.Rowley, *From Joseph to Joshua*, London [2]1951; Y.Kaufmann, *The Biblical Account of the Conquest of Palestine*, Jerusalem [2]1953; G.E.Mendenhall, 'The Hebrew Conquest of Palestine', *BA* 25, 1962, 66-87; J.A.Soggin, 'La conquista israelitica della Palestina nei secoli XIII e XII a.C. e le scoperte archeologiche', *Prot* 17, 1962, 193-208, ET in *OTOS*, 11-30; M.Weinfeld, 'The Period of the Conquest and of the Judges', *VT* 17, 1967, 93-113; P.W.Lapp, 'The Conquest of Palestine in the Light of Archaeology', *Concordia Theological Monthly*, 38, 1967, 283-300; M.Weippert, *The Settlement*, 1971, 1-15; S.Yeivin, *The Israelite Conquest of Canaan*, Leiden and Istanbul 1971 (cf. my review in *OA* 13, 1974, 75-8); H.J.Franken, *CAH* II, 2, [3]1975, 331ff.; G.Wallis, 'Die Sesshaftwerdung Altisraels...', *ZAW* 83, 1971; G.W.Coats, 'Conquest Traditions on the Wilderness Theme', *JBL* 95, 1976, 177-90; Y.Aharoni, 'Nothing Early and Nothing Late – Re-Writing Israel's Conquest', *BA* 39, 1976, 55-76; J.M.Miller, 'Archaeology and the Israelite Conquest of Canaan: Some Methodological Observations', *PEQ* 109, 1977, 87-93; S.Yeivin, 'On the Number of Israelite Tribes', *EI* 14, 1978, 37f. (Hebrew, with an English summary); A.J.Hauser,

'Israel's Conquest of Palestine: A Peasants' Rebellion?', *JSOT* 7, 1978, 2-19, and the response by T.L.Thompson, 'Historical Notes on "Israel's Conquest of Palestine: a Peasants' Rebellion"', ibid., 20-7; M.Weippert, 'The Israelite "Conquest" and the Evidence from Transjordan', in *Symposia...ASOR*, Cambridge, Mass 1979, 15-34; A.Malamat, 'Israelite Conduct of War according to the Biblical Tradition', ibid., 35-55; S. Japhet, 'Conquest and Settlement in Chronicles', *JBL* 98, 1979, 205-18; N.K.Gottwald, *The Tribes*, passim; J.A.Soggin, 'I testi vetero-testamentari sulla conquista della Palestina', *RiBib* 28, 1980, 45-57; A.Rolla, 'La conquista di Canaan e l'archeologia palestinese', 89-96; S.Loffreda, 'L'insediamento israelitico nel Negev alla luce dei recenti scavi', *BeO* 22, 1980, 254-63; V.Fritz, 'Die kulturgeschichtliche Bedeutung der früheisenzeitlichen Siedlung auf dem ḥirbet el-mšaš und das problem der Landnahme', *ZDPV* 96, 1980, 121-35, ET *BASOR* 241, 1981, 61-73; B.Mazar, 'The Early Israelite Settlement in the Hill Country', ibid., 75-85; A.G.Auld, *Joshua, Moses and the Land*, Edinburgh 1980; Z.Kallai, 'Territorial Patterns. Biblical Historiography and Scribal Tradition – A Programmatic Survey', *ZAW* 93, 1981, 427-32; H.D.Lance, *The Old Testament and the Archaeologist*, Philadelphia 1981. For the case of Jericho cf. J.A.Soggin, 'Gerico – anatomia d'una conquista', *Prot* 29, 1974, 193-213 (French *RHPR* 57, 1977, 1-17) and 'The Conquest of Jericho through Battle', *EI* 16, 1982, 215*-217*.

1.1 First of all we have what we might call the official, canonical version of the 'conquest'. This is also the best known. It appears in Joshua 1-12 and presents the events as essentially a single enterprise.

1.2 A more fragmentary version, which the tradition now seeks to present as the continuation and conclusion of Josh.1-12 and the following chapters appears in Judg.1.1-2.5. However, as we shall see below (2.1), things are much more complicated.

1.3 Scattered here and there in the Hebrew Bible, especially in the Pentateuch and the Former Prophets, are other passages which can be connected more or less certainly with the conquest. These are:

1.3.1 The attack made by Simeon and Levi on the central Palestinian city of Shechem, present-day *tell balāṭa* (coord. 177-179), in the eastern suburbs of Nablus (Gen.34): this does not seem to have been followed by any permanent results.

1.3.2 The expedition against the southern hill-country, which is now presented as an exploration led by Caleb (Num.13-14; Deut.1.22f.). This also seems to have had no lasting effects; that is, unless we have an independent note about Caleb's conquest of its own territory. The group was later absorbed into Judah (cf. Josh. 14.6-15//Judg.1.12-15; Josh 15.13-20).

1.3.3 The expedition against Arad (coord.152-069 or 162-076) and other places in the north-eastern Negeb (Num.21.1-3, cf. Judg. 1.17), ending with the defeat of the Canaanites at Hormah, according to Aharoni the present-day *tell em-mšaš*, Hebrew *tell mašōš* (coord.146-069). However, this identification has been questioned seriously by Fritz (1980/81). The texts do not indicate any permanent results, but the information that the Canaanites were defeated makes this probable. It could be that a note to this effect was suppressed because it contrasted with the official version.

1.3.4 The conquest of its own territory by Dan, in the extreme north of the country, setting out from a region in the centre or the south-east which it is difficult to identify (Judg.17-18; cf. Josh. 19.47f.).[1]

1.3.5 Judges 1.27-35 (cf. fragments in Josh. 15.63// Judg.1.21f.; Josh.16.9ff.; 17.11-18) gives a series of places and regions which Israel did not succeed in subjecting during the conquest; that happened at a later stage, 'when Israel became stronger' (Judg.1.28). We have seen (above III.7.1.3) that this period is probably to be identified with the reign of David.

1.3.6 In Josh.8.30-35; 23; 24, cf. Judg. 8.29-35; 9, Israel seems to be settled peacefully in the region of Shechem, cf. above 1.3.1. The texts all come from the Deuteronomistic redaction and are therefore relatively late, though we cannot rule out the possibility that they go back to an ancient tradition: the absence of reports of wars in a source which includes among its themes that of the 'holy war' is at least a significant omission.

1.3.7 In II Sam.5.6-9, as we have seen (above III.6.1.1), there is an account of the conquest of Jerusalem by David, who made it the capital of the united kingdom.

1.3.8 In I Kings 9.16ff. Solomon receives as a dowry from his father-in-law, the Pharaoh, the ruins of the cities of Gezer (above IV.4.6).

1.3.9 One particularly complex theme is that of the settlement of Israel in Transjordan (Num.32;34). We shall deal with that below, 2.10.

2 The fragmentary and often incoherent nature of the sources shows the complexity of the problems with which we have to deal. Sometimes they do not fit in with the rest of the tradition, often they relate only to particular sectors. And it is precisely this complexity that the unitary, pan-Israelite version in Josh.1-12 tries to disguise or at least to reduce.

We must recognize that to a large degree it has succeeded; when people talk about the conquest, in fact they seem to be thinking of the account in the book of Joshua, and only very rarely of other versions. Again, a number of scholars argue that the unitary version is quite compatible with the rest of the information that we have, so e.g. Isserlin (below, 5).

2.1.1 According to this version, the conquest was a large-scale operation carried out in accordance with the pattern begun by the narratives in Exodus, under the leadership of Joshua, Moses' successor (Josh.1.1). Often it seems more like a procession than a military expedition: at its head goes the ark, escorted by the priests, and followed by the tribes, as had happened in the wilderness. Only in the case of Jericho are there still traces of an early version which envisages a military conquest (Soggin 1982).

2.1.2 The tribes are said to have crossed the Jordan coming from the 'plains of Moab' (above VI.8.4.1: Num.36.13; Deut.34.1), a region which is also called Shittim, 'acacias'. We do not know whether this is an alternative designation or whether it is the name of a district or a locality (cf. Num.25.1; Josh.2.1; 3.1). The crossing takes place in the region of Jericho, present-day *tell es-sulṭan* (coord.192-142), a few hundred yards north of the modern city. The tribes which had been allotted territory in Transjordan (Reuben, Gad and the eastern part of Manasseh, below, 2.10), are said to have taken part in this expedition to help their 'brothers' (Josh.1.12ff.), returning to their own territory after the conquest (Josh.22.1ff.).[2]

2.1.3 However, an examination of the geography and topography of Joshua 1-12 immediately brings out a remarkable fact: with only four exceptions (7.26, a marginal text; 8.30-35, which is set in Shechem; 10.1ff., where we are in the southern hill country; and 11.1-15, where we are in Upper Galilee and the problem of the itinerary followed is left open, or we have yet another formerly independent tradition of the conquest), the text refers exclusively to the territory of the tribe of Benjamin, which is one of the smallest tribal areas. And this still holds, despite the objections made by Y.Kaufmann(1953). Gilgal is a typically Benjaminite sanctuary and all the expeditions leave from there; all the ceremonies and all the rites connected with the crossing of the Jordan, which is effected in virtually the same way as the crossing of the Reed Sea (above VI.7.1), take place nearby; and the processions which the texts connect with the fall of Jericho also take place near the sanctuary of Gilgal. There is also mention of Gilgal outside the texts dealing with the conquest: in I Sam.11.1ff. it is said to have been an important sanctuary in the period before the monarchy when Saul, a Benjaminite (above III.4.1), was chosen as king. These observations raise the question whether the sanctuary of Gilgal was not the area in which the traditions of a unitary conquest arose and were handed down, so that they became the official version of events. This is a question which, in the present state of research, cannot be answered, but which is the only one which presents the problem in the right way.

2.2 In Judg.1.1-2.5 we have a more fragmentary account of the conquest; it is now recognized to be closer to the events,[3] although it, too, is expressed in terms of a military conquest.

2.2.1 *Select bibliography*: N.H.Rösel, 'Die Überleitungen vom Josua-ins Richterbuch', *VT* 30, 1980, 342-50; J.A.Soggin, *Judges*, 17-33.

However, what forms the introduction to the 'body' of the book of Judges is not a unitary work either. All the sections are held together by the fact that each time Israel leaves from Gilgal, and this is more a literary than a historical feature.

2.2.2 It appears from the text that Judah and Simeon, the south, are depicted in the act of conquering their own territory, which now includes that of Caleb (above 2.4), so that we already find ourselves in a later stage of the tradition. We hear nothing of the other tribes in this context. The conquests of Judah, however, are limited to the hill-country; in the plain (and the cities of Gaza, Ashkelon and Ekron, which later belonged to the Philistine pentapolis, above III.5.3.1, are mentioned, though we hear nothing of the pentapolis itself), Judah and Simeon did not succeed in gaining the upper hand. It is difficult to say whether the texts preserve the memory of the situation before the arrival of the Philistines, or whether this is simply a repetition of the scheme used for the tribes of the centre and the north; the latter alternative appears to be more probable, given that in the south there were no fertile, densely populated plains, which would be worth the trouble of conquest. So we cannot obtain any certain information from the texts, and even the mention of 'chariots of iron' (this of course means chariots plated and armed with iron) seems to be a feature of the literary genre rather than the reminiscence of an actual fact.

2.2.3 To begin with, the tribes of the centre are presented under the collective name 'Joseph', i.e. Ephraim and Manasseh, but Bethel, the place which is conquered, belongs to the former of the two tribes. The terms in the narrative seem generic, from the mention of Joseph to that of the city founded by the fugitive traitor to whose collaboration Israel owed its entry into the city. The traitor is said here to have founded another city 'in the country of the Hittites', the usual name for Syria-Palestine from the ninth century BC onwards, especially in neo-Assyrian and neo-Babylonian inscriptions. Excavations carried out in the place (usually identified with the modern Arab village of *beitīn*, coord.172-148),[4] have not produced any appreciable result, perhaps also because, as we have seen (above IV.1.4.1) it is impossible to carry out rigorous excavations under an inhabited centre.

2.2.4 The list of the places which the tribes of Benjamin, Manasseh, Ephraim, Zebulun, Asher and Naphtali did not succeed in conquering is very important because it is generally considered to be ancient (the case of Dan is less clear, since the tribe seems to have been added at a later stage). As we have seen, the period of their incorporation into Israel (however that happened) is associated with the reign of David (above 1.3.5; cf. III. 7.1.3).

2.2.5 The conclusion (2.1-5) is probably part of the latest phase of Dtr and is the aetiological legend of an unknown sanctuary, which the LXX prefers to associate with that of Bethel. The text is a reflection on the disobedience of the people, a feature for which the mention of the sanctuary is only a pretext; it has little or nothing to do with the conquest.[5]

2.2.6 The problem of the relationship of this prologue to Judges with the end of the book of Joshua has been tackled and, I believe, resolved, in Rösel's study (1980). This adopts and develops a theory once put forward by O.Eissfeldt, arguing that Josh.24 is continued in Judg.1.1ff.; Josh.23 in Judg.2.6ff.

2.3 The account in Gen.34, where Simeon and Levi attack Shechem, is often regarded as a conquest, or at least an attempt at a conquest. This is a unitary and self-contained narrative like the Joseph story, in which a search for sources has not led to any appreciable result.[6] It could be that here we find the record of an ancient enterprise which turned out badly.

Select bibliography: M. Noth, *Pentateuchal Traditions*, 86f.; G. von Rad, *Genesis*, OTL, London and Philadelphia 1972, 329ff.; C.Westermann, Genesis, BK I, 2, Neukirchen 1981, ad loc.; for monographs cf. S.Lehming, 'Überlieferungsgeschichte von Genesis 34', *ZAW* 70, 1958, 228-50; A de Pury, 'Genèse XXXIV et l'histoire', *RB* 76, 1969, 1-49; W.T.In der Smitten, 'Genesis 34 – Ausdruck der Volksmeinung?', *BO* 30, 1973, 7-9; F.C.Fensham, 'Gen.XXXIV and Mari', *JNSWL* 4, 1975, 87-90; W.Kevers, 'Étude littéraire de Genèse XXIV', *RB* 87, 1980, 38-86; J.A.Soggin, 'I testi', 47-50.

2.3.1 The story of the attack by two of the patriarchs on Shechem in a period which is not defined but is connected with the traditions of the time of Jacob, when the sons were already grown up, is a typical family narrative like that of Joseph. Jacob's only daughter, Dinah (cf. Gen.30.21), has been abducted and raped by the eponymous hero of the city of Shechem, son of Hamor; the population of the place is said to be Hivite, an ethnic group which the tradition associates with the Horites, with whom they are sometimes confused (LXX in fact translates the term ὁ Χορραῖος).[7] The text introduces this population as 'uncircumcised', a designation often used to denote populations of Indo-European origin. Another text which deals with the area, Judg.9, presents the Shechemites as Hamorites, literally 'asinine'. The episode is well known and need not be recounted here.

2.3.2 What are we to make of a text like this? First of all, it should be noted that an event which must have been of primarily political importance is again seen exclusively in a family context, within a framework of love and death, of marriage negotiations and betrayal, which seems to rule out any truly political basis. Obviously this does not exclude the possibility that behind the episode is the recollection of some expedition by the antecedents of Israel against Shechem. It was destroyed at least three times during the second millennium BC: at the end of the eighteenth century, in the middle of the sixteenth century and at the end of the twelfth century. However, there is nothing, not even a hint, to suggest that these are events which could be connected with our text. Moreover, the requirement of circumcision as a *conditio sine qua non* for the beginning of a relationship is much more reminiscent of the conversions to Judaism in the Hellenistic period (below XIII.7.5.6), in which circumcision (and the physical consequences of circumcision) was the order of the day, than of the proto-history of Israel. Albert de Pury has tried to associate Simeon and Levi with the aggressive *ḥapīru* (above V.3.2.4 and below 4.2) mentioned in the el-'Amarna letters; he wants to identify them with a group which he calls 'proto-Israelite', but his attempt seems rather improbable. It seems better, rather, to speak in terms of tribal traditions with a theme similar to that of the Trojan war in Greek epics.

2.4 Numbers 13-14; cf. Deuteronomy 1.22f. describes an expedition coming from the south.

Select bibliography: M. Noth, *Pentateuchal Traditions*, 130ff.; *Numbers*, OTL, London and Philadelphia 1968, ad loc.; F.Stolz, *Jahwes und Israels Kriege*, ATANT 60, Zurich 1972, 69-72; E.Cortese, *La terra di Canaan nella tradizione sacerdotale del Pentateuco*, Brescia 1972, 27-35; J.A.Soggin, 'I testi...', 1, 50f.

In its present form the text sets out to give an account of a reconnaissance mission sent by Moses from the region of Kadesh, where 'Israel' was at the time, to the country of Canaan. The orders received by the explorers are: 'Go up into the Negeb; then go up into the hill country, and see what the land is, and whether the people who inhabit it are strong or weak...' (vv.17f.). So the aim of the expedition is only to reconnoitre the southern sector of Canaan, i.e. the northern Negeb and the southern hill country, though v.21 seems to mention places located in the extreme north, on the frontier of the Davidic empire. And since the text speaks (14.22) of Caleb and Hebron and of the three 'giants' living there, it is evident that the story has links with Josh.14.6-15//Judg.1.10-15, cf. Josh.15.13-20. Joshua 14.7 is obviously connected with Num.14.24, while in Num.13.21 the territory 'explored' clearly coincides with the descriptions in Josh. 15.13f.; Judg.1.10 (above 1.3.2). So, since the texts in Joshua and Judges speak of the conquest of Hebron by Caleb (a group later absorbed into Judah, which also incorporated its traditions about the conquest), it seems reasonable to suppose that Num.13-14 also originally referred to the same incidents. Of course later, in the economy of the pan-Israelite conquest (above 2), the invasion was launched through Gilgal and Jericho, and therefore could not also go independently through the south, so the conquest is turned into an 'exploration'. It is here that Caleb behaves valiantly, receiving his reward in due time.

2.5 Numbers 21.1-3, cf. Judges 1.17, however, speaks of an expedition against Arad, a place situated in the eastern Negeb (coord.152-069 or 162-076). It ends with the defeat of the Canaanites at a place which is then called, aetiologically, Hormah, 'the ban' (for other information see above, 1.3.3). We are not in a position to say whether the expedition had lasting results, and if so, what they were. If we accept the information that the Canaanites were defeated, we might think that the defeat had lasting consequences, though we do not know what they might have been. Here too we could have the remains of a report of a local conquest, which was later supplanted by the offical one.

2.6 The conquest by the tribe of Dan of its own territory in the extreme north of the country is reported in detail in Judg.17-18, and there is an allusion to it in Josh.19.47.

Bibliography: J.A.Soggin *Judges*, ad loc. (with bibliography); M.Rose, *Deuteronomist und Jahwist*, ATANT 67, Zurich 1981, 147ff.

2.6.1 The migration of Dan towards the north was prompted by circumstances for which our texts do not give an adequate explanation, just as we do not seem to be able to determine precisely the region in which Dan had lived earlier. However, there is a reasonable explanation for this last feature: evidently Dan did not succeed in settling permanently in the centre and south (cf. Judg.1.34), and with the arrival of the Philistines in the region its position there became increasingly problematical. The grotesque traditions of the Samson epic could well have preserved, even if in a totally distorted way, the memory of the first struggles that the group had with the Philistines (Judg.13-16).[8]

2.6.2 However, the purpose of this account is not strictly historical, either; it in fact sets out to ridicule the cult of the sanctuary of Dan (present-day *tell el-qādī*, coord. 211-294), whose sacred image is said to have been stolen from an Ephraimite who in turn had made it with precious metal which was the proceeds of a theft.[9] And that is the case despite the proud claim of its priesthood to have descended directly from Moses, without Aaron as an intermediary (Judg.18.30f., cf. the inverted *nun* which is meant to turn *mšh* [Moses] into *mnšh* [Manasseh]). However, there is no reference to the 'golden calf' which according to I Kings 12.29 Jeroboam I had placed in the sanctuary of Dan after the break-up of the personal union between Israel and Judah (below, IX.1.2.3.2).

2.6.3 At all events, the redaction of this passage was later than the invasion of the region by Tiglath-pileser III of Assyria (II Kings 15.29 and the Assyrian annals in *ANET* 283b), which took place in 733-732 BC (below X.3.4.4). The text regards the invasion as a well-deserved punishment for the ancient misdemeanours which had been perpetrated in the sanctuary. On the other hand, this redaction seems to be earlier than that of Dtr, since here the sin of the Danites is not 'the sin of Jeroboam', i.e. placing the 'golden calf' in the sanctuary.

2.6.4 What we might call this concern for edification in the texts also limits them as sources for the historian, all the more so as it also reproduces the pattern typical of the narratives of the exodus and the conquest.

2.7 One large section (Judg.1.21,27-35, with parallels in Josh.15.63; 16.10; 17.11-13,14-18, part of which we examined above, 1.3.5) lists the places which Israel did not succeed in occupying in the course of the conquest. As we have seen (above III.7.1.3), it was probably at the time of David that these places were incorporated into the empire, however that may have happened.

Bibliography: J.A.Soggin, 'I testi . . .'; and *Judges*, ad loc.

2.7.1 The places mentioned have one characteristic in common: they are all in the plains, either the plain of Jezreel (Hebrew *yizrᵉʿʾēl*) or the coastal plains of the centre and the north. This is a region which the el-'Amarna letters show to have been densely populated and subdivided into many city states which exercised political and economic control over the area.

2.7.2 Again in the last years of the second millennium BC, in the brief and contested reign of Eshbaal, son of Saul, it is said that the young king had control of Gilead in Transjordan; Ephraim, Manasseh and Benjamin in the centre; and perhaps also over Asher and even the place Jezreel (usually identified with the ruins of the Arab village of *zerʿīn*, coord.181-218), a few miles north-west of the mountain chain of Gilboa, on the northern spur of the central hill-country (II Sam.2.9).

2.7.3 The same places later appear within Solomon's system of districts (cf. above IV.5,1), and some of them were actually fortified and restored by him (IV.1.4.2–3). It therefore seems reasonable to suppose that they were incorporated into the empire under David ('when Israel became powerful', Judg.1.28//Josh.17.13). It is probable that this was achieved peacefully, by means of treaties.

2.8 Shechem, capital of the northern region of the hill-country, as is Nablus (the modern city) to the present day, appears in Israelite hands in Josh. 8.30-35, clearly a Deuteronomistic text, and in chs.23 (late Dtr) and 24 (revised by Dtr). However, we have no idea how this came about, even if it seems to have happened peacefully. So the situation would seem substantially different from that in the episode recounted in Gen.34.

Bibliography: J.A.Soggin, *Joshua*, and R.G. Boling, *Joshua*, AB 6, Garden City 1982, both ad loc.; J.A.Soggin, 'I testi...'(1 above), 53. For an attempt to attribute these two texts to P, cf. J.G.Vink, 'The Date and Origin of the Priestly Code in the Old Testament', *OTS* 15, 1969, (1-144) 63ff. The relations between Shechem and Gilgal have been discussed by O.Eissfeldt, 'Gilgal or Shechem?' in *Proclamation and Presence* (FS G.Henton Davies), 90-101; R.Smend, 'Josua 23', in *Probleme biblischer Theologie – FS G. von Rad*, Munich 1971, 501-4.

2.8.1 Only in Josh.24 do we find material earlier than Dtr, and it is doubtful whether the other two texts mentioned are anything more than a Deuteronomistic composition.

2.8.2 Relationships with the population of the region of Shechem and its surroundings always seem to have been good, and to have included not only business dealings but also marriages, if we can accept what is said in Judg.8.29-31; 9.1ff. The second of these texts, however, suggests a deterioration in these relationships, though only for a short period, and this was followed by the destruction of the place.

2.8.3 The implicit indication that Israel made a peaceful settlement in the area, with the full agreement of the local populations, is interesting; this contrasts with the official version of the conquest, though that says nothing about the central and northern hill-country, and with another official theory that Israel had to drive out or exterminate the population of Canaan. However, we cannot say more than this.

2.9 I have already dealt with the problems connected with the conquest of Jerusalem (II Sam.5.1ff.) and the gift of Gezer by the Pharaoh who was Solomon's father-in-law (I Kings 9.15; III.6.1.1; IV.4.6).

2.10 The problem of the Israelite settlement in Transjordan is particularly complex, and can only partially be resolved; that is also because of the changing fortunes of those involved in this settlement (cf. above VI.10.1).

Select bibliography: N.Glueck, 'Explorations in Eastern Palestine, I-IV', *AASOR* 14, 1934; 15, 1935; 18/19, 1939; 25/28, 1951 (the classic surface exploration of the region); M.Noth, 'Das Land Gilead als Siedlungsgebiet israelitischer Sippen', *PJB* 37, 1941, 50-101; 'Israelitische Stämme zwischen Ammon und Moab', *ZAW* 60, 1944, 11-57; 'Die Nachbarn der israelitischen Stämme im Ostjordanland', *BBLAK*

(= *ZDPV* 68, 1946-51), 1-50; 'Gilead und Gad', *ZDPV* 75, 1959, 14-73 (all collected in *ABLAK*, 347-90, 391-433, 434, 475, 489-543); id., *Joshua*, HAT I,6, Tübingen ²1953, 78-83 (these are now all classical studies of the topography of the region); M.Wüst, *Untersuchungen zu den siedlungsgeographischen Texten des Alten Testaments*, I, *Ostjordanland*, Wiesbaden 1975; A.G.Auld, *Joshua, Moses and the Land*, Edinburgh 1980, 2ff. (among other things a critique and completion of Wüst's monumental work, 1975); M.Weippert, art.cit., 1; Z.Kallai, 'Conquest and Settlement of Transjordan', *ZDPV* 99, 1983, 110-18; J.F.A.Sawyer and D.J.A.Clines (ed.), *Midian, Moab and Edom*, JSOT-SS 24, Sheffield 1983 (on arguments based on archaeology).

2.10.1 This time the complexity of the problem stems not only from the nature of the sources. It also has an objective basis in the complexity of the features of the Israelite settlement in the region over the centuries, especially in the first half of the first millennium BC. The main biblical texts are Num.21.1ff.//Deut.3.12-20; Josh. 1.12-18; 13.8-22; 22.1ff. Another complicating factor is that all the settlements in the south seem to be late.

2.10.2 The tribes concerned are Reuben, a group which has left no appreciable traces in the historical period (it is mentioned only in one early text, Judg.5.15f., while in Gen.49.3f. it seems to have lost all importance. In Deut.33.6, it even seems to be in process of extinction.). According to Judg.3.1ff., its territory has some obscure connection with the northern part of Moab, but this is an area in which the Israelites found it difficult to gain a footing, following their immigration from the west. Under David, and down to the end of the ninth century BC, the area remained in the possession of Israel, but after that it succeeded in regaining its independence,[10] as we know from the stele of Mesha, king of Moab (above II.7.4 and below IX.3.4.3).

2.10.3 The same inscription tells us that the 'men of Gad' had remained in the region of *'aṭṭarōt* (present-day ḥirbet *'aṭṭārus*, coord.213-109), 'from time immemorial' (*m'lm*), line 10. This information also appears in Num.32.34f., so it is to be preferred to the attempt to locate Gad in Gilead, in the northern region of the modern Hashemite Kingdom of Jordan. Also according to the Mesha stele, the Gadites will have been subjected to the ban and exterminated, in honour of Chemosh, the nation deity of Moab.

2.10.4 We know virtually nothing about the eastern part of Manasseh, which perhaps immigrated into the region after the difficulties it encountered in settling west of the Jordan. At all events, the members of this tribe seem to have been the principal victims of the Aramaean wars during the ninth century and at the beginning of the eighth (cf. Amos.1.3-5, 13-15; 6.13f;[11] cf. below IX.2.2f.).

2.10.5 Numbers 21.21-31 mentions struggles between Israel and Sihon, king of Heshbon (present-day *ḥešbān*, coord. 226-134) and the conquest of Jazer in Moab (v.24; this is perhaps present-day *ḥirbet eṣ-ṣār*, coord. 228-150),[12] near the boundary with Ammon. This is probably an ancient tradition, perhaps transmitted by E, except that v.30, the key passage, is corrupt.[13] It could be an Israelite song of conquest, but it could also be a song from elsewhere which has been attributed to Israel. At all events, it reflects the changing fortunes in relationships between Israel and Moab.

2.10.6 However, we find a different situation in the episode with Og, king of Bashan, the 'last of the Rephaim', an original, mythical population of ancient Canaan associated with the spirits of the dead (to which the root *rāpā'* normally refers, particularly in Ugaritic).[14] The episode aims 'to legitimate the claim of the eastern part of the tribe of Manasseh to a region which the Israelites in fact had never possessed'.[15]

3 The comments I have made so far now allow us to examine the territories which the tradition of Israel thought to have been in the hands of the people towards the end of the second millennium BC, between the reigns of Saul and David. For a bibliography cf.1 above.

3.1 If we leave aside the unitary account of the conquest given in Joshua 1-12, we immediately become aware of the fragmentary character of the Israelite occupation of the region. Precisely this feature shows that Judges 1-2 cannot originally have been the continuation of Josh.23-24, which is what the present redaction means us to believe. So what we have here is not the individual tribes going to take possession of the territories which have already been conquered and then assigned to each of them by lot (cf. Josh. 1-12; 13-21). As I have already indicated (above 1.2, and 2.2), this is an alternative version of the facts which the official narrative has tried to replace. Granted, the information given in Judg.1 differs widely in historical value, but as we have seen, it seems probable that the list in 1.21,27-35 goes back to an ancient and trustworthy tradition, perhaps to a public document of some sort. What picture, then, emerges from the information we are given about the conquest?

3.2 The region of Hebron was occupied by Caleb (a group which was later assimilated to Judah, above 2.4). This was probably an independent operation, in which they came from the south and not from the east (it would be interesting if we had more details either about the course of this invasion or about the economy, population and cities in the region). Otherwise, the conquest always began in sparsely populated regions, on the edge of the steppes and in the hill-country. By contrast, the coastal regions and the plains, which were all densely populated and particularly fertile, and were were organized into a mosaic of city-states, remained outside the Israelite sphere of influence. This happened, first because Israel had no interest in them, and secondly because it did not have the military capacity to conquer them. So we know nothing about the relationships between the city-states and the invaders.

3.3 The situation seems to have been different on the edge of the steppes and in the the hill country. The city-states were few and their territories extensive. The steppe and the woodland, the scrub and the large amount of uncultivated land lent themselves very well to extensive itinerant grazing. This is the pattern that we find, for example, Joseph's brothers observing in Gen.37.12-17. They seem to follow a constant itinerary and Joseph has no difficulty in meeting up with them. Moreover, in Gen.34.23, a passage which I have already cited, we hear that the local populations did not have any difficulty in admitting the newcomers, who could populate almost uninhabited areas and were far from penniless on arrival! In other words, these were regions little suited for agriculture, given the lack of water in the spring and summer, though the discovery of techniques for lining cisterns towards the end of the thirteenth and twelfth centuries bc made it possible to conserve water so that small groups of people could settle and keep sheep and goats[16] throughout the year. Moreover, the increasingly widespread use of iron made it possible to fell trees and introduce new building techniques.

3.4 Three areas are particularly interesting in this connection:

3.4.1 The southern hill-country with Hebron as its capital.

3.4.2 The central hill-country, beginning immediately north of Jerusalem and ending at its last northern spurs before the plain of Esdraelon, including the Gilboa chain and the village of Jezreel.

3.4.3 Finally, upper Galilee, the region around Hazor (*tell el-qēdaḥ*, coord.203-269) and the mountains of the region.

We do not know whether these three regions were in communication with one another and if so, to what extent, However, the south was cut off from the centre by the enclave of the city-state of Jerusalem and its territory. (Those who made the journey from Jerusalem to Bethlehem between 1949 and 1967 will know the difficulties of a route which along the road following the watershed takes two or three hours on foot.) The centre was cut off from Galilee by the more powerful enclave of the city-states of the plain.

3.5 A final problem is posed by two institutions: the 'levitical cities' and the 'cities of refuge'. It is not in fact easy to find a precise historical or sociological setting for these two institutions, not just in the context of the conquest but even in the history of Israel generally.

Bibliography: J. Wellhausen, *Prolegomena to the History of Israel* (1886), ET reissued New York 1957, 159ff.; M.Löhr, *Das Asylwesen im Alten*

Testament, Halle 1930; W.F.Albright, 'The List of Levitical Cities', in *Louis Ginzberg Jubilee Volume...*, New York 1945, I, 49-73; M.Noth, *Das Buch Josua*, HAT I, 7, Tübingen 1953, 100ff.; A.Alt, 'Festungen und Levitenorte im Lande Juda', *KS* II, 306-15; Y.Kaufmann, *The Biblical Account of the Conquest of Palestine*, Jerusalem 1953; B.Mazar, 'The Cities of the Priests and of the Levites', *SVT* 7, 1957, 193-205; M.Haran, 'Studies in the Account of the Levitical Cities', *JBL* 80, 1961, 45-54, 156-65; A.Cody, *A History of the Old Testament Priesthood*, AnBibl 35, Rome 1969, 159ff.; R. de Vaux, *Ancient Israel*, 366f.; T.N.D.Mettinger, *Solomonic State Officials*, CB-OTS 5, Lund 1971, 97ff.; Y.Aharoni, *The Land*; J.L.Peterson, *A Topographical Surface Survey of the Levitical Cities of Joshua 21 and I Chronicles 6*, Diss. Chicago Institute for Advanced Theological Studies and Seabury-Western Theological Seminary, Evanston, Ill. 1977; J. de Vaulx, 'Refuge, villes de', *SDB* IX, 1979, 1495-8; A.G.Auld, 'Cities of Refuge in Israelite Tradition', *JSOT* 10, 1978, 26-40; id., 'The Levitical Cities – Texts and History', *ZAW* 91, 1979, 194-206; id., *Joshua, Moses and the Land*, Edinburgh 1980, 79ff.; Z.Kallai, 'The System of Levitic Cities: A Historical-Geographical Study in Biblical Historiography', *Zion* 45, 1980, 13-34 (Hebrew, with an English summary); and the commentaries on Joshua and Chronicles.

3.5.1 The levitical cities are listed in Josh.21.1-42; cf.Num.35.1-8; I Chron 6.39-66. This is a list of forty-eight places assigned to the Levites as grazing land. The idea behind this is that because the tribe of Levi did not receive a tribal territory of its own, its descendants, the Levites, were given cities instead, to provide an income on which they could live. Num.35.1-8 indicates that each one of them was to be surrounded by territory forming a square of 2000 cubits (rather over 1000 yards). The cities of refuge appear in Josh.20; cf. Num.35.9-34; Deut.19.1-13, and are meant to serve as sanctuary for those who have killed someone and are pursued in vendettas by the families of their victims, hence the name. The cities of refuge are all contained in the list of levitical cities, not vice versa, since there are only seven cities of refuge. That would suggest that there is some sort of relationship between the two types of city.

3.5.2 It is impossible here to go into the complex discussion about the dating of the two institutions (granted that they in fact existed and functioned, which not all scholars would accept).

3.5.2.1 It is enough to recall that in fact Wellhausen, 1886, already pointed out the clearly artificial character of any system which marks out a thousand-yard square around each place. Such a project would be quite impossible to carry out in a largely mountainous country like Palestine!

3.5.2.2 Others (M.Löhr 1930, W.F.Albright 1945, B.Mazar 1957, T.D.N.Mettinger 1971, Z.Kallai 1980) date the two institutions at the time of the united monarchy.

3.5.2.3 Yet others (A.Alt, 1952; M.Noth, 1953; A.Cody, 1969) prefer a much later date: the post-exilic period or, at the earliest, the time of Josiah's reform (below XI.4).

3.5.2.4 However, as in other cases, the Israeli Y.Kaufmann argues that this is a utopian project, though the idea for it dates from the time of the conquest.

3.5.2.5 M.Haran 1961 does not fix on a particular date but sees the list as a geographical and topographical 'priestly' system (thus implying that it is late), with many utopian elements (cf. Y.Kaufmann in the previous section); however, he believes that one cannot rule out *a priori* the possibility that the Levites lived in such places. The position of de Vaux seems similar: he believes that the list reflects utopian concepts but is probably based on ancient documents; and it is also possible that in origin it reflects a real situation.

3.5.3 In this flurry of contrasting opinions the results of Peterson's 1977 surface study, his doctoral thesis, are particularly interesting. He also provides an annotated biography on the question. Between August and October 1971 he carried out surface examinations on seventy-one tells relating to the Late Bronze Age, all connected with the cities in question (only two tells in Syria, one in Lebanon and two in Jordan were not examined because of *force majeure*), and two from the Iron Age. This survey has made it possible to establish that few, less than half, of these are places already attested as occupied in the tenth century BC, and not many are attested in the ninth century. The majority do not appear before the eighth century BC. In other words, here we find a relatively certain *terminus a quo*: it is only relative, because later discoveries could always modify the partial results of this research. Certainly a place could not be a 'levitical city' or a 'city of refuge' before its foundation. And since the assignation of a locality to a particular social group presupposes that this place has already existed for some time, given that the institution really existed, it cannot be earlier than the reign of Hezekiah (below XI.2) or, probably, of Josiah (XI.4.1.1).

4.1.1 It therefore seems easy to verify the basic validity of Albrecht Alt's theory[17] that in reality, at least in its first phases, the occupation resulted from peaceful settlement in the territories of the most extensive and least populated city-states by groups grazing their herds there. The phenomenon could have lasted for decades and perhaps centuries, and seems for the most part to have had the approval of the local population. Only in the final stages could things have become more violent, but this brings us down to the time of Saul and David; even then incidents are always local.[18] About twenty-five years ago,

S.Moscati[19] rightly observed that if we leave aside the Islamic conquest, an atypical phenomenon in both its extent and intensity, we never find a conquest in the ancient Near East which takes place as a result of 'one or more invasions'; by contrast, we have to talk in terms of 'a... periodical infiltration of groups in the predominantly peaceful form demonstrated by ethnology'. 'There is no indication of a violent invasion at one particular time...' That is certainly the case with the Amorites in Mesopotamia during the first half of the second millennium BC and the Aramaeans and the Israelites in Syria and Palestine in the second half of the second millennium. It is only with Saul that we begin to hear of situations of conflict, and these are not so much conflicts with the indigenous populations as with neighbouring people or immigrants who try to occupy or to subject regions inhabited by Israel.

4.1.2 If we leave aside the official version, the biblical sources, examined critically, support this basic view of events: the process must have begun soon after the el-'Amarna period, ending with the reign of David and the incorporation of the city-states into the empire, and with Solomon and his possession of Gezer. In the light of this reconstruction of events the mention of 'Israel' on the stele of Pharaoh Merneptah from the last quarter of the thirteenth century BC takes on new significance: in fact Israel already existed as a people but not yet as a nation, even if we are not in a position to establish with even minimal precision its size, its composition and the territory it occupied. We have also seen that in the economy of the stele, Israel appears located rather north of the Sea of Galilee: however, we have also noted the historical problems that the stele presents (above II.7.3.1).

4.1.3 R. de Vaux*, II, 523-680, has made a different proposal which attempts a synthesis between the theories of Alt and Noth on the one hand and Albright and his followers on the other.

Bibliography: C.Schäfer-Lichtenberger, *Stadt und Eidgenossenschaft im Alten Testament*, BZAW 156, Berlin 1983, 187-90.

First of all, de Vaux uses the French term '*installation*', 'settlement', instead of others like 'conquest', because it is more neutral and more in accordance with the course of events; he then picks out four different regions, each with a distinctive type of settlement. He had produced a sketch along similar lines, though only in embryonic form, in 1962.

4.1.3.1 The first region is the south, and comprises the tribes of Judah, Simeon and Levi and the groups of Caleb, Othniel, Jerahmeel and the Kenites, all of whom were later absorbed into Judah. Here the settlement took place from the south, from Kadesh and from north Arabia. The ancestors of these groups could have been in Egypt, but before Moses. The settlement was essentially peaceful, except when the groups moved towards the hill-country (Hebron), which was populated by the Canaanites.

4.1.3.2 The second region is Transjordan and includes Reuben, Gad-Gilead and Manasseh-Machir, the last of which arrived at a later stage; it, too, left from Kadesh and was led by Moses.

4.1.3.3 Then we have the region of the central hill country, where we find Benjamin and Joseph (i.e. Ephraim and Manasseh), led by Joshua; the settlement of these tribes was essentially peaceful.

4.1.3.4 Finally there is the northern region, Galilee, whose groups – Asher, Naphtali, Zebulun and Issachar – had been in the region for an indeterminate time. They were never in Egypt. Asher and Zebulun ended up by being employed as manual workers in the region; Issachar was originally part of Zebulun. In the battle of Merom (Josh.11ff.), they are then said to have succeeded in defeating Jabin king of Hazor, occupying and destroying the city.

4.1.4 However, it is hard to see how far this synthesis actually works. According to the theories of Albright and his disciples, the central region, which is mentioned chiefly in the book of Joshua, was the scene of the main encounters. Moreover, de Vaux, too, rejects any large-scale association of the settlement with the destruction evident from the excavations, while that is the basic argument put forward by Albright and his school. To say more, it would be necessary to make a detailed examination of each individual theory of the great historian and archaeologist, and that is something which would clearly have to be done in a monograph rather than here.

4.2 Now about twenty years ago, a new theory about the conquest dominated discussions, especially in the United States. This argued for a conquest from within, arising out of a revolt against the authorities of the city-state by the exploited rural population. The first to formulate it was George E. Mendenhall in 1962.

Bibliography. G.E.Mendenhall, 'The Hebrew Conquest of Palestine', *BA* 25, 1962, 66-87; id., *The Tenth Generation*, Baltimore 1973, ch.VII; J.A.Soggin, 'La conquista israelitica' (above, 1), 208; M.Weippert, *The Settlement*, 55-62; M.Liverani, 'Introduction' to *La Siria nell'età del bronzo*, Rome 1969, (3-14) 8ff.; the articles by A.J.Hauser, T.L.Thompson and A.Rolla cited in 1 above; N.K.Gottwald, *The Tribes*, passim; my review of Gottwald in *Bibl* 62, 1981, 583-90.

4.2.1 To begin with, Mendenhall's study, presented modestly in a non-specialist review, was heavily criticized.[20] But any criticism, however legitimate, should not obscure one evident datum: Mendenhall, recently followed by his pupil N.K.Gottwald (author of a monumental, if rhetorical and repetitive volume on the question), in fact puts forward an alternative version both to the traditional theory of an invasion and a large-scale conquest and to the theory of a gradual penetration into peripheral regions which were sparsely inhabited.

4.2.2 So we have a fourth position which needs to be included in the debate, that of the revolt in the rural areas, a view which regards the others as being deficient in basic respects.

4.2.2.1 Mendenhall rightly finds particularly problematical some deductions which are often made from the division of Israel into tribes, e.g. that this division presupposes that Israel had a nomadic, or better semi-nomadic, origin. Mendenhall points out that we find divisions into tribes in ancient Greece and ancient Rome; and even today there are still Arab-Palestinian villages with these structures, which show no traces of any kind of nomadism. This example of the Arab village is particularly interesting: here there is a widespread practice of migrant grazing with the village as a base, but no nomadism. The tribal organization serves rather to denote the self-awareness of the group, what Anglo-Saxon sociologists call the 'in-group'; and in the ancient Near East, too, this structure was connected on an economic and productive level with grazing, along with regular transhumance. So the antagonism which is supposed to have existed between sedentary populations and nomadic populations is simply a creation of scholars. The antagonism between the urban nucleus of the city-state, the seat of political and economic power which, though not productive, controlled the wealth of the region, and the rural villages which, while producing the greater part part of the wealth, had no control over them, seems much more real because it is based on economic and political factors like exploitation and oppression. This contrast often leads to the rebellion of the rural group, and its secession from the capital, a course of action which places it outside the law. For Mendenhall, this last position corresponds to the legal state of the *ḫapīru / 'prm* (above V.3.2.4), the category which, as we have seen, some scholars in the past have wanted to use to identify growing Israel.

4.2.2.2 Mendenhall goes on to point out that in fact the el-'Amarna letters refer to frequent rebellions against the authority of the various city-states nominally subject to Pharaoh, culminating in some instances in the expulsion of the sovereign and other authorities, and sometimes, in extreme cases, in the destruction of the city. Now the Israelite conquest will also have been the product of revolts of this kind. The leading elements in the countryside, reinforced by groups coming from the wilderness, will have regrouped in an alliance (Hebrew *bᵉrīt*), an alliance among themselves and also between the people and the one who was then to become the God of Israel.

4.2.2.3 In other words, the new faith of the group of outsiders coming from the wilderness, which had experienced the power of God in the events of the exodus, will have given the rebels an ideology which brought them unity.

4.2.2.4 This movement will have developed in Transjordan, and then have spread through Cisjordan until the liberation was complete. In some regions, e.g. in the central hill-country, it will have caused virtually no conflicts; elsewhere, the signs are that the conflict was much greater.

4.2.2.5 Mendenhall's basic idea has since been developed recently by Gottwald. However, he adds virtually nothing new except the theory of the 'conversion' of the rebels to Yahwism, the new faith which was brought to them from the eastern desert.

4.2.2.6 In this way the rebels, having obtained their liberty, will have become 'Israel';[21] and their new faith will have been the typical product of their new social reality, all this according to the Marxist theory enunciated by Gottwald, to the effect that Yahwism is the symbol of the Israelite social and economic revolution.[22]

4.2.3 If Mendenhall's and Gottwald's proposals proved historically acceptable, they would resolve a series of problems.

4.2.3.1 First of all, there is the problem of the obvious ethnic and linguistic continuity throughout the region during the transition from the Bronze Age to the beginning of the Iron Age.[23] This continuity is difficult to explain if, with the biblical tradition, we assume another people to have arrived in the region and to have taken the place of the native inhabitants. If we were dealing with substantially new settlements, this sort of continuity could not manifest itself without some form of explanation for it.

4.2.3.2 Again, there is the problem of the command, often given in the biblical texts, to destroy the cities and their inhabitants, while nothing of this kind is said about the villages; this could be a recollection of political opposition between the urban and rural nuclei within the city-state.

4.2.3.3 There is the problem of the survival of the majority of the Canaanite population and its religion down to Josiah's reform.

4.2.3.4 There is the problem of the term '*brīm*, 'Hebrew', as applied to ancient Israel by its adversaries (above V.3.2.4).[24]

4.2.4 However, there are also many questions which these proposals leave unresolved; there are more of them, and they are rather more serious.

4.2.4.1 First of all, Israel was always aware of not having originally been native to Palestine, but of having come from abroad (above, 1). Of course this awareness is expressed in theological rather than historical and ethnic terms, but it is difficult to deny that it has a real basis.[25] Perhaps it was because this awareness contrasted so markedly with the right which Israel had always claimed to what was its Promised

Land. Attributing to a divine gift what it could have claimed as the consequence of a situation which had existed from time immemorial, would have removed from its claim that very element which even now seems to be its distinguishing feature (cf. the importance of the theme in the ideological discussion of the Arab-Israeli conflict today).

4.2.4.2 Moreover, a look at the el-'Amarna letters shows that, rather than arising from the relationship in the city-state between the urban nucleus and the countryside (which can easily be conceived of in terms of exploiter and exploited), the conflicts which are mentioned developed specifically within the ambit of the structures of the urban nucleus itself (above I.8.4). One instance would be a revolt of the assembly of nobles against the palace. In cases where the *ḫapīru* are mentioned, as we have seen above (V.3.2.4), they are never an ethnic group, nor can they be identified with rural groups. Rather, according to Landsberger's 1930 theory which was taken up and developed by Liverani in 1965, they were refugees.

4.2.3 Again, while the patriarchs indeed appear as breeders of herds of small cattle, they are never connected with any kind of village. Yet the patriarchal traditions (and not those of the liberation experienced during the exodus) are the ones which provide Israel with 'the ideological foundation for the possession of the fertile land east and west of the Jordan'.[26]

4.2.4.4 Finally, the reference made by Mendenhall and particularly by Gottwald to the *ḫapīru* and to the 'God of the fathers' seems more a case of an explanation of *obscura per obscuriora* than a clarification. As to the concept of the covenant which is supposed to have cemented the alliance of the groups among themselves and with their new God, we have now known for more than a decade that the term *berīt* and the concept which it expresses are not older than Dtn and Dtr;[27] Mendenhall could not yet have been aware of this in his first paper, but he should not have ignored it subsequently, nor should Gottwald.

4.2.5 The alternative theory of the conquest developed by Mendenhall and particularly by Gottwald does not, then, constitute a valid alternative theory to that of Alt. Of course Alt's theory must constantly be updated and revised to take account of new discoveries and new methods, but it remains basically valid. On the other hand, what the two American studies say about the sociology of Israel and the need to examine it thoroughly remains completely valid; too often, in fact, a lack of sociological training on the part of biblical and Near Eastern scholars has meant that the sociological side of the history of Israel has been obscured. So we should make a careful examination of, for example, the implications of the usual translations of the Hebrew terms *šebet* and the less frequent *maṭṭeh* as 'tribe'[28] (below 7.1.1); or of the sociological and economic implications of the frequently-used term 'semi-nomads', which is evidently not so much a social condition as a mode of production. We must ask how important for ancient Israel was the clash between city and countryside, so dear to Marxist scholars. That is, of course, provided that such research is practicable in the light of our sources: I have in fact repeated many times that we have few economic texts at our disposal, in contrast to our knowledge of the Mesopotamian world and the northern Syrian society of Ugarit.

4.2.5.1 The approach to the problem by Mendenhall and Gottwald has shed light on another feature: as we have seen, in central-northern Palestine the conquest seems to have taken place without a blow being struck. Nor are we told that the incorporation into the Davidic empire of the city-states of the plain was the result of operations of a military kind (this last feature certainly contrasts with the rebellion theory!). So we have to think in terms of a series of agreements with the resident populations. That seems a necessary hypothesis in the case of Shechem and also appears probable for Gibeon; here Josh.9, a text which has now been distorted by apologetic, has retained the memory of the alliance made between the citizens and the invaders. II Samuel 21.1-14 makes independent mention of the violation of such a treaty; here David placates the anger of the Gibeonites by handing over to them the sons of Saul, the guilty one, so that the Gibeonites can be avenged. Cases of this kind may have been much more frequent than the texts now admit, even if the theological concept of the covenant seems much later.

The following modifications, among others, are to be made to the theory put forward by Alt (see Appendix I below). These are not semi-nomadic groups, involved in transhumance, but groups which have past history in the cities; it would seem to be a foregone conclusion that such groups originated in the territories of the city states, which would rule out any form of nomadism. That would be partial confirmation of the theory put forward by G.E.Mendenhall and N.K.Gottwald, but would certainly not confirm a revolt: more simply, groups of city-dwellers will have left the territory of the city states, probably because they were oppressed by taxation and demands on personal services, and will have occupied the uninhabited areas in the hill country, possibly joining forces there with semi-nomadic groups involved in transhumance. Everything will have happened very peacefully.

4.2.5.2 We have only partial information on the other regions, so I do not propose to deal with them here.

5 From the end of the last century onwards, Palestine has been the scene of innumerable campaigns of archaeological excavations, far more so than any other area in the world. At least in the early days, these campaigns often set out to prove the truth of what is said in the Bible in a historical context, just as some years earlier there had been

attempts to demonstrate the truth of the Bible in the sphere of the natural sciences (this was indeed the aim of the expedition of the 'Beagle' with Charles Darwin on board, though it was Darwin himself, with his intellectual honesty, who recognized the impossibility of this approach, so that the result of the expedition demonstrated precisely the opposite to what its sponsors had hoped for). Others simply wanted to illustrate the biblical text, an aim which is stated, for example, in the original statutes of the British Palestine Exploration Fund.[29] From the start, however, the confusion in intentions and the failure to define aims adequately has not prevented biblical archaeologists from refining their techniques, abandoning all claims of an apologetic kind and rightly adopting the generally accepted methodology of archaeological research. This has happened to such an extent that it is now becoming increasingly clear that we should no longer talk of 'biblical archaeology' or 'Old Testament archaeology', but rather of Palestinian archaeology or even the archaeology of Syria and Palestine, thus covering the whole region on both sides of the Jordan and as far as the boundaries with Turkey and Iraq. This is a basic problem which we cannot discuss here, but it shows the direction that archaeological studies have been taking for more than a decade. Meanwhile the methods and techniques of excavation have been perfected to such an extent that it is possible to date very clearly and precisely the various strata of a *tell*, the charac-teristic hill of ruins distributed throughout the Near East (in Turkish and cognate languages it is called a *tepe*); the dating is arrived at by means of an exact classification of finds of pottery, an indestructible material which cannot be modified chemically. It is impossible here to give the reader even a synopsis of the archaeological excavations which have been carried out so far, the discoveries that have been made, or even of the general pattern of results; I shall simply try to provide some information about the best attested of them and seek to draw what may be regarded as reasonably trustworthy conclusions from them.

Select bibliography: W.F.Albright, *The Israelite Conquest*, above 1; id., *The Archaeology of Palestine*, Harmondsworth [4]1960; id., *Archaeology and the Religion of Israel*, Baltimore [3]1963; J.A.Soggin, 'Ancient Biblical Traditions and Modern Archaeological Discoveries', *BA* 23, 1960, 95-100; 'La conquista israelitica', above, 1; H.J.Franken and C.H.Franken-Battershill, *A Primer of Old Testament Archaeology*, Leiden 1963; P.W.Lapp, 'The Conquest of Palestine', above 1; A.v.R.Sauer, 'The Meaning of Archaeology for the Exegetical Task', *Concordia Theological Monthly* 41, 1970, 519-41; H.H.Schmid, *Die Steine und das Wort*, Zurich 1975; M.Weippert, *The Settlement*, ch.IV; H.J.Franken, *CAH* II, 2 [3]1975, 331ff.; id., 'The Problem of Identific-ation in Biblical Archaeology', *PEQ* 108, 1976, 3-11; J.M.Miller,

'Archaeology and the Israelite Conquest of Canaan: Some Methodological Observations', *PEQ* 109, 1977, 87-93; K.M.Kenyon, *Archaeology in the Holy Land*, London ⁴1979; F.Crüsemann, 'Alttestamentliche Exegese und Archäologie', *ZAW* 91, 1979, 177-93; A.Rolla, 'La conquista', above 1; V.Fritz, 'Die kulturhistorische Bedeutung...', above 1; S.Loffreda, 'L'insediamento', 1; V.Fritz, 'Bibelwissenschaft: I. Altes Testament, I, 1, Archäologie', *TRE* VI, 1980, 316-45; H.D.Lance, *The Old Testament for Archaeologists*, Philadelphia 1981; W.G.Dever, 'The Impact of the "New Archaeology" on Syro-Palestinian Archaeology', *BASOR* 242, 1981, 15-29; G.W.Ramsey, *The Quest for the Historical Israel*, Atlanta 1981- London 1982; Y.Aharoni, *The Archaeology of the Land of Israel*, London and Philadelphia 1982 (this is now the most recent and up-to-date work on the theme by one of the most famous of modern archaeologists); P.J.King, 'The Contribution of Archaeology to Biblical Studies', *CBQ* 45, 1983, 1-16; J.M.Miller, 'Site Identification: A Problem Area in Contemporary Biblical Scholarship', *ZDPV* 99, 1983, 119-29; B.S.J.Isserlin, 'The Israelite Conquest of Canaan. A Comparative Review of the Arguments Applicable', *PEQ* 115, 1983, 85-94 (with bibliography; he defends the credibility of an armed conquest). For a detailed study of the archaeological question see Appendix I below, 357-67.

5.1 A first basic recommendation made by the professional archaeologists to the 'non-professionals', and often repeated, is that they should take the utmost care in evaluating discoveries and especially in connecting reports of discoveries with texts and in drawing historical conclusions from the discoveries, precisely because this process might suggest that they were objective. The reason for this is that when archaeology does not produce epigraphical discoveries or is not supported by relevant historical texts, it is an exact science to the extent that it is practised professionally by competent people, but is also a mute science.

5.1.1 Two examples must suffice. When a place in Palestine seems to have been destroyed, let us say, between the thirteenth and the twelfth century BC (a date fixed by pottery finds), how do we go about identifying its original name with certainty – and we have to do that if we are to connect it with any ancient texts that may be at our disposal – if this name does not emerge from the finds? Granted, it is possible that the original name of the place has been retained in the modern Arabic name, but it may happen that this is transferred to other places nearby. Thus the present-day *'anāta*, coord. 175-136, retains the name of the biblical *'ⁿnātōt*, the home of the prophet Jeremiah, but the original biblical place is to be located on *raś el-ḥarrūbe*, coord.174-135, in its immediate vicinity. So in this case, to excavate under the place whose name corresponds to that in the Bible, in the expectation of finding its remains, would not lead anywhere. To cite a different example: the Syrian locality of *tell mardiḥ* has been conclusively identified with ancient Ebla of the cuneiform texts, thanks only to the discovery in the second half of the 1960s of an inscription dedicated to a king of Ebla;[30] this identification was then confirmed some years later by the discovery of the library and archives. (For this set of problems cf. Franken 1976.)

5.1.2 Again, without adequate epigraphical discoveries or historical texts, the excavation cannot indicate who or what occurrence was the cause of a possible destruction. So the hypothetical Palestinian locality mentioned above, destroyed between the thirteen and the twelfth centuries BC, could very well have been destroyed as a result of internal factors (a rebellion or a civil war between factions) or by natural causes (a fire or an earthquake); however, it could also have been destroyed by the Israelites or the Philistines and, if it were situated in the eastern region, by the Ammonites or the Moabites. I Kings 9.15 says of Gezer that it was destroyed by the Egyptians, who handed it over to Solomon, but without this text how could we come to know this if we found signs of destruction in the stratum corresponding to the tenth century BC?

5.1.3 Now Palestine has produced little epigraphical material of historical relevance worth noting,[31] while its humid winter climate has prevented the conservation of papyrus and parchment texts. It is no coincidence that the writings of *wādī ed-dalīyeh* and Qumran (below XII.6.1 and XIII.11.4), the former from the second half of the first millennium BC and the latter from around the end of the first millennium BC and the beginning of the first millennium AD, were found in the desert region of the Jordan and the northern shore of the Dead Sea. So we have an enormous range of archaeological discoveries, the fruit, as we have seen, of more than a century of intensive excavation.[32] However, this is material which for most of the time is difficult to relate to the biblical texts, despite the initially optimistic evaluations, especially in the United States and in Israel, by scholars ranged around the person of W.F.Albright (above V.2.3.5). (We have already considered the problematical historical character of these texts in ch.II.) In other words, 'there are no pure archaeological facts as such, but only interpreted facts'.[33]

5.2 One of the facts that we may consider to have been established over the last ten to fifteen years is that the transition from the end of the Bronze Age to the beginning of the Iron Age in Syria and Palestine was not characterized by any breaks in continuity worth noting, at least in those regions which had been populated for a long time. The only truly new element is provided by Philistine pottery, from the beginning of the twelfth century BC. Its style can easily be connected with the pottery predominant in the Aegean world. Moreover, and I have stressed this often, there are no relevant traces of the settlement of a new population in the region, alongside or in place of the indigenous population (Miller). On the other hand, the transition from the Bronze Age to the Iron Age is characterized by considerable turbulence, and rapid changes accompanied by numerous cases of destruction throughout the region, not only in Palestine. Now it is certainly legitimate to affirm that a situation of this kind provided ideal conditions for the settlement and later the seizure of power by an alien population. However, it seems illegitimate to identify the disturbances and the destruction in question with the work of the Israelites whom the biblical tradition presents as invaders, or even with that of their immediate ancestors. That is all the more the case since, as we have seen, the Bible itself excludes a number of places from the conquest in the narrower sense (Judg.1.21,27-36), and in another instance explicitly affirms that with the exception of the *tell* of Hazor, the places 'situated on their tell' (Josh.11.13, cf. above 1.3.5; 2.7) were not destroyed. As Miller has indicated, the reality presented by the biblical sources seems to have been much more modest. Only four places are said to have been destroyed: Sepath/Hormah (probably *ḥirbet el mšaš*, Hebrew *tell mašōš*, coord. 146-069), Jericho (*tell es-sūlṭān*, coord. 192-142), Ai (*et-tell*, coord. 174-158) and Hazor (*tell el-qedaḥ*, coord. 203-269), the second and third in circumstances which we shall examine below (5.2.2.3).

5.2.2 So the reality seems to be more complex than an examination of the texts might suggest. However, this reality is influenced by the unitary view of the conquest which appears in Josh.1-12. And it is certain that the places investigated in the course of the last half-century (since techniques have been refined) almost all present a series of problems which I shall try to examine.

5.2.2.1 Some sites, in fact destroyed in the transitional period between the Bronze Age and the Iron Age, have not yet been identified with any place mentioned in the Bible. Thus we have *tell el-ḥeṣi* (coord.124-106), identified by some scholars with Eglon, and *tell er-rabūd* (coord.151-093), perhaps Debir, which proves not even to have been destroyed during this period. *tell bēt mirsim* (coord.141-096), which until his death Albright thought to be Debir, an identification which is now generally abandoned, has not been identified even hypothetically, though this was destroyed.

5.2.2.2 It does not follow from the texts that Bethel, present-day *beitīn* (coord.172-148), was in fact destroyed, and to claim that its destruction seems to be implied in the text begs the question. The same is true of Lachish, *tell ed-duweir* (coord.135-108).

5.2.2.3 Other places, Hormah (above 5.2.1), Jericho and Ai,

mentioned explicitly as having been conquered and destroyed in the conquest, were not even inhabited in the period in question; the same is true of Arad (coord.152-069, 162-076), Gibeon (*ej-jîb*, coord.167-139), and Yarmuth (probably *ḥirbet el-yarmūk*, coord.147-124).

5.2.2.4 However, another place seems certainly to have been destroyed by an earthquake and not in warlike operations, i.e. *tell deir-'alla*, probably ancient Succoth (coord.208-178), a little after 1200.

5.2.3 Again, as I have already stressed on several occasions, Palestine is not the only region where there is evidence of destruction of this kind. Syria, too, proves to have had considerable disturbances, and the ensuing destruction is generally attributed to the 'the Sea Peoples' (above III.5.2). Moreover, Pharaoh Merneptah (above, II.7.3.1) also claims to have 'plundered Canaan with every evil', a statement which is followed by a list of the places involved. If the information is historical, in all probability this was in the course of attempts to regain Egyptian control over Palestine.

5.3 However, the situation is different in the areas which were originally sparsely inhabited, the hill-country and the steppes.

5.3.1 Here we find considerable traces of settlement by new populations, living in unfortified villages (in the northern Negeb). All this can be explained on the ecological level by the discovery of a new mortar for sealing cisterns and making them impermeable; the discovery made possible extensive grazing where originally those with flocks of sheep and goats were at best transient (above 3.3).

5.3.2 In these two areas, then, the hypothesis of a conquest by a foreign population does not even appear necessary, though according to Alt's hypothesis, they are precisely the ones where the first Israelite settlements took place, peacefully (note that the villages were unfortified villages).

5.4 Thus it should be remembered that we find only one instance in which there might be a parallel between what is said in the biblical texts and the archaeological discoveries, in that we find a destruction that can be verified: Josh.11.10-13 and the fall of Hazor which is narrated there. As we have seen, Jericho and Ai prove to have been abandoned at that period, and at best they had tiny, insignificant populations. Moreover, there is nothing historical about the texts which speak of their destruction: the account of the fall of Jericho is more reminiscent of a liturgical celebration with processions,[34] while in the case of Ai we have a dissertation on obedience to the word of God and a threat of the punishment which will fall upon those who are rash enough to disobey. Furthermore, as we have seen, the place called Hormah does not even seem to have been inhabited in this period.

5.4.1 That makes the hypothesis put forward by W.F.Albright from the 1930s onwards, and accepted, though with some criticisms and modifications of points of detail, by his pupils J.Bright[35] and G.E.Wright, seem at least hasty and probably imprudent. Albright argued that the destructions and other disturbances which mark the transition from the Bronze Age to the Iron Age in all probability illustrate, even if they do not prove, e.g. the claim in Josh.1-12 of a large-scale military conquest by all Israel. (Albright is fond of using the term 'external evidence', which is considered to be objective, as opposed to the 'internal evidence' of the texts, which is supposed to be more susceptible to the subjective evaluations of scholars.) So far, and clearly we cannot here go into the details of a debate which took place in the now distant years of the 1940s, 1950s, and 1960s,[36] the only place which could validly be incorporated into this theory is the *tell* of Hazor (Josh.11), which was destroyed, as the excavations suggest, at the end of the thirteenth century BC. However, even in this case, the most favourable of all, this is not the only possible explanation, but only one of a great many probable explanations which would fit in with the information at our disposal.[37] If this has any validity at all, it could hold for Upper Galilee, and explain the presence of new villages with pottery and other very rough artefacts. In this region it is in fact possible to accept the presence of situations of the el-'Amarna type, which could have led to a progressive impoverishment of the city-state, resulting in increasingly high taxation and the gradual exodus of large sectors of the rural population, who were not skilled in the techniques of the specialist craftsmen in the cities.

5.5 What remains to be achieved (and here Mendenhall and Gottwald are certainly right, though cf. already M.Liverani and recently W.G.Dever and the so-called 'new archaeology' in the United States!) is what we might call a 'sociological' and 'economic' reclassification of the discoveries. In the absence of political, economic and historical texts, archaeology can provide evidence of ethnic and sociological changes which have taken place; it can give first-hand information about the economy, about demography, states of health, production, food, or the use of domestic animals by the inhabitants of a particular area, thus allowing synchronous and diachronous comparisons with other areas. This is work which for the most part is still to be done and will take at least a generation, if not more; it should be embarked on as a matter of principle when new excavations are planned. So far, archaeologists have been chiefly interested in chronological problems, in an attempt to reconstruct the history of a place; the fact that such attempts have produced very inconsistent results suggests that we should try another approach, in which in all probability new discoveries can be made.

5.6 And it is specifically here (see Appendix I below) that archaeology is in the process of demonstrating a substantial change in the transition from the Bronze Age to the Iron Age (thirteenth to twelfth centuries BC): the mosaic of city states in the plains and the largely uninhabited hill-country was supplemented and partly replaced by hundreds of agricultural and pastoral settlements in the hill-country, with little or no fortification.

6 One of the facts that we can take to have been established by modern biblical and Near Eastern scholars is that, as far as we can trace their history, the tribes of Israel were constituted as such in Canaan, i.e. after the settlement of those groups which came to make them up. We have seen the obstacles that stand in the way of an exact and detailed reconstruction of events, but some facts seem to be reasonably certain:[38]

6.1 We know of the existence of a 'mountain of Judah', the hill-country which extends from Jerusalem southwards until it reaches the northern Negeb; and of a 'a desert of Judah', the region which falls from the northern Negeb towards the Dead Sea (cf. Josh.11.21; 20.7; 21.11; II Chron.27.4; Judg.1.16; Ps.63.1). This is interesting because we know that the first area includes Hebron, a place which is said originally not to have been inhabited by the Judahites (above 2.4). Terms like 'Bethlehem in Judah' (Judg.17.7) indicate the region rather than the tribe.

6.2 In the central hill-country we know of the existence of a 'Mountain of Ephraim' (Josh.20.7; 21.21; cf. I Kings 4.8, where this is the name of one of Solomon's districts – and there are other passages). Probably this included the greater part of the central hill-country. Benjamin also appears as a district in I Kings 4.18.

6.3 There is a 'Mountain of Naphthali' in Galilee (Josh.20.7; I Kings 4.15, where it appears as a district of Solomon). In this connection we have numerous places with the designation 'of Naphtali' , e.g. Kedesh-naphtali in Judg.4.5. In I Kings 4.16, both Asher and Issachar appear as districts of Solomon.

6.4 So it seems reasonably certain that at least some tribal names are directly derived from the names of the regions in which the tribes were formed, and are names which are continued in those of Solomon's districts. No regions are named after tribes, as the reader of the texts might suppose. If there are still some uncertainties, this is only because the names have not so far appeared in biblical texts.

6.5 It seems that only Dan gave its name to the territory which it occupied: the relevant texts in fact indicate that its capital originally had another name, Laish or Leshem (Josh.19.47; Judg.17-18).

7 Another problem which has interested scholars now for more than half a century is that of the common element which united the tribes of Israel once they had settled in their territories, the north under the name of 'Israel' (which later was also to be extended to the others), and

the south as Judah. One alternative designation for the north is 'house of Joseph'. We have already seen that Israel and Judah were probably originally distinct and separate entities (above, III.1.1). And it is here that we come up against the hypothesis of the 'tribal league', also, and wrongly (as we shall see), called the 'amphictyony'. This is a feature illuminated for the first time by Max Weber*, passim, who spoke of the 'confederacy' (*Eidgenossenschaft*), and by other authors at the end of the First World War and afterwards.[39] This view was then presented in a systematic form by M.Noth in one of his first, and rightly famous, works. Despite its clearly hypothetical character, Noth's theory has held the field for more than thirty years and still has a number of supporters even now, though all of them have their reservations. However, in some respects it has proved to be increasingly problematical.

Select bibliography: M.Noth, *Das System der zwölf Stämme Israels*, BWANT IV, 1, Stuttgart 1930; *Pentateuchal Traditions*, passim; and other later writings by him; A.Alt, *Die Staatenbildung der Israeliten in Palästina*, Leipzig 1930 = *KS* II, 1-65; G.Buccellati, *Cities and Nations...*; E.Smend, 'Zur Frage nach der altisraelitischen Amphiktyonie', *EvTh* 31, 1971, 613-30; this has, however, been disputed by G.Fohrer, 'Altes Testament-"Amphikyonie" und "Bund"', *TLZ* 91, 1966, 801-16, 893-904; id.,*Studien*, BZAW 115, Berlin 1969, 84-119; A.D.H.Mayes, *Israel in the Period of the Judges*, SBT II 29, London 1974, and in Hayes-Miller*, 297-308; R. de Vaux*, II, 695-716; G.Fohrer, *Theologische Grundstrukturen des Alten Testaments*, Berlin 1972, 211ff.; G.Weingreen, 'The Theory of the Amphictyony in Pre-Monarchial (sic!) Israel', *JANESCU* 5, 1973, 427-33; H.Weippert, 'Das geographische System der Stämme Israels', *VT* 23, 1973, 76-89; K.Namiki, 'Reconsideration of the Twelve-Tribe System of Israel', *AJBI* 2, 1976, 29-59 (with synoptic tables); P.Lemche, 'The Greek "Amphictyony" – Could it be a Prototype for the Israelite Society in the Period of the Judges?', *JSOT* 4, 1977, 48-59; C.H.J. de Geus, *The Tribes of Israel*, Assen 1976; O. Bächli, *Amphiktyonie im Alten Testament*, Basle 1977; F.Crüsemann, *Der Widerstand gegen das Königtum*, WMANT 45, Neukirchen 1978, 10-28; C.Meyers, 'Of Seasons and Soldiers: A Topological Appraisal of the Premonarchical Tribes of Galilee', *BASOR* 252, 1983, 47-59.

7.1 As I have already stressed on many occasions, the biblical tradition which claims to be normative presents for the period of the conquest and that immediately following the image of an 'Israel' which operates as a single group, on a large scale. The theory reappears, as we shall see in the next chapter, in connection with the period of the 'judges'. In both cases its historicity seems problematical.

7.1.1 The unitary character of Israel, according to the official theory, is counterbalanced by its division into what we call 'tribes': the Hebrew terms are *šebet* and, more rarely, *maṭṭeh*. Both mean 'staff' or 'rod' or simply objects which have that shape; again, they are virtually synonymous. I have briefly stressed the sociological problems in translating them 'tribe' (above 4.2.5).

7.1.2 One thing is relatively certain: for ancient Israel the 'tribe' was made up of people who had a common ancestor, an eponymous hero, in this case a son of Jacob. The members of a tribe thus accepted one another as kindred in the broadest sense of the term. However, we know that genealogical concepts of this kind do not reflect so much a fact as a social position; they are a status symbol (above V.2.3.1). St Paul regarded himself as a member of the tribe of Benjamin when one could no longer speak of the tribe in any way in the social sense of the term (Rom.11.1f.; Phil.3.5).

7.2 Now the most interesting attempt to combine the biblical tradition with the information obtained from modern research is certainly that made by Noth in 1930; he never abandoned it but kept putting it forward again in a revised form. Even shortly before his premature death in 1968 he still thought that he could present an up-to-date version of his hypothesis,[40] though in the meantime it had been questioned by the majority of critics.

7.2.1 The analogy which Noth put forward and developed systematically, after others had made similar proposals, took its starting point in the ancient Hellenic and Italic amphictyonies. These were unions of intrinsically autonomous groups around the cult of a common sanctuary, i.e. something like sacred alliances. And it is precisely this element which Noth also detected in the lists of the tribes in the Old Testament: lists of the male children of Jacob in Gen.29-30, and lists of tribes as they appear in Num.1; 26. These lists of the names of members could vary, but the number twelve remained constant, like the sons of Jacob. Noth made another important distinction: the lists which indicate that Levi was still a tribe were earlier, and the lists in which Levi either did not appear or appeared only as a priestly caste, without a particular tribal territory, were later. In Gen. 49 Levi still appears as a tribe, whereas in Deut.33 it only exercises priestly functions.

7.2.2 The main parallel in the West is provided by the amphictyonies of Apollo at Delphi and by Demeter at Phyle; they were composed of tribes opposed to the city-state. Then there are also Etruscan and Italic amphictyonies. However, we also find similar structures among neighbouring peoples (cf. Gen.22.20-24; 25.2,13-16; 36.10-14, also characterized by a number of members which remains constant).

7.2.3 For Noth, the real history of Israel begins with the birth of the tribal league, and that is why he starts his account with the league, regarding the narratives which precede it as 'traditions of the league' (cf. above, II.5.2). He has recently been followed by G.Buccellati (1967), while A.Malamat (*Die Frühgeschichte*, 1983) arrives at similar results beginning from different presuppositions.

7.2.3.1 As far as we know, all the the amphictyonies took the form of a union of the tribes or groups around a common sanctuary by means of the institution of an alliance; each tribe was then responsible for the upkeep of the sanctuary for one month in the year.

7.2.3.2 Furthermore, each member was obliged to provide adequate representation whenever the assembly discussed matters of mutual interest.

7.2.3.3 Again, the central sanctuary seems to have formed a first step in the direction of unity, this time no longer conceived only in religious, but also in political terms.

7.2.4 According to Noth (and the theme was soon taken up again by G.von Rad, for whom the league was no longer a working hypothesis but an obvious theory),[41] the Israelite amphictyony was founded in circumstances described in a text which was basically thought to be old (Josh.24). Here the 'house of Joseph', the last group to arrive in Palestine, persuaded the other tribes to accept the worship of YHWH, thus giving rise to the tribal league and making Shechem its central sanctuary. Here the representatives of the tribes mentioned in Num.1.5-15, who bore the title of *nāśī*, literally 'prince', met at more or less regular intervals.

7.2.5 The most important object in the cult was the sacred ark (above III.6.1.2), probably the central shrine of the tribes in the narrower sense (whereas the place where they met could change). This explains why we find the ark at different sanctuaries.

7.2.6 One of the functions of the league – and here we find its political relevance – was that of making decisions in any disputes which might arise among its members. One instance appears in Judg.19-21; here the tribes proceed to punish Benjamin, which is guilty of having refused to hand over to the tribunal of the league the perpetrators of a particularly savage crime. The nearest phenomenological parallel, even if it comes from much later, is that of the Amphissaean war, when a member of a Greek amphictyony was punished for refusing to hand over those who had committed sacrilege. The war, fought in 339 BC, led to the punishment and expulsion of the guilty party.

7.2.7 On this theory, the so-called 'minor judges' will have been the officials of the league, charged with implementing mutual projects.

7.2.8 The days of the alliance were numbered in Israel once it proved inadequate to cope with the concentrated attacks of the Philistines and the peoples of the East. Then it had to yield to the monarchy. However, the monarchy inherited a number of features of the tribal league, for example in its early years the precarious status of the person who bore the title of king, which was clearly more dependent on something like charismatic gifts (a term which I use here with the significance attached to it by M.Weber) than on clearly defined institutions.[42] As I have argued in the past, to begin with the monarchy was rather like the institution of the dictatorship in the Roman Republic, a position which arose from temporary needs which more democratic forms of government could not cope with adequately, and which increasingly became the foundation for the rise of the empire as a result of the prolongation of the position throughout the life of its holder.

7.3 Noth's proposal, always meant as a hypothesis, originally had marked advantages which it still retains:

7.3.1 First of all it succeeds in combining the biblical tradition and modern research in a single complex. This also explains why the theory was accepted virtually *en bloc*, almost without criticism or hesitation: even W.F.Albright in the United States and his pupils[43] adopted it unconditionally, despite their other criticisms of Alt and M.Noth, going on to put particular stress on the aspect of the covenant which is supposed to have united the tribes among themselves and with God.[44]

7.3.2 Again, it was, and still is, a brilliant solution to the historical problem of a period about which we otherwise know little or nothing.

7.3.3 It also provided a reasonable explanation of the origin of the earliest sources of the Pentateuch and Deuteronomistic history,[45] and perhaps even of the milieu in which Deuteronomy came to be formed, and therefore also of the origins of Josiah's reform.[46]

7.3.4 It also gave a clear indication of where we should seek the origin of Israelite worship, of the struggle between Canaanite religion and syncretism, of Israel's monotheistic faith and the concept of the covenant.

7.3.5 Moreover, for G.Buccellati[47] the league was the institution which allowed the transition from the settlement to the state; in one way it already actually formed a kind of state.

7.4 However, in recent decades the disadvantages of the proposal have also become increasingly clear.

7.4.1 First of all, the very concept of the 'amphictyony', which is already an obscure term for the classical world, as Lemche has recently pointed out, presupposes that the members reside around the sanctuary, and that is also indicated by the etymology of the term. Now it has often been supposed that such a sanctuary served as a meeting-place for Israel (for example, by those who identify it directly with the ark, which will have been moved from one temple to another), but no convincing proof has ever been given, nor does that seem likely in the present state of the sources. Rather, the Hebrew Bible stresses the regularity in the number of members (though even this does not always happen in practice, cf. also 7.4.3), a feature which is of secondary importance in the Greek and Italian amphictyonies; here the number of the members could also vary. For this reason Buccellati, who otherwise defends the concept of the tribal league,[48] proposes that the term amphictyony should be dropped because it is inappropriate. That would leave only the phenomenological parallel, which is clearly essential.

7.4.2 The distinction between the lists of tribes, depending on whether Levi is mentioned as a tribe or as a priestly caste, is valid on the level of the history of the traditions, but not in historical terms. Moreover, Num.1 and 26 are not ancient texts but, notoriously, belong to P and reflect later priestly adaptations which favour Judah and its position after the exile generally. Again, the problem of Levi as a tribe or as a priesthood is particularly complex, and there are reasons for claiming that the levitical priesthood has nothing to do with a tribe of Levi, on the grounds that this last never existed in history. The biblical tradition which seeks to explain the transition from ethnic group to priesthood makes more sense if it is understood as a later rationalization rather than as a recollection in the tradition of real events.

7.4.3 Nor does the number twelve, which, as has often been observed, in fact denotes totality and completeness rather than an actual figure, appear as consistently as Noth would like: the song of Deborah (Judg.5), the earliest phase of which cannot be dated earlier than the ninth century BC,[49] mentions only ten tribes, and Judah and Simeon are certainly absent from the list; perhaps also Gad (if we cannot identify it with Gilead), Manasseh (provided that it is not identified with Machir), and of course Levi. On the one hand that excludes all the south (which is what we would expect), but on the other hand, if we include the south, it produces a number larger than twelve, if all the tribes we know are mentioned. Noth never dealt with this problem raised by the song of Deborah.

7.4.4 Another of Noth's theories is that the figure of Saul is little different from that of the judges who preceded him;[50] however, there is a basic shift between the judges and the first king, a break in continuity with the past.

7.4.5 Finally, there seems to be no justification for the speculations about the instruments and officials of the league which were current in the 1950s and 1960s, giving the league a truly bureaucratic organization.

7.5 Some fundamental conclusions follow from all this.

7.5.1 In a later period Israel regarded its structure at the time before the monarchy as having been a tribal alliance and reconstructed it in those terms. In some cases it also tried to include Judah, but the whole of the south seems to be absent from Judg.5, which is certainly an early text. So it seems evident that the memory of the league is based on different and often contradictory traditions.

7.5.2 On the other hand, the hypothesis of a tribal league does not appear manifestly absurd or anachronistic; so much so, that Buccellati considers it the institution by means of which Israel came into being as a state. A scholar like Rudolf Smend, who is certainly no conservative, rightly indicated that to rule out the theory of the league would leave us with virtually no information about a period which the tradition of Israel seems to have considered formative and therefore basic to the history or at least the prehistory of the people. And in even more recent times, a critical scholar like F.Crüsemann has also pointed out that a reappraisal of the hypothesis which led to its rejection would leave an effective void in the earliest history of Israel, a void which he would prefer to fill by comparing Israel before the monarchy with the so-called 'segmentary' societies of Black Africa. (I have already referred to this theory above, III.6.5.) In that case Israel would not have been directed by any central institution, but would have had an essentially centrifugal tendency, constrained to provide itself with central instruments of government only under the pressure of external stimuli.[51]

7.5.3 However, it is clearly impossible to verify either the theory of the tribal league or that of the segmentary society in any way. The former has the obvious advantage of having the biblical tradition behind it; the latter is based on a comparison with analogous structures in contemporary societies, comparisons which have clear limits given the chronological and geographical distances involved. Still, it remains sufficiently certain that Noth's hypothesis, especially as it was developed later, cannot bear the weight which is placed on it. Meyers' recent study accepts the existence of a tribal league in Galilee in the period before the monarchy.

7.5.4 As I already stressed at the beginning of this study (II.4.2.3), the theory of a proto-historical tribal league, a kind of theocratic government around a central sanctuary which is defined in only very vague terms, corresponds much more closely with the post-exilic situation, where the one central sanctuary is now a reality. It does not matter at this point that the post-exilic hierocracy must be dated more than 200 years after the date which is traditionally attributed to it (below XII.5.3.5). It seems only logical that the concept of the tribal league would be taken up, revised and reformulated at this particular period. However, we have no information about whether it ever really existed in history; moreover, in the present state of research it is not even possible to weigh up the probabilities.

VIII

JUDGES

1 In the historical scheme of the Hebrew Bible, the book of Judges follows the narratives of the conquest. The theme which the work seeks to present to its readers is that of the loss of the territory gained in the previous operations as a result of enemies at home (the Canaanites of the city-states) and abroad (the neighbouring peoples). The Philistines do not appear anywhere, so we could suppose that these are traditions either prior to their arrival in the region or perhaps arising out of a fairly precise redaction, intent on avoiding anachronisms, unlike for example the redaction of the patriarchal narratives (above V.1.2.4).

Bibliography: Since I have recently written a commentary on the book of Judges I shall confine myself to referring to this work, adding studies which have appeared since its publication. J.A.Soggin, *Judges*; D.W.Gooding, 'The Composition of the Book of Judges', *EI*, 1982, 70*-79*.

1.1.1 The title of the book might deceive the reader unfamiliar with the meaning of the term *šōpēṭ* in the Western Semitic world: the judges of Israel are in fact virtually never involved in activities connected with administering the law. Only once is this the case, in 4.4f., where Deborah is acting in the setting of a court of law; but that happens before she is even called to be a judge! On the contrary, the functions of the judges always seem to be connected in some way with government; at least, that is the case with those who for convenience are called 'major' judges. These always function as leaders in a political or military context.

1.1.2 Other judges are called 'minor' judges; we have brief notes about them which are anecdotal and reminiscent of folklore, which do not tell us precisely what their office was or why their stories have been handed down. A few years ago[1] I tried to explain this by conjecturing that their function was similar to that of the 'eponymi' in the Punic world, i.e. that it was connected with dating; thus we should suppose that, as at Carthage, dating would be done by means of phrases like, 'in the days of the judge (or the judges) x and y', but here we cannot do more than guess.

1.1.3 However, as I have just said, unless the reader has been forewarned, the translation 'judges' does not reflect the real situation, even if it is as old as the LXX rendering κριταί. The Hebrew term *šōpēṭ*, plural *šōpᵉṭīm*, also appears in Phoenicia and Carthage and has been transcribed as *suffetes* by the Roman historians of the time of the Punic wars, where it denotes the chief magistrates of the Carthaginians. This connection of the root with the supreme magistrature already appears among the West Semitic semi-nomads of whom there is evidence at Mari on the Euphrates in the eighteenth century BC, in Ugarit and also in Hebrew, though there it is an archaism. In other words, in the reconstruction which Israel tended to make of its own past, the members of the tribal league will have elected a leader with full powers in cases of grave danger; his task was to confront the danger and to coordinate communal forces. The conferring of full powers evidently signified that the tribes renounced all their own autonomy and independence, though only for a certain time. And, as some authors would suppose, it was precisely from the roots of this institution that the monarchy came into being, with Saul as a transitional figure. However, we have also seen how problematical this reconstruction of events is: obviously, what Israel thought of its own past is one thing, and what we can (or rather, most of the time, cannot, because we do not have adequate sources) reconstruct of it with scientific critical-historical methods is another.

1.1.4 Now the narratives which originally formed the nucleus of Judges have been subjected to a further revision which attempts to find 'charismatic' figures, figures endowed with the 'spirit of YHWH'. This definition is clearly meant in a very different sense from the one that the term acquired much later in the primitive Christian church, and even more different from the way in which the term is used in some modern religious movements. It is used with the connotations that it had for Max Weber.[2] The following texts are involved: Judg.3.10; 6.34; 8.3; 11.29; 13.25; 14.6,19; 15.14; all of them say that the 'spirit of YHWH' came upon the person of one of the judges. This explanation clearly seeks to remove the human element from their role and to attribute everything to a direct divine intervention. So rather than being tested and recognized by the assembly of the league, these leaders are invested with power conferred directly by God. Clearly these are no reminiscences of a past era, but a theological explanation of what will originally have been presented as a purely secular fact: that some allied groups will have chosen a common leader in a particular difficult situation. This revised view of the judges fits in perfectly with the central theory of the 'body' of the book (2.6-16.31): here each individual episode is framed by an introduction and an epilogue. The former explains the appearance of the person concerned as the divine response to the cry of grief which goes up from the oppressed people, in terms clearly drawn from Deuteronomistic theology; moreover, this oppression is said to be a divine punishment for the people's guilt in that God himself delivered them into the hands of their enemies. This example is enough to show how the Deuteronomistic historians worked.

1.2 Chronology is one of the major difficulties, as we find elsewhere in the legends of the proto-history of Israel. I have dealt with it in detail in my commentary, so that it wil be enough to present a brief summary of the question here.

Bibliography: Soggin, *Judges*, 6-12; W.Brueggemann, 'Social Criticism and Social Vision in the Deuteronomic Formula of the Judges', in *Die Botschaft und die Boten. Festschrift Hans-Walter Wolff*, Neukirchen 1981, 101-14.

1.2.1 The chronology of the judges as presented by the book is given either in stereotyped figures (the number forty, its multiples or divisions, as usually happens in the Deuteronomistic history) or in figures which are now quoted out of context. The former go with the historical and theological reconstruction undertaken by Dtn and Dtr to explain to the generations of the exile and the return the reasons for the deportation, the fall of the reigning house (which was never to rise again) in 587/86, and finally the loss of political independence: these were national tragedies which seemed to annul all the divine promises of the past and instead to support the theory that the God of Israel had been defeated by the conquerors. The Deuteronomistic history argues that, on the contrary, the judgment was a product of the strength of YHWH rather than his weakness: God had wanted to punish the people for its unfaithfulness, which could already be seen in its proto-history, even before the beginning of the monarchy. And it is this theological doctrine of history that is the chief motivation behind the accounts of the judges presented here.[3]

1.2.2 Now if it is no longer possible to reconstruct a chronology of Israel before the monarchy, we can at least try to see in what way and on what criteria the material handed down to us has been collected. In my commentary I have given first of all the chronological information which appears in Judges and then tried to make a systematic reconstruction of the way in which it fits into the general context of the chronology from the patriarchs to the first kings.[4] In this way it is possible to see how we arrive at the various figures, with very few left over.

2.1 A first enemy, mentioned in 3.7-11, bears the name Cushan-rishathaim and is confronted by the judge Othniel. Despite attempts to identify the former of these figures, the narrative does not seem to have any foundation in the history of the ancient Near East.

2.2 The episode of Eglon and the judge Ehud (3.12-30) seems more important.

2.2.1 The account smacks of the Grand Guignol, with elements of a scatological humour which is rather heavy for our taste. Its topography is not very precise; Jericho is not mentioned by name, but is paraphrased as the 'City of Palms' (v.13), perhaps to make the story fit in with the narrative in Josh.6. Ethnically, too, the story does not seem to be very precise; as well as the Moabites, the Amalekites and the Ammonites are both mentioned in the same verse.

2.2.2 There is also often a lack of incisiveness in the description of people; the enemy appears ridiculous and clumsy; he is fat and stupid, with a burlesque name that one could translate 'little calf'. In fact here it is precisely those features which are the main literary characteristics of the account which make it historically suspect.

2.2.3 So it is difficult to recover any historical information from the story, for example to establish whether at a given period of its history, and certainly close to the time of its settlement, Moab had tried to advance westwards so as also to take in the territory west of the Jordan around Jericho, and to what extent it had taken possession of the territory in Transjordan which the biblical tradition attributes, rather, to Reuben (above, VII.2.10.2). On the other hand, if we eliminate the Deuteronomistic framework from this account, we have an almost complete narrative, perhaps lacking some details at the beginning and rather more at the end. It is difficult to say how far Ehud could be considered the main character of a heroic narrative; at present the preponderance of humorous features suggests that we should be cautious.

2.3 Shamgar ben Anath is an unknown person (here it is not easy to establish whether the name of the Canaanite deity indicates descent from her or, more probably, the fact that the person came from one of the many places which had this as part of a composite name). Despite these difficulties, Shamgar is interesting because it is with him that we have the first mention of the Philistines. He defeated them. The reference could be to a Canaanite alliance with Israel to fight against the common enemy, just as later we find a Canaanite coalition, probably led by a Philistine, fighting against Israel (chs.4-5; below 3). However, we cannot establish any more precise details: even the origin of the name is uncertain, so much so that some scholars think it is of Hurrian derivation, while others argue for its Canaanite origin. So Shamgar is a problematical figure on the historical level.

3 By contrast, the battle fought in the Jezreel valley between Israel

and a Canaanite coalition made up of members who are not mentioned by name, under a certain Sisera, is an episode which is very important for its political implications and the deductions that can be made from it. It is described in chs.4-5.

Bibliography: D.F.Murray, 'Narrative Structure and Technique in the Deborah-Barak Story (Judges IV 4-22)', *SVT* 30, 1979, 155-89; A.J.Hauser, 'Judges 5: Parataxis in Hebrew Poetry', *JBL* 99, 1980, 23-41; Soggin, *Judges*, 60-101; id., 'Bemerkungen zum Deboralied', *TLZ* 106, 1981, 625-39; id., 'Amalek und Ephraim, Richter 5,14', *ZDPV* 98, 1982, 58-62.

3.1 For the details, here too the reader must consult the works listed. I shall content myself to drawing attention to the following features:

3.1.1 Although chs.4-5 obviously refer to the same event, they differ in their lists of the groups involved in the battle. In 4.6,10 only Zebulun and Naphtali are mentioned, whereas in 5.14ff., in addition to them we have Ephraim, Benjamin, Machir (perhaps Manasseh) and Issachar; Reuben, Gilead (perhaps Gad), Dan and Asher, however, did not reply to the summons. So in the second instance we have a total of ten tribes, with the absence of the whole of the south and of Levi.

3.1.2 The topography of the battle varies from one version to the other. 4.6 mentions the environs of Mount Tabor (coord.137-232), on the south-eastern border of the two tribes involved; however, 5.19 speaks of the neighbourhood of Taanach (coord.171-214), i.e. about thirty miles further to the south-west as the crow flies, not an insignificant distance to cover on foot or in a war chariot.

3.1.3 In 4.14 there is an attempt to make the battle an episode in a holy war, and so the battle proper is described in colourless terms; however, this approach does not appear in 5, where the battle is described in epic and heroic tones.

3.1.4 Thus the episode is narrated twice, but with remarkable differences, and it is not always possible to say which of the two accounts reflects the earliest tradition. As a text the song is clearly the earlier, but matters are not in fact so sure at the level of history and tradition.

3.1.5 In 5.6-8 we have some useful information about the reason for the battle, that is, if we accept the translation that I have suggested for this difficult text (see the studies cited above). If it was the case that before the battle, 'the traders had ceased, and those who went on journeys chose devious routes', and the leaders of Israel could not cope with the emergency, then evidently the aim of the battle (and probably of the war of which it was part, though we hear nothing of that) was to re-establish communications between the tribes in the central hill-country and those in Galilee, communications which passed through the plain and thus through the unoccupied territories of the city-states.

3.1.6 The details of the death of Sisera also vary from one version to another (cf. 4.22; 5.26); however, in this case it seems probable that the former has misunderstood the difficult text and archaic and poetic expressions of the latter.

3.1.7 Another obscure feature is the relationship of 4.2, with Jabin of Hazor, who bears the improbable title 'king of Canaan', to Josh.11.1ff. This is probably a Deuteronomistic editorial addition.

3.2 The two texts do not give us any chronological information, so it is difficult to find a place in which to locate the battle. The majority of scholars put forward a date about 1125 BC, without giving any substantial reason. However, attention should be paid to the proposal made by A.D.H. Mayes at the end of the 1960s and confirmed in the 1970s[5] that the battle should be removed from this indeterminate context and put, rather, in the context of the struggle between Israel and the Philistines.

3.2.1 The starting point for this view is the name of the leader, Sisera, which is certainly not Semitic and probably Luvian in origin, i.e. from an area in Asia Minor. In that case it would seem that he should probably be connected with the 'Sea Peoples' (above, III.5.2) and that Israel's enemy in the battle should be identified as a a Canaanite coalition led by a Philistine.

3.2.2 In that case, however, it seems reasonable to put the battle shortly before the one narrated in I Sam.4, i.e. in the last decades of the second millennium BC, about a century after the date mentioned above. I Sam.4 describes how Israel suffered a heavy defeat at the hand of the Philistines in which even the ark was captured by the enemy; this marked the beginning of the process which in a short time was to lead Israel to become a monarchical state (above III.1.5.2).

3.2.3 In other words, Israel will have originally won a crushing victory over the coalition, not so much by any superiority on its part as by an unforeseen factor: a heavy downpour (something that is very rare in the region, cf. above I.4.2) will have hindered any movement of the Canaanite and Philistine war chariots, turning the battlefield into a bog. There was no alternative for the occupants than to flee on foot, only to be overtaken and massacred either by the Israelites or by nomadic groups which circulated in the area (cf. the episode of Sisera and Jael, 4.15ff.; 5.20ff.). This is the only possible explanation for the flight of the defeated enemy on foot, when the use of their chariots would have given them an evident advantage. It is not surprising that the event was considered a miracle by Israel.

3.2.4 However, as I have said, the Israelite success must have been short-lived; communications between the centre and Galilee seem to have been re-established, but the Canaanites and Philistines soon recovered (above III.4.3), and the monarchy arose out of the heavy defeat. The battle on the heights of Gilboa in which Saul and three of his sons lost their lives (above III.4.4) and the army of Israel was completely defeated also shows that there was almost certainly an alliance between the Canaanite city-states and the Philistines or at the least that relationships were so good that the Philistines were able to pass freely through the region and obtain provisions for their troops. So they could attack Israel whenever and wherever they thought it most opportune. This situation only came to an end, in circumstances unknown to us, at the time of David (above III.1.3).

4. Judges 6-8 describes Gideon's actions against Midianite bandits and their allies from Transjordan who invaded the territory of Israel to destroy the crops and steal the cattle.

Select bibliography: Soggin, *Judges*, 102-61.

4.1 The Gideon traditions present considerable difficulties to anyone attempting to analyse them, and for details the reader must consult the commentaries and monographs. The main problem is posed by the variety of themes and motives they contain, often only very loosely connected with Gideon, together with the manifest contradictions which arise from later elaborations.

4.1.1 A first insertion into the narrative is the account of the found-ation of the sanctuary of Ophrah (perhaps *eṭ-ṭayībe*, coord. 192-223, or *'appūlā*, coord.177-223)[6] in 6.11-24. This is a tradition which appears to be pre-Deuteronomistic, since Josiah's reform (below XI.4) eliminated this kind of sanctuary, and it would be difficult to explain any Deutero-nomistic interest in the text.

4.1.2 Another theme is that of Gideon's fight against syncretism: he demolishes and desecrates the local sanctuary of Ba'al (6.25-32). This feature could be ancient, even if it is probably not earlier than the time of Elijah and Elisha, when the problem of syncretism seems to have begun to be acute (below IX.3.4.1.1). However, as the narrative now stands, before beginning his campaign Gideon performs a series of acts of purification and propitiation which qualify him before God and men as a hero of the faith.

4.1.3 Another complicating factor in the story is that the hero has a double name – Gideon and Jerubbaal. The latter is important because of the episode of Abimelech which follows (ch.9). This name would have been given him after the desecration of the sanctuary of Ba'al on the basis of a popular etymology which connected him with the action he had performed.

4.2 The battle against the Midianites and their allies is described only after we have heard of a series of hesitations and postponements.

However, literary and theological factors rather than any other will have prompted the delay in the time of attack. First of all there is the need to find a place within the pan-Israelite tradition for the form of the tradition that was evidently handed down, to the effect that the battle had been fought only by Gideon and his 300 Abiezrites (7.1-8); then glory had to be given only to God, and not to human strength and skill. Once the problem has been resolved, in an equally literary way, the battle can finally begin.

4.3 In 7.16-22 Gideon goes over to the attack, using a stratagem which prompts the Midianities to fight among themselves and the surivivors to flee in terror.

4.3.1 The starting point for the operation is the spring of Harod (in present-day Hebrew *'ēn ḥªrōd*, and in Arabic *'ein jālūd*, coord.184-217), above Gideon's camp, and the hill of Moreh (probably *jebel nebī-dāḥī*, coord.184-225), with the Midianite camp at its foot, i.e. on the northern spurs of the central hill-country. The topographical details are not always precise and the text is often corrupt; what is said here is based on a reconstruction of the text.

4.3.2 The defeated enemy is pursued across Cisjordan and Transjordan, and its leaders are killed. The text envisages a campaign which covers a considerable amount of ground, if we can identify the Karkor of 8.4-35; 10 with *qarqār* near Petra (coord.205-020) or even with *qaraqīr* in *wādī sirḥan*, in the northern Hegiaz, on the great caravan route.

4.4 At the end of the enterprise, returning home in victory, Gideon is said to have refused the crown offered to him (8.22-32).

4.5 It is difficult to make a historical assessment of Gideon's enterprise. It is interesting to see how the text itself rules out the official pan-Israelite theory (7.1ff.) and reduces the battle and the expedition to a purely local episode, limited to the groups in the area. Moreover, there should be no difficulty in accepting that certain groups in Israel which had just settled will have had problems with other populations (here presented essentially as groups of bandits coming from Transjordan) over traditional rights of grazing and transhumance; these rights will have been put in doubt by the settlement of a new ethnic nucleus. Since this was a question on which the subsistence of these groups depended, no wonder that life-and-death struggles developed. So it is hardly strange that an episode from these struggles should have been handed down, even if the tradition now has a notably different tone from that of the original.

5 Judges 9, which is about Abimelech, king of Shechem, is set in a totally different context. To begin with, the protagonist has nothing to do with the judges, but is the ruler of a Canaanite city-state for which there is also evidence outside the Bible, especially in the el-'Amarna letters; moreover, he does not hold any position in Israel.

Bibliography: S.Springer, *Neuinterpretationen im Alten Testament*, Stuttgart 1979, 16ff. (vv.26-29); J.A.Soggin, *Judges*, 162-94; V.Fritz, 'Abimelech und Sichem in Jdc IX', *VT* 32, 1982, 129-44; N.H.Rösel, 'Überlegungen zu "Abimelech und Sichem in Jdc IX"', *VT* 33, 1983, 500-3; E.F.Campbell, 'Judges 9 and Biblical Archaeology', in *The Word of the Lord Shall Go Forth – Essays in Honor of D.N.Freedman*, Philadelphia 1983, 263-71.

5.1.1 The redactors of the book of Judges inserted the episode of Abimelech at this point because they identified Gideon with Jerubbaal (above, 4.1.3), who was in turn the father of the hero of the narrative. The transition to ch.9 now takes place in 8.29, a text which associates Gideon-Jerubbaal with the place Shechem (present-day *tell-balāṭa*, coord. 176-179, an eastern suburb of Nablus), through the figure of the anonymous Shechemite *pīlegeš* of Jerubbaal. The term *pīlegeš* is usually translated 'concubine', but is certainly to be connected with a superior form of concubine since the woman was considered to be a legitimate wife, though of a lower class, and the union conveyed special rights on descendants.[7]

5.1.2 This kind of connection between people and narratives of very different kinds seems frequent throughout Near Eastern and early Western literature, and is almost always secondary.

5.1.3 Abimelech became king over the city state by means of a plot in which, with the complicity of the assembly of the notables of Shechem (above I.8.1), he is said to have succeeded in eliminating the seventy sons of Gideon, his half-brothers,[8] thus ascending the throne.

5.1.4 So the strange characteristic of this story, compared with other narratives in Judges, is its essentially political theme: a plot which leads to the coronation of a sovereign; an assembly which has the right to decide who will be their new king (the presumption is clearly that the throne was vacant and that there were no successors); and a series of rebellions against the new king, in the last of which he is killed. The scene of the episode is a city-state, Shechem, and the main characters are on the one hand the new king and on the other the assembly, which seems to have quite specific rights in the constitutional field, e.g. those of nominating or deposing a ruler. So it seems probable that at least in the earliest stratum this is an account which could go back to an old chronicle of events and which allows us at least a brief glimpse into the internal constitution of a Canaanite city-state at the time of the Israelite conquest or soon after.[9] However, this tradition now seems to have been substantially elaborated by novelistic features and a fairly discreet Deuteronomistic redaction, to which we probably owe the transmission of this important text.

5.2.1 Having obtained power in this way, the king soon antagonized the city assembly for reasons which we can now only guess at; and the break was followed by open rebellion. Verse 22 gives us some interesting chronological information: the reign is said to have lasted only three years. In any case, the king succeeded in quelling the rebellion by two expeditions against the city (vv.30-41, 42-45) which left it in ruins.

5.2.2 The king himself then fell, killed during the siege of a western (or northern? see below) suburb of Shechem, the Tower of Shechem (*migdal šᵉkem*, vv.46ff.), which is certainly to be distinguished from the capital, though it was part of the territory of the city state.[10] I have tried to identify it, purely hypothetically, with *tell ṣufār* (*ṣufān*), situated on the western limits of present-day Nablus (coord.173-182).[11] Now, after the campaign of excavations on Mount Ebal, north of Nablus (coord.182-177) in 1982 and 1983, I could be persuaded that it should be identified, rather, with a complex consisting of an enclosed area containing a temple-tower (*migdāl*) dating from the beginning of the Iron Age. However, we need to await the publication of the information by the Israeli expedition (oral communication from B.Mazar).

5.3 The excavations carried out by the American Drew-McCormick and ASOR expedition in the 1950s and 1960s attest the destruction of Shechem towards the end of the twelfth century BC;[12] and we must seriously take into account the possibility that this was the one described in the present chapter.

6 With Jephthah, we are taken for the first time in the Book of Judges to Transjordan, to the northern region which according to tradition was the scene of battles between Israelites and Ammonites. The texts are in Judg.10.6-12.6 and have Jephthah as their main character.

Bibliography: J.A.Soggin, *Judges* 201-22; H.(N.) Rösel, 'Jephta und das Problem der Richter', *Bibl* 61, 1980, 251-5.

6.1.1 As things stand, the places mentioned at the beginning of the text, in 10.17, have not yet been identified.[13] Tob in 11.3 is often identified, but always hypothetically, with present-day *eṭ-ṭayībeh*, coord.266-218.

6.1.2 Not only are the topographical details vague, but the story also has an anecdotal character; it is rather like a fairy-tale. The hero, who has been driven out by the family because he is illegitimate (11.1-3), is later recalled and nominated commander of the troops of Israel. However, the Deuteronomistic prologue (10.6-16) contains reflections of a theological kind, and they occasionally appear elsewhere, though never in relation to the figure of the hero. We have no names of any Ammonites, in contrast to the accounts e.g. in I Sam.11.1ff; II Sam.10.1ff.

6.2 The way in which Jephthah is introduced seems rather contradictory; on the one hand he acts with great circumspection, and on the other we see him throwing caution to the winds.

6.2.1 He acts with circumspection when in 11.12-28 he enters into direct negotiations with the Ammonites, with the aim of settling the dispute with them peacefully. However, the text which describes the negotiations is a composition which essentially reflects Deut.2 and the last chapters of Numbers, features of which it tends to combine without noting the contradictions that ensue.[14] Theological reflection predominates in the narrative, evidently the product of consideration of the text of P, so that it is probably later than P. That makes it difficult to detect anything other than generalized historical, geographical and topographical features in this section: the whole passage seems to be an edifying novel rather than a narrative with a historical basis.

6.2.2 Jephthah throws caution to the winds when in 11.29-40 he vows to sacrifice the first person to come out of his house to meet him on his return. As we know, this fate befalls his only daughter, who is never mentioned by name. Here the narrator's interest evidently lies on the one hand in the family drama and on the other in the custom of lamenting the unfortuate girl, rather than in details connected with the history and the topography of events. So we hear of the battle and the victory only in 11.33; here, too, however, there are problems. It is impossible to infer anything from the text other than the probability that the battle was fought around Rabbath-ammon, present day Amman (coord.238-151), capital of the Hashemite Kingdom of Jordan.[15]

6.3 The story of Jephthah ends with an episode of civil war between Ephraim and Jephthah's group in which the latter are victorious. However, there are many obvious parallels with 8.1-3, and while in Judges 8 the account fits closely with the facts narrated, that is not the case here.

It does not make much sense to raise the question of historicity in cases like this, given that the traditions which describe them do not even seem to be ancient.

7 The legends which have grown up around the person of Samson take us into yet another context.

Bibliography: J.A.Soggin, *Judges*, 225-59; J.L.Crenshaw, *Samson*, Atlanta, Ga and London 1978; J.C.Exum, 'Aspects of Symmetry and Balance in the Samson Saga', *JSOT* 19, 1981, 3-29; R.Wenning, 'Der siebenlockige Samson', *BN* 17, 1982, 43-55; R.Mayer-Opificius, 'Simson, der sechslockige Held?', *UF* 14, 1982, 149-51.

The territory in which the events described take place is in what we have seen to be a problematical region, situated to the west of Benjamin (above VII.2.2.4). Samson himself almost always has grotesque, Pantagruel-esque features, and hardly ever seems to perform any of the functions which the other texts connect with the office of judge. The chronology is also confused: cf. 13.1 with 16.31. Nor is there ever any mention of the troops which the hero is supposed to have commanded in his work for Israel, and there is also a complete absence of the pan-Israelite approach which we have seen to be characteristic of the other episodes. So the whole complex gives the impression of being an artificial construction[16] rather than going back to ancient traditions, and that probably makes these texts relatively unimportant for the historian.

8 An episode which now appears as an appendix in Judges concerns the civil war between the league and Benjamin, which was guilty of having refused to hand over the perpetrators of a particularly violent crime. For the conquest by Dan of its territory in the north of the country (Judg.17; 18), cf. above VII.2.6.

Bibliography: S.Springer, *Neuinterpretationen im Alten Testament*, Stuttgart 1979, 19ff.; J.A.Soggin, *Judges*, 279-305; H.W.Jüngling, *Richter 19 -Plädoyer für das Königtum*, AnBibl 84, Rome 1981; S.Niditch, 'The "Sodomite" Theme in Judges 19-20: Family, Community and Social Disintegration', *CBQ* 44, 1982, 365-78.

8.1 At first sight this narrative seems to be a unity, a feature which appears to go far beyond the anecdotal character of some of its episodes. However, on closer consideration there seems to be at least one major contradiction.

8.1.1 The pro-monarchical formula in 19.1; 21.25, which already appears in the preceding episode (17.6; 18.1), is prompted by the story of the violence suffered by the Levite and his concubine (like that of the violence evident in Danite territory in the previous narrative), and suggests that under the monarchy, the guardian of law and order, such things no longer happened (nor would they have happened had the institution already existed then). While this view is compatible with the episode of the migration of Dan, in the present episode it clashes with the appearance in ch.20 of the tribal league, whose institutions watch zealously over order and public morality to the point of taking strongly repressive measures against those who might transgress the law.

8.1.2 There are also other discrepancies in the text: the great dispropo-rtion between the crime and the punishment, between the relatively petty offence and the number of those who are exterminated; the incongruity between the proceedings of a political kind, culminating in the civil war against Benjamin, and the eminently domestic question of the levite and his concubine (for her social position cf. above 5.1.1) and of the attack on the couple by a group of hooligans. Again, there is an obvious parallel between 19.22-28 and Gen.19, though in the latter case the theme is developed coherently; moreover, the symbolism of the woman who is cut in pieces is also an evident reflection of I Sam.11.9, but there the gesture is in its proper place and the invitation connected with it is clear: here its function seems doubtful. So the themes of Judg.19-21 seem to be largely secondary, a sign of the artificial character of the account.

8.2 On the other hand, the narrative of the civil war could have preserved the recollection of something that really happened (now, of course, revised by the tradition in various ways, to adapt it to different purposes). Benjamin was indeed a group famous for its bravery but, as a look at the map will show, it was caught between Ephraim, Judah and the city-state of Jerusalem, so that it could not expand in any way. It might therefore have developed a degree of aggressiveness towards its neighbours and have been semi-destroyed in a vain attempt to expand its own territory.[17] In that case the basis of the narrative might be an essentially political event which the tradition then translated first into individualistic categories of crime and punishment and later into praise of the order and security provided by the monarchy, and after its fall, by the tribal league.

8.2.1 Another feature in which we might perhaps encounter the memory of a real situation is that of the relations with Jabesh in Gilead (21.1-14). In I Sam.11 the messengers from the besieged town go straight to the tribe of Benjamin and are met there by Saul (here it should be noted how the concept of the tribal league acting together seems to be absent!); and again it is the people of Jabesh who give burial to the mutilated bodies of Saul and Jonathan (I Sam.31.11-13). These are features which support the hypothesis of a very close relationship between the city of Jabesh and the tribe of Benjamin. We do not know where the place may have been, perhaps *tell el-maqlūb*, coord.214-201; the *wādī yābiś*, a tributary on the left of the Jordan, coord.201-209, has preserved the name in Arabic down to the present day.

9 To conclude this chapter on the judges and to look back on the persons and events which the tradition connects with them I might point out:

9.1 The tradition now presents each judge as leader of the troops of all Israel; the only exceptions are Jephthah and – most notably – Samson.

9.2 The people who are nominated judge come from different tribes, as though there were a kind of rotation between the individual groups, and each one of them in turn was responsible for providing a nomination for the supreme magistrature. It should be obvious that a concept of this kind is artificial; we need only imagine an emergency in which a judge had to be nominated quickly, to see how impossible it would have been to organize matters in accordance with a predetermined rotation!

9.3.1 At all events, if, as far as we can see, this is the basic theory of the texts, it not only seems unnecessary, but does not even appear to be the most logical explanation of the institution, provided always that we in fact accept its historicity.

9.3.2 On the other hand, the hypothesis of a greater or lesser degree of contemporaneity between two or more judges seems to be more plausible. The episode of Ehud could very well have taken place at more or less the same time as that of Gideon, and the Jephthah episode could have begun before the others ended, even while Abimelech, ruler of Shechem, but not a judge, was on his throne. The stereotyped chronology of Dtr, and the fact that each judge seems to work in a different territory, makes this suggestion possible.

9.4 We have been able to say virtually nothing of the so-called 'minor' judges. For an explanation of their functions, a feature which for the most part escapes us, see the beginning of this chapter, 1.1.2.

PART THREE

A House Divided

IX

THE TWO KINGDOMS TO THE TIME OF THE ASSYRIAN INVASION

1 We know that the united kingdom of David and Solomon did not last long; even if the empire that Solomon left to his successor seemed powerful and splendid from the outside (if we disregard the loss of some peripheral areas, above IV.3-4), in reality the state was economically on the verge of collapse, with many sectors of the population, especially in the North, oppressed and exploited (Noth*, 226). So on the death of Solomon the united kingdom which had existed for two generations will have needed a ruler endowed with more than usual capacities. Instead, it collapsed, leaving traces only in the memory and imagination of posterity. The ancient, and original, dualism existing between Israel and Judah (above III.1.2) dominated all other considerations, in a short space of time producing two second-rate states (Bright*, 1981, 229): it had never really been overcome, but only kept down by repression.

However, it is interesting that from the time of the 'schism' onwards we have a relative chronology. The years of the reign of the sovereign of a kingdom are calculated synchronously with those of the parallel sovereign in the other kingdom. This causes considerable difficulties in points of detail: often we do not know the absolute figures; we do not know whether different calendars and different systems of dating were used in the two nations, or whether there may be periods of co-regency the figures relating to which are added to those of the actual reigns. Nor do we know the method of calculating the reign of a sovereign who was considered legitimate in relationship to the years in which there was also a usurper. Moreover the Hebrew text, the Greek text of the LXX and Josephus' history often have different figures. However, despite these negative factors, the figures at our disposal are now relatively certain, with at worst discrepancies of not more than about ten years. For the various systems of calculation see the tables by H.Tadmor, 'Kronologia', *EncBib* IV, 1962, (245-310) 301ff. (Hebrew); recently brought up to date, especially in connection with method, in 'The Chronology of the First Temple Period', *WHJP* IV, 1, Jerusalem and London 1979, 44-60, 319f.; this study appears as an appendix to the present book by kind permission of the publishers, Massada Press, Jerusalem. The problem of the chronology of Kings is an old one; it was already felt by the Greek translators in the second century BC, then by Josephus, and finally by the rabbinic tractate Seder Olam Rabbah, from the third century AD; cf. also the appendices in Hayes-Miller*, 1977, 682, in Soggin, *Introduction*, 490-9; Jagersma*, 1982, 124-6; Gunneweg*, 1982, 173-97. For an examination of the different figures cf. J.D.Shenkel, *Chronology and Recensional Development of Kings*, Cambridge, Mass. 1968.

So from the death of Solomon, which took place in 926 or 922, we find Israel and Judah again as two separate entities, and this situation lasted till the end of the northern kingdom, with rivalry assuaged only by alliances. This rivalry was to continue in the post-exilic and New Testament periods in the hostility between Jews and Samaritans, and is still attested in the earliest rabbinic writings.

Select bibliography: A.Alt, 'Das Königtum in den Reichen Israel und Juda', *VT* 1, 1953, 2-22 = *KS* II, 116-34; A.Malamat, 'Kingship and Council in Israel and Sumer: A Parallel', *JNES* 22, 1963, 247-53; id., 'Organs of Statecraft in the Israelite Monarchy', *BA* 28, 1965, 34-65; J.A.Soggin, *Das Königtum*, 90ff.; G.Buccellati, *Cities and Nations*; J.Debus, *Die Sünde Jeroboams*, FRLANT 93, Göttingen 1967; D.W.Gooding, 'The Septuagint's Rival Version of Jeroboam's Rise to Power', *VT* 17, 1967, 173-9; id., 'Jeroboam's Rise to Power – A Rejoinder', *JBL* 91, 1972, 529-33; H.Seebass, 'Zur Königserhebung Jerobeams I', *VT* 17, 1967, 325-33; J.Conrad, *Die junge Generation im Alten Testament*, Berlin DDR 1970; S.Herrmann, 'Geschichte Israels – Möglichkeiten und Grenzen ihrer Darstellung', *TLZ* 94, 1969, 644-50; R.W.Klein, 'Jeroboam's Rise to Power', *JBL* 89, 1970, 217f.; E.Lipiński, 'Le récit I Rois XII 1-19', *VT* 24, 1974, 430-7; J.Trebolle Barrero, *Salomón y Jeroboán*, Salamanca 1980; M.Weinfeld, 'The Council of the "Elders" to Rehoboam and its Implications', *Maarav* 3.1, 1982, 27-53. For an examination of the texts see the commentaries by J.A.Montgomery-H.S.Gehman, ICC, 1951; M.Noth, BK IX, 1, 1968; J.Gray, OTL, ²1970.

1.1 The sources which describe the break in the personal union or, from their perspective, the secession of the North which came about on the death of Solomon appear almost exclusively in I Kings 12; 13; 14; they therefore belong to the Deuteronomistic history work. When we take into account the unconditionally pro-Judah bias in this work it is no surprise that, with after some scant attempts at understanding, the action of the northern tribes is presented as politically wrong and theologically sinful. Despite this obviously partisan attitude, however, they are ready to recognize that the requests made by the North were originally legitimate and thus attribute a major part of the process which led to the break to the political incapacity and the immaturity in human relationships of the king designate, Rehoboam (although he was already forty-one years old, I Kings 14.21). Again, according to the Deuteronomistic theory, the will of God underlies the event (cf. also 1.2.2.1). One element which emerges very clearly from the account of the negotiations is what must have been the economic and social situation at least in the North during the united kingdom, and we shall deal with this question later. The situation seems very different from the triumphalist tone of the information with which the court chronicles and the later celebrations of the kingdom are abundantly furnished (cf. above IV. 3.2-4 and 5).

1.2 The texts that we have are as follows: I Kings 12.1-9, a markedly romanticized chronicle of the events which led to the breakdown in negotiations and thus to the dissolution of the kingdom; I Kings 11.29-40; 12.21-24; 14.1-18, a series of prophetic legends connected with the event and probably reported by DtrP; finally I Kings 12.25-31; 14.21-31, which some would want to consider extracts from the annals of the kings of Israel and Judah (if the existence of these is accepted, or rather, if it is accepted that such material could have been preserved and handed down to us; cf. above, IV.1.1), now enlarged by Deuteronomistic comments, which set out to show us the perspective from which the text should be read.

1.2.1.1 In Jerusalem and in Judah the accession to the throne of Solomon's older son Rehoboam does not seem to have posed a problem; the South was strictly tied to the house of David, a bond which was to last until the exile in 587/86, despite occasional difficulties. The South also seems to have been less harassed than its northern neighbour and therefore harboured fewer resentments; another reason for this will have been that the South was an eminently poor region with little to offer, composed as it was almost exclusively of steppe and hill-country, far from the great lines of communication by land and sea.

1.2.1.2 The situation of Israel, the North, was different. Near to the great lines of communication, with substantial means of production in the spheres of agriculture, cattle-rearing and crafts, especially in the plains under the control of the city-states, the North obviously had a series of features which almost cried out to be exploited. However, it seems improbable that there was a 'charismatic' concept of kingship in the North, a kind of continuation of the activity of the judges (above VIII.1.1.1) as presented by Dtr (thus the basic study by A.Alt 1951, followed by Soggin 1967 and many others). On the contrary, Buccellati (1967, 195-21) has demonstrated that in the North, too, the rulers tried to found a dynasty, and the dynasty of Omri (below, 3.3) remained justly famous throughout the ancient Near East. That they did not succeed here is due essentially to a series of circumstances for the most part beyond their control, which I shall try to explain in due course. Be that as it may, at all events the North was the key area in economic terms, and could therefore be exploited; we can also deduce from all this that on the political and cultural plane, too, at least to begin with it probably had a far greater importance than the South. Moreover, we shall not be far wrong in supposing that it was only because of its isolation that the South succeeded in maintaining itself for a century and a half after the North had fallen. At the same time, though, it succeeded in concentrating on itself, its dynasty and the temple, the most vital ideological and theological features of Israel, features which have assured its survival right down to the present day.

1.2.1.3 As I have said, the first account, which is markedly anecdotal, is probably romanticized, but it presents some features of considerable interest.

1.2.1.3.1 In the first place, at least in the North, it seems that the succession to the throne was anything but automatic; the oldest son of the dead monarch did not necessarily succeed to the throne; the question was more complex. Rehoboam, the designated successor, is said first to have had to go to Shechem (a place which evidently functioned as the capital of the North, at least in the administrative sense of the term). There 'all Israel', a formula which this time is meant to refer only to the North, met in assembly to crown him. The text does not explain why Rehoboam had to go personally to the assembly instead of summoning it, say, at Jerusalem or in another locality of his choice: in II Sam.5.1ff., 'all the tribes of Israel' appear before David at Hebron. For this reason, basic doubts have been raised about the verisimilitude of the scene (Debus 1967, 28). Again, the negotiations are said to have taken place when the rebel Jeroboam had already returned home; indeed, he even took part in them (so much so that Debus, and also Lipiński, think that vv.2-3a, 15,17 were added later). The events described all seem improbable and could be part of the romanticized element in the narrative. However, this note does tell us that Judah and Israel, as in the time of David, each crowned its own sovereign and that in this respect each had remarkable prerogatives and marked autonomy. Such information is obviously not downright absurd.

1.2.1.3.2 The text also says that the coronation of the new king was preceded by negotiations which could also, as in this case, be laborious and end up inconclusively. That would suggest that the North had succeeded in maintaining a structure in which certain democratic elements could still find a voice (Soggin 1967, 92ff.) and that no monarch could ignore them with impunity.

1.2.1.3.3 We do not know the composition of the assembly and we cannot ascertain whether and to what point it was already ill disposed towards Rehoboam from the start, resolving to lay down conditions calculated to make the negotiations fail, so that it could then lay the blame for the failure on the inexpert and arrogant candidate. H.Donner*, 1977, 384 and S.Herrmann*, 1981, 189f., seem disposed to believe this, and the information according to which Jeroboam is said to have returned from Egypt, where he had taken refuge (above IV.4.4) after a revolt against Solomon that had evidently failed, even taking part in the negotiations as a spokesman for the assembly (vv.2-3a), suggests that this was also the opinion of the later tradition. However, it should be noted that the requests made to the candidate by the assembly were neither extravagant nor provocative: 'Your father made our yoke heavy. Now therefore lighten the hard service of your father and his heavy yoke upon us, and we will be your loyal subjects' (literally: 'we will serve you', 12.4). It follows clearly from these words that the North, and not the South, felt oppressed. After this the scene changes to the deliberations between the sovereign designate and his counsellors.

1.2.1.3.4 Here the texts show the king involved with two groups of counsellors; however, it does not seem possible to maintain that this is some form of institution with two chambers, as Malamat suggested in 1963, on the basis of an apparently analogous system existing in prehistoric Sumeria (in the meantime the alleged parallel has proved to be extremely doubtful, cf. Soggin 1967, 138ff.). If we accept the usual explanation, the situation is much simpler. On the one hand we find the older and therefore more expert counsellors, 'who had grown old in the service of Solomon' (Donner*, 384); these recommend moderation to the young king. On the other hand we have the younger and therefore inexpert counsellors, some of them the king's childhood companions (12.8). However, it is worth considering Lipiński's 1974 proposal: in his view the 'elders' will have been those among the people who had already opposed the king in the time of Solomon (this is how the expression '*md 'et pᵉnē NP* should be understood), whereas the 'youths' will have been those in the retinue of the monarch and therefore more ready with their adulation. In that case the fault of the sovereign designate will have been to have neglected the advice of the representatives of the people in favour of that of his own followers. Be this as it may, the older men recognize the legitimacy and indeed the moderation of the request made by the assembly and the correctness of the form in which it is presented, and exhort the king to accept the conditions that are put forward. So this is not, as Weinfeld would have it in his most recent study, the concept of the monarchy as being at the service of the people, a precursor of the similar Western concept: here 'serve' means 'submit', 'accept certain conditions', and derives from the language of international treaties. So what v.7 is saying is: 'If today you submit yourself to this people, accepting its conditions and responding to it with good words, its members will be your subjects for ever.' In fact 'speak well', 'respond with good words' means 'accede to someone's request', as Weinfeld has shown on the basis of instances from the ancient Near East. These requests were essentially for exemptions from taxes, typical in places which were the sites of sanctuaries. By contrast, the 'young' exhort the king not to yield; indeed they tell him to reply to the assembly in a particularly arrogant and crude way (v.10b uses a downright obscene expression, a paraphrase for the *membrum virile*, Debus 1967, 23; Noth 1968). Fortunately Rehoboam in fact only gives part of this reply. So it is to the young that the candidate yields, precipitating the disaster. Here, too, we have stereotyped expressions: the elders, sage and tolerant; the young, silly, impulsive and arrogant. The text also observes that all this came about as a result of divine intervention (12.15).

A first attempt by Rehoboam to settle the dispute (12.18-19) fails, and the king only escapes by fleeing from what must in fact have been an attempt on his life. His lieutenant Adoram, the person whom we find in the time of David and Solomon as superintendent of forced labour with the name of Adoniram (III.8.2.7), is not so fortunate: having been ordered by the king to carry on the negotiations he is stoned to death.

1.2.1.3.5 The result of the failure of the negotiations between the assembly and the king was the break-up of the personal union and the re-establishment, in Canaan, of two Israelite groups, as they had existed before the time of David. Benjamin seems very soon to have gone over to Judah (12.21), following the conflicts which I shall discuss below (2). The reasons for this territorial change are difficult to determine, but they are certainly connected with the fact that Judah could not tolerate a northern frontier which ran only a few hundred yards north of the capital (cf. below 2.4).

It should be noted that Judah never wanted to accept this break, so that a reunion of the two groups became the goal of the rulers of Judah, and even an eschatological hope (Isa.9.1-6 [EVV 9.2-7]; Jer.3.1ff.; 23.5-6; Ezek.37.15-22; and other passages). The North never seems to have been particularly anxious for it.

1.2.2 As I have indicated, the prophetic legends in 11.29-40; 12.2-24; 14.1-18, probably deriving from DtrP, in part attempt to attribute to Jeroboam something like a divine election.

1.2.2.1 The first is connected with the abortive revolt against Solomon led by Jeroboam when he was an official in the united kingdom, in charge of forced labour (above IV.4.4), cf. I Kings 11.26-28. According to this narrative, he was met on the road by the prophet Ahijah of Shiloh, who had invested him with rule over the ten tribes of the North. This presupposes that Benjamin was already part of the South. The rule over these tribes is said to have been taken away from Solomon because of his impiety. However, Dtr is anxious to point out that this investiture was conditional on the obedience of the candidates to the divine commandments. The revolt seems to have failed and its leader was forced to flee abroad, to Egypt; from there he returned home on receiving news of the death of Solomon. According to the sources as we have them, he took part in the Shechem assembly. So the text quoted, I Kings 12.15, sees the attitude of Rehoboam as a product of divine intervention, thus fulfilling the promise made to Jeroboam before his flight. Again according to this source, the prospect held out to Jeroboam therefore seems to have been rather like that which Dtr held out to David over against Saul in I Sam.16.1-13 (above III.3.1.2.1): as a punishment, the kingdom is taken away from the man who had received it and is given to others more worthy.

1.2.2.2 The second of these texts, which seems to be a relatively late composition, shows Rehoboam intent on re-establishing the unity of the empire, if necessary by force. He raises an army to move against those whom he considers rebels, but is dissuaded from launching the expedition by a divine oracle delivered by the prophet Shemaiah. After that he withdraws his troops and disbands them. The note contained in 14.30, which is almost a passing remark in its present context, seems more realistic: 'There was continually war between Rehoboam and Jeroboam' – a situation which seems to have been perpetuated during the life of the two monarchs and under their successors, Asa of Judah and Baasha of Israel (15.16).

1.2.2.3 The third text presents Jeroboam on his sick-bed in the act of sending his own wife to Shiloh, to consult Ahijah. The prophet delivers a divine oracle to the woman: YHWH is angry with Jeroboam because he has been unfaithful; therefore the king must die and his dynasty be exterminated. The kingdom will totter and Israel will have to go into exile, where it will be dispersed. The allusion to the events of the last quarter of the eighth century is obvious (below X.4.1).

1.2.2.4 These texts show what we might call the ambiguous attitude of Dtr towards the northern kingdom, an attitude which probably varies depending on individual strata: on the one hand it has Jeroboam designated king by a prophet and protects the new state from an invasion by the South; moreover, it recognizes the legitimate character of the request by the North during the course of the Shechem assembly. On the other hand it considers Jeroboam a sinner, essentially because of his religious policy, a feature which we shall consider below. For this reason his destiny, along with the kingdom in which this infidelity is perpetuated, can only be disastrous. DtrP also follows the general line of Dtr with its inexorable condemnation of the North.

1.2.3 Finally we have two texts which, according to some scholars, could go back to the annals of Israel and Judah – that is, if we accept their existence and suppose at least part of them to have been handed down (12.25-31; 14.21-31).

1.2.3.1 The first text begins by mentioning the new fortifications built at Shechem (in the hill country, *tell-balāṭa*, coord.176-179), at Penuel (in Transjordan, probably at *tulul eḍ-ḍahab*, coord.215-176) and at Tirzah (*tell el-far'ah*, coord.182-88) by Jeroboam; he also moved the capital of the kingdom to Tirzah. Details of the religious schism follow immediately after this information without any break in continuity; they led to the North also being separated from the South in the cultic sphere.

Select bibliography: M.Weippert, 'Gott und Stier', *ZDPV* 77, 1961, 93-117; M.Aberbach and L.Smolar, 'Aaron, Jeroboam and the Golden Calves', *JBL* 86, 1967, 129-40; J.A.Soggin, 'Der offiziell geförderte Synkretismus im 10. Jahrhundert', *ZAW* 78, 1966, 179-204; H.Donner, 'Hier sind deine Götter, Israel', in *Wort und Geschichte – Festschrift K.Elliger*, AOAT 18, Neukirchen 1973, 45-50.

1.2.3.2 At Bethel, immediately north of Jerusalem (the present-day *beitīn*, coord. 172-148) and at Dan, in the extreme north (the present-day *tell el-qāḍī*, coord.211-194), Jeroboam is said to have instituted a schismatic form of cult. This was expressed in the image of a golden bull, to which the text refers in a derogatory way as a 'golden calf'. This is the Canaanite image of a bull, the symbol of male sexual potency; in Israel, though, the bull seems to have served as the pedestal for the invisible God of Israel, just as the ark in Jerusalem served as his throne. That this was the case is clearly shown by the announcement (13.28b): 'Behold your God, O Israel, which brought you up out of Egypt'. This worship was presented as an alternative to that practised at Jerusalem, a sanctuary to which Jeroboam, understandably, no longer wanted the people of Israel to go. And despite many authoritative statements to the contrary, it seems that the term *'elōhīm*, which in Hebrew could be rendered either 'god' or 'gods' (and even 'goddess' and 'idol'), was understood to be singular and not plural: the reference is in fact to the 'golden calf' instituted by Aaron himself in Ex.32.1ff., a narrative which originally gives every indication of having been the cultic legend for Jeroboam's provisions. It is interesting that the first verses of Ex.32.1ff. are not in fact polemical: it was only later (vv.7ff.) that polemic came into the text, probably introduced by the redactors.

1.2.3.3 By contrast we hear nothing of the territories annexed under David. We know that towards the end of the reign of Solomon some peripheral parts of the empire had begun to detach themselves, partly with Solomon's agreement, partly through rebellions. It is probable that this process was continued throughout the last part of the tenth century and the beginning of the ninth century BC. We know from I Kings 15.18-20//I Chron.16.2-6 that Damascus remained bound to Israel for some time by a treaty of alliance, which was later abrogated. And we learn from the annals of Shalmaneser III of Assyria (*ANET*, 376ff.) that Ammon had again become independent by 854 BC, while the stele of Mesha of Moab affirms that Moab also regained its independence at the end of the ninth century. However, the text implies that Moab had already obtained this independence earlier, and then lost it briefly at a later stage (3.4.3 below). Only Edom seems to have remained under Judah.

1.2.3.4 We hear virtually nothing from the biblical texts about the administrative measures adopted by Jeroboam (who had to reconstitute the greater part of a state administration). However, we can deduce from the Samaria ostraca (*KAI*, 183ff.; *SSI* I, 5ff.; *ANET*, 321ff.; cf. Soggin, *Introduction*, 477) that the fiscal system and system of districts inaugurated by Solomon (above IV.5) had remained fully in force (Noth*, 194, 237), thus resulting in the paradox that a system first considered unjust, because it was oppressive and exploited the people, later proved to be the only practicable one on an administrative level. This happens quite often in history.

1.4 The second of the texts to which I have referred speaks of the reign of Rehoboam, his kinsfolk, his works and his failings, with marked Deuteronomistic redactional elements. However, at the end we find a very important note reporting an invasion by Pharaoh Shishak, the Egyptian Shoshenk I from the Twenty-second Libyan Dynasty (14.25-28//II Chron.12.2-9,11).

Select bibliography: M.Noth, 'Die Shoshenkliste',*ZDPV* 61, 1938, 277-304 = *ABLAK* II, 73-93; B.Mazar, 'The Campaign of Pharaoh Shishak to Palestine', *SVT* 4, 1957, 57-66; S.Herrmann, 'Operationen Pharaos Schoschenk I im östlichen Ephraim', *ZDPV* 80, 1964, 55-79; D.B.Redford, 'Studies in the Relationship between Palestine and Egypt during the First Millennium BC: II – The Twenty-Second Dynasty', *JAOS* 93, 1973, 3-17; G.Garbini, 'L'impero di David', *ASNSP* III, 1983, 1-20.

We do not know what prompted the Pharaoh to begin his campaign; we might speculate that it was to reaffirm his sovereignty over a region which traditionally belonged to the Egyptian crown. And it is also possible that Jeroboam, when he had taken refuge in Egypt, had made promises to the Pharaoh in this connection, enticing him with the vision of re-establishing Egyptian sovereignty over the region in exchange first for political asylum and then for Egyptian help in regaining power, promises which he did not keep. But here we find ourselves in the realms of sheer conjecture. It is also important that this is the first Egyptian ruler that the Hebrew Bible mentions by name: *šošak* in K and *šišāk* in Q, and that he is only given the title 'king of Egypt', not 'Pharaoh'.

However, Rehoboam succeeded in making the Egyptians withdraw from his frontiers by giving the Pharaoh a large part of the treasures of the temple and the palace. So the South does not appear at all in the list of the localities conquered, which is in the great temple of Karnak in Egypt. In the north the Pharaoh invaded the plain of Jezreel and penetrated into Transjordan, i.e. the economically most important region. We know nothing of the reaction from Jeroboam I to an invasion which must have caused a number of difficulties on the economic and political plane (Donner*, 1977, 389); that is, unless the fortifications mentioned at 1.2.3.1 and the transfer of the capital to Tirzah were a reaction to these events.

For G.Garbini this expedition will, however, have taken place some decades earlier, still in the reign of Solomon, so it is necessary to revise the chronology of the Pharaohs. The event, which was clearly catastrophic, will later have been put in the time of Jeroboam I and Rehoboam, so that it contrasts with the splendour of Solomon's reign and could readily be interpreted as retribution for the 'sin' of the break-up of the kingdom.

1.5 II Chron.11.5-10 gives a list of fortifications which Rehoboam is said to have had built to protect Judah in the south and the west. Contrary to previous views, some scholars, especially the historians and topographers (Herrmann*, 1973, 197; Gunneweg*, 1979, 90; Aharoni, *The Land*, 330f.; Donner*, 1977, 388 and Bright*, 23), argue that this list must be very old. Moreover, we learn from it that the frontier now ran a little south of Hebron, thus excluding virutally all the Negeb including Beersheba, the coastal plain, and also sectors of the southern hill country. So Judah would have continued to be cut off from the sea and the lines of communication. However, not everyone is of this opinion and some of the most recent studies still argue that the list is late.[1]

Be this as it may, from then on Judah, apart from the interruption caused by the Egyptian invasion and the difficulties over the wars with Israel, could live in peace, focussed entirely on the elect dynasty of YHWH and his temple.

2 *Select bibliography*: M.F.Unger, *Israel and the Aramaeans of Damascus*, London 1957 and reprints, chs.V-X (a conservative, but useful work); J.M.Miller, 'Geshur and Aram', *JNES* 28, 1969, 60f.

The struggles between the two Hebrew kingdoms are the main feature of the first decades of their independent existence. They arose out of the strategic necessity for Judah to extend its own frontiers further to the north, since they were only a few miles north of Jerusalem; in fact, even with the incorporation of the greater part of Benjamin (but cf. below 2.3), these frontiers only extended to just north of the two places known today as Ramallah and el-Bireh (coord.170-145), i.e. about twelve miles north of the capital. The available sources are all in the books of Kings and therefore have undergone a Deuteronomistic redaction, or in the books of Chronicles, and therefore must be used with care. In both cases the orientation is essentially religious, and the texts have little interest in problems of a political and economic kind. Finally, all the material lends itself to divergent interpretations.

2.1 The wars between the two kingdoms, often referred to as fratricidal wars, began with a series of successes on the part of the North. This is not surprising if we remember its economic and productive capacity, which was so superior to that of the South (above, 1.2.1.2). Moreover, as we know, the North now included the greater part of the Canaanite city-states, with their economic structures and their armies, and these had war chariots. So instead of seeing the South extending its own boundaries northwards, we find the troops of the North advancing further south. This state of war continued through the reigns of kings Rehoboam (*c*.992-915 or 926-910), Abijah (*c*.915-913 or 910-908) and Asa (*c*.913-873 or 908-868) of Judah, and Jeroboam I (*c*.922-901 or 926-907), Nadab (*c*.901-900 or 907-906) and Baasha (*c*.900-887 or 906-883) of Israel. In fact it seems that the troops of Israel succeeded in penetrating as far as Ramah (present-day *er-rām*, coord. 172-140), about five miles north of Jerusalem (I Kings 15.16f.//II Chron 16.1ff.)!

2.2 Confronted with a situation which could easily turn into a catastrophe, Asa, king of Judah, asked for help from the Aramaeans of Damascus. As we have seen (above IV.4.3), these had already detached themselves from the empire under Solomon, but had remained bound to Israel by a treaty (above 1.2.3.3). The texts report that Asa sent a delegation to 'Ben-Hadad, son of Tab-rimmon, son of Ḥezion' (I Kings 15.18-20//I Chron.16.2-6, i.e. to Bar-Hadad I (*c*. 900-875 or 885-870); the chronology is purely conjectural, and in the opinion of some scholars (Aharoni, *Land*, 335) the name may be only a title.[2] Asa succeeded in persuading the Aramaeans, though only by paying them a substantial amount of tribute (what remained from the ransom paid to Shishak of

Egypt), to break off their alliance with Israel, to make common cause with Judah, and to attack Israel from the rear.

2.3 This, then, was a surprise attack on a region which had been almost completely undefended. The effects were immediate and serious: the Aramaeans rapidly took possession of three key frontier posts: Abel Beth-maacah (present-day *'abil el-qamḥ*, coord.204-296), Ijon (*tell ed-dibbin*, coord.205-308) and Dan (*tell qāḏī*, coord.211-294), and also of 'all Chinneroth' (*ḥirbet el-'oreimeh*, coord.200-252) and the 'land of Naphtali', i.e. a substantial sector of Eastern Galilee. According to Y.Aharoni (*The Land*, 333), I Chron.2.23 also alludes to Ben Hadad's campaign: 'But Geshur and Aram took from them Havothjair, Kenath and its villages, sixty towns.' This is the area immediately south of the Jarmuk in Transjordan, in northern Gilead, the place that is now called *qanawāt* (coord.302-241). In other words, Israel's last remaining possessions in Transjordan will also have been lost, quite apart from the fact that the Aramaeans succeeded in penetrating the territory of Israel in depth. So the wars between Israel and its neighbours began in the north-east, and for more than a century bloodied the frontiers between the two countries, causing Israel great difficulties. However, the information at our disposal is so sparse that we cannot even establish when and on what conditions the Aramaeans went back to their country on this occasion. It seems improbable that they did so voluntarily and of their own free will! 'This was the first – and not the last – time that Israel's external enemies were able to turn its domestic disputes to their own advantage' (Gunneweg*, 94).

2.4 Compelled to throw his own troops into the breach, Baasha speedily abandoned Ramah, leaving in place the material with which he intended to fortify it; Asa was able to profit from this, immediately advancing northwards, occupying Ramah, and using the material he found there to fortify Mizpah (*tell en-naṣbeh*, coord.170-143) and Geba of Benjamin (present-day *jiba'*, coord.175-141). The excavations on *tell en-naṣbeh* have revealed that the place had originally been a fortress built by the North against the South, but it was soon reorientated by means of some improvised adaptations northwards.[3] From then on, the boundary between the North and the South remained virtually unchanged. According to A.Alt, followed by H. Donner,[4] the territories thus obtained by the South will not have been incorporated into Judah but added to those of the city-state of Jerusalem; this could be the explanation of the note contained in II Kings 12.21, according to which Benjamin went with Judah. What we in fact see here, then, is a partition of Benjamin: part went to the South as a result of these wars and the rest stayed with the North. That also explains how some centuries later Josiah was able to desecrate the 'high places' from Geba to Beersheba, while in II Chron.11.10 Aijalon (present-day *yālō*, coord.152-138), which in I Kings 4.9 belongs to a district of the North, appears as a fortress of Rehoboam.

2.5 At this point there seems to have been peace between Israel and Judah. However, despite its apparent victory, there is no reason to believe that the South succeeded in prevailing over the North, even if it had obtained a more favourable frontier. Granted, the North, at grips with the Aramaeans on its north-eastern frontier, did not even try to advance south again; but it is also the case that it continued to exercise a *de facto* control over its southern neighbours. Donner* 1977, 391, does not hesitate to call this 'a veiled vassal relationship of Judah towards Israel'.

2.6 The texts (I Kings 15.9-15//II Chron. 14.1-4) also report that Asa introduced a religious reform. However, this is described in the stereotyped terms typical of the Deuteronomistic history and Chronicles, so it is impossible to establish whether it in fact took place, and if it did, what it comprised. There is also a somewhat cryptic note to the effect that Asa had to depose his own mother (I Kings 15.13-15//II Chron.15.16-19); the queen mother in fact had a special constitutional position, expressed by the title of $g^e b \bar{i} r \bar{a}$.

Bibliography: G.Molin, 'Die Stellung der G^{e}bīrā im Staate Juda', *TZ* 1954, 161-75; K.Donner, 'Art und Herkunft des Amtes der Königmutter im Alten Testament', in *FS Johannes Friedrich*, Wiesbaden 1985, 105-45; N.E.A.Andreasen, 'The Role of the Queen Mother in Israelite Society', *CBQ* 45, 1983, 179-94.

The title, which we could translate literally as 'the (great) lady', was borne by the queen mother. Her functions and prerogatives at court in Israel and in Judah are far from clear; however, if we accept the information we can glean from the courts of the ancient Near East, these were connected with the regency in cases where it was impossible for the candidate to the throne to exercise his rule. And that seems quite possible in this case. Later (3.8.1), we shall be considering another instance in which the queen mother was even directly involved in a *coup d'état*: the queen mother concerned was Athaliah in the South. Whatever may have happened, Asa succeeded in averting the damage; he deposed the lady on the pretext of some cultic offence which is not more closely defined.

3 With Omri, king of Israel, we have another attempt to form a dynasty in the North, where this had failed earlier. The king only succeeded in ascending the throne after about five years of disorders, proof of the difficulty which always existed in Israel at the constitutional level. However, the dynasty of Omri did not last long, even if it rightly achieved enduring fame, as we shall also see (below 4.1.4.3).

3.1 The reign of Omri was preceded by that of some monarchs whose reigns were of very short duration: Ela (*c.* 877-876 or 883-882), Zimri (*c.* 876 or 882), who was perhaps not of Israelite origin, and finally Tibni (*c.*876-873 or 882-878). Ela and all his family were killed by Zimri; Zimri committed suicide when he was besieged by Omri, commander of the army which was laying siege to Gibbethon (present-day *tell-melat,* coord.137-140), a place south-east of Gezer which seems to have been Philistine. Omri was acclaimed king by the army; as we might put it, 'in the field' (16.16). However, another sector of the people (the texts say half) chose Tibni instead (I Kings 16.8-14,15-20,21,22). All these episodes are ignored in Chronicles. The reign of Tibni must have lasted about four years, since Zimri (who reigned only a few days, v.15) became king in the seventeenth year of Asa of Judah (v.15), while Omri ascended the throne in his thirty-first year (v.23).

3.2 *Select bibliography for Tibni*: J.M.Miller, ' "So Tibni Died" (I Kings XVI 22)', *VT* 18, 1968, 392-4; J.A.Soggin, 'Tibni, re d'Israele nella prima metà del IX sec a.C.', *RSO* 47, 1972, 171-6, *OTOS*, 50-5; E.Puech, 'Athalie, fille d'Achab et la chronologie des rois d'Israël et de Juda', *Salamanticensis* 28, 1981, (117-38) 134ff.

The case of Tibni and his brief reign is more interesting than might seem at first sight. After a series of *coups d'état* accompanied by political assassinations, Tibni is said to have been elected by 'half the people' of Israel (v.21), whereas the other half supported Omri. Now as we have seen, Omri had been acclaimed by his army; it therefore seems reasonable to suppose that the 'half' which had elected him was composed of the army. By contrast, we never hear mention of troops in connection with Tibni, so despite the argument to the contrary by Puech, it seems reasonable to suppose that here we have yet another attempt by the assembly of the North (above, 1.2.1.3.2-4) to nominate its own ruler. This attempt did not succeed because of the intervention of Omri's troops. And after the killing of Tibni, no one could now oppose Omri's ascent to the throne. The incident seems symptomatic, not only because it is evidence of the increasing complexity of the political situation in the North but also because it shows how there could be two kings side by side, with the chronology of the first included in that of the second (see above 1).

3.3 With very few exceptions, the biblical texts have nothing but negative comments to make about Omri and his son Ahab. However, we shall see that the 'house of Omri' was judged differently by the Assyrians (cf. below 4.1.4.3). For Omri cf. the following:

Select bibliography: A.Jepsen, 'Israel und Damascus', *AfO* 14, 1941-44, 153-72; C.F.Whitley, 'The Deuteronomic Presentation of the House of Omri', *VT* 2, 1952, 137-52; A.Alt, *Der Stadtstaat Samaria*, Leipzig-

Berlin DDR 1954 = *KS* III, 258-302; H.J.Katzenstein, 'Who Were the Parents of Athaliah?', *IEJ* 5, 1955, 194-7; M.F.Unger, *Israel and the Aramaeans of Damascus*, London 1957; M.C.Astour, 'Metamorphose de Baal – Les rivalités commerciales au IXme siècle', in *Evidences* 10, 1959, 75, 34-40; 77, 54-58 (not available to me; I know it through B.Lang (ed.), *Der einzige Gott*, Munich 1981, 58f. and the bibliography in the appendix); W.W.Hallo, 'From Qarqar to Carchemish', *BA* 23, 1960, 33-61; B.Mazar, 'The Aramaean Empire and its Relations with Israel', *BA* 25, 1962, 97-120; H.L.Ginsberg, 'The Omrid-Davidic Alliance and its Consequences', in *Proceedings of the Fourth World Congress of Jewish Studies, Jerusalem 1965*, Jerusalem 1967, I, 91-3; R. de Vaux, 'Tirzah', in D.W.Thomas (ed.), *Archaeology and Old Testament Study*, London 1967, 371-83; E.Lipiński, 'Le Ben Hadad II de la bible et de l'histoire', in *Proceedings of the Fifth World Congress of Jewish Studies, Jerusalem 1969*, Jerusalem 1973, I, 147-9; H.Donner, 'Adad-nirari III und die Vassalen des Westens', in *Archäologie und Altes Testament – FS Kurt Galling*, Tübingen 1970, 49-59; M.C.Astour, '841 BC: The First Assyrian Invasion of Israel', *JAOS* 91, 1971, 383-9; M. Elat, 'The Campaign of Shalmaneser III against Aram and Israel', *IEJ* 25, 1974, 25-35; H.Tadmor, 'Assyria and the West: The Ninth Century and its Aftermath', in H.Goedicke and J.J.M. Roberts (eds.), *Unity and Diversity*, Baltimore 1975, 36-48; N.Na'aman, 'Two Notes on the Monolith Inscription of Shalmaneser III from Kurkh', *TA* 3, 1976, 89-106; J.A.Brinkman, 'A Further Note on the Date of the Battle of Qarqar and Neo-Assyrian Chronology', *JCS* 30, 1978, 173-5; S.Timm, *Die Dynastie Omri – Quellen und Untersuchungen zur Geschichte Israels im 9. Jahrhundert vor Christus*, FRLANT 124, Göttingen 1982; C.Schäfer-Lichtenberger, *Stadt und Eidgenossenschaft*, BZAW 156, Berlin 1983, 9.3.1, 9.3.2. For a list of the main fortified places in the time of the dynasty of Omri, cf. D.N.Pienaar, 'The Role of Fortified Cities in the Northern Kingdom during the Reign of the Omride Dynasty', *JNWSL* 9, 1981, 151-7.

For the Samaria excavations cf. J.W.Crowfoot et al., *Samaria-Sebaste*, I-II-III, London 1938-1957; J.B.Hennessy, 'Excavations at Samaria-Sebaste, 1968', *Levant* 2, 1970, 1-21.

3.3.1 Omri (*c*.876-869 or 878-91) – the name is perhaps not even Israelite (Gunneweg*, 1979, 94f.) – must have been confronted almost immediately with a series of grave problems at home and abroad, which had remained in suspense for some years.

3.3.1.1 At home there was a pressing need to re-establish law and order after about five years of *coups d'état*, proscriptions and civil war; abroad, Omri had to put an end as quickly as possible to the long conflict with Judah and also arrive at a solution for the Aramaean war, perhaps the chief threat posed to the new régime, since the war with Judah had now been dormant for some years. We know very little about the Aramaean kingdom, as I have already said (2.2). Nor do we know whether the war continued under Omri and Ahab, and if it did, to what extent. Perhaps the Aramaeans had achieved their aims; perhaps, too, pressure from Assyria was beginning to make itself felt on their north-eastern frontier, so that some caution was advisable; this pressure did not yet pose a threat to Israel. Be this as it may, it seems that the war was not pursued with the same vigour as before, and perhaps, as we saw, it was even broken off.

3.3.1.2 Ending the war with Judah does not seem to have been a difficult matter: it had already languished for a number of years and the frontier had been stabilized. The treaty which was soon concluded was sealed, moreover, by the marriage of Athaliah, daughter, or probably better niece of Omri (II Kings 8.26//II Chron.22.2) to Joram of Judah, a fact to which we shall return in due course (below, 3.7.1).

3.3.2 However, Omri has gone down in history especially as the founder of a new city, Samaria (Hebrew *šōmᵉrōn*). He founded it in the sixth year of his reign, i.e in about 871 or 873, to become the new capital (16.24ff.), and sited it on a hill that had hitherto been uninhabited. It is now beside the Arab village of *sebasṭiye*, coord.168-187. The region took one of its designations, Samaria, from the name of the city; in the Assyrian annals it is referred to as *samerīna*. In the post-exilic period, Samaria continued to be used as the name of the Persian province and its inhabitants, and it was passed on to the Jewish sect which still exists today (see also XIII.4). The excavations carried out on the tells of Tirzah and Samaria broadly confirm this course of events.

3.3.2.1 The king's aims in founding a new capital are not indicated in the sources and seem anything but clear. The theory generally accepted is that of H.Donner*, 407ff., on the basis of Alt's 1954 study; according to this, Shemer, the landowner who sold the site to Omri, will have been a Canaanite, so that the transaction will have been in accordance with Canaanite, not Israelite law (Donner*, 402). However, this theory seems rather doubtful; first, the name is not necessarily Canaanite: in I Chron. 6.31; 7.34 we find a Levite by this name, while Shimrith appears in II Chron 24.26 as the name of a Moabite woman. Moreover as Schäfer-Lichtenberger, 396ff., rightly observes, since we know absolutely nothing about 'Canaanite law', to use it as an explanation only makes matters more obscure. The theory put forward by Alt and Donner goes on to argue that the city will have received a status similar to that of Jerusalem from the time of David onwards, except that it was never a real city-state (as we have seen, Schäfer-Lichtenberger, following Buccellati, rejects this theory also in the case of Jerusalem, cf. above III.7.4.3). Thus Samaria is supposed to have been the capital belonging to the dynasty, as a city-state, and not to the nation as such, and it was because of this status that Ahab built a temple in it, dedicated to Ba'al and not to YHWH (I Kings 16.32)! In other words, here too we would have a personal union, between the Canaanite population with Samaria as a capital, and the Israelite population, which will have had another capital, Jezreel (now the abandoned Arab village of zer'in, coord.181-218), in the south-east of the plain of Jezreel. This arrangement will have recognized the primary importance of the Canaanite population in land-ownership and the economy. Jezreel must have taken the place of Tirzah, which had been destroyed shortly before by Zimri (I Kings 16.18). We next hear of it in the Elijah (I Kings 21) and Jehu (I Kings 9-10) traditions.

However, this theory, too, can be challenged. First of all we know nothing about a second capital for Judah, so that there is no parallel. Nor is it ever said that Jezreel was a second capital: it appears only as a residence for the reigning house during certain periods of the year (for the second argument, cf. recently Schäfer-Lichtenberger, ibid.). So, popular though the theory may be, it does not stand up to close analysis, and we are therefore forced to recognize that we know nothing of the reasons why Omri founded the city.

3.3.3 We also know that the dynasty of Omri was particularly concerned to cultivate the alliance with the Phoenicians, a relationship which perhaps goes back as far as David, and certainly to Solomon (above III.6.2; IV.3.3). The marriage of Ahab to Jezebel, daughter of Ittobaal (king of Tyre, following Josephus, VIII. 324, and not king of Sidon, as I Kings 16.31 suggests) was the natural seal on this alliance, too.

3.4 The traditions of Ahab now seem to be combined with those of two prophets presented as his inexorable enemies: Elijah (I Kings 17; 18; 19; 21; II Kings 1.2-17; and Elisha (I Kings 19; II Kings 2.1-25; 3.4-8, 15; 13.14-21). Another two narratives which seem independent of Dtr have as their theme the Aramaean wars in which he is said to have engaged (I Kings 20; 22). Again, we have the account of Jehu's revolt (II Kings 9.1-10.27), and finally scattered notes here and there in the text, perhaps drawn from the court annals, the problems associated with which we examined above (IV.1.2). There are therefore many difficulties in obtaining relatively certain information: the two prophetic narratives are esentially interested in their own heroes and their struggles against their enemies; among the latter, the king and queen occupy a privileged position. The two chapters on the Aramaean war seem originally to have been anonymous and connected only at a later stage with the figure of Ahab (Donner*, 400).

Select bibliography: A. Alt, 'Das Gottesurteil auf dem Karmel', *Fest-*

schrift Georg Beer, Stuttgart 1935, 1-18 = *KS* II, 135-9; K.Galling, 'Der Gott Karmel und die Ächtung der fremden Götter', in *Geschichte und Altes Testament – Festschrift Albrecht Alt*, Tübingen 1953, 105-26; O.Eissfeldt, *Der Gott Karmel*, Berlin DDR 1953; H.H.Rowley, 'Elijah on Mount Carmel', *BJRL* 43, 1960-61, 190-219 = *Men of God*, London 1963, 37-65; K.Baltzer, 'Naboths Weinberg (I Kön.21)...', *WuD* 8, 1965, 73-78; F.I.Andersen, 'The Socio-Juridical Background of the Naboth Incident', *JBL* 35, 1966, 46-57; J.M.Miller, 'The Elisha-Cycle and the Accounts of the Omride Wars', *JBL* 35, 1966, 441-54; id., 'The Fall of the House of Ahab', *VT* 17, 1967, 307-24; 'The Rest of the Acts of Jehoachaz (I Kings 20.22,1-38)', *ZAW* 80, 1968, 337-42; O.H.Steck, *Überlieferung und Zeitgeschichte in den Elia-Erzählungen*, WMANT 26; G.Fohrer, *Elia*, ATANT 53, Zurich ²1968; H.-C.Schmitt, *Elisa...*, Gütersloh 1972; P.Welten, 'Naboths Weinberg (I Kön. 21)', *EvTh* 33, 1973, 18-32; J.A.Soggin, 'Jezabel, oder die fremde Frau', in *Mélanges bibliques et orientaux en l'honneur de M.Henri Cazelles*, AOAT 212, Kevelaer 1981, 453-59.

3.4.1 Once we manage to strip off from them all the folklore and material relating to the history of religion, the prophetic legends about the activity of Elijah and Elisha indicate that there must have been marked tension between certain Israelite religious groups, with the cult that they practised, and the Israelite court and its religious policy.

3.4.1.1 It is not easy to say whether and to what point the details given about this conflict are historically reliable. One would certainly expect there to have been rivalry between the two ethnic groups which made up the northern kingdom, which could even develop into intense hostility (as also happens in modern times in any multi-ethnic state). Nor does it seem manifestly absurd that religion, a basic element in ancient society, and nowadays in countries with a traditional orientation, should have been one of the forms in which this expressed itself. However, it is in no way possible to discover the content and form of Israelite religion in the ninth and eighth centuries BC. The fact that in the North, as elsewhere, the image of a gilded bull served as a pedestal for the deity (above 1.2.3.2), though he was thought of as being invisible, would suggest a faith with a relatively orthodox content (measured by later criteria), even if it was ready to make some important concessions in terms of form. In this case Elijah and Elisha would have been the representatives of an even more orthodox Yahwistic current, which necessarily came into conflict not only with the cult of the Canaanite population but also with those Israelites whose religion was expressed in more or less syncretistic forms. The declaration in I Kings 19.18 that only seven thousand people (evidently a round figure) remained in Israel who had not compromised themselves in some way

ne great wrath upon Israel; and they withdrew from him
home' (literally 'to their own land', v.27). So here, too,
empt to indicate a victory, the note states that Israel had
ther words, that it lost the war, because of 'a great (divine)
was unleashed on it as a result of the human sacrifice.
contrast to what is said on the stele, the king involved
'son' of Omri (who would have been Ahab), but his
Moab succeeded in regaining its own independence
'or other information about II Kings 3 and the stele, cf.
Land, 336-40, and the map there; also G.Rendsburg, 'A
n of Moabite-Israelite History', *JANESCU* 13, 1981, 67-73.
silence of the stele about Joram, the sparseness of the
bout him generally, coupled with the brevity of his reign
ive character, have suggested to the author of a recent
and the king of Judah with the same name (below, 3.6.2)
the same person, so that Israel and Judah were united
1. We do not have enough information to confirm this
f nothing else, it shows the difficulties caused by the
nces of homonymy and affinity between the kings of Israel
Judah.

gs 6.8-23 speaks of another Aramaean war. The protagon-
mous, but the mention of places and of the prophet Elisha
ough; according to vv.24-31 the Aramaeans even besieged
the view that this is the same episode as I Kings 20, cf.

ing to our sources, the dynasty of Omri was overthrown
coup d'état, headed by a certain Jehu, who then became
an interesting note that the movement developed out of
movements headed by Elijah and Elisha (I Kings 19.15-
9.1-10) and was connected with similar movements in
where Hazael (*c.* 843-806?) was put on the throne in
the reigning sovereign, thought by some scholars to be
ad III (*c.*845-843, successor to Ben/Bar Hadad II, *c.* 875-
es and the sequence of figures remain hypothetical and
to verify them comes up against the inadequacy of the
ems improbable that there was a genuninely historical
e. that a revolt at Damascus should have been prompted
te prophet Elisha; and this also casts doubt on events in
ver, it would not be surprising for the rebels to be backed
orthodox element, discontented with the religious policy
of Omri and supporters of an integral Yahwism. We shall
ures below (4).
situation was difficult in the North, it was not easy in the
even if its greater isolation, its clearer boundaries and the

with Canaanite paganism might well be an illustration of this last
assertion.

3.4.1.2 The legends about the prophets Elijah and Elisha introduce
some of the salient features of these struggles.

3.4.1.2.1 They begin with the long drought of I Kings 17.1ff., which
according to the hagiographer was a kind of challenge as to whether it
was YHWH or Ba'al who gave the rains and therefore made the soil
fertile (for this question cf. above I.4.2). As we know, the dispute was
resolved in favour of YHWH (I Kings 18), in the divine judgment on
Mount Carmel (the location of *muḥrāqa*, coord.158-231), today the site
of the small Carmelite convent, on the south-east side of the mountain,
is very likely to be the right place). The narrative probably preserves a
distant and pale reminiscence of the change of sovereignty over Carmel
from Tyre to Israel, following the treaty made by Omri with Ittobaal,
and sealed by the marriage of Ahab to the princess of Tyre (Donner*,
1977, 403).

3.4.1.2.2 Another episode, this time with social as well as religious
dimensions, is that of Naboth's vineyard (I Kings 19). In its present
version the story has been considerably expanded by novelistic
elements. It deals with what would seem to be the clash between the
Israelite land law and that of Canaan, in that the former had come into
conflict with the claims of the crown. However, a comparison with II
Kings 9.21, where the field does not seem to have been incorporated
into crown property, shows that additions have been made to the
narrative. It is difficult to establish what actually happened, or whether
reminiscences of any actual event underlie the story; in itself the story
could be one of a number in circulation seeking to discredit Ahab and
his wife. This possibility is strongly suggested by its resemblance to
another analogous episode, that of the prophet Nathan and David after
his adultery with Bathsheba and the killing of her husband (II Sam.11.2-
12.15, above III.7.1.1). (In the latter case the king is converted after
listening to the invective and personally escapes; that also happens
here, I Kings 21.27ff.). Besides, as we have seen above, we know
nothing of Canaanite law, whether it relates to property or not (above
3.3.2.1), nor are we in a position to check whether the obvious reference
in I Kings 21.4 to Lev.25.23-31 is only an anachronism of the later
redactor or could amount to proof that a rule of this kind was already
in effect in the ninth century BC: that is how little we know of Israelite
law at this time!

3.4.2 As I have indicated, Ahab's Aramaean wars (I Kings 20; 22)
present complex chronological problems. Scholars are now inclined to
see these incidents as episodes in which the person of the monarch
involved was originally anonymous, and which will have only at a later
stage been supplemented by the insertion of the names of Ahab and

his counterpart Jehoshaphat of Judah (for which see below, 3.7.2: Jepsen 1941-44, Miller 1966 and Donner*, 400). That is because all the signs are that under the dynasty of Omri relationships between Israel and the Aramaeans had improved to the extent that the two countries had in fact become allies against Assyria (cf. further 3.4.4). The first account is of a battle near Aphek, perhaps the present-day *fīq*, on the ascent to the Golan Heights, coord.216-242, east of the Sea of Galilee. This ended in an Israelite victory over the Aramaeans, who had besieged Samaria shortly beforehand (I Kings 20), The second is an Israelite defeat at Ramoth-gilead, present-day *tell rāmīt*, coord.244-210, east of the lake. However, this second narrative is not so much interested in political and military history as in the theological problems of true and false prophecy (which we know to have been very much alive about the time of the exile, cf. below, XI.6.3) and prophetic inspiration. Now the first of the two texts could in fact refer to Israelite victories which will have led the Aramaeans to abandon the Israelite territories which they had conquered earlier (2.4) and to sue for peace. But this must have happened before the reign of Ahab; moreover he was not mortally wounded in battle, as I Kings 22.35// II Chron. 18.34) affirms, but according to I Kings 22.39f. died peacefully. However, for a post-dating see below (4.2). Against all these proposals see H.Tadmor, Appendix II below.

3.4.3 The rebellion of Moab must have begun in the reign of Ahab. We know from the stele of the Moabite king Mesha (above II.7.4) that this was a real war of liberation, as we would call it today. The stele, one of the most important extra-biblical historical documents in our possession, in fact tells us that Dibon, present-day *dibān*, coord. 224-101, in Transjordan, the birthplace and/or the residence of the king, had already fallen into Moabite hands before the conflict (line 3). The text mentions Omri many times as the one who reconquered the country (line 7) and also speaks of one of his sons without mentioning him by name. We shall see other features below, 3.5.

3.4.4 With the dynasty of Omri Israel entered the scene of the major international politics of the time, especially those of Assyria. For a bibliography cf. above on 3.3 and 3.4.

3.4.4.1 Asshur-nasir-pal II (*c.* 884-858), acting with skill and decisiveness, succeeded in reaching the Mediterranean and conquering the Aramaeans and the Phoenicians. In the annals of Shalmaneser III (*c.* 858-824), Omri is mentioned for the first time in the Assyrian records. One might say that Shalmaneser specialized in campaigns westwards, towards Syria and Palestine; so much so that we hear of at least six of them, in the sixth, tenth, eleventh, fourteenth, eighteenth and twenty-first years of his reign (cf. the texts in *ANET*, 278-80). This brings us to the time of Ahab and his successors.

3.4.4.2 The same annals speak o of Palestine and Syria formed by Hadad-idri; this is probably Ben/Ba conjectural dates, cf. below 3.5), Israelite'. The battle took place at I the Orontes in 853, a date recen study. The Assyrians claim to l not improbable; however, we can advantage from their victory. Sha against the same alliance in 849, 848 the theory that Omri and Ahab relations with the Aramaeans, However, we know of this battle or Hebrew Bible is completely silent a

3.4.5 The person chiefly reponsib the biblical texts condemn severe Jezebel, a person to whom I have name is perplexing, to say the l and therefore can hardly have b constitutional (if one can use this intervenes directly in affairs of sta the illicit advantage of the crown persecuted and sometimes killed. literary figure, connected with an a who, because she was a foreigne religion, was considered guilty of a well be the case. At all events, eve temple dedicated to Baal at Samaria that he must have remained Isr theophoric names to his sons: Aha

3.5 Ahab was succeeded to the Ahaziah (I Kings 22.52-54), and Ahaziah's brother Joram or Jehor reigned respectively in 850-849 or 8

3.5.1 Both were mediocre: we l connection with the latter are toi against Moab begun under his fat from the Moabite side by the Mesh campaign appears in II Kings 3 interesting ending. The king of Mo besieged in Kir-heres, also elsewhe *el-kerak*, coord.217-066). Since the under the attack of the besiegers, th to reign in his stead, and offered hir

And there c and returne despite an a to retreat; in wrath' whic However, i was not th grandson. completely. Aharoni, *T* Reconstruc

3.5.2 The informatior and his pas study[5] that were one a in this peric theory, but various inst and those o

3.5.3 II Ki ists are ano are precise Samaria. Fc above 3.4.2

3.6 Accor by a militar king. There the prophe 18; II King Damascus, succession Ben/Bar Ha 843). The d any attemp sources. It connection, by the Israe Israel. How by the ultra of the hous see other fe

3.7 If the South eithe

greater stability of the Davidic dynasty avoided constant conflict abroad, and at home prevented a series of *coups d'état* along with the problems over legitimacy which they created (below 3.8.2).

Select bibliography: W.F.Albright, 'The Judicial Reform of Jehoshaphat', in *Alexander Marx Jubilee Volume*, New York 1950, 61-82; W.Rudolph, 'Die Einheitlichkeit der Erzählung vom Sturz der Atalja (2 Kön. 11)', in *Festschrift für Alfred Bertholet*, Tübingen 1950, 473-8; A.Alt, *Bemerkungen zu einigen judäischen Ortslisten des Alten Testaments*, BBLAK (ZDPV 68, 1949-51), 193-210 = *KS* II, 289-305; M.Liverani, 'L'histoire de Joas', *VT* 24, 1974, 438-53; W.Shea, 'Adadnirari III and Jehoash of Israel', *JCS* 30, 1978, 101-13; H.-D.Hoffmann, *Reform und Reformen*, ATANT 66, Zurich 1980, 93ff.; E.Puech, 'Athalie, fille d'Achab et la chronologie des rois d'Israël et de Juda', *Salamanticensis* 28, 1981, 117-38. Cf. also H.Tadmor, artt.citt., above III n.9; C.Levin, *Der Sturz der Königin Atalja*, SBS 105, Stuttgart 1982; J.Trebolle Barrero, 'La coronación de Joás (2 Re. 11)', *Estbíb* 41, 1983, 5-16 (these last two articles do not take account of the study by M.Liverani 1974). For the 'people of the land' cf. E.Würthwein, *Der 'amm hā'āreṣ im Alten Testament*, BWANT IV, 17, Stuttgart 1936; J.A.Soggin, 'Der judäische *'am hā'āreṣ* und das Königreich im Juda', *VT* 13, 1963, 187-95; R. de Vaux, 'Le sens de l'expression "peuple du pays" dans l'Ancien Testament et le rôle politique du peuple en Israël', *RA* 58, 1964, 167-72; E.W.Nicholson, 'The Meaning of the Expression *'m h'rs* in the Old Testament', *JSS* 10, 1965, 56-66; S.Talmon, 'The Judaean *'am hā'āreṣ* in Historical Perspective', in *Proceedings of the Fourth World Congress of Jewish Studies, Jerusalem 1965*, Jerusalem 1967, I, 71-76; C.Schäfer-Lichtenberger, *Stadt und Eidgenossenschaft im Alten Testament*, BZAW 156, Berlin 1983, 391ff.

3.7.1 Only the biblical texts which form part of the Deuteronomistic and Chronistic history provide material for reconstructing the period which extends from the end of the tenth century to the middle of the eighth century BC in the kingdom of Judah. We have seen (above, 2) how, after a series of defeats, the war between Israel and Judah, aimed at giving Judah a northern frontier which could be defended strategically, ended in victory for Judah; however, this victory was achieved by persuading the Aramaeans of Damascus to attack Israel on its flank. Mizpah, the present-day *tell en-naṣbeh*, coord.170-143, at one time a bulwark of the North against the South, was transformed by King Asa into a bulwark of the South against the North. From then on the frontier between the two Hebrew kingdoms stayed virtually static, and although peace was not officially made, it became an established fact, especially in the period of the dynasty of Omri, during the reign of Jehoshaphat of Judah (*c.* 873-849 or 868-847). Of course it is possible (as Donner*, 391, argues) that the two sides simply confirmed the situation legally and maintained a peace which had already begun *de facto*; at all events, Judah too was soon involved in the enterprises of the North, i.e. the Aramaean wars, cf. I Kings 22.2-4 (but cf. above, 3.4) and II Kings 8.28; 9.14 (below 4.1.1). In II Kings 3.4-8 we see Judah fighting beside Israel against Moab (above 3.5.1). Relationships between Israel and Judah were sealed by the marriage between Joram, son of Jehoshaphat of Judah, and Athaliah, sister, or more probably daughter (thus already Noth*, 236, and recently Puech 1981) of Ahab of Israel. We have already looked at the problem of the relationship between the two Jorams (above 3.5.2).

3.7.2 We know very little about Jehoshaphat, nor are we told much about his successors Joram (*c*.849-842 or 847-845) and Ahaziah (with the same name as the ruler of the North; *c*. 842 or 845: II Kings 8.6-19; 8.25-28//II Chron. 22.1-6 respectively). Ahaziah is said to have been wounded in Jehu's revolt, while staying with Joram of Israel, and to have died as a result of his wounds (II Kings 9.27-29). He had already lost Edom, which had rebelled (II Kings 8.20-24//II Chron 21.8-10), only succeeding with some difficulty in extricating his troops from being encircled by the enemy by means of a hasty flight.

3.7.2.1 So there is little information about Jehoshaphat. In I Kings 22.41-51//II Chron. 20.21-31 there is a report that on the basis of an agreement with Ahaziah king of Israel (above 3.5) he tried to establish trade on the Red Sea, but apparently without any great success.

3.7.2.2 The texts also indicate that Jehoshaphat attempted a religious reform (I Kings 22.47f.), probably directed against Canaanite religion; however, the whole passage is expressed in Deuteronomistic terminology, so that it is difficult to say what really happened. Moreover, II Chronicles 17.1-9; 19.1-11 report that he initiated a reform of public administration, the cult and the army; according to Albright, 1950, he also reformed the legal system. However, here, too it is impossible to establish whether or not the Chronicler was using ancient traditions about the events, so that we do not know precisely what happened (Donner*, 391f., against Albright 1950; for an important recent discussion see H.G.M.Williamson, *I and II Chronicles*, New Century Bible, 1984, ad loc.).

3.8 The killing of Ahaziah, king of Judah, in the course of Jehu's revolt in the North, after a very short reign, left the throne of David vacant. The legitimate successor was Joash, the infant son of the dead king, but because of his age he needed a regent.

3.8.1 According to established practice (above, 2.6), Athaliah the queen mother became regent. She exploited the position of strength which her new position automatically gave her, by eliminating all the heirs to the throne of David. According to our account (II Kings 11//II

Chron.22.9-23.21), only the boy Joash succeeded in escaping. He was rescued by an aunt, sister to the dead king, who is said to have hidden him in the temple. The usurper reigned for about six years, *c.* 842-837 or 845-840, without realizing this. Then one sabbath at the end of this period, the priest Jehoiada summoned the temple guard, armed them, and occupied the sanctuary. After producing the boy, he anointed him king and had him acclaimed by the army and the 'people of the land'. The queen, who had meanwhile arrived at the temple, was arrested, taken to the palace and killed there. In this way the Davidic dynasty was saved and the legitimate succession maintained without the continuity being broken.

3.8.2 However, Liverani's 1974 study has shown that the situation was more complex. On the basis of biblical and especially Near Eastern parallels, he shows the theatrical character of the narrative and its scenes, the way in which it is centred on the small heir to the monarchy, whose legitimate election to the throne is meant to annul the earlier usurpation. But the scene seems historically most improbable, given that the theme is frequent in popular tradition; in the ancient Near East the best known case is that of Idrimi of Alalakh, who also emerged 'from nowhere' to claim the rule over the city state which is said to have been his by right. In the Old Testament itself, in Judg.9.5b, 'the youngest of the sons' of Jerubbaal (above VIII.5.1.3) escapes the slaughter to give an exhortation to the rebels. So in reality it would seem that the Davidic dynasty, too, was interrupted and was only reconstituted later, somewhat precariously, by means of a boy chosen by the priesthood and the sister of the dead king in the temple, and then acclaimed by the army and the 'people of the land'. However, this is the only such instance attested in the South, so that it is the exception which proves the rule of the institutional stability of this country. Moreover, the continuity of the dynasty was preserved, albeit only legally and formally.

3.8.3 In all these events a group called the 'people of the land', Hebrew '*am hā-'āreṣ*, appears for the first time in the biblical narrative. In later Judaism (below XIII.11.3.1; cf.XIV.3.4) the expression denoted the ignorant masses, incapable of study, and therefore of observing the law. However, in the pre-exilic period, the 'people of the land' was something like a landed aristocracy, a group descended from the ancient usufructuaries of the tribal lands and therefore economically independent; this group seems to have backed the Davidic dynasty to the hilt, even if it does not seem to have had any independent role within the legal system (Schäfer 1983). The Deuteronomistic historian recognizes the character of this group as supporters of the traditional Yahwistic faith of Israel, and therefore often contrasts it with the population of Jerusalem, the majority of which was still Canaanite, and with the court there. It defends the dynasty against the latter groups.

3.8.4 We know little about what happened next. Given Joash's age, the young king must have had a tutor-regent; as II Chron. 24.2-3, 15-22 (Donner*, 394) suggests, this was the priest Jehoiada. Chronicles also connects the initial piety of the young man closely with the fact that the priest was his guardian; when Jehoiada died, Joash is said to have ceased to profess his faith. II Kings 12.1-22//II Chron.24.1-16, 23-27, gives an account of his reign. The texts present him as a supporter of the restoration of the temple, financed by offerings which were collected in a coffer introduced during his reign. The sums needed for the rebuilding and maintenance of the temple were taken from it and given to the builders.

3.8.5 There is a report from this period of an attack by the Aramaeans against Jerusalem; Hazael was already their leader. This attack was only bought off by the payment of a large sum (II Kings 12.18ff.). The Aramaeans are also said to have already occupied Gath, perhaps as allies of the Philistines. However, we know little about the event and therefore find it hard to understand. Still, the fact that the Aramaeans could again attack in force indicates that the Assyrian danger which had led them into an alliance with Israel and Judah must have come to an end.

3.8.6 Joash fell victim to an assassination (II Kings 12.21-22), but the succession was assured by his son Amaziah (c.800-783 or 801-787). Amaziah is reported to have won a victory over the Edomites in a 'valley of Salt' which is otherwise unknown (however, its title suggests that it should be located in the vicinity of the Dead Sea, II Kings 14.7); in this operation he is said to have captured Sela (this is not the present-day Petra, as is often claimed, but rather *es-sela'*, coord.205-020). That was probably an ephemeral success, which did not change the political structure of the region in any way.

3.8.7 The texts also report that Amaziah fought a battle against Joash of Israel near Beth-shemesh (present-day *tell er-rumeileh*, coord.147-128); he was taken prisoner and brought to Jerusalem, where the Israelites demolished part of the walls and sacked the temple (II Kings 14.8-14//II Chron. 25.17-24). This information, like the episode as a whole, seems suspect (Donner*, 395) and we do not know when or how it came about, given that for some time there had been lasting peace between the two kingdoms. Amaziah, too, was assassinated in the course of a palace conspiracy, at Lachish (*tell ed-duweir*, coord.135-108), where he had taken refuge (II Kings 14.19-21//II Chron. 25.25-28). However, the 'people of the land' were on their guard and put his son on the throne. The new king is given a double name, Uzziah or Azariah.

4.1 With the revolt of Jehu, as I indicated above (3.6), we have another attempt by the North to establish a dynasty.

4.1.1 As I pointed out, the texts associate the revolt with the prophets Elijah and Elisha, but in this account there are a number of problematical features: the main one is that the two prophets are also supposed to have incited Hazael of Damascus to revolt (Hazael was a ruler who later caused a number of difficulties for Israel and Judah, above 3.8.5 and below 4.3). At all events, an Assyrian stele (*ANET*, 280) confirms that Hazael took power. He is called 'son of no one' (a title reserved for usurpers), which would confirm that this was a *coup d'état*.

4.1.2 The account of Jehu's revolt appears in II Kings 9-10. Jehu, commander of the Israelite army stationed at Ramoth-gilead (present-day *tell rāmīt*, east of Lake Tiberias, coord. 244-210), a region in which there seem to have been endemic clashes between the Israelites and the Aramaeans, was invested with the crown by an emissary of Elisha and acclaimed by the troops. He conspired against Joram of Israel, marched on the royal residence at Jezreel, first killed the king of Israel, and then also mortally wounded Ahaziah, king of Judah, who had been his guest, on his flight southwards. So he exterminated all the royal family, including Jezebel. The texts (II Kings 10.15) also show him in alliance with the Rechabites, an extremist Hebrew sect which rejected agriculture and its products, considering them the produce of Canaan and therefore pagan; its members led an itinerant existence as cattle rearers and craftsmen, and especially as tinsmiths and armourers.[6] The biblical tradition, confirmed independently by Jer.35, presents them as an extremely fanatical group, exclusive worshippers of YHWH, and this characteristic makes it probable that they were connected with the revolt and with prophetic elements.

4.1.3 Thus Jehu had succeeded in taking possession of the royal residence; he still had to seize the real capital, Samaria. First of all he sent a message (II Kings 10.1ff.) and obtained the submission of the city: 'We are your subjects (literally servants), and will do all that you bid us' (10.5). In a second message Jehu then called on the inhabitants of Samaria to hand over to him 'the heads of your master's house' (correction following some Hebrew manuscripts and LXX), bringing them (with LXX) to Jezreel(10.6ff.); the text makes a play on the Hebrew *rō'š*, 'chief, ruler' and 'head'. The inhabitants of Samaria took the invitation in the most literal sense and sent him the heads of the Omrides.[7] Jehu then went on to kill the surviving Omrides, having also occupied the capital. He then summoned the faithful of Ba'al to the temple, on the pretext of wanting to continue to practise the cult, had them massacred and profaned the sanctuary.

4.1.4 That is what the sources tell us. However, in his important studies mentioned in the bibliography above on 3.3, M.C.Astour (1959 and 1971) has suggested a very different reconstruction of the historical and political context within which Jehu moved; while this reconstruction does not deny the importance of the religious element, it puts it on a subsidiary level. Astour's study (1971) makes the following three points.

4.1.4.1 Hosea 10.14 mentions a certain šalmān, whom he wants to identify (as do almost all scholars today) with Shalmaneser III of Assyria. In the course of his campaign westwards in 841 (above 3.4.4), Shalmaneser first besieged Damascus, without succeeding in conquering it, and then destroyed a number of other places including Beth-arbel, mentioned in Hos.10 (the present-day Irbid in Jordan, coord.229-218).

4.1.4.2 From here, as the Assyrian annals tell us (*ANET*, 280), in his eighteenth year Shalmaneser went 'to the mountains of ba'li ra 'si, which is a promontory'. This is probably Carmel (though others think in terms of a place further north, in Lebanon), and in those days Carmel was the boundary between Israel and Tyre (above 3.4.1.2.1). Thus Shalmaneser must have crossed the plain of Jezreel in Israel. For Aharoni, *The Land*, this identification is certain; M. Noth*, 248, thinks rather of Lebanon.

4.1.4.3 On this interpretation, Jehu's revolt would simply have been the product of a coup arranged by the pro-Assyrian faction in Israel, intent on eliminating the Omrides, who until then had been the leading light in the resistance to the Assyrian penetration westwards (above 3.6). In that case, the theory of a connection with a similar movement in Damascus also appears much more acceptable than it might seem at first sight. Be this as it may, soon afterwards, while at Tyre, Shalmaneser received the homage of the pro-Assyrian faction friendly to Assyria and the new king. Jehu is called 'king of the country of Omri',[8] a tribute to what had been a great dynasty, even if the tribute was probably unintentional and the dynasty itself did not receive due recognition in Israel. The account has found immortality by being recorded on the 'black obelisk' of Shalmaneser III and is well illustrated there; the new king of Israel is shown prostrate, face to the ground, before his lord (*ANEP*, 355).

4.1.5 While Damascus was locked in struggle with Assyria, Israel enjoyed a short respite. And since, as we have seen, Jehu was probably put on the throne by the pro-Assyrian faction, it is reasonable to suppose that the anti-Assyrian alliance with the Aramaean kingdoms, one of the key elements in the foreign policy of the Omri dynasty, was also terminated. This must have rekindled the ancient hostilities. In this new context Hazael now becomes the enemy *par excellence*, and he appears in this role not only in II Kings 8.11ff. but also in later prophetic texts like Amos 1.3-5; Isa.9.11.

4.2 It is only logical that the first objective of the Aramaeans should have been the Israelite settlements in northern Transjordan; Israel seems to have lost virtually all of them (II Kings 10.32f., a text in which the numbers involved were probably increased when it came to the south). We then find the Aramaeans probably allied with the Philistines (above 3.8.5, II Kings 12.17f.), and only kept away from Jerusalem by the payment of a substantial ransom.

4.3 From that time and for many years, the independence of the two kingdoms 'was overshadowed by severe struggles in Syria which broke out among the city states there' (Herrmann*, 230). The Aramaean wars must have caused substantial losses to Israel and Judah in men, material and goods, all the more since they usually ended with the defeat of the two Hebrew kingdoms. Only once do we hear of a victory: II Kings 13.4f., 22ff. shows Jehoahaz (*c.* 815-801, 818-802) and his son Joash (*c.* 801-786, 802-787) victors first over Hazael and then over his son Ben/ Bar Hadad III or IV, indicated in the Assyrian annals only by his title *mari'*, 'Lord' (*ANET* 282, 806? – 775?). Some scholars would want to associate these victories with I Kings 20 and 22 which, as we have seen, have been anachronistically connected with Ahab and Jehoshaphat (above 3.4.2).

4.4 However, better times also came for Israel. At the end of the ninth century BC the Assyrians under Adad-nirari III (*c.* 810-783) marched westwards at least four times: in 806, 805, 803 and 797 BC (*ANET*, 281f.). Probably in the course of the last campaign, they forced Damascus first to submit (stele of *tell er-rimāt*[9]) and then to accept Assyrian sovereignty. In the act of submission Joash of Samaria is mentioned explicitly, along with other rulers of the region.

4.5 It was Jeroboam II (*c.* 786-746 or 787-747) of Israel who profited greatly from the elimination of Damascus from the political scene. He succeeded in reconquering all of Transjordan that had traditionally belonged to Israel: from the Dead Sea to *mᵉbōʾ ḥāmāt* (present-day *lebwe*, coord.277-397), also including *qarnayim* in the east (present-day *tell ʿaštāra*, coord.247-249) in his conquests, as II Kings 14.25; Amos 6.13 indicate.[10] The passage which seems to tell us that he even succeeded in occupying Damascus (14.28) is textually uncertain and historically most improbable. The reign of Jeroboam must also have brought a time of economic prosperity, even if, to judge from Amos' invective, the riches were now spread very unevenly between the various social classes. As a result of this, Jeroboam II, himself a notable monarch, is painted with dark colours in the biblical text. For an example of riches in Israel cf. below X.3.2.

5 Uzziah or Azariah of Judah (*c.*783-742 or 787-736 BC) was only a little younger than his contemporary Jeroboam II: his chronology is very complex and therefore controversial.

Select bibliography: H.Tadmor, 'Azriya of Yaudi', *ScrHier* 8, 1961, 232-71; J.A.Soggin, 'Das Erdbeben von Amos 1,1 und die Chronologie der Könige Ussia und Jotham von Juda', *ZAW* 82, 1970, 117-121; id., *Il profeta Amos*, Brescia 1982, 17, 48ff.; N.Na'aman, 'Sennacherib's "Letter to God" on his Campaign to Judah', *BASOR* 214, 1974, 25-39; A.Zeron, 'Die Anmassung des Königs Ussia im Lichte von Jesajas Berufung', *TZ* 1977, 65-68; G.Garbini, 'L'impero di David', *ASNSP* III, 13, 1983, 1-20.

5.1 For the question of the double name of the monarch see Tadmor's 1961 article.[11] At least for a short time, reasonably good conditions were also restored in Israel (II Kings 15.1-7//II Chron. 26.1-23). Under the leadership of Uzziah, Judah seems also to have succeeded in recovering its own southern boundaries, extending them as far as the Red Sea (II Kings 14.22), where Uzziah rebuilt the port of Elat (today the port of Aqaba in Jordan, coord.150-882). In the more extensive text in Chronicles it is said that he fought with success against the Philistines, the Arabians and the Meunites (not the Minaeans of the Hellenistic period in southern Arabia, but a tribe between present-day Petra, coord.020-225, and *ma'an*, coord.952-220) and the Ammonites (cf. I Chron. 4.41; II Chron.26.7, R.Borger and H.Tadmor, 1982, cf. the bibliography to X.1). This is probably the context of a series of fortifications recently excavated right across the Negeb, the southernmost of which seems to be Kadesh-barnea (shades of Moses! – this is present-day *'ain el qudeirat*, coord.098-007, cf. above VI.8.2.1.2). If we accept the substantial historicity of the information given in Chronicles at this point,[12] these fortifications are to be attributed to Uzziah, along with the strengthening of the fortifications of Jerusalem (II Chron. 26.11-15). The settlements in the Negeb were combined with important agricultural settlements, employing specialized techniques for dry farming;[13] and the techniques used have proved to be basically effective down to the present day, with the improvements made to them by modern agricultural technology.

5.2 Relations seem to have been good between Jeroboam II and Uzziah. Taken together, the boundaries of the two kingdoms were now very close to those of the empire of David and Solomon at its greatest extent (above III.7.3), and in the reign of Uzziah Judah must have achieved its greatest splendour. This is the monarch in whose reign G.Garbini puts the maritime expedition and the trading operations which the texts attribute to Solomon (above, IV.3.2).

5.3 The texts also report that Uzziah was smitten with 'leprosy' (II Kings 15.5// II Chron.26.16-21). We do not know for certain what illness is indicated by the term usually translated in this way, but it seems certain that rather than being 'Hansen's disease' it was some kind of skin disease, contagious but not fatal;[14] this also seems to be suggested by the fact that the Hebrew *ṣāra'at* is also used in connection with fabrics and leather (i.e. to denote some form of mould) and with walls (a kind of saltpetre). Chronicles, followed by Josephus, IX, 222-227, adds that this was a divine judgment on a sacrilegious offering made by the sovereign in the temple, an episode which Josephus associates with a violent earthquake that took place about 760 BC. This is the same earthquake referred to in Amos 1.1 and some centuries later in Zech.14.5, that seems to have produced the valley which now separates the Mount of Olives from Mount Scopus. While the synchronism between the king's illness and the earthquake seems historically acceptable, as A.Zeron has recently demonstrated, the Chronicles narrative, later taken up by Josephus, presupposes the vision of Isaiah in Isa.6.1ff., so it is obviously an artificial construction. At all events the illness made the sovereign impure and therefore incapable of running the affairs of state, so that he had to live 'in isolation to the day of his death' (II Kings 15.5//II Chron.25.21). That is how the expression *bēt ḥopšīt* is usually interpeted; the second term of this phrase comes from a root which normally denotes liberty (here a euphemism for liberty from affairs of state?); but in Ugaritic, *ḥapṯt* (Gordon 995, Aistleitner 107) is used to denote the underworld; thus an incurable disease appears as the antechamber of death!

5.4 There is an interesting note that Uzziah's son Jotham became what must have been to all intents and purposes a regent on behalf of his father.

5.4.1 Uzziah remained king in effect, except that he was unable because of his disease to implement affairs of state in person; for want of any direct information it is reasonable to suppose that Jotham continued to be regent until the death of his father and that the succession then passed to him. In the first of the two chronologies which I am using (that of the American schools), that would be from about 750 to 742; in the Begrich-Jepsen chronology, Uzziah would in fact have survived Jotham, so that his successor, Jehoahaz or Ahaz (*c.* 735-715 or 736-729/25), would also have been regent for a short time. If nothing else, this shows the difficulties confronting any study of the chronology of the kings of Israel and Judah.

5.4.2 The mention in the annals of Tiglath-pileser III of Assyria (*c.* 744-702) of a certain '*azriyahu* of Judah' (*ANET*, 282f.) has caused considerable uncertainty. This king is said to have headed an anti-Assyrian coalition in 743, and the name would seem to correspond almost exactly to that of Uzziah-Azariah.[15] It has been understood in this way by many scholars. However, it is not easy to imagine the king, sick and in isolation, involved in an enterprise of this kind. We cannot, of course, rule out the possibility that his name appears as that of the sovereign who legitimately exercised power at the time, though *de facto* this power was delegated to others; however, Na'aman has made a more probable suggestion. He argues that the stele, the text of which in fact is mutilated at many important points, really refers to the rebellion which took place some decades later, under Hezekiah of Judah (below XI.2).

5.5 In the year of Uzziah's death, Isaiah is said to have had his vision (Isa.6.1). It is also at this period that the great prophets of Israel and Judah arose: Amos, Hosea, Isaiah and Micah. I have dealt with them in detail elsewhere,[16] so I refer the reader to these studies.

X

THE ASSYRIAN INVASIONS

1 The Assyrian armies which had invaded both Aram and Israel and the Phoenician city-states after Jehu's *coup d'état*, making them all vassals of the great king, were to become the dominant feature of the second half of the eighth century BC and the beginning of the seventh. And while under the dynasty of Omri of Israel it had been possible for the little states of Syria and Palestine to contain, if not to repel, the threat of the great Eastern empire (above IX.3.4.4) by means of a series of coalitions, which had proved sufficient for the purpose, the occupation of the throne of Israel by a reigning house that was probably pro-Assyrian (above IX.4.1.1) destroyed a balance which had been laboriously achieved and maintained by the nations of the region for decades, albeit with the purely negative aim of resisting the invader. It also reopened, though only for a short time, the conflict between Israel and Damascus. This in fact made the way free for the Assyrian armies to move westwards. When resistance was offered at all, it tended to be essentially local; at other times, as we shall see (below 3.4.3), there was no resistance at all, and in one case the Assyrian intervention was even requested. The region became the theatre of engagements between whatever Mesopotamian power was in the ascendant and Egypt, a force which never seems to have renounced its sovereignty over Canaan. Moreover, first for Assyria and later for Babylon, as for Egypt, Canaan was either the launching pad for an attack or an indispensable advanced defensive position.

Select bibliography: R.H.Pfeiffer, 'Assyria and Israel', *RSO* 32, 1957, 145-50; W.W.Hallo, 'From Qarqar to Carchemish', *BA* 23, 1960, 33-61; D.B.Redford, 'Studies in the Relations between Palestine and Egypt during the First Millennium BC: II. The Twenty-Second Dynasty', *JAOS* 93, 1973, 3-17; B.Oded, 'The Historical Background of the Syro-Ephraimite War Reconsidered', *CBQ* 34, 1972, 153-65; id., 'The Phoenician Cities and the Assyrian Empire in the Time of

Tiglat-Pileser III', *ZDPV* 38, 1974, 38-49; H.Tadmor, 'Assyria and the West: The Ninth Century and its Aftermath', in H.Goedicke and J.J.M.Roberts (eds.), *Unity and Diversity*, Baltimore 1975, 36-48; H.Barth, *Israel und das Assyrerreich in den nicht-jesajanischen Texten des Proto-Jesaja*, Hamburg theol.dissertation 1974; id., *Die Jesaja-Worte in der Josiazeit*, WMANT 48, Neukirchen 1977; H.Cazelles, 'Problèmes de la guerre syro-ephraimite', *EI* 14, 1978, 70*-78*; H.Spieckermann, *Juda unter Assur in der Sargonidenzeit*, FRLANT 129, Göttingen 1982. For the prophets of Israel and Judah in this period cf. H.Donner, *Israel unter den Völkern*, SVT XI, Leiden 1964. For Assyria, its policy and its army cf. e.g. W. von Soden, 'Die Assyrer und der Krieg', *Iraq* 25, 1963, 131-44; H.W.F.Saggs, 'Assyrian Warfare in the Sargonide Period', ibid., 145-54; E.Vogt, 'Die Texte Tiglat-Pilesers III uber die Eroberung Palästinas', *Bibl* 45, 1964, 348-54; M.Cogan, *Imperialism and Religion. Assyria, Judah and Israel in the Eighth and Seventh Centuries BC*, Pittsburgh 1971; B.Oded, *Mass Deportations and Deportees in the Neo-Assyrian Empire*, Pittsburgh 1971; J.McKay, *Religion in Judah under the Assyrians*, SBT II 26, London 1973; H.Tadmor and M.Cogan, 'Ahaz and Tiglath-Pileser in the Book of Kings: Historiographic Considerations', *Bibl* 60, 1979, 491-508; R.Borger and H.Tadmor, 'Zwei Beiträge zur alttestamentlichen Wissenschaft aufgrund der Inschriften Tiglatpilesers III', *ZAW* 94, 1982, 244-51; F.Malbran-Labat, *L'armée et l'organisation militaire de l'Assyrie*, Paris 1982. For the Assyrian names in the Hebrew Bible cf. A.R.Millard, 'Assyrian Royal Names in Biblical Hebrew', *JSS* 21, 1976, 1-14.

1.1 All these factors, taken together, very soon led to the incorporation into the Assyrian empire first of the Aramaean kingdoms, and then, bit by bit, of Israel. Finally, Judah became a vassal, first of Assyria and then, after the brief interregnum of Josiah (below XI.4), of Babylon, before it finally and definitively lost its independence in 587/86 (below XI.6).

1.2 Babylon had been the cultural centre of Mesopotamia from time immemorial. However, it was Assyria, a region situated on the upper Tigris, which for some centuries controlled the destinies of the region and of adjacent territories: from the last years of the second millennium BC to the seventh century BC. Its rise to power was gradual, but it led to 'an empire of a completely different type, an unparalleled power structure...' (Donner*, 416). Its chief characteristics were, first, a permanent and professional army equipped not only with war chariots but also with mounted cavalry, a novelty for the period, and then a complete lack of scruples which led Assyria to perpetrate cruelties which terrorized the whole region. Furthermore, it sacked cities and wrought destruction in a way which left little behind in an enemy country. Isaiah 5.26-29 on the one hand indicates the efficiency and capability of this army, and on the other illustrates how it could be compared with a horde of savage beasts. Of course it is open to question whether and to what extent this reputation for cruelty was based on fact, on events which actually happened, or whether it was not rather the result of skilful propaganda aimed at discouraging any resistance from the start (von Soden, and Saggs 1963), thus making the enemy more malleable and easy to deal with.

1.3 Babylon was the only nation to which the Assyrians seem to have shown some respect. Assyria recognized its intellectual debt to Babylon and the Babylonian contribution to civilization generally. So although Babylon had submitted under Tiglath-pileser III, it was allowed a degree of autonomy by means of a form of personal union, and the governor, an Assyrian, was always of royal blood. This situation, with privileges extending up to a certain point, did not prevent the Assyrians from dealing extremely harshly with their *alma mater* where they thought it necessary.

2.1 At the end of the previous chapter (5.4.2), I mentioned Tiglath-pileser III (*c.* 745-272), who ascended the throne under the name of *pūlu*, hence the Hebrew *pūl*. He was to 'lead the neo-Assyrian empire to the height of its power, bringing it to perfection on a systematic and conceptual, if not a territorial, level' (Donner*, 418).

2.1.1 At home, Tiglath-pileser reformed the structure of the state, changing the great provinces, which were difficult to administer, into smaller, manageable districts, with a much simplified organization.

2.1.2 Towards neighbouring nations, Assyria inaugurated 'a new imperialistic foreign policy, the effectiveness of which cannot be emphasized strongly enough' (Donner*, ibid.).

2.1.2.1 Characteristic of this new foreign policy was the abandonment of the traditional concept of vassalage; instead, the preferred treatment was to incorporate peoples directly into the empire and occupy their territory.

2.1.2.2 Donner* (419) shows how this would normally happen in three successive stages.

2.1.2.2.1 The establishment of a traditional vassal relationship with the nation in question, modelled on the practice of previous Assyrian sovereigns: limited sovereignty, a foreign policy completely dependent on that of Assyria, and a demand for heavy tribute.

2.1.2.2.2 At the first sign of rebellion, there was direct military intervention, with the nomination of a pro-Assyrian ruler, though he might come from the reigning dynasty. The operation was often combined with drastic changes of frontier, followed by the incorporation of the new territory thus obtained into the empire; alternatively, the land was ceded to faithful vassals. All this went with a marked increase in the tribute exacted.

2.1.2.2.3 At the least sign of any form of opposition, there was again decisive military intervention, the deposition of the ruler responsible and his replacement by an Assyrian governor. The remaining territory was incorporated into the empire, and the leading class was deported so as to leave the country leaderless. New ethnic groups were imported.

2.1.2.2.4 Finally, one notable characteristic of the system was its flexibility: it was not applied in a inflexible or dogmatic way, but from time to time was adapted to circumstances. This made it particularly effective.

2.2 Assyria achieved its greatest expansion under Esarhaddon (680-669), who in the course of three campaigns succeeded even in conquering Egypt. However, this was the splendour preceding the decline: even under Asshur-bani-pal (669-627), the Sardanapalus of Greek legend, to whom we owe the famous library which has handed down the majority of Mesopotamian literature, we see Assyria now preoccupied with predominantly defensive wars. In 655, under Psammetichus I (663-609), the founder of the Sixteenth Dynasty, Egypt regained its independence; between 652 and 648 there was war with Babylon, from which Assyria emerged victorious but much weakened. On the death of this literate and wise king, it was only a question of time, a few years, before the empire collapsed without leaving any trace.

2.3 Here one might point out the intrinsic weakness of all these empires, a feature which led to the rapid decline of all but Assyria: they were practically all made up of a multitude of nations which had been subjected in a more or less brutal way, and inhabited by different populations. Common to all, however, was hostility towards the dominant power, so that the trend in the empires was basically centrifugal. And the very mass of people who had to be controlled, coupled with the the extent of these empires, which had grown up in a completely irrational way, and the difficulties and slowness of communications, made them virtually ungovernable after a certain time: their administration was increasingly inefficient, slow and muddled. Increasing resources had to be devoted to repression, with a consequent waste of men and means and the destruction of riches.

3 At the time of Tiglath-pileser III, we have in Palestine what has traditionally, from Luther onwards, been called the 'Syro-Ephraimite war', although in reality it also involved Judah.

Select bibliography: A. Alt, 'Hosea 5,8-6,6. Ein Krieg und seine Folgen in prophetischer Beleuchtung', *NKZ* 30, 1919, 537-68 = *KS* II, 163-87; id., 'Das System der assyrischen Provinzen auf dem Boden des

Reiches Israel', *ZDPV* 83, 1929, 220-42 = *KS* II, 188-205; J.Begrich, 'Der syrisch-ephraimitische Krieg und seine weltpolitische Zusammenhänge', *ZDMG* 83, 1929, 213-37 = *GS* 99-120; H.Donner, *Israel unter den Völkern*, SVT XI, Leiden 1964; E.Vogt, *Die Texte Tiglat-Pileser III, über die Eroberung Palästinas'*, *Bibl* 45, 1964, 348-54; E.M.Good, 'Hosea 5:8 – 6:6: an Alternative to Alt', *JBL* 85, 1966, 173-81; P.R.Ackroyd, 'Historians and Prophets', *SEA* 33, 1968, 18-54; B.Oded, art.cit., 1972, above 1; L.D.Levine, 'Menahem and Tiglath-Pileser – A New Synchronism', *BASOR* 206, 1972, 40-42; M.Weippert, 'Menahem von Israel und seine Zeitgenossen in einer Steleninschrift des assyrischen Königs Tiglathpileser III. aus dem Iran', *ZDPV* 89, 1973, 26-53; A.Vanel, 'Tabe'el en Is VII 6 et le roi Tubaîl de Tyr', *SVT* 26, 1974, 17-24; N.Na'aman, cf. on IX. 5; W.H.Shea, 'Menahem and Tiglath Pileser III', *JNES* 37, 1978, 43-9; W.Dietrich, *Jesaja und die Politik*, Munich 1976; E.Asurmendi, *La guerra siro-efraimita*, Valencia 1982; M.E.W.Thompson, *Situation and Theology*, Sheffield 1982.

3.1 The Syro-Ephraimite war, which was an event of only local importance, could have been the product of an extreme attempt to revive the anti-Assyrian alliance that had proved to be such a good thing about a century before: at that time, the primary aim, that of containing the Assyrian advance westwards, had been completely achieved. We are reasonably well informed about it, though again the information is ultimately inadequate and sometimes contradictory. Among the biblical texts cf. II Kings 15-16; Isa.7.1-7; 8.1-15; 10.27; 17.1-11; Hos.5.1ff.; 5.8-6.6; 8.7-10; but these texts contain a number of often basic contradictions, so that the details often seem very obscure (Donner*, 430). Finally, there are the Assyrian texts from the annals and inscriptions of Tiglath-pileser III, *ANET*, 282-4. I have already pointed out that the chronology of the period is complex (IX.5.4.1), especially in connection with the problems of the regency of Jotham and the death of Uzziah of Judah; in addition there are the problems of the death of Ahaz and therefore of the accession of Hezekiah to the throne (II Kings 16.20; 18.1). So we find marked discrepancies between the two systems of chronology which I am using.

3.2 In Israel the death of Jeroboam II (746 or 747 BC) was followed by the accession to the throne of his son Zechariah (*c.* 746-45 or 747); he was killed by a certain Shallum (745 or 747, II Kings 15, 8-12, 13-16), who was in turn eliminated by a certain Menahem (*c.* 745-738 or 747-738, II Kings 15.17-22), a citizen of the former capital Tirzah. Menahem succeeded in pacifying the kingdom by using very strong repressive measures (15.16); this presupposes that he had control over the army. However, Tiglath-pileser (*pūl*) 'invaded the country' (15.18b-20), having subjected and annexed Hamath in central Syria (present-day *ḥama*, coord.312-503), and Menahem, together with the other rulers of the region, hastened to send a substantial tribute (a thousand talents of silver) as a sign of submission. In this way Assyria carried out the first stage of the process of submission which we have just considered (above 2.1.2.2.1). The Assyrian annals mention him explicitly along with the king of Damascus – *raḥyānu* or *raṣūnnu*, in the Hebrew Bible always *reṣīn*; the same names appear on a recently published stele, which was found in Iran.[1] The biblical sources tell us that Menahem obtained the money by taxing landowners at fifty shekels (11.424 grams each) a head, so that if the ordinary talent amounted to 3000 shekels (the royal talent had 3600 shekels), there must have been a good 60,000 of these landowners, and all of them thriving (Noth*, 258 n.2; Donner*, 424). The rather high figure is an obvious sign of prosperity, and moreover is one of the few economic data we have at our disposal.

3.3.1 Tiglath-pileser III seems to have been content with the tribute and the submission he had thus obtained without striking a blow, and Israel enjoyed some years of peace. However, in 734 the Assyrians reappeared in the region, campaigning against the Philistines,[2] and especially against Gaza, whose king took refuge in Egypt. Later he returned from there, having been pardoned, but this was an exceptional case. The Assyrians very soon arrived at the border with Egypt and established themselves there: this was the traditional 'brook of Egypt', the present-day *wādī el-'arīš*, from time immemorial the frontier between the two regions. This move must have pre-empted any attempt on the part of Egypt to assist possible rebels, and cut off all contact with Egypt.

3.3.2 The campaign does not seem to have had any consequencs for Israel, nor are we told that Tiglath-pileser annexed any territory: some scholars think that the Assyrian province of *dū'ru*, the coastal region around Dor (the present-day *ḥirbet el-burj*, coord. 142-224), which had originally been Philistine (above III.5.3.1), was annexed on this occasion: others, however, think that that happened after the Syro-Ephraimite war. In Israel political chaos again reigned: Pekahiah, the son of Menahem (*c.* 738-737 BC or 737-736, II Kings 15.23-26) ruled for only a few months and was deposed by Pekah, the son of Remaliah (*c.* 747-732 or 735-732, II Kings 15.27-31), who directly assumed the reins of power.

3.4 So in 738 Assyria had reduced Israel and Damascus to the state of vassals, but stopped at this first phase.

3.4.1 Very soon, Rezin of Damascus and Pekah of Israel thought of forming another anti-Assyrian coalition (we do not know exactly when) probably watching the way in which the Assyrians could rush around the region as they liked. If the garrisons left along the frontier with Egypt were to be neutralized, so that their flanks were covered, it was clear that Judah, too, would have to join the alliance; moreover, that would also have convinced those in the region who had not yet joined the alliance to do so as soon as possible.

3.4.2 However, Ahaz of Israel rejected this proposal, though we are not told why. Still, the reason is easy enough to guess: first of all, he was not a vassal of Assyria and therefore not burdened by tribute like his northern neighbours; nor did he feel threatened in any way. Again, having observed from close to what had happened at Gaza, he probably saw that the chances of success for an alliance of this kind were very remote. Of course the others regarded this attitude as a betrayal, since it made the alliance weak in its southern sector; so the two kings of Damascus and Israel tried something very like a *coup d'état*, seeking to replace the king in power with someone who supported their own plans. The choice fell on an Aramaean called 'the son of Tabeel'. We have no precise information about this person, and in addition the reading of the text is uncertain; however, it has been supposed that he was a member of a highborn family from Transjordan, close, if not actually related, to the reigning house of Judah. The suggestion has been made[3] that he was perhaps connected with what in the post-exilic period was to be the family of the Tobiads, which was to make things so difficult for the people returning from exile (Neh.2.19 etc.) and for the faithful of Judah before the Maccabean revolt (below XII.6.2.1; XIII.7.6.1.3). This theory, put forward in 1957 by the Israeli archaeologist and historican B.Mazar, was developed independently in 1972 by the Israeli B.Oded, who argued that Israel and Damascus certainly did not march on Jerusalem just to force Judah to join in the alliance; the wars between the two Hebrew kingdoms were always aimed at defining the frontiers between the two countries. In this case the aim seems to have been to regain territories of Israel, and in Transjordan which Judah had gradually occupied over previous years, profiting from the internal difficulties of Israel. (Cf. II Kings 15.37, which reports the beginning of hostilities at the time of Jotham, and especially II Chron. 27.5-6, which speaks of Jotham's victories over the Ammonites.) Of course, for Oded these two texts are historically trustworthy and need to be taken seriously, which not all scholars would accept. Clearly it is not possible to provide definitive proof; it is, however, worth pointing out that the two theories are only minimally incompatible: the attempt to reconquer Transjordan and the territories of Israel which Judah may have occupied could fit in perfectly with the attempt to set another king, favourable to this anti-Assyrian alliance, on the throne of Judah. Another suggestion made by A.Vanel 1975, that this figure is to be identified with Tubal, king of Tyre, mentioned in a list of kings subjected by Tiglath-pileser and quoted by L.D.Levine 1972, has not found much of a following as far as I can see, not least because we know nothing about the king concerned.

In order to put their plans into effect, the two armies marched on Jerusalem to besiege it (II Kings 16.5-18; Isa. 7.1). To begin with they must have made good progress, according to Hos.5.8ff., in the now classic interpretation by A.Alt (1919);[4] Isa. 7.1ff. describes in humorous tones the panic which seized the court and the government. The situation was all the more threatening since in the south the Edomites had reconquered Eilath, driving out the Judaeans (II Kings 16.6: emended text, read $^{e}d\bar{o}m$ for $^{a}r\bar{a}m$, a confusion between *reš* and *dalet*, two very similar letters, and delete 'Rezin', with all the commentaries, as an erroneous gloss on 'Aram': the region around the Red Sea is too far from Syria, but is on the southern frontier of Edom). Moreover, according to II Chron. 28.18, the Philistines had made a deep penetration into the south-west of Judaea (cf. below, XI.2.2).

3.4.3 However, Ahaz and his counsellors seem to have completely lost their heads: despite the advice to the contrary which the traditions attribute to Isaiah and a prophecy that exhorted him to keep calm, Ahaz took a decision which set in motion a dynamic that was to shape the history of Judah for about a century: he asked help from Assyria, offering his own submission and sending a substantial amount of tribute (II Kings 16.7). Indeed, he did more: he made his submission in person and, as a sign of particular devotion, seems to have introduced into the temple of Jerusalem an altar modelled on the Assyrian altar which he had seen at Damascus. He did this without having been requested to do so by Tiglath-pileser himself, who never imposed his own religion on his vassals (Cogan 1971, cf.1 above; McKay 1973, at XI.3, and Spieckermann, 322ff., though he has a different view, namely that Assyria would have imposed its own religion on its vassals: II Kings 16.10).

3.4.4 The coalition between Israel and Damascus, attacked in the rear by the might of Assyria, had to withdraw its troops with great speed and throw them against the attacker; so even if Jerusalem was in fact besieged, it was not in any danger. However, their efforts were in vain. Damascus resisted until 732 and was conquered; its king was killed; and its territory was transformed into an Assyrian province after the deportation of a group of its most skilled inhabitants. Israel lost all Galilee, whose ruling class was deported, so that it was reduced to the central hill country.

3.4.5 Once again Israel lapsed into chaos: Pekah was killed in a plot arranged by a certain Hoshea ($h\bar{o}š\bar{e}^{a'}$, not to be confused with the prophet of the same name, II Kings 15.30), who was immediately confirmed by Tiglath-pileser III as a vassal: in this way Israel started to suffer the second phase of subjection.

3.4.6 That was the end of the Syro-Ephraimite war; we cannot say precisely when it began. It is difficult to suppose that the beginning was before the advent of Pekah (*c.* 737 or 735); it is also hard to see how it would have been possible to achieve any concentrations of troops during the Assyrian expedition of 734. It does, however, seem probable that diplomatic negotiations with a view to an alliance had already been in progress for some years. The only tangible result of the war seems to have been that it left Judah and what remained of Israel vassals of Assyria, while the Aramaean kingdoms and especially Damascus were completely incorporated into the empire.

4.1 Hoshea reigned over Israel from about 732 to 724 (II Kings 17.1-4), to begin with as a faithful vassal of Assyria, punctual in the payment of tribute (*ANET*, 283f., Borger-Tadmor 1982).

4.1.1 *Bibliography*: S.Talmon, 'Polemics and Apology in Biblical Historiography – 2 Kings 17.24-41', in R.E.Friedman (ed.), *The Creation of Sacred Literature*, Berkeley 1981, 57-58.

Having been a faithful vassal for some time, Hoshea then decided to rebel against Assyria, where in the meantime Shalmaneser V (*c.* 726-722) had come to the throne; indeed, following a practice which is well attested throughout the ancient Near East, Hoshea could well have rebelled at the time of Shalmaneser's succession to the throne. He refused to go on paying tribute and entered into direct negotiations with Egypt, an action which which was at all events forbidden to a vassal. Moreover, this was a premature move: the situation in Egypt was again chaotic, as the Twenty-Fifth 'Ethiopian' Dynasty was laboriously rising to power and attempting, though as yet without success, to reunite its own territory, which had been divided between various rulers. So it is possible that Hoshea will have had dealings with one of the kings who governed the Delta, though we do not know whether this was in fact the case. II Kings 14.4 speaks of a certain So, whom scholars have tried to identify as either a Pharaoh or a general, but their attempts have not produced any result; the name does not seem to correspond to any person known to us.[5]

4.1.2 We do not know what prompted Hoshea to his imprudent action: the tribute was certainly heavy, but he was taking on an enemy at the zenith of its political, economic and military power, and no crisis was looming on his horizon. Moreover, as we have seen, Egypt was again in difficulties, and could not provide any help that he could rely on. Assyria intervened without hesitation; a last attempt at submission on the part of Hoshea was rejected, because Israel was continuing its own negotiations with Egypt. In fact, Shalmaneser had Hoshea captured, perhaps during an attempt at submission, and put him in prison.

4.2. Samaria, the capital of the kingdom, resisted for two years after the fall of the rest of the kingdom and according to the Assyrian annals fell to Sargon II (*c.* 721-705, *ANET* 284ff.); according to the biblical texts (II Kings 17.5f., and especially 18.9-11) it fell to Shalmaneser V. The biblical texts are probably right, even if Sargon II always claimed to have been the successful conqueror.

4.3 Under the name of *samerīna*, Samaria became a province of the Assyrian empire; its ruling class was deported and replaced by persons appointed *ad hoc*. We know very little about the final fate of the region (cf. Alt, 1929): according to II Kings 17.7-41, which explains the tragedy in terms of Deuteronomistic theology, the result was that the region came to have a semi-foreign population with a syncretistic religion, in which YHWH, too, is said to have been worshipped alongside the deities of the new ruling class. This note does not so much give us factual information as anticipate the post-exilic polemic against the Samaritans: it is aimed at casting aspersions on their religion, because the Jerusalem priesthood considered the group heterodox and heretical. We shall consider this question again in due course (below, XIII.4).

XI

JUDAH TO THE EXILE

1 The surviving kingdom of Judah, politically and economically the less important of the two Hebrew states, away from the main lines of communication and from the sea (above IX.1.2.1.1-2), continued to live for rather less than one hundred years in the shadow of the conflicts between the great powers: first as a vassal of Assyria, a condition from which it never succeeeded in freeing itself, despite repeated attempts at the end of the eighth century; then, shortly, of Egypt; and finally of Babylon, which succeeded Assyria at the end of the seventh century BC. Attempts to steer a middle course between the great powers, characteristic of the politics of Judah during this period, only led to continued defeats and finally to the fall of the kingdom (from which it was never to rise again), the loss of political independence (recovered only for about a century between the second and the first centuries BC under the Hasmonaeans and their successors, see below XIII.9), the destruction of the temple and of Jerusalem, and the deportation of the most qualified elements of its population in 597/6 and 587/6. Part of this last group succeeded in returning home at the time of the fall of Babylon (after 539/38) and rebuilt the capital and the temple, re-establishing a very reduced autonomous province of Judaea under the sovereignty of Persia.

Select bibliography: D.J.Wiseman, *Chronicles of Chaldaean Kings*, London 1956; H.Tadmor, 'The Campaigns of Sargon II of Asshur: A Chronological-Historical Study', *JCS* 12, 1958, 22-40, 77-100; W.W.Hallo, 'From Qarqar to Carchemish', *BA* 23, 1960, 33-61; N.K.Gottwald, *All the Kingdoms of the Earth*, New York 1964; M.Broshi, 'The Expansion of Jerusalem in the Reigns of Hezekiah and Manasseh', *IEJ* 24, 1974, 21-6; E.Stern, 'Israel at the Close of the Monarchy', *BA* 38, 1975, 26-54.

1.1 In the last quarter of the eighth century, Judah had remained one of the few independent nations in the region, a survivor of the Assyrian invasion. Although a vassal of the empire, in the first phase of subjection (above X.2.1.2.2.2.1), by way of compensation it had no enemies in the north, though the fact that the territories of the north belonged first to Assyria and later to Babylon obviously ruled out any attempt at reconquest. On the other hand, Judah could now rightly be considered to be the only heir to the religious tradition of Israel and its worship, as well as to the Davidic ideology and state. Indeed, it is generally accepted that it was in this period, immediately after the fall of the kingdom of Israel, that a good deal of the material which had originated and had been handed down there, like the E source of the Pentateuch, the earliest parts of Deuteronomy and the works of the prophets Amos and Hosea, were transferred to the South and incorporated in what was later to become the Hebrew Bible. As we have seen (above IX.1.2.1.3.5), the South had never accepted the separation of the North from the united kingdom; now, to an even greater degree, it could regard itself as having been entrusted with the task of representing all 'Israel': it had to liberate the North from its foreign yoke, an indispensable condition for the restoration of the kingdom of David. That this aim did not meet with success was due not so much to any lack of will and capability on the part of Judah as to the international situation, in which there was clearly no place for a third great power between Mesopotamia and Egypt.

1.2 The position of Judah as a buffer state between the Mesopotamian empire and that of Egypt, newly independent from 655 on (above X.2.2), was difficult – one might say precarious – but certainly not desperate. That both empires needed the region, either as a bulwark of defence or as forward base for an attack (above X.1), provided skilled diplomats with a number of possibilities of playing off one rival against the other: it was certainly a dangerous game, but the prize was well worth the risks involved: the retention of political independence and sovereignty, limited though this may have been. However, we shall see how in the end Judah lost the game, which resulted in its destruction as an independent political entity (below 7).

1.3 As sources, we again have the Deuteronomistic texts of II Kings 18-25 and the parallels in II Chron. 28-36; we also find parallels to II Kings in Isa.36-39 and Jer.52. In addition, we have first the Assyrian and then the Babylonian annals (*ANET*, 287ff., 563ff., respectively; for the latter cf. also Wiseman 1956).

1.4 Finally, it is interesting to note how, throughout the ancient Near East, the seventh century BC was a period of cultural and religious revival. I have already mentioned (above, X.2.2) the work of Asshur-bani-pal, to whose collection we owe the survival of most of the Mesopotamian literature which has come down to us: similar collections were made later in Babylon by Nebuchadnezzar II (*c*. 605-561), a ruler with whom we shall be dealing in more detail below (5.3). In Egypt, too, under the Twenty-Fifth and especially the Twenty-Sixth dynasties, we can see attempts at collecting ancient material.[1] Something of this kind also seems to have happened in Phoenicia, if we accept the testimony of a certain Philo of Byblos, though this is often at second or even at third hand; Philo quotes a certain Sanchuniaton, who lived in the seventh century. It would in fact seem only logical that we should see the beginnings of the movement which led to the reform carried out by king Josiah of Judah and to the re-editing and preservation of texts from the tradition of Israel and what we are accustomed to call the 'Deuteronomist' (below 4.2) in such a context.[2]

2 The person of King Hezekiah, Hebrew *ḥizqīyāh(ū)* (*c.* 715-687 or 728/25-700 [Tadmor 727/6]) immediately raises a chronological problem, as can be seen from the differences in the dating offered by the systems of calculation which I have used. The sources in II Kings 18.1-8 tell us that three important events took place in his reign: a religious reform; wars with the Philistines; and finally, anti-Assyrian revolts, all ending in defeat. In the Deuteronomistic history and in Chronicles, Hezekiah is considered one of the greatest monarchs that Judah ever had, along with Josiah; however, a political judgment which considers the performance and the results obtained by a ruler rather than his intentions and his religious faith must certainly be more severe: outside the capital, which in any case was suffering the after-effects of a long siege, Hezekiah left the country carved up and in almost total ruin, and this situation could not fail to have repercussions on the religion of Judah, among other things undoing the effects of the reformation which he is said to have undertaken.

Select bibliography: A.Alt, 'Neue assyrische Nachrichten über Palästina', *ZDPV* 67, 1945, 128-46 = *KS* II, 226-41; B.Mazar, 'The Campaign of Sennacherib in Judaea', *EI* 2, 1953, 170-5 (in Hebrew with an English summary); J.Bright, 'Le problème des campagnes de Sennachérib en Palestine', in *Hommage à Wilhelm Vischer*, Montpellier 1960, 20-31; H.H.Rowley, 'Hezekiah's Reform and Rebellion', *BJRL* 44, 1961-62, 395-431 = *Men of God*, London 1963, 98-132; J.A.Brinkman, 'Merodach Baladan II', in *Studies... A.L.Oppenheim*, Chicago 1964, 6-53; F.J.Moriarty, 'The Chronicler's Account of Hezekiah's Reform', *CBQ* 27, 1965, 399-406; E. van Leeuwen, 'Sanchérib devant Jérusalem', *OTS* 14, 1965, 145-171; S.H.Horn, 'Did Sennacherib Campaign Once or Twice against Hezekiah?', *AUSS* 4, 1966, 1-28; R. de Vaux, 'Jérusalem et les Prophètes', *RB* 73, 1966, 481-509 (498ff.); B.S.Childs, *Isaiah and the Assyrian Crisis*, SBT II 3, London 1967; O.Kaiser, 'Die Verkündigung des Propheten Jesaja im Jahre 701', *ZAW* 81, 1969, 304-15; A.K.Jenkins, 'Hezekiah's Fourteenth Year', *VT* 26, 1976, 248-

98; J.Rosenbaum, 'Hezekiah's Reform and Deuteronomic Tradition', *HTR* 72, 1979, 23-43; P.Welten, *Die Königs-Stempel. Ein Beitrag zur Militärpolitik Judas unter Hiskia und Josia*, ADPV, Wiesbaden 1969; N.Na'aman, art. cit. (IX.5); H.Haag, 'Das Mazzenfest des Hiskia', in *Wort und Geschichte – Festschrift K.Elliger*, AOAT 18, Kevelaer 1973, 87-94; W.Zimmerli, 'Jesaja und Hiskia', ibid., 199-208 = *GA* II, 88-103; H.G.M.Williamson, *Israel in the Books of Chronicles*, Cambridge 1977; H.-D. Hoffmann, *Reform und Reformen*, ATANT 66, Zurich 1980, 146ff.; G.Garbini, 'Il bilinguismo dei Giudei', *Vicino Oriente* 3, 1981, 209-23; M.Hutter, *Hiskija, König von Juda*, Graz 1982; id., 'Überlegungen zu Sanheribs Palästinafeldzug im Jahre 701 v.Chr.', *BN* 19, 1982, 24-30; A. Catastini, 'Il quattordicesimo anno del regno di Ezechia (II Re 18:13)', *Hen* 4, 1982, 257-63; H.Spieckermann, op.cit., 170ff.; H.Tadmor and M.Cogan, 'Hezekiah's Fourteenth Year: The King's Illness and the Babylonian Embassy', *EI* 16, 1982, 198-201 (in Hebrew with an English summary). An important posthumous study on the whole question is E.Vogt, *Der Aufstand Hiskias und die Belagerung Jerusalems 701 v.Chr.* (in preparation, Pontifical Biblical Institute, Rome). For an examination of the text of II Kings, Isaiah and Chronicles see the commentaries by H.Wildberger, III, 1982, ad loc.; O.Kaiser, *Isaiah 13-39*, OTL, London and Philadelphia 1974, ixff., 367ff.

2.1 According to the text of II Kings 18.3f., Hezekiah initiated a religious reform: he suppressed the 'high places', demolished other kinds of pagan or syncretistic sanctuaries, and destroyed the bronze serpent, a relic which the tradition attributes to Moses (cf. Num.21.6-9). The text of II Chron.29-31 describes this reform in much more detail: the king is said to have restored and purified the temple; to have offered sacrifices, especially of expiation; to have celebrated the Passover in the temple (more probably, according to Haag's 1973 study, only the feast of unleavened bread); and reformed the cult. It is interesting that the North, which had recently been occupied by Assyria, is also said to have been involved in this reform (II Chron.30.1). According to Williamson 1977, 119ff., however, the Chronicler will have had the inauguration of the temple of Solomon in mind. It is difficult to verify the authenticity of this information: it could well be a projection of later attempts back on the past, to give them greater authority. Yet other scholars[3] see these as in fact themes which anticipate Josiah's reform, making it the final phase of a process begun just under a century before (below 4.2-3). Others, however, are more cautious: details of a reform presented in II Kings in Deuteronomistic terms seem doubtful; it is more probable that the writer wanted to concentrate religious life on the temple of Jerusalem, which would then inevitably become the sole national sanctuary for the South as for the North, marking a step towards a restoration of the Davidic empire. For H.Spieckermann 1982, 174ff., this is ultimately an artificial historical construction. Be this as it may, Hezekiah's involvement in reform makes it probable that he should be identified with the Emmanuel (Hebrew *'immānū'ēl*) announced by Isa.7.14f. cf. 9.1-6. In that passage a devoted and pious king is to succeed the wicked Ahaz, who is on the throne; and that is the case regardless of whether or not the oracle is by Isaiah. As we know, it was reinterpreted in messianic terms by the New Testament and applied in the infancy narratives to the birth of Christ (Matt.1.23).

2.2 II Kings 18.8 says that Hezekiah defeated the Philistines as far away as Gaza, thus succeeding in reincorporating into the kingdom of Judah some of the territories which had been lost in the time of Ahaz (II Chron. 28.18, above X.3.4.2). Perhaps, too, I Chron 4.34-43, which describes the expansion of Simeon, in fact refers to this episode (whether or not that is the case, though, *gērār* is to be read with LXX instead of *gēdōr* in v.39; there is confusion between the similar letters *daleth* and *reš*, cf. Oded 444f.). This notice seems to be confirmed in the Assyrian annals, *ANET*, 287; here we read that the people and the nobles of Ekron (present-day *ḫirbet el-muqanna'*, coord.136-131), a Philistine city, had rebelled against their king, handing him over to 'Hezekiah the Judahite'; and from a 'letter to the deity' by Sennacherib we hear that a royal Philistine city had been occupied by Hezekiah (Na'aman 27). So Hezekiah seems to have profited from the campaigns of Tiglath-pileser III (above X.3.2–3) and of Sargon II[4] to fight and subject the traditional enemy, though it was now much weakened (cf. below 2.3.3.1).

2.3 The problem of the campaigns of Sargon II and Sennacherib (*c.* 704-681) in Palestine, and the attitude of Hezekiah to Assyria, seems to be very complex.

2.3.1 There can be no doubt that, at least to begin with, Hezekiah had continued the pro-Assyrian policy of his father Ahaz (above, X.3.4.2). A first anti-Assyrian coalition, formed in about 720 by some city-states of the region, supported by Egypt, and also including what remained of the Aramaean kingdom of Hamath and the Philistine kingdom of Gaza, along with some of the subject peoples of Samaria, does not seem to have included Judah in its number if the silence of the Assyrian sources (*ANET*, 285) and the lack of biblical texts which can be connected with such an event are anything to go by. Be this as it may, the coalition was defeated and the few remaining independent states were annexed. The repression seems to have been harsh everywhere.

2.3.2 However, Hezekiah's attitude was different in the revolt of 713-711, when, under the leadership of the Philistine city of Ashdod

(ʾašdod, coord. 117-129), other Philistine cities, and Edom and Moab in Transjordan, rebelled against Assyria. This time Judah is explicitly mentioned in the Assyrian annals (*ANET*, 286f.). This time, too, the coalition was supported by Egypt, where the Twenty-Fifth 'Ethiopian' Dynasty had reigned from 716. Perhaps the Pharaoh was already Sabako; his dates are uncertain (possibly 716-702). Two passages of Isaiah are often connected with this rebellion: 20.1-6, where at the time of the conquest of Ashdod the prophet performs a symbolic action meant to represent the impending exile; and 18.1-8, where he presents an picture of the foreign policy of Judah in rather frenzied terms. Azotus was annexed, but the other countries in the coalition seem to have been saved by withdrawing in time.

2.3.3.1 In 705, on the death of Sargon II, his successor Sennacherib found the empire in revolt; he had a hard struggle to secure the throne. This time Hezekiah seems to have taken the initiative; in addition, the allies handed over to him the king of Ekron, another Phoenician city which had not wanted to join in the alliance (above 2.2; *ANET*, 217f.). Hezekiah again relied on Egyptian help, despite what seems to have been advice to the contrary from Isaiah (30.1-5; 31.1-4). This time, once again, the Egyptian help did not arrive.

2.3.3.2 II Chron. 32.31 and other texts also report that Hezekiah entered into negotiations with Merodach-Baladan (Marduk-apal-iddina, *c*. 721-710, king of Babylon, II Kings 20.12-19//Isa. 39.1-8//II Chron., which has the more exact text in 32.25-39). He, too, had rebelled and proclaimed his own independence. So the coalition comprised a majority of the ancient Near East. Sennacherib, however, succeeded in taming the Babylonian revolt; he then turned westwards where he reduced first the Philistines and then, moving north-east (the battle of *altāqu*, Hebrew *ʾeltᵉqeʾ*, perhaps the present-day *tell eš-šallāf*, coord.128-144, captured by the Assyrians), he laid siege to Judah from the south (*ANET*, 287f., cf. Isa.1.1-9 for the consequences). He succeeded in occupying most of the territory in a short time. Only Lachish (*tell ed-duweir*, coord.135-108) and Jerusalem succeeded in resisting; the former was soon destroyed (cf. the famous reliefs in the British Museum in London, *ANEP*, 372ff.). Jerusalem had been adequately fortified and its water supplies reinforced; it is still possible today to inspect a water course which brings water from the Gihon, a spring at the foot of the eastern side of the city, to within the city walls (II Kings 20.20; II Chron.32.1-4; Isa.22.9b; Sir.48.17, for this watercourse cf. above III.6.1.1).[5] Moreover, Jerusalem has a very good strategic position (it could only be attacked from one side, the north), so it succeeded in resisting.

2.3.3.3 We have a good deal of information about the conclusion of this campaign, but it is contradictory and therefore inadequate. In II

Kings 18.13-19.36//Isa.36-39//II Chron.32.1-19 there is an account of the siege of the capital which is probably late and certainly romanticized. Jerusalem is said to have been saved at the last moment by a miraculous divine intervention (Childs 1967, Garbini 1981). However, in the annals of Sennacherib we read (*ANET*, 288): 'As to Hezekiah, the Jew, he did not submit to my yoke. I laid siege to 46 of his strong cities, walled forts and to the countless small villages in their vicinity, and conquered (them) by means of well-stamped (earth-)ramps, and battering-rams brought (this) near (to the walls) (combined with) the attack by foot soldiers, (using) mines, breeches as well as sapper work... Himself I made a prisoner in Jerusalem, his royal residence, like a bird in a cage.' However, the Assyrian annals, too, say nothing about a conquest of the capital. It is probable that Sennacherib was content to receive substantial tribute from Hezekiah, as the annals report (*ANET*, 288): 'Hezekiah... deserted by his irregular and elite troops, did send me, later, to Nineveh, ...a tribute.' He then describes the tribute in detail: it differs only in some points from what is said in II Kings 18.13-15. Still, the fact that Sennacherib was now at Nineveh shows that he had lifted the siege (otherwise Hezekiah could not have gone with the tribute). That leads us to suspect that other factors, probably political, prompted him to raise the siege, return home and accept the tribute and submission of Hezekiah. As things are, we do not know what these factors may have been.

2.3.3.4 Thus the capital, Jerusalem, managed to emerge unscathed from what had evidently been a catastrophe which virtually destroyed the nation. Isaiah 22.1-14 protests against the victory song sung by the people of Jerusalem as the siege was lifted.

2.3.4 The apparent contradiction between the passages which speak of a miraculous deliverance of Jerusalem and those which mention the tribute paid to its besiegers has led some modern scholars to postulate two campaigns by Sennacherib in Palestine, which the biblical sources are supposed to have combined into one: the first would have ended in 701 with the payment of tribute and the act of submission; the second, about 688, would have ended with the miraculous deliverance. W.F.Albright argued consistently in favour of this theory all his life,[6] and his pupil John Bright took it over in his *History* (1960 and recently 1981*, 281f.). Its merit is that it resolves a series of problems of detail, but it has two basic disadvantages: there is no mention of a second campaign in the Assyrian annals, which know only the expedition of 701; and it introduces complications into the identification of the various Pharaohs. This is so much the case that even Bright himself (1981*, 309) admits that there is no evidence for the theory. Most recently Hutter (1982), too, has come out very strongly against the theory of a second campaign.[7] It seems most likely that we should suppose that Sennacherib's acceptance of the tribute and Hezekiah's submission, which was quite unexpected, became a miraculous divine intervention in the various legends (Noth*, 268 n.3). Once it is accepted that the report is the product of later theological interpretation of an otherwise inexplicable fact, there is not much point in either rationalistic explanations of the miracle (for example that a plague broke out among the besiegers[8], a theory based on the details given by Herodotus in II, 141, that the camp had been invaded by rats, the carriers of bubonic plague) or attempts to provide a historical explanation (the Assyrians will have left in haste because of the outbreak of new disorders in Babylon).

2.3.5 According to II Kings 19.37// Isa.37.28, Sennacherib was killed by two of his sons in a temple at Nineveh. This is confirmed by the Assyrian annals (*ANET*, 288f.). He was succeeded by a younger son, Esarhaddon (680-669), who was also skilful and determined.

3 In the decades between the Assyrian invasions and Josiah's reform we find two kings on the throne of David, Manasseh and Amon, both of whom the biblical history condemns as impious and wicked because they do not match up to the theological ideals established by Deuteronomy.

Select bibliography: L.W.Fuller, *The Historical and Religious Significance of the Reign of Manasseh*, Leipzig 1912; A.Malamat, 'The Historical Background of the Assassination of Amon, King of Judah', *IEJ* 3, 1953, 26-9; E.L.Ehrlich, 'Der Aufenthalt des Königs Manasse in Babylon', *TZ* 21, 1965, 281-6; E.Nielsen, 'Political Conditions and Cultural Development in Israel and Judah during the Reign of Manasseh', in *Proceedings of the Fourth World Congress of Jewish Studies, Jerusalem 1965*, Jerusalem 1967, I, 103-6; J.McKay, op.cit. (X.1); H.Spieckermann, Juda unter Assur in der Sargonidenzeit, FRLANT 129, Göttingen 1982, 160ff., 307ff.; M. Broshi, art.cit., 1; M.Cogan, op.cit. (above X.1).

3.1 King Hezekiah, whom the biblical texts describe as having been just and pious, left a bitter legacy. It was passed on to his son Manasseh (*c.* 687-642). The sources are unanimous in saying that Manasseh reigned for fifty-five years (II Kings 21.1-18//I Chron.33.1-10). The youthful age at which he ascended the throne makes it necessary to conjecture either a regency or some other form of tutelage in connection with affairs of state, at least for about ten years. So it will have been under this provisional form of government that those developments in the religious and political sphere will have taken shape which the biblical history is unanimous in condemning. In Manasseh's reign, syncretistic or even pagan cults are said to have flourished as never before, even in the Jerusalem temple, and again in his reign 'innocent blood' is supposed to have been shed (II Kings 21.16). We do not know what the biblical authors are alluding to, but the tone of the account suggests that, as in the time of Ahab of Israel (above IX.3.4), those faithful to YHWH were persecuted.

3.2 II Chronicles 33.11-17 adds another episode to Manasseh's biography, this time an edifying one; he is said to have been taken to Babylonia (sic!) by the Assyrians after the failure of a rebellion, and there to have been converted. On his return to Jerusalem, he is said to have purified the temple of the foreign objects which he had had placed there. This theme proved popular; a deutero-canonical work, The Prayer of Manasseh (which was not included in the Roman Catholic canon), presents words which he is supposed to have used on this occasion.[9] This time, too, the reality seems to have been more prosaic: Manasseh was a faithful vassal and he appears many times in this guise in the annals of Esarhaddon, king of Assyria (*ANET*, 291). Later, under Asshur-bani-pal, at the beginning of the campaign against Egypt in 667, the so-called 'C cylinder' I, line 24 (*ANET*, 294), mentions Manasseh among the other vassals (there are twenty two of them!). He arrived in the capital, not in chains, but to deliver to the sovereign the annual tribute and contingents of troops for the campaign. It is from this journey, probably repeated at intervals, that the narrator in Chronicles has constructed the edifying story of Manasseh's imprisonment and conversion, as a result of his experiences. So this is not a passage which provides us with any historical information.

3.3 In fact the problem which preoccupied the biblical authors at this point was of another kind; they had to reconcile the long reign of Manasseh, regarded as an obvious proof of the divine favour, with his wickedness. And since it seemed impossible that God could have favoured a notoriously wicked ruler, they resolved the difficulty by showing him as a person subject to serious crises of conscience, who was then converted and led to repent. Some scholars[10] have tried to explain the narrative in a different way, accepting that it contains an element of history, then amplified at a second stage in a romanticized form. Under Shamash-shum-ukin, brother of the king and governor of Babylon, in 652-648 Babylon rebelled against Assyria. As we saw above (X.2.2), in 655 Egypt had regained its own independence in an alliance with Gyges, king of Lydia. It is certainly attractive to try to connect the failed rebellion of Manasseh with one of these moves. However, even if we accept that, it must be recognized that the narrative that we have is theologically distorted, so that its original significance is now quite unrecognizable.

3.4 Despite the scarce and inadequate information, we can obtain a fairly clear idea of Manasseh's reign. Judah continued to survive in what we have seen to be the second phase of subjection (above X.2.1.2.2.2); it was still a vassal, though in an extreme state of vassalage:

the sovereign retained a certain freedom of action, but this was minimal. The Assyrian sources state that a good deal of Hezekiah's territory was taken from him, to be distributed to faithful allies and vassals of the empire, especially the Philistines; in effect, he was left with only the territory of the city-state of Jerusalem. However, a large part of the territory of Judah seems to have been restored to Manasseh later, though we do not know on what conditions and in what circumstances. In the circumstances, the reform begun by Hezekiah, connected as it was with the Davidic ideology (above 2.1) and the hope of the liberation of the North, had to be abandoned completely, leaving the position as it had been before. So we do not need to suppose, as scholars have often done in the past, that the Assyrians intervened in the cult of Judah on a large scale; J.McKay 1973 and M.Cogan 1974 have amply demonstrated that Assyria was not accustomed to interfere in this way (but see now Spieckermann, 307ff.). However, it is quite understandable that Judah should have tried to retain the good will of the conqueror in every possible way; the country was economically on the verge of ruin, most of its towns were destroyed, and some important cities were occupied by the enemy. For example, Philistine troops were stationed at Lachish (coord.135-108) under the command of Assyrian officials, and other places may well have suffered the same fate. Soon afterwards, with its conquest of Egypt, Assyria reached its greatest territorial expansion: in 671 Esarhaddon defeated the Pharaoh Tirhakah and occupied Memphis; in 667, Esarhaddon's son Asshur-bani-pal defeated him. On the other hand, Egyptian resistance never ceased altogether, and despite the death of Tirhakah, the Assyrians again had to march southwards. They even conquered Thebes; this episode must have made a marked impression in Judah as well, as is witnessed by the mention of the fact in Nahum 3.8-10. So no politician with any sense could even have thought of rebelling and regaining national independence. This was probably the worst period in the history of Israel before the exile.

3.5 It is reported of King Amon (*c.* 642-640) that in every respect he followed in the footsteps of his father Manasseh (II Kings 21.19-26//II Chron. 33.21-25). Amon was killed in the course of a palace conspiracy ('the ministers of Amon') which was perhaps organized by anti-Assyrian elements (A.Malamat, 1953, cf. the previous bibliography), but the 'people of the land' punished the assassins and proclaimed Josiah king in his place. According to the Deuteronomic history, Josiah was the most important king of Judah after David.

4 Josiah, who now succeeded to the throne (*c.* 640-609 or 639-609, Tadmor 639/608), was the reforming king *par excellence.*He was to achieve the crystallization of faithfulness to the God of Israel, as found in various groups and headed by the prophets, into a political option.

At a slightly later date these groups will have found their fullest expression in the book of Deuteronomy and, a little later still, in the Deuteronomistic history work.

4.1 At the same time, evidently in connection with his religious reform, according to our sources Josiah gave priority to the Davidic ideology and proceeded to reincorporate the territories of the North, which had now been reduced to Assyrian provinces, into the kingdom of Judah. That proved possible since the empire was slowly but surely disintegrating (below 4.4.1) under the pressure of the subject peoples from within and the assaults of various enemies who were attacking it from the outside.

Select bibliography: A.Alt, 'Judas Gaue unter Josia', *PJB* 21, 1925, 100-16 = *KS* II, 276-88; H.L.Ginsberg, 'Judah and the Transjordan States from 734-582 BC', in *Alexander Marx Jubilee Volume*, New York 1950, 347-68; F.M.Cross and D.N.Freedman, 'Josiah's Revolt against Assyria', *JNES* 12, 1953, 56-8; D.J.Wiseman, *Chronicles* (above 1); A.Jepsen, 'Die Reform des Josia', in *Festschrift F. Baumgärtel*, Erlangen 1959, 97-108; F.M.Cross and D.N.Freedman, 'Epigraphic Notes on the Hebrew Documents of the Eighth-Sixth Centuries BC', *BASOR* 165, 1962, 34-46; E.W.Nicholson, 'The Centralization of the Cult in Deuteronomy', *VT* 13, 1963, 380-9; M.Weinfeld, 'Cult Centralization in Israel in the Light of a Neo-Babylonian Analogy', *JNES* 23, 1964, 202-12; H.Tadmor, 'Philistia under Assyrian Rule', *BA* 29, 1966, 86-102; H.Cazelles, 'Sophonie, Jérémie et les Scytes en Palestine', *RB* 74, 1967, 24-44; E.W.Nicholson, *Deuteronomy and Tradition*, Oxford 1967; S.Loersch, *Das Deuteronomium und seine Deutungen*, Stuttgart 1967; S.B.Frost, 'The Death of Josiah: A Conspiracy of Silence', *JBL* 87, 1968, 369-82; P.Welten, *Die Königs-Stempel. Ein Beitrag zur Militärpolitik Judas unter Hiskia und Josia*, ADPV, Wiesbaden 1969; E.Nielsen, art.cit. (3 above); M.Weinfeld, *Deuteronomy and the Deuteronomic School*, London 1972; H.D.Lance, 'The Royal Stamps and the Kingdom of Josiah', *HTR* 64, 1972, 315-32; R.P.Vaggione, 'Over All Asia? The Extent of the Scythian Domination in Herodotus', *JBL* 92, 1973, 523-30; W.E.Claburn, 'The Fiscal Basis of Josiah's Reform', ibid., 11-22; A.Malamat, 'Josiah's Bid for Armageddon', *JANESCU* 5, 1973, 267-78; E.Würthwein, 'Die josianische Reform und das Deuteronomium', *ZTK* 73, 1976, 395-423; W.Dietrich, 'Josiah und das Gesetzbuch', *VT* 27, 1977, 13-35; M.Rose, 'Bemerkungen zum historischen Fundament des Josia-Bildes in II Reg.22f.', *ZAW* 89, 1977, 50-63; G.S.Ogden, 'The Northern Extent of Josiah's Reforms', *AustBR* 26, 1978, 26-34; H.-D.Hoffmann, *Reform und Reformen*, ATANT 66, Zurich 1980, 169ff.; H.G.M.Williamson, 'The Death of Josiah and the Continuing Development of the Deuteronomic

History', *VT* 32, 1982, 242-8; M.Delcor, 'Reflexions sur la Pâque du temps de Josias d'après II Rois 23,21-23', *Hen* 4, 1982, 205-19; H.-D.Preuss, *Deuteronomium*, Darmstadt 1982; H.Spieckermann, *Juda unter Assur in der Sargonidenzeit*, FRLANT 129, Göttingen 1982.

4.2 II Kings 22-23 and II Chron. 34-35 give us information about Josiah's life and his religious reform.[11]

4.2.1 Although they have many features in common, the two texts are not parallel, as we shall soon see: they show significant differences in questions of primary importance. Their main interest is in the cult and its reform, a development which II Kings connects with the discovery in the temple, during the work of maintenance and restoration, of a scroll which had apparently been hidden there and which is called 'the book of the Torah'. It should be noted that the book is given the definite article, *sēper hattōrāh*, 'the book' and not 'a book'. The reader of II Kings is given the impression that very little time elapsed between the discovery of the book and the reform, and that the first event was the direct cause of the second, both taking place in the eighth year of the king's reign; this therefore implies that there was a relationship of cause and effect between the two. What II Chronicles tells us is different: the account is more precise and yet at the same time paler, and the Spieckermann's recent study has confirmed the historical improbability of the book of Chronicles. The two sources agree on the fact that Josiah ascended the throne at the age of eight; again, as at other times (above 3.1), this made a regency necessary, responsible for the conduct of affairs of state. Now Chronicles has the young king converted in the eight year of his reign and beginning the reform in the twelfth, i.e. still under the regency; moreover the reform is not limited to 'Judah and Jerusalem' but is extended to 'the cities of Manasseh, Ephraim, and Simeon, and as far as Naphtali, in their ruins round about' (the last term is critically uncertain and I follow the Qere, 34.5f.). By contrast, the reference in II Kings 23.19 speaks of 'all the cities of Samaria'; this is the first time that this term does not denote the city but the region of the same name. So according to the Chronicler, the reform had nothing to do with the finding of the book of the law, but is related, rather, to the reconquest of the territories of the former kingdom of Israel and, in the south, of those lost to the Philistines during the Assyrian invasions, i.e. Simeon. However, in Chronicles, too, 'the book of the Torah' is discovered in the eighteenth year of Josiah's reign, i.e. at the end of the development I have just mentioned, and must therefore have been important only in connection with the renewal of the covenant (34.29ff.) and the solemn celebration of the Passover. So the religious reform will have taken place independently of the discovery of the book.

4.2.2 Compared with its predecessors, Josiah's reform was characterized by its radical and uncompromising nature, at least in theory. Every kind of pagan cult, every type of syncretism, had to be suppressed; the cult had to be centralized on the sanctuary in Jerusalem, suitably purified of objects, persons and cults connected with the Canaanite world. And all this was to be followed by the destruction and therefore the elimination of the local sanctuaries and their cults. Obviously a programme of this kind would come up against all sorts of resistance, and therefore would be difficult to put into effect; nor is it surprising that about this time and even later we have references to sanctuaries which were not eliminated. From archaeological excavations in *'ārād* in the Negeb (above IV.2.3.2, coord.162-076),[12] we know of the existence of a sanctuary dating from the time of Solomon, while in the early post-exilic period there is evidence of Israelite temples at Lachish (coord.135-108),[13] and in Egypt at Elephantine, an island in the Nile on the border with Nubia, at the level of the First Cataract, near the present-day Aswan Dam. Elephantine was the site of a small garrison of Jewish mercenaries down to the end of the fifth century BC (below XII.8.5).[14] So there seems much to be said for Oded's conclusion (460ff.) that even if the reform was supported by the court and endorsed without reservations by the prophets and those of the Israelite population who were more mature in religious matters, as well as by the priesthood of Jerusalem, it did not meet with universal favour. Alternatively, and this appears even more likely in the provinces, it was not carried out with the zeal and the intransigence that the sources would have us believe. Thus a few centuries later we see that the relationships of the Elephantine community and the priests of its temple with the authorities in Jerusalem were constant and cordial; this is certainly a disconcerting fact, given the principles stated.

4.3 After more than a century and a half of critical studies of the question, there is still discussion as to the precise nature of the 'book of the law', and it cannot be said that we are even on the way to a solution. The following points have been established.

4.3.1 The book has evident contacts with Deuteronomy, if we note the actions which, according to II Kings, were taken after its discovery; however, we cannot talk of any form of dependence in either direction, let alone an identity of the two.

4.3.2 Josiah's reform also had evident connections with Deuteronomy, as was rightly pointed out many centuries ago by some church fathers. This is especially true of its concern to eliminate the pagan and syncretistic cults and the centralization of the cult at Jerusalem.[15] So much is this the case that it does not seem rash to affirm that both came into being in the same circles.

4.3.3 The understanding of the relations between Israel and YHWH, now a God conceived of in an absolutely monotheistic way, in terms of a 'covenant', Hebrew *bᵉrīt*, between God and his people, is another typical element of both the reform and of Deuteronomy.

4.3.4 Otherwise, given the silence of the sources, it is only possible to construct hypotheses about the origins of the book and of the reform (it is probable that both came at the end rather than the beginning of a fairly lengthy development). Among the most probable theories is the one which sees the origins of the book in the North, in Israel, among the country levites, who had been expelled from the official cult at the time of Jeroboam I (cf. I Kings 12.31, above IX.1.2.3.2); they had then fled to the South in 722-20.[16] However, it is impossible to say more than this.

4.3.5 We are not even in a position to establish whether the list of the objects and persons removed from the temple and the practices abolished (II Kings 23.4-15//II Chron.34.3-5) are either based on authentic documents (or at least traditions), or are reminiscences of actual occurrences, or whether they are, for example, simply items of polemic. We have seen (above III.10) that before the reform the cult was probably much closer to Canaanite paganism than the later sources are inclined to admit; so the lists in question could represent an interesting insight into how things actually were. On the other hand, it is equally certain that Josiah and the reformers had to provide some justification for their wholesale intervention in the traditional cult of the state, instituted under David and Solomon, so we can well understand that they will have exaggerated somewhat in their descriptions. It also seems clear that the theme of the discovery of the book, which appears to lie at the heart of the matter in II Kings (though as we have seen, Chronicles seems to want to ignore it), leaves a number of questions unanswered. What book was it? Why was it hidden? How was it related to the rest of the Pentateuch, which is also called *tōrāh*? Was it known beforehand, and if so by whom? Moreover, the discovery theme is reminiscent of popular traditions and not accounts of historical events: indeed, a number of scholars have spoken of a 'pious fraud' on the part of the Jerusalem priesthood to endorse their own prestige! (Spieckermann, op.cit., 156ff., is the most recent scholar to challege the theory of fraud.)

4.4 Now quite apart from these issues, which as things are cannot be resolved, there remains the problem of the political dimensions of the reform. As in the case of Hezekiah (above 2.1), this problem seems to be of fundamental importance.

4.4.1 First there is Josiah's attitude towards the territories of the former kingdom of Israel. As we saw above (2.2-3), the Assyrian empire was in an advanced state of disintegration: in 625, Nineveh, its capital, was besieged for the first time by the Medes under Cyaxares (625-585

BC, *ANET*, 362-5); Babylon, under Nabo-polassar (625-05), had newly become independent and aspired to succeed to the empire. In the north, tribes from the mountains wrought havoc and destruction, cutting lines of communication which were already precarious because of the size of the empire, and the Arabians in the south were doing the same thing. Under the onslaught of the Medes, the Babylonians, the barbarians from the north and indeed Egypt under Psammetichus I (664-610), Assyria was now reduced to a rump. The *coup de grâce* came in 612, when the capital fell under the concerted attack of the Medes and the Babylonians; these are the assaults to which the prophet Nahum alludes.[17] So the territories of the former kingdom of Israel had thus in fact become a no man's land, and Josiah had succeeded in occupying a good part of them, in circumstances which are not recorded. As we have seen, II Chron.34.6b even states that the reoccupation extended as far as Naphtali, so that it would have included a substantial part of Upper Galilee as well; however, we cannot check the accuracy of the statement (cf. Ogden, 1978). The Deuteronomistic theory of a reconquest of the north by Josiah has been again put in question by Spieckermann's most recent study (112ff., 150ff.), which regards it as wishful thinking on the part of the redactors. The reason for this view is not only the character of the statements about it, which give every indication of being merely redactional notes, but also the lack of any trace of archaeological discoveries, and the fact that the defeat of Josiah at Megiddo (below 4.5) shows clearly that the king did not have at his disposal an army of sufficient size for an enterprise of this kind.

Jerusalem, the seat of the temple, in which the cult had now been completely centralized, thus also became the religious capital of what was intended to be a kind of restoration of the Davidic empire.

4.4.2 The artefacts and inscriptions discovered in the archaeological excavations carried out in *'ārād* in the Negeb, mentioned above (coord.162-076), at Yabneh-Yam on the Mediterranean (*mēṣād ḥašab-yāhū*, coord.145-121) and at *'ēn-gᵉdī* on the Western shore of the Dead Sea (coord.187-097), show that Judah had again extended its boundaries far to the south, while the ostraca of *'ārād* and the Hellenistic pottery discovered at Yabneh-yam indicate the presence of Greek mercenaries in the service of Judah, rather like those in Xenophon's *Anabasis*. A confirmation of this expansion is also provided by some biblical texts: Josh.15.21-63, to be supplemented by an insertion preserved in LXX at v.59, gives a list of twelve districts of Judah. To date it to the time of Josiah, as was proposed by A.Alt in 1925, has so far proved to be the most reasonable overall explanation of this topographical section (cf. above IV.5.2). On the basis of archaeological excavations, especially those carried out during the restoration of the Jewish Quarter of the

Old City, it is evident that Jerusalem, too, underwent substantial expansion in this period, as would only be expected in the capital of a great kingdom (Broshi 1974, above 3).

4.4.3 Finally, Claburn's 1973 analysis seems to be especially interesting. He argues on the basis of texts like Deut.12.3-6; 14.24-26 and others that the requirement for tithes to be taken to the temple in Jerusalem indicates that one of the aims of the centralization of the cult was clearly fiscal. So it is no coincidence that precisely in this period we find hundreds of seals on amphoras with the sign *lmlk, lammelek*: 'for the king' or 'of the king'. Not all the details are yet clear; for example, the seal could indicate that the amphora represented some official measure, legally current in the kingdom, or that it was reserved for provisions for the palace and the fortresses administered by the crown. It could also indicate that the place concerned, which is often also mentioned on the seal, was responsible for providing provisions for fortresses and other public buildings.[18]

4.5 A small, surviving Assyrian nucleus had barricaded themselves in the region of Carchemish (present-day *jerablūs* on the Upper Euphrates), and an Egyptian expeditionary force under the command of Pharaoh Necho II (609-594), the successor of Psammetichus I, tried to bring it aid. This might seem paradoxical, but it was in the interest of the Egyptians that there should be two nations in Mesopotamia instead of one united empire, which would again have constituted a danger for Egypt.

4.5.1 The biblical texts relating to this episode, in the course of which Josiah lost his life, are II Chron.35.13,20; II Kings 23.29 (the latter, however, read erroneously that Necho went 'against the king of Assyria' (*'al melek 'aššūr*). However, to reach the north of Syria the Pharaoh obviously had to cross the territory of the former kingdom of Israel, which the sources believe to have been liberated by Josiah and now part of his new state. Now Egypt traditionally considered this region as being within its sphere of influence. Josiah decided to oppose the passage of the Egyptians, either simply to defend the sovereignty of his own territory or because he was allied to the enemies of Assyria and was therefore also an enemy of Egypt. It is even possible that he acted for both reasons, since they are not mutually exclusive. Near Megiddo (coord.167-221, perhaps temporarily transformed into an Egyptian military base, Malamat 1973), there was a confrontation, though we cannot establish precisely what happened. II Kings 23.29 says enigmatically of Josiah that Necho 'had him killed in Megiddo' (*wayᵉmītēhū*); II Chron. 35.19-25 reports first a delegation sent to Josiah by Necho, urging him to submit (perhaps this is a recollection of negotiations aimed at obtaining passage, Williamson 1982), and then the king's refusal: he preferred to give battle. Mortally wounded, he died a little later at Jerusalem, where he had been taken. Some scholars[19] are uncertain whether a battle like this ever took place, and think rather that Necho succeeded in capturing Josiah, having him put to death when he discovered that he would not submit. Others (Bright*, 324f.), however, suppose that the battle was historical. Frost 1968 has pertinently spoken of a 'conspiracy of silence' over the death of Josiah on the part of the ancient sources.

4.5.2 With the death of the reforming king, for the moment the attempts at religious reform and the ambitious plans to restore the Davidic empire seem to have come to an end. However, post-exilic Judaism took over the principles of the reform, from Deuteronomy and the Deuteronomistic history, and on the basis of them constructed a theology which faithfully reproduced the elements referred to above (4.3.2-3), now incorporating them into a society which no longer had political independence. However, the imperialistic plans returned in the ideology of apocalyptic (below XIII.5), now closely connected with the expectation of cosmic eschatological catastrophe and the coming of the kingdom of God.[20] These are completely different areas of discourse, and we shall consider them in due course.

5 The last twenty years of the kingdom of Judah, which Malamat 1975 rightly calls 'the twilight of Judah', were characterized by two kings, Jehoiakim (*c.* 609 – 598) and Jehoiachin (*c.* 597), and a regent, Zedekiah (597-587/6), all of somewhat mediocre stature. The chief events were the two sieges of the capital followed by the deportation of the nobility and, in the second instance, by the destruction of the city and the temple. In 587/586 the kingdom ceased to exist, and only regained its independence for about a century during the period of the Hasmonaeans and their successors (165-63 BC, below XIII.9ff.). However, they ruled without belonging to the Davidic dynasty. In 63 BC Judah finally lost its independence, for about two millennia (XIII.10.7).

Select bibliography: M.David, 'The Manumission of Slaves under Zedekiah', *OTS* 5, 1948, 63-79; M.Noth, 'The Jerusalem Catastrophe of 587 BC and its Significance for Israel', in *The Laws in the Pentateuch*, Edinburgh 1966, 260-80; D.J.Wiseman, op.cit. (above, 1); H.Tadmor, 'Chronology of the Last Kings of Judah', *JNES* 15, 1956, 222-30; M.Greenberg, 'Ezekiel 17 and the Policy of Psammetichus II', *JBL* 76, 1957, 676-96; M.Noth, 'Die Einnahme von Jerusalem im Jahre 597 BC', *ZDPV* 74, 1958, 135-57 = *ABLAK* I, 111-32; M.Tsevat, 'The Neo-Assyrian and Neo-Babylonian Vassal Oaths and the Prophet Ezekiel', *JBL* 78, 1959, 199-204; G.Larsson, 'When did the Babylonian Captivity Begin?', *JTS* 18, 1967, 417-23; A.Malamat, 'The Last Kings of Judah and the Fall of Jerusalem', *IEJ* 18, 1968, 137-56; K.S.Freedy and D.B.Redford, 'The Dates in Ezekiel in Relation to Biblical, Babylonian and Egyptian Sources', *JAOS* 90, 1970, 462-85; J.M.Myers, 'Edom and Judah in the Sixth-Fifth Centuries BC', in *Near Eastern Studies... W.F.Albright*, Baltimore 1971, 377-92; S.S.Weinberg, 'Post-exilic Palestine: An Archaeological Report', *IASHP* 4, 1971, 78-97; H.Cazelles, 'Le roi Yoyakin et le Serviteur du Seigneur', in *Proceedings of the Fifth World Congress of Jewish Studies, Jerusalem 1969*, Jerusalem 1973, I, 121-6; E.Kutsch, 'Das Jahr der Katastrophe: 587 v.Chr.', *Bibl* 55, 1974, 520-45; A.Malamat, 'The Twilight of Judah: In the Egyptian-Babylonian Maelstrom', *SVT* 28, 1975, 123-45; E.Stern, 'Israel at the Close of the Monarchy: An Archaeological Survey', *BA* 38, 1975, 26-54; A.R.Green, 'The Fate of Joiakim', *AUSS* 20, 1982, 103-9; A.Schenker, 'Nebuchadnezzars Metamorphose – von Unterjocher zum Gottesknecht', *RB* 89, 1982, 498-527; H.Cazelles, '587 ou 586?', in *'The Word of the Lord Shall Go Forth': Essays in Honor of D.N.Freedman*, Philadelphia 1983, 427-35.

5.1 The death of Josiah ruined the plans of those who had hoped for a reform of belief and the cult along monotheistic lines, on the basis of the message of the prophets; it also dashed the hopes of those who thought that Judah could exploit the hostility between Egypt and Mesopotamia politically, to its own advantage.

5.1.1 Judah had succeeded only in becoming a vassal. First it was subject to Egypt, as its north-eastern outpost; and a little later to Babylon, as its south-western bastion. Its attempts to lean now one way, now the other, exploiting the conflict between the two to its own advantage, all failed, as they had done before (above 1.2 and 2.3). Despite its ambitious plans, the room for manoeuvre was now very much reduced.

5.1.2 Meanwhile Necho II had gone on to Carchemish to bring his own plans to completion and the 'people of the land' had crowned a son of Josiah king: his name was Jehoahaz; he is also called Shallum in Jeremiah and in I Chron 3.15; II Kings 23.30//II Chron.36.1. However, Necho deposed him a few months later and replaced him with another son of the dead king, Eliakim, who, as a sign of obeisance to Necho, changed his name to Jehoiakim (II Kings 23.31-34//II Chron.36.3f.; cf. also Jer. 22.10-12; Ezek.19.4).

5.2 The new ruler is presented in the biblical history as a tyrant: he taxed the people heavily, and will have been utterly tied to Egypt (II Kings 23.36-24.7; II Chron.36.5-8; cf. also Jer.22.13-19). On the other hand, in his reign Judah seems to have succeeded in regaining the territories which it had under Manasseh (above, 3.1), while the serious fiscal measures can be explained by the need to fulfil the demands imposed by victorious Egypt. The case of Jeremiah's preaching in the temple (chs.7; 26), however, is a good indication of the risks to which anyone who opposed government policy was subject.

5.3 Judah remained a vassal of Egypt until 605 BC, when Nebuchad-nezzar II of Babylon (605-561, usually, and more exactly, written Nebuchadrezzar in the book of Jeremiah, Babylonian *nabū-kudurri-uṣur*), son of Nabo-polassar, defeated the Egyptians at Carchemish, thus forcing them to withdraw from Syria and Palestine. The battle, which is referred to in Jer.46.2, was followed by a period of Babylonian domination over the region. Judah also automatically came under this domination, as is indicated in a text revised by the Deuteronomist (Jer.25.1ff.); the episode mentioned in 36.1ff. is presented as having taken place on this occasion (cf. also II Kings 24.1ff.; II Chron. 36.5-8). In a letter sent to the Pharaoh by a certain *'ādōn*, perhaps a Phoenician, but more probably a Philistine king of Ashkelon and Ekron, along with other rulers of the region,[21] which was discovered at Saqqara in Egypt, the sender exhorts the Pharaoh to hasten to their help: if nothing else, this shows the uselessness of Egyptian aid, since Ashkelon was destroyed, an event referred to in Jer.47.5-7.

5.3.1 Jehoiakim remained the faithful vassal of Babylon until 601/600, when Necho II again invaded Judah from the south, and succeeded in occupying Gaza (*ANET*, 564).[22] The king seems immediately to have sided with Egypt, despite the advice of the prophet Jeremiah. Nebuch-adnezzar was only able to set out in 598, with an expeditionary force composed of Babylonians and Ammonite, Edomite and Moabite allies, and laid siege to Jerusalem. Jehoiakim died during the siege, though we do not know in what circumstances, and his son Jehoiachin (also called Jeconiah), succeeded him on the throne (II Kings 24.8-17// II Chron.36.9f.). The new king seems to have surrendered almost immediately to the Babylonians, on the second of the month of Adar (15-16 March 597). This is recorded in the Babylonian Chronicle, which, while not mentioning the name of the king, basically confirms the facts (*ANET*, 564). Nebuchadnezzar deposed the newly enthroned king and deported him to Babylonia: here, however, he enjoyed favoured treatment, living at court[23] with a personal retinue. On the death of Nebuchadnezzar he was admitted to the hospitality of the Babylonian court as though he were an allied sovereign, though he was not allowed to return home (II Kings 25.27-30 and *ANET*, 308). In his place Nebuchadnezzar nominated another son of Josiah, Mattaniah, chan-ging his name to Zedekiah. So the information given in Dan.1.1 is chronologically incorrect. The Babylonians deported part of the ruling class; those deported also included the prophet Ezekiel. The figures vary: II Kings 24.14 speaks of 10,000; 24.16 of 8,000, while Jer.52.28 mentions 3,023. So it is not possible to establish just how many were deported (Malamat 1975).

6 Zedekiah's situation was anything but easy.

6.1 On the one hand, the legitimate king was still alive, though he was prevented from exercising his powers because he had been deported. Thus Zedekiah was only a regent, with limited authority. Consequently Ezek.1.2 counts the years from the date of Jehoiachin's deportation, while Jer.28.4 shows that he was expected to return at any moment, on the basis of prophecies which have not come down to us. The country was again divided into factions: the pro-Egyptian faction, which sought to continue the political line begun by Jehoiakim, that had already led the country to disaster once before, and the pro-Babylonian faction, begun by Jehoiachin, which accepted the sovereignty of Nebuchadnezzar; the latter was also supported by the prophet Jeremiah. Moreover, it seems sufficiently clear that Zedekiah did not have the strength of character and clarity of ideas and aims called for in such difficult conditions. Thus, according to Jer.37-38, on the one hand he consulted the prophet Jeremiah after he had been arrested, and once even saved his life; on the other hand he was incapable of saving the prophet from ill-treatment. Nor could he impose on the factions his own line, which largely coincided with that of the prophet.

6.2 In 594/3 Zedekiah tried to form an anti-Babylonian coalition along with other rulers of the region, strongly opposed by Jer.27-28 (but read ṣidqīyāhū for yᵉhōyāqīm in Jer.27.1!). Egypt again seems to have been behind the coalition; under Psammetichus II (594-589) it was trying to regain a footing in Asia. For reasons unknown to us the plan came to nothing and the king submitted, sending a delegation to Babylonia (Jer.29.3; 51.59).

6.3 The attempt was repeated in 589/88, and this time again Egypt, under Hophra (Hebrew ḥoprāh, Greek Ἀπρίες, 589-570), seems to have been involved in the enterprise; the third Lachish ostracon (*ANET*, 322; *KAI*, 193) mentions the passage through the stronghold of a delegation on its way to Egypt. Josephus (*Contra Apionem* I, 21) reports that Tyre, too, joined the revolt and probably Ammon also participated in it (according to Ezek. 21.24-25). Edom seems to have been part of it as well, though with little enthusiasm; indeed, it was so unenthusiastic that as soon as it saw how things were turning out it joined the side of the victors. Now as Oded* rightly points out, 'Nebuchadnezzar was at that moment at the height of his power and it would have taken more than a coalition of two or three kings to remove the power of Babylon from Phoenicia and Judaea' (472). Internal divisions also continued: on the one hand was the pro-Egyptian party, supported by the army and those prophets who announced the inviolability of the temple and the return of the exiles (called 'false prophets' in Jer.5.12; 14.13; cf. chs.7; 26; 28ff.); on the other was the group, including Jeremiah, which counselled submission to Babylon. In a moment of euphoria the

'Hebrew' slaves (for 'Hebrew' cf. above V.3.2.6) were emancipated (Jer.34.8-22) in the hope of making the army stronger; however, as soon as the immediate danger was over, their owners seem to have gone back on their word. Jeremiah denounces them for this (David, 1948; Malamat, 1968, 152).

6.4 Nebuchadnezzar struck without hesitation (II Kings 25.1ff.// Jer.52.1ff.; II Chron 36.1; Jer.39.1-14). Probably in December 587 (the ninth year of Zedekiah's reign, but the chronology is uncertain, cf. below), Jerusalem was besieged. It was destroyed in August 586, having received no help from the Egyptian alliance, on which Judah had again counted and to which Jer.37.5,11; Ezek.17; 29-32; cf. Lam.2.17 allude. The Egyptian troops were defeated by the Babylonians before they could reach Jerusalem (for the co-ordination between the prophetic texts and the events referred to, a complex problem because of the biblical texts are often very general and only allude to what is happening, cf. M.Greenberg, 1957; M.Tsevat, 1959; K.S.Freedy-D.B.Redford, 1970; J.M.Myers, 1971).

6.4.1 Even the problem of the precise year in which the capital fell has not yet been resolved satisfactorily, because of the inaccuracy of the sources. A discrepancy is already evident in the Bible: II Kings 25.8 has the nineteenth year of Nebuchadnezzar, but Jer.52.29 speaks of the eighteenth year. To attribute this only to different chronological calculations does not seem to me to do justice to the complexity of the problem (Malamat, 1968, 150); both the texts come from Judah and therefore presuppose the same calendar. Scholars vacillate between 587 (E.Kutsch, 1974; J.Bright*, 330; Y.Aharoni, *Archaeology*, 407) and 586 (Malamat, 1968, with a detailed discussion, and 1975; cf. again Tadmor, 1956; Freedy-Redford, 1970; Cazelles), and it is impossible to make a decision.

6.4.2 Again, as at the time of the Assyrian invasions, the enemy route first went south and then did a U-turn northwards. So there were sudden sieges of Lachish (coord.135-108, cf. the fourth ostracon, *ANET* 324; *KAI*, 194) and then Azekah (*tell zakariye*, coord.144-123). The imprisonment of Jeremiah also becomes understandable in this context: as a supporter of the pro-Babylonian party (the Deuteronomistic redaction has even made the prophet call Nebuchadnezzar 'servant, minister of YHWH', *'ebed Yhwh*, 25.9; 27.6; 43.10), he was suspected of treachery. When he tried to leave the besieged capital to go to one of his properties (Jer.37.11-15) he was arrested, accused of treachery, dealings with the enemy and desertion (crimes which always carry the death penalty in time of war), and imprisoned.

6.5 The texts tell us that as soon as the Babylonians succeeded in making a breach in the walls of Jerusalem, Zedekiah sought salvation in flight (Jer.39; 52.6; II Kings 25.3-7).

6.5.1 He was captured, together with his family; his family was killed and the king himself was blinded and taken to Babylon, where we lose trace of him.[24] Jerusalem was sacked, and after any furnishings of value had been carried off, the temple was burnt; the fortifications of the city were dismantled. A similar fate befell many places in Judah. In the south the Edomites seem to have had taken considerable advantage of the situation in Judah: they succeeded in settling in the Negeb and were able to sack the cities of Judah (cf. Ezek. 25.12-14; Obad.10; Lam.4.21f.; Ps.137.7).

6.5.2 Again, part of the leading class and some craftsmen were deported. Jeremiah 52.28-30 speaks of 832 people, and later (below 7.2.3) goes on to mention another 745. So if these figures are correct, this was quite a modest quantity. In accordance with the Babylonian system, which differed from that of the Assyrians (above X.2.1.2.2.3), a governor was nominated who was drawn from the local nobility. His name was Gedaliah (Jer.40.7; II Kings 25.22ff.), and he was perhaps the son of the Ahikam who years before had protected and probably saved Jeremiah (26.24). He lived at Mizpah (coord.17-143, cf. above IX.2.4). Moreover the Babylonians began an interesting form of colonization by means of local elements of the population: they distributed the lands of those who had been deported to what we might call the sub-proletariat of the city and the country (Jer.39.10; II Kings 25.12// Jer.52.16; cf. Ezek. 33.21-27). By this method the Babylonians created a class of small landowners who were not imported from abroad and whose rights were not based on inheritance or purchase, but derived from the intervention of the occupying power; they owed everything to it and therefore were unconditionally faithful. However, this approach inevitably created major problems during the restoration, when the deportees who had returned home reclaimed their own lands, or an adequate indemnity for them (cf. below, XII.7.8.2, where I shall discuss the problem in detail).

6.5.3 A Hebrew seal which reads '(belonging) to Gedeliah, superintendent at the palace',[25] makes it probable that the governor already held an important post (a kind of minister of the royal household) in the time of Zedekiah.

7 The destruction of Jerusalem, its fortifications and temple, followed by the deportation of the most prominent members of the population, led to about half a century of total eclipse for Judah in its own land. This is what is usually called 'the exilic period'.

Select bibliography: A.Alt, 'Die Rolle Samarias bei der Entstehung des Judentums', in *Festschrift Otto Procksch*, Leipzig 1934, 5-28 = *KS* II, 316-37; J.N.Wilkie, 'Nabonidus and the Later Jewish Exiles', *JTS* NS 2, 1951, 36-44; G.Cardascia, *Les Archives de Murašu*, Paris 1951;

H.L.Ginsberg, 'Judah and the Transjordan States from 734 to 582 BC', in *Alexander Marx Jubilee Volume*, New York 1950, 347-68; C.F.Whitley, *The Exilic Age*, London 1957; E.Janssen, *Juda in der Exilszeit*, FRLANT 69, Göttingen 1956; D.W.Thomas, 'The Sixth Century BC: A Creative Epoch in the History of Israel', *JSS* 6, 1961, 33-46; P.R.Ackroyd, *Exile and Restoration*, London 1968; E.Zwenger, 'Die deuteronomistische Interpretation der Rehabilitation Jojachins', *BZ* 12, 1968, 16-30; S.S.Weinberg, *Pre-exilic Palestine* (above, 5); L.Perlitt, 'Anklage und Freispruch Gottes', *ZTK* 69, 1972, 290-303; M.D.Coogan, 'Life in the Diaspora: Jews at Nippur in the Fifth Century BC', *BA* 37, 1974, 6-12; P.R.Ackroyd, 'An Interpretation of the Babylonian Exile', *JTS* 29, 1975, 171-80; M.D.Coogan, *West Semitic Personal Names in the Murašu Documents*, HSM 7, Cambridge, Mass. 1976; R.Zadok, *The Jews in Babylon during the Chaldaean and Persian Periods*, Tel Aviv 1976 (in Hebrew); id., 'Notes on the Early History of the Israelites and Judaeans in Mesopotamia', *Or* 15, 1982, 391-3; R.W.Klein, *Israel in Exile*, Philadelphia 1979.

7.1 For reasons which are easy to imagine, those who were deported considered themselves to be the better part of Israel, the 'elect remnant' announced by the prophets. They were in fact the ruling class, more educated, and they were also probably those who collected and edited what had been salvaged of the traditions of their people.

7.1.1 This explanation was repeated many times and later systematized into polemic against the Samaritans by Chronicles. It also seems probable that an important part of the Deuteronomistic history work was at least conceived, if not composed, during the exile,[26] among the exiles. For the moment, none of the theories which challenge this hypothesis is convincing. If there is a problem, it is at the technical level: how could a work of this size have come out in a period (much earlier than that of the great Hellenic and Hellenistic histories) characterized by works on a much smaller scale?[27]

7.1.2 Contrary to Assyrian practice, the Babylonians did not disperse those whom they deported in an attempt to liquidate them ethnically and politically; they settled them in compact groups, especially in the southern region of Babylonia, near to the 'great canal', the watercourse which brought the waters of the Euphrates near to Babylon, passed by Nippur and reentered the Euphrates near Uruk (Hebrew *'erek*, present-day *wārka*). In Hebrew it is called *nᵉhar kᵉbār*, a transcription of the Accadian *narukabāru*, probably the present-day *šaṭṭ en-nīl* near Nippur (cf. Ezek.1.1ff.; Jer.29.5ff.; Ezra 2.59//Neh.7.61 mention other places). The place called Tel Abib is probably the Hebrew distortion of an unknown Accadian name. In this region the exiles could meet freely, buy land, build houses and communicate with the homeland.

7.1.3 All this presupposes that those who had been deported had achieved some degree of prosperity in a relatively short time. The archives of the Murashu bank discovered at Nippur during the excavations by the University of Pennsylvania at the end of the last century confirm this situation (though they come from the fifth century). Among the bank's clients we find many Jewish names, recognizable as such because they have YHWH as an element in them; this is a sign that after little more than a century the situation of some of those who had been deported was even prosperous. So while it is appropriate to speak of 'deportation' or 'exile', to use terms like 'captivity' does not fit the facts.

7.1.4 However, despite this, the exile has always been felt by Israel to have been one of the great, fundamental breaks in its long history, one of the worst catastrophes;[28] not only was it the end of political independence, but the dynasty which had once been promised that it would last for ever had fallen, and with it had collapsed the underlying ideology of the people of God enjoying happiness in their promised land. For this reason the prophets of the exilic period, first Jeremiah and then Ezekiel, tried to keep alive among the people the hope of a restoration to their homeland. Ezekiel 40-48 is simply a large-scale and detailed programme for the rebuilding of the temple, the restoration of its worship and the reconstitution of the state. However, the head of the state was no longer to bear the title king, *melek*, but only that of prince, *nāśi*, and was virtually subject to the demands of the cult.[29] Here we have the first signs of what would be called the 'hierocracy', even if, as we shall see, this must be dated much later than has usually been the case (below XII.5.3.5-6; XIII.1.3; 7.6.1.3). At all events, after the attempt by Zerubbabel to re-establish the dynasty (below XII.5.3.4), the figure of the prince disappears and we have only that of the civilian governor.

7.1.5 It is probable that during the exile the practice of circumcision, sabbath observance and the whole system of dietary laws became particularly important: they were visible signs by which even foreigners could recognize the faith of Israel (Noth*, 297). Some scholars argue that during this period the institution of the synagogue took shape and was developed, though this is still a controversial matter (to which I shall return later, XII.8.4.2). Be this as it may, it is certain that through the exiles Judah was subjected to a strong Babylonian influence; it adopted the Mesopotamian calendar, the months of which are still the same today. People took Babylonian names, as we can clearly see from the lists of the names of those who led the restoration. Even more important, however, was the influence of Aramaic, which rapidly became the *lingua franca* of the region. Israel adopted the Aramaic alphabet (the so-called square alphabet, still in use today) in place of the Phoenician alphabet; it also began to make increasing use of the language, which rapidly took the place of Hebrew for reasons which were closely connected with the cult and theological discussion.[30]

7.2 The situation of those who had remained behind was difficult, probably more difficult, even if many of them had been favoured in the distribution of land made by the Babylonians (above 6.5.2).

7.2.1 While some people enjoyed a remarkable improvement in social conditions and an increase in personal riches, the destruction of social and economic structures in which they were supposed to express themselves and develop was a great liability. Also at home, and perhaps even more there, there was the trauma of the destruction of the sanctuary, the ruling house and the state; and it is clear in Lam.1-2; 4-5 that these were difficult things to bear. That was so much the case, that even now the ninth of the month Abib (July-August) remains a day of national mourning: the divine promise, and with it the ideological foundation of the nation and the people itself, had been lost.

7.2.2 Gedaliah immediately began a programme of reconstruction, inviting those who had survived the catastrophe and the deportation to repopulate the cities and to resume everyday activities.

7.2.3 Gedaliah's legal position does not seem completely clear from the sources. Was he the governor nominated by the Babylonians for the autonomous province of Judaea, as II Kings 25.22//Jer.39.5ff. seems to indicate? Or was he simply the person in charge of Jewish affairs in a major province, the Samaria of the Assyrian empire, to which Judah will have been added? In that case Gedaliah will have been an ordinary official dependent on the governor of Samaria, as A.Alt (1934) thought was the case in the post-exilic period (below XII.5.4.4; Y.Aharoni, *The Land*, 409, now advances the same argument). We cannot say anything definite, and when in doubt it is probably better to keep to the texts. That would also follow from what, in the light of most recent research, proves to have been the situation in the Persian period. Again, we know little about Transjordan, though a few pieces of information indicate that some cities of Phoenicia and Philistia will have succeeded in retaining their own autonomy (Aharoni, 408). According to Josephus (*Antt.* X, 181f.), Nebuchadnezzar ended the political existence of the kingdoms of Ammon and Moab in his twenty-third year, i.e. 582; in the same year there was a further deportation from Judah, amounting to 745 people (Jer.52.30, cf. also, on the Babylonian side, the inscription by Nebuchadnezzar in the *nahr el-kalb* in Lebanon, *ANET* 307, the text of which seems to refer to these events).

7.2.4 Gedaliah's government, which will probably have helped the region at least towards economic recovery and will have provided provisional administrative and social structures, did not last long. Gedaliah was killed by a certain Ishmael, son of Nethaniah, son of

Elishama, a member of the royal family (II Kings 25.25ff.; Jer.40.11-41.10). He had gathered around him groups of ultra-nationalistic refugees from neighbouring countries, according to Jer. 40.14 at the instigation of Baalis, king of Ammon. We do not know in what capacity he was acting and what he planned, but at all events it seems logical to connect the last deportation made by Nebuchadnezzar with these events. Perhaps Ishmael thought that the Jewish population would revolt and give a hand in driving out the occupying forces. However, nothing of this kind happened; we saw earlier why a large number of the population had an interest in remaining peaceful. Moreover, some preferred to flee, taking refuge in Egypt, against the advice of Jeremiah (cf. chs.42f.). At all events, they took him with them.

7.3 When we read the biblical texts and the Babylonian annals we get the impression that the whole country was now a heap of ruins, that very few of its inhabitants had remained behind, in particular only the poorest, who had benefited from the distribution of land, and that among the few who did remain some deliberately went into exile on the death of Gedaliah. Archaeological excavations also bear witness to heavy destruction at this time, so much so that W.F.Albright[31] asserts that 'archaeologically speaking, the country was a *tabula rasa*'; he argued that not more than 20,000 inhabitants can have been left behind. At most there is evidence only for a few very poor rural communities.[32]

7.3.1 However, all that is only partly true. The economic structure of the country had obviously been severely damaged and its people had suffered heavy losses; the state apparatus only functioned in a minimal way and in some areas must have ceased altogether; but we must be careful about making too sweeping generalizations. Ezekiel 33.24 clearly speaks of 'those living in these ruins in the country of Israel', while Jer.41.5 mentions a pilgrimage to the temple of Jerusalem by the inhabitants of Shechem and Shiloh, i.e. the inhabitants of the territory of the former northern kingdom, which had been reoccupied by Josiah. This makes it reasonable to suppose that the temple, too, was not competely destroyed and that some form of worship, however minimal, was practised there. After all, the interest of Babylon was in destroying Judah as a military base, as a bridge for Egyptian attacks, and therefore in dismantling fortifications; but that clearly also caused the destruction of other buildings whose purpose was not military.

7.3.2 At all events, the information is sparse and not specific. The spiritual centre of Jerusalem and Judah was transferred to Babylon, and there it remained for some decades, until the first of the exiles returned home. The situation is described in theological terms in Ezek. 1;10, where 'the glory of YHWH' leaves the temple. However, it was those who returned from Babylonia who began the reconstruction and set the tone for it, and they soon established what was to be the Judaism of the restoration and the post-exilic period generally.

PART FOUR

Under the Empires of East and West

XII

UNDER THE PERSIAN EMPIRE

1 The rule of Babylon did not last long – less than a century. Nebuchadnezzar II, 605-561, made no further conquests, and after his death it began to decline rapidly.

Select bibliography: A.Alt, 'Die Rolle Samarias bei der Enstehung des Judentums', in *FS Otto Procksch zum 60. Geburtstag*, Leipzig 1934, 5-28; id., 'Zur Geschichte der Grenzen zwischen Judäa und Samaria', *PJB* 31, 1935, 94-111, both in *KS* II, 316-37 and 346-62; R.de Vaux, 'The Decrees of Cyrus and Darius on the Rebuilding of the Temple', in *The Bible and the Ancient Near East*, London and Garden City, NY 1971, 63-96; K.Galling, 'Der Tempelschatz nach Berichten und Urkunden im Buch Ezra', *ZDPV* 60, 1937, 177-83; id., *Studien zur Geschichte Israels im persischen Zeitalter*, Tübingen 1964; E.Bickerman, 'The Edict of Cyrus in Ezra 1', *JBL* 65, 1946, 249-75; W.Rudolph, *Esra und Nehemiah*, HAT I, 20, Tübingen 1949; S.A.Cook, 'The Age of Zerubbabel', in *Studies in Old Testament Prophecy... T.H.Robinson*, Edinburgh 1950, 19-36; F.I.Andersen, 'Who Built the Second Temple?', *AusBR* 6, 1958, 1-35; J.M.Myers, *Ezra-Nehemiah*, AB 14, Garden City NY, 1965; A.Dietrich-G.Widengren-F.M.Heichelheim, *Orientalische Geschichte von Kyros bis Mohammed*, Leiden 1966; C.G.Tuland, 'Josephus Antiquities Book XI', *AUSS* 16, 1966, 232-5; P.R.Ackroyd, *Exile and Restoration*, OTL, London 1968; R.Mayer, 'Das Achämenische Weltreich und seine Bedeutung in der politischen und religiösen Geschichte des alten Orients', *BZ* NF 12, 1968, 1-16; W.Zimmerli, 'Planungen für den Wiederaufbau nach der Katastrophe von 587', *VT* 18, 1968, 229-55 = *GA* II, 156-91; F.M.Cross, 'Papyri from the Fourth Century BC from Daliyeh', in D.N.Freedman and J.C.Greenfield (eds.), *New Directions in Biblical Archaeology*, Garden City, NY 1969, 45-69; P.-R.Berger, 'Zu den Namen *ššbṣr* und *šn'ṣr*', *ZAW* 83, 1971, 98-100; K.-M. Reyse, *Zerubbabel und die Königserwartungen der Propheten Haggai und Sacharja*, Berlin DDR – Stuttgart 1972;

F.M.Cross, 'A Reconstruction of the Judaean Restoration', *JBL* 94, 1975, 4-18 and *Int.* 29, 1975, 187-201 (without the final table); P.W.and N.Lapp, 'Discoveries in Wādī ed-Dalīyeh', *AASOR* 41, 1976; W.S.McCullough, *The History and Literature of the Palestinian Jews from Cyrus to Herod*, Toronto 1976; D.E.Gowan, *Bridge between the Testaments: A Reappraisal of Judaism from the Exile to the Birth of Christianity*, Pittsburgh 1976; S. Talmon, 'Ezra and Nehemiah (Books & Men)', *IDB-SV* 1976, 317-28; N.Avigad, 'Bullae and Seals from a Post-Exilic Judaean Archive', *Qedem* 4, 1976; G. Widengren*, 1977, ch. IX; A.H.J.Gunneweg, 'Zur Interpretation der Bücher Esra-Nehemia', *SVT* 32, 1981, 146-61; id., 'Die aramäische und hebräische Erzählung über die nachexilische Restauration – Ein Vergleich', *ZAW* 94, 1982, 299-302; S.Japhet, 'Sheshbazzar and Zerubbabel – Against the Background of the Historical and Religious Tendencies of Ezra-Nehemiah', *ZAW* 94, 1982, 66-98; E.M.Laperrousaz, 'Le régime théocratique juif a-t-il commencé à l'époque perse ou seulement à l'époque hellénistique?', *Sem* 32, 1982, 93-6; W.Schottroff, 'Zur Sozialgeschichte Israels in der Perserzeit', *VuF* 27.1, 1982, 46-68; B.Reicke, *The New Testament Era*, London 1969; E.Stern, *Material Culture in the Land of the Bible in the Persian Period, 538-332 BC*, Jerusalem and Warminster 1982 (which I have not been able to use fully); A.K.Kuhrt, 'The Cyrus Cylinder and Achaemenid Imperial Politics', *JSOT* 256, 1983, 83-97; P.-E.Dion, 'ššbṣr and ssnwry', *ZAW* 95, 1983, 111f. For the complex problem of the relationship between the books of Ezra-Nehemiah, Chronicles, the deutero-canonical III Ezra and Josephus, cf. H.G.M.Williamson, *Israel in the Books of Chronicles*, Cambridge 1977, with a complete bibliography. For the legal position and the treatment of the Jews in the Persian empire cf. B.Meissner, *Die Achämenidenkönige und das Judentum*, Sitzungsberichte der Preussischen Akademie der Wissenschaften, Berlin 1938, 6-32.

1.1 In Babylon itself, the last king, Nabonidus (*nabū-nā'id*, 555-539), ascended the throne after seven disturbed years which saw three different sovereigns on the throne before him. We must, of course, take into account the possibility that the picture given of his reign in the sources is coloured by hostile polemic. Be this as it may, he seems to have been an eccentric, little interested in affairs of state but zealous in his interventions in the cult,as in his private piety; he was a devotee of Sin, the moon god, whose sanctuaries he restored throughout the country. Where possible he strengthened the cult, favouring it in every way. This activity soon antagonized the all-powerful priesthood of the national god Marduk. For ten years Nabonidus even withdrew to northern Arabia, leaving the government in the hands of Belshazzar as his viceroy; Belshazzar is the main character in the legends related in Dan.5.1ff. This was probably with the intention of strengthening or even extending the empire towards the south.

1.2 Abroad, however, the empire was confronted with the growing power of the kingdom of Media, which a few years previously had played so great a part along with Babylon in the fall of Assyria (above XI.4.4.1). Media was extending slowly but surely westwards, incorporating not only the Assyrian territory conquered at the end of the seventh century but also Armenia and central Asia Minor. In the south-east it had subjected the Persians, a nation governed by the Achaemenid dynasty, the ancient rulers of Elam.

1.3 Now Nabonidus, understandably preoccupied with the expansion of the ancient allies of Nebuchadnezzar and Nabo-polassar, made an alliance with the Achaemenids of Persia: their ruler, Cyrus II (559-530), overthrew Astyages, son of Cyaxares (the conqueror of the Assyrians) and then had himself crowned king of Media and Persia with the support of the Median nobility.

1.4 Thus in place of the kingdom of Media there arose a much greater and more powerful empire, whose brilliant and dynamic ruler continued the expansionist policy of the Medes, both westwards and eastwards. In vain Nabonidus allied himself with Lydia and Egypt; now it was difficult to stop the advance of the Medes and Persians.

1.4.1 At the beginning of the second half of the sixth century BC, Cyrus conquered the Western part of Asia Minor, Lydia, whose king Croesus has gone down in Greek legend for his conspicuous, albeit useless riches.

1.4.2 To the east, Cyrus conquered what remained of eastern Iran. In this way Babylon was clamped in an enormous pincer movement which extended from the south-east to the north-west; the Persians increasingly had the strategic advantage of occupying territory situated in the hill-country and the mountains, from which they dominated the plains of Mesopotamia.

1.4.3 This is the period in which the message of the anonymous biblical prophet called Deutero-Isaiah (Isa.40-55) is usually set. He proclaimed to the Judaeans in exile, in the context of a clearly universalist and monotheistic message, that YHWH the God of Israel is the Lord of the universe and of history and had raised up Cyrus of Persia as a 'redeemer', *gōʾēl*, the liberator of the people of God in exile (44.28; 45.1). These features were then expanded in a grotesque way by Josephus (XI,5), who argued that Cyrus had even read and meditated on the prophet Isaiah! Liberation, then, was imminent, through the fall of Babylon (47.1).

1.5 Cyrus' attack on Babylon was only a few years in coming. In 539 the army of Nabonidus was defeated in the battle of Opis on the Tigris, and a little later Cyrus entered the Babylonian capital, where he was welcomed in triumph.[1] Soon he also took the crown of Babylon, so that Syria and Palestine automatically became part of his kingdom.

1.6 In 525 Cyrus' successor Cambyses (530-522) also occupied Egypt, so that the Persian empire achieved an extent comparable to that of Assyria at the beginning of the seventh century.

2 The kings of Media and Persia adopted a completely new policy towards their subject peoples, especially in comparison with that of Assyria, and indeed of Babylon. There were no more deportations to distant lands, no more attempts to shatter the ethnic structure of their subject peoples (thus constantly being confronted with new attempts at resistance on their part); these were now treated with considerable respect. This was probably not so much an expression of what Noth (302) calls a form of 'benevolent tolerance', seeing that the power remained formally in the hands of the court and officials appointed by it and was not delegated. The main reasons will have been the practicality and therefore economy of such an approach; it was simpler, and cost less, for the Persians to obtain the spontaneous collaboration of their subjects at a local level than to have to impose their sovereignty by force. The 'Cyrus Cylinder' (*ANET*, 316) states the policy explicitly, though without mentioning the Judaeans.

2.1 One evident sign of this new attitude appears in the royal inscriptions. Traditionally composed only in the language of the conqueror, they now appear in multi-lingual form, in Persian, Elamite and Babylonian, and they were also written in Babylonian cuneiform.

2.2 The government appears to have been even more liberal in official correspondence and public acts: here, too, other languages were allowed, and in Syria-Palestine and Egypt Aramaic now predominated, a development to which I have already alluded (above XI.7.1.5). Aramaic is a Western Semitic language attested in inscriptions from the ninth century onwards; it was introduced into the region by Aramaean migrations at the end of the second millennium BC. Disseminated by traders, it had rapidly become a kind of *lingua franca* in the region. That had happened by the end of the seventh century, as is evident from the letter of *'ādōn*, ruler of Ekron or Ashkelon, shortly before the exile (above XI.5.3).

2.3 It seems that in the second half of the sixth century, Aramaic now rapidly took the place of the various Canaanite dialects and Hebrew. As we have seen (above XI.7.1.5), the latter was destined to remain predominantly the language of the temple, the cult and religious discourse generally, even if it never became completely extinct as a spoken language.[2] Thus a new phase of Aramaic began, usually called Imperial Aramaic.

3 The Persian attitude, which was very liberal for its time, also

appeared in their religious policy. There was no longer any pressure from above, and the decrees which limited freedom of religion or worship were annulled; the statues of the gods and the sacred vessels which had been taken from the temples and carried off to Babylon were restored to the cults of the countries from which they had come. Cambyses also took a similar line in the empire and in Egypt, although he was a more authoritarian and less tolerant ruler, not averse to repressive actions and sometimes unnecessary cruelty (Josephus, XI, 26 even describes him 'evil by nature'). The policy of Darius I Hystaspes (522-486) was again liberal (cf. below, 5).

3.1 Chief among the sources for the restoration are the books of Ezra and Nehemiah, though the problem there is the same as that for Chronicles generally;[3] we also have the prophets Haggai, Zechariah, Trito-Isaiah and Malachi.[4] Another important source is a pseudepigraphical book, I Esdras,[5] probably the source of Josephus, Book XI, and parallel to the biblical text of II Chron.35.1 – Ezra 10 with Neh.7.73-8.18. In addition, we have the papyri of the Jewish military colony of Elephantine,[6] from the end of the fifth century, some of which are included in *ANET*; these give us important information about the religious authorities of Jerusalem and the Persian authorities of the time.

3.1.1 The account of an edict by which Cyrus authorized the rebuilding of the temple in Jerusalem is of interest in connection with the history of Israel. We have two versions of its text. The first, in Aramaic, is preserved within Ezra 5.6-6.12, a passage including a correspondence between the Persian court and the satrap in charge of the province of 'Transeuphrates' (cf. above II.3.3.3), the capital of which is located, as one might expect, at Damascus.[7] The second is to be found in Ezra 1.2-4, in Hebrew, and is mentioned in connection with the return of the first exiles. We shall look at both these texts in turn.

3.1.1.1 The majority of scholars today accept that the first document, now inserted, as we saw, in the context of a correspondence about the rebuilding of Jerusalem, is authentic (representatives of this view include Bickermann, in his classic 1946 study, and now Cross 1975, 15; S.Talmon 1976, 321; cf. also Gunneweg 1982, 150). Gunneweg argues that here we have quotations from authentic documents, but that these are contained in a Judaean narrative which in turn quotes its own sources. However, that the documents are authentic is not as certain as some scholars think (the complex explanation given by Gunneweg is an indication of this); among other things there is a certain confusion in them over the sequence of the kings mentioned. So there are those who, like O.Kaiser,[8] endorse the harsh judgment given decades ago by G.Hölscher in 1923; according to them the letters are simply a 'crude falsification', and they conclude that the so-called Decree of Cyrus on the rebuilding of the temple (Ezra 6.3-5) is to be considered a fantasy, like that relating to the return of the exiles (1.2-4).

3.1.1.2 The second text of the decrees appears in Ezra 1.2-4 and is almost certainly apocryphal, even if Bickermann, 1946, defends its authenticity. On the most favourable interpretation this is a paraphrase of the decree, made by the author of the text in his own words.

3.1.2 It also appears highly unlikely that in the first year of his reign (5.13: i.e. in 538, if we understand this to be the first year of his rule over Babylon, which seems to be the obvious interpretation) Cyrus was particularly preoccupied with a remote and tiny corner of his empire, a region which he had never visited. On the other hand it is quite possible that the edict goes back to a standardized formula in which the official in question inserted at the appropriate points the people and the country to which it referred; in that case the text about the Judahites and Judaea would simply be an instance of the detailed implementation of the general policy.

3.2 Be this as it may, for the first moves towards restoration by the first exiles to return we must look to the context of Cyrus' policy towards the deported nations, a policy which authorized all the people in question to return home, to rebuild their sanctuaries and re-establish their patterns of worship. The first group to return must have been quite a small one, seeing that in the desolate state in which it had been for many years, the country was clearly not in a position to take in substantial groups of new inhabitants at all rapidly. Confirmation of this also comes from the considerable number of Judaeans who remained in Babylon, 'not wanting to abandon their own goods' (Josephus XI, 8).

4 The texts also report that a certain Sheshbazzar was commissioned by the Persian court to return the sacred vessels which had been taken away from the temple by Nebuchadnezzar (5.15; cf. 1.8.11).

4.1 We know only the name of this person and nothing else; moreover, we do not know even that with complete certainty (cf. the various versions of it in the Greek of LXX, of III Ezra and Josephus). However, whatever may be the case, it seems improbable that a Babylonian, as his name indicates, should have been a Persian official and that he should have been entrusted with such a delicate mission. So he could have been an authoritative figure among the exiles from Judah who arrived in Judaea with a small group of those who had chosen to return. W.F.Albright[9] always argued that this Sheshbazzar is identical with the Shenazzar of I Chron.3.17, the grandson of Jehoiakim, and with the Σαναβάσσας of III Ezra and Josephus, this being the transcription of a Babylonian name *sin-ab-uṣur* (which is not, however, otherwise attested) or perhaps better (Herrmann*, 304), *šamaš-apla-uṣur* (Albright is now followed by J.M.Myers 1965, 18;

F.M.Cross 1975; N.Avigad 1976; and Y.Aharoni, *The Land*, 413). Although there is no decisive proof, these proposals have the advantage that, if used as working hypotheses, they solve most of the problems. In that case the official will have been an uncle of Zerubbabel. P.-R. Berger 1971, however, challenges this identification; he argues that it is possible to find a Babylonian archetype for the first name and that the second would be different. P.-E.Dion in his recent study confirms Berger's theory, on the basis of the recently published inscription of *tell-feḥeriah*. Again, the text gives him a title which is generally translated 'satrap', Hebrew *peḥah*, but its meaning is still obscure, seeing that it is also used to denote governors or prefects of a province.[10]

4.2 Thus we cannot establish precisely what Sheshbazzar's commission involved, since his title is so uncertain: was he governor or prefect of a more or less autonomous province of Judah? Or was Judah administratively dependent on Samaria, and through Samaria on the satrapy of Transeuphrates? Was Sheshbazzar only an official with a particular task, whose title refers to a function which he performed elsewhere? On the basis of the discoveries published by Avigad in 1976, the first possibility seems the most likely one, and we shall consider it later (5.3.2), when looking at a similar problem.

4.3 Nor are we in a position to establish the authenticity or otherwise of the lists of the sacred vessels which were restored (Ezra 1.7-11) and of the people who returned home (Ezra 2.1-70//Neh.7.6-72), appropriately called Zionists by the *Bible de Jérusalem* (Ezra 1.7-11). And it is in connection with the lists of those who returned that we are reminded of the earliest genealogies and their value for the historian, a problem discussed in V.2.3.1.

4.4 Anyway, to keep to the sources, the stimulus produced by these events will not have led to the return of much more than a small group of those who had been deported and the restoration of the foundations of the temple (Ezra 3.6ff.; 5.16; Zech.4.9; cf. Hagg.1.1-11).

4.4.1 The sources attribute the start of this rebuilding to Sheshbazzar or Zerubbabel, without indicating which; it is possible that the two were sometimes confused, as they already are in Josephus XI,13 (some scholars in fact want to identify the two, cf. the discussion in Talmon 1976, 319ff.). However, in the light of what is said in 4.1, while confusion seems possible, an identification of the two men is certainly not. It seems more likely that Sheshbazzar was active for only a short time, in fact setting the work of rebuilding in motion, but that the real protagonist in it was Zerubbabel. The problem is made even more complicated by the fact that the root *yāsad*, which normally means 'lay the foundations', can also mean 'restore', 'repair', 'rebuild' (Andersen 1958, Gelston 1966).

4.4.2 However, the sources have a plausible explanation for the failure of the work to progress: the economic crisis, aggravated by drought, locusts, and difficulties with the local population. Moreover, those who returned home had to have somewhere to live, and this was a priority. The local population (Ezra 3.3), whom Josephus anachronistically calls 'Samaritans' (or perhaps he only meant to say 'inhabitants of Samaria'?), could have been those people of Judah to whom Nebuchadnezzar had given the land of the deportees (above XI.6.5.2); they could also have been others who had settled in the semi-abandoned territory. Further complications, perhaps to be seen in the context of the rebellions which I shall discuss below (9.5), in which Judah did not take part (Aharoni, *The Land*, 412), make the people say that the time was not ripe for such a demanding enterprise as the rebuilding of the temple complex, that it was both technically and economically premature. They therefore needed something more to create an atmosphere to goad them to carry on with the work (Noth*, 310).

5 This atmosphere was created by a complex of events which the prophets and the people interpreted in eschatological terms: the disorders which erupted in 522 when Cambyses died without leaving a direct heir to the throne. The succession passed to Darius son of Hystaspes, from another branch of the Achaemenids, a group which had already been completely incorporated into the court of Cambyses, but which had yet to be recognized.

5.1 In fact, Darius first had to deal with a series of rebellions which broke out in various parts of the empire. This was something which often happened in the ancient Near East when a new ruler succeeded to a throne, especially if his legitimacy was not competely clear.

5.1.1 The rebellion of a certain Gaumata seems to have been particularly serious. Gaumata passed himself off as Bardia, Cambyses' younger brother, who in fact had been secretly killed in order to eliminate a dangerous rival to the throne. The rebellion of Gaumata/Bardia involved the Medes and the Babylonians, who were also joined by some of the peripheral regions, hopeful of regaining their independence.

5.1.2 After about a year of hard and not always victorious struggles, Darius succeded in overcoming his enemies, thus assuring, towards the end of 521, his uncontested right to ascend the throne. His achievements have been listed in the trilingual text and the relief carved on the rock of Behistun in Persia, near to the present-day route which links Baghdad to Teheran; there are also translations of it, one into Aramaic (there is a reproduction in *ANEP*, no.249).

5.2 In Judaea, the events which must have shaken the empire to its foundations in 522/21 gave the impression that the world was about to end and that the 'day of YHWH', already attested in Amos 5.18[11] and expected with a mixture of hope and fear, was about to arrive: the kingdom of God would soon be inaugurated on the ruins of all the earthly kingdoms. Whatever else, it now seemed vital and particularly urgent to prepare a worthy reception for the Lord who was about to arrive on 'his' day, and to welcome his kingdom. What could be more appropriate than to prepare an adequate dwelling, a place where he could reside (in whatever way that might have been conceived), i.e. the temple?

5.2.1 These are the sentiments which appear clearly in the preaching of the prophets Haggai and Zechariah,[12] though in their books we find indications of two different phases of the same events.

5.2.1.1 With Haggai, we find ourselves at the beginning of the year 521/520, i.e. shortly after the consolidation of the empire, or when that consolidation was in its final phase. However, news of this does not seem to have arrived among those who had returned to Jerusalem, so their expectation of the imminent end remained unchanged. Haggai exhorted the people to rebuild the partially ruined sanctuary as soon as possible and thus to bring to completion the enterprise embarked on when the foundations were laid. The kingdom was indeed on the way.

5.2.1.2 In Proto-Zechariah the situation already seems to be different: the first vision (1.7ff.) shows that the people of Judah were disheartened. Everything was peaceful; the revolutions had finished; the cataclysms which heralded the imminence of the end had not taken place. However, the rebuilding had to continue, even if under other auspices; the cult had to be re-established for its own sake; the divine judgment on the nations was imminent.

5.3 Ezra 3-5, Haggai and Zechariah give several important pieces of information about the composition and the functioning of this first community of those who had returned about the year 520.

5.3.1 The priesthood now seems to be limited to the 'priests the levites, the sons of Zadok', according to the rules laid down in Ezek. 44.15; a tradition recorded in I Chron. 6.34ff. gives Zadok a genealogy going back to Aaron. It is always difficult to talk in terms of truth and falsehood in documents of this kind, but this genealogy in fact seems to use parts of the genealogy of Abiathar, who was deposed by Solomon (cf. above, III.8.1; IV.2.3.5). The figure of the High Priest also appears; mentions of him in the pre-exilic period seem to be anachronistic, since this ministry was probably exercised by the king (above IV.2.3.6).

5.3.2 Alongside the High Priest there also appears the representative of secular power, the 'prince', Hebrew *nāśī'* (cf. Ezek. 45.7ff., and above XI.7.1.4). We see Joshua and Zerubbabel respectively discharging these two functions; the latter was the last of the house of David, and probably also returned with the group of ex-deportees. His name, in Hebrew *zᵉrubbābel* and in Babylonian *zēr-babili*, is clearly Mesopotamian, like that of Sheshbazzar.

5.3.3 However, as with Sheshbazzar, it is impossible to establish the precise function and thus the powers of Zerubbabel, who is also called *peḥah*, 'satrap'. Josephus presents him as a personal friend of Darius and sent by him (XI, 32); it is probable that in this capacity he would have been directly responsible to the court, thus by-passing the hierarchical chain of command which went through the governor of Samaria and the satrapy of Transeuphrates. Of course, this interpretation does not give us any indication of his specific official functions. Was he only the official charged with carrying through the work of rebuilding the temple (thus Galling 1937) or was he, rather, the commissar in charge of resettling those who returned (Sacchi*).[13] We shall return to this question later (5.3.5–6); a plausible solution for it is provided by the discoveries published by Avigad in 1976.

5.3.4 Soon afterwards, however, we find that Zerubbabel unexpectedly disappears, and we do not know what happened to him. He could simply have returned to court, his mission accomplished; others, however (there is a discussion in J.Bright*, 371), think that he was quietly eliminated to avoid the rise of a new form of Judaean nationalism, for which the presence of a member of the house of David could have formed an important focal point. Although this theory is not intrinsically improbable, there is no proof for it.[14] In fact the two possibilities are by no means contradictory; a summons to court could well have been a good occasion for the unobtrusive removal of someone who in the meantime had become an embarrassment to the Persian court. At all events, Zech.6.9-15, a text which Sacchi*, 32, pertinently calls 'a very early and deliberate correction',[15] speaks of two crowns, each of them originally and obviously destined for one of the two figures. Now the High Priest has to wear both!

5.3.5 Anyway, no member of the house of David was ever again called to function as a satrap. It is easy to prove this: I Chron.3.19-24 gives us a genealogy of the house of David down to about the end of the last quarter of the fifth century; and the names inscribed on seals and coins allow us to trace the names of the governors (among whom Ezra and Nehemiah do not appear!) down to about the third quarter of the fourth century BC. No member of the house of David appears among them as governor;[16] we do not know whether a satrap who was not a member of the house of David still bore the title prince. However, this seems improbable, since Ezek.45.7ff. presupposes that this title belonged to David alone. Hence contrary to what was thought a few years ago (e.g. Sacchi*, 32, 47), a dualism between religious and civil power continued down to the end of the Persian period; there are valid reasons for supposing that it continued down to the reign of Antiochus IV Epiphanes (below XIII.7) at the beginning of the second century BC; Laperrousaz 1982 is right to ask whether the theocracy (the term comes from Josephus but seems inappropriate; 'hierocracy' is better) did not begin as late as the Macedonian conquest (or better, I would add, a century and a half later).

5.3.6 The discoveries published by Avigad in 1976 allow us again to solve another problem: on the material in question the Persian officials all have the title *pḥw'* in Aramaic, or *hpḥh* in Hebrew (cf. also the Persian title *hattiršātā'*), attested in Neh.7.65. There are also many seals inscribed with *yhwd* (= *yᵉhūd*), while in Ezra and Nehemiah the region is often designated *mᵉdīnāh* in Hebrew and *mᵉdīnātā* in Aramaic, a term characteristic of an independent regional administrative entity. Thus there seem no grounds for a theory put forward by A.Alt in 1934, and widely accepted,[17] that in practice Judah was annexed to Samaria and that Sheshbazzar and Zerubbabel will only have been charged with a special mission, while only Nehemiah will have been governor. It is in fact clear that both Sheshbazzar and Zerubbabel, and all the figures whose names appear in the inscriptions published by Avigad, were governors. The title *paḥat yᵉhudāh* given to Zerubbabel thus seems quite legitimate, even if the province which he governed was very small, as Bright*, 383ff., rightly points out.

5.3.7 On 23 Adar of the sixth year of Darius (i.e. 12 March 515), the rebuilding of the second temple was finished. Jewish writers therefore call the post-exilic period down to AD 70 'the period of the second temple'.

6 We have virtually no direct information from the period between the rebuilding and inauguration of the temple in 515 and about the middle of the fifth century, although the archaeological discoveries published by Avigad in 1976 and other texts allow us to reconstruct the genealogy of the High Priests, the house of David, and the Persian governors of Judaea and Samaria down to the end of the fifth century and of other families even later.

Select bibliography: A.van Hoonacker, 'Néhémie et Esdras: une nouvelle hypothèse sur le chronologie de l'époque de la restauration', *Le Muséon* 9, 1890, 151-84, 317-51, 389-401; C.C.Torrey, *Ezra Studies*, Chicago 1910; A.Alt, art.cit. (1 above); M.Noth, *Uberlieferungsgeschichtliche Studien*, I, Halle 1943, 110-79; H.Cazelles, 'La mission d'Esdras', *VT* 4, 1954, 113-40; J.Morgenstern, 'Jerusalem – 485 BC', *HUCA* 27, 1956, 101-79; 28, 1957, 15-47; 31, 1960, 1-29; and 'A Further Light from the Book of Isaiah on the Catastrophe of 486 BC', *HUCA* 37, 1966, 1-28; B.Mazar, 'The Tobiads', *IEJ* 7, 1957, 137-45, 229-38; A.Pavlovský, 'Die Chronologie der Tätigkeit Esdras - Versuch einer Lösung', *Bibl* 38, 1957, 275-305, 428-56; S.Mowinckel, *Studien zu dem Buche Ezra-Nehemia*, three vols, Oslo 1964-65; K.Galling, *Studien* (above, 1); C.R.North, 'Civil Authority in Ezra', in *Studi* *in onore di Edoardo Volterra*, Milan 1972, VI, 377-404; W.T.In der Smitten, 'Nehemias Parteigänger', *BO* 29, 1972, 155-7; id., *Esra: Quellen, Überlieferung und Geschichte*, Assen 1973; C.G.Tuland, 'Ezra-Nehemiah or Nehemiah-Ezra?', *AUSS* 12, 1974, 47-62; F.M.Cross, 'A Reconstruction...', (above 1); S.Talmon, ibid.; P.Sacchi*, ch.III; W.Vischer, 'Nehemia, Sonderbeauftragter und Statthalter des Königs', in *Probleme biblischer Theologie. FS Gerhard von Rad*, Munich 1971, 603-10; R.W.Klein, 'Ezra and Nehemia in Recent Studies', in *Magnalia Dei...Essays G.E.Wright*, Garden City, NY 1976, 361-76; N.Avigad, art.cit. (1 above); A.H.J.Gunneweg, 'Zur Interpretation der Bücher Esra-Nehemia', *SVT* 32, 1981, 146-61.

6.1 We learn indirectly that something serious must have happened in the eighties of the fifth century BC, probably a new, though partial, destruction of Jerusalem, which did not affect the temple. J.Morgen-stern 1966 even talks in terms of 'catastrophe' in the year 486/5. The information appears in a message sent from Jerusalem to Susa in the month of Chislev (November-December) of the twentieth year of king Artaxerxes I Longimanus (464-423, i.e. in 445 BC) and is amplified and supplemented with circumstantial details by Josephus, XI, 159ff. Elephantine papyrus Cowley no.30, dated in the year 408,[18] proves that this was the ruler at the time, rather than others of the same name (Artaxerxes II Mnemon, 404-360, and Artaxerxes III Ochus, 360-338, or even Xerxes I, 486-464, as Josephus always calls him). The papyrus mentions the 'sons of Sanballat, governor of Samaria', who is certainly Nehemiah's opponent (2.10,19 and elsewhere). The papyri from *wādī ed-daliyeh*, discovered in the 1960s and not yet published (cf. Cross 1969, 1975, above 1), allow us to trace much of the dynasty of the Sanballatids down to the end of the period in question (tables in Cross 1975 and Talmon 1976).

6.1.1 The message said: 'The survivors there in the province who escaped exile are in great trouble and shame; the wall of Jerusalem is broken down, and its gates are destroyed by fire' (Neh.1.3). We are not in a position to say what had happened; it is certain that the text cannot be a generalized reference to the ruins left by the Babylonians more than a century before and not yet rebuilt, because it would be quite notorious were that the case. So there seems to have been some recent happening, as is also confirmed by the reactions which the text attributes to Nehemiah (Neh.2.1-2). Again, the damage must have been relatively modest if Nehemiah could have it repaired in less than two months (fifty-two days, Neh.6.15). There could have been an attack in force by some of the neighbouring peoples or even conflict between those who had returned and claimed their land back, and those who, having remained in the country, had been given the land by the Babylonians and did not intend to hand it over. We are in the dark. In any event, as P.Sacchi* rightly observes (42), if the details have been lost the event can only have been of secondary importance.

6.1.2 One appropriate situation would certainly have been the rebellion of Egypt on the death of Darius I in 486 (Aharoni, *Land*, 412) and the revolts that followed, all of which took place during the Persian expeditions against Greece. However, we have no information, and unless new sources are discovered, we shall never know.

6.1.3 The book of Malachi,[19] probably composed shortly before Nehemiah's mission, reveals a number of cases of neglect and prevarications on ethical and cultic issues; this is another reason why someone should have taken matters in hand. The fact remains that Nehemiah felt the need to investigate the situation at first hand, and succeeded in convincing the king to send him on a mission.

6.2 So in the year 445 Nehemiah arrived in Judaea for the first time, with a commission from Artaxerxes I, whose cupbearer he was. It is not clear whether this marks the intervention by the intransigent Jewish diaspora in the internal affairs of the community of Judah, which was much more pragmatic and took the inhabitants of the region into account (thus Sacchi*, 39f.), or whether we have an initiative on the part of the Persian court to bring some order to a region which the Persians had to control if they were to dominate Egypt, which was often rebellious; basically, these two factors are not mutually exclusive. At all events, the biblical texts are cautious in attributing an official commission to Nehemiah: in Neh.5.14 he appears with the title *peḥam*, a term of unknown meaning in this context which many scholars take to be a corruption of *peḥah*, a word which appears in 12.26. (North, 1972, in fact argues that he did not have an official commision at all.) However, after the discoveries published by Avigad in 1976, it would not be surprising had he been a 'satrap' in the sense mentioned at 5.4.3-4 above, though as we have seen, his name does not figure in the discoveries. According to the sources, Nehemiah remained at Jerusalem for twelve years, only returning to Persia in 533 (5.14; 13.6). He is then said to have returned a second time in 532 (13.7). As things are, we have no reason to doubt this chronology.

6.2.1 Whether or not Nehemiah's commission was official, at all events he was a plenipotentiary. Though at the Persian court he had only been a page (albeit a well-placed one, Herodotus III.34, so that Sacchi* even makes him 'a powerful minister of the emperor'), his powers, conveyed directly by the king, in fact by-passed the authority of the satrapy of Transeuphrates and of the local governors.

6.2.2 So it is hardly surprising that these last should be first obstructive and then hostile, clearly being accustomed to dealing with people of little prestige and power. Nehemiah 2.10 mentions Sanballat the

Horonite, whom we have already come across; the letter from Elephantine quoted above explicitly calls him governor of Samaria. He was probably a Yahwist by religion, since his two sons had theophoric names with Yahweh as an element; we also come across 'Tobias the Ammonite slave', again with a Yahwistic name; here, however, it is probably better to understand the term *'ebed* as 'official' or even 'minister', rather than as 'slave' (in a derogatory sense).[20]

6.2.3 The opposition of the local authorities is therefore understandable, though we should rule out the theory in the text that this was essentially due to the fact that at last 'someone had come to seek the welfare of the children of Israel'; cf. also 2.19; 6.1-6, where the two officials mentioned are joined by a certain 'Geshem the Arab'. Some scholars want to identify this figure with the father of a certain *qyn*, king of Kedar, the owner of a silver cup with an inscription mentioning both of them, and which is certainly earlier than 400 BC.[21] Hostile reactions were not slow in coming: Ezra 4.11 speaks of a letter sent to Artaxerxes, who accused the Judaeans of subversion; this was followed by the injunction to Nehemiah to suspend all work. By all accounts Nehemiah had already inspected the walls with a view to rebuilding them (2.11-15).

7 The problem of Ezra's mission is much more complex. As things are, we can say that it is insoluble. There is a good account of the problem in J.Bright*, 391-402.[22]

7.1 In Ezra 7.12 we read that Ezra, for whom 7.1-5 provides a genealogy going back to Aaron, and whom 7.7 describes as a 'priest…, scribe of the law of the God of heaven', had come to Judaea along with a group of ex-deportees, again with a direct commission from Artaxerxes. However, while this direct relationship to the king seems probable in the case of Nehemiah, a page in the personal service of the king, the situation is different with Ezra. The text says only that '…the hand of Yahweh, his God, was with him, so that he granted all that he desired' (7.6). The text thus provides an explanation of the success of Ezra which is clearly the fruit of later theological reflection, while giving no indication of the circumstances which led to the conferring of the commission on him. Be this as it may, here too the sources clearly envisage the reign of Artaxerxes I, so his mission will have begun in 458.

7.2 Thus according to the chronology adopted by the redactors of Ezra and Nehemiah, Ezra will have arrived in Jerusalem about thirteen years before Nehemiah. That would make it inevitable, or at least probable, that their stay overlapped (though many scholars regard the references to Ezra as an interpolation).

7.3 However, what we might call the traditional theory comes up against some difficulties, so much so that S.Talmon 1976, 320, speaks of a 'disconcerting' question.

7.3.1 First of all there is nothing in the book of Nehemiah (whose chronology is, as we have seen, more reliable), to suggest that Ezra had already been at work for some time when Nehemiah arrived. Again, the dates given would seem to exclude this, and also the co-ordination of their work.

7.3.2 Moreover, there seems to be some question as to the relationship between Ezra and the governor in office on his arrival, who was probably, according to Avigad's discoveries, a certain 'aḥzay. We could certainly insert Ezra between him and Nehemiah (e.g. Talmon 1976, 327, does this, if only in parentheses), but in that case the invective of Neh.5.15 would also apply to him; this accuses 'the governors who were before me' of having oppressed the people, exacting unjust taxes from them.

7.3.3 So the situation seems to exclude, rather than presuppose, the fact that Ezra and Nehemiah coincided and therefore worked together, though we should recognize that this is essentially an argument from silence. Moreover Talmon, 1976, 320, rightly points out that though Haggai and Zechariah were contemporaries and worked in the same city, neither ever mentions the other in their texts.

7.3.4 Again, according to Ezra 10.6, Ezra spent the night fasting, at the house of a certain Johanan ben Eliashib; however, in Neh.12.22-33 Eliashib is a contemporary of Nehemiah and has a grandson by the name of Jonathan. But this argument, too, is inconclusive; it has recently been attacked by F.M.Cross 1975, 9ff., who argues that there will have been an Elyashib I, father of Yohanan I, a contemporary of Ezra, and an Elyashib II, father of Yohanan II, a contemporary of Nehemiah. One of the two pairs, father and son, will have been omitted by haplography, which often happens in connection with papponymy, in which the sons had the names of their paternal grandfathers. This theory seems to have the unconditional support of A.F.Rainey in Y. Aharoni, The Land, 423 n.105, but is severely criticized by Widengren*, 505ff., because of its obvious inadequacy on the critical level and because of an error of fact (though he recognizes its 'persuasive and attractive character', 509; cf. also Bright*, 402).

7.4 In 1890 the Belgian scholar A. van Hoonacker of Louvain suggested that the solution to the various problems lay in accepting that Ezra probably came not under Artaxerxes I but under Artaxerxes II (404-358), so that the seventh year would have been in 398. The abuses which we find at Elephantine would then have been some of those which Ezra eliminated (Fohrer*, 214ff.). Van Hoonacker's theory has been adopted by many scholars;[23] a few of them have even suggested Artaxerxes III (360-338), i.e. in 354.

7.5 A different proposal is that of Pavlovský, 1957; he argues that Ezra will have come, not in the seventh but in the thirty-seventh year of Artaxerxes I, i.e. in 428, during Nehemiah's second stay. This explanation presupposes an error in the text: the figure thirty will have fallen out. However, there is no evidence for this, so we can discard this view.[24]

7.6 It would seem, then, that despite everything there are also a number of features in favour of the traditional theory that Ezra came to Jerusalem before Nehemiah; they include the opinion of the redactors of the two books and the chronology that they present. Or rather, the chronological problem of the relationship between the two is so complex because of the redactional and editorial work that it cannot be resolved simply by recourse to essentially mechanical operations.

7.7 To this already sufficiently confused situation we must add a theory put forward for the first time in 1910 by C.C.Torrey, some features of which have recently been taken up again by G. Garbini (personal communication). According to this view Ezra never existed: his person is the *ad hoc* creation of the redactors of the two books, the Chronicler or whoever, who sought in this way to legitimate their own theory of what must have been the composition, the organization and the faith of the new community of the restoration. This comprised a prohibition against marrying non-Jewish wives (below, 7.9.2: Ezra 9.1-10.17); the imposition of the 'law' by means of a personal pledge on the part of every member of the community (Neh.8.1-9.3); and its sanctioning as the law of the state. However, such a radical theory also presupposes the rejection of much of the tradition that we possess as being an artificial construction; moreover, the arguments used are anything but conclusive (e.g. the lack of any mention of Ezra in Sir.49.13, where Nehemiah appears alone). There is a good survey of the various possibilities which have been proposed in Fohrer*, 208ff.

7.8 At all events, then, whatever may have happened (and without the discovery of new documents we shall never have precise information), it seems that around the middle of the fifth century BC, and after some unspecified catastrophe which had happened some years before, the Jewish community in Jerusalem underwent a rigoristic religious reform, the leading light behind which was someone sent by the Babylonian diaspora, Nehemiah. Nehemiah was against any form of compromise in the sphere of faith and against any integration with the other peoples in every day life (Neh.10.29; cf.Sacchi*, 38ff., who also points out, 44, that ch.10 is probably based on contemporary documents); thus the reform touched on faith, public worship and everyday conduct.

7.8.1 First of all, this reform gave rise to new stimuli in the life of the nation: under the leadership of Nehemiah the walls of the capital were rebuilt (Neh.2.11-3.32), despite the hostility to the project on the part of the local authorities. The texts mention Sanballat the Horonite, Tobias the Ammonite, and the Ammonite and Philistine populations (Neh.3.33-4.17). For this reason the enterprise had to be brought to a conclusion by armed labourers (4.10ff.). The city was then repopulated through the settlement of new inhabitants who came from the country (7.4-5; 1.1-2). In the end the new walls could be inaugurated with a solemn religious rite (12.27ff.).

7.8.2 To give the population a fresh start, without any kind of burdens and debts, Nehemiah ordered a general remission of debts (Neh.5.1-13). This text seems to refer not only to ordinary debts, for example those which the farmer often contracted for seed and repaid some months later after the harvest; as I have already pointed out (above XI.6.5.2), the solemnity of the texts seems to indicate rather more. As a conjectural explanation I would like to suggest that the provision brought to an official conclusion all the law suits which had arisen over the lands of the exiles which Nebuchadnezzar had distributed to those who had remained behind and which were reclaimed by the exiles when they returned (this suggestion was already made, implicitly, by M.Noth*, 326f.). A conflict of this kind threatened the very existence of the tiny community; it will have been ended by allowing the properties concerned to remain with those who had cultivated them for more than a century.

7.8.3 Another feature seems historically certain: at the end of the so-called edict of Artaxerxes (Ezra 7.12ff., though its authenticity is open to dispute) we find an important assertion: the 'law' becomes the law of the state and is administered with the aid of public powers. Ezra 7.25-26 in fact says: 'Whoever will not obey the law of your (the text is addressed to Ezra in the second person) God – which is the law of the king – let judgment be strictly executed upon him, whether for death or for banishment or for confiscation of his goods or for imprisonment!' And from then on the codified norms of the Pentateuch became the law of the state. This soon gave rise to the rendering of *tōrāh* with the Greek νομός. Conversely, in the temple, prayers were made 'for the life of the king' and sacrifices were offered at state expense (Ezra 6.10); the people of Judah paid direct taxes like everyone else (if we can understand Neh.9.37 in this way), and sometimes extraordinary tribute, which on one occasion was punitive (Josephus XI, 297ff.).

7.9 What motives prompted Nehemiah to return to Judaea in 432 BC? We have no precise information.

7.9.1 One reason could have been that the high priest Eliashib was pursuing an autonomous policy, aimed not at separation from but rather at accommodation with the other governors of the region. He was, as the texts say, 'close to Tobias', an expression which probably indicates that he was related to him. He was also related to Sanballat, since one of his grandsons had married a daughter of Sanballat (Neh.13.28). Eliashib had allowed Tobias to use a room in the temple precinct - we do not know on what grounds and for what purpose (13.7). So it is possible that one of the reasons for Nehemiah's return was to oppose any tendencies towards laxity in this sphere.

7.9.2 At the same time, Nehemiah eliminated other abuses that he had not succeeded in eradicating during his first stay: priests who neglected their ministry (Neh.13.10; cf.Mal.1.6ff.); tithes which were not paid (10.12ff.; Mal.3.6ff.); failure to observe the sabbath (13.15ff.); and marriage with foreign women (13.23ff.; Mal.2.10ff.), an abuse which, as we have seen, did not stop even at the family of the high priest.[25]

8 The centralization of worship in the Jerusalem temple, which took place during the last quarter of the seventh century BC under Josiah (above XI.4), and the emergence in the post-exilic period of the figure of the high priest, surrounded by the Zadokite priesthood, are the main characteristics of the religion of Israel in this period; many of its distinguishing features can be deduced indirectly from the P source of the Pentateuch and later from Chronicles. Despite the presence for about 200 years and probably even more of a civil governor who was by nationality a Judaean (the only exception, the Persian Bagoas at the time of the Elephantine papyri, confirms the rule), the influence of religious power seems to have grown rapidly. On the one hand, in fact the governor represented first Persia and then the other occupying powers, and was accountable for his mandate only to the court which had appointed him. On the other hand, the temple was the only place in which Judah could still exercise any form of self-determination, limited though it was; in this respect, too, it was helped by the religious tolerance of the Persians. Moreover the temple had come to have significant economic importance because of the contributions which it regularly received from the Diaspora in its own currency (the obol) and because it performed functions which we might regard as those of a bank (below XIII.7.2). There is therefore nothing strange in the fact that the religious authorities came to acquire increasing importance alogside the civil government, not only in matters of cult and belief but also in everyday life.

8.1 That came about despite the reduced extent of the territory now occupied by the community: from Jerusalem it was possible to reach the frontier of the governor's lands in one or two days' march. In the north the frontier ran close to Bethel (*beitīn*, coord.172-148) and Baal-hazor (*tell 'aṣūr*, coord.177-153); eastwards it extended to the Jordan and the Dead Sea, including En-gedi (coord.187-097); southwards it extended to Beth-sur (*ḥirbet eṭ-ṭubbīqe*, coord.159-110); and northwards to Azekah (*tell zakariye*, coord.144-123), Gezer (coord.142-140) and to Ono (coord.137-159; Y.Aharoni, *The Land*, map 34).

8.2 However, 'Israel' extended far beyond these wretched bounds. A large part of Palestine was inhabited by people loyal to Jerusalem, though perhaps already excluding Samaria; and the capital was not only the main town of an insignificant province of the empire but also the seat of the temple and therefore of Israelite worship. In this capacity it was the focal point of a vast diaspora in Babylon which sent men and financial means (Zech.6.9-10), though on the other hand, as in the case of Nehemiah, it also intervened in what might otherwise have been thought to be internal affairs of the community.

8.3 We know little of the character and the content of the cult at this period, so that we can proceed only by deductions and suppositions.

Select bibliography: H.H.Schaeder, *Esra der Schreiber*, Tübingen 1930; H.Cazelles, 'La mission d'Esdras', *VT* 4, 1954, 113-40; U.Kellermann, 'Erwägungen zum Esragesetz', *ZAW* 80, 1968, 373-85; S.Mowinckel, *Studien...* (cf.1 above), Vol.III; K.Koch, 'Ezra and the Origins of Judaism', *JSS* 19, 1974, 173-97; G.Widengren*, 514ff.; H.G.M. Williamson, 'The Composition of Ezra I-VI', *JTS* 33, 1983, 1-30.

8.3.1 The process of reforming the cult begun under Josiah and perhaps already under Hezekiah was thus carried forward in a radical way in the post-exilic period. The agricultural character of the traditional festivals, typical of the Canaanite world, had been eliminated and replaced by what has often been called 'historicization', i.e. the festivals had been associated with events in the sacred history of the people, which they thus helped to celebrate.

8.3.2 As M.Noth*, 340f., pertinently pointed out, the divine judgment which had only just come to an end was one of the key concepts in the interpretation of past history. With it went a great fear of violating the commandments and a constant desire for purity and integrity before God. That explains the importance of the rites of purification and expiation in this period, chief among which was the great 'Day of Atonement', *yōm kippūr*, celebrated on 10 Tishri (September-October: Lev.23.27-32; 25.9ff.; but cf. the much earlier text Lev.16).

8.3.3 In the past one often came across the theory that Ezra had brought the P source of the Pentateuch from Susa to Judaea. The foundation of it was Ezra 7.12, 14: '...according to the law of your God which is in your hand' (as we have seen, the edict is addressed to Ezra in the second person). Moreover, it was thought that this was the period in which the redaction of the Pentateuch was completed, on the basis of P. The first of these two theories is improbable: the expression quoted does not in fact mean that Ezra actually brought a document, far less one which can be identified with part of the Pentateuch (Noth*,

335; for the supporters of the theory see Kellermann, 1968, 374ff). A number of modern scholars (e.g. Cazelles, 1954; Sacchi*, 44) think rather of Deuteronomy. That is more likely, though there is no proof for it; moreover, it would not be strange for the Aramaic expression *dātā' dī-'elah šemaiyā'*, 'the law of the God of heaven', to denote the now completed Pentateuch, the first part of the canon and the most important element in the Hebrew Bible in the making.[26]

8.3.4 In this way the Pentateuch, as a norm for faith and life, for meditation, study and daily living, and at the same time the state law for the province of Judaea, began its own canonical career which in a short time was to make it the sacred scripture *par excellence* of both the Hebrews and the Samaritans (for the latter cf. below XIII.4).

8.4 The vast Hebrew dispersion must also have had its own local worship, and that is also true of the communities of Palestine, which were now remote from what was the only sanctuary, the temple: for these, too, a journey of several days once or more a year to reach Jerusalem was clearly an impossibility. However, the situation was even more serious for those in Mesopotamia or in Persia, and later in Egypt and in the West.

Select bibliography: P.Lifschitz, *Donateurs et fondateurs dans les synago-gues juives, Cahiers RB 7*, Paris 1967; L.I.R(abinowitz), 'Synagogue', *EncJud* 15, 1971, 579-84; K. Hruby, *Die Synagoge – Geschichtliche Entwicklungen einer Institution*, Zurich 1971; J.Swetnam, 'Why was Jeremiah's New Covenant New?', *SVT* 26, 1974, 111-15; E.M.Meyers, 'Synagogue', *IDB SV*, 1976, 842-4; F. Hüttenmeister and K.Galling, 'Synagoge', *BRL*, ²1977, 327-32; H.Shanks, *Judaism in Stone*, New York 1979.

8.4.1 So it is probable that the period between the edict of Cyrus and the governorship of Nehemiah saw the birth of that communal institution commonly called the synagogue, in Hebrew *bēt kenesset*, 'house of reunion'; it served for prayer, communal reading and study of the scriptures and other writings, singing, and as a centre of social activity.

8.4.2 We do not know when and where the first synagogue was founded; however, it is certain that the institution spread rapidly wherever there was a sufficiently large group of Jews, even in the holy land in places remote from Jerusalem. Swetnam sees an allusion to the foundation of the synagogue as early as Jer.31.31ff., in the 'new covenant'; Rabinowitz in the 'small sanctuary' of Ezek. 11.16 (though this is an uncertain text which some scholars correct, or understand differently). Be this as it may, there were certainly synagogues in the first century BC, and one in Egypt even seems to go back to the third century BC (Shanks); there are therefore significant indications that the

synagogue grew up independently of the destruction of the temple in
AD 70.

8.5 We are relatively well informed on one sector of the Diaspora,
though this is a special case: the Jewish community and military colony
of Elephantine, situated near the present border between Egypt and
the Sudan, at the level of the First Cataract and the Aswan dam.

Select bibliography: A.E.Cowley, *Aramaic Papyri of the Fifth Century BC*,
Oxford 1923; E.G.Kraeling, *The Brooklyn Aramaic Papyri*, New York
1953; B.Porten, *Archives from Elephantine*, Berkeley 1968. Cf. also
G.Widengren*, 532-5; Soggin, *Introduction*, 486ff.; Fohrer*, 212ff.

8.5.1 The colony was probably established at the time of the Persian
conquest of Egypt under Cambyses in 525 (above 3), and we have
substantial parts of its archives. The earliest letter dates from 495 BC,
i.e. about thirty years from its foundation. The colony disappeared
shortly after 400 BC, probably in the course of one of the many revolts
of Egypt against Persia (above, 6).

8.5.2 The distinctive feature of the cult of the community is that it
has a temple of its own, and its worship included sacrifices, as at
Jerusalem. Furthermore, its beliefs seem to have been polytheistic, or
at least syncretistic; alongside the God of Israel, whose name is almost
always written *Yhw*, we have the cult of two other deities, *'anat-bēt-'ēl*
and *'ašīm-bēt-'ēl*; however, this last may perhaps already be mentioned
in Amos 8.14, where it appears as *'ašmā** (in the construct, *'ašmat*),[27]
perhaps a hypostasis of the divine name connected with the sanctuary
of Bethel. In that case there will have been only two deities. One
plausible explanation of the phenomenon would seem to be that the
Jews of Elephantine had been stationed there before they could be
affected by Josiah's reform, so that their worship had remained Jewish-
Canaanite.

8.5.3 Finally, it is interesting that relations with the priesthood in
Jerusalem were good and frequent, without a single reproof from the
priesthood of the capital. According to Fohrer*, 224ff., one of the
specific tasks of Ezra, who is said to have arrived under Artaxerxes II,
would have been to put an end to abuses of this kind, and the same
could also be said about the return of Nehemiah (above 7).

9 The Persian empire lasted just over two centuries: the expeditions
against Greece which ended in the defeat of the Persians by sea and
land dealt a heavy blow to the political and military prestige of the
empire and led to a series of revolts. These were almost continuous in
Egypt, a country which succeeded in regaining its liberty for long
periods; often they took place among the Phoenician cities who had
neverthless provided the fleets for the expeditions against Greece.
There were also conflicts between the satraps themselves; one particu-

larly serious one occurred between 368 and 360. Artaxerxes III Ochus (360-338) managed to take over the reins of power, but only for a short time. In 345 he subjected the Phoenician cities and in 341 he reconquered Egypt; in this way he was able to provide some reinforcement for the tottering power of Persia. However, he was assassinated, and with his death the recovery ended: now the end was only a few years in coming. For a survey of the little information available on this period cf. recently O.Kaiser, 'Zwischen den Fronten – Palästina in den Auseinandersetzungen zwischen Perserreich und Ägypten in den ersten Hälfte des 4. Jahrhunderts', in *FS J.Ziegler*, Würzburg 1972, II, 197-206.

XIII

UNDER THE MACEDONIANS AND DIADOCHI

Select bibliography: F.-M.Abel, *Histoire de la Palestine depuis la conquête d'Alexandre jusqu'à l'invasion arabe*, Paris 1952; V.Tcherikover, *Hellenistic Civilization and the Jews*, Jerusalem 1959; O.Plöger, *Theocracy and Eschatology*, Oxford 1968; S.K.Eddy, *The King is Dead*, University of Nebraska 1961; S.Zeitlin, *The Rise and the Fall of the Judaean State*, Philadelphia I, 1962; II, 1967; III, 1978; E.Bickerman, *From Ezra to the Last of the Maccabees – Foundations of Post-Biblical Judaism*, New York 1962; D.S.Russell, *The Jews from Alexander to Herod*, London 1967; O.H.Steck, 'Das Problem theologischer Strömungen in nachexilischer Zeit', *EvTh* 28, 1968, 445-58; M.Smith, *Palestinian Parties and Politics that Shaped the Old Testament*, New York 1971; O.Plöger, *Aus der Spätzeit des Alten Testaments*, Göttingen 1971; G.Delling, 'Perspektiven der Erforschung des Hellenistischen Judentums', *HUCA* 45, 1974, 133-76; O.Kaiser, 'Judentum und Hellenismus', *VuF* 27.1, 1982, 68-88; M.Hengel, *Judaism and Hellenism*, London and Philadelphia 1974; P.Schäfer, *Die Juden in der Antike – Geschichte des Judentums von Alexander dem Grossen bis zur arabischen Eroberung Palästinas*, Tübingen 1982. For the movements, thought and doctrine and the political groups between the third century BC and the first century AD see the exhaustive study by C.Thoma, *Christliche Theologie des Judentums*, Aschaffenburg 1978. For Zech.9.1-8 cf. K.Elliger, 'Ein Zeugnis der jüdische Gemeinde im Alexanderjahr 332 BC', *ZAW* 62, 1949-50, 63-115 (not in *KS*); H.Delcor, 'Les allusions à Alexandre le Grand dans Zach. IX. 1-8', *VT* 1, 1951, 110-24. For the Zeno papyri cf. V.Tcherikover annd A Fuks, *Corpus Papyrorum Judaicorum* I, Cambridge, Mass. 1957; they are not included in M.Stern, *Authors*, I-II.

1 In 333 BC, at the battle of Issus, near to present-day Alexandretta, Alexander, the son of Philip II of Macedon won the title 'Great' with

which he has gone down in history by defeating the Persian army of Darius III Codomannus (335-332). He then occupied Syria and Palestine in 332 and attempted to reach Egypt as quickly as possible. Tyre resisted for a good six months, Gaza for two. In the Palestinian territories the (future?) Samaritans welcomed Alexander; Josephus tells us (XI, 325ff.) that to begin with, Jerusalem resisted in order to remain faithful to the Persians; it was then miraculously saved and the high priest submitted. On his return from Egypt, Alexander was able to pass undisturbed through the region on his way to Mesopotamia, where in 332 he defeated the survivors of the Persian army at Gaugamela near Arbela. Samaria, seat of the satrapy, rebelled against him later (Josephus, XII, 7) and was punished by being settled with a Macedonian colony, in 331. In the course of this revolt, groups of nobles to whom the *wādī ed-dalīyeh* papyri have been attributed will have fled from Samaria and taken refuge in the Jordan valley (F.M.Cross, oral communication; cf. above, XII.6.1).

1.1 Unlike the previous conquests, in the course of which one Eastern nation conquered others, this time, with the Macedonians, it was the West that erupted victoriously eastwards, and Hellenistic civilization that was superimposed on all the local civilizations. Thus began the process of the Hellenization of the region, which was to continue under the Diadochi, Rome and Byzantium, and was only to end with the Islamic conquest in AD 634/5. So we may rightly talk of the end of one era and the beginning of another. The period in which the whole of the vast region of the East seems to have been culturally autonomous and intact was at an end, and it rapidly began to become progressively Westernized; however, this process came up against heavy resistance, and not just in Israel. Yet even Jewish Palestine was profoundly affected by it, as is evident from the fact that at the beginning of the second century AD the ultra-nationalist movement of Bar Kochba (below XIV.6.3) in some cases used Greek in its own correspondence.

1.2 There is nothing about this crucial period in the proto- and deutero-canonical writings of the Old Testament: Chronicles does not go beyond the Persian period except in genealogies, and Maccabees only considers it in the broadest of terms. So we are completely dependent on Josephus, and on scarce and peripheral comments by classical authors. All the relevant texts have been collected in the monumental work by M.Stern (quoted often). In a prophetic passage, Zech.9.1-8, there could be an allusion to the passage of Alexander through the region (Elliger 1950 and Delcor 1951).

1.3 We know from Josephus XI, 337ff., that Alexander continued the religious policy begun by the Persians. Judaea was left alone and the inhabitants were allowed to live in accordance with the law; and it is probable that this continued to be the law of the state.

1.3.1 We do not know what happened to the civil governor. The last civil governor to appear in the material published by Avigad in 1976 (above XII.5.3.6) was called *yḥzqyh*, i.e. *yᵉhezqīyāh*, Hezekiah, to be dated about 330; he was thus a contemporary of the high priest Onias I. So it seems that the institution of the civil governorship also continued to exist in the Macedonian period and that therefore in this respect, too, the transition from one regime to another took place without undue disturbance. However, we cannot establish whether the institution of the governorship continued further, and if so under what conditions, though there are some indications that it did. Probably the Tobiads (below 2.3) in Transjordan succeeded in taking over this function until they were expelled by Onias III at the beginning of the second century BC (cf. below 7.6.1.1). At all events, it is clear that with the importance assumed by the temple, the power of the high priest and thus the religious power was on an equal footing with the civil power, and in terms of prestige was evidently superior to it.

2 Alexander the Great died in 323, leaving open the question of the succession. He had two sons, one legitimate and the other illegitimate, but both of them were minors, so this made a regency necessary. Alexander's generals assumed responsibility for this, each of them for the time being becoming governor of a region of the empire. They were called, or later came to be called, 'Diadochi', in Greek 'successors', a term which reflects their *de facto* position. One was given the European territories, Macedonia, Greece and Thrace; another had Egypt; a third Asia Minor; and the fourth Babylonia. Following a pattern which now went back over a thousand years, there was a dispute between Babylon and Egypt over Syria and Palestine.

2.1 The death of the sons of Alexander in 310 and 309 (they were probably assassinated) left things as they were, legitimating the *de facto* power of the Diadochi. Each of them held on to what he had and founded a dynasty, trying at the same time to enlarge his own territories.

2.2 Almost immediately, Palestine came under the Ptolemies of Egypt (sometimes called Lagides because the first Ptolemy was the son of Lagus). Ptolemy, the ex-governor with a seat at Alexandria, the city founded by Alexander the Great on the Mediterranean to the west of the Delta, occupied Palestine and Phoenicia, taking them from the Seleucids of Mesopotamia. This operation caused him some difficulties with the other Diadochi, but the Ptolemies succeeded in retaining control of the region. Jerusalem was occupied in 312. Information about the community in Judah in this period is, as we saw, non-existent. We do, however, know of a substantial Jewish diaspora at Alexandria, which according to Josephus XII, 7, probably came about as a result of a deportation after the conquest of Jerusalem in 312 and was then enlarged by continuous immigration. Relationships between the Jews of Alexandria and the Ptolemies were always good, and it was under Ptolemy II Philadelphus (285-246) that the translation of the so-called Septuagint (LXX, named after the number of scholars involved in it, in fact supposed to have been 72), will have been begun.[1] This translation is an obvious example, if we needed one, of the degree of Hellenization arrived at by the Jewish community, at least in Alexandria, and of its assimilation at least on the linguistic level, a development which was furthered by the incorporation into the community of a large number of 'proselytes' (literally 'those who have joined'), people who had never been Hebrew or Aramaic speakers (below 7.5.6).

2.3 *Select bibliography*: B.Mazar, 'The Tobiads', *IEJ* 7, 1957, 136-45, 229-38.

As far as we can see, the region enjoyed considerable prosperity under the Ptolemies, even if it was subjected to heavy taxation. We get some information about the period from the 'Zeno papyri'; Zeno was a senior Egyptian official who had travelled through Palestine and Transjordan between 260 and 258 BC, i.e during the reign of Ptolemy II, and we have some of his accounts. Zeno did not have any contact with the religious authorities, but only with Tobias; the name is Yahwistic and therefore Jewish. Tobias exercised civil power (Josephus XII, 160). He belonged to a famous house, one of whose members is probably mentioned in Zech.6.9-16; 9; 14 as having come from Babylon to Judaea about 520-515; another member of the family appears as one of the opponents of Nehemiah (above XII.6.2.2). According to Mazar's study (236ff.), the family may have been descended from the Tabeel mentioned in Isa.7.6 (above X.3.4.2). All this would seem to presuppose that Tobias was a civil governor on behalf of Egypt rather than a private individual.

3 At the beginning of the second century BC, after a series of hostile encounters, Syria and Palestine passed from the Ptolemies to the Seleucids of Babylon. This dynasty had been founded in 312 by Seleucus I Monophthalmos, called Nicanor. Under Antiochus III the Great (223-187), an ally of Philip V of Macedon and a friend of Hannibal, to whom he gave sanctuary at his court after the battle of Zama (202 BC), the Seleucid empire extended as far as Asia Minor and the adjoining cities. This soon led to conflict with Rome. Before that, however, in 198 BC, Antiochus was able to occupy Syria and Palestine, defeating Ptolemy V Epiphanes at the battle of Panaea (or Panaeum, present-day *banyās*, later Caesarea Philippi, coord.295-215). The conflict with Rome, whose power Antiochus had evidently underestimated, ended at the battle of Magnesia (between Sardis and Smyrna) with a disastrous defeat (190 BC). Antiochus was forced to make peace on very harsh

terms: he had to abandon all Asia Minor and the Greek cities, pay a heavy fine, give hostages to Rome, including his own sons Antiochus and Demetrius, send war elephants and the fleet, and to extradite Hannibal (Hannibal in fact succeeded in escaping). Antiochus died during an attempt to sack a temple, with the aim of obtaining the money needed to pay Rome.

3.1 To begin with, the community in Judah did not suffer in the transition from the Ptolemies to the Seleucids; it seems, rather, that because of the Ptolemies' fiscal demands they welcomed the change, even if as a result Palestine was cut off from its diaspora in Alexandria. Moreover, Josephus XII, 138-44, mentions some edicts of Antiochus III which benefited the community of Judah.

3.2 Antiochus III was succeeded by his son Seleucus IV Philopator (187-179). The new ruler was not a brilliant man, but sufficiently able to be able to cope with the difficult situation he inherited from his father. He too was hampered by the debts from the war with Rome and tried to take money from the temple treasure in Jerusalem; in other respects, however, he seems to have been more friendly than hostile to the people of Judah. II Maccabees 3.3 in fact says that he made a contribution to the expenses of the temple cult from his personal funds. He also succeeded in ransoming some of the hostages which his father had had to give to Rome, including his brother Antiochus; Demetrius, however, was left behind. Seleucus was assassinated by his minister Heliodorus, and the succession passed to Antiochus, who was on his way back from Rome.

4 Josephus (*Antt.* XI, 304ff.) connects the Samaritan schism with the rigoristic measures of Nehemiah and especially Ezra.

Select bibliography: H.H.Rowley, 'The Samaritan Schism in Legend and History', in *Israel's Prophetic Heritage – Festschrift J.Muilenburg*, New York and London 1962, 208-22; id., 'Sanballat and the Samaritan Temple', *BJRL* 38, 1955-56, 166-98 = *Men of God*, London 1963, 246-76; J.Macdonald, *The Theology of the Samaritans*, London 1964; G.E.Wright, 'The Samaritans at Shechem', in *Shechem*, New York 1965, 170-89; F.M.Cross, 'Aspects of Samaritan and Jewish History in Persian and Hellenistic Times', *HTR* 59, 1966, 201-11; J.D.Purvis, 'The Samaritan Pentateuch and the Origins of the Samaritan Sect', *HSM* 2, Cambridge, Mass. 1968; P.Sacchi, 'Studi samaritani', *RSLR* 5, 1969, 413-40; M.Smith, *Palestinian Parties* (see 1 above), 148-92; H.G.Kippenberg, *Garizim und Synagoge. Traditionsgeschichtliche Untersuchungen zur samaritanischen Religion der aramäischen Periode*, Berlin 1971; A.L.(oewenstamm), 'Samaritans', *EncJud* 14, 1971, 725-57; R.J.Coggins, *Samaritans and Jews. The Origins of the Samaritans Reconsidered*, Oxford 1975; F.M.Cross, art.cit. (above XII.1);

J.D.Purvis, 'Samaritans', *IDB SV*, 1976, 770f.; S.Talmon, art.cit. (above XII.1).

4.1 There was a certain Manasseh, brother of the high priest Jaddua mentioned in Neh.12.11,22, a contemporary of the governor Bagoas (the only governor, as we have seen, to have been a Persian rather than a Judaean), who is also mentioned in the Elephantine letters (above XII.8.5); he therefore lived towards the end of the fifth century BC. Against his brother's will he married a non-Jewish woman. This case is similar to that in Neh.13.28, where one of the sons of the high priest Jehoiada had married a daughter of Sanballat, the governor of Samaria (the similarity is so great that some scholars, like Sacchi*, ch.IV, would regard this as one and the same case); other instances of mixed marriages appear in Josephus XI, 312. To escape the rigours of Jerusalem orthodoxy, Manasseh is said to have taken refuge in Samaria with Sanballat, probably the second to bear that name, and therefore the grandson of Nehemiah's opponent. Here I prefer to follow the chronology of Talmon 1976, and not that of Cross 1975, 5ff.; Cross puts the episode in the time of Sanballat III, who died about 332 BC, i.e. at the time of the Macedonian conquest.

4.2 In this way there will have emerged in the region of Samaria a Jewish community made up of Zadokites, which had a place of its own in Shechem. Ezra will have had dealings with them for a certain time (Cazelles 1954; Sacchi* 54f.). These relations did not last long because of the incompatibility of the respective positions of the two parties.

4.2.1 Now it seems more than likely that a community like this will have come into being following a conflict between rigorists and non-rigorists, and that it will soon have become a focal point for those who were discontented with the turn of events in Jerusalem seems all too probable (Purvis 1976), especially since the north had a population which was Yahwistic by faith and which with some reason regarded itself as heirs to the ancient kingdom of Israel. This provided what we might call the foundation for an eventual policy of religious independence over against Jerusalem.

4.2.2 Moreover, the Samaritan traditions which have come down to us tend to blame Ezra and his provisions as the effective cause of the religious separation of the two groups (Widengren*, 511).

4.2.3 Finally, there was a degree of hostility among the dynasty of the Sanballatids, who governed Samaria on behalf of Persia, towards the Judaeans, especially because of the characteristics they had acquired since the reforms of Nehemiah and Ezra, as we saw above (XII.6.2.2), so that any separatist movement could also count on the support of the local public authorities. If we add to all this the evident political skill of the Sanballatids, who succeeded in keeping the governorship of

Samaria in the family for at least six generations (as far as we know; it could have been for many more), we have an almost complete picture of the situation.

4.3 Thus with the reforms of Nehemiah and Ezra, Judaea became an enclosed community of marked orthodoxy. However, paradoxically it was precisely this development which proved capable of keeping intact the fundamental values of Judaism, those basic features which have allowed it to survive over the millennia.

4.3.1 The situation among the Samaritans seems to have been different.

4.3.1.1 First of all, we must clarify a philological point. P.Sacchi*, ch.IV, has connected the name of the Samaritans with the root *šāmar*, 'observe' (a law), hence the ancient pronunciation *šāmerīm*, 'the observant'; the term evidently lent itself to confusion with *šōmᵉrōn*, 'Samaria'.

4.3.1.2 However, the community which was thus born out of a desire for liberty and opennness found itself, equally paradoxically, in a conservative role. Bound up with a traditional religious attitude which seems to have been only superficially affected by Josiah's reform and was therefore 'at an earlier stage of religious development' (Widengren*), it remained open to the pressures and customs of popular piety.

4.3.2 The break did not come about in a spectacular way, nor are we in a position to establish just when it happened. We do not even know of one or more events which may have caused it. Also, as Coggins (1975, 164), followed by Widengren*, points out, relations between the two groups were only broken off at a very much later stage.

4.3.2.1 Certainly the building of a temple on mount Gerizim (present-day *jebel eṭ-ṭūr*, coord.178-175) south of Nablus involved the community in a *de facto* break with Jerusalem, as it was an obvious alternative to the sanctuary of Zion. It seems possible to date this building fairly accurately; since the Persians had always clearly favoured the cult at Jerusalem, it is likely that the Gerizim temple was authorized later, in the Macedonian period.

4.3.2.2 This information gives substance to the largely legendary account in Josephus XI, 321-4 (Noth*, 355, against Bright*, 209), according to which the Samaritans immediately submitted to Alexander the Great (above 1), and were therefore authorized to build their sanctuary, while to begin with Jerusalem had vacillated, invoking its loyalty to the Persians (Josephus, 325f.), and therefore obtained no more than confirmation of its previous status.

4.3.2.3 Be this as it may, the existence of the Samaritan temple on Gerizim is confirmed by II Macc.6.2 for the first half of the second century BC, and the fact that the text names it along with that of Jerusalem shows that by then it already had some tradition behind it.

4.3.2.4 So we shall not be far from the truth if we connect the founding of the Samaritan temple, and therefore the formalization of the schism, with the transition from Persian to Macedonian rule, between the third and last quarters of the fourth century BC.

4.4 Jerusalem always considered the cult and the community of the Samaritans to be illegitimate. According to many scholars, Chronicles, completed towards the end of the fourth century,[2] seems to have the Samaritans in mind in its constant polemic against the north; in the theology of Chronicles the Jerusalem temple stands at the centre of the spiritual history of the people, and the kingdom of Israel, considered to be the predecessor of the sect, is not even once given a favourable mention. However, the latest phase of Deuteronomy, DeutN (II Kings 17.24-41), already presents the population and the religion of the North after the events of 722-20 (above X.4.3) as the product of an ethnic mix, practising a syncretistic cult. There is no proof of this, so the description must be taken to be polemical. In the Fourth Gospel, the response given by Jesus to the Samaritan woman (John 4.22) goes in the same direction, even if immediately afterwards there are clear signs that the antagonism is overcome: 'You worship what you do not know; we worship what we know, for salvation is from the Jews.' This text, too, clearly implies the illegitimacy of the Samaritan cult and doubts about the quality of their faith.

4.5 The Samaritans were a particularly important group over the centuries, a real alternative community to that of Jerusalem, i.e. to Jewish orthodoxy. However, with the Islamic conquest a gradual process of involution, and therefore of decline, seems to have begun. That was also furthered by the character of Samaritan belief, which was at the same time both popular and conservative: its acceptance only of the Pentateuch, the one canonical biblical text at the time of the separation, left the movement outside the prophetic message and that of the other biblical books; the exclusion from the great debates which troubled but also purified Judaism and constantly brought it up to date, fixed Samaritanism in an archaic form of piety. This attitude also emerges from their ancient form of writing, derived from the Phoenician, which is still in existence today, not because it is more practical but simply because it is traditional.

4.6 The Samaritans survive today in the persons of a few hundred individuals around Nablus, overlooked by their sacred mountain Gerizim, in territory administered by the Israeli army after 1967, and at Holon, a south-eastern suburb of Tel-Aviv.

5 The end of the Persian period and the beginning of the Macedonian period saw the progressive exhaustion and extinction of what had been one of the most characteristic and creative movements in ancient Israel: prophecy.[3] In its place, and for some time parallel to it, there appeared

another movement, basically esoteric and speculative in content, i.e apocalyptic.

Select bibliography: D.S.Russell, *The Method and Message of Jewish Apocalyptic*, London and Philadelphia 1964; G.von Rad, *The Message of the Prophets*, ET London and New York 1968; P.D.Hanson, *The Dawn of Apocalyptic*, Philadelphia 1979; J.A.Soggin, 'Profezia ed apocalittica nel Giudaesimo post-esilico', *RiBib* 30, 1982, 161-73 (with bibliography); P.Sacchi, 'Riflessioni sull'essenza dell'Apocalittica: peccato d'origine e libertà dell'uomo', *Hen* 5, 1983, 33-61.

5.1 From the start, those who returned from exile had been helped, comforted and even rebuked, first by the prophets Haggai and Zechariah, then by Trito-Isaiah and finally, shortly before the arrival of Nehemiah and Ezra, by Malachi; Trito-Isaiah and Malachi are, of course anonymous figures. Another two, Joel and the anonymous Deutero-Zechariah (Zech. 9.1-8 perhaps bears witness to the coming of Alexander the Great), preached in a period we cannot date but which was probably at the end of the fourth century BC. We know of no prophecy after them, and the quality of this post-exilic prophecy seems notably inferior to that of its pre-exilic predecessors. That is also because the lack of political independence left little room for a preaching which often had a good deal of political and social content.

5.2 Parallel to the progressive extinction of prophecy, however, there arose a new movement which derived from it, a kind of illegitimate child, apocalyptic. Its texts are to be found for the most part in the pseudepigraphical books (so-called because they are attributed to people from the proto-history and history of Israel who were certainly not their authors); they never came to form part of the Hebrew canon, apart from the book of Daniel and brief sections here and there in the prophets.

5.2.1 Apocalyptic has much in common with the prophets, so it is legitimate to assume an affinity between them. Both share a faith in the God of Israel who is the Lord of history and brings it to its end, its fulfilment, and who elects Israel as his instrument to pursue his own plans in this history. They see election not as a privilege but as a responsibility; and they are certain that the exile in Babylon was the judgment *par excellence* on the sin of the people, quite apart from any judgment to come.

5.2.2 However, there are so many basic differences between prophecy and apocalyptic that the latter is really a bastard child. In apocalyptic the message is secret, entrusted to someone who receives the revelation and publishes it only 'in the last times'. So the apocalyptists are not preachers, whereas the prophets were precisely that; the apocalypses were repositories of revealed truths which were to remain hidden. In apocalyptic, election also appears as a destiny established in time immemorial by an individual gift, which is withheld from many; all apocalyptic discourse, which speaks predominantly of the end of time and the catastrophes which will usher in the kingdom of God, is esoteric discourse, atemporal, and makes use of mythical material. Moreover there is a strong intellectualist approach, a highly speculative way of advancing the arguments, to such a degree that a scholar like von Rad[4] would prefer to derive it from, or at least connect it with, biblical wisdom.

5.3 The catastrophes of the years AD 70 and 135 (below XIV) discredited apocalyptic: instead of bringing the kingdom of God to the community purified by suffering, this period had brought dispersion and disaster. Thus it was easy for rabbinic Judaism to extinguish apocalyptic almost completely, so that it only remained in marginal movements.

6 So Antiochus IV (175-164), brother of the dead Seleucus IV and former hostage at Rome, ascended the throne. He took the title Epiphanes, 'God revealed': we do not know whether he meant it to convey just that, or whether it was just a piece of rhetoric. However, it will have been provocative to orthodox apocalyptic and Judaism. Like his father Antiochus, he seems to have been a brilliant man, endowed with remarkable skills, even if these sometimes seem to have been mitigated by a form of extravagance (he loved pomp and satisfied it by spending a good deal badly); he was also fickle (it is said that he flitted from one philosophical school to another). However, these were certainly not the problems which disturbed his kingdom.

6.1 He was soon in conflict with Egypt which, as from time immemorial, laid claim to Syria and especially to Palestine; these regions had in fact been under Egyptian sovereignty down to the beginning of the second century BC.

6.1.1 The clash degenerated rapidly into open conflict and in 169 Antiochus invaded Egypt, profiting from the neutrality of Rome, which was involved in the war against Perseus of Macedonia. He succeeded in occupying the Nile delta but, aware of the impossibility of keeping the whole vast country under his control, contented himself with backing Ptolemy VI, who was in combat with his brother (later to become Ptolemy VII). In this way he hoped to settle a sovereign favourable to himself on Egypt. However, the plan failed: the two brothers made common cause against the invader.

6.1.2 So a year later, in 168, Antiochus thought that he should invade Egypt again. However, he had not taken account of Rome. Rome, having brought the war against Perseus to a victorious conclusion, instructed Antiochus, through its legate, to withdraw immediately and unconditionally. As well as the damage done by the interrupted campaign, Antiochus thus had the added humiliation of being forced to recognize that to all intents and purposes a Roman legate had greater powers than he did. We might ask whether the attitude of Rome, while it was not very correct on the level of protocol, was not deliberate: Rome clearly wanted to humiliate Antiochus.

6.2 Precluded from expanding southwards or westwards, Antiochus IV turned eastwards, to Armenia and Persia, inhabited by the Parthians; here he died in 164/3, according to I Macc.6.8ff.; II Macc.9.5ff., after a serious illness and no longer completely sane.

7 The policy of Antiochus IV towards his Jewish subjects has become the classical example of religious persecution in antiquity. In Jewish apocalyptic literature he appears as the personification of the attack of the forces of evil against the 'righteous' (cf. Dan.7.25); in primitive Christian apocalyptic he appears as the type of the anti-Christ.

Select bibliography: E.Schürer, *Geschichte des jüdischen Volkes in Zeitalter Jesu Christi*, Leipzig ⁵1920, brought up to date and revised as *The History of the Jewish People in the Age of Jesus Christ (175 BC – AD 135)*, ed. G.Vermes and F.Millar, Edinburgh I, 1973; II, 1979; III in preparation; J.Bonsirven, *Le judaïsme paléstinien au temps de Jésus Christ*, Paris 1935; E.Bickermann, *Der Gott der Makkabäer – Untersuchungen über Sinn und Ursprung der makkabäischen Erhebung*, Berlin 1937; id., *From Ezra to the Last of the Maccabees*, New York 1949; H.H.Rowley, 'Menelaus and the Abomination of Desolation', in *Studia Orientalia Joanni Pedersen...dicata*, Copenhagen 1953, 303-15; A.Giovannini and H.Müller, 'Die Beziehungen zwischen Rom und den Juden im 2.Jhdt. v.Chr.', *Museum Helveticum* 28, 1971, 156-71; R.Hanhart, 'Zum Wesen der makedonisch-hellenistichen Zeit', in *Festschrift J.Ziegler*, Würzburg 1972, I, 49-58; M.Hengel, *Judaism and Hellenism*, ET London and Philadelphia 1974; id., *Jews, Greeks and Barbarians*, ET London and Philadelphia 1980; Y.Tsafrir, 'The Location of the Seleucid Akra in Jerusalem', in Y.Yadin (ed.), *Jerusalem Revealed*, Jerusalem 1975, 85-9 (with a discussion of the locality); O. Mørkholm, *Antiochus IV of Syria*, Copenhagen 1976; J.A.Soggin, *I manoscritti del Mar Morto*, Rome 1978; cf. also the commentaries on I Maccabees. For relations between the Maccabees and Rome cf. W.Wirgin, 'Judah Maccabee's Embassy to Rome and the Jewish-Roman Treaty', *PEQ* 101, 1969, 15-20; T.Fischer, 'Zu den Beziehungen zwischen Rom und den Juden im 2.Jh.v.Chr.', *ZAW* 86, 1974, 90-3; and recently D.Flusser, 'The Kingdom of Rome in the Eyes of the Hasmonaeans and as Seen by the Essenes', *Zion* 48, 1983, 149-76 (Hebrew; summary in English).

7.1 Now while I would not want to deny the importance of the religious factor in the persecution of the people of Judah by Antiochus

IV, it is important that we should rid ourselves of the presupposition that this factor was the only or even the predominant one. As far as we can see, political and especially economic factors are far more important than a first glance at the sources might suggest.

7.1.1 I have already drawn attention to a first, eminently political factor; with the Seleucid conquest of Judaea, the Jerusalem community found itself cut off from the diaspora in Alexandria (above 3), whose relations with the Ptolemies had always been cordial. Once the break between the Seleucids and the Ptolemies had been formalized, with the wars that followed, relations between the religious authorities of Jerusalem and the community in Alexandria automatically became suspect.

7.1.2 Many economic factors came into play; for example, the attempts by the Seleucids to appropriate sums belonging to the temple treasure in Jerusalem. These were not just attempts at theft, as one might suppose, the more serious because they were also sacrilege; we have already seen a first instance in the reign of Seleucus IV (above 3.2), a ruler whom the sources present as having been in other respects well-disposed towards the Judaean community. The Seleucids were also spurred on by the heavy war debts which Antiochus III had contracted with Rome and which they needed to pay.

7.1.3 The economic situation of Antiochus IV was no better; if anything, it was worse, aggravated as it was by the expenses of his interrupted campaign in Egypt. His attempts to get sums of treasure from the temple are therefore not so much sacrilege as economic and political moves, prompted neither by contempt or hate for the Jewish faith and worship nor by religious intolerance generally, so as to be an expression of religious persecution: Antiochus had no greater respect for the sanctuaries of other deities (cf. Polybius XXX, 26ff., in Noth*, 364), which were all the repositories of substantial riches.

7.2 The temple of Jerusalem was also an important centre of economic power in the country, if not the only one; among other things it performed the functions which banks, savings banks and pawnbrokers do today. So what the faithful might regard as sacrilege might appear to others to be no more than a compulsory loan, an expedient like so many others to replenish the depleted state coffers!

7.3 The first attempt, mentioned above (3.2), to which we shall return in detail in due course (7.6), came up against the resistance of the high priest, Onias III, and the mass of the people. They feared not only the consequences of the sacrilege, but also the possible loss of the sums they had deposited there (cf. II Macc.3, which reports a compelling miracle). However, what we find here is the licence, the excess of power, of an official rather than the consequences of a policy of persecution.

7.4 Still, if we accept the theory put forward by the sources, with the accession of Antiochus IV to the throne, feelings at court towards Judaea seem to have changed for the worse.

7.4.1 Under Antiochus, the Hellenization of the country will have been accelerated in a coherent and systematic way, without resorting to violence where persuasion proved insufficient and the inducements did not achieve their aim.

7.4.2 However, this policy did not grow up out of a void; its vehicle was a pro-Hellenistic party of which Jason (probably a Hellenized form of Joshua) was a member; he was a brother of the high priest Onias III, and was for a long time at odds with him. Jason, assured of the backing of the court in his own candidature for the high priesthood, did not hesitate to promise Antiochus substantial sums for state funds, to be paid from the temple treasure (II Macc.4.8); he also guaranteed his collaboration in the work of Hellenization.

7.4.3 At this point, an examination of the sources reveals a disconcerting fact: the pressure of this political group was a basic element in the political approach adopted by Antiochus over Hellenization. In other words, as we shall see, it is reasonable to suppose that without the offer of money from the pro-Hellenists of Jerusalem, Antiochus would probably have behaved in a more discreet, more moderate, more cautious way (Bickermann 1937, Hengel 1974 and Bright*, 419). As we shall see, it was the certainty of having some of the Jews on his side that prompted Antiochus to his excesses. This is confirmed by Sacchi*, 96ff.: 'It is difficult to believe that Antiochus intended a religious persecution'; he simply wanted to ensure the military security of Jerusalem, a city which was near the border of the kingdom with Egypt. And Menelaus and the Hellenists hoped that this would be a way of eliminating, not so much Judaism generally as the Judaism of Nehemiah and Ezra. So Tcherikover's theory (1959, 191,196) that the revolt will have begun even before the persecution proper would seem to be quite plausible; it was originally aimed more at the Hellenists than at the Seleucid state which supported them (cf. Schäfer, 562ff.). In other words, here we would have what was originally a struggle between the Hellenist faction and the traditionalist group within Judaism which later, as a result of the active support given by the Syrian army to the Hellenists, turned into a struggle for national independence (Sacchi*, 106).

7.5 A project like that of Hellenization, enforced upon a country, might seem paradoxical to the modern reader; it could appear absurd, if not a downright contradiction, that a movement which was intrinsically open and tolerant in religious matters should also try to impose its own philosophical ideas and religious faith on others.

7.5.1 Again, the reality seems to be more complex than the theories that we might produce about it. In the East, as in the confrontations with Rome, Hellenism presented itself as the culture *par excellence*, and therefore as an alternative to traditional culture. This was the problem faced by all the people of the region, and not only by the Jews. However, Judaism, with its monotheistic belief, was the one religion which did not fit in well with the polytheistic schemes which could have worked in other circumstances.

The generic term used by the Greeks to describe those peoples who differed from themselves was 'barbarians'. In origin this was not necessarily an offensive term; rather, it was an ironic and onomatopaeic designation, referring as it did to a language that they thought to be incomprehensible. Little by little, however, the word became increasingly charged with connotations more like those which we attach to it today; in this way it was a derogatory epithet: the barbarian is someone who speaks an incomprehensible language, has different and disconcerting customs, and eats strange or even repugnant food. He does not rule by just laws, and is ignorant of art and the various forms of culture.

7.5.2 Moreover, little was known of the East in Greece and ideas about it were often quite fantastic. Virtually nothing was known of the Jews.[5] It is difficult to respect those whom you do not know or whom you do not know properly, when for a variety of reasons you also feel them to be culturally inferior.

7.5.3 In other words, in the past the Hebrews had experienced violent experiences like deportations and wholesale oppressions; however, these events were felt to be a punishment and a heaven-sent trial rather than anything else; they had not damaged Israelite faith, but rather strengthened it. The religion of those who had persecuted Israel had not had any attraction for a member of the people of God. However, in the confrontations with Hellenism, which presented itself as an alternative world-view, people had to make a choice: either to remain a Jew or to embrace the new doctrine. The Hellenists among the Jews thought that they could do both, while remaining within the bounds of good faith; according to the orthodox, they had in fact chosen Hellenism.

7.5.4 Now compared with that of the 'barbarians', the Greek language presented itself as the universal language *par excellence*; moreover, Greek philosophy and religion also seemed to be universal, apart from some local variants; Greek literature and science, jurisprudence, decorative arts and music were also universal. And all found expression in new centres: in the new, monumental cities, the philosophical schools, the baths and the circuses.

7.5.5 Over against this stood the austere Jewish faith, aniconic and therefore with little interest in the decorative arts. From Deutero-Isaiah onwards it, too, was universalist (above XII.1.4.3), though through the mediation of the concept of the people of God. It was endowed with social institutions which were unique in antiquity, like the sabbath rest and the emancipation of those who had been enslaved for debt after six years of service. And it had a code of ethics which could not fail to appear remarkable even to the most acute modern reader, along with an unsophisticated but efficient legal system which lacked cruel punishments and did not offend human dignity. Moreover, all this was clearly directed against a society which behind its impeccable facade had marked elements of corruption and cruelty: an urban wilderness, prostitution, cruel spectacles, sadistic punishments, parasitism, riches based on the exploitation of paid workers, and endemic slavery.

7.5.6 Not only did Judaism go over, as it were, to the counter-attack; among those groups from which the Pharisees would originate later it adopted a markedly missionary and proselytic attitude. A saying of Jesus brings out the zeal of the Pharisees: '...you traverse sea and land to make a single proselyte' (Matt.23.15), a text which shows that at the beginning of the first century AD their practice was common knowledge, so the same could be true of a much earlier period.

7.6 Now while it is easy to criticize the corruption of the Hellenistic world behind its fine facade, the atmosphere around the Jerusalem temple and the Zadokite priesthood also left a good deal to be desired, even if all the indications are that this corruption was limited to small sectors of the ruling classes, those which were the most enthusiastic supporters of Hellenism. Already under Seleucus IV the situation had reached the point that Sacchi*, 93f., could speak of symptoms of decay.

7.6.1 II Maccabees 3.4 reports that '...a man named Simon, of the tribe (= priestly class) of Bilga (corrected with V Lat and Arm., cf. F.M.Abel, *BJ*; LXX has 'Benjamin', a wrong reading, because a layman would then have been appointed to a senior post in the temple – for the class of Bilga cf. I Chron.24.14), in being made captain (προστατής) of the temple', clashed with Onias III over a question connected with the city market.

7.6.1.1 In reality, the apparently trivial motive cloaks a struggle for power: Simon was connected with the Tobiads, the family which for generations had held the post of civil governor of the region, first under the Ptolemies (with whom they continued to have very close connections) and then under the Seleucids. Having failed to get anywhere with Onias, Simon went to Tarsus, to the governor-general. He told him that there were enormous riches in the temple, far too much for the needs of the cult and therefore probably the fruit of corrupt dealings. He suggested that he might offer adequate compensation, were he to be nominated high priest in place of Onias. However, an inspectorate sent to Jerusalem to check on the accuracy of the denunciation and if possible to remove some of the treasure, was confronted by Onias with arguments which were hard to refute: the temple held deposits belonging to widows and orphans, and also funds deposited by Hyrcanus the Tobiad, which therefore in all probability belonged to the public administration. So these sums could not be touched (above 7.1.2). The attempt to make an inventory with a view to possible future proceedings also came up against such resistance from the priests and the population that the inspector called a halt, while a miracle set a seal on things.

7.6.1.2 We have seen that talk of a religious persecution is out of place: there had been a straightforward denunciation on the part of a senior official, and the governor responsible had gone ahead with a check to see whether or not there were irregularities in administration. Having established the manifest inaccuracy of the accusation, the official in charge had in all good faith tried to make an inventory of the goods in question; only in this last respect does he seem to have acted in an arbitrary way. Be this as it may, this project, too, was immediately abandoned, after encountering some resistance. On the other hand, as Sacchi* and others have rightly seen, Simon's action in offering a payment in order to obtain the high priesthood began a practice which for a while was to become commonplace. There were constant attempts to obtain the office by intervening in the organs of state, profiting from the financial difficulties of the crown and promising payments from the temple treasure.

7.6.1.3 This is probably the time in which we are to put the expulsion of the Tobiads from Jerusalem; as we have seen, they were probably the civil governors of Judaea as well as Ammon. They had already been given this office under the Ptolemies of Egypt (above 2.3), and then under the Seleucids.

7.6.1.4 Their expulsion left the high priest absolute master of Jerusalem (*BJ* I, 31), so that it is only from this time onwards that we can speak of a 'hierocracy' proper.

7.6.2 On the promise of a much more substantial offering than that made by Simon, Jason secured the high priesthood and the deposition of Onias III. We should probably see the intrigues of the exiled Tobiads behind this move (II Macc.4.7ff.). Among the various promises made was one that a gymnasium and an ephebate would be established in Jerusalem. In 175/4, then, Onias III was deposed, an unprecedented intervention in an internal question relating to worship within the Jewish community. He was exiled to Antioch, and Jason took over his post. It was easy for him to introduce the two institutions mentioned above, all the more so since many of the priests were interested in them. They neglected their duties simply so that thy could take part in the games (4.11ff.). Some participants in the games are said to have gone so far as to have undergone plastic surgery in order to hide their circumcision (I Macc.1.15; *Antt*.XII, 241, cf.II Macc.4.16, which speaks quite generally of 'awkward situations').

7.6.3 II Maccabees 4.18ff. reports that on another occasion Jason sent through intermediaries a contribution from temple funds to the sacrifice offered to pagan deities in connection with the games at Tyre.

7.6.4 Antiochus, who passed through Jerusalem for the first time during a journey in the region (perhaps on his return from Egypt in 169, though the chronology of these events is confused, cf. below, 8) was received in triumph (II Macc.4.21f.). Might he have realized, then, that Hellenization affected only a minuscule, albeit powerful, sector of the population? That is quite possible, just as it seems likely that Antiochus looked for a pretext to intervene directly and turn matters to his advantage.

7.6.5 Three years after his nomination as high priest, Jason sent a certain Menelaus to the king with a gift of money and to complete various transactions. (According to Josephus, Menelaus is a Hellenization of Onias, or perhaps of Menahem.) Menelaus was a brother of the Simon who has already been mentioned (above, 7.6.1); he had set in motion the mechanism through which the office of high priest will have been bestowed on the candidate on payment of a sum of money.

7.6.5.1 If the reading which I have suggested for II Macc.3.4 is correct, Simeon and Menelaus were of a priestly family, contrary to what is often affirmed (Widengren*, 582; Soggin, 1978, 71), though it will not have been Zadokite. But instead of carrying out his mission, Menelaus offered the king a large sum to be proclaimed high priest instead of Jason (II Macc.9.23ff.). This time the involvement of the Tobiads in the project seems clear, anxious as they were to eliminate the last representative of the dynasty of Onias. Jason had to flee and hide (II Macc.4.23ff.).

7.6.5.2 However, it was not easy for Menelaus to keep the promises he had made to the king (II Macc.4.27b merely states the fact without giving explanations). There could have been a variety of reasons: for example that he had promised more than he could reasonably fulfil, since it was not possible to make unlimited payments from the treasury. And there is another reason, which appears in the following verses: in 4.28ff., it is said that a royal official had been installed on the 'acropolis' (certainly the temple complex), who received the taxes directly without their passing through the temple treasury; and this official seems to have caused a number of difficulties for Menelaus.

7.6.6 At the same time Onias, from exile, did not cease to intrigue against Menelaus: he censured his malpractices and abuses. Menelaus took advantage of the absence of the king on campaigns to persuade the viceroy of the kingdom to have Onias killed (II Macc.4.30ff.). His murder, which took place in 171/70, was also unprecedented, and it is probable that there are references to the event in Dan.9.26: 'After the sixty-two weeks an "anointed"one shall be cut off, without there being any fault in him' (emended text) and 11.22: 'Finally, the prince of the covenant shall be killed' (obscure text). Antiochus also seems to have been taken by surprise and even angered by the act: II Maccabees indicates that he punished the regent of the kingdom by executing him, after stripping him of office. Perhaps Antiochus was really horrified by the crime, which went far beyond what he was prepared to countenance – or was it just that he was holding Onias in reserve to blackmail Menelaus, a plan which Onias' assassination ruined? We shall never know.

8 So the situation continued to get worse until it reached the point when Antiochus had the pretext for intervention for which he had been waiting. However, from Antiochus' (first?) visit to Jerusalem (above 7.6.4) onwards the chronology is in disorder and the dates are controversial; so it seems impossible to provide a clear diachronic account of what happened. What I shall say, therefore, is conjectural in this respect. We know about most of the events in some detail, since they are reported in I Macc.1.20-23; II Macc.5.1-26; Dan.11.28-31; Josephus, *BJ* I, 31ff., and *Antt.* XII, 239-50; on the other hand, we do not know their precise sequence and therefore how they are connected (there is an important discussion of the problems in Schäfer*, 564-8).

8.1 A first event, the forerunner of later conflicts, was the discovery that there had been some sacrilegious thefts in the temple in 169, during the first expedition of Antiochus to Egypt (above 6.1.1). Lysimachus, brother of Menelaus, was thought by popular opinion to be the thief and the people seized him and killed him (II Macc.4.39ff.). Thus far things could have gone smoothly, since death was the penalty provided for in cases of sacrilege. However, the elders of Jerusalem sent an account of events to Antiochus, who was at Tyre, and also accused Menelaus of complicity. However, Menelaus sent a large sum of money to the king, who absolved the high priest of blame and sentenced the members of the delegation to death (II Macc.4.43ff.).

8.2 During the second campaign in Egypt in 168 (above 6.1.2), ruined because of the intervention of Rome, there was an sudden rumour that the king was dead (5.1ff.), accompanied by apocalyptic signs and various miracles. Jason immediately came out of hiding and attacked Menelaus and his supporters with about a thousand men. This undertaking was at first crowned with success and was followed by the killing of many collaborationists, but then it failed and Jason had to flee again; the texts, which do not show much sympathy for him, make him wander from city to city as far as Arabia, where he was assassinated.

8.2.1 The rebellion gave Antiochus the pretext that he sought for direct intervention. The king did not consider this in the slightest as an internal matter within Judaism but as an act of high treason in time of war. So with the troops returning from Egypt he besieged and conquered Jerusalem, venting on its inhabitants the anger and sense of frustration which had accumulated in Egypt. He killed those he believed to be hostile and, guided by Menelaus, occupied and sacked the temple thoroughly (I Macc.1.21ff.; II Macc.5.15ff.). He then returned to Antioch, leaving behind a garrison with orders to finish the matter off.

8.2.2 In the next year, 167, he issued a series of decrees aimed at the compulsory Hellenization of Judaea, and sent an army under the command of a certain Apollonius to implement his orders (I Macc.1.29; II Macc.5.24). They succeeded in reconquering the city, this time by a stratagem: first they came in friendship and then entered the defenceless city on the sabbath, sacked it, and killed or sold into slavery a large number of citizens. They partly dismantled the walls and with the materials thus obtained built a fortress (the Acra) the location of which is still uncertain; according to the first suggestions made by modern scholars it was perhaps to the north of the temple, on the site later occupied by the Antonia (below XIV.2.5), but more recent conjectures put it to the east (though in that case, where? In the Kidron valley? There is a discussion in Schäfer*, 554ff.). However, it seems logical that it will have been near the temple, a complex which it was aimed at controlling. A garrison was posted in the fortress made up of pagan soldiers (I Macc.1.33a says: 'sinners, outlaws'); the city was now under military occupation.

8.2.3 Soon afterwards, once the military problems had been resolved, officials arrived, charged with supervising the implementation of Hellenization and ensuring that everyone made the compulsory sacrifice to the new deities. They worked in commissions, and controlled the whole country.

8.2.3.1 The temple was desecrated and transformed into a sanctuary dedicated to Zeus Olympius, whose image was called 'the abomination of desolation' (Hebrew *šiqqūṣ mᵉšōmēm*) by the Jews; this is a word-play on *ba'al šāmēm*, the Canaanite deity identified with Zeus Olympius (cf. I Macc.1.54; Dan.9.27; 11.31; 12.11; and, in the New Testament, Mark and parallels). The dedication took place on 15 December 167, and on 25 December sacrifices were offered to the Sol Invictus, whose resurrection was celebrated on that day – the deity perhaps being identified with Antiochus IV himself. Of course all forms of Jewish worship were done away with (in any case they could not have taken place in contaminated places); not only was public worship abolished but the domestic observance of the sabbath was also forbidden, along with that of the Jewish festivals and the practice of circumcision: those who violated the new laws were threatened with death, and many scrolls of sacred books were destroyed.

8.2.3.2 The Samaritan temple on Gerizim was also desecrated and dedicated to Zeus Xenius. So it seems probable that as a religious community the Samaritans were treated like the Judaeans, and that the same laws also applied to them.

8.3 Many Jews gave in to the enticements, pressure and threats. Others, however, resisted, and some, when up against it, chose martyrdom rather than 'lead an infamous existence' (II Macc.6.19).

8.3.1 II Maccabees 6.18ff.; 7.1ff. tell two stories of people who preferred to die confessing their faith rather than be apostates: Eleazar, the 'doctor of the law', and the anonymous mother who was tortured to death after her seven sons had suffered the same fate: all, the sources tell us, in the presence of Antiochus himself. Hebrews 11.35ff. in the New Testament probably alludes to the two episodes.

8.3.2 Yet others chose to take to the hills, in the uninhabited parts of the country (I Macc. 2.29ff.), and here and there acts of open resistance to the king's regulations began. Early on, the resistance had to decide whether or not to observe the sabbath rigidly (I Macc.2.39-41), since the Syrians took advantage of this practice to attack and kill them; it was decided that armed defence in cases of this kind was a necessity and that in such instances practising Jews were exempt from the laws which governed the sabbath (below 11.5.3). Organized resistance was soon to grow out of these barely coordinated groups.

8.3.3 According to I Macc. 2.29, quoted above, those who took to the hills included 'many who... went down to the wilderness to dwell there, they, their sons, their wives, and their cattle'. As far as we know, this note refers to two categories of people, those who were content to escape the persecution, trying only to live a life in accordance with their faith, e.g. those who were to become the Qumran sect,[6] and those who hastened to take arms against the oppressor whenever there was a favourable opportunity.

8.4 'Triumphant Hellenism made the mistake, not uncommon to victors, of underestimating its foe. Victorious in its chief objectives, the cities, Hellenism failed to pay sufficient attention to the desert, partly because of the greater difficulty which this would involve, and partly because its importance was not properly understood' (Ricciotti*, II, 236).

8.4.1 This is a mistake often made by all occupying forces: to believe that the control of some key localities is enough to have the whole country in hand. Then the resistance comes out of the scrub, soon involving the cities and ultimately occupying them. And in this case there were abundant regions suitable for partisan war: the territories on the eastern side of the hill country dropping down towards the

Jordan valley and the Dead Sea, and the valley of the Jordan itself and the Dead Sea. The areas on the borders between the hill-country and the Shephelah (above I.3.5.1) offered good occasions for those who wanted to undertake guerrilla activities.

8.4.2 The resistance, whether active or passive, was given a significant name, the 'faithful', the 'pious', Hebrew *ḥassīdīm*, transcribed into Greek as Ἀσιδαῖοι; the accent was on faithfulness to the covenant and the norms which regulated it. Now a trifling incident was enough to unite the various groups which had formed and for a large part of the active population to be involved in organized resistance.

8.5. An occasion arose very soon. The priestly family of the Hasmonaeans, the descendants of a certain Jehoiarib, mentioned in I Chron. 24.7, had established themselves at Modein (coord.148-148), a place on the edge of the Shephelah, at the latitude of present-day Ramla. Their leader was an old man, Mattathiah, who had left Jerusalem and the temple in which he could no longer exercise his ministry. He was accompanied by his five sons: Jonathan, Simon, Judas (surnamed Maccabaeus, probably hammer or hammerer, *Antt.* XII, 365ff.), Eleazar and John.

8.5.1 We are told by I Macc.2.15 that one day in 167/6, probably during the dry season, since the events take place in the open, 'the king's officers who were enforcing the apostasy came to the city of Modein to make them offer sacrifice'. According to the text, a number of people submitted, while others, gathered around Mattathiah, kept apart.

8.5.2 They repeatedly refused the demands of the royal officials, and when he saw a Jew on the point of offering sacrifice, Mattathiah killed him; then he also killed the royal official and destroyed the altar. Thereupon 'he and his sons fled to the hills and left all that they had in the city' (I Macc.2.28).

8.5.3 The priest and his sons (who continued his work after his death) immediately became a focal point for those who hitherto had chosen only forms of passive resistance as well as for those who were already activists. Mattathiah died the next year, and Judas was appointed in his place (I Macc.3.1).

9 This is not the place to follow in detail the campaigns of the Hasmonaeans, their victories and their defeats, to the point at which they achieved final victory after about thirty years of fighting. For these details see the careful analyses by Ricciotti*, II, 245ff.; Noth*, 359ff.; Schäfer*, 585-96, who also deals with the problem of sources. Here I shall give only the broad outlines of events, emphasizing some important points.

9.1 After a series of victories at a local level which, while not being decisive, were enough to show the Jews that it was possible to resist the enemy and conquer him (and which provided the resistance with the arms that they needed – they took them from the enemy), Judas succeeded in gaining possession of a large part of Judaea. One reason for his success was that Antiochus IV, engaged in the war in the East, could not throw all his forces into the fight against the rebels. Despite that, his troops remained superior to the rebels in quality, quantity and equipment; however, the rebels were more mobile, knew the ground perfectly, and had the advantage of being on the attack. Moreover, they had a far superior motivation, and all their victories were interpreted as an obvious sign of divine favour.

9.2 Judas' campaigns ended in the capture of all of Jerusalem but the Acra, though they succeeded in besieging the surviving troops of Antiochus and the collaborationists there. He then devoted himself utterly to the purification and restoration of the temple, installing Zadokite priests who had not been compromised by the régime. He removed from it anything that had come in contact with the pagan cult, including the altar of sacrifice, which was totally rebuilt. On 25 Chislev (November/December) 164, about three years after its desecration, the temple was solemnly rededicated (the feast of Hanukkah, 'dedication', still celebrated today) and protected by the installation of a small garrison.

9.3 The death of Antiochus IV in the East, in the spring of 164/63, liberated Israel from its declared enemy, but not from the laws which he had promulgated nor from the garrison which remained in the Acra. Moreover, the Seleucid sovereignty outside Judaea remained unchanged.

9.3.1 To remove these hindrances, Judas launched a series of campaigns, above all in those areas which were inhabited by Jews faithful to Jerusalem, i.e. in Galilee and Transjordan. Unable to hold on to these regions because of his inadequate resources, he evacuated the Jewish population to Judaea. Then he turned southwards, occupying Idumaea, which had been settled by the Edomites from 587/86 onwards (above XI.6.5.1), and moved towards Philistine territory. His aim was not to occupy this territory, but to discourage any attempt at aggression on the part of these traditional enemies of Judah.

9.3.2 Having defeated his Seleucid enemy in battle and purified the temple, Judas Maccabaeus laid siege to the Acra. The garrison called for aid from the successor to Antiochus IV, Antiochus V Eupator (164-161), but he was still in the tutelage of his guardian, the general Lysias, who had nominated himself regent of the kingdom, ignoring the wishes of Antiochus IV, who had nominated a certain Philip.

9.3.3 With the troops in the East which in the meantime had been freed for action, and which gave the Syrians overwhelming superiority,

Lysias and Antiochus V launched an attack southwards; Judas Macca-baeus was defeated in a series of encounters which forced him to raise the siege of the Acra; and in the battle of bēt zᵉkaryāh (the present-day bēt iskariye or el-'āzar, about six miles south-west of Jerusalem, coord.118-163), the Syrians claimed a crushing victory, thanks also to the use of war-elephants. They laid siege to the capital and encircled it. Provisions soon began to run out.

9.4 However, catastrophe was avoided through an unforeseen event: Philip, the royal tutor and regent of the kingdom, appointed by Antiochus IV and ignored by Lysias and Antiochus V, arrived at Antioch with an army to assume power in the name of his protégé, and Lysias and Antiochus had to hasten to confront him. So they offered honourable and acceptable terms of peace to Judas Maccabaeus. Among other things, he was guaranteed complete freedom of conscience and worship. Judas had no other choice than to accept; the aim of the rebellion seemed to have been achieved. Meanwhile Menelaus had been killed on the orders of Lysias and Antiochus, probably in connec-tion with the negotiations. So the high priesthood remained vacant.

9.5 But a fourth figure appeared in Antioch, having also decided to come into the limelight: this was Demetrius, the other son of Seleucus IV and another possible contender for the throne. He had once been sent as a hostage to Rome and never ransomed (above, 3), but succeeded in escaping. Perhaps this was with the complicity of the Roman authorities, who were still hostile to the Seleucids and wanted to create difficulties for Antiochus V (Gunneweg*, 154). On his arrival home, he succeeded in having both Lysias and Antiochus V killed by the troops, and had himself crowned as Demetrius I Soter (161-150).

9.5.1 Immediately, representatives of the Hellenistic Jewish party came to him to ask for the post of high priest to be given to their candidate. This was a certain Alcimus (perhaps a Hellenization of Eliakim). They managed to convince the new king; the nomination took place, and the new high priest went to Jerusalem accompanied by a Syrian army under the command of a certain Bacchides.

9.5.2 This new situation led to a division among the Hasidaeans.

9.5.2.1 Some, those whom we might call the pacifists, thought that the essential aim of the rebellion, the re-establishment of religious liberty, had been achieved; after all, the country had been under foreign domination for centuries without having being caused any great inconvenience, so this was nothing to get alarmed about. The Hellenists also put forward similar arguments, though for very different reasons.

9.5.2.2 However, the supporters of the Hasmonaeans did not agree: if all was peaceful and their aims had been achieved, why had Alcimus come with an army?

9.5.2.3 As Ricciotti* saw well (II, 244), it was naive to think that orthodox Jews and Hellenists, Hasidaeans and collaborationists, members of the resistance and Seleucid troops could suddenly 'live together in Jerusalem, side by side, without disturbing each other'. That would not have been easy even without the army; its presence clearly destroyed what little trust there still was.

9.5.2.4 Alcimus soon found himself in difficulties, though we do not know what caused them. Resorting to repression, he had several dozen orthodox Jews killed. It is possible that they had accused him of being more an official of the king than a guardian of the temple, but we cannot say anything more precise than that. All we know is that Bacchides gave Alcimus his full support, and that Alcimus continued to intrigue at court against the Hasidaeans and to ask aid from the king.

9.5.3. Demetrius sent an army to help Bacchides, but it was defeated, so that the king felt compelled again to intervene in force. Israel was heavily defeated in the battle of Elasa, a place which has not yet been identified, and Judas himself fell in the battle.

9.5.4 As a result of these events, the Hellenists gained the upper hand, if only for a short time, while the Hasmonaeans again took to the hills, choosing Jonathan as Judas' successor. The fights continued with varying results, though on the whole with Hasmonaean victories; however, they were only local, and there was no chance of final victory: the enemy was too strong for them even to be able to hope for that.

9.5.5 Nor did the negotiations with Rome begun by Judas Maccabaeus shortly before his death bring any relief, even if, as we have seen, Rome probably had a hand in the return of Demetrius to Antioch (above 9.5). Be this as it may, regardless of whether or not it brought any immediate advantage, the rebellion was now a recognized part of the wider international political scene.

9.5.6 The death of Alcimus in 159 robbed Bacchides of a person and institution to protect and aid. The post of high priest remained vacant for seven years.

9.6 As had already happened once in the past (above 9.5), salvation came unexpectedly to Israel from dissensions among the Seleucids.

9.6.1 In 153, war broke out between Demetrius I and Alexander Balas (150-145), a pretender to the Seleucid throne who claimed to be the natural son of Antiochus IV, whom he resembled. He was also the son-in-law of Ptolemy VI Philometor of Egypt, who gave him unconditional support.

9.6.2 Bacchides was immediately summoned home, while Demetrius offered Jonathan peace on reasonable terms. The Syrians withdrew virtually everywhere, leaving only a garrison in the Acra and at Beth-zur. However, Alexander Balas also courted the favours of Jonathan, and gave him the post of high priest, though he was not of Zadokite descent. In the course of the autumn festival of 152 Jonathan was consecrated and took up residence in the temple.

9.6.3 Alexander Balas achieved complete victory over Demetrius and in fact made Jonathan governor. Jonathan thus combined both civil and religious power in his own person, a somewhat unorthodox development, but in practical terms remarkably effective, especially in view of what was to happen.

9.7 The alliance between the two continued for some time. In 147, Demetrius, son of Demetrius I, rebelled and tried to seize the throne, and Jonathan took advantage of this to lay siege to the Acra and occupy a large part of Samaria.

9.7.1 Demetrius proved victorious and was crowned as Demetrius II Nicator (145-38, 129-125); Jonathan could expect the worst but was able to defend his cause with such skill that he obtained from the new king confirmation both of his own personal position and of the ancient privileges granted to Hebrew worship along with the concession of substantial exemptions from taxes for the Jewish community. He was also given three districts of Samaria whose population had remained faithful to Jerusalem and had not gone over to the Samaritans. However, he had to raise the siege of the Acra.

9.7.2 However, Jonathan's political dexterity proved to be his downfall (Noth*, 378); when Demetrius II refused to withdraw his troops from the Acra and Beth-zur, Jonathan allied himself with yet another pretender to the throne, this time Antiochus, son of Alexander Balas, who was supported by the general Diodotos Trypho; in reality, Trypho wanted the kingdom for himself and used the young prince as a cover. The general, a skilful politician, immediately took account of Jonathan's power and therefore thought that he should eliminate him. He succeeded with some skill, having him imprisoned by a stratagem, and then killed in 143. However, before that, Jonathan had already renewed negotiations with Rome, and had begun others with Sparta.

9.8 The Hasmonaeans chose Simon, Jonathan's brother, who renewed contacts with Demetrius II.

9.8.1 Demetrius, who needed help from Judaea to liquidate Trypho as a rival, gave the country *de facto* independence. In the middle of 141, Simon finally succeeded in seizing the Acra. Then he again renewed negotiations with Rome and Sparta and extended the frontiers of Judaea in a series of campaigns.

9.8.2 Simon was also made high priest; his anomalous position was finally regularized in 140, when the line of Onias III (whose son had been declared unworthy to succeed because he had founded a temple in Egypt) was declared defunct. However, despite the fact that it exercised civil power *de facto*, the monarchy was never recognized, since the expectation was of a descendant of the house of David. In that respect, technically speaking, he was a usurper.

9.8.3 Simon also continued contacts with Rome, and in I Macc.12; 14; 15; *Antt.* XIV, 143, we find documentation of these negotations, though it is of doubtful authenticity.

9.8.4 In 139 Demetrius II became the prisoner of Mithridates, king of Pontus, and his brother Antiochus VII Sidetes (138-129) was appointed in his place (I Macc.14-15; *Antt.* XIII, 184ff.).

9.8.5 Simon died in 134, assassinated at Jericho by his son-in-law along with two of his sons. Some scholars suspect that this happened at the instigation of Antiochus, the regent in place of Demetrius, who was a prisoner (I Macc.16.11-24).

10 With John Hyrcanus (134-104, the second name probably derives from the Persian *Vurkān*) a real Hasmonaean dynasty began. As the years went by it proved to be increasingly tyrannical and decadent, progressively moving away from what had been the ideals of its first founders. Again we must make use almost exclusively of material from Josephus and classical authors, as there is no biblical information about the Hasmonaeans and events connected with them.

10.1 John Hyrcanus was the third son of Simon; he escaped the massacre in which his father and brothers died because he had not gone to Jericho with them.

10.1.1 He too resumed contacts with Rome (*Antt.* XIII, 259-66; XIV, 247-55 provides important documentation, though there is a dispute over its dating).

10.1.2 At the beginning of his reign John had to face an invasion from Antiochus VII who, after a number of victories, succeeded in laying siege to Jerusalem. Since the previous year had been a sabbatical year, a year during which no work was done on the land and therefore there was no harvest, the countryside and especially the besieged capital soon found themselves in difficulties over food supplies. John was very soon forced to yield, and while Antiochus offered him quite acceptable terms, the country again came under Seleucid sovereignty.

10.1.3 However, the Seleucids resumed fighting against the Parthians, by whom they were severely defeated. Antiochus VII also died, in 129, and Demetrius II, who had meanwhile been released from prison (above 9.7.1), returned to the throne. He was immediately involved in a series of internal conflicts and was assassinated not long afterwards, in 125.

10.1.4 All this in fact freed John Hyrcanus from the tutelage of Syria, and he dedicated the rest of his life to the aggrandisement of his own country. He conquered Samaria and destroyed the temple on Mount Gerizim (above 4). In 108 he succeeded in conquering the capital, Samaria. He then 'converted' the Idumaeans, compelling them to be circumcised. (They had settled in Judaea from their original homeland in Edom, in Transjordan, from the south, following the events of 587/ 86 BC, above 9.3.1 and XI.6.5.1.)

10.1.5 John had originally been a disciple of the Pharisees (see below 11.3), but later went over to the Sadducees, probably because the former, ethically more rigorous and consistent, criticized the concentration of civil and religious power in the hands of the same person, and also his tyrannical attitude, that of a Hellenistic ruler and not a Jewish priest (*Antt.*XIII, 288ff.). These accusations were not without foundation, when we remember that John planned formally to assume the title of king. Finally some of his administrative arrangements, like the use of pagan mercenaries, seemed incompatible with the Jewish faith.

10.2 Aristobulus I (104-103) succeeded John. He had his mother, who was to have been regent, and his brother Antigonus assassinated. His other brothers, among them Alexander Jannaeus, were imprisoned. He was such a supporter of Hellenism that he changed his original name, Judas, into one which did not even have the same assonance. Josephus (*Antt.* XIII, 318) therefore calls him 'Philhellene'. Again according to Josephus, *BJ* I, 78ff.; *Antt.* XIII, 311 , remorse hastened his end. He, too, converted by force – in this case the inhabitants of Ituraea, a region either in the north of Galilee or in southern Lebanon (XIII, 318).

10.3 Aristobulus was succeeded by his brother Alexander Jannaeus (104-76), who had previously been imprisoned for a period. Alexander resumed the expansionist politics of his father.

Select bibliography: C.Rabin, 'Alexander Jannaeus and the Pharisees', *JJS* 7, 1962, 3-11.

10.3.1 Alexander, too, was hostile to the Pharisees, probably for the same reasons; they even reached the point of calling for Syrian intervention. And the Syrians came, under the command of their king Demetrius III Eucarius (94-88), defeating the troops of Alexander near Shechem.

10.3.2 The Pharisees, however, having seen that Demetrius aimed at re-establishing Seleucid supremacy over Judaea, gave up the alliance and Demetrius returned home. Their actions certainly served the country well, but they themselves were now completely unprotected. They endured severe repression under Alexander Jannaeus (*Antt.* XIII, 377-82): Josephus in fact says that several hundred of them were crucified and their families killed before their eyes. This was the first time that such punishment was meted out by Jews to other Jews and did not fail to cause considerable consternation among the people, a number of whom took to the hills. The event is probably referred to in the Qumran commentary on Nahum 2.12f. (4QpNah = 4Q169, I,1ff.), which says: '[...]*trws*, king of Greece, who sought, on the counsel of those who seek smooth things, to enter Jerusalem [lacuna...]'; it then goes on: '[lacuna...] concerns the furious young lion [lacuna...] on those who seek smooth things and hangs men alive, a thing *never done formerly* in Israel. Because of a man hanged alive on [the] tree, He proclaims' (a reference to Deut 21.22f. follows).

Now the first name, incomplete because of a lacuna, is generally completed as *dmy-trws*, i.e. Demetrius, while 'those who seek smoooth things' are the Pharisees, who were also enemies of the Dead Sea sect; the 'furious young lion' is clearly Alexander, who first 'hung men alive' (Soggin, 1978, 102f.). The whole passage is an eloquent testimony to the immrpression that the episode must have produced.

10.3.3 In reality Alexander was only 'the lowest type of Hellenistic soldier' as Ricciotti, II, 292, rightly points out, going from one war to the next and obtaining results which can only be considered modest compared with the means expended. At all events, he kept the territory he received and in Transjordan succeeded in enlarging it at the expense of the Nabataeans. He died of an illness, probably also contracted becaus of his dissolute life.

10.4 Alexander was succeeded by his widow Alexandra Salome (76-67); before he died, Alexander proposed that he should make peace with the Pharisees (*Antt.* XIII, 403) because they enjoyed so much popular support. This he did, and Josephus, *Antt.* XIII, 187, says that on his death they mourned him as a 'just king'. His conversion is reported in the Talmud, bab.Qidd 23a.

10.5 Alexander Jannaeus left two sons, Hyrcanus II, the older, who was rather lazy, and Aristobulus, skilful and enterprising.

10.5.1 First of all Alexandra gave a free hand to the Pharisees, who had hoped to be able to have their revenge on their erstwhile persecutor, though as Josephus says, they had forgiven him. At all events, Hyrcanus became high priest and Aristobulus commanded the army. On the death of Alexandra, when Hyrcanus came to the throne, Aristobulus had no difficulty in making his inept brother abdicate in his favour after only reigning for three months. He thus became king as Aristobulus II (67-63).

10.5.2 Very soon Aristobulus' reign, which from the outside seemed very solid, was disturbed by a serious conflict: Antipater, the skilful governor of Idumaea, rebelled, aided by the Nabataeans of southern Transjordan (their capital was Petra, still justly famous, coord.210-020). He promised them that the territory taken from them by Alexander Jannaeus would be restored. He tried to enlist Hyrcanus in his cause, inciting him among other things to revoke his abdication. He gained some military successes and laid siege to Jerusalem. However, underlying the conflict there was also the contention between the Pharisees and the Sadducees: the former were supporters of Hyrcanus and the latter of Aristobulus. With military operations at a stalemate, both sides appealed to Rome, which in 64/63 had annexed Syria (in the Qumran texts it appears as *kittīm*), and Rome decided in favour of Aristobulus, ordering the others to withdraw.

10.6 However, Hyrcanus appealed directly to Pompey, who had arrived in Damascus in 63. At the same time, a delegation also arrived from Jerusalem, which asked the Romans to put an end to the rule of the corrupt and incompetent Hasmonaeans. The delegation proposed a 'hierocratic solution': politically the country would be under the sovereignty of Rome, but internally it would be governed by the temple priesthood.

10.7 Pompey was favourably disposed towards Aristobulus, but Aristobulus left him, taking refuge in his own fortress; then he,too, sought peace, He obtained it, but on harsh conditions: he had to hand over his fortresses and the capital to Rome. He refused to hand over the capital and it was besieged; it fell after three months, in 63. The Romans penetrated the temple and Pompey himself entered the Holy of Holies, which only the high priest could enter, and then only once a year: understandably, this caused consternation among the faithful. Pompey found nothing in the Holy of Holies; Tacitus, *Hist.* V,9 (Stern II, no.281) says that Pompey saw *vacuam sedem et inania arcana*; we know that Israel did not worship images and sacred objects.

10.8 Hyrcanus was nominated high priest and 'ethnarch'; the title of king was dropped. Aristobulus had to follow Pompey's triumph to Rome. However, the real victor seems to have been the skilful Antipater, of whose family we shall hear more later. From then on, in fact, the country was under the sovereignty of Rome, though it was often governed by rulers who thought themselves to be more or less independent.

11 At the end of the first millennium BC, Judaism, which had undergone Josiah's reform and then those of Nehemiah and Ezra, refined by the sufferings of the exile, foreign occupation and the struggle with Hellenism, began to show clear signs of some of the characteristics which have distinguished it down the centuries and still do today.

11.1 Not all these characteristics were already clearly present. Judaism as we know it today has clearly been shaped by another tragedy, the destruction of the temple in AD 70 at the climax of the war with Rome, followed by the deportation of the majority of the Jewish population of Palestine. It eliminated one of its basic elements, the central sanctuary, where the worship and piety of Israel was concentrated.[7] In the period in which we are interested here, the centre of Jewish religious and cultural life was the temple: it was towards the temple that the Jew directed his prayers (Dan.6.11; cf. I Kings 8.14,18, a late text); to Jerusalem that he went in pilgrimage (Tob.1.6, cf. also the Gospels). For anyone who lived in the country at that time, the temple was also an important centre for the conduct of political affairs, as we have seen (7.6); moreover, it was also important on an economic level, exercising the functions which are now performed by banks (7.2). However, if we leave aside the presence of the temple, we begin to form an impression in this period of the basic elements of the thought and practice of later Jews. The one great difficulty lies in the unorganized nature of the sources and their sparseness.

11.2 *Select bibliography*: A.C.Sundberg, 'Sadducees', *IDB* IV, 1962, 160-2; K.Schubert, *Die jüdische Religionsparteien im neutestamentlichen Zeitalter*, SBS 1970, 48ff.; J.Le Moyne, *Les Sadducéens*, Paris 1972; E.Bammel, 'Saduzäer und Sadokiten', *ETL* 55, 1979, 105-15.

In the temple, ministry was exercised by priests who claimed descent from Zadok, called in Greek Σαδδουκαῖοι, hence our Sadducees (above XII.5.3.1). They are also well attested, as we know, in the New Testament.

11.2.1 Characteristic of the Sadducees was on the one hand their strongly traditionalist interpretation of the faith, as is common in any conservative religious group. On the other hand, however, they were ready to make considerable concessions at a practical level, with an openness which could arrive at compromises with contemporary authorities and currents, e.g. Hellenism; it certainly went far beyond anything called for to achieve security (above 7.4.2). However, perhaps this presentation, drawn from I and II Maccabees, is too partisan, and we should think rather of a continuation of the line of the opponents of Nehemiah and Ezra (above 2.3, cf. Sacchi*, 96ff.), a line which, moreover, sought agreement rather than confrontation with the local population. At all events, the fact that some of the Sadducees went beyond a general openness, adopting customs, beliefs and practices from the surrounding pagan world, and allowed the nomination to the high priesthood in fact to be delegated to the royal court, which favoured the best offer, should not shut our eyes to the other equally obvious fact, that the phenomena of corruption affected only a few of, and not all, the sectors of the Sadducean priesthood. Some of its members voluntarily exiled themselves from Jerusalem simply to live out their own faith without compromise, though at considerable economic and personal sacrifice, once it had become impossible for them to exercise their ministry in the desecrated temple.

11.2.2 So it is not surprising, at any rate, to find the Sadducees active in dealings with the various occupying powers, first the Seleucids, then the members of the Hasmonaean dynasty, and finally the Romans. One instance of this can be found in one of the few elements in the course of the trial of Jesus that can hardly be contested: there was a close relationship between the Sanhedrin and the Roman procurator Pilate, a relationship which, although being anything but cordial (below XIV.3.4), presupposes a close and regular collaboration over the years, if we are to believe the Gospels.

11.2.3 In the sphere of faith, the traditionalism of the Sadducees made them reject almost all the doctrines which were not attested, or were only scantily attested, in the Hebrew Bible:

11.2.3.1 The resurrection of the dead, which appears for certain only in a few passages which are always late: Isa.26.14; Dan.12.2-4; II Macc.12.44ff., cf. also various passages in the New Testament.

11.2.3.2 Other doctrines like the development of angelology and demonology, characteristic of Judaism between the Testaments and especially of apocalyptic.

11.2.4 With the destruction of the temple in AD 70, the Sadducees lost both their social and their religious functions, along with the economic basis of their existence as a class, so their ministry came to an end. Because the temple was not rebuilt, no priesthood has arisen again in Israel, though the descendants of the priests mark their origins with names like Cohen and Levi and various derivatives, not all evidently Sadducaean. They must observe special laws of ritual purity, but do not exercise any function other than that of blessing the synagogue community on various occasions.

11.3 *Select bibliography*: W.Beilner, 'Der Ursprung des Pharisäer-tums', *BZ* 3, 1959, 235-51; C.Roth, 'The Pharisees in the Jewish Revolution of 66-73', *JSS* 7, 1962, 63-80; L.Finkelstein, *The Pharisees*, Philadelphia ³1962; A.Michel – J.Le Moyne, 'Pharisiens', *SDB* VII, 1966, 1022-1115; K.Schubert, *Die jüdischen Religionsparteien...*, 22-47; J.Neusner, *The Rabbinic Traditions about the Pharisees before 70*, three vols, Leiden 1971; M.Man.(soor), 'Pharisees', *EncJud* XIII, 1971, 363-6; E.Rivkin, 'Pharisees', *IDB-SV*, 1976, 657-63; H.-F.Weiss, 'Pharisäismus und Hellenismus', *OLZ* 74, 1979, 421-33.

The problem of the origin of the Pharisees seems far more complex. At least in part they were heirs of the Hasidaean movement (above 8.4.2). It seems that they had already emerged at the time of Jonathan Maccabaeus (160-143: *Antt.* XIII, 171, above 9.5.4ff.), and in the end made a final break with the Hasidaeans at the time of John Hyrcanus (134-104: *Antt.* XIII, 288, above 10).

11.3.1 The title seems to derive from the Hebrew *perûšîm*, 'separate', i.e. probably from the ignorant and rough masses, the *'am-hā'āreṣ*. This expression, which at the time of the monarchy indicated a traditionalist group favourable to the Davidic dynasty in Judaean society (above IX.3.8.3), now took on what was clearly a negative significance, meaning ignorant, boorish.

11.3.2 The characteristic feature of the Pharisees was their extremely zealous observance of the Torah (below 11.5.4), in which they did not accept compromise of any kind. This was a form of observance which followed directly in the footsteps of Ezra and Nehemiah (Beilner 1959, Sacchi*, 96ff.), rejecting all contact with the pagans other than that aimed at their conversion. The law was observed punctiliously, and St Paul (Phil.3.5f.) still recalls his own Pharisaic origins and the zeal with which he had observed the various rules in the past.

11.3.3 On the level of doctrine, however, the Pharisees were much more positive. At least to begin with, they did not reject dialogue with the apocalyptists (above, 5), though they rejected a good deal of apocalyptic belief; for the Pharisees, eschatology consisted in the observance of the law, because only sin delayed the coming of the kingdom of God (*Mishnah*, Aboth III, 15). Nor did they reject *a priori* all new doctrine. For example, the notion of the resurrection of the dead, followed by universal judgment, and the development of angelology and demonology, features which in part came from apocalyptic, entered and formed part of their belief. And alongside the written Torah, the Pentateuch, there developed a Torah formed by the collecting together of summaries of discussions, interpretations and updatings of the biblical tradition with a view to the new situation in which they were to be applied. These were the elements which, towards the second century AD, came to be codified definitively in the Mishnah, and then, still later, in Talmudic treatises and commentaries. Jesus is probably referring to this position adopted by the Pharisees when he criticizes them because they set the law at nought by means of their tradition (Matt.15.3 par.).

11.3.4 Precisely because of their rigour, but also because of their openness, the Pharisees had a large following among the people; in this way they became the natural spiritual and civil leaders of the people, especially when the catastrophes of AD 66-74 and 132-135 had destroyed the priesthood as a social class and discredited apocalyptic. It was in fact the Pharisees who gave to Judaism at the time of the destruction of the temple both the canon of the Hebrew Bible and that traditional collection of exegetical and ethical norms which updated it for later reading. Only thanks to them, one might say, did Israel succeed in surviving for almost two millennia of diaspora.

11.3.5 The regulations which the Pharisees presented to the people could be summed up in one basic principle: not only the priesthood of the temple but the whole of the people of God must be holy, since according to Ex.19.6, all Israel, and not just a group of the elite, is called 'a kingdom of priests – a holy nation' (Neusner 1971, 671). Or to put it in the words of a Talmudic text: 'While the temple existed it was the altar which atoned for Israel; now the table of any man atones for it', Talmud bab., Ber.55a, an allusion to the importance that the dietary laws were increasingly assuming.

11.3.6 The refusal of the Pharisees to talk with pagans could lead to positions of the utmost intransigence. On the other hand, the Pharisees always rejected any form of zealotism (Roth, 1962), and their attitude was generally pacifist, even if some of them did not hesitate to particpate in war once it had broken out. In the time of the Hasmonaeans, therefore, the Pharisees wanted to end hostilities once religious liberty had been obtained (above 9.5.2.1). That was in no way a sign of weakness, or of a lack of interest in what was going on around them: their courageous and critical attitude towards members of the Hasmonaean dynasty (above 10.3) led them to martyrdom, simply in order to proclaim what they felt to be the norm for the conduct of the people of God.

11.3.7 Moreover, they believed in a kind of free will, which they did not find difficult to reconcile with the sovereignty and the prescience of God. In all probability the origin of the dualistic doctrine of human nature in which a good impulse and an evil impulse are constantly in conflict is to be sought among the Pharisees. In their view, human beings could help the good impulse to fight the evil impulse by means of the study and practice of the Torah.

11.3.8 It therefore seems difficult to accept in a historical context the judgment which the New Testament apparently wants to pass on the Pharisees almost lock, stock and barrel, namely that they were hypocrites in that they feigned a piety which they did not have, simply to maintain their control over people's consciences. But it is interesting to note that the New Testament is not the only document to accuse them in this way. As we saw earlier (above 10.3.2), the Essenes called them 'those who seek falsehood', and elsewhere they appear as 'masters of hypocrisy'. For the Essenes the explanation is easy. The Qumran sect accused them of laxity and saw their hypocrisy as consisting in the fact that while their precepts were strict, they were content with a much less radical observance of them. Thus, for example, in the question of divorce, the Damascus Document of the sect (CD IV, 20ff.) takes the wording of Gen.1.27 literally and affirms the unconditional indissolubility of marriage, and virtually the same position is taken by Jesus (Mark 10.2-9; Matt.19.3-8 – and in his footsteps even today by the Christian churches which reject the remarriage of divorced persons). However, the Pharisees were much more pragmatic; indeed there were at least two schools among them, one more strict and the other less so. The anti-Pharisaic polemic in the New Testament is therefore to be seen, at least in origin, as the result of discussions, debates and probably also polemic between the Pharisees and their opponents, the Sadducees, the Essenes and soon also the embryo Christian church, *but always within Judaism*, of which Jesus and his disciples were still an integral part. Later, the first Christians and, following in their footsteps, the early church, exploited these features not only against the Pharisees but also against the Jews generally, which was completely against their intention.

11.3.9 Finally, akin to, but not immediately identical with, the Pharisees were the so-called scribes and the 'doctors and teachers of the law'.

11.4 Another group, which we have begun to know in detail only since 1947, from the discoveries at the Dead Sea, is that of the Essenes.

11.4.1 Bibliography: G.Vermes, *The Dead Sea Scrolls in English*, Harmondsworth ²1975; id., *The Dead Sea Scrolls*, London 1977; J.A.Soggin, *I manoscritti del Mar Morto*, Rome 1978, and the bibliographies there.

Because of their withdrawal from public life and the virtual monasticism of at least the group which formed their nucleus, we formerly knew only the little that Josephus and later Philo of Alexandria and some classical authors reported about this group, and their accounts are often coloured by basically moralistic and edifying considerations, aimed at making the community exemplary for its virtue.

11.4.2 Some of the Essenes were organized into what we might call a 'monastic' community, living a celibate life in their 'monastery' located near the north-western shore of the Dead Sea, at Qumran (coord.128-194). Others, who did not practise celibacy, continued to live in their ordinary places of residence, though they made frequent pilgrimages to the 'monastery'.

11.4.3 The origin of the sect is to be sought among those Sadducees who chose to join the Hasidaeans because their way of life had been compromised by Hellenism. The date of this is usually thought to be about the middle of the second century BC, i.e. at the time of Alexander Balas (c.150-145) and Jonathan Maccabaeus (160-143). Their Sadducean origin, combined with their rigorism, would explain their opposition to the Pharisees (above 10.3.2; 11.3.6). They, too, seem essentially to have been pacifists, although they developed a marked aggressiveness in their doctrines and the way in which they expressed them (the final apocalyptic struggles between the 'sons of light' and the 'sons of darkness'). For other details cf. Soggin 1978 and Vermes.

11.5 Despite this marked diversity in trends and orientations, there were some constants in the Judaism of this period.

11.5.1 First of all we must rid ourselves of the prejudice that sees

Judaism in this period as being doctrinally fossilized and ethically attached to a cold and legalistic observance of the dead letter, unmindful of the real and more important problems, in short, a Judaism which had fulfilled its own mission and waited only to be replaced by another movement which had incorporated its most valid points. This seems to be the view of Judaism sometimes presented by the primitive church, and it then became the judgment that the Christian tradition handed down on Judaism and its values. Who can forget the mediaeval iconography in which the synagogue is represented as an ugly, blind-folded hag, while the church is depicted as a beautiful woman with her eyes open? To debunk this image we need only remember the readiness with which thousands of Jews took up arms to defend their faith and their practice of worship, or their readiness for martyrdom, from the time of the Maccabees to that of Bar Kochba; and also the fascination which Judaism has always had for many areas of the pagan world, a fascination which has found tangible expression in many conversions to Judaism (above 7.5.6). Paradoxically, the New Testament often seems to be behind this negative image; however, as we have seen (above 11.3.8), most of the time the New Testament is reflecting internal debates and discussions within Judaism; at other times we have texts which represent polemic not so much against Judaism as against the demands made by Jewish Christians, who argued that it was necessary to become a Jew before becoming a member of the Christian church. Moreover, as we have seen, the Judaism of the time had a multitude of facets, varying from extreme rigorism to laxity, from exclusivism towards other peoples to mission and proselytism, from absolute exclusion to openness.

11.5.2 And if for a moment we leave aside the most rigid groups, like the Dead Sea sect, it is clear that practising Judaism did not seem the slightest bit worried over a casuistry of commandments and prohibitions, but rather lived out a life based on the certainty that it was performing the divine will. It was doing everything possible to fulfil its own mission, accepting the gifts of divine grace (of which the Torah was certainly the greatest), and trying to respond to them in the least inadequate way, certain that obedience to the divine will was the best way of creating a more just society, ready to accept even martyrdom when its faith came up against, or in any way conflicted with, the demands of other powers, including those of the public authorities. In other words, Judaism seems to have resolved what St Paul saw as the conflict between 'the law' and 'the gospel' by seeing the Torah as the means by which it was possible to realize the divine will on earth.

11.5.3 After the example I gave above (11.3.8) of marriage and repudiation, I would like to introduce another, that of sabbath observance, which is one of the focal points of discussion in the New Testament.

11.5.3.1 I do not think that there is any need to point out that a law which requires the cessation of labour and therefore of production for a seventh part of the week is a social as well as a religious law: in fact it ensures that everyone, Jew or non-Jew, free or slave, man, woman or animal, has to break off every activity for rather more than twenty-four hours each week. In basically family and patriarchal enterprises, it was evident that those who did not work still had to be kept, even if they did not produce anything on that day. And this characteristic also explains why there were attempts to violate this law, attempts to which indirect witness is already borne by the casuistry of the Decalogue (Ex. 20.8-11//Deut.5.12-15). As we have seen, the Hasidaeans originally found themselves confronted with the problem whether they should violate the sabbath to fight (above 8.3.2), or whether they should allow themselves to be massacred on that day by an enemy which did not have such scruples (I Macc.2.32-38, cf. II Macc. 6.10f.). It is also interesting to note how among the majority of classical authors we find a complete ignorance of the nature of sabbath observance when they should be concerned with it; the sabbath is frequently explained in terms of the laziness of the Jews, while we can find nothing but the most complete lack of interest in its obvious social dimensions (one could hardly expect them to have an interest in Jewish theology).

11.5.3.2 The matter was debated for a long time and often violently, as we might well imagine, until it was settled by a series of rules. We find an echo of these debates in the New Testament, the texts of which are obviously to be read on this basis. *Mishnah* Yoma VIII, 6 says: '...whenever there is doubt whether life is in danger this overrides the sabbath.' And the following section (VIII.7) quotes the example of a building which has collapsed: if there is even the slightest suspicion that someone might be under the debris, it is necessary to go on removing it, even on the sabbath. Similarly, *Tosephta* Shab.V.22 says, 'But if there is any mortal danger, there is nothing which comes before such danger.' Thus it is quite in order to summon the help of a midwife on the sabbath (Shab. VIII,3); to kindle or put out lights for fear of attacks by humans or demons, to help a sick person to rest, but not to economize on oil or wicks (Shab.II, 5). And R. Akiba, tortured by the Romans in AD 132, ruled that it is not lawful to violate the sabbath to do things that could have been done the day before; however, the sabbath has not been violated when there was no such posibility (Shab.XIX.1). Because 'the sabbath has not been given for you, but you have been given for the sabbath' (*Mekilta* ad Ex.31.13; cf. Jesus in Mark 2.27).

11.5.3.3 However, the attitude of the Essenes seems to have been very different because of their rigoristic interpretation of the issue: the Qumran Damascus Document (CD XI, 13-16) prohibits giving help to any animal in travail on the sabbath, or taking it out of a ditch or a well by any means.[8] Where Jesus seems to go beyond his own contemporaries is when he extends the criterion of mortal danger to the healing of a sick person which in fact could have been performed on any other day of the week; this is a criterion which the Jewish tradition never accepted. So it is evident that to speak of legalism in a context like this is inappropriate: the whole question, bound up as it is with production, is much more complex. Paradoxically, if there is to be any talk of legalism it should be in connection with those who did not weary of finding excuses and sophistries aimed at circumventing the one social law which existed in antiquity.

11.5.4 One factor which basically governs the Jewish piety of the time and of successive ages is Holy Scripture. It was already more or less complete in the form and dimensions in which we know it; however, it is certain that the Pentateuch was already in existence, and indeed a large part of the Prophets and the Psalms. The Pentateuch, the Torah *par excellence*, as ever enjoyed the utmost prestige, the utmost canonicity.

11.5.4.1 Torah is too often translated 'law', because from Ezra onwards it had also become the law of the state (above XII.8.3.4). In fact it comes from a root which means 'teach', 'instruct', so it was understood to mean simply 'teaching', 'training' (*par excellence*). Moreover, the term is clearly used with this meaning in the Psalter. In Pss.19.7; 37.31; 119.97 the term is equivalent to what we would now call the 'word of God', i.e Holy Scripture. In Ps.1.1, too, the 'just' (as opposed to the unjust) 'meditates day and night', not on a 'law' but on the divine word. So the term has various meanings: 'word of God', Pentateuch, law of the state, depending on the context and the usage.

11.5.4.2 In this period we begin to have ample evidence of the implementation of the dietary laws; as we saw earlier (11.3.5), this was a decisive feature in the practice of the Pharisees aimed at ensuring a pure table, especially after the fall of the temple. In Dan.1.8ff., Daniel and his friends, deported to the Babylonian court, take great care not to be contaminated by eating the food put before them at the king's table, and prefer vegetarian food and only water to drink. It is clear that the problem is concerned with more than the question of eating pure animals, which are suitable as food, and impure animals, which are always forbidden food. Ritual slaughter was also a factor, and this was obviously not carried out in connection with the food eaten at court. Daniel and his companions also do not seem to have wanted even to drink wine; that is probably a sign that for them this would have had to be, and was not, ritually pure. See also Tobit 1.10-12, where all those who have been deported eat pagan food, while the hero and his family keep to the rules for pure food; in Judith 10.5, however, the bread is pure, and therefore made in accordance with rabbinical rules.

XIV

UNDER THE ROMANS

1 The beginning of Roman domination in the region coincides with the civil war between Pompey and Caesar, an event which involved Palestine only marginally. At all events, it ushered in a rather unstable period. The sources are essentially Josephus, *Antt.*XIV-XX (up to AD 67) and *BJ*, even if in them the author is often dominated by the need to make an apologia for the Jewish cause generally and himself in particular. Be this as it may, scholars are agreed that when Josephus is somewhat inaccurate, it is more through the omission of facts than by deliberate distortion.

Profiting from the disorders, Aristobulus several times tried to regain the throne and once even succeeded in escaping from his Roman imprisonment. Finally peace returned and, with Caesar's victory, Hyrcanus was confirmed high priest and ethnarch, while Antipater was nominated procurator of Judaea.

Select bibliography: A.Momigliano, 'Ricerche sull'organizzazione della Giudea sotto il dominio romano (63 a.C - 70 d.C.)', in *ASNSP*, III, 3, 1934, 183-221, 347-96; S.Perowne, *The Life and Times of Herod the Great*, London 1956-59; J.Jeremias, *Jerusalem in the Time of Jesus*, London and Philadelphia 1967; E.Lohse, 'Die römischen Statthalter in Jerusalem', *ZDPV* 74, 1958, 69-78; M.Hengel, *Die Zeloten*, Leiden 1961; S.Zeitlin, op.cit. (above XIII.1); S.Sandmel, *Herod: Profile of a Tyrant*, Philadelphia 1967; S.G.F.Brandon, *Jesus and the Zealots*, Manchester 1967; E.M.Smallwood, *The Jews under Roman Rule*, Leiden 1976; A.Schalit, *König Herodes. Der Mann und sein Werk*, Berlin 1969; M.Smith, 'Zealots and Sicarii, their Origin and Relation', *HTR* 64, 1971, 1-19; H.Guevara, *La resistencia contra Roma en la época de Jesús*, Meitingen 1981; J.P.Lémonon, *Pilate et le gouvernement de la Judée*, Paris 1981; P.-G.Antonini, *Processo e condanna di Gesù. Indagine storico-esegetica sulla motivazioni della sentenza*, Turin 1982; E.Bammel and C.F.D.Moule (eds.), *Jesus and the Politics of His Day*, Cambridge 1983.

In addition to the traditions reported by Josephus, we have for the Roman period the texts of Tacitus, *Histories* and *Annals*, now reproduced in Stern* II, nos. 273-94. There is some extremely important material, of relevance to the whole of this period, in *Jewish and Christian Self-Definition*, ed. E.P.Sanders with A.I.Baumgarten and Alan Mendelson, London and Philadelphia 1981; cf. also E.Schürer, *The History of the Jewish People in the Age of Jesus Christ* II, revised and edited by Geza Vermes, Fergus Millar and Matthew Black, Edinburgh 1979.

1.1 Antipater, who, as we have seen, had been the real victor in the contest between Hyrcanus and Aristobulus, first involved his own sons in government, putting them in positions of power. Phasael, the older, became commander of the military region of Jerusalem, and restored its fortifications, while Herod, the younger, was given the command of the northern military region, despite his youth. Both were to distinguish themselves because they were brilliant, dynamic and endowed with great skills, especially Herod, who succeeded in freeing Galilee from the bands of robbers which had formed there during the disorders. Despite this, they were not popular with the people, first of all because they were of foreign origin (the Idumaeans of southern Judaea had been forcibly converted and circumcised by John Hyrcanus, above XIII.10.1.4) and also because they were wilful and violent. Be this as it may, this was how Herod entered politics and for the first time took up an important position.

1.2 On the death of Caesar in 44 BC and the outbreak of the second civil war, Antipater, at first a supporter of Caesar, unexpectedly found himself under Cassius, who ruled Syria. He immediately went over to his side. However, he was killed in 43 BC and Herod, after avenging the death of his father, succeeded him to the throne although he was the younger son. He managed to strike a skilful balance between Cassius and Antony, from the latter of whom he obtained for himself and his brother the ethnarchy of Judaea; therefore only the high priesthood remained to Hyrcanus.

2. During the invasion by the Parthians in 40 BC, Antigonus, son of Aristobulus, was able to recover his father's throne for a short time; he succeeded in keeping it even when the Romans regained the country in 39 BC. However, Herod, who had taken refuge in Rome and had been given the title of king by Antony and Octavian, returned under the protection of the two triumviri and, with the aid of Roman troops, had no difficulty in regaining his own territory, including Jerusalem, which fell after a short siege. Antigonus, who fled to Antioch, was killed by Herod in 37. In the same year Herod married Mariamne, granddaughter of Aristobulus II and Hyrcanus II and sister of Anti-

gonus, and therefore the last heir to the Hasmonean throne. Thus Herod also acquired a certain dynastic legitimacy.

2.1 Herod, whose ability had been proved on the death of Caesar, confirmed his dexterity by manoeuvring skilfully between Antony and Octavian. In relations with Rome his criterion was never to allow himself to be directly involved in the struggles for power, but always to appear beside the victor at the right moment, and therefore never with the loser. In 32, however, when the conflict between Antony and Octavian broke out again, he took sides with the former, but did not play an active part in the war. Then, after the battle of Actium in 31, he managed to go over to the other side, submitting in person to Octavian when he was in Rhodes, in 30 BC. However, before that he had gone so far as to have Hyrcanus killed and Mariamne and her mother imprisoned, ordering that both should be killed if he did not return from his mission. His self-defence before Octavian was conducted with discretion and skill: he openly confessed that he had taken Antony's side, and succeeded in convincing Octavian not only to confirm him in his office but even to give him other territory: among this was Samaria and Peraea, the regions to the east of the Sea of Galilee.

2.2 In 29 he had his mother-in-law and his wife Mariamne killed, and later, in 12/11 BC, two of his sons by her, Alexander and Aristobulus; shortly before his death he had yet another one, Antipater, killed. The Pharisees and their disciples also suffered harsh persecution under him. He died in 4 BC.

2.3 The Gospel according to Matthew puts the birth of Jesus of Nazareth shortly before his death, Jesus whom the primitive church then proclaimed after his death to have been the expected Messiah of Israel, the Davidic king who was to liberate the people of God from their oppressors and inaugurate the kingdom of God on earth (in Hebrew *māšîah*, Greek Χριστός, 'anointed', the title first of the kings of Judah and then of the high priest). Matthew 2.16-18 connects the birth of Jesus with the so-called 'massacre of the innocents', a legendary incident, but one which shows what popular opinion thought Herod capable of!

2.4 It is possible, as a number of scholars believe, that Herod was not completely sane, disturbed by serious persecution mania and an inferiority complex. This last characteristic seems to have been especially important in connection with Mariamne, whom he loved and hated, and who moreover did everything possible to stress her royal origins and her husband's plebeian lineage. Persecution mania must have pursued him all his life, making him see plots and treason everywhere, even among his closest friends.

2.5 Extremely skilful in foreign policy, as we have seen, Herod was equally so in governing of his own country. A superb administrator, he managed to use state funds for some remarkable buildings and other public works. He had the temple of Jerusalem rebuilt, substantially enlarging it (what is now called the 'west wall' or the 'wailing wall' is simply the supporting wall of the temple mount); and on the north side of this he built a fortress which he called the Antonia, after his first protector. Its remains can now be seen at the beginning of the Via Dolorosa, in the Franciscan Monastery of the Flagellation and the Convent of the Sisters of Notre Dame of Zion. He also built a number of palaces: the Herodion, south-east of Bethlehem (coord.119-173), and Massada, near the west shore of the Dead Sea (coord.080-183); there were also others, even in Transjordan. At Massada it is possible that the round building on the intermediate terrace, the functions of which have never been adequately explained, was the tomb of Mariamne.[1] In honour of Augustus, Herod first restored Samaria, calling it Sebaste, i.e. Augusta, and then had the port of Caesarea built, a few miles south of Mount Carmel (coord.141-212). He had some fortresses built and restored the western gate of Jerusalem, giving it three towers called respectively Phasael (in honour of his brother), Mariamne (in honour of his wife) and Hippicus (in honour of a friend), and there he built his own palace. The towers are still in existence today, and have been incorporated into the Turkish fortress at the Jaffa gate, rebuilt, along with the walls, by Suleiman II the Magnificent in the sixteenth century. Under Herod's administration the country was more prosperous than ever before and had hardly any unemployment. However, what we might call 'the good government' of Herod was not enough to win him the sympathy of his subjects, who continued to see him as a stranger and, moreover, a violent and cruel man.

3 From 4 BC to AD 6, after Herod's death, the country went through a chaotic decade. Archelaus, a surviving son of Herod, reigned for a short time, but the region was the scene of various revolts, against either the Herodians or the Romans or both. They were all quelled in blood.

3.1 In AD 6, Judaea became directly dependent on Roman administration and was governed by prefects (later procurators), apart from the brief interregnum of 'king' Agrippa I (AD 41-44), son of Aristobulus IV, the second son of Herod by Mariamne, whom Herod had had killed along with his brother Alexander (above, 2). However, Transjordan, Peraea and Galilee continued to remain under Herod's successors.

3.2 Although Roman administration was the form of government which the people of Judah themselves had asked for in the first place, weary as they were of the Hasmonaeans and then of Herod, it soon proved to be very burdensome and often disturbed by some odious factors.

3.2.1 From a religious point of view Judaism certainly continued to enjoy its traditional autonomy, and the ethnarch (the title borne by the high priest) had ample powers in the civil sphere as well. Rome respected Jewish worship, and did not interfere in it, but all too often this was a purely formal respect which did not preserve the people of Judah from acts and ceremonies which they considered provocative, like the erection of statues dedicated to the emperors or the parade of military standards, all connected with some deity. For example, Pontius Pilate held a parade of this kind at the beginning of his rule in AD 27 (*Antt.* XVIII, 60ff.; *BJ* II, 175ff.). And despite the way in which the Gospels present Pilate (as an honest albeit not very intelligent and courageous bureaucrat), he was a cruel and rapacious man, one of the worst prefects the country ever had. Moreover the Romans hardly disguised their contempt for Jewish worship: one might recall the words of Tacitus quoted above (XIII.10.7) on the absence of images in the cult.

3.2.2 Furthermore, the prefects were always men who neither knew anything about the Hebrew cult nor were interested in it, and who exercised their own functions in an authoritarian and therefore repressive way. Add to this that they were often venal and corrupt, preoccupied more with their own personal enrichment than with the public good, and we have a complete picture of the situation.

3.3 That explains the almost endemic state of disorder, often flaring up into open rebellion, which existed from the death of Herod onwards. As often happens in situations of this kind, it is difficult to say what are political rebellions and when we have more or less obvious forms of banditry. At all events, groups again took to the hills, and new movements of armed resistance began to develop. We know of a certain Judas of Galilee, who also appeared in Judaea in AD 6/7, preaching revolt against the census ordered by the Romans for fiscal reasons. This is the census mentioned in Luke 2.1-5, where it is connected with the governorship of P.Sulpicius Quirinus in Syria. We do not know why Luke then connects it with the birth of Jesus, which according to the text of Matthew will have taken place about a decade earlier, given that Herod was still alive (Leaney*, 638). Some Pharisees also became followers of Judas of Galilee. Judas is also mentioned by Gamaliel in Acts 5.37; he was killed and the revolt was suppressed, but out of it grew the Zealots (Aramaic *qanānā'*, from the root *qinnā'*, 'be zealous for', hence 'be pledged to a cause'). Zealots are also well attested in the New Testament: in Matt. 10.4//Mark 3.18 a Simon wrongly called 'Canaanite' is even one of the Twelve; Luke 6.15, the other parallel passage in the Synoptics, rightly has 'Simon the Zealot'. A later offshoot of the Zealots was the group called Sicarii; armed with a kind of dagger (*sica*), they performed individual acts of terrorism against the Romans and against Jews who were thought to be collaborationists. Perhaps the second part of the name of Judas Iscariot, the disciple of Jesus who betrayed him, is a distorted form of Sicarius. Josephus (*Antt.* XVIII,1ff.) mentions the Zealots alongside the Sadducees, the Pharisees and the Essenes, so there must have been many of them, forming a group with their own characteristics. It is possible that Barabbas, the assassin whom Pilate pardoned instead of Jesus on the request of the mob, had in fact been a Zealot or even a Sicarius, and therefore was regarded with some sympathy, even if not without reservations.

3.4 We can only deal with Jesus here in passing; he belongs more to the history of the church than to that of Israel. Charges were brought against him by the Jewish authorities to the Roman procurator (after a trial the description of which in the Gospels is so full of inaccuracies and even absurdities that it is difficult to believe it goes back to an authentic tradition)[2] as a social agitator. He had been an itinerant preacher for a short time, especially in Galilee and around the shores of the Sea of Galilee, and had then gone to Jerusalem with his disciples, according to the Gospels, to present his messianic claims there. The Gospels also say that he was welcomed by the crowds there. It is difficult to say precisely what led to the break with almost all the Jewish authorities, first with the Pharisees and then with the Sadducees in the temple. One possible explanation could be that in his preaching he spoke chiefly to the '*am hā-'āreṣ*, which all the other groups despised because they were rough and ignorant (above XIII.11.3.1), while in his criticism he did not spare the leading groups; indeed he aimed his criticism at them. Our main problem lies in the fact that virtually the only sources we have are the texts of the Synoptic Gospels, which almost never adopt a historical and biographical approach (and that is even truer of the Fourth Gospel),[3] so that they can be used only with the greatest caution. On the Jewish side we have very little, indeed virtually nothing: a brief reference in Josephus, *Antt.* XX, 200 (a much more extended text, XVIII, 163, is considered to be a later Christian interpolation with apologetic aims). The silence of the earlier rabbinic sources is also complete.[4] So it is reasonable to suppose that the preaching of Jesus, far from having had the impact that the Gospels attribute to it on the Judaism of the time, passed virtually unobserved, as did everything that he did (though of course it obviously was sufficiently notable to lead to the foundation of the first Christian church). This was because it was in competition with the activity of other preachers and 'prophets'; moreover, it took place in a peripheral region, inhabited by a mixed Jewish and pagan population, and was therefore hardly noticed by the rabbis and the Hebrew sages of the time. Thus the affirmation implicit in the title of section 34 of Noth's *History*, 'The Rejection of Christ', seems unacceptable on the historical plane, quite apart from being doubtful theology.

3.5 The sources abound in lists of incidents between the Romans and the people of Judah, all sparked off by religious issues. There was one revolt in AD 41 because the Romans tried to put an image of the emperor in the temple; they may well have had no intention of causing offence, far less of provoking the Jews, since this was common practice among pagans. On another occasion, in the course of a reprisal against a village near where a Roman patrol had been attacked, the Torah scrolls of the local synagogue were treated with scant respect. These instances could be multiplied (see Leaney*, 644ff.).

4 One thing seems certain; given the situation that had come into being, it did not take much for the local revolts to degenerate into a general uprising, of the kind that had happened in the time of the Maccabees under Antiochus IV (above XIII.6ff.).

The occasion was provided by some actions of the procurator Gessius Florus in AD 67. He was probably the most corrupt of the officials sent by Rome. It is therefore possible (as a number of scholars accept) that Gessius had deliberately provoked the incidents so as to be able to hide his own misconduct behind the punitive provisions. However, we are obliged to make exclusive use of the only source at our disposal, the writings of Josephus, and these clearly favour the Jewish cause: there is no representation of the Roman point of view, though that ought to be heard. On the other hand, the corruption in the Roman administrative system is well known, so that there is nothing strange about Gessius' attitude; however, it had remarkable consequences, not only for Israel but also for Rome. This was obviously the occasion that the Zealots had been awaiting for years.

4.1 Of course a rebellion like the Jewish revolt did not begin from a single isolated act. For some years there had already been tensions between Jews and pagans in areas where there were mixed populations. For example, in Caesarea, the seat of the Roman procurator, the Jewish element and the non-Jewish element had been at daggers drawn for years and minor incidents continually occurred until the Jews, in order to put an end to the constant provocations, decided to leave the city *en masse*, taking with them their scrolls of sacred scripture and the objects which were used in synagogue worship. Soon afterwards, in May 67, Gessius had the remarkable sum of seventeen talents taken from the temple treasury.

4.1.1 The response from Jerusalem was not long in coming and it was not what one could call diplomatic or even correct: the procurator was publicly jeered at and insulted. By way of reprisal he allowed the troops to ransack a particular district, and the troops made full use of his permission, putting a section of the Holy City to fire and sword. Then the procurator demanded that the population should give a triumphal welcome to two cohorts arriving from Caesarea.

4.1.2 The high priest, along with a good many of the Sadducean priests and the Pharisees, urged the people to yield and do what was asked, but when the two cohorts did not respond to the salute of the crowds, the mob again let fly against the procurator, and the soldiers took up arms.

4.1.3 The people of Jerusalem then occupied the temple and cut off communications between it and the Antonia. In vain Agrippa II and his wife tried to intervene. Agrippa II was the son of Agrippa I, to whom the Romans had given territory that originally belonged to Herod, in Transjordan and in Lebanon, to compensate for the loss of Judaea, which had been restored to procuratorial administration; however, Herod continued to spent most of his time in Jerusalem, where he had retained the right to nominate the high priest. While the people would have been ready to make concessions, they were now unwilling to submit to Gessius Florus, and there was little or no way of proceeding against him by administrative or judicial means.

4.2 Meanwhile the Zealots had begun to occupy the various fortresses of Herod, all more or less unguarded; there they also captured a considerable amount of arms and equipment. Thus they took possession of the palace fortress of Massada and of Herodion (above 2.5) and the old palaces and fortresses in the Jordan valley and in Transjordan.

4.2.1 At the same time, Eleazar, son of the high priest, occupied the temple. The sacrifice for the emperor, deriving from a practice begun under Ezra (above XII.7.8.5), was suspended, and a prohibition was issued against offering sacrifices for aliens.

4.2.2 In vain the high priest pointed out that these were customs which had gone on now for centuries, and his attempts to subdue the rebellion from within were also vain, though they were supported by the majority of the priests and the Pharisees. Infact the leading class in Israel seems to have been clearly aware of the impossibility of victory in any direct confrontation with Rome. However, the troops sent by Agrippa II proved insufficient to quell what had become a popular revolt, so that the rebels soon found themselves masters of the situation, having taken possession of the city, including the temple and the Antonia. This also amounted to a formal sanctioning of the break with Rome, which the authorities had tried to avoid with all the means at their disposal: as Noth* points out (436), 'all that remained now was a struggle to the death'.

4.2.3 The high priest was killed, and Herod's palace at the western gate and that of the Hasmonaeans were set on fire; a Roman cohort which had been barricaded in the former, and had been given a safe conduct to leave the city, was massacred. Similar disorders flared up in all the great centres, and on the whole the insurgents gained the upper hand. Only at Caesarea, Scythopolis (formerly Beth-shean),

Ptolemais (formerly Acco, Acre) and Ashkelon did the pagans get the better of them. Finally there were also serious disorders between the two groups in distant Alexandria, in Egypt.

4.3 That same year C. Cestius Gallus, Roman legate in Syria, seeing that the movement was increasingly taking on the characteristics of a general uprising by the Jews against Rome, moved south with a legion.

4.3.1 He had no difficulty in occupying the whole of the coast, where in cities with pagan populations the Jews had been suppressed; then he moved against Jerusalem, camping on Mount Scopus (coord.134-173), the hill to the east-north-east which in modern times (since 1924) has become the site of the Hebrew University. But he immediately saw that his troops would not be enough to reduce a strongly fortified city defended to the last, so he decided to withdraw. However, his troops fell into an ambush near Beth-horon (present-day *bēt 'ūr*, coord.160-143) and were defeated; the survivors in fact had to flee, leaving a good deal of their arms and equipment behind on the ground.

4.3.2 So the Zealots remained masters of the field, and all hope among the moderates for a negotiated solution was gone. The leaders therefore began to organize the defence, and many of the moderates, seeing that the conflict had begun, joined the fighters.

As one can imagine, the organization almost always left much to be desired. It was impossible to make soldiers out of the undisciplined Zealots and therefore to organize trustworthy troops; it was impossible to coordinate production and to concentrate forces in a population which in some regions was mixed and partly not even pro-Jewish and anti-Roman. However, now the rebellion had taken the road of no return, burning its bridges. Finally, the movement lacked arms, equipment, military instruction, qualified officers and technique.

4.3.3 The country was divided into military districts and Galilee was entrusted to the command of a certain Joseph, son of Mattathiah, later to become the historian Flavius Josephus. He was a moderate and had not yet lost hope of arriving at some kind of understanding with Rome, given the absolute impossibility of a victory; because of this pragmatic view he had to suffer the abuse of various of the Zealots. In other words, the country had arrived at a kind of polarization of national political life which much resembled that existing before the Maccabean revolt; the only difference was that the the conflict had been between Jews faithful to the Torah and Hellenistic Jews, whereas now all were against Rome, though one group, aware of the impossibility of a victory, sought some kind of compromise, while the other trusted in its own valour and force of arms.

4.3.4 Unfortunately for the rebels, this division soon showed itself in real internecine struggles during the periods of calm, periods which would have been better used by them in reinforcing their effectiveness or seeking a compromise. From the beginning this laid a heavy burden on the cause of the rebels, whose chances of victory were in any case, as we saw, very slight.

4.4 Given the dimensions the revolt had now assumed, Nero resolved to launch a massive attack. He sent one of his best generals, T.Flavius Vespasianus, who in 43-44 had distinguished himself as a commander during the invasion of Britain. And Vespasian, through a skilful campaign, soon succeeded in reconquering a good deal of the country, especially those regions with mixed populations: Galilee, northern Transjordan and the plain of Jezreel, so that the rebels saw themselves reduced to holding only tiny Judaea. It was at this point that Josephus, having been taken prisoner, went over to the enemy, taking the name of Flavius in honour of his Roman protector.

4.4.1 Months of relative calm followed for the rebels. Vespasian temporized, waiting to see what happened in Rome, where, on the death of Nero, Galba, Otho and Vitellius were claimants to the throne, all nominated by the army. The troops in the East also nominated as their emperor Vespasian himself, after Vitellius had been killed in December 69. Vespasian came to the throne in the summer of 70, but meanwhile had entrusted the command of the army to his son Titus.

4.4.2 The rebels had not made good use of the months of relative calm; their factions continued to fight one another, armed to the teeth, especially around Jerusalem: Zealots fought against moderates, and partisan bands came out of the wilds to fight the Zealots. So when Titus launched his final attack the rebels were not only divided but also notably weakened by internal struggles.

4.4.3 Titus laid siege to the capital in the spring of 70 with at least four legions and numerous auxiliaries. He too camped on Mount Scopus, shortly before the Hebrew passover. In the face of the imminent danger the internal struggles largely ceased and the final defence of the city began. To show how unprepared the rebels were, it is enough to point out that the public celebration of the passover took place that year in the usual way, with the presence of thousands of pilgrims who had come to the city for the feast. In the besieged and overpopulated city, hermetically sealed by the circumvallation of the besiegers, the food situation soon became critical and not long afterwards, desperate; Josephus narrates a series of horrifying episodes, all caused by the famine. At all events, the defenders succeeded in maintaining discipline in the city, though only by resorting to very harsh repressive measures.

4.5 The work of the besiegers was in any case very difficult. On the east, south and west sides the walls of Jerusalem formed a complex that jutted out over the drop to the valleys of Kidron and Gehenna, so that the city could be taken by assault only from the north. And there three successive walls had been built, the innermost wall connected with the Antonia (cf. above 2.5).

4.5.1 However, the besiegers were not new to these problems. With their advanced siege tactics they succeeded in taking the three walls one after the other. Then, in July, they captured the Antonia, and in August the temple, which went up in flames in the fighting (against an explicit order by Titus, but now it was not longer possible to hold back the soldiers); finally, in September the western part of the city also fell. This was completely razed to the ground, except for what remained of Herod's palace (above, 2.5) and some of the western fortifications, where the Roman troops were quartered.

4.5.2 The various surviving fortresses were reduced one after the other and the last, Massada, fell only in 74 (earlier it was thought to have fallen in 73),[5] after a long siege and desperate resistance on the part of those inside it, which culminated in their collective suicide. It was probably during this siege that the community of Essenes established on the north-west shore of the Dead Sea, at Qumran, was also destroyed (above XIII.11.4).

4.5.3 According to the information provided independently by Josephus and Tacitus, more than 600,000 Jews will have been killed in the course of the military occupation, about twenty-five per cent of the population, and many others will have been taken prisoner and sold as slaves. Thus it would seem possible that something like half the Jewish population had been physically eliminated. The Arch of Titus in the Forum at Rome gives a picture of the triumph of the future emperor in which there is a reproduction of the candelabrum captured from the temple.

5 Despite the seriousness of the rebellion, the Romans do not seem to have nurtured any particular hostility towards Judaism as a religion; evidently it was enough to have quelled the revolt and established conditions which made it impossible for it to be repeated.

Select bibliography: J.Neusner, *Life of Yohanan ben Zakkai*, Leiden ²1970; id., *Development of a Legend: Studies on the Traditions Concerning Yohanan ben Zakkai*, Leiden 1970; id., *From Politics to Piety*, Leiden 1973; Neusner*, 663-77.

5.1 Thus the Romans allowed Judaism to continue as a *religio licita*, probably in the hope that it would be a focal point for the more moderate elements. So they did not oppose a Pharisee, Johanan ben Zakkai, said to have been arrested and taken to Titus' camp in romantic circumstances, when he set up a house for study in the locality of Jabneh, Greek Jamnia (coord.126-141).

5.2 With the destruction of the temple, the Sadducees' social function and economic basis had disappeared; moreover a large number of them had perished in the burning of the sanctuary. The Palestinian nuclei of other groups like the Essenes had been dispersed and the first Christians, too, are said to have taken flight temporarily to Pella in Transjordan (present-day *tabāqat fāḥl*, coord.206-207).[6] So only the Pharisees remained. Because they were not tied to official structures, while they had suffered severe losses, their organization had remained intact. At Jabneh they immediately took up the work of reorganizing the Jewish community in the Holy Land. Very soon the school of Jabneh, which collected together what people and traditions it could, was also recognized by the Diaspora. 'From politics to piety' is the effective definition which Neusner 1973 gives of this development: from a political point of view Israel had certainly been destroyed, but it remained as the bearer of a faith and practice.

5.3 Johanan and his followers succeeded in overcoming the shock and the disorientation prevailing among the survivors, feelings which are quite understandable after the catastrophe. Because in the past the temple had too often been the centre of intrigue and collaboration with the occupying forces, it had lost much of its prestige even before the catastrophe; that explains why there was virtually no thought of rebuilding it, though that had been a priority for those returning from exile in the second half of the sixth century BC (above XII.4.4 and 5.4.6).

5.4 In this way the doctrine and life-style of the Pharisees (see above XIII.11.3) became what we are accustomed to calling normative Judaism, which has governed Israel for centuries in a diaspora which was later to extend from the Yemen to the Baltic and from Russia to America and Australia. And it is in this context, even if we have no precise information, that the canon of the Hebrew Bible was closed and the 'oral Torah' began to be collected. The latter gradually grew into the great exegetical works and commentaries. But all this now belongs to another, later phase of the history of Israel.

6 Once the first revolt had been quelled, the region became a province of the Roman empire. Temple worship was not resumed nor was the building restored; the obol destined for it was instead sent to the sanctuary of Jupiter Capitolinus, a measure which was obviously insulting on the political level and provocative in religious terms. However, that came about only twenty-five years later, under Nerva (AD 96-98).

Select bibliography: S.M.Baron, *A Social and Religious History of the Jews*, II, 2, New York 1952, 89-122, 368-77; M.Noth*, 448-54; S.Perowne, *Hadrian*, London 1980, passim, esp. 149ff.; A.Fuks, 'Aspects of the Jewish Revolt in AD 115-117', *Journal of Roman Studies* 51, 1961, 98-104; J.A.Fitzmyer, 'The Bar Kochba Period', in *The Bible in Current Catholic Thought – Gruentaner Memorial Volume*, New York 1962, 133-

68 = *Essays on the Semitic Background of the New Testament*, London 1971, 305-54; H.Mantel, 'The Causes of the Bar Kochba Revolt', *JQR* 58, 1967-68, 224-42, 274-96; Y.Yadin, *Bar Kochba*, London and New York 1971; J.Neusner*, 863ff.; P.Schäfer, *Der Bar Kokhba Aufstand. Studien zum zweiten jüdischen Krieg gegen Rom*, Tübingen 1981.

6.1 The sources are almost completely silent about the events between the first and second Jewish wars. Also, with the end of Josephus' work at the events of AD 74, they thin out drastically. It is therefore difficult to establish the precise causes of the second Jewish revolt in 132, more than sixty years after the destruction of the second temple.

6.1.1 One explanation put forward by some scholars is that there were those in Judah who, as the seventieth anniversary of the destruction of the sanctuary drew near, began to think of an imminent end of the times, and thus of the end of the pagan rule over the Holy Land. For the figure we have the announcements in Jer. 25.11; 29.10 and the speculations of Dan.9.1ff., and those of other apocalyptists from the time of the Maccabees and later.

6.1.2 Another explanation, which appears more probable, combines economic and political information with the former point. According to this, as at the time of the first rebellion, developments which the Jews regarded as provocations were combined with a theology of the zealot and apocalyptic kind, in which war was simply the beginning of the catastrophes which ushered in the imminent end of the times and the coming of the messianic kingdom. At all events, we know from two apocalyptic and pseudepigraphical books, the Apocalypse of Syriac Baruch and IV Esdras respectively, that the destruction of the temple had caused a serious collective uneasiness (above 5.3), and that there was a great longing to re-establish the temple cult.[7]

6.1.3 We shall not be far from the truth, though, if we postulate that the motives which prompted Judah again to rebel will have been basically those which led to the first revolt. These will hardly have diminished with time. It is unimaginable that the Roman administration, avaricious and corrupt as it was, should suddenly have become solicitous, generous and honest, all the more so since the emperors of the Flavian dynasty – Vespasian (69-79), Titus (79-81) and Domitian (81-96) – are hardly likely to have been better disposed to the people of Judah after the bloody campaign. Only in fact under Nerva did the situation begin to get rather better. But clearly there were still a number of factors which, given the right moment, could have precipitated events.

6.2 From the little information that has come down to us it is also clear that the Diaspora, too, was far from tranquil. In fact there was a series of rebellions about 115, and even if they were evidently unconnected with the events of 132-5, they show that things were already coming to the boil.

6.2.1 During a campaign by Trajan (98-117) against the Parthians, a revolt broke out in 115 among the Jews of Cyrene and Alexandria, Cyprus and even Mesopotamia, i.e. near to the front. We are in the dark about its causes and aims; however, we shall not go far wrong in recalling that disorders between Jews and pagans had already become common in cities with mixed populations. A.Fuks 1961, who has made the most precise analysis of this movement, based on recent papyrological discoveries, points out that the revolts were always brutal in character, with the extermination of populations, leaving scorched earth behind, especially in Cyrenaica, Cyprus and Egypt; in Mesopotamia, on the other hand, a revolt seems to have come about with the approval of the local population. At all events, Trajan did not hesitate to crush all these revolts, but the fact that this took him some years and that the repression continued under Hadrian shows that it must have been a hard task. We do not know whether the rebellion extended to Judaea, but we do know that Lusius Quietus, who had just crushed the revolt in Mesopotamia, was soon afterwards nominated governor of Judaea. If this is a coincidence, it is quite a remarkable one; was this move perhaps to re-establish order there too? This is what Noth*, 449, supposes.

6.2.2 The last great revolt broke out under Hadrian (117-138); from the little we know, its dimensions were similar to that of 67-74. Otherwise, here too our information is also very sparse, and moreover we have apparently contradictory information about its origins. We are dependent on the only two authors who recorded it: Dio Cassius, LXIX, 12-14 (Stern II, no.1440) and Eusebius, HE IV, 6 (Noth*, 449).

6.2.2.1 According to Dio, the Jews rebelled because of the foundation by Hadrian of Aelia Capitolina on the ruins of Jerusalem and the inauguration there of a sanctuary dedicated to Jupiter Capitolinus, and took up arms.

6.2.2.2 However, according to Eusebius the revolt broke out because a law promulgated by Hadrian had equated circumcision with castration, a practice forbidden by Roman law, though we do not know from when. Anyway, a few years later, under Antoninus Pius (138-161), circumcision was again allowed as a legitimate exception to the law on castration, together with other Jewish practices prohibited after the second revolt.

6.2.3 These two pieces of information seem contradictory, but are only apparently so; they fit in well with what we know of the period.

6.2.3.1 Hadrian travelled to the East in 130/131 and during his travels had some cities built. He certainly went to Gerasa (present-day *jāraš*, coord.188-258) in Transjordan. We do not know whether he also went to Jerusalem, though this seems likely; at all events, even a plan to go there would have been enough to create considerable tension among the survivors of Palestinian Judaism, even if it were not actually carried out.

6.2.3.2 As to the prohibition of circumcision, that clearly affected all the peoples of the Roman empire who practised it, and not just Israel, so it can hardly be considered in itself as a measure against the Jews. In fact, however, it was a heavy blow to Israel's faith, of which circumcision was (and still is) a distinctive feature.

6.2.3.3 So in both cases there were marked points of conflict: the desecration of holy places and intolerable interference in matters of faith. In the past, in the time of the Maccábees and the first revolt, both these things had led to rebellion, and so they did now.

6.3 At the head of the rebellion we find a certain Simon *ben kōsība'*, soon acclaimed by his own followers in Aramaic as *bar kōkbā'*, 'son of the star', according to Num.24.16 understood messianically: '...a star arises from Jacob'. Later the rabbis caricatured the name as *bar kōzība'*, 'son of the lie'. Here we find a true charismatic as the term is used by Max Weber (cf. above VIII.1.1.4); his authority was in fact immediately recognized by all without the internal struggles which had characterized the first revolt (above 4.3.4). Finally the venerable R.Akiba, who had originally opposed the revolt, was convinced and fascinated by him, proclaiming him to be the Messiah (*Jerus*. Ta'an.68d).

6.4 Meanwhile Hadrian had returned to Rome. To begin with, he does not seem to have been very concerned about the revolt. So it was easy for the rebels initially to gain considerable successes: they recaptured Jerusalem and succeeded in liberating a large part of the country, which Simon governed from the ancient capital, minting his own coinage. Every series of coins was characterized by a cipher denoting 'the year of the liberation of Israel'. Moreover, he must have restored temple worship, since on one of the coins a priest with the name of Eleazar appears; according to some scholars he will also have begun to rebuild the temple.

6.5 However, this time again, once Rome had decided to make a serious intervention, the struggle soon proved hopeless, though the rebels followed more partisan tactics, avoiding combat in the open. However, the Romans, skilfully led by Julius Severus, who had distinguished himself in Britain, where he had been governor, arrived in the country with overwhelming force and decided to follow a similar tactic: the rebel strongholds were besieged one after the other and the rebels overcome with hunger and thirst.

6.5.1 We know of the sieges of *bēt-ṭēr*, near the Arab village of *bittīr* (the last station on the railway line to Jerusalem), on *ḥirbet el-yehūd* ('ruin of the Judahites', coord.126-162), a fortified place which after a heroic but vain resistance was overcome through hunger and thirst, along with the usual siege techniques. It was probably here that Simon perished.

6.5.2 The last of the rebels took refuge in the complex of caves above the *wādī murabbā'at*, in Hebrew *nahal ḥeber* (coord.093-182), which flows down to the Dead Sea, hoping that they would be able to continue their guerrilla warfare from there; however, in the arid region they were soon blockaded and reduced by hunger and thirst. Archaeological discoveries, now on display in the Museum of Israel in Jerusalem (the region and especially the caves were excavated in 1960-61) indicate that the majority of those besieged preferred death by starvation to capture.

7 Thus yet again, final resistance ceased. Again the Jewish population were subjected to severe trials; there are reports of about 850,000 dead (Fohrer*, 230). Many teachers were also killed, those who had been laboriously reshaping Judaism on the ruins of the first revolt; they included R.Akiba, who was tortured by the Romans despite his advanced age.

7.1 Jerusalem was made a colony and called Aelia Capitolina; it was rebuilt with all the urban characteristics of a Roman city: Jews were forbidden to enter it. The celebration of Hebrew ceremonies was also forbidden, as was circumcision and the production or possession of scrolls of the Torah. This time, then, as opposed to 70-74, we have a series of measures also aimed against Judaism as a religion (but cf. above, 6.1).

7.2 The traditional name Judaea was replaced with that of Palestine, from the name of the Philistines who had lived in the south west of it. As Noth*, 454, rightly observes, the surviving Jews had become strangers in their own traditional homeland, just as they were strangers in the regions of the diaspora.

8 That brings to an end the biblical and immediately post-biblical period of the history of Israel. However, as we know, this history does not stop there (though some scholars would prefer from now on, or even earlier, to talk in terms of the history of Judaism).

8.1 In the Diaspora, which now, as we have seen, also included the desecrated holy land, Israel continued not only to survive but even to develop and flourish, keeping alive over the millennia the remembrance of the region which it continued to regard as its real homeland. The passover salutation, 'Next year in Jerusalem', must have arisen at this time. In the synagogue liturgy there continued to be prayers for rain and harvest in the distant 'homeland', connections with which never ceased, not least because especially in Galilee, which was little affected by the war, numerous communities continued to exist.[8]

8.2 In the Diaspora, it could be said that Israel consciously or unconsciously followed the exhortation which according to tradition

Jeremiah had addressed to his fellow countrymen who had been deported to Babylon in 587: 'Build houses and live in them; plant gardens and eat their produce. Take wives and have sons and daughters; take wives for your sons, and give your daughters in marriage, that they may bear sons and daughters... Seek the welfare of the city where I have sent you into exile, and pray to the Lord on its behalf, for in its welfare you will find your welfare...' (Jer.29.4-9). With these guidelines Israel has continued to survive now for almost two millennia, almost always the object of discrimination (as was only to be expected in the non-pluralist societies of former days); sometimes this took the form of persecutions which even went as far as the expulsion or the killing of Jews locally or nationally. In other cases, especially in the Arab world at the time of its greatest expansion, it was possible for the Jews to develop, always adapting themselves to the new situations which arose.

8.3 In the Diaspora, Jews have always tried to reconcile the duties of being good citizens with those imposed by their faith. Often, in periods of tolerance, we see them studying not only their own scriptures and religion but as doctors, philosophers, philologists, grammarians, mystics and musicians; later as psychologists and sociologists. Some have even become the counsellors of kings. However, that, along with the development of philosophy, belongs to another era of the history of Israel.

List of Plates

List of Figures

1. Sinai, Palestine, Jordan, and Arabia with the Red Sea in a modern satellite photograph

2. Town gate in unbaked brick from the nineteenth-eighteenth century BC, Tell Dan (by courtesy of the Hebrew Union College, Jerusalem)

3. Megiddo. To the right, the ruins of the temple, and to the left an altar from the late Canaanite period, end of the Bronze Age (by courtesy of the Department of Antiquities and Museums of the State of Israel, Jerusalem)

4. Megiddo, 'Solomon's Stables' reconstruction (by courtesy of the
Department of Antiquities and Museums of the State of Israel, Jerusalem)

5. Megiddo, 'Solomon's Stables' (by courtesy of the Department of
Antiquities and Museums of the State of Israel, Jerusalem)

6. Tell Arad during the excavations (by courtesy of the Archaeological
Institute of the University of Tel-Aviv)

7. The temple of Tell Arad (by courtesy of the Archaeological Institute of the University of Tel-Aviv)

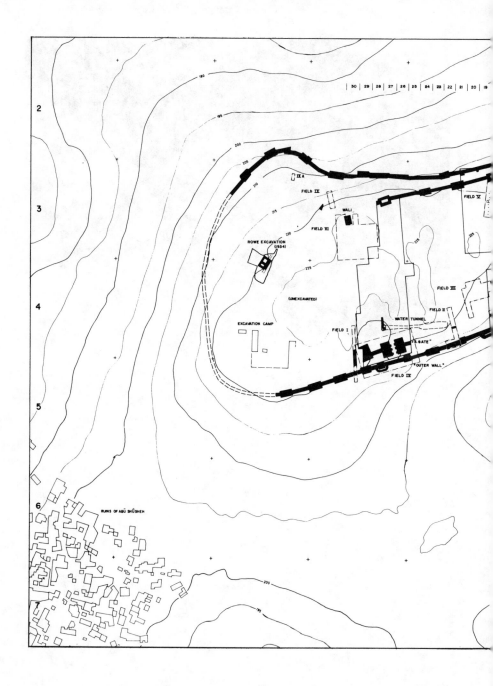

| 30 | 29 | 28 | 27 | 26 | 25 | 24 | 23 | 22 | 21 | 20 | 19 |

IX A

FIELD IX

FIELD V

WALL

FIELD VI

ROWE EXCAVATION
(1934)

(UNEXCAVATED)

FIELD XII

FIELD II

EXCAVATION CAMP

WATER TUNNEL

FIELD I

"S.GATE"

"OUTER WALL"

FIELD IX

RUINS OF ABŪ SHŪSHEH

8. Gezer. Plan of the sites of excavations made between 1964

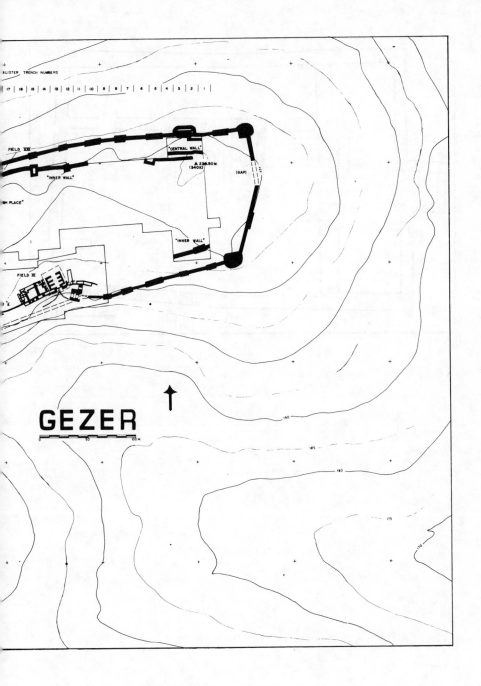

FIELD VII

"CENTRAL WALL"

Δ 234.50 M.
(340K)

(GAP)

"INNER WALL"

GH PLACE"

"INNER WALL"

FIELD III

GEZER

↑

0   50   100 M.

190

185

180

175

170

and 1973 (by courtesy of the Hebrew Union College, Jerusalem)

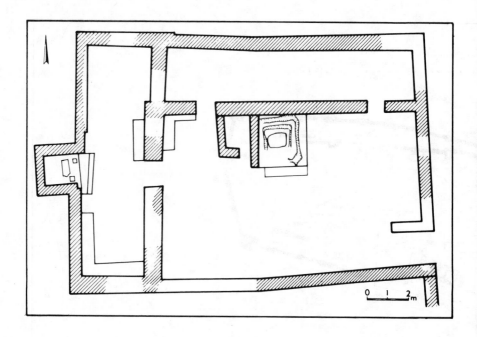

9. Plan of the temple of Tell Arad (by courtesy of the Archaeological Institute of the University of Tel-Aviv)

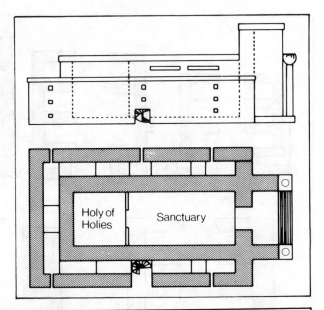

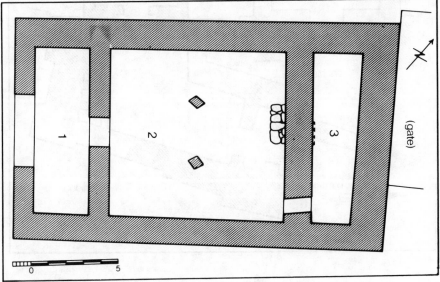

10. Reconstruction and plan of the temple of Solomon (from W.G.Dever, 'Monumental Architecture in Ancient Israel', in T.Ishida (ed.), *Studies in the Period of David and Solomon*, Tokyo 1982, 262-306, fig.11 – the original is in *IDB* IV, 1962, 537 fig.7)

11. Schematic plan of 'Temple 7300' of Shechem, MB-IIC (*c.* 1650-1550 BC) (from W.G.Dever, 'Monumental Architecture in Ancient Israel', in T.Ishida (ed.), *Studies in the Period of David and Solomon*, Tokyo 1982, 269-306 – the original is in W.G.Dever, *BASOR* 216, 1974, 40 fig.10)

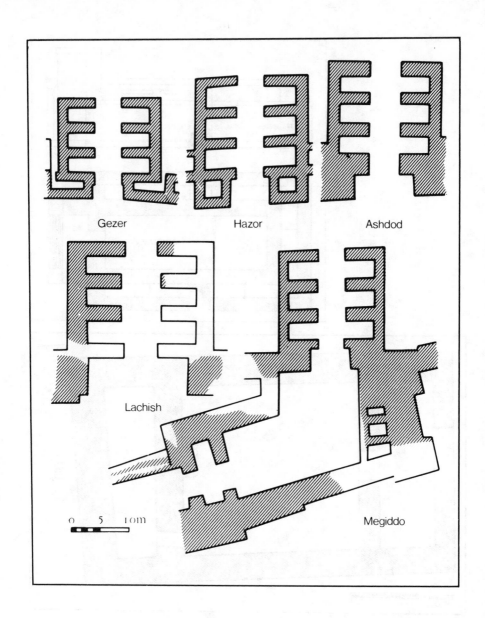

Gezer   Hazor   Ashdod

Lachish

0   5   10m

Megiddo

12. Town gate from the tenth century BC, the time of the united monarchy (from W.G.Dever, 'Monumental Architecture in Ancient Israel', in T.Ishida (ed.), *Studies in the Period of David and Solomon*, Tokyo 1982, 269-306, fig.11)

13. Gate from the time of Solomon, tenth century BC, looking south-south-
    eastwards. Note the large drainage channel which runs across the street
    (by courtesy of the Hebrew Union College, Jerusalem)

14. The *tell* of Beer-sheba during the excavations (by courtesy of the Archaeological Institute of the University of Tel-Aviv)

15. The western quarter of the *tell* of Beer-sheba, with typical houses from the Israelite period (by courtesy of the Archaeological Institute of the University of Tel-Aviv)

16. The altar with four 'horns' discovered during the excavations on the *tell* of Beer-sheba (by courtesy of the Archaeological Institute of the University of Tel-Aviv)

17. Remains of the northern wall of Jerusalem, from the end of the eighth century BC (by courtesy of the Israel Exploration Society, Jerusalem)

18. Remains of a tower inserted in the northern wall of Jerusalem, from the seventh century BC. Note on the left hand side the building that uses it as a foundation, which comes from the time of the Maccabees (by courtesy of the Israel Exploration Society, Jerusalem)

APPENDIX 1

An Introduction to the Archaeology of Syria and Palestine on the Basis of the Israelite Settlement

Diethelm Conrad

I. Theory

1. Definitions

The meaning of the term 'archaeology' has shifted in a number of ways between the Greek period and the present day. To begin with, as in Josephus, it denoted the narration of ancient history, i.e. the description of historical developments, including the habits and customs of particular peoples and times. After the Enlightenment, subject-matter like individuals, states and religions of antiquity (and in the case of the Bible, biblical questions) came to be dealt with under this heading. It is only with the rise of an active programme of excavation in the last third of the nineteenth century and during the twentieth century that the term has now come to be understood to refer above all to field archaeology in (Syria and) Palestine. Now as in addition to 'the archaeology of (Syria and) Palestine', terms like 'biblical archaeology' and 'archaeology of the land of Israel' are also used and – especially over the last decade – have become the subject of vigorous discussion, I must first venture a few definitions to clarify matters.

1.1 In content and method, the archaeology of (Syria and) Palestine is a special division of Near Eastern archaeology, limited to the region of Syria and Palestine, i.e. to the sphere in which biblical history ran its course. Because of the historical and cultural contacts between the cultures of Syria and Palestine and the cities and cultures in the north and south of this region, it is of course essential to look beyond its limits, e.g. to Mesopotamian and Egyptian archaeology. However, apart from the coasts, above all in the north-east, Syria comes closer to Mesopotamia than to Palestine, i.e. to a wider horizon, so that in our case it is more accurate to speak simply of Palestinian archaeology or the archaeology of Palestine. Chronologically, Palestinian archaeology extends from the Stone Age (the earliest history) to the present. Numerous scholars are now working to clarify developments here, especially in Israel and Jordan, but also in

America and Europe. In principle, the term 'archaeology of the Land of Israel' has the same meaning; it is used especially by Israeli scholars.

1.2 German-speaking scholars in particular still prefer the term 'biblical archaeology'. This, too, is a specialist division of the archaeology of the Near East, the location of which is limited to the sphere of (Syria and) Palestine and the time-span to the second and first millennium BC. Biblical archaeology keeps to a methodically controlled correlation of archaeological finds and written sources (essentially the biblical text).

1.3 Objections are made by each perspective to the other, and also come from a third perspective. Those who favour 'biblical archaeology' over against 'Palestinian archaeology' object that in the latter the correlation of archaeological discoveries and written sources is either not controlled at all or not controlled by an adequate method. Those who favour 'Palestinian archaeology' over against 'biblical archaeology' argue against the limited time-span of the latter. As biblical archaeology often relates only to the Old Testament period, objections to it are made by New Testament scholars. In fact the period between the Testaments and the first centuries of the Christian era should also be included here, as neither Christian nor Byzantine archaeology covers this period (though Palestinian archaeology does!). American scholars also rightly object to the term biblical archaeology because it is associated with a fundamentalist approach according to which biblical archaeology confirms or even proves the historical reliability of the biblical traditions. However, if biblical archaeology is understood in accordance with the definition given in 1.2, this fundamentalist conception can be rejected.

2. Branches of work

The scientific discipline of Palestinian or biblical archaeology came into being in the course of the nineteenth century as a result of the growth of historical interest in the land of the Bible as well as in other areas. Three different branches can be established: they were there from the beginning and are not just the result of specialization. These are: surveys, archaeological fieldwork carried out through excavations, and systematic archaeology. One special branch of the subject which has developed in recent years in Palestinian archaeology as elsewhere is marine archaeology, distinctive because of the special technical equipment needed.

2.1 By covering the country systematically and evaluating select pottery finds, surveys discover settlements and how long they lasted, and lead to a history of the settlement of the land (topography) and occasionally to the identification of sites with places known from written sources (toponomy).

2.2 Excavations (often called 'dust' or 'dirt' archaeology) disclose the remains of buildings and enable the collection of artefacts from the daily life of their inhabitants over a period (above all pottery fragments). These are data for a history of settlement and culture, which also has social, economic and religious dimensions.

2.3 By collecting, examining, sorting, classifying and interpreting the facts which are produced by surveys and excavations, systematic archaeology (often also called 'armchair archaeology') attempts to bring these together into a history of the settlement, culture and society of the people of Israel and of earlier and neighbouring cultures, though so far only a beginning has been made on this (in the form of a lexicon).

2.4 Marine archaeology investigates sites on the coast of Palestine, especially submerged harbour installations (Caesarea, Dor, Acco, etc.) and other remains connected with seafaring.

3. Methods

In the course of the history of the discipline, extending over more than a century, specific methods have been developed for the branches of archaeology mentioned above, each of them appropriate to the work to be carried out. These are widely recognized today and guarantee the scientific character of the discipline. Treatment of the pottery (finds) is particularly important. Catalogues of types and forms are constantly refined and allow the origin and dating of ceramic vessels and their sherds to be determined with increasing accuracy. To this degree pottery is a kind of fossil, providing a chronological guide.

A whole spectrum of methods can be used not only in carrying out archaeological investigation but also in planning it and evaluating it. It should be stressed that nowadays all excavations are done with special attention to stratigraphy. In other words, during excavation the shifting of earth and the levels which together make up a stratum of settlement are carefully noted and described in both the horizontal and the vertical plane. It goes without saying that methods are constantly developed and refined, and techniques from the natural sciences are increasingly being incorporated into them. Such techniques are useful in prospecting (aerial archaeology, electrical and magnetic techniques), dating (dendrochronology, archaeomagnetism, thermo-luminescence and obsidian dating) and in the determination of origins (pollen analysis, palaeo-biology, analysis by röntgen fluorescence, neutron activation and electron microscopes). Computers must increasingly be involved in mastering the mass of data which is produced in this way, and also for statistical investigations. As these techniques are very expensive, a cost-analysis is very important here. Nowadays, sociological methods are used for formulating questions and evaluating and interpreting results, and ethnological data are used for comparisons. However, the discussion over the nature and extent of their use is far from over.

4. The problem of interpretation

All the data produced by surveys and excavation are mute unless they are accompanied by textual discoveries – and this happens only very rarely. That means that the data have to be elucidated and interpreted. Thus our understanding of archaeological data is an understanding of their interpretation and therefore has 'only' the status of a hypothesis. This shows how important methodology is in interpretation, if agreement over results on an objective basis is to be achieved. Consequently the subjective presuppositions of the interpreter, whether historical, cultural or religious, have also to be taken into account. However, it is impossible to put too much stress on the importance of knowledge of the environment of any datum or object to be interpreted. This demonstrates the great importance of geographical knowledge of Palestine in the broadest sense. It includes physical geography, geology, climate (rainfall), flora and fauna, topography, communications (for trade and travel) and historical geography, along with all kinds of written documents: the Bible, texts from surrounding nations, epigraphical texts (inscriptions) on stone, clay, papyrus, leather and so on from Palestine itself. However much the texts may speak for themselves, they, too, need interpretation. This applies above all to biblical texts, as a result of the special circumstances surrouding their origin, collection, transmission and purpose. The interpretation of them is the task of biblical exegesis.

This brief statement already makes it clear that archaeological data and the text of the Bible cannot be brought together directly: each needs to be interpreted. In the process it has emerged that only on very rare occasions do archaeological data shed direct light on the text of the Bible or vice versa. Thus archaeological data (like the text of the Bible) remain independent sources for conditions (and on occasion also events) relevant to the history of culture, society, economics and religion.

5. *Periods in archaeology and cultural history*

The following table may be regarded as a conventional framework for the identification of periods in any discusion of the history of culture in Palestine:

Up to 4000 BC	Stone Age
Fourth millennium BC	Chalcolithic Age
3200-1200 BC	Bronze Age (divided into:)
3200-2200 BC	Early Bronze Age
2200-1550 BC	Middle Bronze Age
1550-1200 BC	Late Bronze Age
1200-535 (330) BC	Iron Age (divided into:)
1200-1000 BC	Iron Age I : The Period of the Judges
1000-587 BC	Iron Age II: The Period of the Monarchy

587-535 BC	Iron Age III, also the Babylonian period
535-330 BC	(often still Iron Age III:) Persian Period
330-65 BC	Hellenistic Period
65 BC-AD 324	Roman Period (including Herod, 37 BC-AD 4)
AD 324-634/40	Byzantine Period

All these periods are further subdivided, depending on cultural changes. This is partly a historical and partly a cultural phenomenon, often connected with changes in technology and society. The individual periods initially represent only a relative chronology, which becomes an absolute chronology only through datable synchronisms. So in this area, too, archaeology is also an auxiliary discipline for historians.

II. Example: The Israelite Settlement

In view of the state of our literary sources, i.e. the text of the Bible, it is still difficult to arrive at a historically accurate picture of the Israelite settlement. So in the present state of research, what can Palestinian archaeology contribute to the clarification of this period, taking into account what I said in I. above? To answer the question we must first look again at the biblical account, previous archaeological evidence and previous models of historical methodology before moving on to more recent archaeological results and their interpretation.

1 The account in Josh.1-12 suggests that the land promised to the Israelites by God was conquered from the east in a rapid expedition with powerful thrusts southwards (e.g. Lachish) and northwards (e.g. Hazor). However, on closer examination we can see that there is very little specific material for this account. Moreover there are other texts, e.g. Judg.1, which contradict both the view of the conquest as an action by all the tribes (here, rather, it is a matter of individual actions) and the extent of the territory conquered.

2 The excavations in Jericho and Ai showed that neither in Jericho nor in Ai did a city exist at the end of the Late Bronze Age, but that both older cities had been destroyed and abandoned long before any possible occupation by the Israelites under Joshua. And whereas Hazor and the cities in the Shephelah show traces of destruction at the end of the Late Bronze Age or the beginning of the Iron Age, so that they may be said to have been destroyed at this time, this evidence in itself does not indicate who destroyed them, and whether the city concerned was destroyed by

military attack, siege or a conflagration; indeed it might have fallen victim to a disaster like a catastrophic fire. Moreover, it should be pointed out that where the traces of destruction can be dated they are distributed over a period of about a century.

3 Because of the uncertain historical facts in the period of the settlement, a historical reconstruction of this era can be made only on the basis of hypothetical models into which these facts fit. The contradictions in the literary sources and the ambivalence of the archaeological evidence and the different judgments passed on it have by now led to very varied models.

W.F.Albright and American scholars following him have been more confident about the biblical texts and have seen the results of archaeology as external evidence which confirms the biblical accounts and the military conquest of the country.

A.Alt, M.Noth and numerous German scholars have seen the settlement more as a peaceful process. Israelite groups are said to have infiltrated the sparsely settled areas in the hill-country and valleys remote from the Canaanite city-states and outside their spheres of influence, and formed themselves into tribes there. Their military conflicts with the Canaanite cities only took place as a second stage.

A third model, first put forward by G.Mendenhall in 1962, which has found supporters since then – often in a modified form - argues that a peasant revolt took place in Canaan in which there was an exodus, an emigration of dissatisfied peasants from the social sphere dominated by the Canaanite city-states. Some scholars already see Yahwism at work in this connection; they claim that the occurrence of 'Israel' on the Merneptah stele, which is now dated about 1207 BC, belongs in this wider connection.

4 In the first half of this century the main interest was in investigating the history, the rise and fall, of the great cities known from the Bible; now, however, archaeologists are more interested in regional studies. A whole series of such projects is under way; the investigations are far from being complete. Results have only been published in a few cases, and then they are mostly provisional. However, these are of great significance for the question of the Israelite settlement, as new facts are emerging. Surveys of particular regions, whether complete or still in progress, have shown that the characteristic of the sudden destruction of the Late Bronze Age city is not so important for the cultural change from the Late Bronze Age to the Iron Age; in the meantime there has also been enough evidence of an uninterrupted development from the Late Bronze Age to the Early Iron Age. The real characteristic of cultural change is that the Late Bronze Age is stamped by a political and social system of city states and their material and religious culture. These cities lie on the coast, on the periphery of the great plains and valleys and on the major lines of communication (there are also a few of them in the hill-country). With the beginning of the Iron Age countless new unfortified villages appear, above all in the hill-country). Of course this great change in the settlement pattern also has political and

social significance. And the question is whether it has anything to do with the settlement of Israelite groups.

There is evidence of a hundred such settlements in the central hill-country of Ephraim and Manasseh; these are often arranged in groups around an ecological feature, like a valley, and can also have a common cultic centre, like the 'bull site' (coord.180-201) between Tirzah and Dothan (coord.172-202). The first settlements are found in the north of this area, and seem to have extended from the north-east to the south-west.

This evidence seems to contradict what J.A.Callaway has said to be the result of his investigations of Ai and Raddana (coord.169-146). Both settlements are supposed to have come into being as early as 1220 BC. Cisterns were constructed below the houses before they were built, with sophisticated arrangements to purify the rainwater flowing into them. Paved streets are just one indication that the new settlers had already lived a sedentary life elsewhere, and had a high degree of technical skill, which they could only have acquired on the coastal plain. That would suggest an extension of settlements from west to east.

In the hill-country of Judah there are no Late Bronze Age cities apart from Jerusalem and Debir, and the same is true of the Negeb. Thus here the Late Bronze Age Israelite settlements are even more sparse than in Ephraim and Manasseh. Countless new villages also came into being in these two areas, in the Negeb first of all from the eleventh century BC. Giloh (coord.167-126) is an example from Judah, but that was abandoned again with the incorporation of Jerusalem under David.

In the valleys of the north (Megiddo and Beth-shean), Canaanite culture extends further into the Iron Age, and only from the tenth century onwards do Israelite settlements appear to any great extent. There are again Early Iron Age settlements in Lower and Upper Galilee, and in Gilead. A special characteristic of these areas is that the earliest settlements occur on the tops of hills, and only later descend to the valleys. Here, too, there are hardly any Late Bronze Age cities.

Virtually all these villages were built in places where hitherto there had been no settlement. There are a few villages on abandoned tells which had been settled in the Middle Bronze or even in the Early Bronze Age (Ai; Arad; Malhata, coord.152-069), but were abandoned for a long time. Finally there is also the transition from the Late Bronze Age city to the Iron Age village (Hazor, also Megiddo).

These villages show a series of common characteristics. The basis of their livelihood is in all cases agriculture and cattle breeding, the latter of both sheep and goats and in some cases of larger animals (oxen, etc.). The villages are unfortified, but there are settlements with an outer ring of houses for defence, both from the eleventh century BC in the south (e.g. Tell Masos, with external entrances; Tell es-Seba'; Tell Esdar, coord.147-064) and also in the north (Megiddo; Hurvath 'Abot in Upper Galilee, coord.193-276). It is already possible to see the construction of terraces in villages in the hill-country. In some settlements the earliest stratum is formed by pits; this is the case in Tel Masos, Tell es-Seba' and also Hazor. Most villages are small and had one or two hundred inhabitants. This would perhaps represent a whole family, a clan. Tell Masos, with an estimated 1500 inhabitants, is an exception. The recently discovered Hurvath 'Aboth also seems to be larger than usual.

Houses with free-standing pillars in the courtyard but also on and in the walls to strengthen the construction are typical of the architecture of these villages. It used to be assumed that this method of building, together with the plan of a three- or four-room house, was a characteristic of the Israelite method of building. However, possibly there is a Late Bronze Age forerunner of it. A further architectural characteristic of these villages is the numerous silos in open spaces between the houses.

The pottery found in these villages is restricted to a few forms. Cooking pots, storage jars and *pithoi* make up about eighty per cent of all types. Three regions can be distinguished which have a varied repertory of forms: Upper Galilee with connections with Tyre; the central hill-country;and the northern Negeb, but they all link up with earlier traditions of pottery and with the pottery of neighbouring regions. On the whole the pottery is cruder and technically less good. Whether the so-called collared rim jar was really a product of Israelite society (as has been assumed since Albright) has recently been rightly disputed.

Documents with alphabetic writing have been found in some of these villages, above all the alphabet of Işbet Şarţah (coord.146-168). There is a tendency to see this as an expression of an egalitarian society in which the democratization of education has advanced.

The result of this brief account may be said to be that a vigorous activity of settlement can be seen throughout the country at the beginning of the Iron Age. Nothing can yet be said on the basis of archaeological evidence about the origin of these settlers or the ethnic groups to which they belonged. However, we may note that the settlers had previously lived in settled communities rather than as nomads. The way in which the settlements developed geographically is not clear. All this implies that the 'settlement' was not a unitary process but must have been much more complex. That also means that none of the models of the process of settlement is adequate in itself to explain the process of the settlement, but rather a combination of them all is needed. If we are to achieve further clarification, new investigations must be carried out. It remains amazing how quickly in this new society people could come to worship a common God, YHWH.

Select Bibliography

On I.1

W.F.Albright, *The Archaeology of Palestine*, Harmondsworth [3]1956
K.M.Kenyon, *Archaeology in the Holy Land*, London [2]1965
S.M.Paul and W.G.Dever, *Biblical Archaeology*, Jerusalem 1973

H.Donner, *Einführung in die biblische Landes- und Altertumskunde*, Darmstadt 1976

V.Fritz, 'Bibelwissenschaft I. Altes Testament, I/1. Archäologie (Alter Orient und Palästina)', *TRE* VI, 1980, 316-45

Y.Aharoni, *The Archaeology of the Land of Israel*, Philadelphia and London 1982

Academic journals

ADAJ	*Annual of the Department of Antiquities of Jordan*
BA	*Biblical Archaeologist*
BASOR	*Bulletin of the American Schools of Oriental Research*
BAR	*Biblical Archaeology Review*
IEJ	*Israel Exploration Journal*
Levant	*Levant, Journal of the British School of Archaeology in Jerusalem*
ZDPV	*Zeitschrift des Deutschen Palästina Vereins*

On I.2

1. H.Donner (cf.I.1), 64-72 (and bibliography)
2. M.Avi-Yonah and E.Stern (eds.), *Encyclopedia of Archaeological Excavations in the Holy Land I-IV*, Jerusalem 1975-78

E.K.Vogel, 'Bibliography of the Holy Land Sites'
I, *HUCA* 42, 1971, 1-96
II, *HUCA* 52, 1981, 1-92
Elenchus biblographicus biblicus. Archaeologia biblica

3. K.Galling (ed.), *Biblisches Reallexikon*, Tübingen ²1977

B.Reicke and L.Rost (eds.), *Biblisch-Historisches Handwörterbuch*, Göttingen 1-3, 1963-1966; 4, 1979

4. E.Linder and A.Raban, *Marine Archaeology*, London 1975

On I.3

R.Amiran, *Ancient Pottery of the Holy Land*, Jerusalem 1969

Y.Aharoni, Z.Herzog, M.Kochavi, S.Moshkovitz and A.F.Rainey, 'Methods of Recording and Documenting', in Y.Aharoni (ed.), *Beer-Sheba* I, Tel Aviv 1973, 119-32

W.G.Dever and H.D.Lance (eds.), *A Manual of Field Excavations. Handbook for Field Archaeologists*, Cincinnati, New York, Los Angeles and Jerusalem, 1978

D.Brothwell and E.Higgs (eds.), *Science in Archaeology. A Survey of Progress and Research*, London ²1969

B.Hrouda (ed.), *Methoden der Archäologie. Eine Einführung in ihre naturwissenschaftlichen Techniken*, Munich 1978

P.Ihm, *Statistik in der Archäologie*, Bonn 1978, Archaeo-Physika, Vol.9

F.G.Maier, *Neue Wege in die alte Welt. Methoden der modernen Archäologie*, Hamburg 1977

N.K.Gottwald, *The Tribes of Yahweh. A Sociology of the Religion of Liberated Israel 1250-1050 BCE*, Maryknoll and London 1979

F.Crüsemann, *Der Widerstand gegen das Königtum. Die antiköniglicher Texte des Alten Testaments und der Kampf um den frühen israelitischen Staat*, WMANT 49, Neukirchen-Vluyn 1978

C.Schäfer-Lichtenberger, *Stadt und Eidgenossenschaft im Alten Testament. Eine Auseinandersetzung mit Max Webers Studie 'Das antike Judentum'*, BZAW 156, Berlin and New York 1983

On I.4

F.Crüsemann, 'Alttestamentliche Exegese und Archäologie. Erwägungen angesichts des gegenwärtigen Methodenstreits in der Archäologie Palästinas', *ZAW* 91, 1979, 177-93

E.Noort, *Biblisch-archäologische Hermeneutik und alttestamentliche Exegese*, Kampen Cahiers No.39, Kampen 1979

Y.Aharoni, *The Land of the Bible. A Historical Geography*, Philadelphia and London ²1979

D.Baly, *Geographical Companion to the Bible*, London 1963

J.B.Pritchard (ed.), *Ancient Near Eastern Texts relating to the Old Testament*, Princeton ³1969

J.B.Pritchard (ed.), *The Ancient Near East. Supplementary Texts and Pictures Relating to the Old Testament*, Princeton 1969

O.Kaiser (ed.), *Texte aus der Umwelt des Alten Testaments*, Gütersloh 1982ff.

On II.1-3

V.Fritz, *Israel in der Wüste. Traditionsgeschichtliche Untersuchung der Wüstenüberlieferung des Jahwisten*, Marburg 1970

M. Weippert, *The Settlement of the Israelite Tribes in Palestine*, SBT II 21, London 1971

On II.4

A.Mazar, 'The "Bull Site" – An Iron Age I Open Cult Place', *BASOR* 247, 1982, 27-42

J.Callaway, 'Excavating Ai (et-tell): 1964-1972', *BA* 39, 1976, 18-30

B.Mazar, 'Giloh: An Early Israelite Settlement Site near Jerusalem', *IEJ* 31, 1981, 1-36

Z.Gal, *The Lower Galilee in the Iron Age* (unpublished PhD thesis), Tel Aviv 1982 (in Hebrew)

S.Mittmann, *Beiträge zur Siedlungsgeschichte und Territorialgeschichte des nördlichen Ostjordanlandes*, ADPV, Wiesbaden 1970

V.Fritz and A.Kempinski (eds.), *Ergebnisse der Ausgrabungen auf der Hirbet el Mšāš (Tell Masos) 1972-1975*, ADPV, Wiesbaden 1983

M.M.Ibrahim, 'The Collared Rim Jar of the Early Iron Age', in *Archaeology in the Levant. Festschrift K.M.Kenyon*, ed. R.Moorey and P.Parr, Warminster 1978, 116-26

A.Demsky, 'A Proto-Canaanite Abcedary dating from the Period of the

Judges and its Implications for the History of the Alphabet', *TA* 4, 1977, 14-27

The Chronology of the First Temple Period
A Presentation and Evaluation of the Sources

H. Tadmor

A. The Sources and Their Value

1. Chronology and chronography

Dating events according to the regnal years of the current monarch was accepted practice throughout the ancient Near East – in Egypt, Babylonia and Assyria[1] – as well as in Judah and Israel. A unified counting system to be used by every city and county in the state is essential to centralized administration. One can therefore assume that from the very inception of the united monarchy in Israel, especially under the rule of David and Solomon, the foundation was laid for a single reckoning system to be shared by both the civil and the military administration. The reckoning would naturally be made according to regnal years, inasmuch as the system of reckoning by era known in Greece or in Rome[2] was foreign to the people of the ancient Near East until the Hellenistic age.

Ostraca of the monarchic period, such as those from Samaria and Lachish, refer simply to the regnal year, e.g. 'in the ninth year',[3] without mentioning the king's name, as do the Egyptian ostraca from the New Kingdom. In official documents written on parchment or papyrus – which have not survived – details were probably listed in full: the king's name, the regnal year, the month, and the day. The ancient chronographers summarized chronological data in extensive chronographic compositions such as 'Chronicles of the Kings of Judah' or 'Chronicles of the Kings of Israel', which are referred to in the book of Kings. The exact nature of these works remains unclear, but they probably recorded not only the length of each king's reign but also his age upon accession to the throne, the name of his father, and in Judah the name of the queen-mother.

After the division of the united monarchy, the chronographers supplement their extensive compositions with synchronisms. Thus the accession year of a king of Israel was juxtaposed to the regnal year of the contemporary Judaean monarch (henceforth, Judaean synchronism), and the year of accession of a king of Judah was juxtaposed to the regnal year of the contemporary king of Israel (henceforth, Israelite synchronism). Because the chronographers considered the separate Hebrew kingdoms two divisions of a single people, whose histories intertwined, they recorded the chronological data synchronistically. Similarly, in Mesopotamia during the Neo-Assyrian period, the intricate connections between the Assyrian empire and Babylonia gave rise to synchronistic literature, the foremost example of which was the 'Babylonian Chronicle'.[4] This work narrated the main events in Babylonia from the first half of the eighth century onward (dating them by the current Babylonian monarchy) and integrated those Assyrian and Elamite kings directly or indirectly involved in Babylonian affairs. The narration takes the form of a synchronous chronicle.

At the end of the First Commonwealth and especially during the Babylonian exile, chronographers composed extensive chronographic works in which they attempted to forge a full and continuous chronological scheme for the entire monarchic period. The exilic redactor of the book of Kings had at his disposal not only extensive chronographic works but apparently older documents, like chronicles and king-lists.[5]

Since the Northern Kingdom had disappeared a century and a half prior to the redaction of the book of Kings, the Israelite chronicles probably did not survive intact for such an extended period. The redactor was often unable to find required data in the available sources and was therefore compelled to add certain details – such as Israelite synchronisms – on the basis of his own calculations or approximations. Because these calculated dates did not always suit the heterogeneous evidence in the sources, they gave rise to some contradictions (fairly common in the Israelite synchronistic data, but relatively rare in the data about the Israelite regnal years). The Judaean data in the hands of the redactor seem to have been more reliable, so that the number of errors in the transmission of the chronological data is relatively small.

Although it is still debated whether the ancient chronological material used by the redactor of the book of Kings was drawn from a 'canonical' corpus, the details of which had already been harmonized, the numerous inconsistencies in the chronological data in Kings seem to indicate that the redactor drew upon divergent sources, often conflicting. Certain passages derive from ancient chronicles and are incorporated verbatim into the book of Kings. These preserve authentic chronological information with which the editor did not tamper. Finally, there is a certain validity to the conjecture that in a significant number of places there have been scribal errors in transmission. Changes in system of writing numerals, as evidenced in Hebrew epigraphic documents, might over long periods have readily given rise to errors.

2. *The history of research*

The study of biblical chronology did not start with modern biblical scholarship: struggles with the contradictory dates in the book of Kings are ancient. Thus in several versions of the Septuagint in Kings – the Codex Vaticanus (= version B of the Septuagint) and the Lucianic recension –

traces of a chronological system different from the one in the Masoretic text (= MT) are distinguishable.

It has been suggested that this residue (in particular the synchronisms between Jehoshaphat and his son Jehoram and the Kings of the Omride Dynasty) reflects the *Vorlage* of the Septuagint, which is considered more reliable than the Masoretic Text in matters of chronology.[6] This question, however, is still unsettled. The problems which arise from the Septuagint version are complex and it has been argued that the Masoretic Text is in fact original and to be preferred, the variants in the Septuagint being no more than later attempts to harmonize the contradictory dates in the Septuagint's Hebrew *Vorlage*.[7] Josephus, in his attempt to settle the contradictory dates, suggested a system of his own, different in certain elements from MT.[8] Furthermore, the authors of the rabbinic chronograph *Seder Olam Rabbah* encountered difficulties in reconciling the contradictory biblical data of the MT.[9] So, too, the mediaeval exegetes Rashi, Ibn-Ezra, and Gersonides offered harmonistic attempts to reconcile the obvious contradictions.

From the middle of the nineteenth century on, biblical scholarship has repeatedly delved into the chronological questions of the reigns of the kings of Judah and Israel.[10] The early investigators preferred to use the regnal years rather than synchronisms; twentieth-century scholars tend to prefer synchronisms. Even here the problem has been tackled in several ways, with a general inclination toward the Judaean synchronisms rather than the Israelite.

The fact is that none of the systems thus far suggested – even the most conservative textually – have succeeded in preserving simultaneously both the synchronisms and the regnal year data. Those who try to uphold the maximum number of biblical chronological data are usually forced into far-fetched assumptions about the possibility of long periods of co-regencies or into other conjectures often devoid of scriptural support.

Opinions also vary about how regnal years were reckoned (below, 4). The most extreme conjecture is that the reckoning system was subject to several changes even within the time-span of a single reign.[11] Such an approach is often motivated by a desire to verify and harmonize as many biblical dates as possible.

3. Questions of methodology

The point of departure for the present study is the assumption that the data concerning regnal years in Israel and Judah does not represent the official reckoning current during the king's reign, and here the present author differs from prevalent systems of biblical chronology. We are confronted instead with data that has already been edited – sometimes painstakingly – by the editors of the chronological framework of Kings. Consequently, assessment of this data for a modern chronologist is entirely dependent on a proper evaluation of the methods employed by those ancient chronologists who prepared that framework.

Before undertaking the analysis of the ancient chronologists' *modus operandi* (below, 6), one must clarify a number of questions inherent in any discussion of dating systems: What type of calendar was used in the biblical period? Was the year a solar year, as in Egypt, or was the calendar lunar-solar as in Mesopotamia (in which the solar year, with 365 days, was adjusted to the twelve-month lunar year by the intercalation of a thirteenth month every few years)? On the one hand the term for month *yrḥ* (moon), or *ḥdš* (new), indicates that the basic unit of the biblical calendar was lunar. On the other hand there is no doubt that the major festivals of the year – the Feast of Unleavened Bread in the month of Abib, Pentecost at the time of the wheat harvest, and the Ingathering Festival 'at the turn of the year' (Ex.34.22) – were determined by the seasons and the agricultural cycle. One can conclude therefore that the calendar in biblical Israel was a lunar-solar one. Nonetheless, we do not know how these two elements – the 365-day solar year and 354-day lunar year – were harmonized. Was it by intercalating a month, as in Babylonia, or by adding ten days at the end of every twelve-month cycle, as in Egypt, or by some other method?[12]

4. The reckoning of regnal years

How were the regnal years reckoned and, in particular, how was the year of accession counted?

Let us first define the term 'regnal year'. Does it refer to an actual calendrical year, counted from the day of the king's ascension to the throne (or from the day of coronation) to the corresponding day in the following year? Or does it refer to the nearest calendrical year following accession or coronation, counted from one New Year's day to the next?

In Mesopotamia and Egypt the regnal year generally coincided with the calendar year. During the New Kingdom in Egypt (the Eighteenth to Twentieth Dynasties), however, regnal years were reckoned from the day of the Pharaoh's coronation.[13] While there is no direct evidence as to which of these two methods was used in Judah and Israel, there are clear, although indirect, indications that in the system used by the editors of Kings the regnal years of every king coincided with the calendar year. The advantage of this system was that both the royal chronographers and the king's officials in the various branches of state administration would have no difficulty in determining when a regnal year began, since New Year's Day – whether in the agricultural or cultic calendar – was simultaneously 'the New Year for kings' in the official reckoning.

The question to be answered next is: How did the king count the year in which he ascended the throne?

The two methods of counting a king's initial year in the ancient Near East were 'post-dating' and 'ante-dating'.[14] In the post-dating system the king's first year begins not with his accession to the throne, but with the following New Year. For purposes of chronological reckoning, the part of the year from the day the king was enthroned until the next New Year was not counted for the new king (i.e., it was a 'zero year', since it was reckoned as the remainder of the last year of the previous king).

In the ante-dating system the first year of the king was reckoned from the day the king ascended the throne or sometimes from the day of the official coronation. In this system it was possible for a king who actually reigned a very short time, e.g. only one month – half before the New Year and half after – to be credited with a reign of 'two years', since the first two weeks would be considered the 'first year', and the second two, from New Year's Day on, the 'second year' of the reign. When setting up a continuous chronological scheme we must reduce by one year the total number of regnal years counted according to the ante-dating system, since the last incomplete year of the king's reign must be included in the regnal years of his successor.[15] Otherwise the same calendar year would be credited to both the old and new kings. In the post-dating system, however, the number of a king's official regnal years was identical with the number of years he actually ruled.

The ante-dating system was current in Egypt during the Old and Middle Kingdoms and reappeared at the time of the Twenty-Sixth Dynasty. The post-dating – or as some scholars designate it, 'the accession year' – system was practised only in Babylonia and fell out of use with the rise of the Hellenistic empires. It grew out of the custom of naming each year of a king's reign. In this system the king's accession year had a special term: 'the year of the start of the reign' (in Akkadian, *šanat rēš šarrūti*), his year 1 beginning only with the following New Year, at Nisan.[16] In Assyria, however, years were counted by the names of specially designated eponyms (*limmu*),[17] and hence the question of counting the accession year separately did not usually arise. The Assyrian royal inscriptions, starting from the middle of the ninth century, counted regnal years according to *palū*, 'regnal period, term of office'. But this count, introduced under Babylonian influence, did not always coincide with the count according to regnal years.[18]

Post-dating enjoyed wide use in Syro-Palestine as a result of the spread of Babylonian administrative practices during the Neo-Babylonian and Persian periods. It is mentioned in II Kings 25.27 as the time when Evil-Merodach king of Babylon freed Jehoiachin from prison: *bišᵉnat molkō*, i.e. during his accession year or *šanat rēš šarrūti* in Babylonian terminology.[19]

For earlier periods, however, it can be assumed that Israel and Judah employed the ante-dating system, since it was both simpler and more natural than the unconventional post-dating. Nevertheless, the chronological data beginning with Manasseh or Amon, kings of Judah, can be suitably explained only by the post-dating system. The uncommon use of post-dating can be accounted for in one of two ways: 1. Amon, or his father Manasseh, introduced the Babylonian post-dating system into Judah; or 2. even though ante-dating was actually used in Judah throughout its history as a kingdom the exilic chronologist edited the data (below, 6), and adjusted the regnal years in the period between Manasseh or Amon and Zedekiah according to the post-dating system (below, B.4).

5. The 'Royal New Year' in the biblical period

A tradition from the Second Temple period (Mishnah *Rosh ha-Shanah* 1.1) distinguished between 'New Year for kings', i.e. the royal New Year, and 'New Year for years', i.e. the calendrical New Year: the former in Nisan and the latter in Tishri. This tradition seems to have reflected the practice of the first century CE. The Hasmoneans, King Herod, and the leaders of the First Revolt against Rome reckoned their years from Nisan, as had apparently been the case in Judah in the biblical period (see below). In the course of the first century CE, however, and especially during the first half of the second century, counting the years from Tishri in matters of economy and religion, prevailed over that of Nisan. Since then 1 Tishri has been the only New Year in the Jewish tradition.[20]

Modern scholarship ever since the end of the nineteenth century has been divided on the question of the start of the year in Judah and Israel in biblical times and the date of the royal New Year. Some hold that only one calendar was used in Israel and Judah, which ran from Nisan to Adar. Others maintain that the oldest calendar in Judah and Israel began in Tishri and that counting from the spring (Nisan) was the result of Assyrian or Babylonian influence. Many believe that the royal New Year in Judah and its counterpart in Israel were half a year apart, but even on this point opinion differs: according to some, the Judaean kings counted from Tishri, and the Israelite kings from Nisan; according to others, they counted from Nisan in Judah, from Tishri in Israel.

The evidence in our sources points to the fact that in ancient Israel there actually were two New Years, the one in the spring – in the first month – and the other in the fall – in the seventh month (in the northern kingdom perhaps in the eighth month; cf. I Kings 12.33). The Gezer calendar, which lists the farmer's yearly agricultural activities, opens with *yrḥw 'sp*, 'the season of ingathering' – the end of Elul Tishri, or the beginning of Marheshvan. The terminology of Ex.23.16, *wᵉhad hā-'āsip bᵉṣē't ha-šānā*, and of Ex.34.22, *wᵉhag hā-'āsip tᵉqupat ha-šānā*, presupposes an agricultural year which begins, or ends, with the Festival of the Ingathering in the fall. Other traditions in the Pentateuch (Ex.12.2; Lev.23-24; Num.23.16; 33.35; Deut.16.1) speak of the month of Abib as the first month. In fact, the months in the biblical period are always counted from the spring. The point can be illustrated from Jer.36.22: in the ninth month the king sat in his winter palace in front of a blazing hearth.

At the same time, it can be conjectured that during and after the united monarchy there were several reckoning systems used in different spheres of life; in commerce and agriculture it was customary to count from the fall, while in the cult – especially in the traditions of the Jerusalem priesthood – it was accepted that the year commenced in the spring. The practice of counting the New Year from the spring as in Mesopotamia has always been followed by the people of Israel, whereas the agricultural year, in the autumn, was taken over from the ancient local tradition of pre-conquest Canaan.

We can now return to the question posed at the outset: When did the kings of Judah and Israel reckon the beginning of their regnal years? Although explicit evidence is exceedingly rare, there are a few indications that in Judah the years were counted from the spring. Thus in Jer.46.2, the battle of Carchemish, when the Egyptian army was defeated by the Babylonians, is dated in the fourth year of Jehoiakim (605 BCE, and see below, the table of fixed dates). One can deduce that at the end of the seventh century BCE regnal years began in the first month of spring.[21] Since reckoning customs tend to be extremely conservative, we can safely assume that even prior to Jehoiakim Judaean kings counted from the spring. This would, in turn, correspond with the practice of the Jerusalem priesthood, mentioned above, whose year started in the month of Abib.

On the other hand, we have no data about the regnal New Year in the Northern Kingdom, and there is disagreement among scholars as to whether it was in the spring or the autumn. However, there is indirect evidence that New Year in Judah did not coincide with that in Ephraim; it is to be found in II Kings 15.8,10; Zechariah, who reigned for six months, ascended the throne in the thirty-eighth year of Uzziah of Judah and died in Uzziah's thirty-ninth year. During these six months a new regnal year had therefore commenced in Judah. At the same time, however, no new year had begun in Israel;[22] if it had, Zechariah's six-month reign would have been counted as two years (cf. the brief reigns of Nadab son of Jeroboam I and Elah son of Baasha of Israel). May one conclude that this half-year discrepancy in matters connected with the regnal New Year existed not only in the days of Uzziah and Zechariah but throughout the period of the kingdoms of Judah and Israel? If indeed, as already noted, the kings of Judah counted their years from the spring and if there is a half-year discrepancy, we are forced to conclude that the Ephraimite kings reckoned their regnal years from the autumn (either from the seventh or the eighth month).[23]

6. The editorial method of the ancient chronologist

We turn to the main problem presented at the outset of our discussion (above, 3): What was the *modus operandi* of the ancient chronologist in constructing the chronological framework of the book of Kings? We believe that he must have used the standard procedures employed by Mesopotamian chronologists in respect to the rounding off of years.[24] Since a main interest of this editor was to synchronize the reigns of the kings of Judah and Israel, he was naturally concerned only with the number of full regnal years. If his sources reported that a certain king of Judah reigned x years plus y months (e.g., David in Hebron: seven years and six months, II Sam.5.5), he would have had to delete the number of months in excess of full years (i.e. the last incomplete year), and count only the complete years. Exactly the same practice would be followed by a modern chronologist who sets out to arrange a synchronistic scheme on the basis of regnal data calculated by ante-dating.

The result is that all of the kings of Judah and Israel, whose regnal years have been rounded off by the editor, actually reigned (according to their own count) one year more than is attributed to them in Kings. Consequently, Rehoboam reigned seventeen years and x months and died in the eighteenth year of his reign; and since Rehoboam and Jeroboam ascended their respective thrones in the same year, Rehoboam died in Jeroboam's eighteenth, not his seventeenth, year. This is indeed recorded in the synchronism in I Kings 15.1: 'Now in the eighteenth year of King Jeroboam the son of Nebat, Abijam began to reign over Judah.' Moreover, the assumption that the editor deleted the extra months, leaving the number of complete years, solves two major chronological problems: the ten regnal years of Menahem of Israel and the single year of Ahaziah. According to the synchronisms, Menahem began to reign in the thirty-ninth year of Uzziah, king of Judah, and died in Uzziah's fiftieth year (II Kings 15.17, 23). Hence, Menahem reigned not ten but eleven or even twelve years (counting by the ante-dating system). The best way to preserve both the figure 'ten' and the synchronisms of II Kings would be to assume that Menahem reigned actually ten years plus x months (i.e., eleven years in his own official count) and that the ancient editor, faithful to his method, deleted the extra number of months fixing Menahem's total to ten full years.

The other difficulty solved by the present assumption involves the single regnal year of Ahaziah of Judah. According to the system of ante-dating, if his reign terminated before a New Year, it would have been considered a zero for synchronistic purposes, in which case the chronologist would have reported the exact number of months of that incomplete year. If his reign had extended beyond one New Year – i.e., into his second official year – he would have been credited with two years. We therefore assume that the editor found in his sources that Ahaziah had reigned one year and a few months, but, in keeping with his system of rounding off, he deleted the number of months and credited the king with one year (II Kings 8.26).

What were the sources used by our editor? It stands to reason that the major portion of the material from Judah consisted of official chronicles, or gleanings from them, which lasted both full regnal years and additional months. By contrast, the Israelite material at his disposal was partly original, partly reworked. It would seem that for the period between Jeroboam and the end of the Omride dynasty, only data about complete regnal years reached him. That is to say, in his source the number of regnal years of the Israelite kings had already been rounded off and only whole years were listed. These numbers were somewhat similar: Jeroboam, twenty-two years; Nadab, two years; Baasha, twenty-four years; Elah, two years; Omri, twelve years; Ahab, twenty-two years; Ahaziah, two years; Joram, twelve years. Rounding off numbers according to cycles of 2 + 22 and 12 years, which indeed was rather close to the actual number of regnal years, was resorted to, it seems, as a mnemonic device (or even may have resulted from contamination). Accordingly the editor did not tamper with these numbers, which had already been rounded off, even though each one of them was one year higher than the actual number of regnal years. The Judaean synchronisms for this period fit this assumption. On the other hand, for the period after the rise of Jehu our editor's data seem to have been more exact. Here he consistently kept to his method of rounding off, so that Jehu's twenty-eight years and Jehoash's sixteen years were in fact twenty-eight years + x months and sixteen years + y months, which in the ante-dating system were counted officially as twenty-nine years and seventeen years respectively.

In contrast with his standard working procedure, our chronologist was precise when dealing with the kings who reigned for less than a year. Here his methods were those of the compilers of the Babylonian kinglists:[25] he recorded the actual number of regnal years, months, or even days. Thus, he recorded for Zimri seven days, Zechariah six months, and Shallum one month, giving Jehoahaz and Jehoiachin of Judah three months each. These figures must certainly derive from chronicles or official records and bring us one step closer to the no longer extant chronological sources.

7. Co-regencies

One other principle which guided our chronologist was the assumption that during the entire period of the Israelite monarchy there were no co-regencies: i.e., the heir to the throne serving as regent during his father's lifetime counted this period as part of his own reign. Our sources do point, however, to periods of co-regency: Jotham 'judged the "people of the land"' during the lifetime of Uzziah his father (II Kings 15.5)[26] and Uzziah apparently was regent for fifteen years during the lifetime of his father Amaziah (II Kings 14.17).[27] Whether the chronologist knew about these and other co-regencies but decided to ignore them, or whether he did not know about them at all – as was probably the case – it is clear that the method he chose has created serious discrepancies in the chronological scheme of the book of Kings.

The assumption that there actually were co-regencies in both Judah and Israel – in itself logical and clearly alluded to in the sources – does much to solve a few of the more serious contradictions.[28]

B. Determining the chronological scheme

1. Fixed dates

The chronological scheme of the monarchic age divides naturally into three periods: (a) From Jeroboam until the rebellion of Jehu; (b) From Jehu until the fall of Samaria; (c) From the fall of Samaria until the destruction of the First Temple. Inasmuch as the chronological data from the last period are the most certain, our chronological considerations begin with the late period and then work backwards.[29]

It is only natural that information from extra-biblical sources will provide absolute dates and serve as 'anchor points'. The following table lists twenty external synchronisms for the First Temple period,[30] drawn on the whole from Assyrian and Babylonian sources. The dates are chronologically absolute (in the Julian calendar), since Assyrian and Babylonian chronologies of the first millennium BCE are based on continuous listing of years down to the Hellenistic and Roman periods, verifiable by astronomical reckoning.[31]

TABLE OF DATES

Event	Synchronism*	Year	Biblical Reference
1. Ahab the Israelite participates in the battle of Qarqar as one of twelve kings of Syria	6th year of Shalmaneser III	853 BCE	—
2. Jehu 'the son of Omri' pays tribute to Assyria	18th year of Shalmaneser III	841 BCE	—
3. Jehoash, king of Israel, pays tribute to Adad-nirari III		796 BCE	—
4. Menahem, king of Israel, pays tribute to Pul (Tiglath-pileser III), king of Assyria	8th year of Tiglath-pileser III	738 BCE	II Kings 15.19–20
5. Campaign of Tiglath-pileser III to Philistia. Ahaz (Jehoahaz) pays tribute ot Assyria		734 BCE	—
6. Conquest and exile of the inhabitants of Galilee and Transjordania by Tiglath-pileser III, during the reign of Pekah		733–732 BCE	II Kings 15.26
7. Death of Pekah; Hosea ascends the throne		732 BCE	—
8. Tiglath-pileser II receives tribute from Hoshea during his campaign in Chaldaea	731 BCE		—
9. 9th year of Hoshea; Hoshea taken captive by Shalmaneser V; siege of Samaria begins		724 BCE	II Kings 17.4–5
10. Capture of Samaria by Shalmaneser V		722 BCE	II Kings 17.6; 18.10
11. Exile of Israelites by Sargon II	2nd year of Sargon	720 BCE	
12. Sargon's campaign to Ashdod	9th–10th years of Sargon	713–712 BCE	Isa. 20.1–2

Event	Synchronism*	Year	Biblical Reference
13. Sennacherib's campaign to Judah	4th year of Sennacherib (his 3rd campaign)	701 BCE	II Kings 18.13:Isa. 36
14. 31st year of Josiah; campaign of Necho; the battle of Megiddo; the reign of Jehoahaz	18th year of Nabopolassar	609 BCE	II Kings 23.29
15. 4th year of Jehoiakim; defeat of Egypt at Carchemish by Nebuchadnezzar	21st year of Nabopolassar	605 BCE	II Chron. 35.20; Jer. 46 (between Nisan and Ab)
16. Capture of Jerusalem by Nebuchadnezzar	7th year of Nebuchadnezzar II	598/7 BCE	
17. Exile of Jehoiachin and of 10,000 men	8th year of Nebuchadnezzar II	597 BCE	II Kings 24.12–14;
18. 10th year of Nebuchadnezzar II	18th year of Nebuchadnezzar II	587 BCE	Jer. 32.1
19. 11th year of Zedekiah; Destruction of the Temple	19th year of Nebuchadnezzar II	7th of Ab, 586 BCE	II Kings 25.8
20. Release of Jehoiachin from prison in 37th year of his captivity	Accession of Evil-merodach	25th or 27th of Adar 561 BCE	Jer. 52.31

* All dates are given in terms of the Assyro-Babylonian year, which began in Nisan (April-May) and ended in Adar (March-April).

2. From the fall of Samaria until the destruction of the First Temple

This is a period of 134½ years, according to the regnal year date for Judaean kings which extends from the sixth year of Hezekiah (inclusive) until the eleventh year of Zedekiah. The half year – three months of Jehoahaz and three months of Jehoiachin – is taken up (in the post-dating system) in the reckoning of complete years, leaving only 134 years. The period is divided into 112 regnal years, from the conquest of Samaria (sixth year of Hezekiah) until the death of Josiah, and twenty-two from the death of Josiah until the destruction of the temple in the eleventh year of Zedekiah.

The dates of the last four kings of Judah – Jehoahaz, Jehoiakim, Jehoiachin and Zedekiah – are determined by the synchronisms between Jehoiakim and Zedekiah and Nebuchadnezzar king of Babylon (see the table above):

Death of Josiah	609
Reign of Jehoahaz and accession of Jehoiakim	609
Reign of Jehoiakim	608/7-598/7
Reign of Jehoiachin and accession of Zedekiah	597

It is difficult to determine the exact date of the destruction of the temple.

The dates 587 and 586[32] have been proposed. Since the corresponding passage in the Babylonian Chronicle which tells of the conquest of Jerusalem and the destruction of the temple is not extant,[33] there is as yet no generally accepted conclusion. The question involves yet another, more difficult, problem: When was the exile of Jehoiachin and when exactly did Zedekiah start counting regnal years – from the spring of 597, the autumn of 597, or only from the spring of 596? The present writer, who adheres to the view that Judah counted the years from the spring, prefers to place the destruction of Jerusalem in 586 in agreement with II Kings 25.8, which synchronizes the eleventh and last year of Zedekiah with the nineteenth year of Nebuchadnezzar (which began 1 Nisan 596). Zedekiah's first year would accordingly begin in Nisan 596, rather than in Nisan 597, immediately after Jehoiachin's exile. The explanation offered for this postponement of one year is that while people were being carried to exile (and no doubt the 10,000 people were carried off *after* 1 Nisan 597), Zedekiah would have refrained from celebrating his accession and hence reckoned his regnal years from the spring of 596. The shortcoming of this suggestion is that it postulated an extremely unusual accession year of 12 plus x months. Therefore one of the following alternatives might be considered: (*a*) that the equation of Zedekiah's eleventh year with Nebuchadnezzar's nineteenth is not reliable (and there is not sufficient reason to assume that), or (*b*) that it was the ancient chronographer who counted Zedekiah's regnal years from (spring) 596 rather than from (spring) 597. In any event, unless additional evidence is unearthed, 586 seems to be a preferable date for the destruction of the Temple.

Since Josiah's death in his thirty-first regnal year has been reckoned at 609 BCE, his first regnal year must have been 639/8 BCE. Between 722 BCE, the date of the fall of Samaria, and 639/8 BCE, the start of Josiah's reign, 83 years elapsed. But the sum of years of Judaean kings from the sixth year of Hezekiah (the year of the conquest of Samaria, according to II Kings 18.9f.) until the first year of Josiah is only 81 years: 24 years of Hezekiah (from his sixth until his twenty-ninth year), fifty-five years of Manasseh, two years of Amon, all according to the post-dating system.

Several solutions to this discrepancy have been suggested:

1. The total number of regnal years of Manasseh and/or of Amon as transmitted by MT is corrupt. Manasseh should be credited with fifty-seven years and/or Amon with four years. All the ancient versions and translations, however, support the figures given in MT.

2. Alternatively it has been suggested[34] that Hezekiah was co-regent during the last two regnal years of his father Ahaz but these two years were not included in his twenty-nine regnal years. The synchronisms which place the start of the siege of Samaria in Hezekiah's fourth year and its destruction in his sixth are numbered from his co-regency. This suggestion raises more difficulties than it solves, especially as it does not accord with placing the death of Ahaz in the year 727, the last year of Tiglath-pileser III (see below, 3).

We propose yet a third solution, in line with our assumption that the ancient editor rounded off years (above, 6): The twenty-nine years of Hezekiah, the fifty-five of Manasseh and the two of Amon represent only the complete regnal years of these kings. Each of them reigned a few additional months which amount, when added together, to two years. Our chronologist deleted, according to his practice, the extra months and recorded only full years.

Another point to be considered is that the regnal years of the last kings of Judah, beginning with Manasseh, were reckoned by post-dating. Was it actually employed during the reign of Manasseh (as a result of Mesopotamian influence?) or did the exilic chronologist apply the post-dating system to the last kings of Judah, starting with Manasseh or Amon? (If so, it would seem that our chronologist had already at his disposal a chronological framework – in the ante-dating system – for the pre-Manasseh period.) For the present, the problem must remain unsolved.

3. From the rebellion of Jehu until the fall of Samaria

If Hezekiah came to the throne in 727/6 BCE, then between this date and the rebellion of Jehu in 842, 115 years would have elapsed. But the total number of regnal years of the kings of Judah and Israel during this period exceeds 115. In Israel the total is 140, a twenty-five year discrepancy, and in Judah 159, a forty-four year discrepancy.

To account for these discrepancies one must assume either that the numbers in MT are corrupt or that some of the kings were co-regents, sharing power and authority during their fathers' liftetime. These possibilities are not mutually exclusive.

Reckoning in both Israel and Judah was done by the antedating system (above, 4). According to our approach the number of regnal years recorded in Kings for this period includes only the number of years allocated to him in Kings (e.g. Jehu died in his twenty-ninth year, Jehoahaz in his eighteenth, Jehoash in his seventeenth, Menahem in his eleventh, etc.).

The absolute date fixed by external synchronism for the end of this period is the fall of Samaria. Even here, however, scholarly opinion is divided. In the past it was customary to accept at face value Sargon's claim in the Khorsabad Annals that he had conquered Samaria and exiled its inhabitants at the beginning of his reign, during his *šanat rēš šarruti*, i.e. between December 722 (or January 721) and April 721. This entry in the Annals is contradicted, however, by a more reliable inscription, according to which Sargon appears not to have undertaken a military campaign before his second year, i.e., not before April 720. The compilers of the royal Annals apparently transferred an event from 720 to 721 in order to open the narrative of Sargon's reign with a great military victory. The biblical reference to the king of Assyria who besieged and conquered Samaria (II Kings 17.5f.) is therefore to Shalmaneser V and should be considered reliable. This tradition is further supported by the Babylonian Chronicle, which states that Shalmaneser V conquered *šamara'in* (the Aramaic form of *šomᵉrōn*/Samaria).[35]

Another vexing chronological problem concerns the date of the accession year of Hezekiah. According to II Kings 18.10, Hezekiah was in his sixth year at the time of Samaria's fall. Confirming this datum is Isa.14.28: 'In the year that King Ahaz died came this oracle: Rejoice not all Philistia, that the rod which smote you is broken.' Breaking the rod which smote Philistia is probably a reference to the death of Tiglath-pileser III, the only Assyrian king from the days of Ahaz worthy of such an epithet. It appears therefore that Ahaz died and Hezekiah came to power in the same year that Tiglath-pileser died,[36] which according to the Babylonian Chronicle was 12 Tebet 727/6 BCE (27 December 727 or 15 January 726).

On the other hand, the heading in II Kings 18.14 (Isa 36.1) states that: 'In the fourteenth year of Hezekiah, Sennacherib king of Assyria came up against all the fortified cities of Judah and took them.' As this event, reported in detail in Sennacherib's Annals, is fixed beyond any doubt as the year 701 BCE, it follows that Hezekiah's acccession took place in 716/5. This date, however, is contradicted both by Isa.14.28, as explained above, as well as by the series of synchronisms between Hezekiah and Hoshea in II Kings 18.1,9f. A modern biblical chronologist, who prefers to rely upon the date in II Kings 18.13, must reject the authenticity of the synchronisms in II Kings 18.[37] It has therefore been suggested[38] that the heading in II Kings 18.13 (Isa.36.1) belonged originally to the tale about Hezekiah's illness and his miraculous recovery (II Kings 20.1-11; Isa.38.1-8) and was placed in its present position by a later editor, who related all the prophetic stories concerning Isaiah and Hezekiah to the fateful year of Sennacherib's campaign and the miraculous salvation of Jerusalem.

4. From Jeroboam until the rebellion of Jehu

The total number of years of the kings of Israel (from Jeroboam I until Joram son of Ahab) is 98, and those of the kings of Judah (from Rehoboam until Ahaziah son of Jeroboam), 95. Inasmuch as Jeroboam and Rehoboam ascended the throne at the same time and Joram and Ahaziah were both killed during Jehu's rebellion, the number of regnal years for the kings of both Judah and Israel must be equal.

We have assumed (above 6) that the data about regnal years of the Judaean kings, even in this period, include only the complete years, without the months of the incomplete last year, whereas the data for Israelite kings include the incomplete final year. If so, in order to work out the chronological table one must decrease by one the regnal years of each Israelite king.

Two external synchronisms are available: 1. The battle of Qarqar, in which Ahab participated, took place in the sixth year of Shalmaneser III of Assyria (= 865 BCE); 2.Jehu paid tribute to Assyria in the eighteenth year of Shalmaneser III of Assyria (= 841 BCE).

The main crux in the chronology of this period concerns the years 853-

841. If Ahab was killed in the battle against Aram (I Kings 22) after he participated in the battle of Qarqar,[39] then in the thirteen years inclusive between 853 and 841 we must be able to account for the following data for the Northern Kingdom:

x = period of time that Ahab reigned from the battle of Qarqar until his death;

2 regnal years of Ahaziah (actually one calendar year);

12 regnal years of Joram (actually eleven calendar years);

y = period of time from Jehu's rise to power until delivery of tribute to Assyria.

The x figure should include at least a few months, for Ahab was Ben-hadad's ally at Qarqar and it is not likely that Ahab would have attacked his former ally at Ramoth-Gilead so soon after Qarqar. The tribute was certainly paid after Nisan 841 BCE, whereas the rebellion seems to have taken place the previous winter while the king was recuperating from his wounds in the Omride dynasty's winter residency, Jezreel.

In addition to the difficulty of accounting for twelve = x = y years in the short interval between 853 and 841 BCE, there are several contradictions between various synchronisms and the totals of the regnal years.[40]

One might perhaps solve the chronological crux by an emendation: if Jehoram son of Ahab reigned not twelve but only ten years (actually nine full years and a few additional months) we are left with about two years for the period of Ahab's reign, between Qarqar and Ramoth-Gilead, and about a year for the period between Jehu's accession and the payment of tribute to Assyria. Add to this, nine or ten years of Jehoram's reign and we arrive at a total of thirteen years (at most) between 853-841 BCE.

However, no system in biblical chronology proposed so far offers a fully satisfactory solution to the conflicting data in this period, especially that which concerns the reign of Jehoshaphat. Here the Greek versions (above, A.2) preserve somewhat different figures, which according to several scholars should be preferred to those of the Massoretic Text.[41]

5. The united monarchy

The length of Saul's reign is unknown. The passage in I Sam.13.1 ('Saul was one year old when he reigned and ruled over Israel two years') is clearly defective. The original reading must have included a reasonable number in each case: Saul was x years old when he began to reign and he reigned y years and 2 years over Israel. Completion of the number in the tens column is a matter of conjecture.

The information in II Sam.5.4; 11.42 about the reigns of David and Solomon is also very scanty.

David: thirty years old when he
began to reign

	seven years over Judah
	thirty-three years over Israel
Total	forty years.
Solomon:	forty years over Israel
Total	forty years.

The forty-year reigns of David and Solomon seem to be approximate and typological figures. David is reported to have been thirty years old when he assumed power and is said to have reigned forty years and six months (II Sam.5.4), making him seventy years old when he died; this is, in all opinions, a typological number signifying an average life-span (Ps.90.10).[42] Nevertheless, the abundance of stories in Samuel about David's career forces us to assume that he had a lengthy reign of at least several decades. Solomon also reigned for an extended period and his successor reached the throne at the age of forty-one (I Kings 14.21). Therefore, just as the chronographer rounded off the 38/39 year reign of Jehoash king of Judah to forty years,[43] so both David and Solomon were credited with forty years, a typological number commonly used in the Bible to indicate a full generation.[44] Likewise, units of eighty, forty and twenty years expressing two, one, or half generations (Judg.3.11,30; 8.28; 15.20; I Sam.7.2) were employed by the chronographer who narrated the period that preceded the establishment of the monarchy.[45] However, by its very nature, such data originating in oral tradition and important as it may be for genealogical chronology, cannot be subjected to strict chronological enquiry.

Notes

I Context

1. This information has been collected, with a commentary, by H.-J. Zobel, 'kᵉna'an', *TWAT* IV, 224-43.

2. *AHw* I, 479.

3. *Ep.ad Rom.Exp.*, 13, PL XXXV, 2096.

4. Cf. B.Maisler (Mazar), 'Canaan and the Canaanites', *BASOR* 102, 1946, 7-12; S.Moscati, op.cit., 67, and 'Sulla storia del nome Canaan', in *Studia Biblica et Orientalia*, AnBibl 12, Rome 1959, 266-9; M.Noth, *OTW*, 49-52.

5. W.F.Albright, 'The Role of the Canaanites in the History of Civilization', in *Studies in the History of Culture. Waldo H. Leland Volume*, Menasha, Wisc. 1942, 11-50, reprinted in *The Bible and the Ancient Near East. Essays in Honor of William Foxwell Albright*, Garden City and London 1961, 328-62; but cf. the critical comments by G.Garbini, *I Fenici*, ch.1. See also S.Moscati, *Il mondo dei Fenici*, Milan 1966.

6. Noth, 'Geschichte des Namens Palästina', *ZDPV* 62, 1939, 125-44 = *ABLAK* I, 294-308.

7. Cf. the passionate if unconvincing defence of the use of 'Land of Israel' and even of *Eretz* (sic!) *Israel* by A.F.Rainey, the translator of Y.Aharoni, *The Archaeology of the Land of Israel*, Philadelphia and London 1982, XIIIf.

8. For these peoples cf. T.Ishida, 'The Structure and Implications of the List of pre-Israelite Nations', *Bibl* 60, 1979, 461-90; N.K.Gottwald, *The Tribes*, 498-503. For the theme in general cf. the exhaustive articles by A.R.Millard, 'The Canaanites', and M.Liverani, 'The Amorites', both in D.J.Wiseman (ed.), *Peoples of Old Testament Times*, Oxford 1973, 29-52, 100-33.

9. R. de Vaux, 'Les Hurrites de l'histoire et les Horites de la Bible', *RB* 74, 1967, 461-503.

10. M.Liverani, 'Ville et campagne dans le royaume d'Ugarit. Essai d'analyse économique', in *Societes and Languages of the Ancient Near East. Studies in Honour of I.M.Diakonoff*, Warminster 1982, 250-2, provides an interesting example of the ruthless exploitation of the country for the building of the royal palace in the city.

11. The first two can be obtained in specialist libraries and bookshops.

II Methodology, Bibliography and Sources

1. 'Historical and Mythical Elements in the Joseph History', *JBL* 37, 1918, (111-43) 113f., and the pertinent observations by T.L.Thompson, *The Historicity of the Patriarchal Narratives*, BZAW 133, Berlin 1974, 8 n.26. For Albright see

now two works: L.G.Running and D.N.Freedman, *Wiliam Foxwell Albright – A Twentieth Century Genius*, New York 1975 (it is a shame that this work, rich as it is in information, too often gets lost in useless detail and generally assumes a laudatory and apologetic attitude which often verges on the ludicrous); P.J.King, *American Archaeology in the Mideast*, Philadelphia 1983, passim.

2. For these problems see my 'Geschichte als Glaubensbekenntnis – Geschichte als Gegenstand wissenschaftlicher Forschung', in *I.L.Seeligmann Memorial Volume*, Jerusalem (in preparation; the typescript was submitted to the editorial committee in 1977!). I cannot go into detail here about the basic problems inherent in any historiography; among the thousands of studies see M.Adinolfi, 'Storiografia biblica e storiografia classica', *RiBib* 9, 1961, 42-58; and S. Accame, 'Il problema storiografica e la critica storica', *Teologia* 6, 1981, 243-77. P.Gibert, *La Bible à la naissance de l'histoire*, Paris 1979, is still important. In all ancient historiography, and especially in classical historiography, to a greater or lesser degree we come up against the attitude which considers *historia magistra vitae*. For Roman history, which many people will probably feel has been treated in a superficial way here, I would refer to the monumental work edited by Hildegard Temporini, *Aufstieg und Niedergang der römische Welt* I, *Von den Anfängen bis zum Ausgang der Republik*, Berlin 1, 1972; 2, 1972; 3, 1973 and 4, 1974. See especially C.G.Starr, *The Roman Place in History* 1, 1972, (3-16) 6, where he refers to the 'conventional picture of the history of Rome': Act 1, the virtue of ancient Rome; Act 2, moral decadence; Act 3, the renaissance of virtue at the earliest period of the empire: *pax Romana*, etc. It is surprising that, despite this approach on the part of ancient historians, there is so much information about the foundation of the state that we can extract from the sources. We find a similar situation in the early sources of the Bible. For an examination of the problems inherent in any documentation and any testimony see the wise collection (part amusing and part tragic) made by R.W.Winks, *The Historian as Detective. Essays on Evidence*, New York 1968 and reprints. Cf. also R.G.Collingwood on the parallel between the historian and the detective, *The Idea of History*, Oxford 1946, 266-8.

3. J. Van Seters, *Abraham in History and Tradition*, New Haven 1975.

4. R.Rendtorff, *Das überlieferungsgeschichtliche Problem des Pentateuch*, BZAW 147, Berlin 1977.

5. R.E.Clements, 'The Prophecies of Isaiah and the Fall of Jerusalem, 587 BC', *VT* 30, 1980, 421-36, and O.Kaiser, *Isaiah 1-12*, OTL, London and Philadelphia 1983 (this last is often excessively sceptical, cf. my forthcoming review in *VT*).

6. 'Aspects of the Double, Controversial Valuation of Egypt in the Old Testament', a lecture given in the University of Rome on 18 May 1981, the publication of which is forthcoming.

7. J.A.Soggin, 'Zur Entwicklung des alttestamentlichen Königtums', *TZ* 15, 1959, 401-18.

8. The Deuteronomistic character of I Sam.8 was already argued for by J.Wellhausen, *Die Composition des Hexateuch*, Berlin ³1898, 243, cf. recently R.E.Clements, 'The Deuteronomistic Interpretation of the Founding of the Monarchy in I Sam VIII', *VT* 24, 1974, 398-410.

9. For the predominantly exilic or post-exilic redaction of the biblical books cf. J. Van Seters, 'Confessional Reformulations in the Exilic Period', *VT* 22, 1972, 448-59, and the observations of a conservative author like D.N.Freedman,

'Son of Man. Can These Bones Live?', *Int* 29, 1975, (171-86) 171: 'As a literary entity the Bible is a product of the exile...' So it is understandable and right that some authors call the exilic period 'the creative era', cf. already D.W.Thomas, 'The Sixth Century BC: A Creative Epoch in the History of Israel', *JSS* 6, 1961, 33-46; P.R.Ackroyd, *Exile and Restoration*, London 1968, 143.

10. For this problem see two recent studies, though they reach very different conclusions: M.Weinfeld, *Getting at the Roots of Wellhausen's Understanding of the Law in Israel*, Jerusalem 1979; and R.Smend, 'Wellhausen und das Judentum', *ZTK* 79, 1982, 249-82. Cf. also recently R.E.Friedman, *The Exile and Biblical Narrative*, HSM 22, Cambridge, Mass. 1981.

11. Thus rightly F.Hesse, 'Zur Profanität der Geschichte Israels', *ZTK* 71, 1974, 262-90.

12. A.Kuenen, *De godsdienst van Israël*, I, Haarlem 1869, 32ff.(ET London 1874, 30ff.), and B.Stade, *Geschichte des Volkes Israel* I, Berlin 1885, 16ff. Hallo's argument on the probable beginning of the history of Israel at the time of the Exodus has been recently and independently revived in the book by H.-J. Zobel and K.-M.Beyse (eds.), *Das Alte Testament und seiner Botschaft. Geschichte – Literatur – Theologie*, Berlin DDR 1981, cf. my review in *TLZ* 108, 1983, 189–91.

13. However, Hallo's attitude (recently followed uncritically by A.Malamat, 1983) can be understood in the context of a naive Sunday-school-like conception of the history of Israel by a writer who is not a biblical scholar; it risks becoming gratuitous and malicious when it is combined with unproven accusations of incompetence (e.g. the charge of using circular arguments) directed against those who hold different opinions.

14. J.M.Sasson and W.W.Hallo, artt.citt. in the bibliography.

15. M.C.Astour, review in *JAOS* 102, 1982, (192-5) 194. This is not a new explanation; it was authoritatively put forward in the 1930s by E.Meyer, *Geschichte des Altertums* II, 2, 1931, which I cite from the Stuttgart edition [3]1953, 253f. n.3. He considers the frontiers of the Davidic empire recorded in I Kings 5.4 to be a 'late fantasy' and connects the Hebrew expression *'ēber hannāhār* with the name of the Persian satrapy *'abār naharā'*. However, one might well ask whether a river like the Euphrates does not form one of these natural boundaries and therefore is not subject to shifts of a political kind; so the argument does not seem to me to be decisive. There is another explanation in A.Malamat, 'Aspects of the Foreign Politics of David and Solomon', *JNES* 22, 1963, 1-17; and *Das davidische und salomonische Königsreich und seine Beziehungen zu Ägypten und Syrien*, ÖAW Sitzungsb. 402, 1983, 19ff.: he thinks that the terminology is late but that the fact it records is ancient. Cf. also G.Garbini, 'L'impero di David', *ASNSP* III, 13, 1983, 1-20.

16. K.A.Kitchen, *The First Intermediate Period...*, 338ff.

17. A.Alt, 'The Settlement of the Israelites in Palestine' (1925), ET in *Essays on Old Testament History and Religion*, Oxford and New York 1967, 133-69; id., 'Erwägungen über die Landnahme der Israeliten in Palästina' (1939), *KS* I, 125-75; also S.Moscati, *I predecessori d'Israele*, Rome 1956.

18. In this book I shall use the term 'proto-history' (like Malamat, 1983) instead of the more usual pre-history: the former can form the object of historical investigation, which is more difficult in the case of the latter. This concept was already known in ancient Israel; passages in Deuteronomistic

style often use the expression 'in ancient days' (Hebrew *mīmē qedem*) for the period before the monarchy.

19. Cf. my *The Book of Joshua*, Introduction,and 'Gerico – anatomia d'una conquista', *Prot* 29, 1974, 193-213, French translation *RHPR* 57, 1977, 1-17.

20. G.Buccellati, *Cities and Nations*, passim.

21. See the recent noteworthy treatment by D.M.Gunn, *The Fate of King Saul*, JSOT-SS 14, Sheffield 1980.

22. J.A. Soggin, *Introduction*, 163.

23. M.Haran, *Temples and Temple Services in Ancient Israel*, Oxford 1978, passim.

24. Cf. my *Das Königtum* and 'Der Beitrag des Königtums zur israelitischen Religion', *SVT* 23, 1972, 9-26 and the works indicated there; also below, III.10.

25. We now have two works on Max Weber: the texts of the contributions to the symposium edited by W.Schluchter, *Max Webers Studien über das Judentum*, Frankfurt am Main 1981, and C.Schäfer-Lichtenberger, *Stadt und Eidgenossenschaft im Alten Testament*, BZAW 156, Berlin 1983.

26. H.Spieckermann,*Judah unter Assur in der Sargonidenzeit*, FRLANT 129, Göttingen 1982, shows the degree of care needed in the examination of these texts from the seventh century BC: all the more care is needed for earlier periods!

27. Cf. n.5 above.

28. W.H.Schmidt, 'Die deuteronomistische Redaktion des Amosbuches', *ZAW* 77, 1965, 168-93, and my *Il profeta Amos*, Brescia 1982, 31ff.

29. A.Schalit, *Zur Josephusforschung*, Darmstadt 1973, and Hayes-Miller*, 1ff. There is a negative evaluation of the work of Josephus in G.Garbini, *I Fenici*, ch.VII.

30. M.Stern, *Greek and Latin Authors on Jews and Judaism*, Jerusalem I, 1974; II, 1980; III in preparation. This lists only pagan authors.

31. S.Moscati, *I predecessori d'Israele*, Rome 1956, 54ff. See also H.Engel, 'Die Siegesstele von Mernepta. Kritischer Überblick über die verschiedenen Versuche historischer Auswertung des Schlussabschnittes', *Bibl* 60, 1979, 373-99; ET in *DOTT*, 137ff.; *ANET*, 376-8.

32. J.Bright*, 114f.; cf. also E.Otto (below n.34), 80 n.1, and A.Lemaire*, 18 n.2. To begin with, O.Eissfeldt argued that the Egyptian *yšr³r* could not be identified with *yśr'l*, but later he accepted the equivalence of the two terms without offering any explanation (cf. *CAH* II, Ch. XXVIa, ²1965, 14, with II, 2 ³1975, 318, 544f., reference J.M.Sasson). The two most recent studies of this important document are those by G.Fecht, 'Die Israelstele, Gestalt und Aussagen', and E.Hornung, 'Die Israelstele des Merneptah', both in *Fontes atque Pontes. Festschrift H.Brunner*, Wiesbaden 1983.

33. J. Bright*, ibid.; my *The Book of Joshua*, 173, and R.G.Boling, *Joshua* AB 6, Garden City 1982, 369 (undecided, but tending to be doubtful). The place is now identified with an abandoned Arab village of *lifta* (coord. 168-133) near to the west exit from Jerusalem.

34. W.Helck, *Die Beziehungen Ägyptens zu Vorderasien im 3. und 2. Jahrtausend v.Chr.*, Wiesbaden 1962, 240f.; S.Herrmann, *Die prophetischen Heilserwartungen im Alten Testament*, BWANT 85, Stuttgart 1965, 72ff., and Gunneweg*, 43f.

35. E.Otto, *Jakob in Sichem*, BWANT 101, Stuttgart 1979, 199ff.

36. Cf. my *Introduction*, 475ff.; *DOTT*, 195ff.

III David

1. Cf. A.Alt, 'The Monarchy in the Kingdoms of Israel and Judah', *Essays on Old Testament History*, 239-59, and R.de Vaux, *Ancient Israel*, London 1971, 133-8. For a defence of the substantial unity existing between Israel and Judah, see Z.Kallai, 'Judah and Israel – A Study in Israelite Historiography', *IEJ* 28, 1978, 251-61. However, the points against this theory seem to me to be stronger than those in its favour, even if everything is hypothetical.

2. Cf. my *Judges*, ad loc.

3. For Mesopotamia see e.g. A.L.Oppenheim, *Ancient Mesopotamia*, Chicago and London 1964, 166; D.J.Wiseman, *CAH* II, 2, [3]1975, 443ff.; for Egypt, K.A.Kitchen, *The Third Intermediate Period*, sections 220, 235f.; J.Černý, *CAH* II, 2, [3]1975, 606ff. In other words, as Malamat, 1983, 10, pertinently points out, 'To use Machiavelli's words, the *occasion* was there, but what lord would have had the *virtue*?'

4. This narrative was 'discovered' and examined by L.Rost, *The Succession to the Throne of David*, ET Sheffield 1982; id., *Das kleine Credo*, Wiesbaden 1965, 119-253; cf. also R.N.Whybray, *The Succession Narrative*, SBT II 9, London 1968; E.Würthwein, *Die Erzählung von der Thronnachfolge Davids – theologische oder politische Geschichtsschreibung?*, TS 115, Zurich 1979; T.Ishida, 'Solomon's Succession to the Throne of David – A Political Analysis', in T.Ishida (ed.), *Studies...*, 175-87. For a predominantly aesthetic and literary analysis see now J.Fokkelman, *King David*, Assen 1981. For this important work see now the detailed (sadly, perhaps too detailed!) review by F.Langlamet, *RB* 90, 1983, 100-48, and my review in *Hen* 5, 1983, 268–72. An attempt to extend the work by including other texts is the recent study by G.Garbini, ' "Narrativa della successione" o "storia dei Rei"?', *Hen* 1, 1979, 19-41. For its earliest sections see now F.Langlamet, 'David, le fils de Jesse', *RB* 89, 1982, 5-47.

5. E.Meyer, *Geschichte des Altertums*, II,2, reprinted Stuttgart 1953, (281-6) 285.

6. For this see my 'Il regno di 'Esba'al, figlio di Saul', *RSO* 40, 1965, 91-106.

7. It seems to me improbable that there is a direct connection between I Sam. 16.13a and I Kings 1.39a, as Mettinger argues, op.cit., 207: the texts both deal with the 'anointing' of a king and are similar in that they describe the same act. M.Kessler, 'Narrative Technique in I Sam. 16.1-13', *CBQ* 32, 1970, 543-54, seems to me now the only one to support the antiquity of this text.

8. This text too is certainly later, probably from the Persian period, as is indicated by the vocabulary (A.Rofé, *Gerusalemme*, verbal communication).

9. Similar proceedings are also well attested in Assyria, cf. H.Tadmor, 'History and Ideology in the Assyrian Royal Inscriptions', in F.M.Fales (ed.), *Assyrian Royal Inscriptions – New Horizons*, Rome 1981, 13-33, and 'Autobiographical Apology in the Royal Assyrian Literature', in H.Tadmor and M.Weinfeld, *History, Historiography and Interpretation*, Jerusalem 1983, 36-57; I have only been able to make partial use of this last important study.

10. M. Weber, *Ancient Judaism*, ET Glencoe 1952; id., *Wirtschaft und Gesellschaft*, Tübingen [4] 1956, I, 140ff.; II, 662ff.

11. H-J.Zobel, *Stammesspruch und Geschichte*, BZAW 95, Berlin 1965, 44-47, with bibliography; for the location cf. my 'Amalek und Ephraim. Richter 5.14', *ZDPV* 1982, (58-62, with a map) 60, and Z.Kallai, 'Timnat Heres', *EncBibl* VII, 598-600 (in Hebrew).

12. F.Crüsemann, *Der Widerstand gegen das Königtum*, WMANT 49, Neukirchen 1978, 200-8.

13. K.-D.Schunck. *Benjamin*, BZAW 86, Berlin 1963, 121, who also comments (wrongly) on the unusual grammatical form; cf. also J.J.Bimson, *Exodus and Conquest*, JSOT-SS 14, Sheffield 1978, 97; both consider the form corrupt. However, M. Noth*, 176f. and now K.D.A.Smelik, *Saul*, Diss. Amsterdam VU 1977, 69ff., regard it as valid. For an analogous case cf. Judg.9.22 and my *Judges*, 177ff.

14. Thus R.Althann, 'I Sam.13.1: A Poetic Couplet', *Bibl* 62, 1981, 241-6.

15. See the text and the commentary cited in n.13.

16. J.H.Hayes, 'Saul: The Unsung Hero of Israelite History', in *Trinity University Studies in Religion* 10, 1975, 37-47, and D.M.Gunn, *The Fate of King Saul*, JSOT-SS 14, Sheffield 1980, passim. For an analytic study of the texts cf. F.Langlamet, 'David et la maison de Saül', *RB* 86, 1979, 194-213, 481-513; 87, 1980, 161-280; 88, 1981, 321-32.

17. W.L.Humphreys, 'From Tragic Hero to Villain: A Study of the Figure of Saul and the Development of I Samuel', *JSOT* 22, 1982, 95-117.

18. N.P.Lemche, 'David's Rise', *JSOT* 10, 1978, 2-29.

19. 1977*, 335ff.

20. S.Moscati, 'L'archeologia cominicia a parlarci dei Filistei', in *Il Messaggero di Roma*, 12 February 1965.

21. A very recent study by A.Loffreda, 'Ancora sul ṣinnōr di 2 Sam.5,9', *LA-SBF* 32, 1982, 59-72, thinks rather that the men of David succeeded in blocking the water conduit, thus cutting off the water supplies and forcing the city to surrender. According to C.Schäfer-Lichtenberger, *Stadt und Eidgenossenschaft im Alten Testament*, BZAW 1983, 385-96, the city will never have been conquered, but occupied by David with the full agreement of the local population, as seems to be demonstrated by the fact that a small contingent of troops was enough to complete the operation.

22. H.Timm, 'Die Ladeerzählung (I Sam.4-5; II Sam.6) und das Kerygma des deuteronomistischen Geschichtswerkes', *EvTh* 29. 1966, 509-26; E.F.Campbell, *The Ark Narrative*, SBL-DS 16, Missoula 1975; cf. also J.A.Soggin 1977*, 336.

23. D.Harden, *The Phoenicians*, London ²1963, 51, 158f.; E.Moscati, *Il mondo dei Fenici*, Milan 1966, 33-36. B.Peckham, 'Israel and Phoenicia', in *Magnalia Dei...Essays...G.E.Wright*, Garden City 1976, 224-48, rightly observes that despite the apparent abundance of material, 'the history of their relationships remains elusive'.

24. For a reconstruction of facts see M.Noth*, 187f.

25. D.J.McCarthy, *Treaty and Covenant*, AnBibl 21-A, Rome ²1978, 143 and passim.

26. M.Delcor, 'Les Kerethim et les Crétois', *VT* 28, 1978, 409-22.

27. A.Alt, 'Das Grossreich Davids', *TLZ* 75, 1950, 213-20 = *KS* II, 66-89. It should be noted that in his recent article G.Garbini thinks that this theory, and therefore this reconstruction of events, is too optimistic; by contrast he thinks of a much smaller entity, including Philistine and Moabite territory in addition to Judah and Israel. Similarly already J.A.Montgomery and H.S.Gehman, *The Books of Kings*, ICC, Edinburgh 1951, 128f., whom he explicitly cites.

28. 'Die Staatenbildung der Israeliten in Palästina' (1930), *KS* II, 1-65, and Soggin*, 349-56. Also A.Alt, 'Das Grossreich Davids', see preceding note.

29. G.Buccellati, *Cities and Nations*, 137ff., 146ff., 160ff. For Jerusalem,

Buccellati has found an ally in the very recent study by C.Schäfer-Lichtenberger, *Stadt und Eidgenossenschaft im Alten Testament*, BZAW 157, Berlin 1983, 381-91, which I was able to use only at the last moment.

30. J.Simons, *The Geographical...*, 317.

31. Y. Aharoni, *The Land*, analytical index s.v. This theory seems to have been confirmed by the excavations by E.D.Oren, 'Ziklag – A Biblical City on the Edge of the Negev', *BA* 45, 1982, 155-66. G.Buccellati rightly points out that the place is included in the lists of the cities of Judah and Simeon (Josh. 15.31; 19.5; I Chron 4.30), so that its legal status was evidently different from that of Jerusalem, which does not appear in such lists. We shall deal with this later.

32. J.A.Soggin, *Joshua*, and R.G.Boling, *Joshua*, cf. above II, nn.17, 30.

33. A.Alt, 'Der Stadtstaat Samaria'(1954), *KS* III, 258-302.

34. For the titles of David's officials cf. A.Cody, 'Le titre égyptien et le nom propre du scribe de David', *RB* 72, 1965, 381-91; T.N.D.Mettinger, op.cit. (above 7.1), 28; B.Mazar, *'Sōfēr hammelek ūbᵉ'ayat happeqīdūt haggᵉbōrāh bᵉmalkūt iśrā'ēl'*, in *Canaan and Israel, Historical Essays*, Jerusalem 1980, 208-21 (in Hebrew). For the problem of the priesthood of the sons of David cf. G.J.Wenham, 'Were David's Sons Priests?', *ZAW* 87, 1975, 79-82.

35. For this division into two periods, one favourable and the other unfavourable, which probably goes back to Dtr, see R.A.Carlson, *David the Chosen King*, Stockholm 1964. It also appears in the case of other monarchs, Saul and Solomon.

36. For the material see my studies, 'Der offiziell geförderte Synkretismus in Israel während des 10. Jahrhunderts', *ZAW* 78, 1966, 179-204, and 'Der Beitrag des Königtums zur alttestamentlichen Religion', *SVT* 23, 1972, 9-26, and Soggin*, 361-3. For the important text II Sam.7 cf. the two very recent studies by A.Caquot, 'Brève explication de la prophétie de Nathan (2 Sam.7.1-17)', in *Mélanges bibliques et orientaux en l'honneur de M.Henri Cazelles*, AOAT 212, Kevelaer, 1981, 51-69, and J.Coppens, 'La prophétie de Nathan – sa portée dynastique', in *Von Kanaan bis Kerela – FS J.P.M. van der Ploeg*, AOAT 211, Kevelaer 1982, 91-100 (with bibliography).

37. G.Garbini, *I Fenici*, Ch.V.

38. 'La religione fenicia nei dati della Bibbia', in *La religione fenicia – matrici orientali e sviluppi occidentali*, Rome 1981, 81-90. Cf. also M.Smith, *Palestinian Parties and Politics that Shaped the Old Testament*, New York 1971, Ch.II; B.Lang (ed.), *Der einzige Gott*, Munich 1981, especially the contributions of B.Lang and H. Vorländer, which argue with ample evidence that only in the exile can one speak of real monotheism in Israel. W.G.Dever, 'Material Remains and the Cult in Ancient Israel. An Essay in Archaeological Systematics', in *The Word of the Lord Shall Go Forth. Essays... D.N.Freedman*, Philadelphia 1983, 371-587, and B.Lang, *Monotheism and the Prophetic Minority*, Sheffield 1983, have meanwhile arrived at very similar results to those put forward here. I have only been able to make partial use of the latter. For recent support for the theory of the contamination of an originally pure religion of Israel cf. D.Kinet, *Ba'al und Jahwe*, Frankfurt am Main and Berne 1977, passim, esp. 209ff.; cf. my review in *Prot* 38, 1983, 110.

IV Solomon

1. J.Liver, 'The Book of the Acts of Solomon', *Bibl* 48, 1967, 75-101, supports the existence of the 'Book of the Acts'; G.Garbini, *I Fenici*, Ch.VII, does not hide his scepticism.

2. G.E.Wright, *Biblical Archaeology*, Philadelphia ²1962, 127.

3. K.M.Kenyon, *Digging up Jerusalem*, London 1974, 99-106.

4. Cf. the provisional reports by Y.Shiloh, *BA* 42, 1979, 165-71; 44, 1981, 161-70. For the problem see recently G.W.Ahlström, *Royal Administration and National Religion in Ancient Palestine*, Leiden 1982, and the brilliant analyses of the discoveries by W.G.Dever, 'Monumental Architecture in Ancient Israel in the Period of the United Monarchy', in T. Ishida (ed.), *Studies*, 269-306.

5. Y.Yadin, 'New Light on Solomon's Megiddo', *BA* 23, 1960, 62-8; id., 'Megiddo of the Kings of Israel', *BA* 33, 1970, 66-96; and 'A Note on the Stratigraphy of Israelite Megiddo', *JNES* 32, 1973, 330. Also J.B.Pritchard, 'The Megiddo Stables', in *Near Eastern Archaeology – FS Nelson Glueck*, Garden City, NY 1970, 268-76. Yadin argues that these were stables, but dates the complex much later. For the palaces of the time of Solomon cf. recently B.Gregori, 'Considerazioni sui palazzi ḥilani del periodo salomonico a Megiddo', *VO* 5, 1982, 85-101.

6. Y. Yadin, *Hazor: The Head of All Those Kingdoms*, London 1972; and *Hazor: The Rediscovery of a Great Citadel of the Bible*, London 1975. Again Y. Aharoni, 'The Building Activities of David and Solomon', *IEJ* 24, 1974, 13f.; W.G.Dever (ed.), *Gezer I-II*, Jerusalem 1970, 1974. Cf. also U. Müller, 'Tor', *BRL* ²1977, 346-8 (with five plans).

7. J.B.Pritchard, *Gibeon*, Princeton 1962, for a provisional account of the excavations down to the end of the 1950s. Cf. also the very recent study by C.H.W.Brekelmans, 'Solomon at Gibeon', in *Von Kanaan bis Kerala, FS J.P.M. van der Ploeg*, AOAT 211, Kevelaer 1982, 53-9.

8. G.R.H.Wright, 'Pre-Israelite Temples in the Land of Canaan', *PEQ* 103, 1971, 7-32; Y.Yadin, op.cit., 1975 (n.6), 79-120.

9. Y.Aharoni, 'Arad: Its Inscriptions and Temple', *BA* 31, 1968, 2-32. Recently, however doubts have arisen over the Solomonic dating of the artefacts (R.K.Amiran, verbally).

10. J.A.Soggin, 'The Ark of the Covenant, Jeremiah 3,16', in P.Bogaert (ed.), *Le livre de Jérémie*, Louvain 1981, 215-21.

11. For this theme cf. J.C.de Moor, *The Seasonal Pattern in the Ugaritic Myth of Ba'lu*, Kevelaer 1971, 60, 113. It is not surprising that, given the circumstances, it has been thought that Solomon will have adapted and restored an already existing Canaanite sacred building for his use (cf. recently K.Rupprecht, *Der Tempel von Jerusalem*, BZAW 144, Berlin 1977). However, interesting though the theory is, it does not seem defensible in the light of the sources we have, cf. my review in *BO* 36, 1979, 83f. Moreover, the proposal is not new: it already appears in Josephus, *BJ* VI, 246, where the building of the temple is attributed to Melchizedek, albeit in a clearly rhetorical context (further V.3.2.1); Gen.14.18ff. (B.Mazar, *The Jerusalem Post Magazine*, 25 March 1983, 6). Another difficulty arises from the unusually large dimensions of the sanctuary in Solomon's temple: it measures over 100 feet by 35 feet, dimensions for which there seem to be no parallels in the region until some centuries later. Does the description refer to the building of a much later time? For the problem cf. recently P.Sacchi, 'Israele e le culture circonvicine', *RSLR* 19, 1983, 216-28.

12. This is how I translate the term šᵉlamīm, instead of the usual 'peace-offerings' as is often done; cf. Zorrell, *Lexicon*, under šelem.

13. Cf. R.Schreiden, 'Les entreprises navales du roi Salomon', in *Annuaire de l'Institut de philologie et d'histoire orientales et slaves* 13, 1955, 187-90; G. Bunnens, 'Commerce et diplomatie phéniciennes au temps de Hiram Iᵉʳ de Tyr', *JESHO* 19, 1976, 1-31. G.Garbini, art.cit., has recently denied the historicity of these passages: if they happened at all, such expeditions are to be attributed to Uzziah/Azariah, about 150 years later (cf. below IX.5ff.).

14. G.Ryckmans, 'Ophir', *SDB* VI, 1960, 744-51; V.Christides, 'L'énigme d'Ophir', *RB* 77, 1970, 240-7, for a summary of the discussion. The US Geographical Survey proposes *mahd ed-d̠ahab*, a place on the sea between Mecca and Medina, an area which is still rich in gold-bearing sand, *BA* 39, 1976, 85.

15. Thus recently, and with good arguments, M. Görg, 'Ophir, Tarshisch und Atlantis. Einige Gedanken zur symbolischen Topographie', *BN* 15, 1981, 76-86.

16. For 'peacocks', W.F.Albright, *Archaeology and the Religion of Israel*, Baltimore ³1953, 212 n.16, proposes 'baboons', a species of animal which he clearly does not suppose to be included in the 'apes' just mentioned.

17. Cf. *BHS* and the commentaries. We now have the basic study on this trading by Y.Ikeda, 'Solomon's Trade in Horses and Chariots in Its International Setting', in T.Ishida (ed.), *Studies*, 215-38.

18. H.Donner, 'The Interdependence of Internal Affairs and Foreign Policy during the Davidic-Solomonic Period', in T.Ishida (ed.), *Studies*, (205-14) 207f., notes the existence of a break between vv.13 and 14 and deduces from this that it is not possible to understand the transfer of this territory in terms of payment and compensation for the debts contracted; however, he does not offer a different, more adequate explanation, although he recognizes that the affair 'was hardly a triumph for Solomon's foreign policy'.

19. S.H.Horn, 'Who was Solomon's Father in Law?', *BiblRes* 12, 1967, 3-7; K.A.Kitchen, *The Third Intermediate*, 235ff.; H.D.Lance, 'Solomon, Siamun and the Double Ax', in *Magnalia Dei... Essays... G.E.Wright*, Garden City 1976, (209-25) 222. F.Pintore, *Il matrimonio interdinastico nel Vicino Oriente durante i secoli XV-XIII*, Rome 1978, 78, examines this problem very succinctly. Here, too, G.Garbini, art.cit., considers the fact highly improbable, given the well-attested customs of the Egyptian court. For the problem of these relationships cf. recently A.Malamat, 'A Political Look at the Kingdom of David and Solomon and its Relations with Egypt', in T.Ishida (ed.), *Studies*, 189-204; and op.cit., above, III.2.1.

20. D.B.Redford, 'Studies in the Relations between Palestine and Egypt during the First Millenium BC – II. The Twenty-Second Dynasty', *JAOS*, 1973, 307.

21. For the theme see the basic studies by A.Alt, 'Israels Gaue unter Salomo', in *Alttestamentliche Studien R.Kittel zum 60. Geburtstag dargebracht*, Leipzig 1913 = *KS* II, 76-89, and W.F.Albright, 'The Administrative Divisions of Israel and Judah', *JPOS* 5, 1925, 17-89. Such explanations have recently been put in question by F.Pintore, 'I dodici intendenti di Salomone', *RSO* 45, 1970, 177-207, who thinks, rather, that the purpose of the system was essentially to organize staging posts and provisions for royal convoys. The proposal has not been taken up, though it is probable that the 'finance officers' also had this

responsibility. Two recent studies largely confirm Alt's work: Y. Aharoni, 'The Solomonic Districts', *TA* 3, 1976, 1-15, and N.Na'aman, 'The District System in the Time of the United Monarchy', *Zion* 48, 1983, 1-20 (in Hebrew with an English summary).

22. D.B.Redford, 'Studies... [n.21] – I. The Taxation System of Solomon', in *Studies on the Ancient Palestinian World – Festschrift F.V.Winnett*, Toronto 1972, 141-56.

23. Cf. my *Joshua* and R.G.Boling, *Joshua*, AB 6, Garden City 1982, both ad loc. and with bibliography.

24. Thus F.M.Cross-G.E.Wright, 'The Boundary and Province List of Judah', *JBL* 75, 1956, (202-26) 224f.; G.E.Wright, 'The Provinces of Solomon (I Kings 4,7-15)', *EI* 8, 1967, 58*-68* and F.Pintore, art.cit (n.22).

25. However, A.Alt, 'Judas Gaue unter Josia', *PJB* 21, 1925, 100-16 = *KS* II, 276-88, is very cautious.

26. Cf. the Hebrew terms and *AHw* II, 1972, 619 s.v.

27. G.von Rad, 'The Joseph Narrative and Ancient Wisdom', in *The Problem of the Hexateuch and Other Essays*, Edinburgh 1966, 293; id., *Old Testament Theology* I, Edinburgh 1966, reissued London 1975, 48-56; G.Gerleman, *Das Hohelied*, Neukirchen 1966, 13ff. G. von Rad has revised his own theory in *Wisdom in Israel*, Nashville and London 1972. The problem is treated afresh by R.N.Whybray, 'Wisdom Literature in the Reigns of David and Solomon', in T.Ishida (ed.), *Studies*, 13-26. For the subject (but without special reference to Solomon) cf. A.Lemaire, *Les écoles et la formation de la Bible dans l'Israël ancien*, OBO 39, Fribourg 1982.

28. R.B.Y.Scott, 'Solomon and the Beginnings of Wisdom in Israel', *SVT* 3, 1955, 262-79.

29. This is the view of the most recent, important study by F.W.Golka, 'Die israelitische Weisheitsschule, oder "des Kaisers neue Kleider"', *VT* 33, 1983, 257-70.

30. R.N.Whybray, *The Intellectual Tradition in the Old Testament*, BZAW 135, Berlin 1974, 15-54.

31. Cf. e.g A.Alt, 'Die Weisheit Salomos', *TLZ* 76, 1951, 139-44 = *KS* II, 90-9; H.-J. Hermisson, *Studien zur israelitischen Spruchweisheit*, WMANT 28, Neukirchen 1968, 115-36; M.Weinfeld, *Deuteronomy and the Deuteronomic School*, Oxford 1972, 244ff.

V Patriarchs

1. Cf. R.E.Clements, *Abraham and David*, SBT II, 5, London 1967, and my *Introduction*, 101ff.

2. W.M.Clark in his contribution to Hayes-Miller*, 1977, 120-48.

3. M.Noth, *A History of Pentateuchal Traditions* (1948), ET Garden City, NJ 1972, reissued Chico, Ca 1982.

4. P.A.H.de Boer, *Aspects of the Double, Controversial Valuation of Egypt in the Old Testament* (in preparation).

5. For this 'Amorite migration' cf. e.g. G.Posener, J.Bottéro and K.M.Kenyon, *CAH* I, 2, ³1971, 532-97 (in favour), and M.Liverani, 'The Amorites', in D.J.Wiseman (ed.), *Peoples from Old Testament Times*, Oxford 1973, 100-33 (against, with convincing evidence), and the bibliographies to both books.

6. Quite different, and rather clumsy, are the attempts at locating them by

the so-called Genesis Apocryphon, cf. J.A.Fitzmyer, *The Genesis Apocryphon*, BiblOr 18, Rome ²1971, ad loc.

7. See the study by A.Rofè, 'La composizione di Genesi 24', *BeO* 23, 1981, 161-5, though this is only a summary of a lecture. For a pre-exilic date, very close to Deuteronomy, see recently F.García López, 'Del "Yahvista" al "Deuteronomista"', Estudio crítico de Génesis 24', *RB* 87, 1980, 242-73, 350-99, 514-59. In no way can the text be considered early.

8. The annals of Tiglath-Pileser I (*c.*1116-1078, low chronology), in *ANET* 275, cf. A.Dupont-Sommer, *Les Araméens*, Paris 1979, 17ff.; de Vaux, *Early History* I, 180.

9. N.K.Gottwald, *The Tribes of Yahweh*, Maryknoll 1979 and London 1980, 437ff., 465ff. and passim. The very recent study by M.A.Morrison, 'The Jacob and Laban Narrative in the Light of Near Eastern Sources', *BA* 46, 1983, 155-64, concludes succinctly (164): 'The story of Jacob and Laban does not contain any of those characteristic details which would allow us to identify it with a particular period. However, it does draw on universal aspects peculiar to specific usages in the economic and social spheres.' He makes this comment in connection with the Near Eastern parallels to the cycle.

10. The study by J.-L.Kupper, *Les nomades en Mésopotamie au temps des rois de Mari*, Paris 1957, is now a classic. I cannot go into detail on the subject; cf. e.g. A.Malamat, 'Mari and the Bible', *JAOS* 82, 1962, 143-50, and 'Mari', *BA* 34, 1971, 2-22. Also T.L.Thompson, chs.III-IV; Gottwald, loc.cit.

11. Gottwald, op.cit., 308ff.

12. A.Malamat, 'King Lists of the Old Babylonian Period and Biblical Genealogies', *JAOS* 88, 1968, 163-73; M.D.Johnson, *The Purpose of the Biblical Genealogies*, SNTS-MS 8, Cambridge 1969, 77ff.; R.R.Wilson, 'The Old Testament Genealogies in Recent Research', *JBL* 94, 1975, 169-89; id., *Genealogy and History in the Biblical World*, New Haven and London 1977; T.J.Prewitt, 'Kingship Structures and the Genesis Genealogies', *JNES* 40, 1981, 87-98.

13. B.Diebner, 'Die Götter der Väter – eine Kritik der Vatersgott Hypothese', *DBAT* 9, 1975, 21-51, points out that there is no archaeological evidence for the sanctuary of Mamre before the exile.

14. K.Galling, *Die Erwählungstraditionen Israels*, BZAW 48, Giessen 1928, 65ff., stresses that the patriarchal narratives are a 'conscious creation', focussed on the 'pan-Israelite conception', and intended to anticipate the date of legal rights over Canaan.

15. H.Gunkel, *Die Genesis*, HKAT I, 1, Göttingen ³1910, Introduction; H.Gressmann, 'Saga und Geschichte in den Patriarchenerzählungen', *ZAW* 30, 1910, 1-34.

16. K.Galling, op.cit. (n.14), 9.

17. For the problem in general cf. the comments in T.L.Thompson, op.cit., 3 n.6.

18. E.g. N.Glueck, *The River Jordan*, New York ²1968, 8f. and passim.

19. W.F.Albright, 'The Israelite Conquest of Palestine in the Light of Archaeology', *BASOR* 74, 1939, 11-23; J.Bright, *Ancient Israel in Recent History Writing*, SBT I, 19, London 1956; G.E.Wright, 'Modern Issues in Biblical Studies: History and the Patriarchs', *ExpT* 71, 1959-60, 292-6 (also against von Rad). For a summary of the discussion see my 'Ancient Biblical Traditions and Modern Archaeological Discoveries', *BA* 23, 1960, 95-100, and R.de Vaux, 'Methods in

the Study of Early Hebrew History', in J.P.Hyatt (ed.), *The Bible and Modern Scholarship*, Nashville and New York 1965, 15-29. For Albright cf. above II n.1.

20. G.E.Wright, 'What Archaeology Cannot Do', *BA* 74, 1971, 70-76. For an evaluation of Wright's work cf. recently W.G.Dever, 'Biblical Theology and Biblical Archaeology – An Appreciation of G.Ernest Wright', *HTR* 73, 1980, 1-15.

21. G. von Rad, *Old Testament Theology* I, ET Edinburgh 1962, reissued London 1975, 105ff.

22. 'Den gammelstestamentliga teologin efter Gerhard von Rad', *SEA*, 1982, (7-20) 9ff., and the article cited in ch.II, n.2.

23. M.Noth, 'Hat die Bibel doch Recht?', in *Festschrift Günther Dehn*, Neukirchen 1957, 7-22; id., 'Der Beitrag der Archäologie zur Geschichte Israels', *SVT* 7, 1960, (262-82) 269ff.; both in *ABLAK* I, 17-33, 34-51.

24. Proposals made initially by C.H.Gordon, 'Biblical Customs and the Nuzi Tablets', *BA* 3, 1940, 1-12, then taken up by E.A.Speiser, *Genesis*, AB 1, Garden City 1965, passim. For criticism see the works by T.L.Thompson, chs.III, X; J. Van Seters, passim; and W.M.Clark*, in Hayes-Miller*, 1977, 120ff., all cited above.

25. T.L.Thompson, op.cit., ch.II.

26. Ibid.

27. Cf.M.Noth, *A History of Pentateuchal Traditions*, passim, and recently C.Westermann, *Die Genesis*, BK I, 2, Neukirchen 1981, ad loc.

28. L.Woolley, *Excavations at Ur*, London [3]1955.

29. J.Bright, 1981*, 90f., who favours this solution; S.Herrmann*, 49, is uncertain.

30. C.H.Gordon, 'Abraham and the Merchants of Ura',*JNES* 17, 1958, 28-31; id., 'Abraham of Ur', in *Hebrew and Semitic Studies... G.R.Driver*, Oxford 1963, 77-84, thinks of a Hittite locality by the name of Ur(a) attested in Ugarit, north of Ḥarrān, but otherwise unknown (*WUS*, 369: 'arᵤ and 'ari); against this, and with valid arguments, H.W.F.Saggs, 'Ur of the Chaldees', *Iraq* 22, 1960, 200-9; R. de Vaux, *Early History* I, 187ff.: Ur is always connected with Babylonia.

31. W.F.Albright, 'New Light on Early Recensions of the Hebrew Bible', *BASOR* 140, 1956, (27-33) 31f.

32. Most recently R. de Vaux*, I, 182-7.

33. J.Bright*, 90, doubtful but favourably inclined; for T.L.Thompson, associations of this kind 'would constitute a serious error in interpretation', 21ff., 87.

34. R. de Vaux*, I, 183, takes this seriously into consideration, but finally rejects it.

35. Cf. my *Joshua*, 19, 237ff.

36. Once more now by W.C.Van Hattem, 'Once Again: Sodom and Gomorrah', *BA* 44, 1981, 87-92, who even suggests locating the whole episode in the late Bronze Age, third phase.

37. An attempt to find the five cities of the valley in an unspecified text from Ebla, made by P.Matthiae and G.Pettinato at the General Meeting of the American Schools of Oriental Research, St Louis, Mo, 29 September 1976, has meanwhile proved erroneous,though it has often been repeated. For the communication cf. D.N.Freedman, 'A Letter to the Reader', *BA* 40, 1977, 2-4, and recently id., 'Ebla and the Old Testament', in T.Ishida (ed.), *Studies...*, (309-55) 328.

38. For the possibility of a connection with Adoni-zedek in Josh.10-13 cf. my *Joshua*, ad loc., and *Judges*, 21f.

39. There is a synopsis in M.Weippert, 76-9.

40. And it is a great pity that this study has remained largely unnoticed, partly because it appeared in Italian and partly because it was published in a journal which was not a Near Eastern review. However, I have made a long summary of it in *ZAW* 79, 1967, 253f. Liverani takes over and develops Landsberger's arguments, bringing them up to date.

41. An interesting comparison between Idrimi of Alalakh, who fled and for some years took refuge among the *ḫapīru*, and David fleeing before Saul, has been suggested by G.Buccellati, 'Da Saul a Davide', *BeO* 1, 1959, 99-128; cf. also *UF* 13, 1981, 199-290.

42. For the sources cf. M.Weippert, 72 n.4. See also M.Liverani, 'Farsi *ḫabīru*', *Vicino Oriente* 2, 1979, 65-77.

43. N.K.Gottwald, *The Tribes*, 213-19, 401-9.

44. G.E.Mendenhall, 'The Hebrew Conquest of Palestine', *BA* 25, 1962, 66-87, and *The Tenth Generation*, Baltimore 1973, V, with a synoptic table of their attestation, 123. For a provisional criticism cf. my observations in *Prot* 17, 1962, 208; M.Weippert, 102f.

45. This is the pivot of Gottwald's argument.

46. Gottwald, *Tribes*, analytical index s.v. 'Converts to'.

47. W.F.Albright*, 1940, 189; ²1957, 248.

48. A.Alt, *KS* I, 26 n.2; O.Eissfeldt, *KS* III, 363 and 392 n.4; R. de Vaux, I*, 269; and recently A.Lemaire, 'Les Bene-Jacob', *RB* 85, 1978, (321-37) 323ff. D.R.Hillers, '*Paḥad Iṣḥaq*', *JBL* 91, 1972, 90-2, rejects the interpretation.

49. P.Garelli, *Les Assyriens en Cappadocie*, Paris 1963, provides a recent and up-to-date treatment of these matters.

50. *ARM* V, Paris 1952, no.20.

51. *KAI* 215, line 22, cf. also 24 line 16; 25 line 6.

52. Cf. my *Judges*, ad loc. For the problem of the association of the patriarchs with sacred trees and their sanctuaries cf. recently M.Liverani, 'La chêne de Shardanu', *VT* 27, 1977, 212-16.

VI   Egypt and Exodus

1. M.Noth, 1959*, 110ff.; A.Alt, *Die Herkunft der Hyksos in neuer Sicht*, Berlin 1954, *KS* III, (72-98) 87; J.Bright*, 1981, 120.

2. Bright*, 121.

3. Cf. my 'I testi vetero-testamentari sulla conquista della Palestina', *RiBib* 28, 1980, 45-57.

4. M.Noth, *Die israelitischen Personennamen...*, Stuttgart 1928, 63. According to the information collected by J.M.Weinstein, 'The Egyptian Empire. A Reassessment', *BASOR* 241, 1981, (1-28) 17ff., in the late Bronze Age and down to the end of the twelfth century BC, this nominal control will have turned into an actual occupation of the territory; that is quite evident from the many buildings of an Egyptian type attested for the period. It makes even more probable the presence of Egyptian names.

5. Y.Aharoni, *The Land...*, 1979, 196, wrongly sees here a quotation of the term '*prw*.

6. For different reasons, D.B.Redford, 'Exodus I 11', *VT* 13, 1963, 411-18,

and, recently, J.J.Bimson, *Redating the Exodus and the Conquest*, JSOT-SS 5, Sheffield 1978 (cf. my review in *VT* 31, 1981, 98ff.) have objected; the latter would date everything one or two centuries earlier. W.Helck, '*tkw* und die Ramsesstadt', *VT* 15, 1965, 35-48, replies to Redford.

7. Rather than from *muškēnu(m)*, to be understood as 'cities (built) with forced labour', as E.A.Speiser would prefer: 'The *muškēnum*', *Or* 27, 1958, 19-28 = *Oriental and Biblical Studies*, Philadelphia 1967, 333-43; but cf. *AHw* 684.

8. For the details cf. recently W.H.Schmidt, *Exodus*, BK II, Neukirchen 1974ff., 34ff., with bibliography.

9. M.Noth, *A History of Pentateuchal Traditions* (1948), Englewood Cliffs, NJ 1972, reprinted Chico, Ca 1982, 208-13; G.von Rad, *Genesis*, OTL, 347ff.

10. A part-volume of *UF*, 13, 1981, 199-290, is now dedicated to the stele of Idrimi. There is useful information on the subject in W.F.Albright, 'Some Important, Recent Discoveries, Alphabetic Origins and the Idrimi Statue', *BASOR* 118, 1950, 11-20, and G.Buccellati, art.cit., V n.41.

11. Von Rad, *Genesis*, 347ff.

12. J.L.Crenshaw, 'Method in Determining Wisdom Influence upon "Historical" Literature', *JBL* 88, 1969, 129-42, and the studies by R.N.Whybray and G.W.Coats already cited.

13. 'Erwägungen über die Landnahme der Israeliten in Palästina', *PJB* 35, 1939, (8-63) = *KS* I, (126-75) 61/173.

14. *Hyksos* (above n.1), 72-98.

15. Again T.J.H.James in the title of his contribution to *CAH* II, 2,1, ³1973, 289ff.; in the text, however, he is much more cautious!

16. The problem of the Hyksos' rise to power and subsequent fall cannot be deal with here. Cf. D.B.Redford, 'The Hyksos Invasion in History and Tradition', *Or* 39, 1970, 1-51, who stresses that these are not alien elements; B.Couroyer, 'Les Aamon-Hyksôs et les Cananéo- Phéniciens', *RB* 81, 1974, 321-54, 481-523. See also N.K.Gottwald, *The Tribes*, 391-4, and the notes to this section, especially 296-7. In general see the histories by M.Noth*, 29-32; R. de Vaux* I, 75-81; and S.Herrmann*, 19f.

17. Cf. the conclusions, 203ff.

18. G.E.Wright, *Biblical Archaeology*, Philadelphia and London ²1962, 54ff.

19. G. von Rad, op.cit. (n.9); de Vaux*, I, 291-6; and Wright, op.cit. (n.18).

20. J.Vergote, op.cit., 203ff., quotes other early examples. For D.B.Redford, op.cit., the Joseph story seems much less well informed on Egypt than would appear at first sight; it also seems to reflect the situation at the court of Judah rather than at that of the Pharaohs! As a *terminus ante quem* he suggests the fifth century BC.

21. J.Vergote, 135ff., and *KB*³, s.v., with bibliography.

22. E.Lipiński, 'From Karatepe to Pyrgi', *RSF* 2, 1974, (45-61) 46; the translation is mentioned with reservations by R. de Vaux*, I, 297f., cf. also S.Herrmann, 'Zu Gen.41.53', *ZAW* 62, 1950, 321. For the problem in general cf. M.Ellenbogen, *Foreign Words in the Old Testament*, London 1962, 3-5.

23. *AHw* I, 3.

24. *ANET*, 259f.; cf. Wright, op.cit (n.18), 56; S.Herrmann, *Israel in Egypt*, SBT II, 27, 25f.

25. J.A.Wilson in *ANET* suggests 'bedouins', but *šws* is better translated 'shepherd', which is what it means. For these peoples cf. R.Giveon, *Les bédouins Shoushou des documents égyptiens*, Leiden 1971.

26. The material on this area is in S.Yeivin, *The Israelite Conquest of Canaan*, Leiden 1971, 243-64 = appendix D.

27. Cf. my *Judges*, 10-12, with bibliography.

28. M.Noth, *Die israelitischen Personennamen*, index; W.F.Albright, 'North-West Semitic Names in a List of Egyptian Slaves from the Eighteenth Century BC', *JAOS* 74, 1954, 222-32; W.H.Schmidt, op.cit., 42.

29. Cf. n.5 above; the text here says nothing either about compulsion in connection with the work or the conscription of whole ethnic groups to it.

30. J.Pedersen, 'Passahfest und Passahlegende', *ZAW* 52, 1934, 1161-75; recently E.Otto, art.cit. (in the bibliography to 6.4), has suggested that the accounts of the plagues indicate that they were recited.

31. I*, 362.

32. For the problems cf. E.Galbiati, *La struttura letteraria dell'Esodo*, Alba 1956, 111-33; U.Cassuto, *A Commentary on the Book of Exodus*, Jerusalem 1967, 111-33.

33. As was already correctly noted by G.Fohrer, 75ff. Recent examples are K.A.Kitchen, *The Ancient Orient and the Old Testament*, London 1966, 157, and A.Ademollo, art.cit.

34. M.Noth, *A History of Pentateuchal Traditions*, 8-41, and Exodus, OTL, ad loc.

35. M.Noth*, 112.

36. For the traditional dating cf. my *Introduction*, 104f.; for a relatively late dating see F.Foresti, 'Composizione e redazione deuteronomistica in Ex. 15.1-18', *Lateranum* 48, 1982, 41-69.

37. H.Cazelles, 'Moïse', *SDB* V, 1957, (1308-37) 1325; Y.Aharoni, op. and loc.cit (8.1), who speaks of places 'all situated in the north-Eastern part of the Nile delta'.

38. Against Noth*, 112; L.H.Grollenberg, *Atlas of the Bible*, London 1956, map 9.

39. G.E.Wright and F.V.Filson, *The Westminster Historical Atlas to the Bible*, London and Philadelphia ²1956, map 5, reproduced in J.Bright*, map III. In both cases the starting-point is the eastern region of the delta.

40. Op.cit., 51f.

41. Noth*, 117.

42. Cf. above n.39.

43. Noth, *Exodus* (n.34), 140.

44. Ibid., 133.

45. The map in Aharoni, *The Land...*, n.13.

46. For the problem cf. my *Judges*, ad loc.

47. See G.I.Davies, *The Way* (above 8), and M.Har-El, *Journeys...*, for other suggestions of places and their respective merits, especially the traditional location. The most recent attempt to identify Sinai known to me is that suggested by the Italian-Israeli archaeologist E.Anati, 'Search for Mount Sinai', *The Jerusalem Post*, 19 August 1983, 5, who wants to identify the holy mountain with Mount Karkum in the Negeb, coord.967-125, which has the remains of an early Bronze Age temple. The proposal has in its favour the fact that it locates Sinai about thirty-five miles from the oasis of Kadesh, so that it could be reached from there in a three-day journey.

48. Y. Aharoni, *The Land*, 198ff., favours the traditional locality and produces quite weighty arguments.

49. Aharoni, ibid., and R. de Vaux* I, 426-39.

50. M.Noth*, 130f.; *Exodus*, 155f.; J.Bright*, 1981, 124; J.Jeremias, op. and loc.cit.

51. Aharoni, *The Land...*, 199-201.

52. M.Noth, art.cit., 6/46; Aharoni, *The Land*, 200f., differs.

53. Aharoni, *The Land*, index of names.

54. G.von Rad, 'The Form-critical Problem of the Hexateuch', in *The Problem of the Hexateuch and Other Essays*, Edinburgh 1966, 1ff.; id., *Old Testament Theology* I, 289ff.; M.Noth, *Exodus*, ad loc., and *136.

55. Cf. my *Judges*, ad loc.

56. Noth*, 135; *Pentateuchal Traditions*, 160; see also H.Cazelles, art.cit (n.37), 1319.

57. J.Bright, *Early Israel in Recent History Writing*, SBT I, 19, 52ff., 105ff.; the quotation comes from 109; id.*, 126.

58. M. Noth*, 136.

59. Loc.cit. The position of W.Eichrodt, *Theology of the Old Testament*, London and Philadelphia I, 289ff., is similar.

60. E.Osswald, *Mose...*, passim; id. 'Moses', *RGG³* 1959, IV, 1151.

61. Bright*, 128f.

VII Conquest

1. Cf. my *Joshua* and *Judges*, and R.G.Boling, *Joshua*, AB 6, Garden City, NY 1982, all ad loc.

2. *Joshua*, ad loc.

3. J.J.Bimson, op.cit. (VI, n.6), in his markedly conservative work, is also ready to accept that this section provides a truer picture of the course of the conquest.

4. But see the alternative identification, supported by good arguments, in J.J.Bimson, op.cit. 215ff.

5. R.Smend, 'Das Gesetz und die Völker', in *Probleme biblischer Theologie...FS von Rad*, Munich 1971, 494-509.

. 6. G. von Rad, and recently W.Kevers, opp.citt., in the following bibliography.

7. E.A.Speiser, 'Ethnic Movements in the Near East in the Second Millennium', *AASOR* 13, 1932-33, 29ff.; R.T.O'Callaghan, *Aram Naharaim*, Rome 1948, 54 n.8.

8. Soggin, *Judges*, 225-59.

9. A.Malamat, 'The Danite Migration and the Pan-Israelite Exodus-Conquest: A Biblical Narrative Pattern', *Bibl* 51, 1970, 1-16. For the variant in Joshua cf. J.Strange, 'The Inheritance of Dan', *ST* 20, 1966, 120-39.

10. For the stele of Mesha cf. my *Introduction*, 475ff., and II Kings 1.1; 3.1ff. (below IX.3.4.1).

11. For these texts cf. my *Il profeta Amos*, Brescia 1982, 15ff., 145ff.

12. M.Noth*, 1959, 62ff., and Aharoni, *The Land*, 278 n.55.

13. R. de Vaux*, II, 564ff., and M.Wüst, 10ff.

14. C.L'Heureux, 'The Ugaritic and Biblical Rephaim', *HTR* 67, 1974, 265-74; J.C. de Moor, 'Rāpi'uma – Rephaim', *ZAW* 88, 1976, 323-45; M.Dietrich – O.Loretz – J.Sanmartin, 'Die ugaritischen Totengeister *rpu(m)* und die biblischen Rephaim', *UF* 8, 1976, 45-52.

15. R. de Vaux*, II, 567.

16. W.F.Albright, *The Archaeology of Palestine*, Harmondsworth [3]1962, 113, 210; R. de Vaux, *Ancient Israel*, London 1961, 240; C.C.McCown, 'Cistern', *IDB* I, 1962, 631; D.R.H(illers), 'Cistern', *EJ* V, 1971, 578f.; S.M.Paul and W.G.Dever, *Biblical Archaeology*, Jerusalem 1973, analytical index.

17. This has recently been opposed, with strong arguments, by V.Fritz, 'The Conquest in the Light of Archaeology', in *Proceedings of the Eighth World Congress of Jewish Studies, Jerusalem 1981*, I, Jerusalem 1982, 15-21, who considers Alt's theory inadequate; in fact we know little or nothing of the actual situation at the time of the 'conquest'; cf. A.Alt, 'Settlement', 150ff.; id., 'Erwägungen' (VI n.13), 137ff.

18. For the sociological problems see the exhaustive work by W.Thiel, 'Die Anfänge von Landwirtschaft und Bodenrecht in der Frühzeit Alt-Israels', *AOF* 7, 1980, 127-141, though it is not very up-to-date on American studies.

19. S.Moscati, 'Chi furono i Semiti?', *ANLM* VIII , 8, 1957, 35ff.

20. W.Thiel, *Die soziale Entwicklung Israels in vorstaatlicher Zeit*, Berlin DDR – Neukirchen 1980, 90ff., considers this conception a 'fantasy'; for other criticisms cf. n.10.

21. Gottwald, *The Tribes*, 555ff. The contrast between the city and the rural world was already pointed out by M.Weber in 1920; details in C.Schäfer-Lichtenberger, *Stadt und Eidgenossenschaft im Alten Testament*, BZAW 157, Berlin 1983, 40ff. Moreover, throughout his own work, Gottwald recognizes his debt to Weber, even if the latter never speaks of revolts.

22. Ibid., 700ff.

23. Liverani, *Introduction*, and H.J.Franken, *CAH* II, 2, [3]1975.

24. There is a survey in Weippert, op.cit., 63-102.

25. Ibid., 102.

26. Ibid., 103.

27. Cf. my *Introduction*, 127-31, and the bibliography there.

28. C.H.J. de Geus, *The Tribes of Israel*, Assen 1976; O.Bächli, *Amphiktyonie im Alten Testament*, Basle 1977; G.W.Rogerson, *Anthropology and the Old Testament*, Oxford 1978, 98-101. The problem is treated in detail again by Gottwald, *Tribes*, passim.

29. 'A Society for the accurate and systematic investigation of the archaeology, topography, geology and physical geography, natural history, manners and customs of the Holy Land, *for biblical illustration'* (my italics).

30. G.Pettinato, in P.Matthiae et al., *Missione archeologica italiana in Siria*, IV, Rome 1972, 1-37.

31. Cf. my *Introduction*, 474.

32. These can be found in the Rockefeller Museum and the Museum of Israel in Jerusalem; in the Louvre in Paris; and in the British Museum in London, to mention only some of the main collections, as well as the many lesser public and private collections.

33. Cf. R.de Vaux* II, 484.

34. J.A.Soggin, 'Gerico – anatomia d'una conquista', *Prot* 29, 1974, 193-213 (French *RHPR* 57, 1977, 1-17).

35. J.Bright*, 137ff., in a much reduced form.

36. See J.M.Miller, in Hayes-Miller*, 262ff.

37. R. de Vaux, 'A Comprehensive View of the Settlement of the Israelites in Canaan', *Perspective* XII, 1-2, 1971, 23-33, and II*, 658ff.; M.Liverani, review, *OA* 15, 1976, 145-59.

38. M.Noth*, 53-68.

39. E.Sellin, *Gilgal*, Leipzig 1917, who speaks of a 'Yahweh coalition' and of 'federation'; A.Alt, 'Eine galiläische Ortsliste in Jos.19', *ZAW* 45, 1927, (59-81) 75ff. For the problem cf. also O. Bächli, 'Nachtrag zum Thema Amphiktyonie', *TZ* 28, 1972, 356; C.H.J.de Geus (n.29).

40. Bächli, art cit.

41. G. von Rad, 'Problem', 1ff., and *Studies in Deuteronomy*, SBT I, 9, 1953. Both studies have rightly remained famous.

42. J.A.Soggin, 'Zur Entwicklung der alttestamentlichen Königtums', *TZ* 15, 1959, 401-18.

43. J.Bright*, ch.IV, esp. 162ff.

44. Gottwald, *Tribes*, index s.v. 'covenant'.

45. M.Noth, *Pentateuchal Traditions*, and G.von Rad, 'The Problem of the Hexateuch'.

46. E.W.Nicholson, *Deuteronomy and Tradition*, Oxford and Philadelphia 1967, 48ff.

47. Op.cit., 111f.

48. Op. and loc.cit.

49. J.A.Soggin, *Judges*, ad loc., and 'Bemerkungen zum Deboralied, Richter Kap.5', *TLZ* 106, 1981, 625-39. For the significance of the number twelve cf. C.H.J.de Geus, op.cit (n.29), 117.

50. G.Buccellati, *Cities and Nations*, 127, 195-200, who rightly disagrees with my earlier studies.

51. C.Schäfer-Lichtenberger, op.cit. (n.22), 333ff., has recently re-examined the problem of the relationships between pre-monarchical Israel and 'segmentary' societies; cf. earlier, F.Crüsemann, *Der Widerstand gegen das Königtum*, WMANT 49, Neukirchen 1978, 200-8, and also A.Malamat, 'Tribal Societies: Biblical Genealogies and African Lineage Systems', *Archives européens de sociologie* 14, 1973, 126-36. This is clearly a direction worth pursuing, given the many analogies we find between the two systems, which are hardly a coincidence.

VIII   Judges

1. Cf. J.A.Soggin, 'Das Amt der "Kleinen Richter" in Israel', *VT* 30, 1980, 245-8.

2. M.Weber, *Ancient Judaism*, Glencoe 1952; id., *Wirtschaft und Gesellschaft*, Tübingen ⁴1956, I, 140ff.; II, 662ff.

3. L.Perlitt, *Bundestheologie im Alten Testament*, WMANT 36, Neukirchen 1969, 7ff., presented a classic formulation of this theory.

4. Cf. W.Richter, *Die Bearbeitungen des 'Retterbuches' in der deuteronomistischen Epoche*, BBB 21, Bonn 1964; and my *Judges*, 8ff., 10ff.

5. A.D.H.Mayes, 'The Historical Context of the Battle against Sisera', *VT* 19, 1969, 353-60; id., *Israel in the Period of the Judges*, SBT II, 29, London and Philadelphia 1974, ch.III.

6. This last theory has been proposed by Y.Aharoni, *The Land*, 263.

7. See the discussion by H.-W.Jüngling, *Plädoyer für das Königtum*, AnBibl 84, Rome 1981, 80.

8. This is a figure which denotes a sizeable quantity and therefore should not be taken literally, cf. Judg.1.7; II Kings 10.1 and the inscription of Panamuwwa II (*KAI* 215; *SSI* II, 14, line 3) from the second half of the eighth century BC. For

the theme cf. F.C.Fensham, 'The Numeral Seventy in the Old Testament and the Family of Jerubbaal, Ahab, Panamuwa and Athirat', *PEQ* 109, 1977, 113-15.

9. This is the theory which I maintained in 'Il regno di Abimelek in Sichem ("Giudici", IX)', in *Studi in onore di Edoardo Volterra*, Milan 1972, VI, 161-89, an article which needs substantial revision after having been delayed over five years between acceptance and publication (it was finished in the late 1960s).

10. See my 'Bemerkungen zur alttestamentlichen Topographie Sichems, mit besonderem Bezug auf Jdc 9', *ZDPV* 83, 1967, 183-98.

11. The almost universal tendency is to identify the two places, most recently Y.Aharoni, *The Land*, 264f., and V.Fritz. However, I have explained in my article (see the preceding note) and in *Judges*, 192f., why these must be two different places; cf. already E.Täubler, *Biblische Studien*, Tübingen 1958, 276-82.

12. G.E.Wright, *Shechem. The Biography of a Biblical City*, New York 1965, 101ff., 122, with an exhaustive account of the excavations and a bibliography on them.

13. An attempt is made by Y.Aharoni, *The Land*, 265, but he does not give the coordinates.

14. For details cf. my *Judges*, 210ff.

15. For details and the various attempts at a solution cf. S.Mittman, 'Aroer, Minnith und Abel Keramim', *ZDPV* 85, 1969, 63-75.

16. Thus rightly M.Noth, *Das Buch Josua*, HAT I, 7, Tübingen ²1953, 14, and on Josh.19.40-49.

17. And O.Eissfeldt's theory, still followed by many scholars: 'Der geschichtliche Hintergrund der Erzählung von Gibeas Schandtat (Richter 19-21)', in *Festschrift Georg Beer zum 70. Geburtstag*, Stuttgart 1935, 19-40 = *KS* II, 64-80.

IX The Two Kingdoms to the Time of the Assyrian Invasion

1. P.Welten, *Geschichte und Geschichtsdarstellung in den Chronikbüchern*, WMANT 42, Neukirchen 1973, 11-13; V.Fritz, 'The "List of Rehoboam's Fortresses" in 2 Chr. 11.5-12 – A Document from the Time of Josiah', *EI* 15, 1981, 46*-53*. The late character of the list had already been argued for in the important study by G.Beyer, 'Beiträge zur Territorialgeschichte von Südwestpalästina im Altertum. I. Das Festungssystem Rehabeams', *ZDPV* 54, 1931, 113-34.

2. Cf. F.M.Cross, 'The Stele Dedicated to Melcarth by Ben Hadad of Damascus', *BASOR* 1954, 1972, 36-42 (but cf. the comments by E.Lipiński, *VT* 25, 1975, 553-612); E.Puech, 'L'ivoire inscrit de Arslan Tash et les rois de Damas', *RB* 88, 1981, 544-62.

3. G.E.Wright, *Biblical Archaeology*, Philadelphia and London ²1972, 148 (with illustrations) and H.Donner* 1977, 391.

4. A.Alt (bibliography to 1), followed by Donner*, 1977, 391.

5. J.Strange, 'Joram, King of Israel and Judah', *VT* 25, 1975, 191-201.

6. Cf. F.S.Frick, 'The Rechabites Reconsidered', *JBL* 90, 1971, 279-87, and H.Donner* 1977, 410f.

7. For the number seventy as a round number cf. above VIII.5.1.3.

8. And not 'son of Omri', which is still usually taken to be the reading, cf.

H.Tadmor, 'The Historical Inscription of Adad-Nirari III', *Iraq* 35, 1973, (141-50) 149. M.Noth*, 1959, 247 n.2, had already suggested 'of the house of Omri'.
    9. S.Page, 'A Stela of Adad Nirari III and Nergal-ereš from Tell al Rimah', *Iraq* 30, 1968, 139-63.
    10. For further details see my 'Amos VI, 13-14 und I,3 auf den Hintergrund der Beziehungen zwischen Israel und Damaskus im 9. und 8. Jahrhundert', in *Near Eastern Studies in Honor of W.F.Albright*, Baltimore and London 1971, 433-41, and *Il profeta Amos*, Brescia 1982, 16ff., 145ff.
    11. There are two roots, '*āzaz* and '*āzar*, which tend to converge in the confession of faith in help from the omnipotent God.
    12. Noth*, 1959, 238 n.4, and Donner*, 1977, 395, have doubts; Aharoni, 1979, 345, is in favour. For the problem of the southern frontiers of Judah cf. C. Meyers, 'Kadesh Barnea: Judah's Last Outpost', *BA* 39, 1976, 148-51.
    13. Cf. N.Glueck, *Rivers in the Desert*, New York [2]1968, ch.VI.
    14. For the so-called 'leprosy', cf. J.F.A.Sawyer, 'A Note on the Etymology of *ṣāra'at*', *VT* 6, 1976, 241-5; E.V.Hulse, 'The Nature of Biblical Leprosy', *PEQ* 107, 1975, 87-105 (a definitive study from the medical point of view). For the biblical texts cf. T.Seidl, *Tora für den 'Aussatz'fall*, S.Ottilien 1982; cf. also the entries in the various biblical dictionaries. For the problem in other countries in the region cf. J.Kinnier Wilson, 'Leprosy in Ancient Mesopotamia', *RA* 60, 1966, 27-58 and 'Medicine in the Land and Times of the Old Testament', in T.Ishida (ed.), *Studies...*, (337-65) 354f., 363ff.
    15. M.Noth*, 257 n.3; J.Bright*, 270; H.Tadmor, art.cit., and many others.
    16. Cf. my *Introduction*, 241-74, and the individual prophets mentioned.

X The Assyrian Invasions

    1. The names may seem very different; in reality the guttural in *raḥyān* indicates the Aramaic '*ayin*, which in turn corresponds to the Hebrew *tsade*, cf. also the Accadian *raṣunnu*.
    2. *ANET*, 272, and Wiseman, D.J., 'Two Historical Inscriptions from Nimrud', *Iraq* 13, 1951, 21-6.
    3. Cf. W.F.Albright, 'The Son of Tabeel (Isaiah 7:6)', *BASOR* 140, 1955, 34f.; for relationships with the Tobiads see B.Mazar, 'The Tobiads', *IEJ* 7, 1957, 137-45, 229-38, a theory accepted by Y.Aharoni, *The Land*, 370, who quotes long sections of the relevant texts.
    4. An interpretation which has not been outdated by E.M.Good's 1966 study.
    5. R.Borger, 'Das Ende des ägyptischen Feldherrn Sib'e = Sô', *JNES* 19, 1960, 49-53; H.Goedicke, 'The End of "So, King of Egypt"', *BASOR* 171, 1963, 64-66.

XI Judah to the Exile

    1. Cf. J.A.Wilson, *The Culture of Ancient Egypt*, Chicago 1951, 294ff.
    2. W.F.Albright*, 314ff.
    3. Y.Aharoni, 'The Horned Altar of Beer Sheba', *BA* 37, 1974, 2-6; Y.Yadin, 'Beer Sheba: The High Place Destroyed by King Josiah', *BASOR* 222, 1976, 5-18.
    4. Cf. Tadmor, 'Philistia under Assyrian Rule', *BA* 29, 1966, 86-102.
    5. Cf. recently N.Shaheen, 'The Sinuous Shape of Hezekiah's Tunnel', *PEQ* 111, 1979, 103-8. R.Wening and E.Zenger, 'Die verschiedenen Systeme der

Wassernutzung im südlichen Jerusalem und die Bezugnahme darauf in biblischen Texten', *UF* 14, 1982, 279-94, is a thorough study of the question of the water system of Jerusalem. For arguments against the identification of Lachish with *tell ed-duweir* see now G.W.Ahlström, 'Tell ed-Duweir: Lachish or Libnah?', *PEQ* 115, 1983, 103f.

6. From the 1930s onwards, cf. 'The History of Palestine and Syria', *JQR* 24, 1933-34, (363-76) 370f., and *The Biblical Period from Abraham to Ezra*, New York [2]1963, 78ff. An extreme attempt to salvage the antiquity and credibility of the biblical narratives has been made by K.A.Kitchen, 'Egypt, The Levant and Assyria in 701 BC', in *Fontes atque Pontes. Festschrift H.Brunner*, Wiesbaden 1983, 243-50. That the biblical tradition now reflects a late state of the tradition seems to have been proved beyond any possible doubt, cf. the commentaries by Wildberger and Kaiser, and the study by Garbini, 1981.

7. In n.4 of this there is a list of those who have recently supported the theory: J.Gray (1964, but no longer in 1970), E.W.Nicholson, R.de Vaux and S.Horn.

8. Thus again recently W.von Soden, 'Sanherib von Jerusalem, 701 BC', in *Antike und Universalgeschichte. Festschrift H.E.Strei*, Münster 1962, (43-51) 45.

9. Cf. J.A.Soggin, *Introduction*, 462.

10. Cf. the article by E.L.Ehrlich, already cited; B.Oded*, 454f.; Bright*, 311.

11. Cf. J.A.Soggin, *Introduction*, 114ff., 185ff.

12. Y. Aharoni, 'Arad: Its Inscriptions and Temple', *BA* 31, 1968, 2-32.

13. Id., 'Trial Excavations at the "Solar Shrine" at Lachish', *IEJ* 18, 1968, 157-69.

14. A.E.Cowley, *Aramaic Papyri of the Fifth Century BC*, London 1923; E.G.Kraeling, *The Brooklyn Museum Aramaic Papyri*, New York 1953. There are other details in Soggin, *Introduction*, 485ff.

15. J.A.Soggin, *Introduction*, 114ff.

16. A.Alt, *Die Heimat des Deuteronomiums' (1953)* = *KS* II, 250-75; G.E.Wright, 'The Levites in Deuteronomy', *VT* 4, 1954, 325-70.

17. Soggin, op.cit., 275f.

18. For the problems connected with these stamps and seals, especially in an economic and topographical context, cf. Y.Aharoni, *The Land*, 394-400.

19. Noth*, 278f.; Herrmann*, 271f.; Gunneweg*, 111 have doubts.

20. Cf. J.A.Soggin, 'Profezia ed apocalittica nel Giudaesimo post-esilico', *RiBib* 30, 1982, 161-73.

21. W.H.Shea, 'Adon's Letter and the Babylonian Chronicle', *BASOR* 223, 1976, 61-4; B.Porten, 'The Identity of King Adon', *BA* 44, 1981, 36-52, who has in mind Ekron and the year 600, cf. on 5.3.

22. E.Lipiński, 'The Egypto-Babylonian War of the Winter 601-600', *AION* 32, 1972, 235-41.

23. The Babylonian texts have been studied by E.F.Weidner, 'Jojachim. König von Juda, in babylonischen Keilschrifttexten', in *Mélanges syriens offerts à M.René Dussaud*, Paris 1939, II, 923-35.

24. F.E.Deist, 'The Punishment of the Disobedient Zedekiah', *JNWSL* 1, 1971, 71f., points out in his brief study that the punishments inflicted on Zedekiah, rather than being an indication of the cruelty of the king of Babylon, were those provided for in the curse on signatories to treaties who fail to fulfil their obligations.

25. S.Moscati, *L'epigrafia ebraica antica*, BibOr 15, Rome 1951, 61.

26. For this question see my provisional study, 'Die Entstehung des deuteronomistichen Geschichtswerkes', *TLZ* 100, 1975, 3-8.

27. Thus G.Garbini, Review, in *AION* 32, 1982, 497.

28. Cf. my study cited above n.25, esp. 161.

29. W.Zimmerli, 'Planungen für der Wiederaufbau nach der Katastrophe von 587', *VT* 18, 1968, 229-55 = *GA* II, 165-91, and G.C.Machholz, 'Noch Einmal: Planungen für der Wiederaufbau nach der Katastrophe von 587', *VT* 19, 1969, 322-52.

30. J.A.Soggin, 'Bilinguismo o trilinguismo nell'Ebraismo post-esilico', *Vicino Oriente* 3, 1980, 199-207.

31. W.F.Albright*, 322f.; id., *The Biblical Period from Abraham to Ezra*, New York 1963, 110 n.180.

32. Thus Weinberg 1971, and K.M.Kenyon, *Jerusalem*, London and New York 1967, 78-107.

XII Under the Persian Empire

1. S.Smith, *Babylonian Historical Texts relating to the Capture and Downfall of Babylon*, London 1924.

2. J.A.Soggin, 'Bilinguismo e trilinguismo nell'ebraismo post-esilico', *Vicino Oriente* 3, 1980, 199-207.

3. J.A.Soggin, *Introduction*, 414ff., 420ff., and Williamson.

4. Ibid., 322ff., 329ff., 335ff., 343ff.

5. Ibid., 471f., and Williamson.

6. For details and critical texts (some in *ANET*), cf. Soggin, *Introduction*, 485ff.

7. I cannot go here into the problem of the structure of the Persian administration; cf. the work mentioned in n.14 and the bibliographies there, also O.Bucci, 'L'attività legislativa del sovrano achemenide e gli archivi reali persiani', *RIDA* III, 25, 1978, 11-93. It is a pity that this important and exhaustive study treats the biblical material uncritically (it quotes Esther, Ezra-Nehemiah and Chronicles).

8. O.Kaiser, *Introduction to the Old Testament*, ET Oxford 1975, 180f., who quotes G.Hölscher, HSAT II, Tübingen ²1923, 491ff.

9. W.F.Albright, 'The Date and the Personality of the Chronicler', *JBL* 40, 1921, (104-24) 108ff.

10. For the term *peḥah* cf. A.Alt 1934, 24/333f. n.2.

11. J.A.Soggin, *Il profeta Amos*, Brescia 1982, 127ff.

12. J.A.Soggin, *Introduction*, 322ff., 329ff.

13. In III Ezra 2.8 we read that he was προστάτης τῆς Ἰουδαίας, which Sacchi wants to correct to τῶν Ἰουδαίων, cf. Josephus XI, 31, who calls him Ἰουδαίων ἡγεμών, and Ezra 6.7, which has the Aramaic *peḥah yᵉdūdāyēʾ*, not to be corrected, as is usually done.

14. A.T.Olmstead, *History of the Persian Empire*, Chicago 1948, 142,

15. J.A.Soggin, *Introduction*, 332f.

16. Against P.D.Hanson, *The Dawn of Apocalyptic*, Philadelphia 1975, 348-52, though at that time he had no access to the documentation published by Avigad in 1976.

17. But cf. the criticism already in M.Noth*, 321, and in M.Smith, *Palestinian Parties and Politics that Shaped the Old Testament*, New York 1971, 193ff. However, it is worth remembering that this reading with *pḥwʾ* is at least controversial:

F.M.Cross, 'Judaean Stamps', *EI* 9, 1969, 20-7, had suggested the reading *phr'*, 'potter', for earlier finds; this would denote the craftsman who had made the vessel. Cf. recently G.Garbini, 'La "storia d'Israele"', *Hen* 5, 1983, (243-55) 250, who doubts the authenticity of all this documentation, which is not only quite extraordinary, but also palaeographically suspect. However, as far as I can see these considerations have not found any support. The problem is not mentioned by Avigad or by others who have made specialist studies of the question, but it should be raised again in the light of recent discoveries, in order to obtain the clarity which is indispensable for the critical use of this evidence.

18. A.E.Cowley, *Aramaic Papyri of the Fifth Century BC*, Oxford 1923 (not in *ANET*).

19. J.A.Soggin, *Introduction*, 343ff.

20. That is, if we do not read *ṭōbīyāh wᵉʿebed hāʿammōny*, 'Tobias and Ebed the Ammonite', with W.F. Albright, 'Dedan', in *Geschichte und Altes Testament – Festschrift Albrecht Alt*, Tübingen 1953, (1-12) 4f., which would be a reference to a Persian governor of Ammon in Transjordan. This is an improbable proposition (Tobias was the governor of Ammon and the family was Ammonite), even if Cross 1975 considers it 'extremely attractive'.

21. Cf. I. Rabinowitz, 'Aramaic Inscriptions of the Fifth Century BCE from a North-Arabian Shrine in Egypt', *JNES* 15, 1956, 1-9; W.J.Dumbrell, 'The Tell-Maskhuta Bowl and the "Kingdom of Qedar" in the Persian Perriod', *BASOR* 203, 1971, 33-44.

22. Cf. J.A.Soggin, *Introduction*, 420ff.; Fohrer*, 208ff.

23. There is a list in Soggin, *Introduction*, 423, but Sacchi, 40ff., is connected with the former rather than the latter. Cf. also Widengren*, 535f., and Fohrer*, 211ff.

24. Cf. J.A.Emerton, 'Did Ezra Go to Jerusalem in 428 BC?', *JTS* 17, 1966, 1-19.

25. For an explanation of the ban, which should not, however, be understood in an ethnic and racialist sense, cf. J.A.Soggin, *Introduction*, 395f.

26. J.A.Soggin, *Introduction*, 11-19.

27. J.A.Soggin, *Il profeta Amos*, Brescia 1982, 182ff.

XIII Under the Macedonians and Diadochi

1. Soggin, *Introduction*, 21f.

2. Soggin, *Introduction*, 414.

3. Soggin, *Introduction*, 211-40.

4. G.von Rad, *Old Testament Theology*, Edinburgh 1965, reissued London 1975, 301ff.

5. Cf. D.Auscher, 'Les relations entre la Grèce et la Palestine avant la conquête d'Alexandre', *VT* 17, 1967, 8-30. For confirmation it is enough to read, even if only superficially, the writings collected in Stern, *Authors*.

6. Cf. J.A.Soggin, *I Manoscritti del Mar Mortto*, 1978, 73ff.

7. 'By three things is the world sustained: by the Law, by the temple service, and by deeds of loving-kindness',*Mishnah*, Aboth I,2 (Simon the Righteous, *c.* 300 BC), ed. H.Danby, Oxford 1933, 446.

8. Soggin, 1978, 135; F.Michelini Tocci, *I Manoscritti del mar Morto*, Bari 1967, suggests a different translation, which would rather authorize the saving of a

human being in this case: but the intrinsically negative context suggests that it should all be understood in negative terms.

XIV Under the Romans

1. Cf. A.Schalit, 'Das Problem des Rundbaus auf der mittleren Terrasse des Nordpalastes des Herodes auf dem Berge Masada', *Theokratia*, 1970-72, 45-50.

2. For the trial of Jesus see e.g. P.Winter, *On the Trial of Jesus*, Berlin 1961.

3. It was the great achievement of Albert Schweitzer, *The Quest of the Historical Jesus*, London 1910, [3]1954, that he demonstrated that the Synoptic Gospels, not to mention other writings in the New Testament, are completely inadequate as a basis for writing a life of Jesus, though attempts are always being made by authors who are not familiar with Schweitzer's work.

4. J.Maier, *Jesus von Nazareth in der talmudischen Überlieferung*, Darmstadt 1978. This is at present the definitive study on the question. But see the review by D.Goldberg, *JQR* 73, 1982–83, 78–86.

5. Cf. W.Eck, 'Die Eroberung von Massada und eine neue Inschrift des L. Flavius Silva Nonius Bassus', *ZNW* 60, 1969, 282-9. The results of this study have now been questioned by B.Reicke 1982, 289 n.24, who suggests Josephus' dating, April 72.

6. Thus Eusebius, *HE* III, 3.3-4; cf. S.G.Sowers, 'The Circumstances and the Recollection of the Pella Flight', *TZ* 26, 1970, 305-20, and Leaney*, 659, with bibliography.

7. For these two apocalyptic writings cf. the study by W.Harnisch, *Verhängnis und Verheissung der Geschichte*, FRLANT 97, Göttingen 1969.

8. An example of Jewish agricultural settlement with a tradition which probably goes back to a time before the two catastrophes is that of *peqi'in*, in Arabic *buq''eia*, in Upper Galilee, coord 261-81. Here the Jewish rural population remained until the Arab rebellion of 1936. They had to flee after that, but managed to return a decade later.

Appendix 2 : The Chronology of the First Temple Period

1. See *WHJP* IV, 1, 63-101, 260-9.

2. See J.Finegan, *Handbook of Biblical Chronology*, Princeton 1964, 108-223; E.Bickerman, *Chronology of the Ancient World*, London 1968, 70-7; G.E.Samuel, *Greek and Roman Chronology*, Munich 1972, 245-8.

3. See e.g. D.Diringer in O.Tuffnell, *Lachish* III, Oxford 1953, 339 (ostracon no. 20); J.C.L.Gibson, *Textbook of Syrian Semitic Inscriptions* I, Oxford 1971, 8f., (Samaria ostraca nos.1, 2, 6, 10, 19).

4. The Babylonian Chronicle: F.Delitzsch, *Die babylonische Chronik*, Leipzig 1906 (= ASGW, phil-hist.Kl. XXV). For the Synchronistic King List from Ashur cf. A.L.Oppenheim, *ANET*, 272-4. On the Egyptian king lists: A.Gardiner, *Egypt of the Pharaohs*, Oxford 1961, 46-69.

5. A.Jepsen, *Die Quellen des Königsbuches*, Halle a/S 1956, 30ff.; E.R.Thiele, *The Mysterious Numbers of the Hebrew Kings* = (*MNHK*[2]), Grand Rapids, Mich. 1956, 174-91; S.R.Bin-Nun, *VT* 18, 1968, 414-32.

6. J.M.Miller, *JBL* 86, 1967, 277-88, and especially J.D.Schenkel, *Chronology and Recensional Development in the Greek Text of Kings*, Cambridge, Mass. 1968.

7. D.W.Gooding, *JTS* NS 21, 1970, 118-31; E.R.Thiele, *JBL* 93, 1974, 174-200.

8. Thiele, *MNHK*, 167-203.

9. See in general *JE* XI, cols. 147-9; *EJ* XIV, cols.1091-3 (including bibliography).

10. For bibliographical survey until 1961, see H.Tadmor, 'Chronology', *Enc.Miqr.* IV, Jerusalem 1962, cols.261-4. Additional studies include: D.N.Freedman, in G.E.Wright (ed.), *The Bible and the Ancient Near East. Essays in Honor of W.F.Albright*, 1961, 203-28; C.Schedl, *VT* 12, 1962, 88-119; J.Gray, *I and II Kings*, London 1964, 55-74; A.Jepsen and R.Hanhart, *Untersuchungen zur Israelitischen-jüdischen Chronologie*, BZAW 88, Berlin 1963, 1-47; V.Pavlovsky and E.Vogt, *Biblica* 45, 1964, 321-47; M.Miller, *JBL* 86, 1967, 276-88; A.Jepsen, *VT* 18, 1968, 31-45; W.R.Wifall, *ZAW* 80, 1968, 317-36; S.Yeivin, *M.Zer Kabod Volume*, Jerusalem 1968, 367-81 (in Hebrew).

11. This was suggested by Thiele in *MNHK*², and more recently by Wifall (above n.10).

12. On the problem of calendar and intercalation in the biblical period, see J.B.Segal, *VT* 7, 1957, 250-307.

13. A.Gardiner, *JEA* 31, 1945, 11-28; id., *Egypt of the Pharaohs*, Oxford 1961, 69-71. It is quite possible that the Persian court practised a similar custom (cf. E.Bickerman, *Chronology of the Ancient World*, London 1968, 90), which may explain the contradiction between the dates in Neh.1.1 and in Neh.2.1. This would also obviate the necessity of emending the text in Neh.1.1 and in Neh.2.1. For previous suggestions, see Tadmor, *JNES* 15, 1956, 227 n.70, and more recently D.J.A.Clines, *JBL* 93, 1974, 35.

14. For these, as well as for the terms 'accession year' and 'non-accession year', see J.Finegan, *Handbook of Biblical Chronology*, 80-6.

15. Cf. the Egyptian practice in the Hellenistic and Roman periods (e.g. 'the thirtieth year' [of Ptolemy XII], which is year 1 [of Cleopatra VII]; T.C.Skeat, *Mizraim* 6, 1937, 8; see also Finegan, *Handbook*, 80f.

16. This practice originated in Babylon during the Kassite dynasty, in the thirteenth century BCE, but it may in fact have started in the fourteenth century; see also J.A.Brinkman, *WO* 6, 1971, 153. The terms *rēšīt malᵉkūt* and *rēšīt mamlᵉkūt/mamleket* used for the reigns of Jehoiakim and Zedekiah (Jer.26.1; 27.1; 28.1; 49.34) are not necessarily exact chronological terms like the Babylonian *šanat rēš šarrūti*, but general terms which indicate the initial period of these kings' reigns, whether it was less than a year, a full year, or more than a year. The Akkadian term *rēš šarrūti*, 'the beginning of the reign', occurs in some literary texts without the chronological connotation. See also Tadmor, *JNES* 15, 1956, 227 n.17; id., *Studies in Honor of Benno Landsberger*, Chicago 1965, 353. For a variant opinion see N.Sarna, *Hagut Ivrit be-America* 1, Tel Aviv 1972, 121-30 (in Hebrew).

17. A.Ungnad, 'Eponymen', *RLA* II, 412-59.

18. Tadmor, *JCS* 12, 1958, 22-33.

19. See Tadmor, *JNES* 15, 1956, 227; *Enc.Miqr.* IV, cols., 267f. The term *šᵉnat molkō* (II Kings 25.27) also appears in a Phoenician inscription from the Persian period. Where Aramaic was predominant, the term used was a translation of *šanat rēš šarrūti*: see now F.M.Cross, 'Papyri from the Fourth Century BC from Dālīyeh', *New Directions in Biblical Archaeology*, ed. D.N.Freedman and J.C.Greenfield, Garden City, NY 1969, 44f.

20. M.Steen, *Compendia rerum Judaicarum ad Novum Testamentum*, I/1, Assen 1974, 62-68, and M.D.Herr, ibid., II, 1976, 843-5.

21. *Enc.Miqr.*, cols 265-6. It is possible that Ezekiel counted the years of Jehoiachin's exile from the spring, although the evidence in Ezekiel is not decisive because it could, in part, conform with the autumn reckoning: see A.Malamat, *IEJ* 18, 1968, 146ff.; id., *VTS* 28, 1975, 125-45; K.S. Freedy and D.B.Redford, *JAOS* 90, 1970, 262-74. Further support for the view that the year in Judah started in the spring has recently been brought by D.J.A.Clines, *Australian Journal of Archaeology* 2, 1972, 9-34; id., *JBL* 93, 1974, 22-40.

22. See Tadmor, *Scripta Hierosolymitana* 8, 1961, 259ff.

23. See Talmon, *VT* 8, 1958, 48-74.

24. For details of the methods employed by the Egyptian and Mesopotamian chronographers, see *Enc.Miqr*, cols.271-4.

25. For a somewhat different view, see J.A.Brinkman, *A Political History of Post-Kassite Babylonia*, Rome 1968, 63-7.

26. See *Enc.Miqr.* IV, col.286; VI, col.126.

27. See *Enc.Miqr.*, I, col.439.

28. See especially E.R.Thiele, 'The Question of Coregencies among Hebrew Kings', in *A Stubborn Faith. W.A.Irwin Festschrift*, Dallas 1956, 39-52.

29. The chronological scheme briefly delineated here has been presented in detail in the present writer's article on biblical chronology in *Enc.Miqr.* IV, cols.274-302; cf. bibliography, ibid., cols.309f. and above, n.10.

30. See ibid., cols.255-9, tables 7-9, and accompanying notes. Two new synchronisms have been added: no.3, see A.R.Millard and H.Tadmor, *Iraq* 35, 1973, 57ff., and Tadmor, ibid., 64; no.8 will be published in our *Inscriptions of Tiglath-pileser III, King of Assyria*, The Israel Academy of Sciences and Humanities (forthcoming). Note also the following new studies on synchronism no.4: L.D.Levine, *BASOR* 206, 1972, 40-2; M.Cogan, *JCS* 25, 1973, 96-9. For synchronism no. 20, see above, n.19. For the problem of Egyptian synchronisms in the biblical period see K.A.Kitchen, *The Third Intermediate Period in Egypt*, Warminster 1973; id., 'Late Egyptian Chronology and the Hebrew Monarchy', *JANES* 5, 1973 (= T.Gaster Festschrift), 225-33.

31. For Assyrian and Babylonian chronology in the first millennium BCE see G.Smith, *The Assyrian Eponym Canon*, London 1876; F.X.Kugler, *Sternkunde und Sterndienst in Babel*, II/2, Münster in Westfalen 1912, 342-61; R.A.Parker and W.H.Dubberstein, *Babylonian Chronology, 626 BC - AD 75*, Providence RI 1956.

32. See A.Malamat, *IEJ* 18, 1968, 135-57; id., *SVT* 28, 1975, 123-45; and *WHJP* IV,1, ch.X. (Basing himself on a Tishri calendar he arrives at 586 for the destruction date.)

33. D.J.Wiseman, *Chronicles of Chaldaean Kings* (626-556 BC) in the British Museum, London 1956, 72.

34. See J.Lewy, *Die Chronologie der Könige von Israel und Juda*, Giessen 1927, 19f., n.3.

35. For details see Tadmor, *JCS* 12, 1958, 33-40.

36. See J.Begrich, *ZDMG* 83, 1929, 213; 86, 1932, 61. For a fundamentally different view, according to which Hezekiah asumed power in 716/5, see Thiele, *MNHK²*, 155-72; id., *VT* 16, 1966, 83-107.

37. E.g. Thiele, above, n.36; W.F.Albright, *BASOR* 100, 1945, 22; also, more recently, J.Gray, *I and II Kings*, OTL, London and Philadelphia ²1970, 58, 74.

38. L.L.Honor, *Sennacherib's Invasion of Palestine*, New York 1926, 70; J.Lewy, *OLZ* 31, 1928, 158f.; Tadmor, *Enc.Miqr.* IV, cols.278f.

39. Jepsen had conjectured that the story of Ahab's death, I Kings 22, should

actually be placed in the time of the Jehu dynasty, and that the king who fell in the battle of Ramoth-Gilead (in a war against Ben-Hadad III son of Hazael) was actually an heir of Jehu (A.Jepsen, *AfO* 14, 1942, 154-8). This view has recently been taken up again and developed by Miller, who contends that the king was Jehoahaz son of Jehu (J.M.Miller, *JBL* 85, 1966 ,441-5; id., *ZAW* 80, 1968, 337-42). We have not adopted these views mainly because they raise more historical and historiographical problems than they attempt to solve.

40. *Enc.Miqr.* IV, cols.289-94.

41. See most recently J.D.Schenkel, *Chronology and Recensional Development in the Greek Text of Kings*, Cambridge, Mass. 1968, 61-108. But see the critical remarks of E.R.Thiele, *JBL* 93, 1974, 182-90.

42. Cf. A.Orr, *VT* 6, 1956, 304, 360; R. Borger, *JNES* 18, 1958, 74.

43. See *Enc.Miqr.* III, col.481; IV, cols.281f.

44. *Enc.Miqr.* IV, cols.247-51.

45. For a possible Sumerian parallel see T.Jacobsen, *The Sumerian King List*, Chicago 1939, 93 n.145 (Mes-anne-pada and his son A-anne-pada, the two early kings of Ur, reigning forty years each). Assigning forty years to a generation is also common in the Greek chronographic tradition; see G.E. Samuel, *Greek and Roman Chronology*, Munich 1972, 241-6. Cf. also D.W.Prakken, *Studies in Greek Genealogical Chronology*, Lancaster, Penn.1943, 20.

General Index

Index of Biblical References

Index of Modern Scholars